Krafft: The Debian System

Martin F. Krafft

The Debian System

Concepts and Techniques

Publisher: William Pollock
Cover Design: Octopod Studios
U.S. edition published by No Starch Press, Inc.
555 De Haro Street, Suite 250, San Francisco, CA 94107
phone: 415.863.9900; fax: 415.863.9950; info@nostarch.com; http://www.nostarch.com

Original edition © 2005 Open Source Press GmbH
Published by Open Source Press GmbH, Munich, Germany
Publisher: Dr. Markus Wirtz
Original ISBN 3-937514-07-4
For information on translations, please contact
Open Source Press GmbH, Amalienstr. 45 Rg, 80799 München, Germany
phone +49.89.28755562; fax +49.89.28755563; info@opensourcepress.de; http://www.opensourcepress.de

Library of Congress Cataloging-in-Publication Data

```
Krafft, Martin F.
   The Debian system : concepts and techniques / Martin F. Krafft.-- 1st ed.
       p. cm.
   Includes index.
   ISBN 1-59327-069-0
1. Linux.  2. Operating systems (Computers) I. Title.
   QA76.76.O63K68 2005
   005.4'32--dc22
                                    2005019963
```

To Aline.

And Peter Gabriel,
for the tunes
which kept me going.

Table of Contents

Appendix

A   Debian flavours and other Debian-based operating systems

B   When is Debian the right choice?

C   Miscellaneous

Introduction

My first reaction to Linux? This defies all logic.
— Ian Murdock

The Debian GNU/Linux operating system is a fully-featured operating system for servers, workstations, and home desktop machines alike. It can serve up web pages, relay email, provide a database backend and file-sharing services, authenticate users, firewall and monitor networks, control appliances and power embedded devices. Debian can also act as a workstation or desktop machine, allowing users to browse the Internet, read and write emails, author documents, calculate spreadsheets, edit images, view multimedia content, play games, write software, or manage schedules, contacts and other personal information. When it comes to Debian (or GNU/Linux in general), the question is usually "how is it done?", rather than "can it be done?". Thus, the Debian system constitutes an excellent basis for most tasks.

The broad range of possible Debian GNU applications is an important part of Debian's undamped growth[1]. Another, perhaps even more important reason for the success of the Debian system, is the stability of its software packages along with the robustness of its administrative tools, and invaluable overall reliability. Furthermore, Debian's support for eleven different processor architectures allows for unified administration across the various platforms that have become popular over the years.

The Debian system owes much of its power to numerous free software projects and movements, most notably GNU and Linux. Debian uses the Linux kernel, so anything that is possible with Linux itself is possible with Debian GNU as well. Over 15 000 Debian packages are available for straightforward installation, offering a great deal of functionality without the burden of manually satisfying dependencies, compiling source code, setting up initial configurations, and keeping programmes up to date. And then again, if you do have to compile a tool, library, or application manually, don't worry; Debian will give you all the tools, and then keep out of your way. This is perhaps one of the most important points about Debian: it is there to assist you, and it is quite successful in being quiet unless explicitly called for. In other words, you control the system, and not the other way around.

Debian package maintainers try to keep the packaged software as identical as possible to the original, upstream source. Instead of introducing major changes, they make sure their packaging work adheres to a strict set of rules designed to allow thousands of Debian packages to form a truly integrated system, rather than merely coexisting side by side, hoping they do not get in each other's way. Therefore, when you install official Debian packages, you install the original software that neatly slots into the system, rather than just working when used in a certain way or specific environment.

When modifications done by Debian are not Debian-specific (and this is often the case), they are usually merged with the original upstream code, improving the software and successfully keeping Debian-specific differences minimal. Even tools developed specifically for Debian are available for the public and often find their way into other distributions. The Debian project has a strong commitment to the free software community and makes all its work available for the benefit of others, just as it uses the produce of others for its own good.

The Debian community is a community of volunteers. Debian developers do not receive direct financial compensation from the project. Nevertheless, the philosophy and technical merits of Debian have always attracted professionals from all over the world who bring problem-solving proficiency to a variety of areas within the Debian project. Every Debian developer has to display a common conception of ethics and an acceptable level of Debian-specific skills before being officially accepted. As volunteers, these people are then free to approach any challenges of personal interest, while working on the same integrated system.

[1]Netcraft determined Debian to be the fastest growing Linux distribution in 2003 and 2004: http://news.netcraft.com/archives/2004/01/28/debian_fastest_growing_linux_distribution.html

Computer users have needs *today* and Debian fulfills these needs successfully while encouraging their implementation in a formal and sustainable manner. Debian may not be universally applicable, but stability and maturity are its keywords. Assuming that these reflect a user's primary needs, the rest is negotiable.

1.1   About this book

Packages in the Debian archive contain a variety of free software, ranging from standard tools to amazing utilities. The Debian-specific tools, which will be our primary focus, form a major subset. This book uncovers those tools, explains the underlying concepts, and highlights potential pitfalls or shortcomings. It explains how the tools should be used, and how they interoperate to offer a robust and consistent means of administering and maintaining Debian installations. I will be focusing on the popular x86 architecture. However, since the functionality and feel of the Debian system is mostly equivalent across all supported architectures (with the notable exception of installation and boot processes), the x86-specific parts of this book are minimal.

This book does not cover Linux in general, nor does it cover specific system administration aspects[2]. It was written to be the source of knowledge about the Debian system and its specifics.

This book is intended to be objective. Debian may be the perfect operating system for some, but that does not make it ideal for everyone. Advocating the use of Debian is a good thing, and every additional user is a significant gain to the project. But nothing is gained if newcomers give up after painfully discovering that Debian does not meet their needs or expectations. Polemic praise of the "universal operating system" is not what prospective users need or want; information should be based on facts, not on advertisements.

The goal of this book is not to be a pamphlet about Debian. Instead, it presents the Debian approach to various system administration tasks and points out common myths and factoids. It highlights those points that make a Debian administrator's life easy and enjoyable, as well as those that cause headaches and the occasional fit of raving madness. All in all, however, the book primarily serves as a platform for the Debian system to speak for itself. It gives you the plain facts, allowing you to compare them with your expectations and either embrace Debian GNU, or move on. In appendix B, you will find a summary and more help in making this important decision with its many practical implications.

---

[2]If you are looking for references on these topics, I can recommend O'Reilly's *Running Linux*, 4th edition, written by Matt Welsh *et al.*. Machtelt Garrels also provides a good online hands-on guide at http://www.tldp.org/LDP/intro-linux/html. Finally, the documentation compiled by *The Linux Documentation Project* (http://www.tldp.org) is a helpful and indispensable reference. Finally, Evi Nemeth *et al.* have written the excellent *Linux Administration Handbook* and the fantastic *Unix System Administration Handbook*, targeted specifically at system administrators providing services to users (http://www.admin.com).

Writing a book about Debian is not easy when you are involved with the project. Whenever I found a problem, I tended to fix (or at least report) it instead of documenting workarounds. Since the inception of this book, I have filed 354 bugs against Debian packages, fixed 68, exchanged about 5500 emails on topics related to the book and spent countless hours on IRC. Undoubtedly, the book would have been completed much faster if I had simply accepted the problems. As it stands, however, I feel that both the book and the project, have benefited from the procedure I followed, which can not be said for my peace of mind.

1.2   Target audience

This book is targeted at people familiar with Unix who are looking to understand what makes Debian different, and how to best put Debian's paradigms and tools to use. It is intended to be a reference for the Debian system, as well as a guide for those that want to go further with the system. Its target audience is broad and can be roughly classified into four groups, which are discussed in the following sections.

1.2.1   The Linux administrator

As the ideal reader of this book, you possess know-how in two main areas. First, you will have profound knowledge of the Linux kernel, the GNU userland utilities, and a general understanding of the Unix operating system as well as the Portable Operating System for Unix (POSIX) standards. Second, you will have practical experience of multiuser system administration. You will have developed an understanding of the scope of daily administration tasks and ideally written many scripts to facilitate the numerous aspects of your job. While it does not hurt to know the do's and dont's of system administration, the book concentrates more on the effective management of stable and secure production systems over long periods of time.

You will find in this book an enticing introduction to the Debian Way of system administration and management. It offers a comprehensive and objective overview of the strengths and weaknesses of Debian and serves as a basis for migrating from another Linux distribution to Debian GNU.

1.2.2   The Unix administrator

If you are an administrator of another Unix operating system, such as BSD or Solaris, you will want to read this book along with a GNU/Linux[3] reference manual. The book is based on Debian using Linux as the kernel. Debian has been ported to

---

[3]See footnote on p. 19.

other kernels, but these ports are not yet as mature as the Linux-based distribution. Nevertheless, a great number of skilled and ambitious developers are working hard to bring these ports up to par, and every additional user ready to help out can speed up the process.

If you are ready to move to the Linux kernel, or would like to continue profiting from your experience of the BSD kernels while entering the world of Debian, you may consider yourself an ideal reader. Debian acts and feels pretty much the same, no matter what the kernel or architecture may be (see chapter 4.5).

1.2.3 The Debian user

If you are already running Debian GNU/Linux, you can still profit from this book. The sophistication of the Debian system keeps a system running with minimal effort, and the maintenance of a single-user workstation does not require in-depth knowledge of the advanced concepts and intricacies of Debian GNU/Linux. Nevertheless, sooner or later new requirements are likely to surface, and this means the Debian user learning more about the system and enhancing it to handle new tasks, or improve the handling of old tasks. The need may arise to give out accounts to family and friends to let them experience the freedom of a Linux system. Or you may at one point consider turning your knowledge and enthusiasm for the system into money by entering the commercial world, assisted by the operating system. Lastly, you may discover that you simply like playing around with Debian and get a kick from its elegant methods, whether you need them or not[4].

If this sounds like you, this book will mainly give you the motivations of the various Debian approaches, as well as showing you some utilities and paradigms that you may not yet have encountered. Unless you are confident of, or not fully dependent on, your production machine, I would recommend testing most of the stuff you read on the following pages on a fresh installation, or within a chroot install (see chapter 8.3.1). When you have understood and mastered each method, you can port it to your main system, if you so desire.

Shameless plug: while thinking about the target audience of this book, it occurred to me that I would *not* have bought it if I had seen it on the shelf. When I started writing, I considered myself an advanced Debian user and well-versed developer, who would not learn much from a printed Debian reference. I was wrong. As I put together the information that now fills these pages, I learnt about ideas and techniques that I had not previously not dreamt of; researching the depths of the Debian system opened up whole new perspectives to me, some of which have since revolutionised the way I work with the Debian system. If your involvement with Debian is anything more than chance, this book is for you.

---

[4]I have always been like that.

1.2.4 The Linux apprentice

This book assumes a good knowledge of the Linux operating system. Consequently, users new to Linux should probably look elsewhere for the basics. Nevertheless, along with a good introductory Linux reference[2], some enthusiasm, and quite a bit of free time, this book can facilitate a clean, bottom-up start into Linux system administration.

This said, Debian may not be the best choice for your first steps in the Linux world. If you are choosing Linux because you have had enough and want to author your documents, compose messages, and browse the Web on a stable, secure, and free operating system from now on, then you may want to consider one of the Debian derivatives (see appendix A.2) or a different distribution at first. These are frequently optimised for specific applications or target a specific user base, which makes them be simpler to learn. For instance, several Debian-based distributions provide simplified installers (or need not be installed at all), or provide a standard selection of common desktop programmes, allowing you to get to work immediately without having to find out how to get there first. These distributions do not need to handle the broad set of applications that Debian supports and can thus do with less flexibility (and complexity). Once you have learnt to walk with one of these, you can always come back to Debian for its maintainability (or any other reason).

If you really want to jump in at the deep end and hop right on the Debian bandwagon, then, by all means, go right ahead. You will find a welcoming community and a helpful crowd, but be aware that you will probably be in for a hard time at first. If the computer you plan to use for your learning experience also serves your productivity, make sure you know what you are doing. For your experiments, it might be wise to invest a small amount of money in another machine, networked to your main machine. Hardware is cheap, and your main computer will almost certainly be capable of sharing Internet access with the hosts on your local network. This allows you to restrict use of your production machine to important work. And should a problem on the Debian machine prevent network access, you can still use your main machine to seek help from the community.

1.3   How to use this book

The amount of information and knowledge you can extract from this book largely depends on how you use it. To harvest its full power, you will need access to a machine on which you can install Debian and ideally experiment to your heart's content without fearing the obliteration of your data or the loss of your computer system. Declining computer prices and Linux' minimal system requirements make this all the easier; you can install Debian on a Pentium II with 64 Mb RAM for this purpose, or even a much less powerful machine. If this is not possible, then you can do with any Linux-based machine, but you need root access. You can use the installation walkthrough in chapter 8.3.1 to set up a working sandbox in which to experiment.

Besides reading this book, try out everything you see and read on your lab machine. Add your own experiments to the ones in this book. Try out everything that comes to your mind. If you hose the machine, just install it again, or set up an installation in a subdirectory of your local hard disk (**chroot**). If the worst comes to the worst, you can restore your lab machine by copying the untouched snapshot over the hosed version from the host system. I will explain how to do that in chapter 8.3.1. Also, there is **pbuilder** to automatically manage an environment in which you basically cannot break anything (see chapter 9.6).

In addition to playing around and experimenting away, you should try to read as much as you can about the concepts introduced. Every Debian system comes with a plethora of documentation and information about the available utilities (see chapter 10). In addition, the Internet is full of useful tidbits (chapter 10.2 lists some starting points), and one of Debian's core strengths is its mailing lists. It is highly advisable to join **debian-user** and to start reading random posts as well as posts of interest even before you get started with this book. The best advice is not to hesitate to write back to the list if you know (or think you know) the answer, or if you can offer valuable input. Chapter 10.4.1 will pick up this topic in greater detail.

If you use Debian partly for the fun (*i.e.* if you like playing around with your system rather than doing actual work[5]), then you may want to stop by the next flea-market or check your neighborhood for old machines and save them from hitting the junk yard. Sun Microsystem's slogan "the network is the computer" holds for Unix in general, and thus for Debian as well. You can have a lot of fun with a single machine; you can have exponentially more fun with a home network, and you do not need fancy equipment for that.

Finally, it is a good idea to take notes during your experimentation. First, it is a good practice to get into, as a meticulously kept log book can be the difference between data loss and data rescue. Second, it will be almost impossible to remember everything you learn during the first few months of your Debian experience. Instead of having to research the same topics time and time again, it is useful to be able to refer to your own notes. I found Wikis[6] to be incredibly helpful for this sort of note taking.

---

[5]Those of you who believe in telekinesis, raise my hand!

[6]A Wiki is a colaborative web page that can be edited by everyone, even though access controls can be put in place to allow for closed-group use. Please refer to http://en.wikipedia.org/wiki/Wiki for more information.

1.4 Final notes

1.4.1 Conventions

Source code and shell interactions quoted in this book follow a standard convention and should be easy to understand. At times, screen output has been simplified for brevity and clarity, so please do not try to match it character by character.

Shell scripts use /bin/bash for interpretation, rather than /bin/sh (which is only used in a few simple cases). The main reasons for this choice are clarity and convenience, as bash supports some useful constructs that standard POSIX shells do not, and thus removes the need for complex workarounds. As bash is installed on every Debian system, it seems sensible to make use of it.

I assume a fresh directory for each example, which is denoted with the tilde (˜). In between approaches and topics, I assume the directory to automagically[7] empty itself.

File contents are usually shown as part of the corresponding cat or grep (or similar) invocation. This establishes the context and allows you to understand and use the examples without having to parse the text for the file data.

1.4.2 Keeping up to date

Debian's open development cycle puts the system into a state of continuous flux. While most tools covered in this book have been around for quite some while and are unlikely to change (with the exception of minor details), there is no guarantee. Software problems are reported and fixed every day, and while I have taken care to introduce the latest Debian developments, by the time this book is printed, some of the concepts may not be entirely state of the art. This said, the usage paradigms of almost all the tools mentioned in this book were established a while back and are unlikely to change. As Debian fixes bugs and adds new features, this book will continue to hold true.

In a fast-paced project such as Debian changes will happen, in fact they are a good thing, and of course I cannot predict the future. I will keep a list of changes at http://debiansystem.info/
changes to complement the book and keep you up to pace with the Debian system. I also do not anticipate this book to be error-free. Whenever I find mistakes, I will publish them at http://debiansystem.info/errata. If you find an error or an unclarity, I would really appreciate your feedback via email to errata@debianbook.info.

---

[7]"Automatically, with a touch of magic."

1.4.3 An urgent plea for feedback

The book you are holding in your hands has completely occupied my life for almost a year. As a result, it is one of the most comprehensive references for the Debian system and the community surrounding it. It would not have been possible to put together all the facts, data, and tidbits you find here without the active help of many members of the community, answering my questions, providing valuable additional information, and letting me know about changes I had not immediately noticed.

It is my goal to keep this book as up to date as possible for future editions. I therefore rely on your help. In addition to spotting errors, I ask you to drop me a line whenever you note a development that you deem relevant to the contents of this book. I have reserved the **feedback@debianbook.info** address for this purpose. Thank you very much in advance!

1.5 About the author

I promise to keep this short, but let me introduce myself. I am a PhD student at the Artificial Intelligence Laboratory of the University of Zurich, Switzerland, researching neurobiologically inspired models of learning in robots. I am also actively involved with RobotCub[8], an international endeavour to develop an open source robotics research platform. To earn my living, I work for the Munich-based AERAsec GmbH[9], teaching network security and privacy protection to professional system administrators.

Linux has been an integral part of my life ever since 1995, and I had my first encounter with Debian in 1997, albeit rather passively. Ever since then, my interest in the project and its operating system has grown exponentially. I became a developer in 2002, after spending at least three years fielding support questions on the **debian-user** mailing list, representing Debian at fairs, and fixing bugs.

My role within Debian is that of a simple developer with special interest in security, support, quality assurance, and public representation of Debian. I have tried hard to concentrate on my real life and reduce the time I spend on Debian, but have always found something to do for the project to keep me from working on my thesis. This book is perfect proof of my lack of discipline. I hope you will enjoy it.

I offer professional consultancy services for Debian and open source deployment with a strong focus on security and integration. I am based in Zurich, Switzerland but would travel within Europe and Asia. My rates depend on the project and its duration. I will donate up to a fifth of all profits to the Debian project and

---

[8]http://www.robotcub.org
[9]http://www.aerasec.de

other related open source projects. If you are interested, please write to me at madduck@debian.org.

1.6 Acknowledgements

First and foremost, I would like to thank all supporters of the Debian project. The beauty of the operating system as well as the spirit of the community made writing this book a marvelous experience! I am proud to be a member of the Debian team and wish all the members of the projects all the best for the future. Hopefully this book will help to improve Debian and its acceptance even further.

The book in your hands is the work of many people. I would not have been able to write it without the regulars of the **#debian-devel** IRC channels, who have put up with my daily presence for months and tried to be helpful all along. In particular, I would like to thank Goswin von Brederlow, Jeroen van Wolffelaar, Thomas Hood, Marco d'Itri, Joey Hess, Roland Mas, Frans Pop, Christian Perrier, Andres Salomon, Martin Michlmayr, Joshua M. Kwan, Colin Watson, Adeodato Simó, Manoj Srivastava, Branden Robinson, Steve Langasek, Andreas Barth, Peter Palfrader, Jaldhar Harshad Vyas, Wouter Verhelst, Thiemo Seufert, Matt Taggart, Junichi Uekawa, Thomas Lange, Peter Grandi, Matthias Klose, Norbert Tretkowski, Piotr Roszatycki, Gerfried Fuchs, Karsten M. Self, Lars Wirzenius, Helen Faulkner, Benjamin Mako Hill, Klaus Knopper, Pierre Morel, Warren Woodford, David Kammerer, Dirk Eddenbuettel, and many others for their cooperation and their help in making sure that I correctly documented their respective domains.

Most of my gratitude goes to the two people who spent countless hours with the manuscript, poked holes at it, and provided me with invaluable feedback: Hanspeter Kunz and Davor Ocelić. In addition, Don Armstrong, Lorrin Nelson, Martin Michlmayr, Sean Finney, and Stephan Beal inspected individual sections and made helpful suggestions; thank you too!

I want to thank the NetBSD team for their operating system, and the various discussions I witnessed on the **#netbsd/freenode.org** IRC channel. The Wikipedia encyclopedia has been most helpful (despite its restrictive licence); thanks to all those people who make it possible.

Outside of the free software community, many people have been instrumental in making this book happen. First of all, I want to thank my girlfriend Aline for her patience and loving support. I am greatly indebted to my parents, and my family and friends for putting up with my endless retreats to the computer screen. The same applies to Professor Rolf Pfeifer and the members of his Artificial Intelligence Laboratory at the University of Zurich: thanks for your understanding! Last but not least, I want to express my gratitude towards my publisher, Markus Wirtz for giving me the opportunity to write this book, and for his patience and advice[10], and Ian Travis for carefully reading over the final version and working with me through errors in my spelling and grammar.

[10]Talking to other authors, I seem to have been given a chance to work with one of the best publishers of the field... thanks for spoiling me on my first book, Markus.

2

The Debian project in a nutshell

If you want to build a ship, do not drum up the men to gather
wood, divide the work and give orders. Instead,
teach them to yearn for the vast and endless sea.
— Antoine de Saint-Exupéry

In this chapter, I introduce the Debian project and everything related to Debian that
is not part of the operating system. If you are anxious to get down to the bones of
the Debian system, skip this chapter. However, the Debian system and the Debian
project are inseparable; this will become more and more obvious as you learn more
about the Debian system. If you decide to skip this chapter for now, please make
sure you read it some time later. It contains many pieces of important information
for the serious Debian administrator.

2.1 A history lesson

When the Debian project was born, the Linux kernel was still in its infancy, but growing at a quick rate. Linus Torvalds, the founder of Linux, was inspired in part by the GNU project when he adopted an open community approach for the development of the Linux kernel. From the very beginning, enthusiastic and capable developers contributed to the kernel code and pushed improvements where they were most needed. The kernel became more and more usable, and the combination with the GNU user-space utilities allowed it to mature at an unforeseen pace, with updates published on a daily, if not hourly basis. Staying up to date became impossible for those interested in working *with* the system rather than *on* or *for* it. Administrators especially, whose task was to provide higher-level services to a group of users, were unable to track important updates (if for no other reason, then because the code was being released faster than it took to compile it on contemporary processors.

With computers becoming more and more integral in academic as well as commercial environments, it became increasingly important to be able to install them in larger numbers without continuously bootstrapping from scratch and compiling the required software by hand. As a result of these developments, several groups of developers teamed up to package precompiled software in a way that would allow for simple installation on end-user systems[1]. Despite the first business models created around the distribution of assorted free software, many of these distributions quickly fell prey to their own cause: with quality control and interoperability, maintaining a distribution was even more time-consuming and harder to handle than expected. As the count of external sources and updates grew, most groups threw in the towel and left buggy collections of aging software behind. In this situation, where bootstrapping and manually compiling a usable system was too daunting a task for the inexperienced, these distributions remained the primary entry point for new users — it is not difficult to imagine the grief that ensued.

In 1993, Ian Murdock, an undergraduate student at Purdue University and an avid user of the SLS distribution, which was similarly struggling at the time, found an answer to the dilemma: if the Linux kernel was developed decentrally by hundreds of people in parallel, then a distribution should be maintained decentrally by hundreds of people in parallel. Following Ian's first announcement[2], dozens of interested users joined forces and set the grounds for the Debian Linux project. In an article for Linux Journal[3], he brought forth a number of ideas, which were later formalised in the Debian Linux Manifesto (see appendix D). A new distribution with the ambitious goal of being carefully maintained and high quality had been born. In January 1994, the public was given a first glimpse at the release of Debian 0.91.

---

[1] Interestingly, recent developments on the distribution market are trying to revive the nostalgia.
[2] http://lists.debian.org/debian-devel-announce/2003/08/msg00008.html
[3] http://www.linuxjournal.com/node/2841; at this point I would like to thank the Linux Journal for deciding to open older articles to the general public without requiring a subscription (confirmed by the editor in chief, 27 January 2005)!

The approach to system administration taken by the Debian project could be poetically described as "academically-inspired applied functionalism." Debian developers approach problems patiently and academically in search of solid, long-term solutions. Consequentially, in the Debian system you will often find tools and concepts that are far more powerful and robust than needed for most situations; at the same time, however, these tools can be put to use in standard and complex scenarios alike, allowing administrators to stay on familiar ground while growing with their tasks.

Despite its academic spirit, Debian is everything but theoretical and inapplicable in the real world. "Applied functionalism" primarily refers to the system development process: the tools and concepts that make up the Debian system were not conceived *ad hoc* and put to use. Instead, they have emerged out of the practical needs of Debian's users. Administrators often struggle to keep their custom solutions synchronised with the rest of the Debian system. To attack this problem at the root, experienced administrators stepped forward and made clever approaches to common challenges available as part of the Debian system. In addition to the usual benefits of being freely available, the software also became an official part of the Debian system and improved the overall integration of its numerous components by enabling the reuse of standard solutions for common tasks.

Half of what makes a good system administrator is the ability to automate repetitive tasks before they become repetitive. The other half is to turn challenges around and reuse simple solutions rather than developing individual solutions for every problem[4]. The Debian system gives you everything you need to work by these principles. Repetitive tasks can be automated in a flexible way. And the universality and simplicity of the existing tools invites you to make use of them, rather than to expend extraneous effort implementing custom solutions that might break.

The project name "Debian" is a conglomeration of the names of Ian Murdock's wife Debra and Ian himself. It is officially pronounced "deb-ee-an" (/'debiən/), yet other pronunciations are common in other parts of the world. Chances are that people will recognise the name.

In the following, you will find a brief account of the history of Debian. The **debian-history** package, which resides in the official archive, also contains some information about the evolution of the project and its operating system. The document is available online[5], too. Note that it makes no attempt to be complete.

The early days

Ian Murdock steered the project from its inception to 1996. By that time, thanks to the invaluable work of Ian Jackson, **dpkg**, the Debian package management tool,

---

[4]Actually, the real trait that identifies the ingenius system administrator is laziness, and the tools to make sure others do not find out.

[5]http://www.debian.org/doc/manuals/project-history

had become an indispensable part of the distribution, and first ports of the Debian operating system to other processor architectures began to surface. Ian Murdock withdrew from the project in favour of his family as well as future plans, and Bruce Perens was invited to be the next leader.

Under Bruce's guidance, about 60 developers migrated all of Debian from the previous a.out to the ELF executable format and in June 1996, Debian 1.1 was released as Debian *buzz*[6] for the i386 architecture.

Debian 1.0 was never officially released because a CD-ROM manufacturer had mistakenly labelled an unreleased version of Debian as 1.0 in December 1995, so this version was skipped to avoid confusion.

The next version, Debian 1.2, codenamed *rex*, followed in December 1996. By that time, 120 developers were maintaining a total of 848 packages; the project had doubled in size since the release of *buzz*. Eight months later, in July 1997, 200 developers released Debian 1.3 *bo* with just under 1 000 packages.

Figure 2.1:
The Debian release
timeline

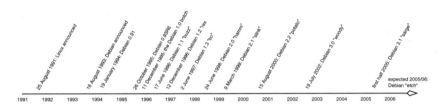

Formalising the endeavour

Bruce Perens, who led Debian through three releases in less than two years, also formalised and published two documents that became substantial to the Debian project: the Social Contract established the priorities and ideals of the project (see appendix E), and the Debian Free Software Guidelines (DFSG) defined the criteria a software's licence must meet in order for the product to qualify for inclusion in the official Debian archive (see appendix F). In addition, Bruce spearheaded the founding of Software in the Public Interest (SPI) as a legal entity to manage the parts of the project which can only be managed by a legal entity (such as trademark applications, as well as monetary funds).

---

[6]At that time, Bruce was an employee of Pixar, the company behind the famous computer-animation movie series *Toy Story*. Starting with Debian 1.1, every Debian release received a code name based on characters from the movie series: Debian 1.1: *buzz*; 1.2: *rex*; 1.3: *bo*; 2.0: *hamm*; 2.1: *slink*; 2.2: *potato*; 3.0: *woody*; 3.1: *sarge*; The next release following *sarge* will be named *etch*, based on the Etch-A-Sketch character of Toy Story. *sid*, the name of the malicious kid from the movie, is used as the code name for the Debian *unstable* repository, since the name is also an acronym for "still in development," or rather, "still in development" is a "backronym" for the code name, as it was coined only after the code name had been used in Debian.

Over the following years, the project grew in number of developers and available packages. By 1997, 400 developers were working together under the leadership of Ian Jackson culminating in the first multi-architecture release, Debian 2.0 *hamm*, in July. This release was fully based on libc6, consisted of 1 500 packages, and officially supported the **m68k** series architectures in addition to the **i386** platform.

Wichert Akkerman took over in the beginning of 1999 and, under his guidance, Debian 2.1 *slink* added support for the **Alpha** and **SPARC** architectures. 2 250 packages required the expansion of the official distribution set to a second CD. Debian 2.1 was released in March and included **Advanced Package Tool (APT)**. To date, **APT** maintains its highly innovative position as Debian's package management interface, providing a means to install software with unheard of simplicity and robustness.

Into the next millenium

One and a half years later, in August 2000, Debian released version 2.2, codenamed *potato*, which featured almost 4 000 packages and additionally supported the **PowerPC** and **ARM** architectures.

The interval to the next official release, Debian 3.0 *woody* was two years, which explains Debian's reputation of being outdated. By the time of the release, the project had grown to 900 developers managing just under 9 000 software packages (7 CDs) that ran equally well on a total of 11 architectures (**IA-64**, **HP PA-RISC**, **MIPS** (big and little endian), and **S/390** were added in these two years). Over this timespan, the project was restructured to accommodate its massive growth, adding the *testing* repository to facilitate the release cycle.

In April 2002, Bdale Garbee was elected project leader and in July 2002, *woody* was the first Debian release to feature internationalisation, and include cryptographic software as well as the popular Desktop environment **KDE**. **KDE** could not be distributed in Debian due to the non-free Q Public Licence of the underlying **Qt** library. It was a major accomplishment for the Debian project when **Qt**'s publisher, Trolltech, agreed to licence the library under the GNU Public Licence (GPL) for non-commercial use.

In 2003, Martin Michlmayr won the Debian project leader election and held the position for two years.

Debian today

At the time of writing, the next official release, Debian 3.1 *sarge* is expected in the first half of 2005. However, as before, this will only happen if the next release is ready by that time (see chapter 2.2.3). Despite great efforts to shorten the release cycle, the high goals for the next release[7] required more work than initially planned. *sarge* will provide a powerful new installation system and feature new versions of core software, *e.g.* GCC 3.3, Perl 5.8, XFree86 4.3, KDE 3.3, Gnome 2.8, and glibc 2.3.

The release following *sarge* will be named *etch*. Several of the developers want to move towards a time-based release cycle for *etch* and its successors. The size and complexity of the Debian project makes this an extraordinary challenge. A time-based release cycle can only be instituted when the entire project reaches a consensus and agrees to work towards a common goal. At this time of writing, such a goal has not been formulated, but a proposal to relax the support of some of the less popular architectures is under discusion[8]. An online brainstorming page about possible future release strategies has been launched on the Debian Wiki[9].

In April 2005, the Debian developers elected Branden Robinson as project leader. In his platform[10], Branden identified the lack of visibility of some of Debian's internal processes as a major source friction within the project, and pledged to increase the level of transparency. He is also a member of the newly-founded "Project Scud", a team of developers who joined forces to support the Debian project leader with his work[11]. This form of group leadership was heavily debated during the time leading up to the project leader election. Some developers feared Debian could split into a two-class society, and lead to the further exclusion of the general public from important processes (such as the release cycle). It remains to be seen whether Branden will succeed in dispelling these fears by establishing a working group leadership model for Debian while making the administrative internals of the Debian project more accessible to all developers.

2.2   The Debian philosophy

During the development cycle that followed Ian Murdock's initial formalisation of the goals, a number of priorities began to crystalise and form the basis for the philosophy by which the project abides. In its foundation documents — the Social Contract (see appendix E) as well as the DFSG (see appendix F) — the project formalises major parts of its philosophy, including the priorities governing the development of the Debian GNU/Linux operating system.

At first encounter, many of the priorities Debian chooses to follow seem purely idealistic and somewhat counter-productive. In fact, when analysing Debian's performance in competing for acceptance among home users, it seems like Debian is

[7] http://release.debian.org/sarge.html
[8] http://lists.debian.org/debian-devel-announce/2005/03/msg00012.html
[9] http://wiki.debian.net/index.cgi?ReleaseProposals
[10] http://www.debian.org/vote/2005/platforms/branden
[11] http://lists.debian.org/debian-project/2005/03/msg00035.html

tied to a stone and refusing to leave the stone behind. The prime example here would have to be the long periods of time between *stable* releases.

However, it is important to understand the philosophy behind the operating system to be able to understand the choice of priorities. When it is referred to as "the universal operating system" (which is Debian's slogan), this universality is available to those who use it, not to those better served by other operating systems. In particular, "the universal operating system" allows an administrator to maintain equivalent systems across a great variety of architectures and kernels (see chapter 4.5 and chapter 5.12.1). Debian does not try to be the best operating system for everyone.

Moreover, Debian does not try to follow or compete with the market leaders in the operating system sector. On the contrary, it often takes the lead by implementing robust, generic solutions and paving the way for standards to be formulated. On the momentous occasion of the tenth anniversary of the Debian project[12], Ian Murdock illustrated his vision of Debian's focus nicely:

> The focus shouldn't be on following the commercial distributions where they want to lead us, but rather on taking the lead — for example, by working with and strengthening existing vendor-neutral, community-owned standards efforts such as the Linux Standard Base (LSB).

Debian supports and participates in the Free Standards Group (FSG), LSB, and File-system Hierarchy Standard (FHS) efforts. In fact, because of its many innovative approaches, Debian is crucial to the development and acceptance of these standards. The Debian developers work very closely with upstream authors who need to ensure compliance with these standards in such a way as to minimise differences between a software and its Debian version. Thus, Debian works actively towards making upstream software LSB-compliant before accepting it, which is the main reason for the delay in LSB certification.

While *woody* came close to LSB 1.3, it did not pass the certification due to a small number of bugs. *sarge* is expected to be fully LSB 1.3 and nearly 2.0 compliant (a few bugs that need to be fixed still remain). Debian achieves LSB compliance through the installation of the lsb package. An LSB-compliant development environment is created by installing the lsbdev package. More information may be found on the Debian LSB status page[13], and there is also a mailing list for LSB issues: debian-lsb[14].

Instead of following commercial distributors who have the resources to influence the market, Debian steers clear of market dependence and focuses on the needs

---

[12]The Debian project turned ten on 16 August 2003, an event which was celebrated all over the globe (http://www.debconf.org/10years).

[13]http://people.debian.org/~taggart/lsb

[14]http://lists.debian.org/debian-lsb

of its users and the improvement of free software products, while meticulously upholding its quality standards. Before you start thinking that you have heard this said many times before: it actually works in practice. Strict adherence to quality standards has been an integral part of the Debian project since the early days and govern major aspects of the project and the development of the Debian GNU/Linux operating system up until the present day. Debian users have come to rely on the system's robustness and stability, and it is top priority for the project to walk the thin line between providing upgrades while keeping the operating system rock solid.

Perhaps one of the most distinguishing factors of the Debian project is that it tries to minimise the differences between the software in its archive and the original versions released by the respective upstream authors. Not having to maintain a patch set for every upstream release certainly eases the maintainer's job, which is one of the main reasons why Debian maintainers like to work closely with the upstream authors; when an improvement is made to a software as a result of its use as part of the Debian system, this improvement is pushed upstream, and the maintainer of the package does not have to worry about it anymore. Staying as close as possible to the upstream version also allows Debian users to find support in the upstream forums. While certain distributions provide heavily modified versions of software in their archives, which are subsequently unsupportable by the original authors, Debian users can profit from resources not specific for Debian.

At the same time, however, Debian developers are not afraid to go their own ways to address the users' needs better than the upstream authors do. At times, the Debian developers develop alternate configuration paradigms to work around limitations of the original configuration mechanisms. If these changes turn out to be improvements, they often flow back into the upstream software and thus become standards.

A great deal of the Debian system is based on the works of other, non-Debian developers. In fact, the Debian system would be nowhere if not for the innumerable achievements in the free software community upon which the Debian developers have always built their system. It is therefore only natural that the Debian developers hand any improvements and derived or original works back to the community to let others profit in similar ways. After all, the Social Contract (see appendix E) places the free software community on the same priority level as all Debian users.

Giving back to the community is thus respresentative of the Debian philosophy. However, it is also the basis for the continued growth of the free software community, for the standardisation of its products, and ultimately for the competitive challenges that Linux and other free software projects have become for commercial vendors. Competition helps to ensure quality; by giving back to the community, the Debian project ensures that users have a choice.

2.2.1   Debian and its users

Debian wants to be the best operating system in the eyes of its users. Nobody is forced to use Debian, but those who choose to use the operating system can do more than install and operate a machine: they can also voice their opinions and initiate change. It is users that steer the project, and they are free of external influences and pressure. The Social Contract carves this mantra in stone: "We will place [our users' and the free software community's] interests first in our priorities" (see appendix E).

Users steer the project

Contrary to popular belief — especially among people with experience mainly in commercial environments — software is not developed by a few pizza-eating geniuses who are unapproachable by mere mortals. In the free software community especially, software is developed by users of the software (who still eat pizza), and the development process encompasses far more than writing code in cryptic languages. Software development also relies on people coming up with ideas, testers, individuals who write documentation, and people playing along with others nicely.

It is here where Debian profits greatly from the close tie-in between users and developers (who are also users). On the one hand, Debian developers are present on the community forums day and night, and users and developers alike work hand in hand to solve problems and clarify misunderstandings. On the other hand, every package has a dedicated developer, or an email address to reach a team of developers for more complicated packages (see chapter 10.5). While package maintainers generally do not have abundant resources to field support requests, they will be happy to listen to your suggestions and consider proposed improvements.

The Debian developers make these kinds of improvements available to the upstream authors to allow the entire free software community to benefit. Similarly, all tools developed specifically for Debian are available to everyone, whether you use Debian or not. For example, APT, which was developed for the Debian operating system and is now optionally available in other distributions, such as Fedora and Mac OS X (Fink).

As stated before, improvements do not necessarily have to involve programming. To give another example, I am notoriously bad at documentating the code I write and cling to the principle that "code is its own best documentation," which is not how most users would see it. In several cases, users of my libraries stepped in to fill the gap and asked for permission to author documentation for my work. At other times, users have contributed valuable comments and suggestions to improve the packaging of some software I maintain. Often, I thought my software was doing everything I needed until a user requested a feature that revolutionised the way I employed the programme.

This exchange of ideas and thoughts is not specific to Debian, it was made possible by the growth of the Internet. What Debian fostered, however, was a large base of people interested in accepting this invaluable feedback and acting upon it. Debian's priorities (users and free software, see appendix E) give the project the ability to listen and incorporate the ideas that are generated, rather than having to follow a strategy or plan. The Debian project actively furthers the evolution of free software by effectively and efficiently closing the gap between the user and the large number of authors responsible for the pieces of software which run on that user's machine.

Open to the public

As part of its commitment to its users, Debian makes operating system development completely transparent to the public. Discussions related to design choices in packaging and other issues are held publicly on the **debian-devel** mailing list[15], and contributions are *not* restricted to developers. In fact, it is quite common for interested users to join these discussions and contribute their thoughts and suggestions. It cannot be stressed enough that Debian would be nowhere if it were not for the massive input the project has received from its user base. Rather than developing for their users, the Debian developers lay open their cards and work on the Debian system together with their users. Of course, participation in the project is not required to use the Debian system.

As an integral part of Debian's development, the Bug Tracking System (BTS) also resides publicly on the Internet (see chapter 10.6). In the Social Contract, the project promises to "keep our entire bug-report database open for public view at all times. Reports that users file on-line will immediately become visible to others" (see appendix E). Along the same lines, Debian does not attempt to hide security problems from its users but works closely with upstream authors and other distributors to protect its users in an optimal fashion (see chapter 7 for the juicy details).

With all the openness, it must be noted that two communication forums remain exclusive to developers: the **debian-private** mailing list as well as the Internet Relay Chat (IRC) channel with the same name, **#debian-private** on irc.debian.org. The main purpose of these forums is for developers to announce leaves of absence, which could be harmful if publicly available (advertising to the world when you are away from your home is inviting intruders to exploit the situation). Other uses include the discussion of problems related to individuals, or financial and organisational issues, where it is deemed that disclosure would not be in the interest of the parties involved. Issues related to the operating system, or otherwise relevant to the user base, are highly discouraged and pushed to open forums immediately.

---

[15]Or a more specific list for a certain topic. For instance, development of packages related to the X server system are commonly found on the **debian-x** mailinglist.

2.2.2 Free beer and free speech

One of the continuously recurring themes in Debian is the topic of free software. Efforts to ensure the freedom of software distributed with Debian enjoy a similarly high priority as users of the operating system. The Free Software Foundation identifies four kinds of freedom[16], namely the freedom to

- run the program, for any purpose.

- study how the program works, and adapt it to your needs.

- redistribute copies so you can help your neighbour.

- to improve the program, and release your improvements to the public, so that the whole community benefits.

For the purpose of the following discussion, these types of freedom can be condensed to produce two categories of software:

- The first category includes software which may be copied and used without payment. The distinction is between commercial and non-commercial providers, that is, between those looking to make money off the software and those who make it available to people without requiring a mite in return. Software must be "free as in free beer" to satisfy this requirement of freeness. Note that it is acceptable to charge for the distribution of free software, but paid copies are governed by the same rules as their free counterparts and may be redistributed for free.

- that can be freely used, copied, studied, modified, and redistributed by the user. This applies to the freedom the user obtains along with the software. Here, the distinction is between proprietary and non-proprietary software, that is between software whose internal workings are protected as intellectual property, and software available to everyone without restrictions. Such software is commonly referred to as "*libre*" (which is the French adjective alongside the noun "freedom"). To comply with this definition, software must be "free as in free speech."

These two definitions may well collide. Many programmes are available at no charge, but the software may only be used, not reverse engineered or distributed in modified form. On the other hand, some companies licence software source code to paying users, but forbid redistribution in non-binary form.

Despite popular belief, free software is not the same as software developed under the open source model. When the term "open source" was coined, it applied

---

[16]http://www.fsf.org/philosophy/free-sw.html

to the same software as the term "free software." A difference started to evolve between the two classes when the supporters of free software increasingly began to emphasise the philosophy behind the freedom of software, while the followers of open source software pragmatically harped on the improved development cycle and cheaper costs.

While open source software is generally available at no cost, it is not always free. A prominent example is qmail, a mail transfer agent. While the source code of qmail is readily available, the author chose to restrict the distribution of modifications in binary form, a restriction that contravenes the principles of free software and violates the Debian Free Software Guidelines (DFSG)[17]. Free software is a subset of open source software. More specifically, free software is always open source, but open source software may well be non-free.

Free software is, however, not totally free of constraints - it is governed by the licence and copyright statement. The software licence aims to give users the flexibility to put the software to productive use, while protecting the rights of the authors, who can carefully but freely choose the licences to govern the release of their works. The copyright statement serves to protect the rights of the author, who chooses the licence and is free to modify it (within the terms of the licence)[18].

Debian and free software

Debian takes an extraordinary and somewhat radical approach to free software. One of the fundamental documents of the Debian project is the DFSG; it regulates the availability of software in Debian according to its licence.

The Debian software pool is separated into three sections, sorted in decreasing order of the freedom of the software they contain[19]:

main

> The *main* archive contains software in full compliance with the DFSG. Furthermore, any package in *main* may only depend on other packages also available in *main*.

---

[17]Since qmail is in violation with the FHS in many ways, it needed to be amended to comply with the FHS for installaton on the Debian system. The licence forbids distribution of a modified version in binary form, so Debian cannot provide the package in its archive. Instead, the maintainer had to create the qmail-src package, which can compile and build the qmail package on the user's system.

[18]Obviously, if an author releases a piece of software under a free licence and then later chooses to commercialise the product, any code previously available continues to remain available under the free licence. Only software in the *public domain* is completely unrestricted and does not have an owner.

[19]The gory details of rules governing the Debian archive are available as part of the policy manual: http://www.debian.org/doc/debian-policy/ch-archive.html

contrib

> Packages in *contrib* are free themselves, but depend[20] on software available in *contrib* or *non-free*. In addition, packages in *contrib* might also depend on software that has not or cannot be packaged. Please note that packages in *contrib* are not actively supported. A maintainer may well support the software, but you should not rely on it. Also, the security team does not tend to the *contrib* archive.

non-free

> Finally, software in *non-free* is not in accordance with the DFSG. As regards support, *non-free* is the same as *contrib*: the archive is not officially supported, and security updates are not provided by the security team.

The *non-US* is a relic of the times of US American export laws, mainly related to cryptographic software. After the export restrictions were relaxed, Debian moved the software from *non-US* to the three official archives (see above), according to their freeness. At this time of writing, only a single package remains in *non-US*, and the archive is likely to be removed in the near future.

Every Debian package installs the licence(s) and copyright statement(s) governing the software it contains in /usr/share/doc/<packagename>/copyright. In addition, you can find discussions of the DFSG-freeness of common licences online[21]. Software that meets the requirements of the DFSG is commonly referred to as *DFSG-free*. Software which does not qualify for inclusion in the *main* archive is called *non-free*.

The importance of free beer

I hardly need to argue the importance of free beer. Beer is an essential nutrient[22], and if it is available for free, then all the better.

Believe it or not, the same holds for software. While in most industrialised parts of the globe, new computer hardware comes with an operating system and programmes for basic needs, this is not the case in a large number of less developed countries. Furthermore, the software accompanying new hardware frequently only covers the bare essentials and additional software must be purchased to accomodate the needs of users or corporations. Standard software prices are typically astronomical in these areas. Unless users have no issue with unauthorised copying of software, they depend on operating systems like Debian, which provide a complete environment at no charge, and will continue to be available in the future. Even if the members of the Debian project officially started to charge money for

---

[20]A dependency here is defined as the union of the relations **Depends**, **Recommends**, and **Build-Depends**, and thus includes dependencies for both running and building the software.

[21]http://wiki.debian.net/index.cgi?DFSGLicences

[22]I was born in Munich and baptised in the brew (no, my parents did not actually dump me in beer.)

their work, the terms of the DFSG ensure that anyone else can continue distributing (and developing) Debian for free.

Debian is committed to servicing every single user independent of background or financial status. The Social Contract promises that the entire collection of software available in the Debian (*main*) archive will be usable without a charge. Furthermore, Debian tries to maintain every software with respect to security problems.

The importance of free speech

The Debian archive has been partitioned into the aforementioned sections for the benefit of the Debian users. The *main* section comprises about 97% of the Debian archive and provides everything needed to run a production system. Therefore, for most users, it is quite sufficient to use only the *main* section of the APT sources to install and maintain their systems. On such systems, the user is free to use, study, copy, modify, and redistribute the software without restrictions[23].

By using only software from the *main* archive, the user can stay on the safe side legally, to the best of Debian's knowledge and efforts, no matter where the software is used. Debian *sarge* installs only components from *main*, if packages from *contrib* or *non-free* are needed, the user has to modify /etc/apt/sources.list accordingly and explicitly request their installation.

The additional ability to use Debian for whatever purpose a user thinks fit is equally important. Debian does not allow any discrimination of persons, groups, or fields of endeavour. Debian may be put to use by anyone for anything, even in morally debateable domains, such as genetic research or warfare. Debian does not attempt to define what is acceptable and what is not because it would put a limit on the freedom of its users.

The importance of free software

Free software also prevents the so-called *vendor lock-in*, a situation in which the user is dependent on a vendor or manufacturer for certain parts of a product and a switch to a different product would encompass unbearable costs. Since Debian's main archive is not specific to Debian, anything you use on a Debian system can also be used on other systems with similar capabilities. Using Debian therefore does not mean being dependent on Debian[24]. The DFSG states that any software in *main* is licenced for free use, and that this licence is not specific to Debian. In short, any package within Debian's *main* archive is also freely usable outside of Debian

---

[23]This does not always hold. For example, some software requires modifications to be distributed alongside the original source, rather than properly integrated with the source code. While Debian does not advocate such restrictions, it tolerates them, as stated in the fourth clause of the DFSG (see appendix F). Therefore, before applying modifications to software with the intent to redistribute the modified version, it is a good idea to check /usr/share/doc/<packagename>/copyright, which every package must provide.

[24]Unless, of course, you start to appreciate the "Debian Way" and become addicted.

under identical terms. However, it is important to keep in mind that Debian is not a legal office, nor does it have professional legal advocates. The above is therefore not a guarantee. Nevertheless, violations are not ignored and the developers will take appropriate action to maintain the freedom of the *main* archive to the best of their abilities.

Free software (and therefore the entire *main* archive) also provides for independence from the respective authors. If a project is moving in a direction unfavourable to you, you are free to team up with others and create a forked edition. As an obvious example, all of Debian's own administrative utilities, such as the package management system, are available for use outside of Debian[25]. Thus, if you ever get sick and tired of Debian but cannot imagine life without **APT**, you are free to go and take it with you.

Free software will not die. This means that everything you **apt-get install** will persist. You can spend time learning every detail of a software, and you have access to the same means as everybody else to keep it working or even improve it. When building systems, you know that you can always reinstall, that the software itself will always be available. Its development may stop (forcing you to possibly fix bugs yourself), but it will always be free software.

Finally, free software packages constitute a software ecosystem. The Debian *main* archive boosts the potential of the Unix principle of modularised toolkits. Small (or not so small) pieces of software serve to provide services which are directly or indirectly usable by other software, without imposing licence restrictions thanks to the DFSG. This can lead to phenomena such as co-evolution and shortened maturation cycles, generally yielding flexible and modular solutions with a comparatively short amount of development.

2.2.3 Debian and the market

Possibly the most frequently asked question related to Debian is when the next version will be released. The answer has always been the same: "when it is ready." While this has driven some users up the wall, others have come to rely on it. As part of the Social Contract (see appendix E), Debian promises to treat its users with the highest priority. Therefore, Debian does not and will not make compromises when it comes to the quality of the distribution. Users who wish to remain on the cutting edge can run *testing* or *unstable* (see chapter 8.2). Those who need a rock-solid system have Debian *stable*.

The Debian system is driven purely by quality, not by the market. A Debian release is made when the goals for the release have been met, all release-critical bugs (see chapter 10.6.3) have been fixed, and the developers can call it *stable* with a clear conscience. No previous Debian release has taken as long as *Sarge* to be-

---

[25]APT has been ported to RedHat Package Manager (RPM)-based distributions, for example.

come *stable*. One of the biggest reasons for the delay was due to designing and implementing the new installation system from scratch (see chapter 3). Building an installation system for eleven architectures is a task second to none. However, it seems as if the **debian-installer** team has succeeded in providing a flexible and extensible base for future enhancements and improvements. Thus, the installer will probably not hold up future release cycles and can still be extended to allow for new architectures and features.

2.3 Licencing issues

Over the years, the Debian project has often been in the news, and some of the time, the news has not necessarily been pleasant. Especially in the period leading up the release of Debian *sarge*, one recurring topic has been Debian's strict adherence to the DFSG and the ensuing problems with licenses that do not meet the requirements put forth in the DFSG. Debian has in the past been forced to remove software that does not meet the requirements of the DFSG from its archive, an action that has had serious ramifications for its users at times.

In fact, to the casual observer it may seem that the Social Contract (see appendix E) contradicts itself. While it promises that Debian will remain free forever, it also establishes the interests of its users as top priority of the project. When software is removed from the archive in an effort to conform to the first promise of the Social Contract, it undoubtedly inconveniences a number of users who rely on the removed software. On the other hand, other users rely on the freeness of Debian's archive and are in favour of the strict enforcing of the DFSG.

Obviously, when any project makes decisions in the interest of its users, it can only make decisions in the interest of the majority of its users. However, Debian has no official way to determine the preferences of its users, or put numbers to them (*c.f.* chapter 5.11.10). The Social Contract promises the freedom of the archive. In order to avoid inconveniencing users of a package that has to be removed due to licencing issues, the package is moved to *non-free* as long as it can be legally distributed and a developer agrees to maintain it there. As a result, the *main* archive gets rid of licence problems; its users can again enjoy freedom without worrying about legal risks. At the same time, those in need of non-free software can install programmes from *non-free*.

Leading up to the release of Debian *sarge*, the project almost shot itself in the foot. As part of an editorial amendment of the Social Contract in April 2004[26], the Debian project reached a general resolution and extended its promise from 100% free software to 100% freeness of all its components. While only few realised the consequences of this change at time of vote, the project was hit all the harder when it became apparent that this change requires the removal of many system

---

[26]http://www.debian.org/vote/2004/vote_003

components that do not meet the requirements put forth in the DFSG. While some purists argue that the change will not affect Debian, it seems obvious that the removal of large numbers of device drivers as well as software documentation could easily inconvenience the majority of users.

Three types of components in the Debian archive seem to be affected by the change: firmware, binary data, and documentation. Firmware refers to the code a driver loads onto an extension card for processing by the card's processor for special features (or full operation). Binary data refers mainly to media files such as images and sounds. Documentation includes manuals and reference documents licenced under the GNU Free Documentation Licence (GFDL), which is non-free[27].

Fortunately, many Debian developers recognised the negative implications of such a move and feared that the removal would unnecessarily delay the release of *sarge* even more. In addition, no other free software project had previously questioned freedom in such a broad sense. Thus, before taking premature actions, the extents of a rigorous approach to freedom such as advocated by the editorial amendment must first be determined. In another vote, it was thus decided to delay the changes to the Social Contract until after the release of *sarge*[28].

Debian is venturing into unknown terrain and it is currently uncertain what will happen with respect to the promise of freeness of all its components. Supporters of the absolute approach of removing everything that is not DFSG-free from Debian can use the Social Contract itself as best argument for the move. Nevertheless, the arguments put forward by their opponents are not to be underrated.

- Firmware does *not* run on the computer processor but is evaluated on a separate device, which does not run Debian. Thus, does the Social Contract apply? Also, what exactly is firmware? In its broadest definition, firmware does not have to be executable but could consist of data to be processed. In this light, would constants and magic numbers not also be considered firmware? If so, what is the source code of a constant or a magic number?

- The DFSG requires the source code to be available for modification and redistribution. What exactly is the source code of an image, or of a sound file? A free licence such as the GPL requires source code to be available in "the preferred format for modification." Of course, you can load a Portable Network Graphics (PNG) file into **The Gimp** and modify it, but due to the lossy compression algorithms, it will be almost impossible to undo that modification in another editing session. The same applies, *e.g.*, to Ogg Vorbis sound files. Would Debian thus have to ship the X Bitmap (XBM) and Wavetable file format (WAV) counterparts for binary data files to be DFSG-free? Is the availability of source code not supposed to enable the recreation of the "final product?" Would the source code

---

[27]The Debian project is working with the GNU project to resolve these problems. Please refer to http://people.debian.org/~srivasta/Position_Statement.html for more information.

[28]http://www.debian.org/vote/2004/vote_004

of an image not rather consist of all the brush strokes and edits to an image? What if a programme was used to generate the image, which in itself is not free or not part of Debian? What if the image was created in **Adobe Photoshop**?

- Among other things, the GFDL forbids the omission or change of "invariant sections." Such sections can only exist as part of "secondary sections," whose contents must not be concerned with the matter documented in the text. Thus, secondary sections hold copyright and acknowledgements, which are arguably to be propagated to derived works. Is the GFDL then really non-free? Still, invariant sections allow for nasty acts[29], so it limits the freedom. On an unrelated note, removing documentation from the system certainly inconveniences many users and makes Debian unusable (or mostly so) to those without permanent or reasonable Internet access. If the Social Contract promises that Debian will honour the desires of its users, how can this dilemma be resolved?

As you can see, a great number of questions remain unanswered[30]. While Debian hopes to exercise its influence and to cause change, *e.g.* a revised GFDL, or vendors releasing their driver firmware under a free and open licence, it is impossible at this moment to forecast the future of such licence issues. The Debian project promises *etch* to be fully conformant to the Social Contract in any case.

The **debian-legal** mailing list as well as the **#debian-legal** IRC channel **irc.debian.org** are the forums dedicated to discussions that focus on freedom and licencing issues. Please make sure you search the list archives[31] before posting. Also, the Debian Wiki has a page on common licences and their DFSG status[32].

2.4   The Debian community

2.4.1   Organisation of the project

The Debian project is organised according to the structure described in its constitution[33], which establishes the decision-making bodies and the processes for making decisions within the project. Figure 2.2 is a rough approximation of the structure of the Debian project. Many groups, subprojects, and individuals cannot be clearly classified or outlined in a meaningful way. However, the image gives an overview of the most important bodies and their relationships. The list of current occupants of the official positions is available on the Web[34].

---

[29] Read http://slashdot.org/articles/03/04/20/1357236.shtml for a few examples.

[30] At http://lists.debian.org/debian-vote/2005/03/msg00152.html, you can find a number of challenging licence considerations for different data types.

[31] http://lists.debian.org/debian-legal

[32] http://wiki.debian.net/index.cgi?DFSGLicences

[33] http://www.debian.org/devel/constitution

[34] http://www.debian.org/intro/organization

As shown, the all-encompassing group is the set of users. Within the Debian project, everybody is also a user of the system, which makes for the close relationship between users and developers and also provides most of the motivation for the volunteers running the project. Users can apply to join the project (see chapter 2.5.2), and if approved, they join the developer body. Alternatively, numerous areas exist in which users can contribute to the project without having to go through the application process (see chapter 2.5.1).

The set of developers makes up the major organisational body of Debian. At the time of writing, the Debian project consisted of about 950 developers, each of whom was taking care of one or more parts of the project, be it package management, documentation, internationalisation, organisation, or infrastructure maintenance, to name but a few. Participation in any of these projects is voluntary, generally without an ironclad commitment, which allows people to dedicate their available time to any project they wish.

Possibly one the most important aspects of the Debian community is its international orientation. Even though the project was founded in the United States, Debian developers live all over the world[35], allowing for diversity and political independence, among other traits. As many aspects of the project are security-sensitive, trust among the developers plays an important part (see chapter 2.4.3).

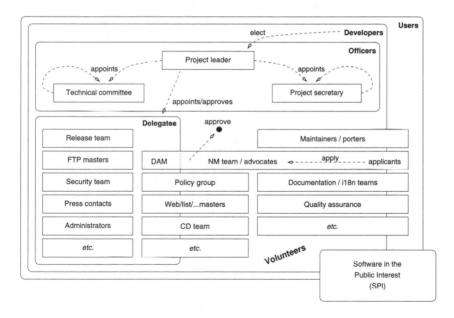

Figure 2.2:
A rough sketch of
Debian's organisation

---

[35]http://www.linuks.mine.nu/debian-worldmap

The project officers

The developer body itself is organised in a flat hierarchy. At the top of the hierarchy sits the project leader, who is elected annually by the developers. Every developer has a vote, and every developer can become a candidate. The project leader guides the project and and is responsible for its coordination. The project leader should be a driving force for new directions and can focus developer attention on specific areas of problems. The leader has various special powers which are rarely used. However, the developer collective may cast a majority vote to overrule the project leader's decision, which has never happened.

Upon being elected, the project leader appoints the officers (together with the previous occupants of these positions) and delegates a number of tasks to chosen individuals and teams. Subsequently, the project leader is free to replace officers and delegates as appropriate. The project leader may be replaced by the chairman of the technical committee together with the project secretary, should it be necessary (*e.g.* in case of death or absence without leave).

Assisting the project leader are the members of the technical committee, fronted by the chairman. The technical committee's task is to monitor the technical aspects of the distribution. In exceptional cases, it may require a developer to take a certain course of action over another, if it is deemed to be in the better interest of the project and its users. The project secretary mainly coordinates elections and other votes. Furthermore, the secretary's job is to resolve disputes on the interpretation of the constitution.

The delegates

The delegates receive deputations from the project leader and are given special powers in specific task domains. For instance, the project leader delegates the task of Debian account maintenance to the Debian Account Manager (DAM), and the job of interacting with the media to the press contact. Within their domain, the delegates have the freedom to act according as they judge best. In addition, to prevent concentration of power, the delegates can make certain decisions which the project leader may not make directly. Such decisions are mainly concerned with project membership.

Delegation is not an official or necessarily visible process. In addition, it need not be an explicit process. Many delegate positions are held by people for years, and the project leader simply accepts their status by not choosing replacements. The delegate must have all the necessary competence in the delegated domain to make decisions (or else should not be chosen as a delegate). The project leader cannot override a delegate's decision once it is spoken. Therefore, it is in the leader's best interest to choose someone trustworthy and capable. The project leader may replace delegates given sufficient reasons. However, a single decision made, possibly in disfavour of the leader, is not a sufficient reason.

Notable delegate positions include the release managers, the security team, and the FTP masters. The release managers set the goals for the next *stable* release, and coordinate and supervise the release process. This involves scheduling freezes and carving the final release date in stone. A separate *stable* release manager then takes over. The security team's job is to cooperate with security teams from other projects to provide security-related fixes to software in the *stable* archive as soon as possible. Finally, the FTP masters are in charge of the Debian archive, deciding what software is allowed into the archive and what must be removed.

The developer collective

At the bottom, albeit all-encompassing, resides the remainder of developers, each acting within their own self-assigned niche of the project. Although it is preferred for a developer to maintain a package (a common but not absolutely necessary requirement for becoming a Debian developer; see chapter 2.5.2), many other tasks call for volunteers. Be it documentation and internationalisation endeavours, user support on mailing lists and on IRC channels (see chapter 10.4.1 and chapter 10.4.3 respectively), or simply fixing bugs and providing ideas on how to improve the distribution, a single developer can take on as many responsibilities as desired. It is important to realise that these responsibilities are by choice as nobody within the project is in a position to order a developer to do something; not even the project leader.

While the individual developer may be perceived to be at the very bottom of Debian's organisational structure, the developer majority can overrule any organisational body within Debian's structure, including the project leader, by way of general resolution. General resolutions are Debian's primary means of reaching a consensus on non-trivial decisions. A general resolution may be proposed by anyone and will be opened for vote when enough seconders back up the proposer's call. Every developer may participate in the vote, and if a majority is reached[36], the resolution takes effect immediately and cannot be overruled (except by means of another general resolution).

The Debian users

The Debian users and the community they form are unquestionably the most important entity for the project. The Social Contract defines its users as the project's top priority (see appendix E). Debian's main purpose is thus to meet the requirements of its user base. Without its users, the project would not have a purpose. Every developer is also a user, but a critical mass of "normal users" is paramount for the Debian system to stay universal and competitive (see chapter 2.2.1).

[36]Debian uses the Condorcet method to allow its developers to voice preferences rather than simple votes; see http://en.wikipedia.org/wiki/Condorcet_method

Even though normal users cannot cast votes, they can influence the direction of the project in a plethora of ways, for instance by participating in discussions on mailing lists (see chapter 10.4.1), filing bug reports (see chapter 10.6), or stepping forward in a proactive fashion to fix problems the way they would like them fixed, before someone else gets around to it.

Ultimately, every Debian user may become a Debian developer after establishing trust and demonstrating familiarity with the rules and proceedings of the projects, as well as skills pertaining to Debian's package management system and tools (see chapter 2.5.2).

SPI — Software in the Public Interest

Without being a part of the Debian project, SPI[37] is part of its organisation. SPI was founded by Bruce Perens to act as a legal entity of the Debian project. In as such, it holds all trademarks for Debian, owns all of its monetary and material assets, and represents the project in legal matters. In addition, SPI embodies an economic entity and can accept tax-deductible donations for the project, at least within the United States of America. SPI has no authority over decisions cast within the Debian project. Along the same lines, Debian claims no authority over SPI other than over the use of Debian property held and managed by the SPI.

2.4.2   Social aspects of the community

The community behind the Debian project is similar to the communities of other comparable projects. Nevertheless, the Debian community has a very strong reputation, which makes it stand out at times. Debian has the largest developer base of all free software distributions, and it constitutes more of a meta project than a simple project, as it consists of a plethora of subprojects whose only common ground in many cases is that they are part of the Debian system. While other projects of comparable size or of comparable diversity exist, Debian is unique in the combination of the two and in the way it organises the production of the Debian system. Those who support the community commonly describe it as unparalleled in terms of it dynamics and competence, and many rank the level of support available from the community as the most important factor in choosing Debian. At the same time, the Debian community is often badmouthed as arrogant and too idealistic for the real world.

It is not the purpose of this book to argue either position. The only way to decide is to get involved with the community and see for yourself. If you are new to the project, it is probably a good idea to get to know the community before it gets

[37]http://www.spi-inc.org

to know you. In the following, I put together some useful facts about the Debian community[38].

First of all, it is important to realise that the community is made up of volunteers. Developers typically work for the project because they use the Debian operating system, believe in its philosophy, and/or otherwise enjoy contributing to a cooperative effort without commercial strings attached, and without anyone ordering them around[39]. The same applies to regular users who contribute to the community. The community welcomes anyone who keeps that in mind, and abides by the usual rules of decency and etiquette expected from people sharing common grounds (even if those grounds are virtual).

Another important point to consider is that members of the community (or "users", for short) try to be helpful whenever possible. Nevertheless, nobody likes to do someone else's work. Thus, you are unlikely to find answers without doing your part first, which means using the available resources before approaching other people for help (see chapter 10). If it is clear from the details you provide that you have thought about the problem, tried to contain it, and gone to search in other places before asking for support, people will gladly offer assistance. Maybe the best way to find answers is by asking the right questions in the right way, and of the right people. Eric S. Raymond has put together a delightful piece on how to ask smart questions[40], which I suggest you read. Having read and understood the text, you need not be afraid of asking stupid questions in a Debian forum.

A nice trait of the Debian community is the equality with which everyone is treated. For new users and veterans alike, the primary focus of attention is the problem at hand[41]. This also means that the Debian community does not consist of a crowd of needy users and a bunch of gurus that answer questions. Instead, everyone is encouraged to partake and provide helpful advice, and people do. On the one hand, people like to show off their knowledge, and if it is helpful to others, all the better. On the other hand, following the community discussions and pitching in advice here and there has proven to be an excellent way to learn more about the operating system, and is advocated as such by many users[42].

---

[38]Please keep in mind that I am not claiming that the Debian community is unique. Much of what follows is equally applicable to other projects. I am just introducing the Debian community and laying out the facts.

[39]It is not that being told what to do is inherently bad, but it often causes quality to give way to market or time pressure, and working on products without the ability to maintain a quality level can be painful.

[40]http://www.catb.org/~esr/faqs/smart-questions.html

[41]Debian would not be Debian if long-standing users did not continuously pull each other's legs and exchange witty and sarcastic comments. However, the problem at hand maintains top priority and after bashing one another for a bit, Debian folks are usually quick to come up with helpful advice.

[42]These two patterns of behaviour are quite common in the open source world. For a complete analysis of their evolution and motivations, I refer you to Eric S. Raymond's book *The cathedral and the bazaar* (http://www.catb.org/~esr/writings/cathedral-bazaar). Another good read for those truly interested is *Understanding Open Source Software Development* by Feller and Fitzgerald (http://opensource.ucc.ie/uossd).

In the community forums (see chapter 10.4), you will find a healthy balance of technical discussion (most), humour (some), unrelated topics (few), and flamewars (rare)[43]. Overall, interactions within the community generally have a high level of productivity, and interesting discussions sometimes ensue once a solution has been found. Frequently, these discussions culminate in improvements made to the system, either on the technical or usability side, or in the documentation. The Debian policy, which will be discussed in great depth in chapter 5.7, plays an important role in the community. The policy standardises the organisation of files and the logic of administrative processes to allow the large developer collective to provide an integrated system rather than an aggregation of different packages. At the same time, the policy also makes sure that the Debian system stays the same across all installations, independent of architecture and minor version. Everyone works with the same tools on the same ground, and solutions can be found rapidly.

To sum this up, the community is made up mostly of users who are members by choice and contributors by conviction. Newcomers are often very eager to help others in an attempt to give back to the community. Others acknowledge their lack of experience with software development and contribute towards the documentation or the maintenance of web pages. The cooperative development found in and around the Debian operating system provides a prolific basis for hobbyists, enthusiasts, and professionals alike to work towards a common goal.

2.4.3   Social aspects of the group of developers

The Debian organisation is very open and flat. Apart from the officers, delegates, and a few other privileged positions, everybody in the developer team has equal rights. The prime example is the openness of the BTS and the Debian archive under equal terms to every single developer. Should one developer neglect a certain package, then another can simply take over and provide a fixed version for official inclusion in the archive without the need to acquire special privileges. When a maintainer is temporarily unavailable, other developers can provide Non-Maintainer Upload (NMU)s to be acknowledged upon return by the maintainer. Note that NMUs are constrained to single, small fixes and cannot be used to push a new upstream release, for example. In any case, when an NMU is made, the package's official maintainer is still in control, and may opt to reverse a fix. Unless such an issue causes harm to the project and thus needs to be resolved by the technical committee, a maintainer's decision is final and irrefutable.

Should a package maintainer's unavailability extend beyond an acceptable period, a developer can announce an intent to take over a package, and claim responsibility for the package if nobody objects. This developer then becomes the new maintainer and custody of the package is fully transferred. The previous maintainer has

---

[43]<humour>If you want flamewars, come to live forums, such as the #debian IRC channel on irc.debian.org! People seem to love flamewars there.</humour>

then lost privileged influence over the package's maintenance, but frequently the involved parties coordinate upon return of the absentee to keep everybody happy.

In any case, it remains the maintainer's responsibility to see to a package's well-being, and to decide on its fate. Within a community of about a thousand developers, many different interpretations of responsibility are inevitable. The core of the project is carried by a smallish number of developers that take Debian very seriously and perform their duties with the same amount of care and devotion (or even greater) as their regular jobs, or true hobbies. The majority of Debian project members treat Debian as secondary to their main life but do their best to properly attend to the responsibilities they have chosen. A number of people have taken on too many responsibilities to be able to properly address them individually, and a few seem to interpret Debian developer status merely as the right to own a Debian email address and otherwise neglect their responsibilities.

Such variety exists in every volunteer organisation of reasonable size. Debian's approach to the coordination of the developers on the path that the project has chosen is to decentralize privileges, as mentioned previously. The openness and focus of self-organisation prevents deadlocks and guards against stalls induced through negligence by single developers.

Debian — a bazaar of cathedrals

Most packages are still maintained by individuals rather than a group of people. In as such, the Debian project can be described as "a bazaar of cathedrals[44]." Although Debian's openness prevents many of the problems described by the cathedral model, not all the issues are properly addressed. When package maintenance is handled by an individual who also maintains the jurisdiction over the package, a situation not too different from the dreaded vendor lock-in surfaces. Even though it is always possible to make suggestions or provide patches via the BTS (see chapter 10.6), the package's maintenance depends on the single maintainer, which is never a good thing.

A number maintainers have taken the lead and moved the maintenance of their packages to public, collaborative platforms, such as Alioth[45] to reduce such dependencies. Whether developed entirely collaboratively or not, many packages list co-maintainers: developers allowed to provide new versions of a package without having file them as NMUs.

---

[44]I read this description on IRC, but did not note its author at the time. It references Eric S. Raymond's definitive account of the dynamics of open source projects[42].

[45]Alioth is Debian's open source development coordination forum, based on GForge: http://alioth.debian.org

Debian — a meritocracy

A few task domains within the Debian project, including the responsibilities of the delegates and officers, remain restricted to a small set of people. Examples are the maintenance of the Debian archive, the management of Debian user accounts, write access to the security archive, and the administration of Debian's infrastructure. Even though every developer can theoretically take part in these tasks and request the necessary privileges, in practice, such positions undergo very few fluctuations.

While the Debian project tries to prevent these jobs from being the domain of single persons by encouraging teams, the effectiveness of such teams depends on the skill levels of its members. Certain tasks, such as the administration of Debian machines, require much experience from their caretakers, and individuals lots of enthusiasm but little experience would do more harm than good.

Within the project, the occupants of positions with greater privileges are chosen on the basis of their abilities and their achievements. Therefore, the form of government that comes closest to the organisation of the Debian project is a meritocracy[46]. To be able to rise in the Debian hierarchy, an individual must have displayed competence and contributed significantly to a domain before being chosen to occupy a position within this domain.

Among the most prominent examples here is membership of the security team. As the security team's work definitely constitutes a core component of the Debian project and the stability of the Debian system, some individuals consider it prestigious to be part of the security team. In lengthy emails they explain their great ideas and elaborate their promises of how they would be an asset to the team. Even though the security team is rather understaffed, such requests are not honoured. Instead, those promoted to the security team have made valuable contributions, helping the team without actually being part of it. Such achievements then serve as the basis for the team to evaluate the individual's ability and decide on possible membership of the team.

In discussions among Debian developers, the term "cabal" may come up from time to time. While more fictitious than a real, the term cabal refers to a group of developers with elevated priviliges or senior status within the project where nobody has the membership details. The term is used mostly jokingly, but may occasionally pop up in criticisms, usually hand in hand with an expressed desire for more openness with some of the project's internal processes. It is a contagious term which is best avoided to prevent insulting people. Cabal members are often said to be unapproachable by others; in most cases this is simply a function of being approached by too many people at once, or of being overloaded with work. The best recipe to deal with alleged cabal members is to be proactive: make sure you have read

[46]The Merriam-Webster dictionary defines a meritocracy as "a system in which the talented are chosen and moved ahead on the basis of their achievement."

the available documentation and prepare concrete questions or proposals which to present to the developers.

Trust among developers

Until recently, Debian was the only operating system that was purely community-driven. While some people like to see Debian as an instance of socialism in action[47], several parts of the project and its infrastructure require legal owners, responsible persons, and proper accountability. SPI shields the project from much of the administrative burdens surrounding an institution of the size as Debian, but many aspects remain that require developers to step in to take responsibilities. Because most of the developers have never met each other, except on mailing lists or IRC[48], it seems surprising that vital parts of the project are laid in the hands of volunteers without much ado.

For instance, the responsibility of managing the Debian infrastructure, and especially the build daemons lies solely in the hands of individuals. Effectively, these individuals ensure the integrity of the Debian archive. The Debian project exists to maintain the Debian archive, and thus the project rises and falls with the propriety of its developers. Here, too, the social dynamics of open source projects, which Eric S. Raymond describes in his book, play an important role. When it comes down to it, people have little incentive to be trustworthy (in general), and there is no profit motive in contributing to Debian. However, people do work for more than immediate gain, and praise and respect amongst peers seem to be the major driving forces behind open source projects, in this case keeping the responsible developers on track.

Similarly, the Debian project does not have a structured funding infrastructure, yet a plethora of users donate money to the project. In some cases, registered organisations have volunteered to shoulder the financial administration and to accept donations for Debian for a specific part of the globe. For most countries, however, Debian does not have such dedicated legal bodies and banking fees for international money transfers are exorbitant. In these cases, developers step in to fill the gap. The sums of money which these people handle for Debian are relatively small, but there are no constraints or contracts. If a trustee decides to abandon ship and throw a party with Debian's funds, the Debian project will have little on its side to prosecute the offender[49].

---

[47]"Everyone bakes a cake and everyone gets a piece..." Davor Ocelić comments: "The point actually gets deeper to a technical side too, as I see it. Current computing power is too great (and develops too fast), and lifetime is too important to any of us to waste time reinventing stuff and making the same mistakes again. Writing software today only pays off with a free software license, because you are giving it a potential to last. This is simply the professionalism of the 'new age.'"

[48]IRC is the Internet Relay Chat, a worldwide chat system where users can meet in pertinent channels for discussion. See chapter 10.4.3

[49]No case of such thievery has come to my attention since I joined the Debian community.

Large parts of the Debian project work on the basis of trust alone. At times, the lack of professional management has caused serious grief (not because of misappropriation, but rather accountability), but most of the time, the trust model has served Debian well. A serious offence or abuse of the rights results in the immediate and typically irrevocable expulsion from the developer team. Apparently, Debian developer status is enough of a reason to do no harm to the project. In addition, Debian developers are non-anonymous; harming the project would seriously tarnish their reputation throughout the open source community. Moreover, given the visibility of open source software development through popular search engines, it is likely that any mischief makes the rounds even beyond the community: a previous employer once confronted me with instances of good and bad conduct I had exhibited on mailing lists and expected me to justify my behaviour or commended me on my actions.

Identification

Anonymity does not exist within the Debian developer team. Identification of developers in cyberspace is handled with GNU Privacy Guard (GPG) keys. Debian developers are free to sign their Debian-related email with a strong, cryptographic signature (and users are encouraged to do the same) for important matters. Uploads to the Debian archive must be authenticated with a signature by a current developer, and signatures are required for other organisational processes, such as voting.

GPG keys are created using software such as **GnuPG**, which is freely available. It is important to realise that the identity information, such as name and email address, are provided to **GnuPG** by the user. As a result, everyone can create keys under any name. To ensure the identity of a prospective developer, it is thus required to have a key approved by an existing developer of the Debian project. This verification requires personal contact and the consideration of an official document of identification. In chapter 2.5.2 you can find more information on the process of becoming a developer.

When developers sign each other's keys, they create a relational network known as the "Web of Trust." As one of the largest groups using digital signatures consistently, Debian forms a large portion of the global Web of Trust. A complete analysis of the trust between Debian developers is available online[50].

Thus, within Debian, every developer's real-world identity is known. While the developers (and parts of the remaining user community) usually refer to each other by their nicknames (especially on IRC), the developer's full name is publicly accessible in the developer database[51]. The developer's address and contact information are not required but are generally available, albeit only to other developers for privacy

[50]http://people.debian.org/~weasel/weboftrust/index.php
[51]http://db.debian.org

reasons. Experience has shown that real names are perceived of as being considerably more trustworthy than pseudonyms[52], and it is trust upon which the entire project is built.

Social gatherings

Social gatherings among Debian developers are quite common. With the help of online resources[51] and mailing lists, users travelling to an area frequently reach out to local Debian users and set up meetings. Usually, the "excuse" is to sign GPG keys, and then to spend many hours getting to know each other. Furthermore, at any Linux-related conference, Debian folks will get together to strengthen their personal relations. Just like the Debian project, these meetings are generally open to the public, and users (as well as other people) are welcome to join.

Debian maintains a rudimentary GPG keysigning coordination page[53]. A better coordination platform, which also supports the coordination of keysigning events and expands beyond Debian's border is Biglumber[54]. The procedure of keysigning is detailed on Debian's web site[55]. For bigger events, fully-fledged protocols exist as well[56]. Debian's **signing-party** package provides **gpg-key2ps**, which conventiently converts the key information to Postscript for printing.

2.5   Helping the Debian project

Users of the Debian system often look for ways to give back to the Debian community. The Debian project is open to everyone and people willing to help will be able to do so. In many cases, it does not matter whether a contributor is a developer or not. Accounts on colaborative platforms, such as Alioth[57] or the Debian Concurrent Version System (CVS) repository[58], can be obtained without developer status. Often, the only difference between developers and non-developers is who has the final burden of making the upload, in addition to other responsibilities that take away time.

---

[52]A reader of the **de.newusers.questions** newsgroup once remarked that the use of real names is favourable over pseudonyms as it allows people to concentrate on the post rather than to have to get engaged in a discussion over the sense or nonsense of these names.

[53]http://nm.debian.org/gpg.php

[54]http://www.biglumber.com

[55]http://www.debian.org/events/keysigning

[56]http://www.cryptnet.net/fdp/crypto/gpg-party.html

[57]http://alioth.debian.org

[58]http://cvs.debian.org

Nevertheless, for an enthusiastic and active contributor, good reasons exist to apply for Debian developer status. Before describing the application process, the following sections lay out some (few) possible ways to contribute to the Debian project. An online document is also available on the Debian web site[59].

2.5.1   Contributing to the project

If you would like to contribute to the Debian project, you will not have a difficult time finding areas in need of help. Since the Debian system is continuously work in progress, it is almost impossible to identify the areas in most need of help. In general, the rule applies that if something is broken, you can contribute by fixing it, and if something is not perfect, you can contribute by improving it.

Always keep in mind that Debian is a meritocracy (see chapter 2.4.3): you step up the ladder and gain authority through work and reputation. Therefore, the road ahead may be a little rough. It is probably a good idea to start small and to make sure that people know you as someone who does what they promise to do and in a timely manner, and as someone skillful enough to produce quality work. With that said, do not forget that Debian is about volunteer work, and that whatever you do should be done because you enjoy it. Nobody will tell you what to do, so you are completely on your own as to how spend your time.

Feedback

Probably the most significant form of contributing to the project is through constructive feedback. If you run into a problem and you have the time and means to investigate further, please do. If you think you have found a problem, do not hesitate to put your findings into a bug report (see chapter 10.6.5). You may be the first to stumble across a problem; by helping to fix it, you are helping others to avoid the pitfalls. Alerting the maintainer to a problem and offering to help with narrowing it down goes a long way towards fixing it. The free software community depends on the continuous flow of feedback to maintain its progressive bearing. Alternatively, do not hesitate to participate in discussions on mailing lists and in discussion forums (see chapter 10.4). When developers need to make decisions, your input can help to improve a product.

User support

On the topic of mailing lists, an equally important domain for contribution to the project is the support of users in these forums. If you can spare the time, listen in to the problems of other users and provide advice if you can. Any constructive

[59] http://www.debian.org/devel/join

help on mailing lists such as **debian-user** will be greatly appreciated. Moreover, fielding questions on such a list can produce incredible learning effects: while you will have little to contribute in the beginning, your expertise will grow as you read what other people have to say. Over time, you will be able to provide valuable information on an ever increasing number of problems. At the same time, you are becoming more and more a master of your own system.

Quality assurance

A large part of Debian's reputation is quality. Maintaining the high quality of the operating system is a never-ending task. The quality assurance team is therefore grateful for any help it receives. Quality assurance mainly entails working on existing bugs, but extends to package adoptions and testing of software and filing bugs accordingly.

If you choose to contribute in this field, you choose to improve free software as a whole. Perhaps the best way to start is to pick a few packages of software that you use often and which you know fairly well. For each of these packages, pull up the corresponding page on the Package Tracking System (PTS)[60] (see chapter 10.6.9) and check the to-do and bug lists. You may want to let the maintainer know what you are doing, but otherwise there is nothing to keep you from taking a stab at addressing to-do items and producing patches for the open bugs. Please make sure you read chapter 10.6 and in particular chapter 10.6.10. If a package's maintainer appreciates your work and you manage to build up trust, this is your chance to become a co-maintainer of a package that you use often.

Rather than concentrating on single packages, you may also wish to simply attack the show-stoppers of the next *stable* release: the release-critical (Release-Critical (RC)) bugs. The coordination page for release-critical bugs is available online[61], as is a general overview of the current situation[62].

Another way to help out is by selecting older bugs and reproducing them; maybe certain problems do not exist anymore in current versions; maybe you can analyse other problems. In all cases, make sure you send your findings to the BTS. If a bug exists in a package's version in *stable* but not in its *testing* version, set the appropriate tag. And if a bug has disappeared from *stable*, you can close it (see chapter 10.6.7).

As an alternative, you may want to help with maintenance of a package. On its web page, Debian maintains a list of packages in need of help[63]. Packages that are in need of a new maintainer (up for adoption, or orphaned) may be worth the effort. On the other hand, if you prefer the challenge of a new package, you could

[60] http://pts.qa.debian.org
[61] http://bts.turmzimmer.net
[62] http://bugs.debian.org/release-critical
[63] http://www.debian.org/devel/wnpp

consider attacking one of the requested packages, or prepare a software that you would like to see in the Debian archive for its inclusion (see chapter 9). Another kind of challenge are packages marked as needing help. In these cases, the current maintainer intends to continue as maintainer but seeks additional people to assist.

Documentation and localisation

If you are less technically versed but enjoy writing, then maybe you can help to improve documentation, both of packages as well as the documents available as part of the Debian Documentation Project (DDP) (see chapter 10.2.1). While changes to the documentation of single packages are best coordinated with the individual maintainers, the DDP documents are available via CVS[64].

Another domain in continuous need for help is localisation[65]; in the interest of non-English-speaking users, software, documentation, and web pages should be available in as many other languages as possible, and each localisation should be of acceptable quality and up-to-date. Translations are coordinated via the Debian international pages[66]. The procedures (which should be followed) are specific to each language group. Interesting references related to localisation include chapter 8 of the Developer's Reference[67] and the "Mini survey of localization in Debian"[68].

Testing

By running the Debian system, you are also testing it to make sure that it works and meets up to its quality standards. However, chances are that normal use will not find obscure bugs or uncover problems that taint the quality of the operating system. Thus, if you have some time to spare and ideally possess a system to experiment, you could try hard to break things on the Debian system which should normally stand up to the stress testing. In addition, if you have special hardware (such as a system with a less-common architecture) or infrastructure, concentrate on related areas. Ideally, you should be running *testing* or *unstable* systems for the experiments. If you find a problem, make sure to check the BTS for whether a corresponding bug has already been filed. If not, read chapter 10.6.5 and submit a problem report.

---

[64] http://cvs.debian.org/?cvsroot=debian-doc

[65] Localisation is often abbreviated l10n as there are 10 letters between the l and the n (a convention started in the mid-eighties at DEC). Internationalisation (i18n) is a related term, and often the two are confused. Internationalisation involves enabling a software to deal with different regional settings ("locales") and provides hooks for translations. Localisation is then the actual process of adding support for a specific region and/or language to the software.

[66] http://www.debian.org/international

[67] http://www.debian.org/doc/manuals/developers-reference/ch-l10n.en.html

[68] http://graal.ens-lyon.fr/~mquinson/debian/l10n-survey

Some of the most important areas in need of testing are the Debian installer and the upgrade process. While problems with the former may put off new (or existing) users, failures during the upgrade process can be fatal on production systems. Therefore it is of utmost significance to walk through the processes multiple times, ideally not following the paved path at all times; experiment, try something new, try to make it fail. And if you succeed, analyse the problem and write a bug report (see chapter 10.6.5).

Security updates

When a security problem is found, it is in the interest of the user base at large to have the problem fixed as soon as possible. While the Debian security team works hard to make this possible, it needs help at times to manage the load of work that comes with the task of security support. Principally, you can help in two ways:

First, you can keep your eyes open and make sure that the security team is aware of new problems as they appear. The team reads the common security announcement forums, so it is not necessary to forward every announcement immediately. However, if you are aware of an outstanding issue and waiting for the security team to take action, it does not hurt to inquire about the status. Please make sure you follow the advice given in chapter 7.1 pertaining to the choice of medium for such inquiries as some security issues may need to be handled non-publicly.

The second way to help the security team is by offering your help in finding solutions to problems, and backporting fixes to the version currently provided in *stable*. If you are serious about helping out in this area, please let the team know and make sure you let actions follow.

Development and improvement

Several components of the Debian system are aged, and while they still do their job just fine today, they need to be improved to be able to meet up to tomorrow's increased requirements. The main examples here are **dpkg** and APT, which are both rather slow and lack consistent support for important extensions, such as cryptographic signatures for **dpkg** (see chapter 7.5.3). Other fields in need of improvement that come to mind include optimisation of the boot initialisation sequence (by introducing policies and dependencies; see chapter 6.3.1), and a modular rewrite of the **ifupdown** system (see chapter 6.8.1; the **netconf** project has been started on **alioth.debian.org** with this goal.). Plenty other possibilities exist, and Debian maintains a list of to-do items online[69]; find your own niche and start working!

---

[69] http://www.debian.org/devel/todo

Infrastructure

Several core components of the Debian project are the work of single developers; the BTS (see chapter 10.6), the PTS (see chapter 10.6.9), and the developer packages overview[70] are just a few examples. These components exist because their authors lacked their functionality at one point in time and decided to change that. If you are looking to provide similar tools but do not know where to start or what to implement, maybe tuning in to the **debian-devel** mailinglist and reading along for a while will spill a hint.

2.5.2   Becoming a Debian developer

A Debian developer enjoys several privileges not available to the regular user:

- Debian uses democratic votes to gain consensus on open issues. Only developers may cast votes to influence decisions on such issues.

- Debian developers have write access to the Debian archive and can upload packages at will. Without developer status, it is still possible to get your own packages into the archive, but you need to have them sponsored by an existing developer who does the actual upload.

- Debian developers have access to the **debian-private** mailing list and **#debian-private** IRC channels. These forums are only used to discuss internal or personal issues and are thus only of importance to developers. Or, put differently: as Debian does not hide problems from its users (see appendix E), you are not deprived of any information by not being able to access these forums[71].

For an enthusiastic contributor, who has been active in the Debian community for a while and managed to build up a reputation, it may be worth to consider applying for Debian developer status. Among the chief reasons that speak for such an application would be a desire to influence the project by participating in the (infrequent) votes. Having write access to the archive is only significant when previous contributions were continuously delayed as they had to wait for sponsors (active developers) to proxy the upload. Remember that plenty of ways exist in which contributions can be made without being a developer: accounts on collaborative platforms do not require developer status, and in many areas, contributions can be made without having to submit anything on a regular basis (such as user support and quality assurance). Access to the private discussion forums should probably not be counted as a reason to become a developer simply because these forums do not produce information relevant to the Debian system.

[70] http://qa.debian.org/developer.php
[71] but you are guarded from endless flamewars about irrelevant topics and inter-developer frictions.

Preparing the application

To become a Debian developer, you have to go through a lengthy and elaborate process, and it is not possible to become a Debian developer "just like that," for reasons related to prestige, or because you want a @debian.org email address. Instead, you should be enthusiastic about the project, and be able to dedicate some of your time to it, now as well as in the future. An online article[72] explains the process, in addition to the following pages.

The process of becoming a Debian developer consists roughly of the following steps and requirements, which are described in detail online[73]:

Identification
> To become a developer, you must possess (and know how to use) a GPG key, which has to be signed by at least one existing Debian developer. Anonymity is not tolerated among Debian developers. This step ensures that you are joining the project under your official identity.

Advocation
> Before you will be considered as an applicant, an existing Debian developer has to advocate you and give elaborate reasons why you would be a worthy addition to the Debian developer team. The best way to find an advocate is by contributing to Debian and building up a good reputation. If the advocate is the same developer that signed your key, you will need another person's signature before you can apply. This person need not be a developer but must be strongly connected to the Web of Trust. This is to avoid fake applicants that exist only in the imagination of the advocate.

Philosophy and procedures
> You must have a thorough understanding of the philosophy of the Debian project, as outlined by the Social Contract (see appendix E) and the DFSG (see appendix F). It is also of utmost importance to understand and be familiar with the community. An applicant must have been actively immersed in the project before being considered. The Developer Reference[74] is a crucial document in understanding the responsibilities and procedures of Debian project membership.

Tasks and skills
> You must be familiar with Debian packages, and the Debian system as a whole. You must know the Debian policy (see chapter 5.7), understand its principles and reasons, and be able to apply it to situations and tasks. You should be familiar with the Debian infrastructure, the BTS, and the various

---

[72]http://programming.newsforge.com/article.pl?sid=05/01/28/1618201
[73]http://www.debian.org/devel/join/nm-checklist
[74]http://www.debian.org/doc/developers-reference

skills of software development. It is not necessarily required to know how to write programmes in languages such as C, but it is almost certainly an advantage to be able to do so.

Leading up to your application, the **debian-mentors** mailing list will be one of the primary resources in learning about the development of the Debian system. Please make sure you read and act according to the **debian-mentors** Frequently Asked Questions (FAQ)[75], which also contains valuable information about the application process. In particular, it details the process of finding a sponsor for your package. Obviously, you are also welcome to participate in discussions on other mailing lists (see chapter 10.4.1).

The Debian Women project hosts a mentoring programme designed to help interested people learn more about developing for Debian in an applicatory and exploratory way way. Active mentors are listed on the Web[76].

The application process

When you meet the criteria of a Debian developer, you can apply for developer status and become a New Maintainer (NM) (technically, you become an applicant, but these are commonly referred to as NMs).

Once you have applied, you can keep track of your application online[77]. At some point, you will be contacted by an application manager, who will test your knowledge of the Debian project, its philosophies, and assess your skills related to Debian packages and the system as a whole. Make sure you are prepared and do not underestimate this assessment. You should also be able to provide a list of your contributions to Debian for reference. Note that this list does not have to be extensive, but it should make it evident that you are interested in continuing to help the project, not just reaching developer status and then fading away. Also, it is of utmost importance to keep in mind that *you* want to join the project. You should therefore try hard to minimise the application manager's workload by providing well formulated and complete answers.

Waiting for DAM approval

If you manage to complete the assessment and have all other requirements in place, it is your turn to wait for approval by the DAM. Applications must be carefully verified before you are given developer status. This can take a long time, especially during times leading up to a release, when the developers are generally overloaded. The Debian NM team is working hard to accomodate the increasing number of

---

[75]http://people.debian.org/~mpalmer/debian-mentors_FAQ.html
[76]http://women.alioth.debian.org/mentoring
[77]http://nm.debian.org

applicants, while maintaining the level of standards and quality required so as not to jeopardise the project and its operating system. The best advice to give is to apply only when you are ready, and to be patient. It will not help if you continuously ask people about your application status, and if you disappoint your application manager with lack of preparation, you are likely to be deprioritised.

Even though this may all sound painful and unnecessary, I do not want to discourage you from applying. The NM process ensures that Debian developers are fully aware of their responsibilities, are capable of handling them, and are dedicated enough to not become a burden to the project. Only with rigorous procedures is the project capable of upholding the quality of its operating system, and the dynamics of the community surrounding it. If you are sure that you want to become a Debian developer, then, by all means, apply. You are in for a rough ride, but the well-prepared, skillful, and patient applicants are the ones to harvest the ripe fruits.

The length of the NM process also ensures that only dedicated developers join the project as impatient or itinerant folks are weeded out by natural selection. If you contribute to the project while waiting for your developer account, you are making a strong point. If you are impatient, you are suggesting that maybe all you really want is a **debian.org** email address.

2.6 The Debian swirl

The official Debian logo is the red swirl hovering above a genie's bottle (see figure 2.3(a)) and may only be used for official parts of the Debian project, or by Debian developers in their official function. Unofficially, the project or operating system may be referred to using just the swirl (see figure 2.3(b)), which is known as the "Open Use Logo." The printed "Debian" is optional for both and shown only as part of the second logo. The logos exist to protect Debian's property from any use which could hurt its reputation.

(a)   (b)

Figure 2.3:
The Debian logos: (a) the swirl from the genie's bottle (official logo); (b) the swirl by itself (public use)

Both logos were designed by Raul M. Silva as part of a logo contest held in 1999[78]. The official source for the logos is on the Debian web site[79]. Note that figure 2.3(b) is actually an unofficial version[80] which more closely resembles the original design published by Raul.

Raul never made an official statement about the meaning or symbolism of the logo (at least I could not find a record of such), so several theories have developed, ranging from the brisk to the esoteric:

- The bottle represents the developer collective, and the result is the magic swirl, symbolising the Debian operating system.

- The swirl has both the containment of a circle, and the flexibility of a spiral, just like the operating system is contained and flexible.

- The swirl symbolises how Debian sucks everything in to be packaged, and the bottle belongs to the Helpful Debian Genie.

- Bruce Perens offers the following description:

  > It's "magic smoke". Electrical engineer lore is that when you burn out an electronic component, you cause the "magic smoke" that makes it work to be released. Once the magic smoke is gone, the component doesn't work any longer. Debian is supposed to be the magic smoke that makes your computer work.

- In Pixar's 1995 animation masterpiece Toy Story, a red swirl decorates the chin of Buzz Lightyear, the space ranger[81]. The movie predates Debian's choice of logo and could have been a source of inspiration.

- The swirl stems from the bass clef used in music scores. The traditional bass key is the 'F', which stands for "Free", "Functional", "Fantastic", "Fun", and "Fine".

---

[78] http://www.debian.org/News/1999/19990826
[79] http://www.debian.org/logos
[80] http://www.hands.com/~phil/debian/logo
[81] For example: http://allearsnet.com/tp/mk/buzz7.jpg; the swirl is also visible on the cover of the French DVD of the sequel: http://aram.free.fr/covers/images/toy_story2.jpg

3

Installing Debian the right way

*joeyh installs debian using only his big toe, for a change of pace.
— Joey Hess, in #debian-boot

Installation mechanisms of common end-user systems try to combine two extremes: while trying to ask as little as possible from the user and automate everything else, they aim at installing all possible features to satisfy the broadest possible user base and leave no desires unmet. These two goals require installation systems to make many decisions based on assumptions, which come in the form of hard-coded defaults, heuristics[1], or expert systems at runtime. Some operating systems do not install everything, but provide a healthy cross-section of programmes instead. The user is left with a usable system and a few extra goodies. Yet another class of operating systems provides basically no installation method and the user is expected to bootstrap the system from scratch.

[1]A heuristic can be described as a simplification or an educated guess, whose goal is to find a less than perfect solution in shorter time than it would take to find a perfect solution.

Debian takes a conceptually different approach to installation than most other operating systems. The Debian installer provides the basics needed to pull up a minimal system, queries for the essential configuration data of the base system, and then leaves the user to the graces of the package management system. The whole process installs a minimal set of packages to enable the use of APT in various environments[2]. Depending on the network connection and purpose of the machine, a number of packages may still be removed from the few that Debian actually installs[3] (see appendix C.3 for a list of packages which can be safely removed).

That is actually Debian's secret: where others try to do a lot and automate whatever needs to be done in between, Debian does very little and leaves only the bare essentials to automation algorithms. At the same time, it provides powerful tools which the administrator may put to use where desired. The result is exactly what Debian aims to be: a strong foundation with robust tools that let the administrator keep control over the system.

3.1   The Debian installer

The Debian installer provided with *sarge* is a new software, developed from scratch to address the shortcomings of the previous Debian installer (**boot-floppies**, also known by the short name "bf"), and to pave the way for easier maintenance and future extensibility. Over the period of four years, the developers have worked their experience from the **boot-floppies** project into a new, unified architecture for the installation of Debian, independent of the source medium. If you're familiar with other install programs, the new Debian installer may surprise you. It introduces Debian's strengths right at the start, and goes a long way towards burying Debian's reputation for being difficult to install.

One of the biggest points of criticism of Debian has always been the awkwardness and complexity of its installation system. While those experienced with Debian could install a complete system within minutes, the uninitiated haplessly tried to follow the path of least resistance, often failing miserably as the system did not provide a straight line through the process. As a result, numerous Debian-based distributions (see appendix A.2) have clustered like pilot fish around a shark, with their main claim to attention being the easy installation that leaves users with a Debian-compatible system. However, these providers only support a subset of the architectures Debian supports (see chapter 4.5), and thus, the Debian system could never integrate the improvements into the main line[4]. Furthermore, language sup-

---

[2]The default minimal installation consists of 123 packages, which take up 97 Mb. This also includes the accompanying documentation, log files, and temporary data.

[3]The smallest Debian system that can still be called a Unix system consists of 89 packages and consumes 84 Mb of space.

[4]For what it is worth, some effort went into using Progeny's installer for the Debian system, but the installation system was not modular and flexible enough to be extended to all eleven architectures.

port has always been a problem. While the Debian system supports almost 40 languages, most Debian installation systems provided English, or a handful different languages at most.

The problems with the previous installation system had far-reaching effects. On the one hand, Debian slowly but strongly gained the reputation of being a distribution for cracks and hackers, and anyone not glued to the keyboard would be unable to use it. On the other hand, those who did succeed at installing the system joined what was perceived to be an elitarian crowd around the Debian project, which apparently did not care enough to make a move and improve their users' experience (and widen their user base).

As it turns out, the Debian project has been aware of the problems and has been working actively to solve them. However, as good things take time, it took four years until all the requirements of a new installer had been met, which has also been among the primary factors of the delay of *sarge*.

3.1.1 Features of the new installer

The new installer continues to be unglamourously text-based, but work on graphical front-ends has begun[5]. The installer does provide many enhancements which should improve users' experience while not limiting the expert — an approach found throughout the Debian system.

The installer is fully documented online[6] for all architectures and the most popular languages. A list of frequently asked questions is also available[7].

The features of the new installer include the following:

Modular architecture
>   The installer is built out of a multitude of modules working hand-in-hand. This allows for easy customisation of the installer (see chapter 8.3.3) and provides for ease of maintenance.

Hardware detection
>   The new installation system uses **hw-detect** and the **discover** hardware detection utility to determine the hardware present in a system. The set of hardware these two can detect is limited to the devices supported by the kernel. While it is likely that a recent 2.4 series kernel will power the *sarge* installer by default, a 2.6 kernel can be used instead to allow detection of newer devices.

Expert mode
>   While the installer allows access to a plethora of parameters to those who

---

[5]http://www.debian.org/devel/debian-installer/gtk-frontend
[6]http://d-i.alioth.debian.org/manual
[7]http://wiki.debian.net/?DebianInstallerFAQ

want it, the number of questions thrown at the average user is kept to a minimum.

Improved partitioning

A new partitioning system combines support for all major filesystems with the ability to move, copy, and resize partitions. Furthermore, Redundant Array of Independent Disks (RAID) and Logical Volume Manager (LVM) volumes can be configured prior to the creation of the filesystems.

Wireless LAN (WLAN) configuration

What worked sporadically in the old *woody* is now an integrated feature: Debian-supported WLAN drivers can be used throughout and for the installation[8].

Architecture support

Support for all architectures has been improved. For instance, installations on **powerpc** run much smoother than before, and **x86** now uses **Grub** as the **bootloader**.

Easy customisation

The installer has been designed with maintainability in mind. In addition to its modular design, this provides an easy way to create customised installers for specific requirements.

Boot media

Also thanks to the modular design, Debian now has ability to support a wider range of boot media. The more advanced include: Pre-boot Execution Environment (PXE) (which is not strictly new, **boot-floppies** already supported it), and Universal Serial Bus (USB) sticks.

Internationalisation

The installer has been translated into 40 languages at the time of writing (and 10 more are under active development). In addition to the language, it also supports the associated character sets. Thus, more than two thirds of the world population can use the installer in their native language.

3.1.2 System requirements

Debian GNU/Linux does not ask much. Nevertheless, some minimum requirements must be met for the system to run. Not essential but very useful is a CD-ROM

---

[8]The set of drivers provided by Debian's kernel includes popular products, featuring chips by Wavelan and Prism, among others. Unfortunately, the Intel PRO Wireless cards, used in many Centrino laptops, are currently not supported for the installation due to licencing problems (see chapter 2.3). The drivers can be easily built for Debian (from **ipw2100-source** and **ipw2200-source**, see chapter 8.1.3) and integrated in a customised version of the installer (see chapter 8.3.3).

or DVD-ROM drive, and a Basic Input/Output System (BIOS) capable of booting from these drives[9]. Debian can be installed using only a network connection, or bootstrapped onto a hard disk temporarily connected to a second computer (both of which will be discussed in this chapter), but the preferred and most popular method is the bootable CD.

To run the Debian installer, you need at least 24 Mb of Random Access Memory (RAM) (and even less on some other architectures). If you are interested in bootstrapping an embedded system with less memory available, it is probably best to use the method laid out in chapter 8.3.1.

For sensible operation of a minimal system, 256 Mb of hard disk space is required for a new partition . It is possible to squeeze the system into a smaller space, but log files and APT and dpkg caches like to have more space available. A system spanning 256 Mb will not provide more than the mere essentials, and a graphical user interface will not fit. A common workspace installation will consume around 2 Gb, excluding data, and leaving little room for additional programmes. For servers, it is advisable to provide more space for /var and/or /srv. Generally, the more the merrier, which should not pose a problem with the storage capacities available these days.

Lastly, the system should have a means to connect to the network. Installing over the network is the smoothest way, and Unix was made for the Net after all. Debian supports Peer-to-Peer Protocol (PPP) and PPP-over-Ethernet (PPPoE), but so-called "WinModems"[10] are not natively supported. Most Ethernet and WLAN adapters are supported, including those found integrated in consumer motherboards. In general, the Debian installer does not provide drivers beyond those available in the kernel. Thus, if it works with Linux, it works with Debian, and *vice versa*.

3.2 The minimalistic approach to installation

If you are used to installation systems commonly found on other platforms and the installation of Debian is your first exposure to the operating system, you are in for an interesting ride. The Debian installer very much embodies the overall philosophy of the operating system, which is to aid but not to impose. It is task-oriented rather than process-oriented: the user does not navigate from one screen to the next with *Next* and *Previous* buttons (or the equivalent), but rather selects from tools to accomplish various tasks during the installation. The installer suggests an

[9]If your system lacks the ability to boot from CD-ROM, an interesting solution is the **Smart Boot Manager**, which can boot from floppy and hand over control to a CD-ROM drive to allow booting from CD even if the BIOS does not support this: **http://btmgr.webframe.org**

[10]Many internal modems are WinModems, which rely on drivers to provide the functionality traditionally found in hardware. The manufacturers generally do not provide specifications to the open source community. **http://www.linmodems.org** is the one-stop resource for support of these devices. Generally, the acquisition of an external modem will be less problematic and save time and thus money.

order, but the user is completely free to go back and forth between the tools[11]. Furthermore, the installer focuses on function rather than looks and is unlikely to win a beauty contest any time soon. However, it is a powerful tool in the hands of those who know what they want or need.

This chapter is for those who are unacquainted with the installation process, or not familiar with Debian as a whole. It also exists to demonstrate how Debian is meant to be installed. Towards the end of the process, the installer will ask you for a method to install packages. New users commonly spend a significant amount of time browsing the available packages, trying to install every package that they will need, think they will need, or imagine that they could need in the future. This unnecessarily lengthens the installation procedure, can be thoroughly confusing, and will result in a system full of cruft right from the start.

Instead, an install-on-demand strategy is often preferred, largely thanks to **APT**. During the installation, no extra packages are installed, leaving the user with a system comprised of only a few packages in addition to the essential ones. When the base system is in place, the various package installation methods can be used to obtain the packages needed to address the system requirements.

3.2.1   Installing the base system

Booting the installer

This section will illustrate a typical Debian installation process. The new system is booted with a Debian CD, which is among the most popular means to install the operating system. Debian provides various different types of installation images:

full

> The official CD image includes everything needed for a standard installation of Debian, and furthermore provides some of the most popular packages. Therefore, network access is not strictly needed for the installation. This would be the preferred and most popular means to install Debian.

netinst

> The **netinst** image is optimised for installations with (fast) network access. It provides everything needed to run the installer and setup a standard Debian system. Any additional packages must be fetched from a Debian mirror via a network connection (which can be any type supported by Debian, including PPP and Digital Subscriber Line (DSL)).

---

[11]Obviously, some restrictions exist. For instance, after installing the core packages, it makes little sense to repartition. The installer will let you do so, but you will not be able to reinstall the basesystem without recreating the root and /usr filesystems.

businesscard

Optimised for size to be able to fit on the small business card CDs, the **businesscard** image provides the installer but requires network access to download the packages needed for the base system. At time of writing, only Ethernet connections are supported. If you are using a modem or DSL, or a specialised network type, you will not be able to use this image.

netboot

This image allows a machine to boot and pull the installation over the network, using PXE and Boot Protocol (BOOTP). See chapter 8.3.2 for more information.

hd-media

The **hd-media** image allows for the booting off a USB stick, or similar. Instructions are available in sections 4.4 and 5.1.3 of the Debian installer manual[12]. Your BIOS must support booting off USB media for this to work.

floppy

The **floppy** images allow a machine to boot from floppies before using a network connection to obtain the base system.

access-floppy

The **access-floppy** image allows the use of a Braille terminal during the installation, to support visually impaired Debian users. Unfortunately, the installation process currently does not configure the system for later use with the Braille terminal. Installing the **brltty** package during the installation and should solve this.

No matter what installation medium is used, the installation process is more or less the same. For some media, the network has to be configured to access the mirror during the installation. However, the major steps are the same, independent of the medium used to boot. In the following, I assume the use of the **businesscard** image.

Your system may require some BIOS tweaks to allow your machine to boot from CD-ROM. If successful, the Debian CD will greet you with the boot screen, and a **boot:** prompt (see figure 3.1). Here, you can select from four different methods by typing the method's name and pressing **[enter]**:

linux

Starts the installer in standard mode atop a recent 2.4 kernel. If you do not specify a boot image (but just hit **[enter]**), this one is selected by default.

[12]http://d-i.alioth.debian.org/manual/en.i386/ch05s01.html#usb-boot

linux26
> Also running the installer in standard mode, this option will cause a recent 2.6 kernel to be used.

expert
> This executes the installer in expert mode, using the same 2.4 kernel as **linux**.

expert26
> Expert mode, with the same 2.6 kernel as **linux26**.

Figure 3.1:
The boot screen

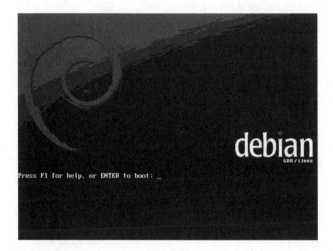

The installation modes — standard and expert — actually map to **debconf** priorities (see chapter 5.8.2). Expert mode configures **debconf** to use **low** while standard mode causes the priority to be set to **high**. Using a boot parameter, it is possible to use other priorities as well. For instance, by passing **debconf/priority=critical** at the boot prompt line, you can effectively reduce the number of questions the installer asks to nine. When inside the installer, the "Change debconf priority" item at the bottom of the menu allows for the priority to be changed at any time during the installation. Chapter 8.3.4 goes into greater depth on what can be specified on the boot prompt.

The 2.6 kernel works fine and should probably be used for support of newer hardware (like **Serial ATA** or newer Gigabit Ethernet adapters). The 2.6 kernel series also improves on many shortcomings of the 2.4 series, such as virtual memory management and the kernel scheduler, making it more powerful than its predecessor. Nevertheless, Debian will continue to default to the 2.4 kernel series, which has been thoroughly tested over the past three years (see chapter 4 and chapter 7 for a discussion of this decision). Only the **powerpc** and (yet unofficial) **amd64** architectures will use 2.6 by default. Finally, the new installer does not support the 2.6 kernel on the **alpha, arm, m68k, mips, mipsel,** and **s390** architectures.

The installer boots a universal kernel which tries to support a large set of different hardware. Unfortunately, many manufacturers ship their systems with broken implementations of standards, which may work fine during day-to-day use, but could wreak havoc in the presence of other drivers or features supported by the installer. Laptops in particular often contain buggy components. If the installer crashes, or the machine hangs, it may be necessary to disable certain parts of the installer's kernel. This can be accomplished through the use of boot parameters, which need to be passed after the kernel command:

```
boot: linux noacpi noapic nolapic
```

Some of the kernel's boot options are listed in the pages accessible by pressing [F5], [F6], or [F7] at the boot prompt. The following are some of the most common options:

Option	Effect
noacpi	Disables Advanced Configuration and Power Interface (ACPI) (which is seldom correctly implemented). Effects of an erroneous ACPI implementation usually result in random reboots or system lock-ups.
noapic nolapic	May allow machines with broken Advanced Programmable Interrupt Controller (APIC)s to work. APIC problems usually translate to spurious and repetitive messages about IRQ problems, and/or simply freeze the machine.
hw-detect/start_pcmcia=false	Disables Personal Computer Memory Card International Association (PCMCIA) support during installation. If your machine hangs after choosing to enable PCMCIA support, this option ensures proper operation.
debian-installer/probe/usb=false	Disables USB probing at boot time (for legacy devices). You may need this option if your machine freezes during the boot phase (*i.e.* before the blue background appears).

Table 3.1: Common boot options for the Debian installer to work around buggy hardware

continued

Option	Effect
debian-installer/framebuffer=false	Causes the installer not to use a frame-buffer. Multi-language support will not be available without a framebuffer. However, if your screen flickers or displays weird patterns when running the installer, this option may help.

In addition, the standard Linux kernel boot parameters[13] can be used. Also, it is possible to initialise the **debconf** database (see chapter 5.8) used for user interaction throughout the installation. More information on this possibility is available in chapter 8.3.4.

If the installer boots up and you manage to get to the language selection screen (or the menu in expert) mode, you will probably have an easy time with the rest of the installation (with the exception of PCMCIA problems). It may happen, however, that you cannot navigate the menus as the keyboard seems to be inoperable. This symptom relates to a problem with the kernel 2.6 USB drivers, which interfere with the keyboard subsystem. Using a USB keyboard, or disabling BIOS USB support ("USB Legacy support") work at times. Another workaround is to generate enough interrupts to keep the keyboard driver active and prevent the takeover: after hitting [enter] at the boot prompt, press the [caps lock] key repeatedly at high frequency until you see the blue background.

Meeting the installer

After the kernel does its thing, the installer presents itself in the gray-on-blue look you will see all over Debian (unless you reconfigure it[14]). The "graphical" installer front-end uses a **framebuffer** to enable non-American Standard Code for Information Interchange (ASCII) characters used in many languages. In case of problems with the framebuffer, the **debian-installer/framebuffer=false** option may be passed at boot-time to work without it.

In expert mode, the installer presents you with the menu shown in figure 3.2. Despite being task-oriented, the installer proposes the next step in the process by selecting it in the menu. The order of proposed steps is the same as the steps taken automatically in standard mode. However, the selection is not binding, and the installer will automatically complete prerequisite steps if one jumps ahead in

---

[13]See Documentation/kernel-parameters.txt in the kernel source tree.

[14]Setting debconf/frontend to text would run the installer in text-mode, although the text front-end is not included in the default image. You will need to provide a custom image if you are a text freak like me (see chapter 8.3.3).

the sequence. In the following, only the differences between standard and expert mode are highlighted, and it is assumed that expert mode users follow the proposed sequence of steps. Users of standard mode should theoretically not be exposed to the menu at all. Nevertheless, in case of an error, the installer will jump to the menu to allow for greatest control of the situation. By default, you just have to press [enter] to repeat the last step, or you can choose other functions from the menu that may clear up the problem.

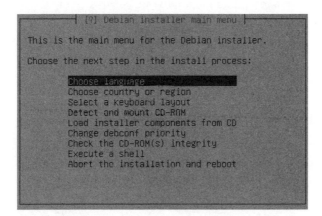

Figure 3.2:
The initial installer
menu in expert mode

Navigating the installer

The normal installer display is character-based, using **newt** for the user interface. All interaction is done via the keyboard, the mouse is not operational in this environment. The graphical installer frontend[5] will allow the mouse to be used instead. Navigation of the dialogs is straight forward, if you are used to keyboard-driven applications. Each dialog usually consists of one or more groups of controls. For instance, figure 3.3 shows a typical dialog with two groups: the country list in one, and the "Go Back" button in the other. With [tab] and [Shift-tab], you can cycle between the groups, while the [left] and [right] arrow keys select the group (logically) to the respective side of the current group.

Within a group of controls, the [up] and [down] arrow keys navigate to the previous or next item (scrolling as necessary), and [Pg-up] and [Pg-down] work as expected. In addition, you can also press a letter key to jump to the first item that starts with this letter.

Hitting [enter] selects an item, and [esc] takes you one step back, the same as hitting the "Go Back" button. Checkboxes can be toggled with the [space] bar.

The user interface of the installation system resides on **tty1**. The key combination [Alt-F2] gives you access to a shell on **tty2**. It should be noted that this is a "convenience shell" used primarily for special purposes, and only if you know what you are doing. You can severely affect and/or disable the installer by doing too much. On **tty3** (key combination [Alt-F3]), you can see the contents of **/var/log/messages**, which contains the output of external programs invoked by the installer. If you want to know what is going on behind the progress indicators, this is the place to look. Finally, on **tty4**, the system scrolls **/var/log/syslog**, which mostly consists of debugging information. You will want to inspect it in case of problems (in addition to **tty3**). With [Alt-F1], you can return to the installer's user interface.

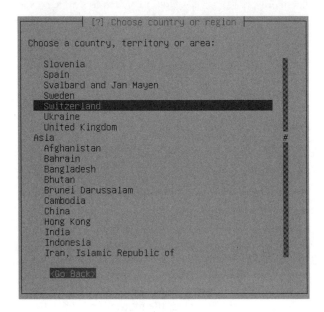

Figure 3.3:
A typical dialog with
two groups of
controls

Beginning the installation

The installer will first ask you to select your country and/or region, your desired language, and the keyboard type and layout corresponding to your hardware[15]. These parameters determine the default language and regional settings (**locale**) used in the installation process as well as the resultant system. At a later point, your choice here determines the selection of the timezone, and it is also used to suggest a Debian mirror.

---

[15]If you are installing a system with a keyboard layout too far removed from the US standard (which is the default until you configure it), you can use the **bootkbd** boot parameter to initialise it to the correct one at boot-time.

Accessing the installation medium

The next step consists of the detection of the hardware necessary to access the installation medium. In the case of a CD-ROM installation, I/O controllers are probed. In the case of a network-based installation, this involves detection of the network hardware. In standard mode, the installer will try all available modules in sequence (you may use the boot parameters to disable single modules if there are problems). The expert mode allows you to specify which modules to load, selecting all by default. If the debconf priority is set to low (which is the case in expert mode), the installer allows you to specify options to be passed to each module, which should not be necessary except for special hardware.

In expert mode, you will also be asked if you want to load the Card Services to enable accessing of CD/DVD drives attached via PCMCIA. This decision can be made at boot-time with the hw-detect/start_pcmcia=false parameter. At time of loading, the installer gives the user a chance to specify resource parameters. Certain machines — laptops especially — require port or Interrupt Request (IRQ) exclusions to prevent the host machine from freezing[16]. At the end of this initial hardware detection process, the installer will have detected the media and installation can proceed.

Installer components

The installer is based on a modular architecture, as previously mentioned. As such, it is a big advance from the previous, monolithic boot-floppies installer. Modules are simple Debian packages, called udeb files. The packages use debconf (see chapter 5.8) to interface with the user, and simple hooks to register with the installer, which then allows access to their functionality from within the installer menu.

The power of this approach is two-fold. First, as the different components of the installer are packages themselves, the installer has (finally) become maintainable. The components integrate with the existing infrastructure, and proven management mechanisms, such as the bug tracking system (see chapter 10.6), allow for greatly simplified development and maintainance. Even though advancement serves to directly improve the user experience in forth-coming versions of debian-installer, you are probably more interested in the second advantage of the component system: it makes the installer extensible. Developers, organisations, and administrators may integrate custom modules into the installer and take care of specific aspects of the target system conveniently during the installation. While additional modules may be loaded from floppies, CDs, or local International Standards Organization (ISO) images, the open architecture of the installer also make it easy

---

[16]A full list of recommended parameters for freezing machines may be found on the pcmcia-cs homepage: http://pcmcia-cs.sourceforge.net/ftp/doc/PCMCIA-HOWTO-2.html#ss2.5

to integrate such components into a customised installation medium, such as a CD-ROM for local use.

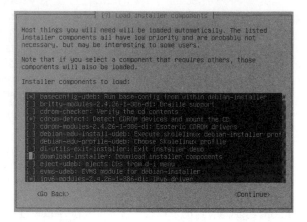

Figure 3.4:
The installer lets you
choose the
components to load
(in expert mode)

While the installer specifically asks expert mode users to choose the additional components to use, users of the standard installation mode can load additional components after the installer loaded a default selection. Figure 3.4 depicts the dialog for component selection. The modules are usually loaded from the installation medium. In addition, the **load-floppy**, **load-cdrom**, and **load-iso/scan-iso** components allow for modules to be loaded off floppies, CD-ROMs, or installer ISO images. Downloading components off the Debian mirrors is not supported by the CD-ROM installation media. Network-bootable or floppy installations allow it through the **net-retriever** component.

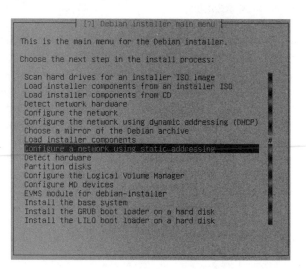

Figure 3.5:
The full menu of the
installer after loading
additional
components

Much in the spirit of Debian, installer components may be loaded at any point during the installation process. Thus, you should probably resist loading most of them right at the start to guard against confusion. Each loaded component expands the main menu (figure 3.2) with items contributed by the module. Figure 3.5 shows a menu after most components have been loaded.

Configuring network access

If it did not do so in the previous step, the installer will now attempt to detect the network hardware[17]. If the system does not have network hardware installed, you can leave the network configuration component with [escape]. If network hardware is installed in the system, but the installer fails to discover the interface(s) (which may happen in the case of ISA cards, or with newer "El-Cheapo" chipsets[18]), a list of available modules is presented, which can be manually loaded. Figure 3.6 shows the dialog. If none of the available modules is appropriate but you have the correct kernel modules on a floppy, you can include them now by opting for "none of the above" in the manual selection list. I usually have a known-to-be-supported network interface (*e.g.* with an RTL8139 or EtherExpress Pro chipset) with me and use that in case of problems.

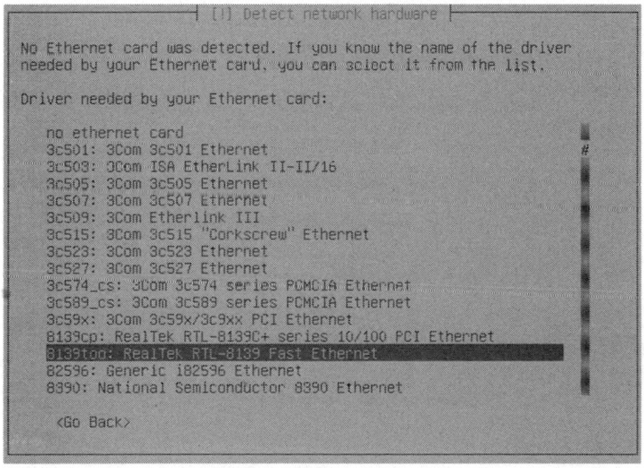

Figure 3.6:
Manual selection of
network drivers

[17]The installer can detect any Peripheral Component Interconnect (PCI) hardware also supported by the kernel. If you have newer hardware, you may have to opt for the 2.6 kernel (see further up for the respective boot options). Most Industry Standard Architecture (ISA) hardware can be autodetected, but some hardware may require manual intervention. More specialised hardware, such as AX.25, Fiber Distributed Data Interface (FDDI), and Micro Channel Architecture (MCA) network cards, are not supported. Integrated Services Digital Network (ISDN) cards are supported, but the (obsolete) 1TR6 protocol cannot be used.

[18]"El-Cheapo" is colloquial for "cheap", used frequently in the domain of computer hardware. Usually, El-Cheapo hardware is somewhat limited, either in features, standards-compliance, warranty, support, or quality.

At time of writing, the installer does not support the use of modems or DSL during the installation. If you are connected to the Internet by one of these means, you should opt not to configure the network during the installation (by selecting "no Ethernet card" from the list of supported cards), and to set up the connection manually using the appropriate tools from **tty2** (see chapter 6.8.4 and chapter 2 respectively). After installing the system, the configuration unfortunately has to be redone. The next stable release of the installer will allow for the proper configuration of PPP and PPPoE through the user interface.

Once the drivers for the network hardware have been loaded, you can select the primary interface. The system will attempt to use Dynamic Host Configuration Protocol (DHCP) to configure the card. If you have multiple interfaces, be careful not to trip over the Linux kernel's interface naming strategy: there is no reliable method of determining which interface name corresponds to which interface. Therefore, a trial and error strategy may be the least painful. After installing the system, you can use **ifrename** or **udev** to assign static names to network interfaces (see chapter 6.8.1 and chapter 6.5.1 respectively). The installer uses DHCP by default to configure network interface parameters. In expert mode, static network addresses may be specified instead. It is even possible to disable the use of DHCP in standard mode, by specifying the **netcfg/use_dhcp=false** option at the boot prompt. Lastly, the **netcfg-static** installer module provides a means to configure static network parameters instead of using the automated DHCP method.

Selection of package source

By default, the installer will pull the packages required for the base system from the installation medium, if it contains the necessary packages. The official Debian CD-ROM as well as the **netinst** image contain these, the **businesscard** image requires network access to obtain the base system.

Figure 3.7:
Selection of the
desired Debian
release

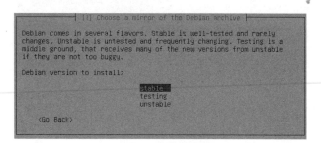

The **choose-mirror** component allows for an online Debian mirror to be used, even if the base system is available on the installation medium. The installer will try to choose the correct country and present you with a list of known mirrors, of which you will want to choose one at random within your region. At this moment, however, packages are not going to be installed. Instead, the installer asks you in expert mode, which release you would like to install (see figure 3.7). Unless you know what you are doing (and have read chapter 4), the release suggested by the installer will serve you well. When run in standard mode, you are not given a choice and the installer will install the current *stable* (but at least *sarge*). When using a physical installation medium, this question might be skipped, since the medium usually contains only one release.

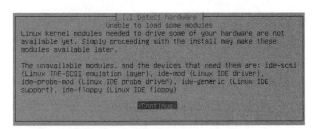

Figure 3.8:
Unless affecting
critical components,
warnings from the
hardware
autodetection can be
safely ignored.

In the next step, the installer goes out a third time to detect hardware, this time loading every driver corresponding to a device in the local system. You may see some error messages at this point (figure 3.8 shows an example). Unless you are running some kind of special controller hardware, these warnings can simply be ignored, as installing the base system files will cure the reported problems most of the time. That said, it is never a bad idea to note down the problems for later reference.

The partition manager

Drivers for all critical hardware have now been loaded. Before the actual installation of packages can take place, the hard disk must be prepared. Much to everyone's surprise, the new installer does not rely on the handy **cfdisk** partitioning tool, but instead provides a newly developed manager application, **partman**. This tool is written in the same spirit as **debian-installer**, providing only a structural foundation for modules to extend the functionality. Various additional modules serve to make **partman** more than a partitioning tool. Its functionality includes:

Automatic partitioning

partman can automatically partition a single drive, or the largest continuous block of free space on a hard drive. Rather than assuming a default, it lets the user choose a scheme and then uses smart heuristics[1] to decide the partition sizes.

Partition table types

partman can create partition table types appropriate for all supported architectures.

Partitioning

> partman can do everything that cfdisk can; in particular, it has the ability to create a partition at the end of free space. In addition, partman can resize existing partitions to create room for a Debian installation. Some aspects directly accessible in cfdisk, such as the hexadecimal partition type, are handled more abstractly by partman.

Filesystems

> partman can initialise partitions with all common filesystems[19]. Additional filesystems can easily be added qwith components. Mount points and file-system flags are also configured within partman.

Multi-device support

> partman can configure Linux Multi-Device (MD) support, including RAID levels 0, 1, and 5.

Logical volume manager

> partman can create volume groups and logical volumes for use by the Linux LVM.

Undo support

> As partman does not write anything to disk until you tell it to, you can have it restore the state of the partition table and undo any changes you have made.

As a separate component, autopartkit provides another automatic partitioner, which preceded partman, but with several shortcomings that partman set out to address. Its functionality has largely been superceded by partman; it is now obsolete and only sparsely supported, if at all. My advice is not to use it.

Guided partitioning

A new system rises and falls with the design of its partition table. Many users do not know the principles of partitioning and thus should not be expected to come up with a table just like that. The partman partitioner provides an automatic partitioner, which is referred to as "Guided partitioning", automatic partitioner, or by the name of the partman component: partman-auto. In simplified mode, partman-auto is automatically invoked whereas in expert mode, you are given the choice. It is always possible to enter "Guided partitioning" from the partman main menu, and when the automatic partitioner has finished its job, it is still possible to manually edit the partition table as it drops you into partman's user interface.

[19]See appendix C.2.2

The automatic partitioner queries the user for the space it should partition (see figure 3.9). Usually, this will be an entire volume (thereby erasing all data on the disk), but **partman-auto** also allows free space to be used, leaving existing partitions untouched.

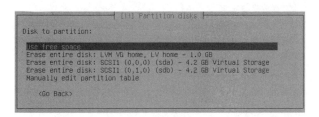

Figure 3.9: partman-auto can automatically partition whole volumes, or just use existing free space.

At this point, it is possible to skip automatic partitioning and enter **partman** directly, even in simplified mode. From within **partman**, it is furthermore possible to resize and move partitions to make space for the Debian installation.

Instead of imposing a typical partition table on the user, **partman-auto** provides a selection of schemes, as depicted in figure 3.10. Here, the user may choose between different high-level descriptions, such as "Separate partition for home directories," or "Multi user system." The resulting set of partitions includes one or more filesystem partitions in addition to a partition for swap space[20]. The filesystem sizes are calculated from the disk size, minimum and maximum sizes, and a priority relative to the other partitions. This algorithm produces very nice results. The syntax used for the scheme definition files is rather straightforward, allowing for easy addition of schemes in a custom installation.

```
┤ [!] Partition disks ├
The disk can be partitioned using one of several different schemes.
If you are unsure, choose the first one.

Partitioning scheme:

    All files in one partition (recommended for new users)
    Separate partition for home directories
    Multi-user system

    <Go Back>
```

Figure 3.10: Partitioning schemes available for automatic partitioning

When the automatic partitioner finished its job, it displays the result, as shown in figure 3.12 in the main **partman** screen. The automatic partitioner leaves you with a pre-configured manual partitioner, so there are no limits on the changes you want or need to make.

---

[20]See http://sourcefrog.net/weblog/software/linux-kernel/swap.html and http://sourcefrog.net/weblog/software/linux-kernel/free-mem.html for interesting discussions of swap space on Linux systems.

If the result is acceptable, the user may select "Finish partitioning and write changes to disk" to move onwards in the installation process. Otherwise, you will need to use partman.

Figure 3.11:
The new and powerful
partition manager

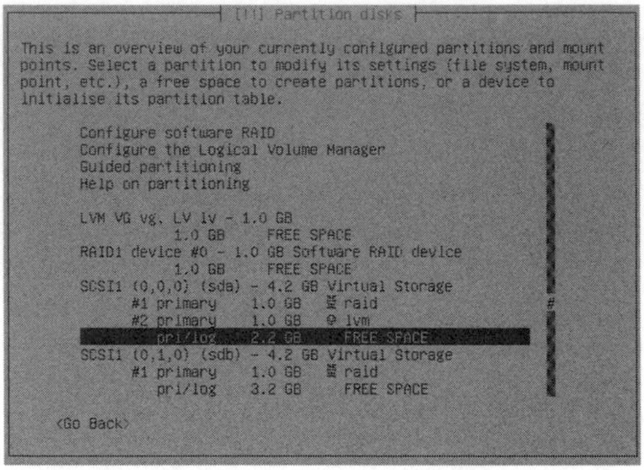

```
                      ┤ [!!] Partition disks ├
   This is an overview of your currently configured partitions and mount
   points. Select a partition to modify its settings (file system, mount
   point, etc.), a free space to create partitions, or a device to
   initialise its partition table.

        Configure software RAID
        Configure the Logical Volume Manager
        Guided partitioning
        Help on partitioning

     LVM VG vg, LV lv - 1.0 GB
                1.0 GB      FREE SPACE
     RAID1 device #0 - 1.0 GB Software RAID device
                1.0 GB      FREE SPACE
     SCSI1 (0,0,0) (sda) - 4.2 GB Virtual Storage
        #1 primary    1.0 GB    K raid
        #2 primary    1.0 GB    P lvm
           pri/log    2.2 GB      FREE SPACE
     SCSI1 (0,1,0) (sdb) - 4.2 GB Virtual Storage
        #1 primary    1.0 GB    K raid
           pri/log    3.2 GB      FREE SPACE

     <Go Back>
```

partman, the partition manager

Your first encounter with **partman** can be somewhat awkward, especially if you have only used the *fdisk up to this point (like me). However, three or four installations should have your skill level back up to par, and you will soon begin to appreciate the new partition manager[21]. In figure 3.11, you can see the partitioner in its new outfit. Note the four items tagged "FREE SPACE", where partitions will be created.

The partitioner consists of three sections. The top is devoted to configuration utilities and hosts tools like the RAID and LVM configurators as well as the auto-partitioner. In the middle are the disks available on the local system, as well as any logical volumes and RAID devices that have been defined. These are referred to as "volumes," a common term for entities holding partitions in the Unix domain.

If your desired destination volume does not show up, make sure the appropriate driver for your controller is loaded. Finally, there are the "discard" and "save" options at the bottom. The partitioner interface uses **debconf** and thus feels similar to the rest of **debian-installer**. This includes the ability to use the various keys for quick keyboard navigation.

Compared to the previous **boot-floppies**, **partman** is task- rather than process-oriented. With **boot-floppies**, admins first had to create the partitions, before

---

[21]At time of writing, a major shortcoming of the partitioner is its slow speed. However, this limitation is being worked on. The partitioner is currently written in **shellcode**, and a rewrite in a compiled language should fix this.

going on to initialise and mount them one by one. If you need to resize a partition later, the whole process had to be redone. With **partman**, everything is configured step by step without an imposed order of steps. The user can go back and change previously configured parameters at any time. When everything is set up and the user chooses to finish the partitioning process, the partition table is written, filesystems are created, and the partitions mounted accordingly. At the same time, the user may opt to undo all changes and restore the partition table to its previous state (by rereading it from the volume).

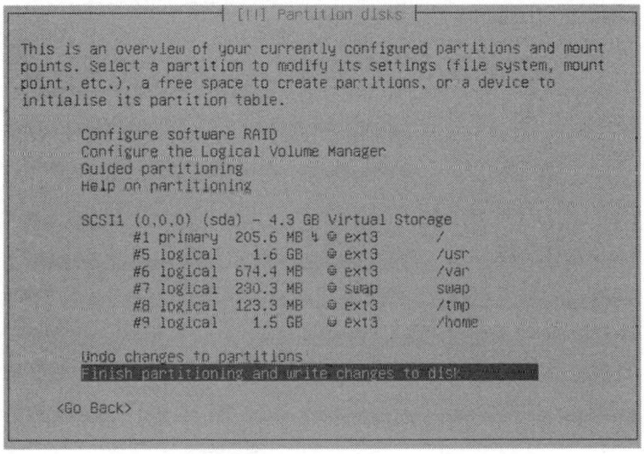

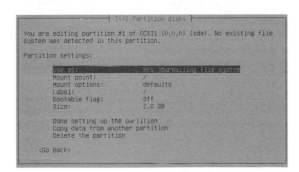

Figure 3.12:
A partition table
produced by the
"Multi-user
workstation" scheme
of the automatic
partitioner

Below each volume, the partitioner lists the defined partitions as well as any free space still available. A new partition table can be created by selecting the desired volume and hitting [enter]. Unless you know what you are doing, the type of the new partition table should be **msdos**, which is standard on the **x86** architecture. You may be able to use other partition table types, but depending on your BIOS and hardware, you might have to jump through hoops. When a new partition table has been created, a new item, "FREE SPACE" should appear.

Existing partitions can be edited, and new partitions created in areas of free space, simply by selecting the partition or chunk of space and hitting [enter]. For existing partitions, this will bring up the partition configuration dialog shown in figure 3.13.

Figure 3.13:
The dialog used to
configure partitions

If you are faced with an existing partition table, and need to free up some space for your Debian installation, the partitioner allows you to resize swap partitions, as well as partitions using one of the following filesystems: **FAT, NTFS, ext2/3**. If the filesystem is supported, its size will be editable in the partition's configuration dialog. Entering a new size into the dialog depicted in figure 3.14 (which also specifies the limits) will cause **partman** to resize the partition and the filesystem accordingly. Take note that resizing a filesystem requires the partition table to be written and all changes made in **partman** so far to be permanently written to disk. Thus it is probably best to first resize all partitions as desired before making other changes in the partition manager.

Figure 3.14:
The new installer can
resize existing
partitions.

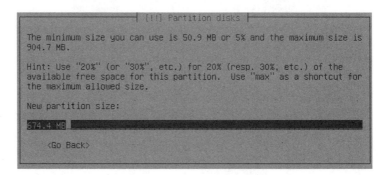

If you are instead creating a new partition, you are first asked to give some more information about the partition you would like to create: what the purpose of the partition will be (*e.g.* swap space, or a regular filesystem), the desired size, the location within the free space, and other parameters relevant to the partition table type you created. In the case of the **msdos** partition table type, it wants to know whether to create a primary or a logical partition (if there are not four primary partitions already). After answering these few questions, the partitioner leaves you with the partition's configuration dialog (see figure 3.13), where you can fine-tune the new partition.

The partition configuration dialog is the heart of the partition manager. From here, you can initialise filesystems, instruct the installer to leave existing partitions untouched, or dedicate partitions to the LVM or MD (RAID) drivers. A partition's destiny is set by its "Usage method." Depending on the selected usage, the list of available options changes accordingly. Common to all usages is the control of the partition's size as well as the state of the "bootable" flag (if applicable to the partition table type). We will return to the bootable flag when we talk about boot managers in a little while.

If you are creating a normal data partition to hold a filesystem, you will need to specify a mount point for the filesystem, and you are given the chance to define a number of boot flags to be used for the filesystem, which the installer automatically writes to **/etc/fstab** for you. It is also possible to copy data from an existing filesystem to the new space[22].

The item "Done setting up the partition" will take you back to the partitioner menu. Remember that all changes you make here are not commited until you tell **partman** to do so. You may come back to the partition configuration dialog of each partition and tweak and polish your partition scheme as many times as you wish.

When the table and partitions have been configured to your liking, you can tell **partman** to "Finish partitioning and write changes to disk" from the main menu. Alternatively, you can tell it to "Undo changes to partitions" and re-read the partition table, reverting all changes.

Configuring RAID

The Debian installer allows for the configuration of RAID volumes prior to the installation, eliminating the need to bootstrap a RAID system from a temporary installation (or live boot medium). Three RAID levels are currently supported:

Level 0
> Also known as striping, this is actually a pseudo-RAID in which the data are spread across different partitions to give the impression of one large partition. If this is what you need, I encourage you to look at LVM (see chapter 17) instead.

Level 1
> What is known as mirroring involves the maintenance of two (or more) partitions with exactly the same data in sync. All writes go to all involved partitions, and reads can be served from any single partition. This level provides highest redundancy, slow write speed, but a high read rate.

Level 5
> In this level, which requires three disks at least, each block of data is spread across all but one disk, and the last disk stores checksumming data that can be used to restore the data on the other disks, if one of them fails. This level can handle the failure of one disk, provides the slowest write speed, and adequate read access.

A RAID volume needs at least two partitions (expediently on two separate physical media, RAID 5 needs three disks), which must be marked for use by the RAID volume. To create such a partition, you follow the usual steps, and select "physical volume for RAID" as the partition's usage method, as shown in figure 3.15.

---

[22]This is accomplished with **libparted**'s function **ped_file_system_copy**. The target partition must therefore be at least as big as the source partition. At the moment, **libparted** only supports partitions with **ext2**, **ext3**, or **FAT16/FAT32**.

Figure 3.15:
Configuring a
partition for RAID

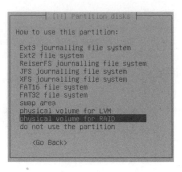

All the partitions used in a RAID volume should be of the same size. The RAID volume will be of the same size as the smallest available partition, thus potentially wasting disk space.

Figure 3.16:
The RAID
configuration tool

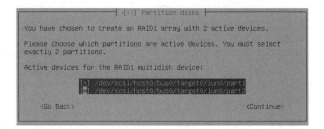

When all partitions that are to partake in the RAID configuration have been prepared, you can start the RAID configuration tool from the **partman** main screen (provided that the **mdcfg** installer component has been loaded). Using the tool (depicted in figure 3.16), you can assemble RAID devices interactively.

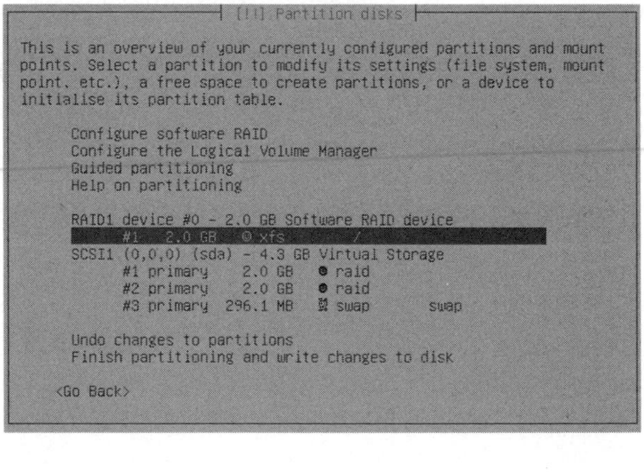

Figure 3.17:
A RAID volume
appears in the
partitioning tool like
a normal partition.

When done, each defined RAID volume shows up as a separate device in **partman**, as shown in figure 3.17. The new device may be used like any other partition to hold a filesystem, or even incorporated as a logical volume into a LVM volume group.

Configuring LVM

The LVM is a device mapper, which logically separates filesystems from the physical disks or their partitions. Without going into too much detail, the gist is that a Volume Group (VG) spans one or more physical partitions. A VG may hold one or more Logical Volume (LV)s. A LV holds a filesystem. The main advantage of a LV is that it can be resized. Furthermore, VGs can be extended with additional Physical Volume (PV)s to accommodate growing LVs. Figure 3.18 shows the schematic relation of the concepts underlying the LVM.

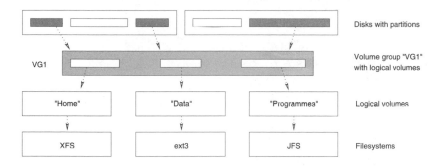

Disks with partitions

VG1 — Volume group "VG1" with logical volumes

"Home"   "Data"   "Programmes" — Logical volumes

XFS   ext3   JFS — Filesystems

Figure 3.18:
A schematic overview
of LVM

To configure the LVM from the installer, the **lvmcfg** component has to be loaded. Furthermore, at least one partition must be designated for use as a PV by the LVM. Therefore, the first step in setting up LVM is usually to create a partition and choose "physical volume for LVM" as its usage method. This partition will serve in a VG. Keeping in mind that it is possible to add and remove PVs from the VG at a later point in time, you probably do not want to spend too much time trying to figure out the layout at this time, unless you already know what you want.

When at least one partition has been configured for the LVM, the VGs can be set up with the item "Configure the LVM" off the partitioner's main menu (or the installer's main menu). This step requires the partition table to be written to disk and will thus permanently write any changes you made so far. A later undo will not be possible. The LVM menu allows you to create VGs and LVs in a straightforward way. Obviously, you must create at least one VG before any LVs can be made. Volume groups are identified by a name of your choice. The name could describe the source of the VGs, such as "IDE_disks".

The creation of logical volumes is equally straightforward. Their names should be chosen to reflect their purpose (such as "Mail spool"). After creating the desired logical volumes, the installer lists the LVs as additional volumes in the main window, as shown in figure 3.19. When creating logical volumes, it is useful to keep in mind that it is typically quite easy to attach additional space to an existing volume, and to grow the filesystem to use it. However, not all filesystems support shrinking, and if a filesystem is full, shrinking it will cause data loss.

Figure 3.19:
The partitioner treats
a LV like a normal
partition.

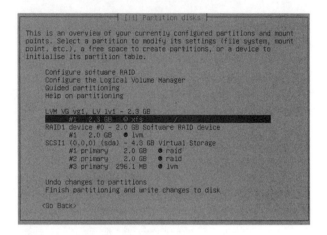

Using the conventional partitioning tools

If you prefer to stick to **fdisk**, **cfdisk** & co. — you will find them installed and usable in **tty2**. Be advised that the installer uses **devfs**, thus you will not be able to locate **/dev/hda** or **/dev/sdb**. Instead, the local hard drives are available under **/dev/discs**, numbered in BIOS order (on Intel/AMD architectures). The entries in that directory are symbolic links, thus you can easily distinguish between them[23]. The actual disc is found as **disc** in the directory the **symlink** references. Thus, to partition with **cfdisk**:

```
~# cfdisk /dev/discs/disc0/disc
```

Once the partitions are created, you have to return to **partman**. Unfortunately, the installer cannot deal with filesystems that you create and mount externally; it expects you to designate desired filesystems and mount points in the configuration dialog shown in figure 3.13.

---

[23]Since **devfs** is deprecated, Debian might release a new installer without **devfs** soon after *sarge*'s release

Installing the base system

When the partitions have been set up, the installer proceeds to install the base system. Again, the default is to pull the required packages from the installation medium. With physical installation media, using the **choose-mirror** component and selecting a mirror causes the installer to automatically use the chosen mirror to obtain the base system. On the other hand, if the **cdrom-detect** package is used to detect local CD-ROM drives during a network installation (**netboot**), and an installation medium is found, this medium will be used. In general, an APT repository available on a locally mounted CD-ROM is preferred over a remote repository.

Now is the right time to take the dog for a walk, or run an errand (or sit and stare at **tty3**) — the base system installation takes a little time to fetch, unpack, install, and configure the packages needed for the base system.

Following the installation of the base packages, the installer configures the kernel of the target system. By default, it installs the same kernel as used during the installation, which ensures maximum compatibility. In expert mode, the user is given a choice of kernels to install. Care should be taken when selecting a different kernel for installation as it may result in an unbootable system. While stepping up a kernel version should generally work, installing an older kernel than used for the installation process is almost always a bad idea.

Installing a bootloader

The final step in the first stage of the installation process is the configuration of a **bootloader**. In standard mode, the installer automatically selects the preferred bootloader and attempts its installation. For Intel and AMD-based architectures, the preferred **bootloader** is Grub. In expert mode, the user can choose not to install a bootloader (which will leave the system unbootable!), or select a different bootloader (such as **Lilo** for **x86**, which has a better grasp of RAID volumes than **Grub** at time of writing).

In addition, if the **/boot** directory is on an **XFS** filesystem, you must use a different bootloader than **Grub** due to a bug in **grub-install**, which could cause the install process to hang indefinitely. You can convert to using **Grub** once the system is up and running. The problem has been identified and a solution is being worked on, although it appears to be a serious bug and may take some time to fix. The installer will warn you about this inconvenience. If you insist on using **Grub**, you may be able to install it manually through the **Grub** shell on **tty2** (see chapter 8.3.1).

Before writing itself to disk, the **bootloaders** for the i386 architecture ask for the destination of the boot block. Usually, this will be the Master Boot Record (MBR), but the presence of another operating system may affect this choice. It is probably a good idea to create a backup of the MBR before overwriting it. The following command, executed in the shell on **tty2** will write the MBR to a file in the **/boot** directory of the new system:

```
~# dd if=/dev/hda of=/target/boot/mbr.backup bs=512 count=1
```

Grub is capable of incorporating and booting other operating systems, so the MBR should generally be the right choice. With a backup of the boot block, one should be on the safe side. If the desired scenario is a **dual-boot** with Microsoft Windows, then letting **Grub** or **Lilo** boot Windows instead of letting **ntldr** load Linux allows for greater flexibility.

If a partition is chosen instead of the MBR, the partition must be marked **bootable** (or **active**). While **Lilo** can do this automatically, **Grub** and other **bootloaders** still require user intervention at present time. Thus, following the installation of the **bootloader** into a partition, you must not forget to return to **partman** and set the destination partition **bootable**. In standard mode, this requires you to "Go back" when the installer displays the dialog shown in figure 3.20, to navigate to **partman** and make the required change. Alternatively, you can enlist **sfdisk**. Assuming you installed the **bootloader** to the third partition on the first disk:

```
~# echo ';;;*' | sfdisk --force /dev/discs/disc0/disc -N3
```

The **--force** argument is necessary because the partitions are already mounted, and **sfdisk** would refuse to change the partition table otherwise. Flipping of the **bootable** flag is a safe modification.

Figure 3.20:
The dialog indicating
the installer's
completion — unless
you did not install
Grub into the MBR.

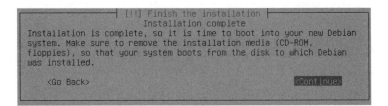

Telling the installer to finish the installation completes its first stage (which takes most of the time). In stage two, we need to configure the base system.

3.2.2 Configuring the base system

When the installer has finished, the new system needs to be rebooted. There are still a few system parameters that need to be set, a task picked up after the first boot by the **base-config** programme. This is commonly referred to as the second installation stage. Using the **baseconfig-udeb** installer component, **base-config** can be run from within the installer during the first stage. The following assumes that the conventional two-stage path is followed.

The **base-config** programme presents itself as shown in figure 3.21. It follows the same usage paradigms as the installer, since it also uses **debconf** (see chapter 5.8).

During its execution, you are free to use consoles **tty2** through **tty6**, which are accessible with the usual [Alt-F2] through [Alt-F6] key combinations. Until you have configured the root password and/or added other users, you can log in as root without a password.

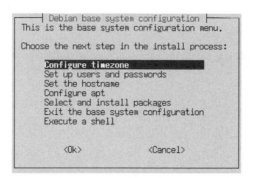

Figure 3.21:
Almost done... the
menu used to
configure to base
system.

The individual steps are straightforward and well documented. Therefore we can skip ahead to the item "Configure apt". To use **APT**, it needs to know where to obtain any packages you ask it to install. Additionally, if you use a modem or DSL connection, you must configure these first. At present, the Debian installer only offers to set up a PPP connection if it was unable to configure an Ethernet device previously. Thus, if you opted not to configure the network before the reboot, **base-config** should bring up **pppconfig** and walk you through the configuration of a PPP connection, as used by most modems. DSL (unless it uses DHCP), or other PPPoE connections are not currently configured by **base-config** and must be setup manually: before configuring APT, change to **tty2** with [Alt-F2], log in, and use **pppoeconf** to configure your setup. Once you have verified that a connection exists (*e.g.* you can ping **debian.org**), the rest of **base-config** (on **tty1**) should complete without any fuss.

While **base-config** could certainly just reuse the repositories specified during the installation, you are given another chance to select them. We will call it a feature, not a bug. The packages can reside on a Debian CD, somewhere on the Internet and accessible via HyperText Transfer Protocol (HTTP) or File Transfer Protocol (FTP). **base-config** walks you through the mirror selection process, using your regional settings to make suggestions. In standard mode, you can only select a single mirror, and security updates are automatically included. Expert mode allows you to add as many APT sources as you want, and choose whether to include security updates, or packages from the *contrib* and *non-free* repositories.

When APT is configured, the most definitive step of the Debian installation is ahead: software installation. After choosing "select and install packages" from the **base-config** menu, you are presented with a screen allowing for the selection of tasks (see chapter 5.5), or given the option to manually select the packages you want installed from the start. The task selection is depicted in figure 3.22 (see also chapter 5.5). If you pick the option to manually select the packages to install, the installer invokes **aptitude** (see chapter 5.4.11), and packages corresponding to the other tasks you selected will be marked for installation. For a minimal installation, you will want to select no tasks and quit **aptitude** without making any selections at this point.

Figure 3.22:
During the
installation, you may
opt to install
collections of
software, or manually
select packages to be
installed.

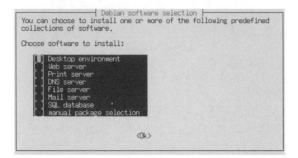

Debian uses **exim4** as its default mail transport agent, and **base-config** allows you to configure it before starting to use the system. You can always modify the chosen configuration with **dpkg-reconfigure exim4-config.**

When done configuring the mail transfer agent, the new Debian system is completely installed, fully configured, and ready for use. **base-config** can be invoked again from the command line, and if not needed, the package can be safely purged. For a suggestion of the first package to install, and to help improve the Debian system, please refer to chapter 5.11.10.

3.3 Configuring the X server

Since the task of configuring an X server is not necessarily specific to the Debian system, Debian provides a set of tools and approaches which an administrator is invited to use. Unfortunately, the rapid developments in the domain of graphics adapters do not correlate well with Debian's idea of stability. As a result, it is often not trivially possible to configure the correct driver to make use of all the features of modern graphics cards.

That said, Debian has come a long way in terms of making the configuration of X as easy as possible. Nevertheless, since one of the most common problems with new Debian installations is the inability to configure the X server; the following section attempts to shed some light on the philosophy, and expose some tricks.

3.3.1 An overview of X in Debian

Assuming a minimal installation (see chapter 3.2), the easiest way to install the **X** server along with core components is through the installation of the **x-window-system-core** meta package (dummy package), which depends on the bare essentials of the **X** server system and thus causes them to be installed as well: that is, the server itself, a basic selection of fonts, fundamental graphics libraries, and the standard set of **X** utilities. The package does not depend on display or window managers, or even a terminal emulator, which need to be installed in addition. An alternative is the **x-window-system** meta package, which additionally pulls in a number of useful but mostly optional components (such as a font server, the **X** print server, proxy services, the **twm** window manager, and the **xterm** terminal emulator).

Both of the **x-window-system-*** meta packages cause the **xserver-xfree86** package to be installed, which in turn depends on the **xserver-common** package. These two packages provide the core of the **XFree86** system and use **debconf** to query the user for configuration data (see chapter 5.8). While the configuration data is limited to parameters governing the invocation of the **X** server (and only shown if **debconf** is configured with a priority of **low**; see chapter 5.8.2), the **xserver-xfree86** package's **debconf** questions concentrate on the hardware and driver configuration.

A typical set of **debconf** parameters for a Swiss Debian installation with a Matrox graphics card, and a USB mouse might be the following:

Parameter	Value	
X server driver	14 (mga)	*Table 3.2:*
X Keyboard (XKB) rules	xfree86	*A typical set of debconf parameters*
XKB keyboard model	pc105	*for the*
XKB keyboard layout	de_CH	*xserver-xfree86*
XKB keyboard variant	nodeadkeys	*package for a Swiss*
XKB keyboard options	ctrl:nocaps	*machine*
Mouse port	/dev/input/mice	
Mouse type	ImPS/2	
LCD device	yes	
Monitor configuration method	medium	
Best video mode	1280x1024 @ 60Hz	
Video modes to use	5 6 7 8 9 10	
Default colour depth	6 (24 bits)	

Once configured, you should be able to start **X** using the **startx** command (avoid running it as **root**). Alternatively, install the **xdm** package for a basic graphical login (which should be preferred over **startx**[24].

3.3.2   Integrating automatic hardware detection

Answering these questions obviously requires knowledge about the available hardware. As such, it may be asking too much of the administrator who concentrates on software and does not particularly care about what powers the machine on the inside. Two methods exist to aid the installing user with answering the questions pertaining to devices and drivers. The first should be enough for most cases and involves the **xserver-xfree86** package to use a few other packages for hardware auto-detection. The second method uses a separate package and a larger set of helpers to seed the **debconf** database.

xserver-xfree86 auto-configuration

The **xserver-xfree86** package suggests (see chapter 5.7.3) three utilities to determine the hardware of the local system: **mdetect** detects where the mouse device is and what protocol it uses, **read-edid** scans the attached monitor for supported modes, and **discover** allows for the automatic discovery of the graphics adapter and its parameters.

If these three packages are installed prior to the configuration of **xserver-xfree86**, the package will use them to aid the user in determining the correct values to use. Any parameter which can be unambiguously determined by these tools will be set accordingly, while **debconf** will skip the associated question. If the tools fail to determine the hardware, the user has to provide the parameter. If a number of possible values exist for a parameter, the user is given the choice; the **xserver-xfree86** configuration script is good at suggestion reasonable defaults.

To make use of the automatic hardware detection, you should install X in the following way (assuming that you will use **x-window-system-core** to pull in the core components):

```
~# apt-get install discover mdetect read-edid
[...]
~# apt-get install x-window-system-core
[...]
```

[24]A problem with **startx** is that it is called from a console login session. A malevolent hacker could circumvent an X screen locker by killing the X server, or by switching to a virtual console and temporarily suspending it. In both cases, the attacker would gain access to the account despite the screen locker. Solutions include running **exec startx** instead (to replace the login shell with the X server, or using a display manager such as **xdm**.

When **debconf** asks you to configure the **xserver-xfree86** package, you can choose to let it attempt automatic configuration of the mouse, screen, and graphics adapter devices and drivers.

xdebconfigurator

The **xdebconfigurator** package provides a tool which ties together a number of hardware detection methods, runs these in turn, and uses the findings to seed the **debconf** database for the **xserver-xfree86** package. It also provides sensible defaults for all other parameters, allowing for automated installs.

To make use of the tool, install and run it prior to the **X** server:

```
~# apt-get install xdebconfigurator hwinfo mdetect read-edid
[...]
~# xdebconfigurator
[...]
~# apt-get install x-window-system-core
[...]
```

3.3.3   Dealing with unsupported hardware

The most common inconvenience experienced by users is the lack of support for their display adapter. Debian continues to provide a very mature but also outdated version of **XFree86** (due to licencing issues), and the new **X** server produced by the X.Org Foundation will not become an official part of Debian until Debian *etch* (although it will become available in *testing/unstable* soon after *sarge*'s release). Therefore, many recent developments in the **X** drivers sector are not available from the Debian **X** server at time of writing, even though some drivers have been back-ported by the Debian **X** maintainers. In addition, an increasing number of vendors are providing non-free, binary drivers to draw the last bits of performance from their devices (which is what competition forces them to do). Due to Debian's commitment to free software, it cannot provide these drivers in its archive (see chapter 2.3).

Still, it is often possible to make **X** work with a particular graphics adapter. This said, a user installing a new Debian system does not necessarily want to spend hours on the virtual console, trying to find a solution. Fortunately, the standard **vesa** driver supports all modern graphics adapters, and can be used to get **X** running with minimal effort and delay (albeit without hardware acceleration or **OpenGL** support).

With a graphical user interface, the familiar browser, and other commonplace tools, it is more convenient to research the challenge of how to make **X** support the installed graphics adapter. In the mean time, the Debian installation can be used for all tasks without complex graphical requirements.

If you prefer to use the modern X.Org server, you can also use the packages prepared by Ubuntu. To prevent other Ubuntu packages from being pulled in, you should probably pin the Ubuntu repository source to a low priority, and select the *hoary* target release explicitly for the installation of the X server:

```
~# cat <<EOF >> /etc/apt/sources.list
deb http://archive.ubuntu.com/ubuntu/ hoary main
EOF
~# cat <<EOF >> /etc/apt/preferences
Package: *
Pin: origin archive.ubuntu.com
Pin-Priority: 50
EOF
~# apt-get update
[...]
~# apt-get install -t hoary x-window-system-core
[...]
```

3.3.4   Customising the X session

The **X** server is usually invoked in one of two ways: a single, local session can be started with **startx** from a virtual console. Alternatively, a display manager such as **xdm** can be used to control the server display and manage login sessions, locally or remotely.

Multiple display managers can be installed; the **debconf**-managed /etc/X11/default-display-manager file contains the path to the display manager executable to be used by default. Debian starts its display managers with **init.d** scripts, rather than by using a special runlevel (see chapter 6.3.1). These scripts only start the corresponding display manager if it is the default.

Following the execution of **startx**, or a successful authentication with the display manager, an X session is created. Traditionally, single sessions started from the console read initialisation commands from the /etc/X11/xinit/xinitrc file, while display managers would use /etc/X11/Xsession. Debian takes a unified approach and uses the latter for both. /etc/X11/Xsession eventually uses **run-parts** (see chapter 6.1.1) to iterate and source all files under /etc/X11/Xsession.d. At various times during the process, /etc/X11/Xsession.options is checked for configuration options, which are detailed in the **Xsession.options** (5) manpage. By default, the following intialisation steps configure a X session on the Debian system:

1.   If **startx** was called with the **failsafe** argument and the **allow-failsafe** is set in Xsession.options, the initialisation sequence merely spawns a terminal

emulator and exits[25]. If **startx** is given the path to an executable, the executable is invoked instead of the usual X session. Client arguments which are not path specifications are passed as arguments to a terminal emulator, which is started instead of the default session.

2. All resources from files in **/etc/X11/Xresources** are merged with **xrdb**. If **Xsession.options** specifies **allow-user-resources**, **~/.Xresources** is also merged.

3. If the **allow-user-xsession** is set, and **~/.xsession** exists, it is executed or sourced, depending on whether the executable bit is set. If the file is not present, **~/.Xsession** is tried. If neither of these two files exists, the process starts the default session manager, or, if absent, the default window manager. If neither is available, a terminal emulator is started.

4. If **ssh** is installed and the **use-ssh-agent** option set in **Xsession.options**, the X session is started as a child of **ssh-agent**.

The Debian archive contains a number of session and window managers, as well as a selection of terminal emulators. In all cases, the default to use is determined with the alternatives system (see chapter 6.1.4). The corresponding canonical service names are **x-session-manager**, **x-window-manager**, and **x-terminal-emulator**, respectively. Thus, to use **fluxbox** as the default window manager, you can issue the following command:

```
~# update-alternatives --set x-window-manager /usr/bin/fluxbox
Using '/usr/bin/fluxbox' to provide 'x-window-manager'.
```

When the **allow-user-xsession** is set, users can override the default by providing a session initialisation script in **~/.xsession**. A simple example follows, which starts **xscreensaver**, prompts for the Secure SHell (SSH) passphrase to register a key with the SSH agent, and executes **fluxbox**:

```
~$ cat <<EOF > ~/.xsession
nice -20 /usr/bin/xscreensaver &

if [ -f $HOME/.ssh/id_dsa -o -f $HOME/.ssh/identity ]; then
  export SSH_ASKPASS=/usr/bin/ssh-askpass
  /usr/bin/ssh-add < /dev/null || exit 1
fi

exec /usr/bin/fluxbox
EOF
```

---

[25]At time of writing, failsafe support was broken (see http://bugs.debian.org/297002). Please execute **startx** /usr/bin/x-terminal-emulator to get the same effect.

4

Debian releases and archives

Look, this is Debian. They don't release things until you have to
fire rockets at the thing to stop it from working.
— MrNemesis on Slashdot

Probably the two most common facts to hear about Debian is that it is hopelessly
outdated and stable as a rock. In the Debian world, these two traits are actually
one and the same, and it would be difficult to argue against either one. Already at
the time of release of a new Debian version, the software it contains is usually not
current. In the world of free software, where improvements, fixes, and new features are added to projects on a daily basis, this may have negative consequences.
However, in productive environments, new features and improvements can often
backfire. Thus, the Debian *stable* release focuses on software stability, rather than
trying to surf the cutting edge with possibly buggy and untested software. Only
security-related bug fixes are allowed in.

Debian *stable* is not the only Debian release. In addition, the archive provides two other ones: *testing* and *unstable*. While these are not really released in the way that *stable* is frozen and termed official, they are publicly available and in use by many people[1]. Before inspecting each of the Debian releases in turn, it is important to define what stability means with respect to Debian, or what instability the name *unstable* is trying to coin.

In the context of a software and distribution archives, stability can refer to one of three aspects:

Software runtime stability

> Most commonly, the term stability is used to refer to the reliability and robustness of software contained in the archive. Stable software is mature software with an extremely low number of bugs (there is no such thing as bug-free software). Runtime stability is what keeps users happy.

Software feature stability

> Stability may also refer to the feature set provided by a software. In this definition, stable software does not introduce drastic changes or radical new features from one release to the next. Administrators appreciate feature stability because it allows them to fix bugs with newer versions without risking unwanted changes to the behaviour.

Archive stability

> A software distribution archive can be termed stable if the set of packages or pieces of software it provides does not fluctuate. Furthermore, archive stability also includes the relationships among the contained packages. A stable software distribution archive does not grow or shrink in size, and updates only affect individual packages, not larger parts of the archive. Archive stability allows for official releases to happen.

The canonical Debian release names "*stable*" and "*unstable*" refer to the second and third definition of stability, although the first sense of stability is implicit to a certain extent. While Debian developers upload new packages to *unstable* on a daily basis, and drastic changes to the packages and pieces of software they provide are possible (albeit rare), once a Debian release becomes *stable*, no packages will be added or removed to or from the set. Furthermore, as a function of Debian's security update policy (see chapter 7), updates to individual packages are limited to security-grade bug fixes and must not affect the feature set (or fix non-security) bugs. Fixes to inconvenience bugs, new versions, and new software as a whole are held back until the next Debian release is promoted to Debian *stable*.

The first of the above three aspects of stability results from the Debian release cycle, which we shall unfold in an instant. For a package to be included in *stable*,

---

[1]The term "release" is frequently used to refer to self-contained archives in the domain of software development.

it must be free of critical bugs and have received several months worth of testing. While the runtime stability of a software is purely in the hands of the upstream author, the rigorous testing and quality control applied throughout the Debian release cycle ensures an acceptable level of runtime stability across all programmes included in Debian *stable*.

The three archives, *stable*, *testing*, and *unstable* are naturally related. A normal package traverses all three (in reverse order). To help understand the process, it is useful to look at a package life cycle, from the moment the maintainer finishes and uploads it until it is immortalised on the media of an official Debian release.

4.1   Structure of the Debian archive

First, let us identify the different directory hierarchies and their purpose in the Debian archive. The archive is split into two main hierarchies, rooted at /**pool** and /**dists**. All the packages and source files reside under /**pool**, whereas the index files are located in /**dists**. This separation was instituted when *testing* was introduced (which happened between the release of *potato* and *woody*). Some packages have equivalent versions in multiple releases and it is less of a waste of space to store packages in a common pool and reference them individually from the release indices.

An excerpt of the structure of a Debian mirror is shown in the tree diagram in figure 4.1.

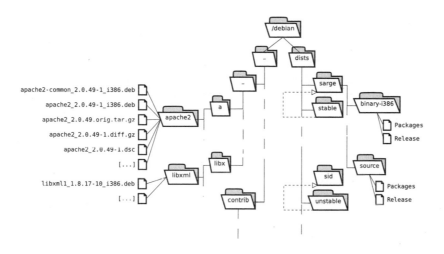

Figure 4.1:
A tree diagram
showing excerpts of
the Debian archive

4.1.1 The package pool

The /pool hierarchy is divided up into three sections: *main*, *contrib*, and *non-free*. The hierarchy is further subdivided at the next level into subtrees according to the first letter of the contained packages. Within each single-letter directory there are directories for each Debian source package. For instance, files related to **apache2** are located in **/pool/main/a/apache2**. An exception is made for libraries, which sort into different subtrees, rooted at **lib?** (where the question mark is a wildcard). For example, binary packages generated from the **libxml** source package are found below **/pool/main/libx/libxml**.

At this point it is useful to identify the two different types of package found in Debian: source and binary packages. At the same time, there are native and non-native or external packages. It will all become clear in an instant! The maintainer transforms a software into a source package. Source packages are not The Debian package format (DEB) files but rather the combination of their source files. In the case of an external (non-native) package, a source package is made up of:

*.orig.tar.gz
>   The .orig file is a **tarball** containing the software in the way its (upstream) author released it.

*.diff.gz
>   The **diff** file encapsulates the changes needed to debianise a software. After applying the patch (a **diff** file is a patch), the software can be packaged for Debian with standard Debian tools.

*.dsc
>   The **dsc** file provides the essential information to describe a source package, including the **MD5** sums of the **orig** and **diff** files. It is signed by the maintainer and authenticates an upload[2].

Software that was specifically written for Debian does not need to be debianised. Therefore, the **diff** file does not exist and the **orig** file is replaced by a **tarball**, which, when unpacked, can be used directly to produce a Debian binary package.

With the information stored in the ./**debian** subdirectory of a debianised source package, the Debian maintainer tools can produce a DEB file containing the software installable on and tailored for a Debian system. A DEB file is always a single binary package. A Debian source package can produce more than (but at least) one binary package. For instance, many libraries are split across three binary packages all generated from the same source package: **libfoo1**, **libfoo-dev**, and **libfoo-doc**.

---

[2]In combination with the **buildd's**, the **dsc** file serves to identify an upload entity. For architectures other than the maintainer's native one, the **dsc** file is signed by the administrator of the **buildd** (see chapter 4.2).

The Debian archive currently contains about 15 000 binary packages generated from about 10 000 source packages.

4.1.2 Package indices

The /dists hierarchy provides the index files needed for **APT** to work and find DEB files to download[3]. A separate index is provided for each combination of the following four parameters:

- the release name, such as *stable* or *sarge*.

- the section, such as *main*.

- the target architecture.

- package type: source or binary.

The archive uses subdirectories to map these parameters to files, so finding the appropriate index file is a matter of climbing down the directory tree rooted at /dists based on these parameters.

On the first level there are the different releases with symlinks for the canonical names. For instance, when *sarge* is released, **stable** will be a symlink to **sarge**. Additional directories at that level include **experimental** and **stable-proposed-updates**. We will return to these in chapter 4.4.1 and chapter 4.4.4 respectively.

Below each release directory there are subtrees for the three sections which resemble the /pool hierarchy. The separation of all files within each release according to their degree of freedom is an important prerequisite to being able to produce or deploy archive snapshots with specific licence requirements. Also in the release directories are the **Contents** files, which map the files installed on the filesystem to the providing package. Tools such as **apt-file** (see chapter 5.4.4) use this information, and **grep** can usually extract all necessary information from this file as well.

In each section's directory, there are several subdirectories for the indices of binary packages as well as the directory for the source index. The index file is called **Packages** in all cases and contains the information of all available packages in the part of the archive identified by the four parameters.

For instance, /dists/stable/main/binary-i386/Packages contains the package descriptions for all binary packages in *main*, which can be installed as part of the *stable* distribution on the i386 architecture. Similarly, /dists/sid/contrib/source/Packages references all source packages in *contrib* which are contained in *sid*. The architecture does not matter for source files.

---

[3]The package indices are not to be confused with the /indices directory found on the mirror; the latter indexes file in the mirror filesystem, while package indices index Debian packages stored therein.

4.1.3   The Release files

The /dists directory of a Debian mirror is home to the index files for the various releases provided by the mirror. Each such release is additionally described by a **Release** file, which contains important data about the release. The **Release** file of the *woody*'s third release looks like this:

```
~# cat Release
Origin: Debian
Label: Debian
Suite: stable
Version: 3.0r3
Codename: woody
Date: Mon, 25 Oct 2004 17:56:29 UTC
Architectures: alpha arm hppa i386 ia64 m68k mips mipsel powerpc s390 sp
arc
Components: main contrib non-free
Description: Debian 3.0r3 Released 25th October 2004
MD5Sum:
[...]
```

The **Release** file is used mainly by **APT**, which determines the architectures and components available from the mirrors specified in **/etc/apt/sources.list** using these files. Also, when mixing releases (see chapter 8.2), the various data can be used to specify criteria for pins. Finally, the file contains the checksums of all index files associated with the release. As shown in chapter 7.5, these checksums can be used to verify the integrity of packages downloaded from a Debian mirror.

4.2   The package upload

A Debian package has a life cycle, and a long way to go before it is distributed as part of the Debian *stable* release. Figure 4.2 illustrates how the different archives and components of the Debian infrastructure work together. You need not understand it all, but it may come in as a handy reference.

Following the debianisation process, a maintainer transfers the source files (along with the DEB file for the build architecture[4]) to one of the available upload queues. On the side of the accepting server, the Debian queue daemon moves the files to the **unchecked** directory at regular intervals. This directory is the domain of **katie** and friends[5], which verify that the uploaded package is signed with a trusted signature, and run a number of sanity checks on the package. On successful verification,

---

[4]This is required to make sure that no maintainer uploads without building the package locally first. At time of writing, the binary packages created by the maintainer directly propagated into the *unstable* archive. For all other (applicable) architectures, the build daemons are expected to generate the binary package(s) from the source package. Please see chapter 7.5 for security implications.

[5]**katie** and friends are a set of scripts named after female celebrities which work hand

the upload is moved to the **incoming** directory, which is accessible over the Web[6], but which should not be used as a package source except in special circumstances.

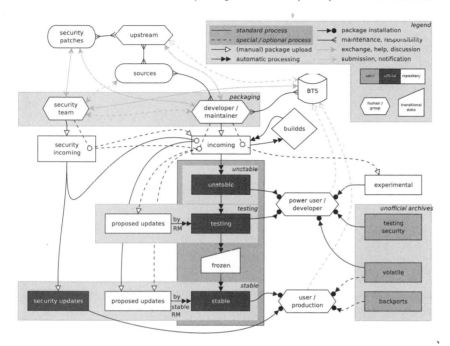

Figure 4.2:
The life cycle of a
Debian package
(based on the work of
Kevin Mark)

When an upload hits **incoming**, the build daemons (referred to as **buildd**) are notified[7]. There is at least one build daemon for each architecture that Debian supports (see chapter 4.5), and its job is to compile the software and produce a DEB file specific to the respective architecture. The resulting DEB is accompanied by a file describing it (the **.changes** file[8], which has to be signed by the administrator of the **buildd**). Finally, the package file is submitted to the upload queue and trickles into unstable as previously noted.

On a daily basis, **dinstall** moves available package files from **incoming** to the appropriate locations of the Debian pool (the **/pool** directory of every Debian mirror). It then updates the index files of the archive. Subsequently, the new packages are available from the *unstable* archive via APT.

in hand on the various tasks surrounding the management of the Debian archive. See http://cvs.debian.org/dak/?cvsroot=dak.

[6]http://incoming.debian.org

[7]The status of the individual **buildds** is available at http://www.buildd.net.

[8]The .changes file is generated as part of the build process for each architecture and identifies a (set of) binary package(s). It must be cryptographically signed by a Debian developer for the package(s) to be considered for inclusion in the Debian archive. See chapter 9.2.12.

4.3   The official releases

Each of the three official Debian releases — *stable*, *testing*, and *unstable* — has specific traits related to the role the release plays during the package life cycle and the overall project. As a package usually enters the *stable* release by way of the *unstable* and *testing* archives, the following sections provide an overview of the three official releases in the same order that a new package encounters them on its way into the Debian system.

A Debian system can be installed and maintained using any of the three releases as package sources. In chapter 5.4.1 you see how a single release is selected, and chapter 8.2.1 describes how they can be combined. Note that all three of the official releases give you archive signatures for the index files of the corresponding archive (see chapter 7.5). In appendix C.1.1 you can find information to help you verify the keys used for the signatures.

4.3.1   The unstable release

As previously mentioned, the *unstable* release is in a state of continuous change. *unstable*, which is also called *sid*[9], is the workspace of Debian development. New packages percolate into the archive and become part of *sid* in a somewhat chaotic fashion. As a result, dependencies between packages break, only to be resolved later, conflicts appear and disappear, and packages possibly do not meet the quality standards of the rest of the archive. Furthermore, while maintainers take care not to inconvenience users tracking the *unstable* release, sometimes drastic changes in the packaged software hit the archive and can cause serious breakage on the target system.

The term "unstable" also applies to the packaging of software. Occasionally, a maintainer uploads a package in a rush, overlooks a detail or makes a mistake in the packaging. The resulting package — if it makes it past the sanity checks — usually does not play ball with the local system, or installs horribly dysfunctional software. Even policy violations are possible. It is important to note that such policy violations are mostly restricted to misplaced files, but it should go without saying that *unstable* is *not suitable* for production environments. Having said that, most Debian developers run *unstable* on their primary machines. If the occasional failed dependency resolution is not fatal, *unstable* is quite a nice way to experience Debian — especially when there is a desire to contribute back to Debian with bug reports or interesting arguments on mailing lists.

In fact, it is unlikely for *unstable* to be more fragile than other operating systems, which are based on young software and whose developers try hard to publish the

---

[9]Sid is the name of the evil boy in Pixar's Toy Story who continuously breaks toys. It is thus an appropriate name for a release that can break a system. Conveniently, *sid* is also an acronym for "Still in development."

system as soon as possible. It goes without saying that short development cycles (such as Debian *unstable*) do not leave much room for testing, and therefore often result in a plethora of bugs.

Note that "unstable" refers primarily to the archive and the packages, and only indirectly to the software itself: software provided as part of Debian *unstable* may in fact be quite stable since packages in *unstable* usually correspond to official releases of the software. Thus it depends on the software author's quality standards how much runtime stability a programme needs to be part of an official upstream release. Often, a software will be available in two versions: an official release (which is often called "stable"), and a development release. If the latter is of any interest (or if the upstream authors are overly conservative with version numbering), chances are that a maintainer will provide pre-release packages for inclusion in Debian *in addition* to the official version. While not a rule, the development version usually comes in *-snapshot packages directly from the version control system to allow Debian users to be truly on the bleeding edge. For example, **gcc-snapshot** provides a bleeding edge version of the GNU compiler, while **gcc** provides a version deemed stable by the **gcc** developers.

As regards security updates, *unstable* enjoys a similar kind of attention as the *stable* release. While the security updates published by the security team might be restricted to the version in the *stable* release, a new and fixed version will usually become available in short time, and the maintainer will attribute special priority to uploading a fixed package to *unstable*.

Dealing with an *unstable* system is not very different from dealing with an installation of Debian *stable*. Upgrades for *unstable* are available through APT, but it is important to keep in mind that package upgrades in *unstable* have received considerably less testing than packages distributed as part of an official upgrade to Debian *stable*.

As the dependency information of packages in *unstable* can change, systems based on packages from the *unstable* archive should be upgraded with **apt-get --show-upgraded dist-upgrade** rather than with the plain APT upgrade mechanism. The **--show-upgraded** option is not needed but advisable to be able to inspect the changes proposed by APT before enacting them. In addition, tools such as **apt-listchanges** and **apt-listbugs** (see chapter 5.11.2 and chapter 5.11.3 respectively) are invaluable in assessing whether an upgrade is worth the trouble or involves unnecessary dangers.

4.3.2   The testing release

An upload to the Debian archive is accompanied with an urgency specification, coded into **debian/changelog** within the package. Normal uploads are of low urgency, while security updates enjoy prioritised treatment due to their high (or even emergency) urgency. The urgency of an upload also determines when the uploaded version of a particular package moves from *unstable* to *testing*.

Depending on the urgency, a given version of a package must have been in *unstable* 10 (low), 5 (medium), 2 (high), or 0 (emergency[10]) days before being considered for testing. When a package is considered for promotion to *testing*, a number of other criteria have to be met before it is moved. If a previous version of the same package already exists in *testing*, the new version must have been built on at least all architectures supported by the previous package, and it must not have more release-critical bugs (see chapter 10.6.3) filed against it than the package in *testing*. Furthermore, all of the package's dependencies must be satisfiable within *testing*, and its declared relations cannot break another package already in *testing*.

When all these criteria have been met, the archive scripts move the package to testing, replacing any previous version[11]. *testing* is therefore generally not affected by the childhood diseases of packages as they hit *unstable*, but it is also not as current as *unstable*.

testing seems like the ideal release for all but the most critical applications. It is not on the bleeding but on the leading edge, and yet its contents has been scrutinised more carefully than the software from *unstable*. It also fluctuates less than *unstable*, which provides for easier maintenance. In the past, the major disadvantage of *testing* was the lack of security support. Security updates may already be delayed when they percolate to the *unstable* archive, and at least another two day delay is imposed before they are accepted into *testing* – provided all other requirements are met. Therefore, security updates in testing are sometimes delayed by several days, which is an important point to consider. Obviously, a home computer with a dial-up line to the Internet still qualified for a *testing* installation, but machines with a permanent Internet connection that offer services to the world, or machines that host multiple untrusted users are probably better off using *stable*, or *unstable* if that is an option.

Leading up to the release of *sarge*, the Debian testing security team has formed to address this shortcoming. At time of writing, the team is still operating unofficially, mainly coordinating through the **secure-testing-team** mailinglist hosted on **lists.alioth.debian.org**. An online record[12] with daily updates keeps track of outstanding security issues that persist in the *testing* archive. Depending on progress, *etch* could be supported with security updates while it is the *testing* release.

Similarly to *unstable*, it is advisable to use **apt-get --show-upgraded dist-upgrade** in place of **apt-get upgrade** because of the fluctuation in the set of packages provided in *testing*.

---

[10] Due to a limitation in the archive management script **britney**, it actually takes a day for emergency uploads to trickle into testing.

[11] Previous releases are available in the daily snapshots of the archive: http://snapshot.debian.net

[12] http://merkel.debian.org/~joeyh/testing-security.html

4.3.3 The stable release

Whenever the goals for the next release have been met[13], *testing* is frozen. During the ensuing freeze cycle, no new features are allowed to enter *testing*, and the developers concentrate on fixing bugs and providing additional translations. Especially bugs with severity above and including **serious** have to be fixed. These bugs are labelled RC and must be solved before a release can be made. Packages with outstanding RC bugs may be removed from the *testing* release during the freeze cycle.

Once *testing* is ready for release, the previous *stable* release is obsoleted (but archived[14], and the *stable* and *testing* symlinks changed to point to the next release generation. For this reason, it is advisable to hardcode the release codename in /etc/apt/sources.list, rather than its canonical name. Specifically, for a *sarge* system, I recommend changing all occurrences of "stable" with "sarge." While Debian release is unlikely to catch you off-guard, using the code names for the APT archive allows an upgrade to the next official release on your own schedule, and not when the symlinks in the archive change. When the next release follows, all you need to do is replace "sarge" with "etch" and then **dist-upgrade** as usual (see chapter 5.4.7).

As soon as a release has become the new *stable*, it becomes immutable. Security updates are kept in a separate repository (see chapter 7.2), and neither the set of packages nor the packages themselves are subject to change until the next official release comes around. It may seem a little peculiar to have security updates kept separate, but as with everything else, there is a reason for this procedure. Not every administrator wants security updates. Larger corporations frequently maintain their own internal release and have policies in place that require the ability to precisely identify the state of their machines. In such a case, fixes first need to be scrutinised before being provided internally. If the underlying archive (*stable*) were to change every other day, it would be impossible to maintain a consistent installation across hundreds of machines and simultaneously provide custom extensions and updates.

At semi-regular intervals, security and other proposed updates (such as trivial bug-fixes) are merged with the last official release to create the next revision of the official release. These revisions ("stable dot releases" or simply "r-releases,") are identified by a specific suffix to the version number of the current *stable* release. For instance, when this book was written, the official Debian release was *Debian 3.0r3*, which is the third revision of the release after *woody* became *stable*. When a new dot release is published, it replaces the previous *stable* archive.

---

[13] http://release.debian.org

[14] http://archive.debian.org is the official archive address, and many mirrors feature /debian-archive as a sibling of /debian, which holds /dists and /pool. At time of writing, the primary site has not been reachable for a long time, and inquiries about its status have remained unanswered. Available mirrors are listed on the distribution archives web page: http://www.debian.org/distrib/archive

4.4   Unofficial APT archives

In addition to the three archives corresponding to the three official releases *stable*, *testing*, and *unstable*, a number of other APT repositories exist, and can be easily integrated with APT on systems that need them. The following sections introduce the most important of these. While it is certainly possible to run Debian systems for all purposes without these archives, the packages they contain may be needed at times. In any case, it is good to know about their existence and purpose.

4.4.1   The experimental archive

The Debian archive also hosts the *experimental* release, which contains packages that are not ready for public use, not even as part of *unstable*. Developers use this space to share packages as part of the development cycle. Unless you want to take part in this development (*e.g.* as a tester, or more actively), you can safely ignore the *experimental* archive.

The following lines in **/etc/apt/sources.list** enable APT to install software from *experimental* (see chapter 5.4.1). As always, please make sure you use your closest mirror instead (see chapter 5.4.1).

```
~# cat <<EOF >> /etc/apt/sources.list
deb     http://ftp.debian.org/debian experimental main
deb-src http://ftp.debian.org/debian experimental main
EOF
~# apt-get update
```

The *experimental* archive contains new major versions for some of the software found regularly in the Debian archive. For instance, APT 0.6 (see chapter 7.5.2) resides in *experimental*, while version 0.5 is available from the three release archives. The *experimental* archive is automatically deprioritised by APT so there is no need to worry about upgrading all your packages to the available experimental versions. This is accomplished with a special directive in the archive's **Release** file. See chapter 8.2.1 for more information:

```
~$ getfile /dists/experimental/main/binary-i386/Release
~$ grep NotAutomatic Release
NotAutomatic: yes
~$ apt-cache policy apt
apt:
  Installed: 0.5.27
  Candidate: 0.5.27
  Version Table:
     0.6.25 0
          1 http://ftp.debian.org experimental/main Packages
 *** 0.5.27 0
```

```
500 http://ftp.debian.org sid/main Packages
100 /var/lib/dpkg/status
```

To install software from the experimental archive, pass the **--target-release ex-perimental** option to APT:

```
~# apt-get install --target-release experimental apt
[...]
Setting up apt (0.6.25) ...
```

4.4.2   The volatile archive

Debian's *stable* archive does not change beyond security updates, and these do not add new features (see chapter 4.3.3 and chapter 7). While administrators generally value this stability highly, certain types of software must change over time, even on the most stable systems. Prime candidates of such software include virus scanners, spam filters, and other tools which operate on data that is expected to change (such as **whois**).

While I was working on this book, a number of Debian developers started to conceive a strategy of how to deal with software that needs to change to remain usable. Such software was termed to be "volatile." A draft of the strategy is available at **http://volatile.debian.net**, which also hosts an **APT**-accessible archive for volatile software.

The goal of the *volatile* archive is to become a parallel to the security archive, and allow administrators to pull in updates with the same confidence with which they use the security archive. Changes will be limited to essential features and will only happen in close cooperation with the respective maintainers. Furthermore, security support for the packages in the *volatile* archive will be available.

To use software from the *volatile* archive, tell **APT** to use one of the mirrors found in the official mirror list[15], and update APT

```
~# cat <<EOF >> /etc/apt/sources.list
deb http://volatile.debian.net/debian-volatile sarge/volatile main
deb-src http://volatile.debian.net/debian-volatile sarge/volatile main
EOF
~# apt-get update
[...]
```

The *volatile* archive uses a custom version scheme designed to integrate and not conflict with the official packages from the main Debian archives (see chapter 5.7.5). All index files in the archive are signed with cryptographic signatures (see chapter 7.5), and information to validate the key used may be found in appendix C.1.2.

[15]http://volatile.debian.net/mirrors.html

4.4.3   The amd64 archive

Even though the **amd64** architecture is not yet officially supported by the Debian project, the port is ready to be used (see chapter 4.5.2). You can find installation and maintenance instructions at the port's web page[16].

Until it can be integrated with the main Debian archive, the **amd64** architecture is available from a separate APT repository. You can find details, as well as a list of mirrors online[17]. The archive's index files are signed with a separate key to ensure package integrity (see chapter 7.5). Information about the key may be found in appendix C.1.2.

4.4.4   The *-proposed-updates archives

The two directories **stable-proposed-updates** and **testing-proposed-updates** provide a way for developers to circumvent the normal package cycle via *unstable* and *testing* into *stable*. Packages uploaded to these directories are considered for manual inclusion by the respective release manager. Specifically, **stable-proposed-updates** serves as the basis for the next dot release of Debian (see chapter 4.3.3).

Even though both directories host proper **APT** repositories, you are herewith discouraged from using them directly. Software in either of these bypasses the regular Debian quality assurance surveillance and does not receive the same amount of testing as software that progresses via *unstable*.

4.4.5   The backports.org archive

Compared to *testing* and *unstable*, the Debian *stable* release often contains outdated software. Furthermore, many packages are not available at all because they have only been packaged recently. Even though single DEB files can be manually downloaded from newer releases, versioned dependencies make this impossible. For instance, upgrading **postfix** to version 2 (*e.g.* for policy server support) is not possible on a *woody* system without pulling in other packages from the next Debian version (*sarge*):

```
~# getfile pool/main/p/postfix/postfix_2.1.5-5_i386.deb
~# dpkg --install postfix_2.1.5-5_i386.deb
[...]
dpkg: dependency problems prevent configuration of postfix:
 postfix depends on libc6 (>= 2.3.2.ds1-4); however:
  Version of libc6 on system is 2.2.5-11.5
[...]
```

[16]http://www.debian.org/ports/amd64
[17]http://amd64.debian.net/README.mirrors.html

Undoubtedly, users of Debian *stable* are not going to be in favour of upgrading libc6; it would be a major change to a system, puting its stability at risk. An alternative would be to download the source and recompile the package against the libraries available in *stable*. If you have to do this more than once, the process becomes tedious and error-prone.

The **backports.org** archive[18] attempts to close this hole and distributes packages that have been recompiled in exactly this way. To get **postfix** version 2 installed on a *woody* system, the following line in /etc/apt/sources.list is needed. Please use the mirrors page[19] to find the mirror closest to you, and use that mirror instead of the main distribution server.

```
~# cat <<EOF >> /etc/apt/sources.list
deb http://www.backports.org/debian woody postfix
EOF
~# apt-get update
~# apt-get install postfix
[...] ·
Setting up postfix (2.1.4-2.backports.org.1) ...
[...]
```

As you may note, the required package is listed as part of the repository specification. The **backports.org** archive contains more than 450 packages, and you probably do not want all your installed packages to be upgraded to the latest backport[20]. Thus, **backports.org** allows you to specify precisely the set of packages you want to include. You can also specify multiple packages on a single line:

```
~# cat <<EOF >> /etc/apt/sources.list
deb http://www.backports.org/debian woody postfix subversion
EOF
```

As we will be discussing the **APT** sources syntax in chapter 5.4.1, you can take the above line as a way of making the *woody* backports for **postfix** and **subversion** available for direct installation with **APT** from the **backports.org** archive. Moreover, the line also ensures that backports of all dependencies can be installed with similar ease, if necessary.

Please note that the packages provided in the **backports.org** archive are not officially endorsed and come without any warranty. **backports.org** is not an official part of the Debian project, even though it is maintained and supported exclusively by official Debian developers. In particular, its packages have not undergone standard Debian quality assurance verifications, and have not received the same amount of testing as official Debian packages.

---

[18]http://www.backports.org
[19]http://www.backports.org/mirrors.html
[20]If you do, you can use the pseudo package name all in /etc/apt/sources.list instead.

That said, the source used to produce the packages in the **backports.org** archive comes directly from the official Debian archive and should therefore be as secure as the original version in the respective archive. Still, it is important to keep in mind that an extra delay exists for security fixes to percolate to the **backports.org** archive.

As a last note, if you are using a backported package from this archive, please refrain from reporting bugs against the Debian BTS. Instead, use the **changelog.Debian.gz** file to figure out the backporter's address to which to submit any bug reports, or send them to the **backports.org** mailing list[21]. The list is also the primary source of support for packages from the **backports.org** archive.

4.4.6   The apt-get.org directory

Setting up an **APT** repository is quite simple (as shown in chapter 9.3). Over the years, unofficial repositories have sprung up all over the place, providing useful Debian packages that are not included in Debian, or which are modified for specific purposes. The web site at **http://apt-get.org** serves as a directory for these sites.

The database can be searched by architecture and package name (or even a regular expression). The result encompasses all matching and registered repositories. For each entry, a short description, the matching package(s) (along with version information), and the necessary lines for **/etc/apt/sources.list** are provided. It is impossible to make an authoritative statement on the security, integrity, or stability of packages in the archives referenced from **apt-get.org** archive directory. If you use packages from sources listed here, you should be aware that they are packaged by people not necessarily connected to or supported by the Debian project. In particular, it would not be difficult to register an **APT** archive containing trojaned software. The directory has no guidelines, restrictions, or quality verification procedures governing the archives it lists. You have to decide for yourself which repositories you want to trust.

4.4.7   Christian Marillat's multimedia archive

Due to the freedom requirements on Debian packages, which the Debian project set in stone in the DFSG, many useful multimedia programmes cannot be distributed with the official Debian archive. Even though Debian is working hard with the respective authors to release the software under a free licence, progress is slow at times.

Christian Marillat, a Debian developer, maintains an unofficial Debian archive with prominent multimedia content. His archive, which is described on his web page[22],

[21] http://lists.backports.org
[22] http://debian.video.free.fr

is host to popular software, such as **Mplayer**, **lame**, **transcode**, and various video codecs. Christian maintains packages for this software unofficially, which is more of an indication of the level of support he can provide, than the quality of the packages themselves. Christian is an official Debian developer, and his archive is signed to allow for integrity verification (see chapter 7.5).

As a side note, **Mplayer** is actually available under a DFSG-compatible license and official packages have been prepared at time of writing of this book. Unfortunately, *sarge* will not include these packages.

4.5 Architecture support

Although the consumer market is full of computers powered (and heated) by derivatives of Intel's **x86** architecture, **PowerPC** machines, and the latest generation of 64 bit processors by AMD and Intel, a significant number of other architectures also profit from the support by the Linux kernel. Linux is gaining popularity as operating system for embedded devices (*e.g.* with **arm** or **mips** processors), professional servers (*e.g.* using **sparc**, **alpha**, and **hppa** chips), and entire mainframes (*e.g.* **S/390**-based). All of these architectures are supported by Debian, as well as some others.

Nevertheless, the Linux kernel does not make up an operating system by itself. The kernel is merely the interface between hardware and the user-space software. As large parts of the common user-space software (as well as the kernel itself) are written in medium-level languages (which require a compiler to generate processor-specific assembly code), sensible support for a processor architecture requires the support by the kernel as well as by the entire user-space software collection that makes up a Unix system. As the "universal operating system," Debian GNU/Linux extends the architectural support of the Linux kernel with the GNU user-space utilities on eleven different processor architectures. More supported architectures are in preparation.

To support an architecture means that all of Debian has been enabled to work on that specific architecture. Moreover, it also means that the installation feels like any other Debian system, independently of the processor architecture powering it. Therefore, the Debian operating system can be seen as a layer of abstraction, allowing unified system administration across different types of machines. With the exception of packages not applicable to all architectures (such as **memtest86**, a memory tester for the **x86** architecture), all packages available in the archive have been built for every one of the eleven supported architectures.

The combination of Debian, the underlying kernel, the user-space collection, and a processor architecture is called a "port" of Debian. The official Debian GNU/Linux ports (the architectures on which Debian GNU/Linux runs)[23] are:

---

[23] http://www.debian.org/ports

i386

Being the first architecture supported by Linux, the IA-32 architecture found on **x86**-compatible chips by AMD, Cyrix, Intel, and others, is also Debian's most popular architecture.

ia64

Together with HP, Intel finally abandoned full **x86**-(backward-)compatibility with the 64-bit IA-64 architecture. Debian started supporting **ia64** with the *woody* release. The **ia64** port allows the use of 32 bit code through software emulation.

powerpc

Out of the cooperation between Apple, IBM, and Motorola grew the PowerPC chip, which powers IBM's RS/6000 line as well as Apple's PowerMac series. Support for the **powerpc** architecture was added in *potato*.

m68k

The Motorola 68000 series of processors powers a wide variety of computer systems, most notably the sun3 workstation series, as well as the personal computers by Amiga, Apple Macintosh, and Atari. Debian added support for the **m68k** architecture with the *hamm* release.

sparc

The Sun SPARC architecture powers the Sun SPARCstation workstation series as well as some models of the sun4 family. Similar to the **powerpc** port, the **sparc** architecture sports a 64 bit kernel but comes with a 32 bit userland. As an add-on to the **sparc** port, the **sparc64** sub-architectures aims to enable 64 bit user-space applications. Debian features support for **sparc** since the release of *slink*.

alpha

Also with *slink* came support for the 64-bit Reduced Instruction Set Computer (RISC) architecture Alpha, developed by Digital (Digital Equipment Corporation, DEC).

arm

The ARM processor is a low-power RISC chip by Acorn and Apple. Later, Digital and Intel joined to produce the improved StrongARM chips based on the **arm** architecture. First supported in *potato*, ARM processors are commonly found in mobile and embedded devices.

mips

Used primarily in SGI machines, Cisco routers and gaming devices by Sony and Nintendo, this RISC chip has been supported since *woody*.

mipsel

> The "little-endian" brother of the **mips** architecture, found primarily in DEC-stations, also joined the Debian architectures family with *woody*'s release.

hppa

> Hewlett-Packard's PA-RISC architecture found support from Debian with the *woody* release. The **hppa** architecture is mainly found in HP machines running HP/UX (or Debian).

s390

> The IBM S/390 mainframe (reborn as eserver zSeries in 2001) was officially adopted by Debian a short time later with the *woody* release. The 64-bit architecture power highly powerful chips optimised for parallel computing.

The advantages of supporting multiple processor architectures are self-evident. First, Debian gives a larger user base the ability to run Linux, as little to none viable user-space collections exist for users of non-Intel processor machines. Second, corporations and institutions, whose IT infrastructure has grown over years with a museum-like diversity of server architectures, are able to deploy Debian as a single operating system across all existing hardware. Thus, the costs of unifying system administration are kept as low as possible with Debian.

4.5.1 80386 – the processor

With gcc-3.3 1:3.3ds6-0pre6 (and also in some versions of **gcc-3.2**), the compiler started using the **bswap**, **xadd**, and **cmpxchg** instructions for code optimisation. These instructions are not available on real **80386** processors, but were added to the Intel instruction set with the **80486** processor series. With the packages for kernel versions 2.4.24 and 2.6.0, Debian added a patch to its Linux kernels to simulate these instructions in software on true **80386** processors. Unfortunately, the patch is known to be buggy and somewhat unmaintained.

The **80386** is an incredibly old and slow processor, but Debian would like to continue its support (it actively supports other architectures that are even less powerful than the **80386**, too). However, the upgrade from *woody* to *sarge* puts systems with true **80386** processors into an unfortunate catch-22 situation[24]: *sarge*'s libc6 and libstdc++5 both use the aforementioned instructions. Updating either of these libraries will hose the system until a new kernel is installed, but a new kernel cannot be installed due to a dependency on **modutils** (2.4 kernels) or **module-init-tools** (2.6 kernels), which in turn depend on a version of **libc6** not available in *woody*.

---

[24]Derived from the (excellent) book "Catch-22" by Joseph Heller, such a situation is an impossible situation where you are prevented from doing one thing until you have done another thing, but you cannot do the other thing until you have done the first.

At time of writing, the project is still discussing the possible steps to take. The suggestion for a special upgrade kernel was dismissed because of complexity and distribution issues. The preferred method to solve this would be the development of some user-space solution to emulate the missing instructions. If such a solution cannot be found, Debian will probably drop **80386** support altogether[25]. Debian *sarge* does not really run properly on one of these chips, largley due to memory requirements that cannot be fulfilled. Users of embedded **80386** machines typically have their own kernels to minimise memory usage.

Should **80386** processor support be dropped, the Debian project will look into to renaming its **i386** architecture to **i486** to indicate the change. However, the change might break existing scripts, as "i386" has been around forever. Further investigation will show. In any case, *sarge* supports the **80386** processor.

4.5.2   The amd64 architecture

While I was writing this book, Debian was ported to the **amd64** architecture. Being a very young port still, it is not distributed as an official port with Debian *sarge* nor contained in the official archive. Still, it is mostly complete and available for installation from its own archive (see chapter 4.4.3). At time of writing, four different ports exist for the **amd64** architecture:

sarge

> the 64 bit port of Debian *sarge*. The Debian **amd64** team is planning to provide security updates until the **amd64** architecture is part of the official archive.

pure64

> the 64 bit port of Debian *etch* and *sid*. This port will be integrated with the main Debian archive in the near future, and the 64 bit port of *sarge* will be merged in.

gcc3.4

> this port is identical to the **pure64** port, rebuilt with version 3.4 of the **gcc** compiler.

multi-arch

> an effort to integrate the multi-arch concept (see below) with **amd64**. Plans are to merge this port with **pure64** once it becomes part of Debian *unstable*.

Currently, the **pure64** port is the recommended port for **amd64** systems. At time of writing, it was not possible to upgrade an **i386** installation on an AMD 64 bit processor to any of the **amd64** ports. However, work is in progress to allow for this.

---

[25] http://lists.debian.org/debian-release/2004/10/msg00027.html

4.5.3 Multi-arch

With the advent of affordable 64 bit processors like the AMD Athlon 64, Debian has intensified its efforts to address the challenge of integrating 32 bit and 64 bit applications on the same system. Most 64 bit architectures support native or emulated 32 bit code execution, but the applications and libraries are incompatible across the two register sizes. Instead of implementing quick hacks or duplicating packages, Debian is trying to work with the LSB to come up with a method of integrating multiple architectures on a single machine in a scalable and well-designed way. Under the working title "multi-arch support", work has begun to address the challenge, and small test environments have already been put in place to help develop a policy[26].

The existing 64 bit architectures (**ia64** and **sparc64**) use separate directories to hold the 32 bit and 64 bit versions of the installed libraries. The approach is commonly referred to as "biarch" and is not free of problems. Apart from breaking the rules of the FHS (see chapter 5.7.4), the approaches differ and do not scale to other architectures, or similar changes in the future. As multi-arch reaches production status, current 64 bit architectures are expected to switch to using it. In addition, with multi-arch, Debian will be able to add full support for other 64 bit architectures, including **powerpc64**, **mips64/mipsel64**, **hppa64**, **sparc64**, and **s390x**, within a short time[27].

Until multi-arch is ready for production use, special arrangements have to be made to run 32 bit applications on 64 bit installations. One good technique is to use of a **chroot** managed by **dchroot** (see chapter 8.3.1).

---

[26]You can find more information about multi-arch at http://people.debian.org/~taggart/multiarch
[27]Some of these architectures (such as **sparc64**) are already supported, but use the deprecated biarch approach.

The Debian package management system

I was attacked by **dselect** as a small child and
have since avoided Debian.
— Andrew Morton

5.1   Requirements

Package management is among the most important features of an operating system. Most users want their machines to Just Work™ and are not particularly keen on spending hours a week keeping them up to date, or jumping through hundreds of hoops when they need a new software installed. Similarly, system administrators tending to a larger number of machines have better things to do than to spend hours on end for each workstation in their care.

Installation footprints

The most basic features of a good package management system are easy installation and removal of packages. The system should keep track of the files it drops onto the filesystem and be able to remove them later without leaving a trace.

For instance, when a bug is found with a programme, the package management system should be able to tell which package provided the programme so that the bug can be filed appropriately. In addition to the files installed as part of the software, the package management system should allow proper handling of files created by the software at runtime. For instance, a database server may drop a bunch of cache files next to its data files. Upon removal, it may be desirable to clean the system of the temporary files but to preserve the data files. After all, we are deinstalling the software, not the data.

Installation and deinstallation hooks

Often, software cannot be simply dropped onto the filesystem, but requires further configuration to work. Similarly, a programme may need to clean up when the user requests its deinstallation. A package management system should allow for custom actions to be taken at various points during the installation and deinstallation processes, allowing the maintainer to harness the full power and flexibility of regular Unix scripts.

Configuration file management

Another crucial factor that separates good from bad package management systems is the handling of configuration files. No matter how the package management system approaches configuration files, it must never overwrite the administrator's changes or the system will not have any friends. At the same time as it preserves modifications it should also allow for unmodified parts of the configuration to be merged with the newer version. However, configuration file management should not impose any limitations on the syntax of the configuration file, or the software configuration options.

Dependencies

Based on the Unix philosophy[1], a typical programme uses a number of libraries and possibly other programmes to accomplish its tasks. A good package management

---

[1] The Unix philosophy is to provide numerous small tools, each of which does no more than its own task and strives to do that in the best possible way. With standard usage paradigms and communication protocols, these tools can be arbitrarily combined.

system should have a full grasp of these relationships, including the automatic resolution of dependencies when a software is to be installed.

Software upgrades

As software evolves and new versions are published, a good package management system should be able to keep a system up to date without too much fuss. New dependencies should be properly resolved (and old ones obsoleted), and upgrade paths paved to provide for smooth transitions to newer releases.

Package format capabilities and package quality

Since a programme's upgrade path is typically very specific to that programme, it is important to realise that even the best package management system will perform really badly if the packages are incompatible across different versions, or if there is simply no upgrade path from one version to the next. Thus, when assessing the quality of a package management system, it is important to realise it needs to take the packages it is supposed to handle into consideration. The role played by the capabilities of the package is just as important as the quality of the packaging itself. If these two are not powerful and flexible enough to encapsulate the flexibility of Unix software, the capabilities of the package management system will be squashed to the largest common denominator.

The Debian package management system

If you have been around fellow geeks or spent enough time on forums and amidst the Linux community, you will have certainly been alerted to the powers of the Debian package management system. In fact, ask anyone for Debian's most important feature and most will respond with some reference to this package management system. They are both right and wrong. They are right, because the package management system is the main interface between an administrator and the Debian system. But they are also wrong because the package management system itself is not what puts the fun back into software installation and system maintenance for many Debian users.

In a nutshell, what makes the Debian system so powerful is the combination of its robust package management system, the Debian policy, which gives the developers the rules needed to produce an integrated system rather than just a set of packages, and the flexible system administration tools which evolved out of the needs of its users. In the following chapters, I will introduce these pieces and help you assemble the big picture of the Debian system. First, you will meet the package management system and its three key components: the Debian package format, the Debian package manager **dpkg**, and APT, the Advanced Package Tool.

5.2   Introducing Debian packages

Most of the Debian system is based on packages: regular software comes in package form just like low-level components, such as the kernel, and device drivers. The files governing the boot initialisation sequence are also managed through the package management system, and the same applies to other administrative aspects of the system which are not really software in the typical sense of the word (*i.e.* executable programmes). Two types of package exist in the Debian world:

Binary packages
> A binary package comes in the form of a file with the **.deb** extension. These files are commonly called DEB files, and usually contain exectuables, documentation, configuration files, and copyright information, or any subset thereof. However, apart from the copyright information (and the **changelog.Debian** file), binary packages can also be empty and serve as transitional or meta packages (also known as dummy packages), whose sole purpose is the satisfaction of dependencies.

Source packages
> Even though the word "package" has the connotation of a single file "packaging" the content, a source package actually consists of two or three files. Together, these files provide everything needed for the package maintainer scripts to create the binary packages generated by the source package. A source package therefore provides the source code of the software as well as the "source code" needed to generate the binary package(s).

A source package is used to create one or more binary packages. In most cases, only a single binary package is generated. However, in some cases, it makes sense to modularise the software at the package level. The binary packages generated from the **xscreensaver** source package include **xscreensaver** and **xscreensaver-gl**. While the first provides the **xscreensaver** application with some savers, the latter contains savers written with **OpenGL**; users without graphics acceleration can thus save space and only install the standard savers.

At present, the Debian archive provides almost 10 000 source packages, which generate about 15 000 binary packages. Debian users generally deal with binary packages, although source packages provide for interesting possibilities even to normal users, as we shall see shortly (see chapter 5.9.1).

5.2.1   Package categories

Every Debian package, binary or source, belongs to a category containing other packages with related functionality. These are not reflected in the directory structure of the Debian archive[2] but governed by the package control files (see chapter 5.2.4). These categories make it easier to find packages for certain applications and provide a logical compartmentalisation of the package pool.

The following categories are defined by the policy:

Section name	Description
admin	Administrative utilities (install software, manage users, etc)
base	The Debian base system
comm	Programs for faxmodems and other communications devices
devel	Utilities and programs for software development
doc	Documentation and specialized programs for viewing documentation
editors	Text editors and word processors
electronics	Programs for working with circuits and electronics
embedded	Programs for embedded systems
games	Games, toys, and fun programs
gnome	The **GNOME** Desktop System
graphics	Utilities to create, view, and edit graphics files
hamradio	Software for ham radio operators
interpreters	Interpreters for interpreted languages
kde	The **KDE** Desktop System
libdevel	Development files for libraries
libs	Collections of software routines
mail	Programs to write, send, and route email messages
math	Numeric analysis and other mathematics-related software
misc	Miscellaneous software
net	Programs to connect to and provide various services
news	Usenet clients and servers
oldlibs	Obsolete libraries
otherosfs	Emulators and software to read foreign filesystems
perl	**Perl** interpreter and libraries
python	**Python** interpreter and libraries
science	Software for scientific work

Table 5.1:
Debian package categories defined by the policy (thanks to aptitude)

---

[2]Up until the *potato* release, each category did have a subdirectory in the archive; since *woody's* release, this has been discontinued.

continued

Section name	Description
shells	Command shells and alternative console environments
sound	Utilities to play and record sound
tex	The TeX typesetting system
text	Text processing utilities
utils	Various system utilities
web	Web browsers, servers, proxies, and other tools
x11	The X window system and related software

5.2.2 Package priorities

The importance of the 15 000 binary packages available in the Debian archive to an average Debian system varies greatly. While a number of packages are absolutely indispensable to even the most basic systems, most packages are optional, or a luxury. Similar to the package categories from chapter 5.2.1, each Debian package — source or binary — specifies a priority, which serves as a measure of the package's importance. The policy defines five priorities:

required
: Packages which are necessary for the system to work properly. These packages may not be removed, or the system's integrity is at serious risk. Systems with only the **required** packages are probably unusable, but they do have enough functionality to allow the sysadmin to boot and install more software.

important
: Important programs, including those which one would expect to find on any Unix-like system, are filed under this priority. The **important** packages are a bare minimum of commonly-expected and necessary tools.

standard
: These packages provide a reasonably small but not too limited character-mode system. A minimal Debian install (see chapter 3.2) consists only of packages from this section (and the two previous ones). Most larger applications are not in this section.

optional
: Software with this priority is what you might reasonably want to install if you did not know what it was and did not have special requirements. This includes the X Window System, a full TeX distribution, and many applications. Note that **optional** packages should not conflict with each other.

extra

> This priority contains all packages that conflict with others in the **required,** **important, standard** or **optional** priority groups, or are only likely to be useful if you already know what they are or have special requirements.

Unfortunately, the distinction between the **optional** and **extra** priorities is not very clear — not even to Debian developers. The default priority for new packages is (and always has been) **optional**, which has led to an overpopulation of the group. Many packages are **optional** but should be **extra**, a situation which undoubtedly has to be rectified somewhere along the line. As a consequence, the **optional** priority *does not* identify a set of packages which anyone may want to install as a whole. In fact, neither **optional** nor **extra** are priorities of real concern to the user.

The different priorities take effect in two ways within Debian. First, the policy dictates that no package may depend on another package of a lower priority. This implies that you can cap a system at *e.g.* the **optional** priority and be sure that no **extra** packages are installed.

Possibly more important is the significance of priorities during the release preparation phase. The base system consists of **required** and **important** packages, and packages of these priorities are frozen first. Since these packages are the ones on which most other packages depend, this procedure allows the archive to stabilise, which is necessary to release a new version of Debian. Next, **standard** packages are frozen, followed by **optional** and **extra** packages just before the release.

5.2.3   Anatomy of binary packages

A Debian binary package resides in a single DEB file, and *vice versa*: a DEB file can only ever contain a single binary package. While the name of this file gives you various information about the package, the package management tools do not actually care about it. Despite this, the files contained in the Debian archive are named according to the following scheme, shown with the **postfix** package as an example[3].

```
postfix_2.1.5-1_i386.deb
   /        |        \
postfix  2.1.5-1   i386
```

As you can see, the package name consists of three fields, separated by underscores. The policy forbids the use of underscores in package name, version, and architecture, thereby assuring the non-ambiguity of these fields. The fields encode the package name, version number and Debian revision, and architecture, for

---

[3]You will see **postfix** pop up quite often throughout this book. You are to read it as an expression of my gratitude to Wietse Venema, the author of **Postfix**, a secure, extensible, and performant mail transport agent: http://www.postfix.org

which the binary package has been compiled, respectively. The architecture may be **all**, which suggests a package containing architecture-independent data files, or programmes written in interpreted script languages which need not be compiled. Nevertheless, the DEB file may also be named **foo.deb** and still install Postfix 2.1.5-1. The control data used by the package management tools are contained within the package. Nevertheless, having the most important data be part of the file name facilitates identification. The **dpkg-name** utility from the **dpkg-dev** package can be used to rename DEB files according to the standard naming scheme:

```
~$ dpkg-name foo.deb
moved 'foo.deb' to './postfix_2.1.5-1_i386.deb'
```

Dissecting a binary package

The DEB package format was designed from the start to be open and compatible with standard utilities. On the one hand, this means that the Debian package management tools did not have to reinvent the wheel but were able to build on existing functionality (much in the Unix spirit). On the other hand, with standard utilities, anyone could inspect and manipulate DEB files without needing a working Debian system. Granted, it is rare that someone will want to manipulate DEB files on a different Unix system, and its even rarer to have a non-functional Debian system, but extra flexibility is never wrong and comes in handy when you need it. We will use standard Unix utilities in the following to learn about the DEB file format.

There is no magic in a DEB file. In fact, it is nothing more than a BSD **ar** archive[4]:

```
~$ ar t postfix_2.1.5-1_i386.deb
debian-binary
control.tar.gz
data.tar.gz
```

These three files encapsulate the functionality of the package and are neatly split according to their content:

debian-binary
> This file simply serves as a "magic" to identify the archive as a Debian package. It contains the version number of the package format used (currently 2.0).

[4]This may come as a surprise, considering that the **ar** programme provided in the Debian archive is a GNU programme. The two differ subtly in the way they represent file names internally. GNU **ar** can be used to extract BSD **ar** files, and DEB files created with GNU **ar** work fine with **dpkg**. However, GNU **ar** is not (yet) supported. Please see http://bugs.debian.org/161593.

control.tar.gz

> This is a tarball of the control information needed by the package management tools.

data.tar.gz

> The data.tar.gz tarball contains the footprint of the Debian package, as placed on the root filesystem. Unpacking this tarball into / is thus almost equivalent to telling **dpkg** to unpack but not configure a package.

Using **ar** and **tar**, it is possible to get at all the files and data stored in a DEB package. If you are curious about the choice of **ar** and **tar** rather than just **tar**, the DEB file is packaged with **ar** to conserve space since **tar** stores more information per file (*e.g.* permissions, owner, date, …), which is just unnecessary in the case of the three files.

```
~$ cp /var/spool/apt/archives/postfix_2.1.5-1_i386.deb .
~$ ar x postfix_2.1.5-1_i386.deb
~$ cat debian-binary
2.0
~$ tar tzf control.tar.gz
config    templates   shlibs      postinst   preinst
prerm     postrm      conffiles   md5sums    control
~$ tar tzf data.tar.gz
[...]
./usr/sbin/postfix
[...]
./var/spool/postfix/
[...]
```

Inspecting a binary package

The **less** preprocessor **lesspipe** knows about DEB files and can extract the most important data about the file. With the environment variable **$LESSOPEN**, **less** can be told how to handle DEB files, when asked to view them directly. It probably makes sense to set the variable startup scripts according to your shell.

```
~$ export LESSOPEN="|lesspipe %s"
~$ less postfix_2.1.5-1_i386.deb
[...]
```

lesspipe is particularly useful in combination with file viewers and other programmes that display information about DEB files. In chapter 5.3.1 we see that **dpkg** provides the same functionality as well; since **less** is integrated into many other programmes, especially viewers and file navigators, the above can come in quite handy.

The mc file navigator, available in the mc package in the Debian archive, provides a virtual filesystem handler to access DEB files and inspect their contents. In mc, you can simply locate the DEB file you wish to inspect, select it, and press enter. The control files will be available in ./DEBIAN and the contents under ./CONTENTS.

Lastly, users of Emacs may appreciate the debian-el package, which allows them to open DEB files in their beloved editor to browse the contents and inspect the control information.

5.2.4   The control files

A Debian binary package consists of payload data (the software and all associated files) as well as control information (see chapter 5.2.3 for the details). The control information is spread across a set of files, known as the control files. The contents of these files are used to control the package management tools, store meta data, such as dependencies (see chapter 5.7.3), and provide general information about the package, such as a description of the included software. The Debian package format specifies the following set of control files, all but one of which are optional:

control

> The file contains the meta information for a package and is used by the package management tools to display information about the package and verify dependencies prior to its installation. This is the only mandatory control file.

conffiles

> All files listed (with their full paths) in conffiles will be treated specially by the package management tools so as to preserve user modifications to these files for package upgrades or if the files already exist (*e.g.* from a previous tarball, non-package installation).

preinst

> The preinst script is run prior to the installation or upgrade of a package. If an upgrade fails, the old version's preinst is given a chance to redo any configuration which was previously removed as part of the upgrade[5].

postinst

> The postinst script is run as part of the configuration process, following the unpacking of a package. Also, if the upgrade, deconfiguration, or removal of a package fails or is aborted, dpkg lets postinst set things straight[5].

prerm

> The prerm script is run prior to removal of a package. If a package is upgraded, the old package's prerm script is also given a chance to run. Finally, if

---

[5]The details of when and how dpkg invokes the four maintainer scripts are described in sections 6.4 and 6.5 of the Debian policy (http://www.debian.org/doc/debian-policy).

a package upgrade or configuration fails, the package is left unpacked, but it is deconfigured. **dpkg** allows the maintainer to take specific error unwinding steps with **prerm** during the deconfiguration or upgrade process[5].

postrm

The **postrm** script is run after a package has been removed from the system. **dpkg** lets the script know whether the package has been deinstalled or purged (see chapter 5.3.5). The script also gets called after a package has been removed in favour of another package, due to a conflict or an upgrade. Finally, **dpkg** invokes **postrm** when an upgrade or installation is aborted[5].

md5sums

This file contains **MD5** sums of all files installed by the package, which can be used for verification of the installed files. Please see chapter 5.11.1 for more information.

shlibs

To support the maintainer utilities, the **shlibs** file lists the libraries and their SONAMEs[6] provided by the package, alongside the package name. During automatic dependency determination, the maintainer scripts use these files installed by all packages to determine which package provides which version of a library. More information about the **shlibs** system is available in chapter 9.4.3.

config

The **config** script's job is to obtain information from the user with respect to the configuration parameters of the package. Responses given by the user are cached in **debconf**'s database for later processing by, *e.g.* the **postinst** script.

templates

Decoupling the configuration parameter descriptions from the logic, the **templates** file defines the questions and notices that **debconf** displays.

The **dpkg-deb** tool can extract all the important information needed for a package from the DEB file prior to installation. Please refer to chapter 5.3.1 for more information.

5.3 Dealing with packages: dpkg

On its manpage, **dpkg** is described as "a medium-level package manager". **dpkg** is the workhorse of the Debian package management system, responsible for instal-

---

[6]A library's SONAME is the name by which the dynamic linker identifies the library and its binary interface version.

lation and removal of packages, for their configuration, and for managing installed packages. In addition, it provides a plethora of toolkits to gather information from, interact with, and manipulate Debian package files. On the **dpkg** web page[7], additional information is available.

The **dpkg** programme keeps an inventory of installed packages in a database. Probably the most important feature of **dpkg** is that it is meticulously careful with the database and guarantees never to leave it in an inconsistent state. As a result, **dpkg** is robust and remarkably graceful in the face of a problem.

dpkg deals with single packages, and the meta data they define. When it executes an action, it ensures that the action does not put the system into a state inconsistent with the inventory that **dpkg** keeps in its status database. In the face of a problem, **dpkg** prevents an action rather than taking additional action required to solve the problem. On the other hand, APT (the topic of chapter 5.4) tries to honour any request, if necessary by taking additional steps to ensure the consistency of the system. While on the topic, another difference between APT and **dpkg** is that **dpkg** does not deal with package acquisition but rather expects packages to be available in the form of a DEB file, or be installed on the local system, whereas APT provides the means to obtain missing packages from external sources.

The dpkg family

dpkg has two siblings, **dpkg-deb** and **dpkg-query**. While **dpkg**'s purpose is the installation and removal of packages, **dpkg-deb** excels at manipulating DEB files, and **dpkg-query** gives you read access to the status database used by **dpkg**. For simplicity, **dpkg** wraps the functionality of its two siblings and thus can be used as an all-in-one programme to harness the full power of the **dpkg** family. Therefore, **dpkg**'s functionality can be divided into four parts:

- inspecting and manipulating DEB files (the domain of **dpkg-deb**)

- installing packages

- querying the package management database (the domain of **dpkg-query**)

- removing packages

In the following, I will use **dpkg-deb** and **dpkg-query** instead of the wrapper interface provided by **dpkg**.

[7] http://www.dpkg.org

5.3.1   Handling binary packages

With **dpkg-deb**, it is possible to extract information and data from DEB files (as opposed to using tools like **ar**, see chapter 5.2.3). To print a package's control information, use the tool as follows:

```
~$ dpkg-deb --info postfix_2.1.5-1_i386.deb
new debian package, version 2.0.
size 798936 bytes: control archive= 42708 bytes.
    191 bytes,     7 lines      conffiles
  10997 bytes,   355 lines  *   config       #!/usr/bin/perl
   1076 bytes,    22 lines      control
   7613 bytes,   119 lines      md5sums
  12842 bytes,   465 lines  *   postinst     #!/bin/sh
    914 bytes,    41 lines  *   postrm       #!/bin/sh
   6702 bytes,   251 lines  *   preinst      #!/bin/sh
    960 bytes,    43 lines  *   prerm        #!/bin/sh
    109 bytes,     4 lines      shlibs
  76002 bytes,  1505 lines      templates
Package: postfix
Version: 2.1.5-1
Section: mail
Priority: extra
Architecture: i386
Depends: libc6 (>= 2.3.2.ds1-4), libdb4.2, libgdbm3,
  debconf (>= 0.5) | debconf-2.0, netbase, adduser (>= 3.48),
  dpkg (>= 1.8.3), debconf
Recommends: mail-reader, resolvconf
Suggests: procmail, postfix-mysql, postfix-pgsql, postfix-ldap,
  postfix-pcre
Conflicts: mail-transport-agent, smail, libnss-db (<< 2.2-3),
  postfix-tls (<< 2.0-0)
Replaces: postfix-doc (<< 1.1.7-0), postfix-tls
Provides: mail-transport-agent
Installed-Size: 1900
Maintainer: LaMont Jones <lamont@debian.org>
Description: A high-performance mail transport agent
 Postfix is Wietse Venema's mail transport agent that started life as an
 [...]
```

If you need single fields from a package's control information rather than the whole load, use the **--field** option[8].

```
~$ dpkg-deb --field postfix_2.1.5-1_i386.deb Version
2.1.5-1
~$ dpkg-deb --field postfix_2.1.5-1_i386.deb Recommends Suggests
Recommends: mail-reader, resolvconf
```

[8]Note that Debian distinguishes between dependency recommendations and suggestions, as shown in the example. More details may be found in chapter 5.7.3.

```
Suggests: procmail, postfix-mysql, postfix-pgsql,
  postfix-ldap, postfix-pcre
```

If your attention is more towards the set of files a package installs, **dpkg-deb** can extract this information from the DEB file as well:

```
~$ dpkg-deb --contents postfix_2.1.5-1_i386.deb
[...]
-rwxr-xr-x root/root  6804 2004-06-22 23:06:27 ./usr/sbin/postfix
[...]
drwxr-xr-x root/root     0 2004-06-22 23:06:08 ./var/spool/postfix/
[...]
```

In addition to extracting information, **dpkg-deb** can unpack and create DEB files. For the unpacking, it is necessary to distinguish between control and data payload:

```
~$ dpkg-deb --control postfix_2.1.5-1_i386.deb
~$ dpkg-deb --extract postfix_2.1.5-1_i386.deb .
~$ ls -F *
postfix_2.1.5-1_i386.deb

DEBIAN/:
conffiles  control  postinst*  preinst*  shlibs
config*    md5sums  postrm*    prerm*    templates

etc/:
init.d/  postfix/  ppp/  resolvconf/

usr/:
bin/  lib/  sbin/  share/

var/:
log/  spool/
```

The **DEBIAN** directory contains the extracted control files. The package's contents have been placed directly in the current directory. Like you would expect, the directory layout of the contents reflects the footprint occupied by the **postfix** package when it is installed.

Apart from extracting information, **dpkg-deb** is also the tool used to create binary packages. A directory with the layout such as the one we just created by extracting the DEB file can be trivially converted (back) into a binary package:

```
~$ mkdir pfpkg
~$ mv --target-directory=pfpkg DEBIAN etc usr var
~$ dpkg-deb --build pfpkg
dpkg-deb: building package 'postfix' in 'pfpkg.deb'.
~$ file pfpkg.deb
pfpkg.deb: Debian binary package (format 2.0), uses gzip compression
```

```
~$
~$ dpkg-deb --field pfpkg.deb Version
2.1.5-1
```

It is thus possible to build DEB files with very simple means. Even though, essentially, every package is created with this method, the package maintainer scripts provide several layers around the programme to facilitate and automate the creation of the above layout from a source directory. We will see how this can be done in chapter 9, which also shows how the package maintainer scripts mostly automate the generation of the control files.

5.3.2 Installing packages

When **dpkg** installs a package, it does so in two phases: first, it unpacks the payload, and then it runs the **postinst** control script (if present). This is known as the configuration step. These steps can be executed separately (see below). Alternatively, **dpkg**'s **--install** option automatically invokes the configuration phase when the software has been unpacked. Note that **dpkg** expects the actual path to the DEB file containing the package as its argument; it does not have the ability to acquire the required package file when given only the names of packages.

```
~# dpkg --install ./postfix_2.1.5-1_i386.deb
Selecting previously deselected package postfix.
(Reading database ... 10088 files and directories currently installed.)
Unpacking postfix (from ./postfix_2.1.5-1_i386.deb) ...
Setting up postfix (2.1.5-1) ...
[...]
```

Unpacking packages

Unpacking is largely accomplished by **dpkg-deb**, **dpkg** merely conducts the process:

```
~# dpkg --unpack postfix_2.1.5-1_i386.deb
Selecting previously deselected package postfix.
(Reading database ... 10088 files and directories currently installed.)
Unpacking postfix (from postfix_2.1.5-1_i386.deb) ...
```

This causes **dpkg** to take the following steps:

1. After verifying that the package is in fact a Debian package (using **debian-binary**), the control information is extracted to a temporary location[9].

    [9]/var/lib/dpkg/tmp.ci

2. The **preinst** script is run (if it exists) to configure relevant bits before installation. Many **preinst** scripts stop relevant services to prevent problems during the installation.

3. **dpkg** now extracts all files listed in the **conffiles** file to a temporary directory and moves them to the appropriate location under **/etc**. At the same time, it appends the **.dpkg-new** extension so that existing files are not overwritten.

4. **dpkg** then unpacks the rest of the **data.tar.gz** tarball in the root directory of the local system (which can be overridden with the **--root=dir** option of **dpkg**).

5. Now, the control files are placed in **/var/lib/dpkg/info**, each file prepended with the package name and a full stop: *e.g.* postfix.conffiles. The **control** file is not installed but used to update the package database.

6. Finally, **dpkg** marks the package as "unpacked" in the package database (see chapter 5.3.4).

A package cannot fulfill a dependency when it is merely unpacked (see chapter 5.7.3). While all files (except for those marked as **conffiles**) are installed in their appropriate places, the software is not guaranteed to work yet.

Configuring packages

After unpacking, the package is given a chance to make modifications that could not be hard-coded into the package's payload. This may be the case when data specific to the local system is needed, or if the user can influence the way the software works at installation time. When **dpkg** installs packages, this step is usually executed automatically. It can also be explicitly requested by telling **dpkg** to configure a single package. Unlike the unpack phase, **dpkg** wants to know the package name (not the name of the DEB file).

```
~# dpkg --configure postfix
Setting up postfix (2.1.5-1) ...
[...]
```

Configuration consists of the following steps:

1. **dpkg** consults the administrator for every configuration file with local modifications. Depending on the administrator's decision, the configuration file is then either overwritten with the version provided in the package, or left untouched (see chapter 5.3.3).

2.   With all configuration files in place, the **postinst** script is run (if it exists). If the package uses debconf, this causes the **config** script to be run. The **config** script uses debconf to obtain parameter values from the user, should these not be already cached by the **debconf** database.

3.   The **postinst** file then takes care of changes to the system that cannot be included in the package directly. This includes enacting the configuration parameter choices made by the user through **debconf**, as well as tasks like creating device nodes and users. Also, services are usually started by **postinst**.

4.   Finally, **dpkg** marks the package as "installed" in the package database (see chapter 5.3.4).

After completing the configuration phase, the package is installed and the software fully operational. If **dpkg** is asked to configure a previously configured package, the above command will exit immediately, but not report an error.

It is also possible to instruct **dpkg** to configure all unconfigured (unpacked) packages in one go. If no packages remain to be configured, the command does not report an error and exits immediately.

```
~# dpkg --configure -a
[...]
```

5.3.3 Configuration file handling

As I mentioned earlier, the package may contain two types of files: those installed and subsequently managed by **dpkg**, and so-called *conffiles* – configuration files which are expected to be modified by the user. When unpacking, **dpkg** happily overwrites existing files of the first type. Configuration files, however, are handled specially:

1.   During the package's unpack phase, **dpkg** installs all files marked as **conffile** to their target locations, but gives each a **.dpkg-new** extension to prevent clashes with any existing files.

2.   When configuring the package, **dpkg** checks each existing configuration file for modifications (using a set of MD5 checksums; see below). If modifications are found, the administrator must choose whether to overwrite or keep the local file.

3.   If the local file is kept, the new configuration file (installed with the **.dpkg-new** extension) is renamed with the **.dpkg-dist** extension.

4.   If the local file is to be replaced by the configuration file from the package, it is given the **.dpkg-old** extension and left in place as a backup.

For example, the abcde package provides /etc/abcde.conf, which is flagged as a configuration file. Thus, dpkg handles it appropriately:

```
~# dpkg --unpack abcde_2.0.3-1_all.deb
(Reading database ... 59575 files and directories currently installed.)
Preparing to replace abcde 2.0.2-1 (using abcde_2.0.3-1_all.deb) ...
Unpacking replacement abcde ...
~# ls -F /etc/abcde.conf*
/etc/abcde.conf  /etc/abcde.conf.dpkg-new
~# dpkg --configure abcde
Setting up abcde (2.0.3-1) ...
Installing new version of config file /etc/abcde.conf ...
```

If the administrator had made changes to the file, dpkg would have asked before taking any action (the first command simply appends a line to the file, thereby simulating a modification):

```
~# echo >> /etc/abcde.conf
~# dpkg --unpack abcde_2.0.3-1_all.deb
(Reading database ... 59575 files and directories currently installed.)
Preparing to replace abcde 2.0.2-1 (using abcde_2.0.3-1_all.deb) ...
Unpacking replacement abcde ...
~# dpkg --configure abcde
Setting up abcde (2.0.3-1) ...

Configuration file '/etc/abcde.conf'
 ==> Modified (by you or by a script) since installation.
 ==> Package distributor has shipped an updated version.
   What would you like to do about it ?  Your options are:
    Y or I : install the package maintainer's version
    N or O : keep your currently-installed version
       D    : show the differences between the versions
       Z    : background this process to examine the situation
 The default action is to keep your current version.
*** abcde.conf (Y/I/N/O/D/Z) [default=N] ? y
Installing new version of config file /etc/abcde.conf ...
```

Identifying change

dpkg only prompts on changed configuration files if it is about to install a configuration file that has changed from the previous version it installed. If the administrator removes a configuration file from the system, dpkg also prevents trouble: if a previous configuration file is not present, it will not reinstall it. If, however, dpkg upgrades a package and installs a configuration file that differs from the previous one, it will prompt. If the user opts to replace the file, everything continues as before. If, however, the user chooses to preserve the local modifications, dpkg will continue to prompt the administrator whenever the package is upgraded, whether the maintainer-provided configuration file changed or not.

In pseudo code:

```
Mp <= stored MD5 sum of configuration file
      from package of previous version
Mn <= MD5 sum of new configuration file,
      extracted from the package
Ml <= MD5 sum of locally installed configuration file

if Mn != Mp
then: # the maintainer provides a new file

  if Ml != Mp:
  then: # the administrator made local changes
    A <= action desired by administrator
    if A == install
    then: # admin chose to replace file
      install new version of configuration file
    end if
  else: # the local file was not changed
    install new version of configuration file
  end if

  let Mp = Mn # make the new version the next previous

else: # the new package does not update the file
  do nothing
end if
```

It is entirely up to the you as the administrator to decide what **dpkg** should do when a new version of a package provides updated configuration files which conflict with the locally modified ones. If you choose to keep your locally edited copy of the **conffile**, **dpkg** will install the new version next to the one you decided to keep, using the **.dpkg-dist** extension to the filename. You may return at a later time to inspect the new configuration file and merge your old configuration into it. If, however, you choose to replace your local file with the new version from the package being installed, **dpkg** saves the file with your changes with the **.dpkg-old** extension, allowing you to refer to the locally modified file later.

The Debian utilities know about the possible existence of these files and ignore them. Therefore, there is no danger in leaving stray **.dpkg-dist** or **.dpkg-old** files around. Nevertheless, when another package upgrade comes around, it *will* overwrite existing **.dpkg-dist** and **.dpkg-old** (if you've edited the configuration since the last update), so it is always a good idea to tend to configuration files and remove the ones with a **.dpkg-*** extension if you will not need them again. A simple command can then help you identify configuration files that need manual migration:

```
~# find /etc -name '*.dpkg-*'
```

Merging configuration files (or not)

Often, users complain that even though **dpkg** preserves changes made to files, it provides no way to merge new configuration directives from updated configuration files provided by newer versions of a package. For instance, take the following configuration file, in which the administrator replaced the previous nickname with "madduck":

```
~$ cat /etc/foo.conf
NICKNAME=madduck
```

In a newer version of the **foo** programme, the configuration file also specifies the server to which to connect. The package includes the following file:

```
~$ cat /etc/foo.conf
NICKNAME=gort
SERVER=barada.nikto.org
```

In an ideal world, **dpkg** would offer to merge the files to produce a version with the (unchanged) server directive, but with "madduck" as the nickname.

Unfortunately, the variety of configuration paradigms found across a Unix system make this virtually impossible; one would have to give **dpkg** knowledge of every configuration file that it should ever merge, including (but not limited to) its structure and its syntax. Then, when a configuration paradigm changes, **dpkg** would need to be updated.

Beyond standardisation of configuration files across all of Unix (which is not going to happen), the only sensible approach to this task is the automatic generation of configuration files from values stored and maintained in a database or registry. Debian purposely does not go down that road because it aims to bring the software to the user with minimal modifications. If you install the **postfix** package, you get the **postfix** mail transport agent in much the same way as if you were to build and install it yourself. A seasoned **postfix** administrator would never consider running a mail server with Debian GNU/Linux if it required configuration through a database, possibly imposing limitations on the configuration syntax.

5.3.4   Interacting with the package database

dpkg meticulously keeps track of all the packages it installs, and even remembers packages that were once installed but previously removed.

In the current incarnation of **dpkg**, the package database is spread across a number of flat files. These are found in **/var/lib/dpkg**, which I will call the **dpkg** database directory. Unless stated otherwise, all files and directories in the following reside below this directory.

The package database stores the following data for packages:

- The state of the package (see below). These data are stored in the **status** file.

- If the package is installed (or removed, but not purged), the database contains the package's full control information (following the state information in the **status** file).

- The alternatives database (see chapter 6.1.4) in **alternatives**.

- The permission override database (see chapter 6.1.2) in **statoverride**.

- Below **info/**, it keeps a record of each package's installed files in *.list as well as its **conffiles** (in *.conffiles). Also, it stores the four hook control script (*.*inst and *.*rm).

- Optionally, **dpkg** stores MD5 sums of all files a package provides in **info/*.md5-sums**. See chapter 5.11.1 for more information.

- **debconf** data is also kept in **info/**: *.config and *.templates. See chapter 5.8 for more information.

- In **available**, **dpkg** stores the list of available packages, which is used only by **dselect** (see chapter 5.3.9).

- **cmethopt** and the **methods** directory are throwbacks from the days when **dpkg** integrated various acquisition means (*e.g.* FTP, HTTP). This is now handled by APT, which is the only default acquisition method of **dpkg**.

One of **dpkg**'s main problems is performance, and the main culprit is the package database. Flat files scale linearly (at best) with the number of installed packages. Among the to-do list entries for **dpkg** is the replacement of the database with a more powerful database format (which would scale logarithmically).

Now let us use the package database. A list of the installed packages can be obtained with the command **dpkg --list**:

```
~$ dpkg --list
Desired=Unknown/Install/Remove/Purge/Hold
| Status=Not/Installed/Config-files/Unpacked/Failed-config/Half-installed
|/ Err?=(none)/Hold/Reinst-required/X=both-problems (Status,Err: uppercase=bad)
||/ Name           Version         Description
+++-==============-===============-============================================
ii  adduser        3.57            Add and remove users and groups
ii  apt            0.6.25          Advanced front-end for dpkg
ii  apt-doc        0.6.25          Documentation for APT
ii  apt-utils      0.6.25          APT utility programs
ii  at             3.1.8-11        Delayed job execution and batch processing
[...]
```

Each line corresponding to a package starts with three columns showing the status of the package. The first column identifies the status desired by the user and is limited to the following five states:

u   The desired state is unknown, meaning that the package is not installed (and has never been) and the user did not request its installation.

i   The user requested the installation of the package.

r   The user requested the removal of the package.

p   The user requested the purging of the package.

h   The user requested that this package should be held at its current version and no automatic upgrades should be attempted.

In the second column, the current state of the package is encoded. The column may list any of the six states. If there is a serious problem (see below), **dpkg-query** uses an upper-case letter to indicate it.

n   The package is not installed.

i   The package is installed and fully configured.

c   The package was previously installed and has since been removed, but its configuration files remain on the system.

u   The package has been unpacked but not yet configured.

f   The configuration of the package has been attempted but failed.

h   The package was installed but the installation failed to complete.

Finally, the third column indicates error conditions and can assume one of four states. The first state indicates no problems and is not marked with a symbol. The other three symbols indicate problems.

h   The package is on enforced hold because another package required in a versioned dependency cannot be upgraded due to a hold.

r   The package is broken and requires reinstallation before normal interaction is possible (including removal).

x   The package is both broken and on enforced hold.

Inspecting single packages

The **dpkg --list** command also accepts standard filename patterns (see your shell manual) to limit the output to matching packages. The filename patterns may need to be escaped or enclosed in quotes to prevent the shell from interfering:

```
~$ dpkg --list ssh
[...]
ii  ssh   3.8.1p1-8.sarg Secure rlogin/rsh/rcp replacement (OpenSSH)
~$ dpkg --list \*finger\*
[...]
un  cfingerd   <none>    (no description available)
ii  efingerd   1.6.2     Another finger daemon for unix
un  ffingerd   <none>    (no description available)
un  finger     <none>    (no description available)
un  fingerd    <none>    (no description available)
un  xfingerd   <none>    (no description available)
~$ dpkg --list \?fingerd
[...]
un  cfingerd   <none>    (no description available)
ii  efingerd   1.6.2     Another finger daemon for unix
un  ffingerd   <none>    (no description available)
un  xfingerd   <none>    (no description available)
~$ dpkg --list '[ec]fingerd'
[...]
un  cfingerd   <none>    (no description available)
ii  efingerd   1.6.2     Another finger daemon for unix
```

Many people use the output of **dpkg --list** in scripts. For instance, the following command should purge all packages that have been previously removed (rc: the package should be removed but still has configuration files on the system).

```
~# dpkg --list | grep ^rc | awk '{print $2}' | xargs dpkg -P
[...]
```

If you try the above, you are likely to see an error. The output of **dpkg --list** is squeezed into the width available on the calling terminal, even if a pipe is attached. Therefore, some package names will not be complete causing the above command to fail. To illustrate this, in the following, a field parser will only be able to obtain "module-init-to" rather than the complete package name **module-init-tools**:

```
~$ dpkg --list | grep module-init 1>&2 | awk '{print $2}'
ii  module-init-to 3.1-pre2-2    tools for managing ...
module-init-to
```

The solution is to override the column width using the $COLUMNS variable. Each line can then be forced to a certain length. Squeezing whitespace characters in the output with **tr** produces usable output since the first three fields are guaranteed not to contain whitespace:

```
~$ COLUMNS=1000 dpkg --list | grep module-init \
  | tr -s ' ' 1>&2 | awk '{print $2}'
ii module-init-tools 3.1-pre2-2 tools for managing ...
module-init-tools
```

Especially for scripts, a query interface provided only by **dpkg-query** is more useful as the displayed fields can be selected individually. If no format is specified, the package name is printed by default:

```
~$ dpkg-query --show postfix
postfix
~$ dpkg-query --show --showformat='${Package}\t${Status}\n' mc
postfix install ok installed
```

In the last example, the status corresponds to the first three columns in the **dpkg --list** output, though the second and third column are reversed: `ii_` (with an empty third column to indicate "ok").

Table 5.2:
Package states and
their mappings to
single letters. The
dots identify the
column in which the
letter may be seen in
the dpkg --list
output. States
prepended with an
asterisk are not
states defined by the
package management
system but rather
emerge out of other
states.

Letter	State
u..	*unknown
i..	install
r..	deinstall
p..	purge
h..	hold
.n.	not-installed
.i.	installed
.c.	config-files
.u.	unpacked
.f.	half-configured
.h.	half-installed
..h	*hold
..r	reinst-required
..x	reinst-required & *hold
..	ok (empty third column)

Thus, a better way to purge all previously removed packages is:

```
~# dpkg-query --show --showformat='${Status} ${Package}\n' \
  | grep ^deinstall | cut -f4 | xargs dpkg -P
```

Speaking of fields, there is an easier way to access the information for an installed package. As you may guess, the field names in front of the colon on (almost) every line in the output of the following command are the same as you can use in --showformat.

```
~$ dpkg --status postfix
Package: postfix
Status: install ok installed
Priority: extra
Section: mail
[...]
Conffiles:
 /etc/init.d/postfix 5fe44b0a0f8e510d10d1633d96b251b4
[...]
```

Essentially, the output of **dpkg --show postfix** corresponds to the output of **dpkg --info postfix.deb**. The first includes some information relevant to the installed package (such as the status), while the second shows some data that only make sense in the context of a DEB file (such as the control files the package file provides).

Along similar lines, the functionality of **dpkg --contents postfix.deb** is also available for the installed **postfix package**:

```
~$ dpkg --listfiles postfix
[...]
/usr/sbin/postfix
[...]
/var/spool/postfix
[...]
```

Another useful tool is **dpkg-awk**, available in the package by the same name. It supports searching for packages which meet certain criteria, and optionally sorts the results. For instance, to print out the package name and status of packages with version numbers 0.01, 0.1, 0.02, or 0.2, sorted by section:

```
~$ dpkg-awk --sort Section Version:^0.0?[12]- -- Package Status
Package: ed
Status: install ok installed

Package: libtextwrap1
Status: install ok installed

[...]
```

Searching the list of installed files

Since the package management tools track each file they install, you can query the database of installed files to figure out which package owns which file. This comes in handy when you need to figure out why a file is on one but not another system, or to find the package and thus *e.g.* its documentation from a single file. The command to search the database also accepts patterns to identify multiple files:

```
~$ dpkg --search /usr/lib/postfix/*d
postfix: /usr/lib/postfix/qmqpd
postfix: /usr/lib/postfix/smtpd
~$ dpkg --search bin/gawk
gawk: /usr/bin/gawk
```

Hence, **dpkg --search *** will list all files installed and managed by the Debian package management tools.

Even though its development stopped years ago, **dlocate** remains to be useful. It claims to be a fast alternative to **dpkg --list** and **dpkg --search**, and provides a set of useful additional functionalities.

dpkg's options **--list**, **--search**, and **--listfiles** are directly available as **-l**, **-S**, and **-L** respectively, which happen to be the same as the short options to **dpkg**. The main advantage of **dlocate** is its ability to feed sets of filenames (all the files in a package, just the **conffiles**, or all the manpages) to tools such as **ls**, **du**, and **md5sum**. For instance, the long listing of all **conffiles** is easily obtained:

```
~# dlocate -lsconf postfix
-rwxr-xr-x  1 root root  2347 Oct 31 04:37 /etc/init.d/postfix*
-rwxr-xr-x  1 root root 21207 Oct 31 04:37 /etc/postfix/post-install*
-rw-r--r--  1 root root 16114 Oct 31 04:37 /etc/postfix/postfix-files
[...]
```

Furthermore, **dlocate** allows you to display and verify the **MD5** sums of installed packages. The following indicates that **/etc/init.d/postfix** differs from the version installed by the package (which is to be not an anomaly since the file is a **conffile**).

```
~# dlocate -md5sum postfix
79ac631ecb6e3cbb1d8684aa6de101fc  etc/init.d/postfix
0f6d12880a5f95b96037f15d658cecb0  etc/ppp/ip-up.d/postfix
0758469f9f1c073a53df50d9dc43c8eb  etc/ppp/ip-down.d/postfix
[...]
~# dlocate -md5check postfix
/etc/init.d/postfix FAILED
/etc/ppp/ip-up.d/postfix OK
/etc/ppp/ip-down.d/postfix OK
```

Putting a hold on packages

Packages can be put on hold to prevent their automatic upgrade. In addition, the package management tools may enforce a package hold because the dependencies of an updated version cannot (yet) be satisfied. Manually putting packages on hold requires a little more than a single command, we will get to know higher-level tools to automate this process soon (see chapter 5.3.9 and chapter 5.4.11), as well as other methods better suited to the task (see chapter 8.2.1). Please note that a hold only affects automatic upgrades. If you explicitly request a held package to be upgraded, **dpkg** will happily comply.

Recall the purpose of the first column in the **dpkg --list** output: to denote the desired (or requested) state of a package. A hold on a package is one of these desired states, and it is possible to manipulate the requested state of each package with **dpkg**, without **dpkg** immediately jumping to meet the request. The tuple linking the package to a desired state is referred to as a "selection" in **dpkg**-parlance. We can use **dpkg** to get the table of selections corresponding to the current status of the packages. Without arguments, **dpkg --get-selections** returns all packages which it knows about (*i.e.* all packages that are currently installed, or were installed at one point and removed later):

```
~$ dpkg --get-selections apt-doc apt-utils at
apt-doc                         deinstall
apt-utils                       install
at                              hold
```

Manipulating the desired states of packages thus simply requires the appropriate modification to the second column for the line corresponding to the package whose status is to be changed. You can either export the list to a text file with **dpkg --get-selections**, modify the file as you wish, and then feed that modified version into **dpkg --set-selections**, or you can simply echo the requests into **dpkg --set-selections**:

```
~# dpkg --list postfix
[...]
ii  postfix      2.1.5-1       A high-performance
~# echo postfix hold | dpkg --set-selections
~# dpkg --list postfix
[...]
hi  postfix      2.1.5-1       A high-performance
```

5.3.5 Deinstalling packages

Debian distinguishes between packages that are deinstalled and packages which have been purged from the system. The difference between the two is that conf-files of a removed (deinstalled) package remain on the system and only purging removes them. By default, Debian will never automatically purge a package. Thus, to remove configuration files from the system, the user has to manually tell **dpkg** to do so. A package can be removed and later purged. If the purging is requested for a currently installed package, the removal will be done implicitly prior to the purge.

To remove a package, **dpkg** is invoked with the **--remove** option and the package to be deinstalled. Other than during installation, removal only needs the package name, not the actual DEB file.

```
~# dpkg --remove postfix
(Reading database ... 10228 files and directories currently installed.)
Removing postfix ...
[...]
```

During removal, **dpkg**

1.   first runs the **prerm** script (if it exists), which can *e.g.* stop processes belonging to the package.

2.   Next, all installed files except **conffiles** are unlinked (removed from the system).

3.   All the control files of the package are removed from **/var/lib/dpkg/info**, with the exception of two: **postfix.postrm** and **postfix.files** remain. **postfix.files** is truncated to the set of **conffiles**.

4.   Finally, **dpkg** changes the package state to **conf-files** with a desired state of **remove** (see chapter 5.3.4).

The **conf-files** state is a well-defined state, which means that the package management tools can be used as shown previously to query the database for information about packages in that state:

```
~$ dpkg-query --list postfix
[...]
rc  postfix       2.1.5-1    A high-performance[...]
~$ dpkg-query --listfiles postfix
/etc/init.d/postfix
[...]
/etc/postfix/postfix-script
/etc/postfix/post-install
/etc/postfix/postfix-files
[...]
~$ dpkg --search /etc/init.d/postfix
postfix: /etc/init.d/postfix
~$ dpkg --search /usr/bin/mailq
dpkg: /usr/bin/mailq not found.
```

The package contents vanish from the package database when the package is purged.

```
~# dpkg --purge postfix
[...]
Purging configuration files for postfix ...
~$ dpkg --list postfix
[...]
pn  postfix         <none>      (no description available)
```

Note the state of the package: **pn**, which indicates that the package is actually purged, but also that the package database has an entry for the package. Therefore, **pn** specifies that **postfix** was previously installed and the package management database has seen it and

1. All remaining files are unlinked (removed from the system).

2. If it exists, the **postrm** script is run.

3. The two remaining files, **postfix.postrm** and **postfix.files** are unlinked from /var/lib/dpkg/info.

4. **dpkg** marks the packages as non-installed in the package management database (see chapter 5.3.4).

For mass removals, an administrator may also resort to the selection interface of **dpkg** and register deinstallation and purge requests before telling **dpkg** to enact them:

```
~# echo postfix deinstall | dpkg --set-selections
~# dpkg --remove --pending
[...]
Removing postfix ...
~# echo postfix purge | dpkg --set-selections
~# dpkg --purge --pending
[...]
Removing postfix ...
Purging configuration files for postfix ...
```

5.3.6   Overriding dpkg's sanity and policy checks

dpkg enforces the Debian policy (see chapter 5.7) wherever and whenever it can. It refuses to overwrite files belonging to other packages, it preserves configuration files, it prevents the removal of essential packages which are needed to provide core functionality of the system, it refuses to install packages when the dependency relations are not satisfied, ... The list goes on and on, and **dpkg** would not be a versatile tool if these checks could not be individually overridden. Overriding **dpkg**'s rules is called "forcing" in Debian speak.

It goes without saying that forcing is to be used with care. Lowrey's Law (a subsection of Murphy's Law[10]) states "if it jams, force it; if it breaks, it needed replacement anyway." Fortunately, the Debian package management tools do not abide by this law. The Debian package database is designed to be robust, and the tools have been carefully crafted to leave the database in a consistent state no matter how they are called, or do whatever they do, or fail. When a user employs forcing, that user is explicitly telling the package management tools to put the system into an inconsistent state. **dpkg**'s forcing method is an acknowledgement that at times, the system must be rendered (temporarily) inconsistent. For instance, third party software may be uninstallable otherwise, or the current state of Debian *unstable* may be inconsistent internally, and thus unusable in the wake of **dpkg**'s strict rules. Nevertheless, the best recipe to destroy a Debian system is to employ forcing without care. Use forcing only when you have no alternative, and try to keep an overview (or better yet, a written account) of what you have forced.

The **dpkg** (8) manpage lists all the available forcing methods. The following are the most commonly used ones:

--force-depends

> This switch causes **dpkg** to ignore *all* dependency declarations during the execution of the requested action. The removal or the installation of a package with this option has grave implications for future interactions with the package database. For instance, forcing the removal of **vim-common** (despite the dependency of the **vim** package) prevents further installations of unrelated packages, in this case **mc**:

```
~# dpkg --remove --force-depends vim-common
dpkg: vim-common: dependency problems, but removing anyway as you
   request:
 vim depends on vim-common (>> 1:6.2).
[...]
Removing vim-common ...
~# apt-get install mc
[...]
You might want to run »apt-get --fix-broken install« to correct
   these:
The following packages have unmet dependencies:
  vim: Depends: vim-common (> 1:6.2) but it is not going to be
   installed
E: Unmet dependencies. Try »apt-get --fix-broken install« with
   no packages (or specify a solution).
```

> The package database is now in an inconsistent state and even though it knows about the source of the problem, **dpkg** cannot continue to service the user's request until the problem is fixed. In chapter 5.3.7, I will be introducing methods to handle situations like this more gracefully.

[10]http://www.murphys-laws.com

It may be better to ignore the dependencies only for a single package. For this purpose, dpkg provides the --ignore-depends=<package> option (which may be given multiple times). With the option, it is possible to forcefully override the dependencies of the specified package. However, dependency relationships of other packages continue to be protected by dpkg during the same operation. Thus, the following allows dpkg to remove netkit-inetd but prevents the removal of adduser (do not try this at home):

```
~# dpkg --purge --ignore-depends=netkit-inetd netkit-inetd adduser
[...]
Purging configuration files for netkit-inetd ...
dpkg: dependency problems prevent removal of adduser:
 ssh depends on adduser (>= 3.9).
[...]
```

Furthermore, if only the version of a versioned dependency must be overridden, --force-depends-version is a better choice.

--force-overwrite

With this switch, dpkg is allowed to overwrite files belonging to another package. This may be necessary with incompatible packages that have no conflict declared between them. This can easily happen when the DEB files are obtained from unofficial sources. In addition, fluctuations in *unstable* may sometimes call for this switch:

```
~# dpkg --install coreutils_5.0.91-2_i386.deb
[...]
Unpacking replacement coreutils ...
dpkg: error processing coreutils_5.0.91-2_i386.deb (--install):
trying to overwrite '/bin/chgrp', which is also in package
  fileutils
dpkg-deb: subprocess paste killed by signal (Broken pipe)
Errors were encountered while processing:
 coreutils_5.0.91-2_i386.deb
~# dpkg --install --force-overwrite coreutils_5.0.91-2_i386.deb
[...]
Unpacking replacement coreutils ...
dpkg - warning, overriding problem because --force enabled:
 trying to overwrite '/bin/chgrp', which is also in package
  fileutils
Setting up coreutils (5.0.91-2) ...
```

From the viewpoint of the package management tools, /bin/chgrp is now owned by coreutils, nor by fileutils. Thus ownership has changed. In certain situations, this can have severe consequences. coreutils is an essential package and therefore its removal is highly unlikely. But assuming we were talking about another package and removed coreutils, dpkg would unlink

/bin/chgrp. fileutils is still installed, but its footprint is now incomplete —
and the package management tools have no way to know that. If the functionality of fileutils depended on /bin/chgrp, the package would be rendered unusable by removing a different package. Obviously, such situations
are extremely rare, but it is important to understand the implications of the
--force-overwrite switch.

Please refer to chapter 5.3.7 for information on how to handle this kind of
scenario.

--force-hold

If this option is given, dpkg will override the request to hold a package and
process it anyhow.

--force-conflicts

This option allows dpkg to ignore Conflicts declarations and install conflicting packages anyhow. This usually requires --force-overwrite and is
generally a good way to shoot yourself in the foot.

5.3.7   Dealing with errors in packages

At times, packages may fail to install due to unsatisfied dependencies or existing
conflicts, files that would be overwritten, or erroneous control scripts. Problems like
this should never occur in the *stable* release (and will be treated as **grave** bugs).
However, on a system running *unstable*, this kind of problem can happen.

Depending on the source of the problem, different techniques must be employed
to restore proper operations. In all cases, it is important to remember that dpkg
notes any problems and remains robust in the face of inconsistencies. Moreover,
dpkg remembers the desired action and attempts to enact it over and over again,
until it finally succeeds. At the same time, actions unrelated to the problematic
packages are not affected.

Correcting dependency problems

In the following example, the administrator attempts the installation of postfix,
but the dependent package netbase is not installed. dpkg registers the desire to
install postfix but cannot fulfill it until netbase is installed.

```
~# dpkg --install /var/cache/apt/archives/postfix_2.1.5-1_i386.deb
dpkg: dependency problems prevent configuration of postfix:
 postfix depends on netbase; however:
  Package netbase is not installed.
~# dpkg --info postfix
iU  postfix       2.1.5-1    A high-performance mail transport agent
```

While the **netbase** is in a broken state, **dpkg** lets the administrator work on other packages. For instance, **apache2** can be installed and purged without problems:

```
~# dpkg --install /var/cache/apt/archives/apache2_2.0.52-3_i386.deb
[...]
Unpacking apache2 (from .../apache2_2.0.52-3_i386.deb) ...
Setting up apache2 (2.0.52-3) ...
~# dpkg --purge apache2
Removing apache2 ...
```

The dependency problem relating to **postfix** can be resolved at any point in time, either by installing the dependent **netbase** package and asking **dpkg** to configure **postfix**, or by removing **postfix**.

Since **dpkg** remembers the administrator's request to install **postfix**, it will retry and automatically complete the installation as soon as the dependencies are fulfilled:

```
~# dpkg --install /var/cache/apt/archives/netbase_4.19_all.deb
[...]
~# dpkg --configure postfix
[...]
```

At times, you may want to use software installed *e.g.* below **/usr/local** to satisfy dependencies in existing software. For instance, you may need a special version of **libsasl2** for use with **postfix**. Rather than forcing **dpkg** to ignore the dependencies, it is better to employ special tools that are designed to convince the package management system to regard a specific dependency as fulfilled (*e.g.* using the **equivs** or **checkinstall** packages, introduced in chapter 5.10.3 and chapter 5.10.2 respectively).

Dealing with file conflicts

dpkg will not let a package overwrite files that belong to another package. As we saw in chapter 5.3.6, it is possible to force **dpkg** to overwrite files in another package, but the use of this feature is highly discouraged. If the problem seems to be of a temporary nature (as is frequently the case with *unstable*), overwriting may be fine. Please consider filing a bug against both packages to make sure that the maintainers know about the problem (see chapter 10.6).

However, if the problem is persistent because you need to install DEB files from external sources, or DEB files build with **alien** (see chapter 5.10.1), then a bug report will not help. Of course, the packager of the external DEB file should be informed, but a fixed version may take forever to appear. In such a case, it is possible to tell **dpkg** to use a different name for the file in one package in favour of the file in another. For instance, if **foo** tries to install **/usr/bin/foobar**, which is also in **bar**, and you want to use **foo**'s version of the file, you can tell **dpkg** to divert all other versions to a different filename:

```
~# dpkg-divert --package foo --rename \
  --divert /usr/bin/foobar.bar /usr/bin/foobar
Adding 'diversion of /usr/bin/foobar to /usr/bin/foobar.bar by foo'
```

Now, foo and bar can coexist, but **/usr/bin/foobar** is foo's version. If **bar** is updated, **dpkg** automatically installs the new **/usr/bin/foobar** file to **/usr/bin/foobar.bar** instead. The **--rename** option causes **dpkg** not only to register the diversion, but also to immediately rename the file on the filesystem.

For more information on diversions, please refer to chapter 6.1.3.

Dealing with broken control scripts during installation

Broken maintainer scripts are another cause of problems. If *e.g.* a package's **postinst** control file contains an error, the package cannot be configured completely by **dpkg**. For instance, in the following (simulated) case, the **netbase postinst** script fails and prevents the installation of the package:

```
~# dpkg --install /var/cache/apt/archives/netbase_4.19_all.deb
[...]
Setting up netbase (4.19) ...
[...]
dpkg: error processing netbase (--configure):
 subprocess post-installation script returned error exit status 1
Errors were encountered while processing:
 netbase
E: Sub-process /usr/bin/dpkg returned an error code (1)
...]
```

Such an error should definitely be reported to the bug tracking system with a **grave** severity (see chapter 10.6). To help diagnose the problem, it may be useful to trace the execution of the offending script. In the case of a shell script, you can simply insert **set -x** right after the first line (**1a** tells **sed** to append a line to the first line of the file):

```
~# sed -i -e '1aset -x' /var/lib/dpkg/info/netbase.postinst
```

postinst scripts may also be written in Perl. Unfortunately, **Perl** does not provide a similar means to trace the execution of the script. Instead, you can use the interactive debugger by appending the **-d** option to the first line of the script (in which the **Perl** interpreter is identified). This will invoke the **Perl** debugger when the **postinst** script is run the next time. The debugger is documented in the **perldebug (1)** manpage. In **perldebtut (1)**, a beginner's tutorial is available.

You are free to modify the **postinst** script in an attempt to correct any errors, but please exercise care when doing so; the script is executed as **root**! If you do find the problem and possibly even fix it, please provide all necessary information (or even a patch) in the bug report. Alternatively, you may opt to force the script to exit successfully by letting it execute **exit 0** in the right place, and then try to configure the package manually. The same holds for the preinstallation script.

Unless you need the package, maybe the best idea is to purge or remove the package and wait for an updated version to be provided in response to your bug report. You can remove packages with broken installation scripts as you would remove any other package.

Dealing with broken control scripts during deinstallation

The option to deinstall a package with broken control scripts does not really exist when a package's removal scripts are the ones causing problems. Even though you could force the removal by causing the offending control script to exit cleanly, this would prevent **dpkg** from cleaning up your system properly, potentially leaving orphaned files behind. Short of fixing the problem (and submitting a patch to the bug tracking system), it is probably best to report the problem (see chapter 10.6) and wait for an updated, fixed version to percolate into the archive. Then, the package may be removed as it should. This only holds for the **postrm** script, however. If the **prerm** script is broken, you will have to simulate its successful completion to make the upgrade to the next package version work.

5.3.8   dpkg configuration

dpkg reads its default options from **/etc/dpkg/dpkg.cfg**, as well as ~/.dpkg.cfg, which takes precedence. The contents of the file are trivial and consist merely of the literal command line options you need as defaults for every invocation of **dpkg**, without the leading dashes. Thus, the following is a good way to ensure your sanity, should it ever come down to it:

```
~# echo refuse-downgrade >> /etc/dpkg/dpkg.cfg
~# dpkg --install /var/cache/apt/archives/bash_2.05b-24_i386.deb
Will not downgrade bash from version 3.0-10 to 2.05b-24, skipping.
```

5.3.9   dselect

If you have some previous experience of Debian, you will probably know **dselect**. To quote its maintainer: "dselect is the venerable user interface to the Debian package management system and archive. It's certainly one of the most uniquely identifiable components of a Debian system."

dselect is a user interface to **dpkg** that supports interactive package selection, and automatic acquisition of packages from various sources, such as CD-ROMs, FTP sites. dselect can also use APT (see chapter 5.4) to acquire and install packages, and can thus also fetch DEB files from any source supported by APT (see chapter 5.4.1). The programme does not, however, make any other use of APT's functionality.

dselect sports its own dependency resolution mechanism. When a package is selected for installation, dselect automatically adds its dependencies to the set of packages to install. In the case of ambiguity (if two or more packages can satisfy a single dependency, for example), dselect presents the user with a resolution screen in which a choice can be made among the possibilities.

Independently of APT, dselect keeps its own list of available software in /var/lib/ available. For dselect to be useful, this list has to be regularly updated, which can also be done at the command line, where Packages is the package index file downloaded from a Debian mirror or another source of Debian packages.

```
~$ dpkg --merge-avail Packages
Updating available packages info, using Packages.
Information about 17877 package(s) was updated.
```

Figure 5.1:
The six steps of
dselect

```
Debian `dselect' package handling frontend.

   0. [A]ccess   Choose the access method to use.
   1. [U]pdate   Update list of available packages, if possible.
 * 2. [S]elect   Request which packages you want on your system.
   3. [I]nstall  Install and upgrade wanted packages.
   4. [C]onfig   Configure any packages that are unconfigured.
   5. [R]emove   Remove unwanted software.
   6. [Q]uit     Quit dselect.

Move around with ^P and ^N, cursor keys, initial letters, or digits;
Press <enter> to confirm selection.   ^L redraws screen.

Version 1.10.22 (i386).
Copyright (C) 1994-1996 Ian Jackson.
Copyright (C) 2000,2001 Wichert Akkerman.
This is free software; see the GNU General Public Licence version 2
or later for copying conditions. There is NO warranty. See
dselect --licence for details.
```

On launching, dselect presents the user with a menu comprising six steps (or seven, depending on whether quitting is a step), depicted in figure 5.1. These steps are designed to be executed in succession and mostly relate to the individual calls to dpkg:

0. Access

In addition to APT, which has become the dselect standard access method since its inception, dselect can also fetch packages from CD-ROM, via Network File System (NFS), from an unmounted or mounted filesystem, or from a floppy.

1. Update

The option causes dselect to retrieve the list of packages provided by the

access media chosen in step 0 and merges them into a single listing with
dpkg --merge-avail.

2. Select

Behind this item hides the interface shown in figure 5.2. **dselect** presents
the packages it knows about according to various sort criteria and allows for
the modification of the requested status of the packages (e.g. installing, or
putting a package on hold).

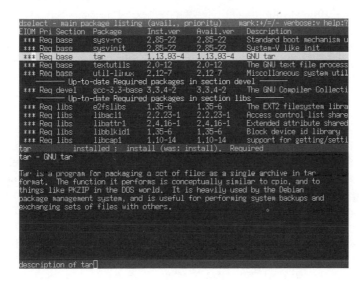

Figure 5.2:
The package selection
screen provided by
dselect

3. Install

This step causes **dselect** to fetch all DEB files whose installation the user
requested in the selection phase from the respective source media, and consequently to unpack all packages. It also automatically configures newly
installed packages and removes those marked for deinstallation.

4. Config

Packages can be explicitly configured with this option, which the install calls
automatically. It is therefore seldom used. The command executed for the
configuration is **dpkg --configure --pending**.

5. Remove

If a user only wants to remove packages marked for deinstallation but post-
pone any pending installations, this menu option should be chosen rather
than Install. It is, however, executed automatically as part of an installation. The command executed when selecting this option is **dpkg --remove
--pending**.

The main interaction with the programme happens through the selection interface. Here, you can scroll the list of packages and select packages for installation, deinstallation, and purging, by pressing the [+] (plus), [-] (minus), and [_] (underscore) keys respectively. A regular expression search over the package names is accessible with the [/] key. The package selection can be confirmed by hitting [enter], and changes can always be reverted with the [R] key.

When you change a package's requested state (*e.g.* select it for installation), **dselect** checks whether the request can be honoured without rendering the system inconsistent. If the request would introduce an inconsistency, **dselect** presents you with a dependency resolution screen, and a suggestion on how to restore consistency. You are free to accept the suggestion with the [enter] key, or to first make any changes, such as using a different package to satisfy a dependency than suggested. If the selection you make in the resolution screen does not correspond to a consistent state (*e.g.* a conflict exists, or a dependency is not met), **dselect** opens a new resolution screen to resolve the new conflict.

The resolution screen can be quite a daunting experience to the new user, who may have a hard time returning to the package selection screen as **dselect** keeps displaying one resolution screen after another. Keep in mind that the selection of packages you make must be internally consistent. Here, **dselect**'s dependency on **dpkg** clearly shows: unless you propose a selection that satisfies all dependencies and introduces no conflicts, **dselect** will not accept it just like **dpkg** would prevent the installation of an offending package. In particular, if you select an alternative package to satisfy a dependency, you must undo **dselect**'s suggestion or the two packages may conflict. The [D] key can be used to erase all suggestions made by the user. The [U] key tells **dselect** to revert all changes since the last suggestion (effectively making the suggestion again). Finally, it is always possible to restore the selection state before the unresolved dependencies or conflicts appeared by pressing the [R] key.

After making any changes (or not, if you are happy with the suggested solution), the [enter] key will take you back to the package selection window, or take you right back into the dependency resolution screen if inconsistencies persist. Remember that **dselect** is not capable of resolving these inconsistencies automatically, it can only make suggestions. It is possible to return to the main package selection without resolving dependencies and conflicts by using the [Q] key. When another inconsistency is found, the resolution screen will simply merge suggestions and alternatives for both inconsistencies into one list, which may be somewhat confusing.

If **dselect** is told to enact a selection that contains inconsistencies, it will skip over any packages with unresolved dependencies or conflicts and put these packages on hold. It is not possible to introduce inconsistencies into the system with **dselect** thanks to the underlying **dpkg**.

While many users swear by **dselect**, my suggestion is to replace it in favour of **aptitude** or another interface to APT (see chapter 5.4.11, chapter 5.4.12, and chapter 6.10). Being based on APT, **aptitude** can resolve conflicts automatically to honour the user's request; it does not impose a sequence of steps on the user: you can mark packages for installation and deinstallation as required and deal with broken packages individually, and whenever you desire. On the other hand, if this is too much trouble, **aptitude** will find a solution for you.

5.4 Managing packages: APT

dpkg is a powerful tool. Its robustness ensures the consistency of a Debian system. Nevertheless, it is far from today's standards in package management, as it lacks automatic dependency resolution, to name just one shortcoming. APT, which is an acronym for "Advanced Package Tool", has been written to fill this gap. It is a high-level tool that deals primarily with the abstract concept of a package, which consists of the following data:

- An identifying name

- The version number

- The Uniform Resource Locator (URL) of the DEB file providing the package

- Dependency information, including conflict declarations (see chapter 5.7.3).

Using this information, APT determines the set of packages needed to fulfill a request, downloads them from a repository (such as the Debian archive), and installs and removes packages from the local system as needed.

Where **dpkg** conservatively prevents an action from taking place, rather than putting system consistency at risk, APT will figure out the additional steps to restore the consistency, and perform those steps. For instance, if a package depends on another, **dpkg** will not install the former without the latter. In contrast to this, APT would automatically install the latter first so that the original request could be carried out.

APT does not install or remove packages itself, but uses **dpkg** for package handling at the system level. APT's job is the acquisition of dependencies as well as the orchestration of calls to **dpkg** in the right order to achieve the desired result without giving **dpkg** a chance to complain.

To accomplish its task, APT maintains a list of available packages, which the administrator regularly updates with the list of packages provided on the Debian servers as well as repositories residing on other media, such as DVDs, the download servers of independent software projects, and local collections. After each update, APT parses the dependency information for each package and calculates a dependency tree using standard graph theory[11], with a specific edge type for each different dependency relation. Figure 5.3 shows selected parts of the dependency tree rooted at the abcde package.

Figure 5.3:
Selected parts of the
dependency tree
rooted at the abcde
package[12]

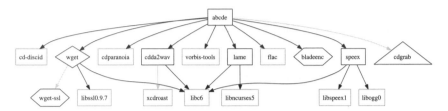

The different symbols and line colours reflect the types of relationships: normal packages are rectangular boxes, virtual packages provided by others are triangles, diamonds denote normal packages also provided by others (**wget-ssl** provides **wget**), and non-existing packages are displayed as hexagons. Boxes with light lines denote leaf packages where the recursion stopped because we told **apt-cache** to only graph the packages explicitly named (**-oAPT::Cache::GivenOnly=true**). Finally, the light lines identify conflicts while the black ones represent normal dependencies (including suggestions and recommendations).

APT is actually a library that provides package handling facilities. An administrator may use this library from the command-line through two front-end programmes, **apt-get** and **apt-cache**.

5.4.1 Specifying repositories

APT sits higher up in the package management hierarchy and does not interact with DEB files directly. In the **APT** domain, packages are referred to by their package name and optionally the version number. APT can handle any number of repositories and merge the list of available packages. Duplicates are resolved in favour of the first encounter. The repositories are identified by lines of the following form in /etc/apt/sources.list[13]:

```
deb ftp://ftp.debian.org/debian sarge main
deb http://nonus.debian.org/debian-non-US sarge main
deb copy:/srv/mirror/debian/debian sarge main
deb cdrom:[title]/ sarge main
```

[11] The underlying algorithm is a topological sort. See: http://www.cs.sunysb.edu/~algorith/files/topological-sorting.shtml

[12] The graph was made with the output of **apt-cache dotty --option APT::Cache::GivenOnly=true abcde wget speex speex lame cdda2wav** fed through **dot** of the **graphviz** package

[13] Please make sure to use a closer mirror instead of ftp.debian.org (see chapter 5.4.1). The full list of mirrors is available online: http://www.debian.org/mirror/list.

Each line encodes the location of the **Packages** on the given medium. The exact syntax definition of a valid line may be found in the **sources.list** (5) manpage. A line has at least three fields which together provide the information necessary to piece together the paths in the archive. The fields are:

package type

> **deb** references binary packages. To access source packages, **deb-src** must be used instead.

source URI

> The Universal Resource Identifier (URI) identifies the source medium and can use any of the following access methods:

> cdrom

>> allows access to local CD-ROM drives and supports media swapping as well as prompting for new media, identified by the title specified between brackets. Use **apt-cdrom** to add CD-ROM entries to **/etc/apt/sources.list**.

> file

>> allows selection of an arbitrary file system location to be used as a repository, such as an NFS mount or a local mirror.

> copy

>> similar to the **file** access method, **copy** uses APT's cache directory[14] to store the files after the download.

> http

>> the fastest and preferred package source using a network connection, honouring the **$http_proxy** variable.

> ftp

>> slightly slower than **http**, the **ftp** method is highly configurable via **/etc/apt/apt.conf**. It may use an optional proxy defined in **$ftp_proxy**.

> ssh

>> given an SSH connection which does not require password entry, **APT** can use a remote mirror via a secure tunnel. **rsh** is also provided but should not be used or enabled for security reasons. For example:

>> ```
>> deb ssh://user@intranet.company.com/srv/debian/ ./
>> ```

distribution

> With standard mirrors, the **distribution** field identifies the Debian release by canonical name (*e.g. stable*) or codename (*e.g. sarge*). It can also be a complete path, in which case it must end with a slash. For instance, lines similar to the following (my staging repository) are frequently found for project or private repositories:

[14]/var/cache/apt/archives

```
deb http://people.debian.org/~madduck/stage ./
```

/stage is a simple directory exported to the web server, which contains the Packages file and only provides a single collection of packages. When the distribution path is not a complete path, it identifies part of the path to the Packages file for the desired distribution, as shown later.

components

The remainder of each line serves to identify the component collections contained in a distribution. For the official mirrors, these correspond to the archives (*e.g. main* and *non-free*) and also specify when *non-US* software is to be used. For unofficial repositories, these can be used to identify components freely defined by the repository administrator (see chapter 4.4.5 for a smart example). APT will create a separate URI for each component. Thus, regular distribution entries require at least one component. Conversely, lines with complete paths do not specify components.

When APT is told to update its understanding of available packages with **apt-get update**, it goes out to fetch the various Packages files, whose locations are encoded in the lines of /etc/apt/sources.list. Each component mentioned in the line corresponds to one Packages file, while lines with distribution set to a complete path only identify a single Packages file and have no components.

An entry in /etc/apt/sources.list of the following form:

```
deb ftp://ftp.debian.org/debian sarge main contrib non-free
```

causes **apt-get update** to retrieve the following Packages files[15], assuming an i386 architecture:

```
ftp://ftp.debian.org/debian/dists/sarge/main/binary-i386/Packages
ftp://ftp.debian.org/debian/dists/sarge/contrib/binary-i386/Packages
ftp://ftp.debian.org/debian/dists/sarge/non-free/binary-i386/Packages
```

A line can also specify a complete path within a repository. Note the final slash, which is mandatory. By using a variable for the architecture, the repositories can be specified in a portable way:

```
deb http://people.debian.org ~madduck/packages/stage/
deb http://intranet.company.com/srv/debian/ $(ARCH)/
```

maps to the following URI:

```
http://people.debian.org/~madduck/packages/stage/Packages
http://intranet.company.com/srv/debian/i386/Packages
```

[15]If available, APT prefers Packages.gz files in the same location as the Packages files.

Binary packages usually depend on the architectures for which they were compiled. When a package provides architecture-independent data (such as documentation), it is labelled with the special architecture **all** and made available in the **Packages** files for all architectures.

The tools **apt-cdrom** and **apt-setup** (from the **base-config** package) can be used to easily add sources to the **sources.list** file:

```
~# apt-cdrom --cdrom /media/cdrom
Using CD-ROM mount point /media/cdrom/
Unmounting CD-ROM
Please insert a Disc in the drive and press enter
Mounting CD-ROM
Identifying.. [1319efb1a0e8df6caed2bd4e0b507933-2]
[...]
Writing new source list
[...]
Repeat this process for the rest of the CDs in your set.
```

apt-setup uses **debconf** and is essentially the same too which **base-config** invokes:

```
~# apt-setup
Apt configuration
-----------------

Please choose the method apt (the Debian package management tool)
should use to access the Debian archive.

For example if you have a Debian cd, select "cdrom", while if
you plan to  install via a Debian mirror, choose "ftp" or "http".

  1. cdrom  2. http  3. ftp  4. filesystem 5. edit sources list by hand

Archive access method for apt:
[...]
```

Finding the closest mirror: apt-spy

The Debian mirror infrastructure is gigantic with over 100 mirrors officially providing the entire Debian archive. In addition, many universities and institutions provide unofficial mirrors, so it is usually a good idea to listen around. While the majority of mirrors are available for worldwide access, it makes sense to use the mirrors closest to your location. This spreads mirror load and bandwidth evenly and ensures fastest download times.

A full list of all mirrors is available online[16]. For most countries, HTTP and FTP access is available from **ftp.xx.debian.org**, where "xx" is the standardised two-letter coun-

---

[16]http://www.debian.org/mirror/list

try code[17]. These mirrors can become very overloaded and choosing a different one generally results in improved access to the archive.

The **apt-spy** tool is designed to find the best mirror by trying out a set and picking the fastest one, automatically writing the result to **/etc/apt/sources.list**. It can restrict its test to servers within a specific country or area (set of countries), can optionally only test a limited number of servers, or run for a specific maximum time. Furthermore, the areas are easily customised in **/etc/apt-spy.conf**. Thus, to find the fastest servers in the region around Lake Constance, and write an appropriate **sources.list** file for *sarge*, the following would do the trick:

```
~# cat <<EOF >> /etc/apt-spy.conf
Bodensee:
AT
CH
DE
EOF
~# apt-spy update
Updating...
Grabbing file http://http.us.debian.org/debian/README.mirrors.txt...
Update complete. Exiting.
~# apt-spy -d sarge -a Bodensee
[...]
```

The above will take about one minute per server, which can be controlled with the **-t** option. Make sure to read the **apt-spy** (8) manpage for further information on this option.

As mirrors can only be selected per country, users in countries with a large number of mirrors (such as the United States) will not find **apt-spy** very useful. It is, however, possible to cap the number of servers to be tested, using the **-e** option. By restricting it to check only a small number of servers, **apt-spy** regains some of its value in large countries.

5.4.2   APT configuration

Most aspects of **APT** can be customised. In fact, in the **/etc/apt/apt.conf** file, you can change the defaults for almost all command line switches. Instead of the default file, the **$APT_CONFIG** environment variable can be pointed to a different configuration file that will be used instead when set.

Configuration parameters are name-value pairs, split into groups according to their application. The name of the group is prepended to the parameter with a "::" separator. The **apt.conf** (5) manpage describes the syntax. Available items are listed in the manpages of the corresponding commands (*e.g.* apt-get (1) and apt-cache (1)).

[17]http://en.wikipedia.org/wiki/ISO_3166-1_alpha-2

```
APT::Cache-Limit 16777216;
APT::Get::Show-Upgraded true;
APT::Get::Default-Release "sarge";
APT::Get::Purge false;
Acquire::Queue-Mode host;
Acquire::Retries 0;
```

Alternatively, group prefixes can be scoped with curly braces. All in all, the syntax is reminiscent of C++ namespaces:

```
APT {
  Cache-Limit 16777216;

  Get {
    Default-Release "sarge";
    Show-Upgraded true;
    Purge false;
  };
};

Acquire {
  Queue-Mode host;
  Retries 0;
};
```

/etc/apt/apt.conf allows you to control the way in which APT invokes dpkg to handle the package files it downloads, or to interact with the package database. For instance, you may let APT instruct dpkg never to downgrade a package and never to reinstall a package of the same version with the following snippet in /etc/apt/apt.conf:

```
DPkg {
  Options { "--refuse-downgrade"; "--skip-same-version"; }
};
```

If switches like this are part of your system administration policy, it is better to set them in dpkg's configuration to prevent them being ignored when dpkg is invoked directly rather than via APT (see chapter 5.3.8).

In addition to /etc/apt/apt.conf, the /etc/apt/apt.conf.d directory may contain files with APT configuration snippets, which will be sourced in lexicographical order (see chapter 6.1.1). It might not be a bad idea to drop local configuration into different files below this directory to logically separate it into chunks at filesystem level.

Furthermore, every APT programme accepts additional settings with the --option command line flag. Thus, the following two commands are equivalent:

```
~# apt-get install --download-only postfix
~# apt-get install --option APT::Get::Download-Only=true postfix
```

Using the APT configuration directives, you can also fine-tune the acquisition of DEB files from the various media. The top-level **Acquire** group of configuration directives allows you to set parameters relevant to the HTTP, FTP, and CD-ROM media. For instance, default proxies for the two network protocols can be specified, including user and password information. The user can override the proxies with the standard $http_proxy and $ftp_proxy environment variables, which take precedence over the APT settings.

APT hooks

APT provides three hooks for the user to run custom commands at various stages of interaction with **dpkg**. Two of these hooks are of particular interest to administrators of specialised systems. For instance, on systems where **/usr** is generally mounted read-only, the following settings cause APT to enable writing to the **/usr** filesystem for installations or upgrades:

```
DPkg {
  Pre-Invoke { "mount -o remount,rw /usr"; };
  Post-Invoke { "mount -o remount,ro /usr"; };
};
```

An additional hook, **Pre-Install-Pkgs** works in a similar way. APT invokes commands specified for this hook even before **Pre-Invoke**, feeding it the names of the DEB files to be installed on **stdin**. This hook is most commonly used by extensions, such as **apt-listchanges** (see chapter 5.11.2).

5.4.3   Installing packages

When the user requests a certain software to be installed, APT uses its dependency graph to find best the way of satisfying the user's request. From **dpkg**, it knows about the set of installed packages and can thus figure out which additional packages must be downloaded and handed to **dpkg** for installation. Similarly, APT identifies conflicts. Where **dpkg** (rightfully) fails in the face of a conflicts, APT suggests the removal of any conflicting packages, giving priority to the user's request (as opposed to refusing the installation due to the conflicts). It is therefore always a good idea to inspect the changes by a utility based on APT before telling it to do its thing (see chapter 5.4.2 about the **APT::Get::Show-Upgraded** option).

For each package that APT needs to install, it enables an appropriate download method to retrieve the DEB file from a repository into its cache directory[18]. If multiple repositories provide the same file, the repository mentioned first in **/etc/apt/ sources.list** will be used.

[18]/var/cache/apt/archives

Finally, APT enlists **dpkg** to remove any conflicting packages and subsequently install the new packages from the DEB files it downloaded to the cache directory. In the following example, the **postfix** DEB file is already in APT's cache directory. The other package files needed to fulfill **postfix**'s dependencies have not been cached, however, and APT thus fetches them from the location associated with the package.

```
~# apt-get install postfix
Reading Package Lists... Done
Building Dependency Tree... Done
The following NEW packages will be installed:
  adduser debconf debconf-i18n ifupdown iputils-ping
  liblocale-gettext-perl libtext-charwidth-perl libtext-iconv-perl
  libtext-wrapi18n-perl libwrap0 net-tools netbase netkit-inetd postfix
  tcpd
0 upgraded, 15 newly installed, 0 to remove and 0 not upgraded.
Need to get 857kB/1636kB of archives.
After unpacking 6550kB of additional disk space will be used.
Do you want to continue? [Y/n] y
[...]
Get:13 http://debian sarge/main tcpd 7.6.dbs-6 [72.6kB]
Get:14 http://debian sarge/main netbase 4.19 [40.2kB]
[...]
Selecting previously deselected package netbase.
Unpacking netbase (from .../archives/netbase_4.19_all.deb) ...
Selecting previously deselected package postfix.
Unpacking postfix (from .../postfix_2.1.5-1_i386.deb) ...
[...]
Setting up netbase (4.19) ...
Setting up postfix (2.1.5-1) ...
[...]
```

As opposed to **dpkg**, APT does not use a database but computes package download locations and dependencies on every invocation (which makes it somewhat slow). Similar to **dpkg**, an optimised rewrite is on the to-do list. To do this, APT uses the files in **/var/lib/apt/lists**, which **apt-get update** had downloaded previously. Thus, to service a request for a binary package, APT reads the **Packages** files in the order of their repositories, as declared in **/etc/apt/sources.list** and computes the URI to be used in each case. It also reads the **MD5** sum for each DEB file from the **Packages** files for later verification of the downloaded data. You can make APT output this information instead of carrying through with the request using the **--print-uris** switch:

```
~# apt-get install --print-uris postfix
[...]
'.../pool/main/t/tcp-wrappers/tcpd_7.6.dbs-6_i386.deb'
tcpd_7.6.dbs-6_i386.deb 72614 08523a7ed8671461cd35c5e02ea14fc9
'.../pool/main/n/netbase/netbase_4.19_all.deb'
netbase_4.19_all.deb 40182 1203c825810b1262ce74c4d9d7676671
```

```
'.../pool/main/p/postfix/postfix_2.1.5-1_i386.deb'
postfix_2.1.5-1_i386.deb 798936 e4062f342b5d77416ae4ef28dfed1ef8
```

You can also tell APT to merely simulate and not actually install:

```
~# apt-get install --simulate
[...]
Inst postfix [2.1.5-1] (2.1.5-1 Debian:sarge)
Conf postfix (2.1.5-1 Debian:sarge)
```

apt-get also accepts POSIX-style regular expressions in place of package names:

```
~# apt-get install libusb-\(0\.1-4\|-dev\)
[...]
Note, selecting libusb-0.1-4 for regex 'libusb-(0.1-4|dev)'
Note, selecting libusb-dev for regex 'libusb-(0.1-4|dev)'
[...]
The following NEW packages will be installed:
  libusb-0.1-4 libusb-dev
[...]
```

APT automatically checks the hash sum of each file it processes against its entry in the corresponding **Packages** file. Only when the **MD5** sums match will the installation proceed. In case of a discrepancy, APT will report an **MD5** mismatch and refuse to install or upgrade a package. In chapter 7.5 we will revisit package hash sums and introduce a means to verify downloads.

Updating the APT database

The **Packages** files, which are integral to APT's operation, must be updated regularly. Even though the *stable* release does not change (other than when a new "r-release" is made), the only way for APT for find out about newly available security updates (or newly available packages, if you are running something other than *stable*), is by checking the registered repositories for updated **Packages** index files. It is probably a good idea to update these files once a day, or at least once in a while, prior to use. The **cron-apt** package provides a flexible framework that allows you to automate this (and other) APT processes (see chapter 5.11.4). Outdated **Packages** files can cause APT to fail when its indices point to files which have been removed in favour of newer versions.

To update the database, you simply run one command:

```
~# apt-get update
Get:1 http://debian sarge/main Packages [3331kB]
[...]
Fetched 3331kB in 0s (24328kB/s)
Reading Package Lists... Done
```

During the update, APT cleans /var/lib/apt/lists of any files belonging to repositories which are not referenced by /etc/apt/sources.list. If you pass the --no-list-clcanup option (APT::Get::List-Cleanup), APT refrains from erasing obsoleted files, which may be handy if you are only temporarily disabling a repository in the sources.list file; you will not have to download it again when you put the repositories back in APT's package sources.

Dependency resolution in action

When resolving dependencies, APT tries to make sane choices. Apart from automatically pulling in packages on which a requested package depends, APT removes conflicting packages that are already installed in an effort to honour any request the user makes. Whenever a request does anything in addition to what the user wanted, apt-get will ask for confirmation after displaying the proposed changes to the package selection. This is to prevent inadvertently deinstalling conflicting packages or pulling in hundreds of dependencies. If no extra actions are required, APT will not prompt.

As shown in chapter 5.4.2, APT can be made to always prompt for confirmation by setting APT::Get::Show-Upgraded true. Similarly, setting APT::Get::Assume-Yes true or specifying --yes in the APT command line causes APT to always bypass confirmation and continue. Avoid this option; confirmations are a good thing in the productivity domain[19].

At times, a package may depend on any one of a set of packages. For instance, apache2 depends on "apache2-mpm-worker | apache2-mpm-prefork | apache2-mpm-perchild", and thus requires any one of these three to be installed. By default, APT will install the first package, unless another one is explicitly requested:

```
~# apt-get install apache2
[...]
The following NEW packages will be installed:
  apache2 apache2-common apache2-mpm-worker libapr0 libexpat1
  libmagic1 mime-support openssl ssl-cert
[...]
~# apt-get install apache2 apache2-mpm-perchild
[...]
The following NEW packages will be installed:
apache2 apache2-common apache2-mpm-perchild libapr0 libexpat1
  libmagic1 mime-support openssl ssl-cert
[...]
```

If the preference is *not* to install one package but pick any other, APT can be told to choose the next one in the row by instructing it not to use the first choice to satisfy the dependency:

[19]You *do* use the -i flag with rm and mv when working as root, right?

```
~# apt-get install apache2 apache2-mpm-worker-
[...]
The following NEW packages will be installed:
  apache2 apache2-common apache2-mpm-prefork libapr0 libexpat1
  libmagic1 mime-support openssl ssl-cert
[...]
```

You can use plus and minus signs to influence APT's decision; appending a minus to a package explicitly removes it (and appending a plus to a package in an **apt-get remove** invocation installs the package, as one might expect).

Debian also knows about the concept of virtual packages (see chapter 5.7.3). You cannot install virtual packages directly, but packages may depend on them.

```
~# apt-get install mail-transport-agent
Reading Package Lists... Done
Building Dependency Tree... Done
Package mail-transport-agent is a virtual package provided by:
  zmailer 2.99.56-2
[...]
  postfix 2.1.5-1
[...]
  courier-mta 0.47-3
You should explicitly select one to install.
E: Package mail-transport-agent has no installation candidate
```

For instance, **at** depends on **mail-transport-agent**. Since every package providing a Mail Transfer Agent (MTA) in Debian includes this virtual package, new MTAs can be used to satisfy **at**'s dependency without requiring a change to **at**. If a package depends on a virtual package, APT chooses a package with the virtual package for installation. To override the choice, you can do the same as above:

```
~# apt-get install at
[...]
The following NEW packages will be installed:
  at courier-authdaemon courier-base courier-mta
[...]
Do you want to continue? [Y/n] n
~# apt-get install postfix at
[...]
The following NEW packages will be installed:
  adduser at debconf [...] postfix
[...]
```

Note that order matters on the **apt-get install** command line[20]. If you were to install **at** and then **postfix**, APT would also pull in **courier-mta**'s dependencies even though it will not install **courier-mta** in the end. Thus, APT scans the command

---

[20]http://bugs.debian.org/122304

line and appends all dependencies, resolving conflicts by giving priority to packages pulled in later.

Reinstalling packages

It may be necessary at times to ask for a package to be reinstalled. Maybe the root user deleted a file by accident, or a modification to the configuration files went out of control. When **APT** is told to install an already installed package, it will not comply with the request:

```
~# apt-get install postfix
[...]
postfix is already the newest version.
0 upgraded, 0 newly installed, 0 to remove and 31 not upgraded.
```

The **--reinstall** switch forces **APT** to perform the installation again, regardless:

```
~# apt-get install --reinstall postfix
[...]
0 upgraded, 0 newly installed, 1 reinstalled, 0 to remove and 0 not
  upgraded.
Need to get 0B/795kB of archives.
After unpacking 0B of additional disk space will be used.
Do you want to continue? [Y/n] y
[...]
```

As long as the required DEB file is still cached (above), you can also use **dpkg** directly for the reinstallation. Thus, the following is equivalent to telling **APT** to reinstall a package:

```
~# apt-get --download-only install postfix
~# dpkg --install /var/cache/apt/archives/postfix_2.1.5-1_i386.deb
```

5.4.4 Searching the APT database

So far so good, installing packages with **APT** is a piece of cake once you know the package name. **APT** provides comprehensive tools to query the package database to obtain the desired package name(s), in addition to various resources online, which will be reviewed in the following sections.

The Debian web page features a section exclusively dedicated to its package pool[21]. The site provides three means to browse the collection of available packages. The "package lists" provide short blurbs for each package, while packages are sorted

[21]http://packages.debian.org

into categories according to their function. By choosing a category, a user can quickly find a set of packages relevant to a certain requirement.

It is also possible to search the package database for package names, package descriptions, or even the contents of all packages to see which package provides a specific file. Further search criteria allow you to filter the set of results, making it easy to retrieve the necessary information for the command-line **APT** tools.

Finally, each package has a dedicated information page on the Debian web site. These pages are accessible through a canonical URL using the binary[22] or source package name[23]. Some more information is available through the package tracking system (see chapter 10.6.9).

Instead of requiring a web browser, all this functionality is also available from the command line, in case you prefer not to go via the web interface. Most work is done by the **apt-cache** interface, which can be used to search the package database, including the package descriptions like so:

```
~$ apt-cache search palm sync command line
autopilot - Monitor the DTR line of /dev/palm and run a command to start
  sync
malsync - Allows a PalmOS PDA to synchronize to a MAL server
pilot-link - Tools to communicate with a PalmOS PDA
```

The arguments to **apt-cache search** are regular expressions themselves, and if more than one argument is specified, all of them have to match for a package to be included in the output. It is also possible to search only the package names with the **--names-only** option (APT::Cache::NamesOnly true). When specifying the **--full** switch (APT::Cache::ShowFull true), the full package information is displayed. This information is also accessible for each package directly and is essentially the same as available via **dpkg --info** and **dpkg --show**:

```
~# apt-cache show postfix
Package: postfix
Priority: extra
Section: mail
[...]
Provides: mail-transport-agent
[...]
Description: A high-performance mail transport agent
[...]
```

Searching the Debian archive for single files

Further search capabilities are available through the **apt-file** tool, available in the package with the same name. **apt-file** is essentially an interface to the **Contents**

[22]http://packages.debian.org/<package>
[23]http://packages.debian.org/src:<package>

file found in **APT** repositories. This file is available for each distribution and contains a list of all files installed by the packages in the specific distribution. Before **apt-file** can be of any use, it has to have access to the **Contents** files the user wants to search. Running **apt-file update** will take care of that and place the downloaded files under **/var/cache/apt**. Now, **apt-file** can be used to search these lists.

The main use of **apt-file** is to determine which package provides a certain file. For instance, if someone told you to use the **/usr/bin/convert** tool to reformat a picture file, you could use **apt-file** to figure out that the **imagemagick** package is what you need to install:

```
~$ apt-file search /usr/bin/convert
imagemagick: /usr/bin/convert
```

Furthermore, **apt-file** is capable of displaying the files associated with a package. This is similar to **dpkg --listfiles** but does not require the package to be installed:

```
~$ apt-file list postfix
postfix: etc/init.d/postfix
postfix: etc/postfix/access
[...]
postfix: usr/lib/sendmail
postfix: usr/sbin/postalias
[...]
```

5.4.5   Inquiring about package dependencies

Returning to **apt-cache**, the programme also provides access to various additional information about packages and the package database. Apart from a package's control data, which can be accessed with **apt-cache show**, **apt-cache** has two methods of displaying the dependency information of a package as well as the list of packages which declare dependency relations for a specific package:

```
~$ apt-cache depends apt-file
apt-file
  Depends: perl
  Depends: gzip
  Depends: libconfigfile-perl
  Depends: libapt-pkg-perl
  Suggests: ssh
    ssh-krb5
  Recommends: wget
    wget-cvs

~$ apt-cache rdepends apt-file
apt-file
Reverse Depends:
  dh-make-perl
```

Alternatively, the two can be combined with general information about a package:

```
~$ apt-cache showpkg apt-file
Versions:
2.0.3-7(/var/lib/apt/lists/...Packages)(/var/lib/dpkg/status)
Reverse Depends:
  packagesearch,apt-file
  dh-make-perl,apt-file
Dependencies:
2.0.3-7 - perl (0 (null)) gzip (2 1.2.4) libconfigfile-perl (0 (null))
  libapt-pkg-perl (0 (null)) ssh (0 (null)) wget (0 (null))
Provides:
2.0.3-7 -
Reverse Provides:
```

For the (forward) dependencies, the values in parentheses following the dependent packages encode the version requirements and directly map to their symbolic counterparts as shown in table 5.3. (null) is a special value to indicate a lack of version dependency. Each reverse dependency lists pairs of depending and dependent binary packages. If the reverse dependency is versioned, the version number is also included.

Table 5.3:
The numeric
representations of
versioned dependency
relations in the
apt-cache showpkg
output

Number	Symbol	Description
0	=	equal to
1	<=	less than or equal to
2	>=	greater than or equal to
3	<<	strictly less than
4	>>	strictly greater than

For further investigation of package dependencies, **apt-rdepends** in the package of the same name can perform recursive dependency listings according to specific criteria. For instance, to show the installed packages suggested by **postfix**:

```
~$ apt-rdepends --state-show=Installed --state-follow=Installed \
  --show=Suggests --follow=Suggests postfix
Reading Package Lists... Done
Building Dependency Tree... Done
postfix
  Suggests: procmail
```

Dependency graphs

There are at least two methods of visualising the dependency graphs used internally by APT. The older of the two uses **apt-cache**, which can be rather inflexible in its use, because it only allows you to specify the nodes to be included and excluded on the basis of the package name. **apt-rdepends** also provides the "dotty" functionality and allows for the same criteria to be used as shown above.

The tools do not output graphs but rather information needed to create graphs. There are a number of tools capable of the latter transformation. The classic tools are **dot** and **neato** from the **graphviz** package. **neato** places nodes all over two-dimensional space while **dot** attempts to create hierarchies. Both can generate an Encapsulated PostScript (EPS) file and **dot**'s result is especially suited for printing (see figure 5.3 on page 164).

```
~$ apt-cache dotty postfix > /tmp/postfix.dot
~$ dot -Tps -o /tmp/postfix.eps /tmp/postfix.dot
```

The resulting graph can become huge quite quickly. It is possible to constrain the set of nodes to include only the packages listed on the command line and their immediate dependencies, and not to recurse further down the resulting tree:

```
~$ apt-cache dotty --option APT::Cache::GivenOnly=true postfix netbase
```

An alternative to **graphviz** is **springgraph** from the package of the same name. It uses a different algorithm to layout the graphs and is specifically useful for larger data sets due to its better use of space. It cannot output hierarchies like **dot**, but it does produce better results in two-dimensional space than **neato**. **springgraph** produces PNG files and is thus less suited for printing:

```
~$ apt-rdepends --dotty postfix > /tmp/postfix.dot
[...]
~$ springgraph < /tmp/postfix.dot > /tmp/postfix.png
```

Both, **apt-cache** and **apt-rdepends** produce the same dotty output and thus either one can be used with any compatible spring graph creator.

5.4.6 Deinstalling and purging packages

Removal (or purging) of packages happens analogously. If the user requests the deinstallation of a package on which others depend, these will also be removed. APT always tries to fulfill the user's request while keeping the number of changes to a minimum. A system may have **postfix** installed to meet the requirement of certain packages for a **mail-transport-agent**. When **postfix** is removed, APT will take those with it, so as to not leave behind packages with unsatisfied dependencies.

```
~# apt-get remove postfix
Reading Package Lists... Done
Building Dependency Tree... Done
The following packages will be REMOVED:
  at mailx mutt popularity-contest postfix
[...]
Removing popularity-contest ...
Removing postfix ...
```

To prevent the deinstallation, the user can specify another package to replace the **mail-transport-agent** functionality on the same command line by appending a plus sign.

```
~# apt-get remove postfix zmailer+
[...]
The following packages will be REMOVED:
  postfix
The following NEW packages will be installed:
  zmailer
[...]
```

Obviously, this has the same effect as simply installing **zmailer**, as its installation will cause APT to remove the conflicting **postfix** package implicitly:

To remove a package's configuration files as well, specify the **--purge** option. On certain systems, it may make sense to always purge by setting APT::Get::Purge **true**.

```
~# apt-get remove --purge mc
[...]
The following packages will be REMOVED:
  mc*
[...]
Removing mc ...
Purging configuration files for mc ...
```

Note the asterisk following the **mc** package, which indicates the impending purge as opposed to a simple remove.

Instead of **apt-get remove --purge**, it is also possible to just use **dpkg -P**, which has the same effect and requires far fewer keystrokes. However, **dpkg** cannot be used to remove a package on which others depend. While APT would offer to remove the depending packages as well, **dpkg** will simply prevent the action and report an error.

Note that APT only removes packages that need to be removed to satisfy a deinstallation request. In particular, if APT installs **bar** to meet the dependency of **foo** during the installation of the latter, it will not remove **bar** automatically when **foo** is removed, even though **bar** may not be needed anymore. If you want automatic deinstallation of unneeded packages, please consider consistent use of **aptitude** (see chapter 5.4.11) instead of APT, or run **deborphan** (see chapter 5.11.5) to identify and remove unneeded packages.

5.4.7 Seamless upgrades

One of the core strengths of Debian is its the seamless package upgrades. Whether APT is asked to upgrade a long-running *woody* server to *sarge*, or an upgrade of the current *stable* release encompasses a number of upgraded packages, APT will not break a sweat.

An upgraded package is defined as a package with a higher version number than the currently installed package (see chapter 5.7.5). From one Debian release to the next, a package's version number can increase deliberately, while upgrades within *stable* are confined to security and non-trivial bug fixes, but may not provide additional functionality. If a security problem is fixed in a newer upstream version of the packaged software, the security fix itself is backported to the software version in *stable* so as to not introduce any further changes. Debian *stable* is guaranteed to be stable.

While the set of packages contained in *stable* may never change, a new Debian release usually contains many additional packages. As a consequence, dependencies within *stable* never change, but a new release could contain renamed or split packages, requiring modifications to the dependency relations of packages. For instance, the **debconf** package in *sarge* introduces a dependency on **debconf-i18n**, which was not needed for **debconf** in *woody*. More precisely, **debconf-i18n** does not exist in *woody* and will never become part of it.

APT provides a powerful dependency resolution algorithm which can handle upgrades from one Debian release to the next. The algorithm involves complex searches of the APT dependency graph and thus is not very powerful. Given that the set of packages within *stable* is immutable, using this algorithm is overkill for keeping a *stable* release up to date. Hence, a simplified version catering specifically for the requirements of Debian *stable* updates is also available.

Upgrading a stable system

Let us inspect the simplified version first, but not before updating the APT package database (see chapter 5.4.3).

```
~# apt-get update
Get:1 http://security.debian.org woody/updates/main Packages [189kB]
[...]
Reading Package Lists... Done
~# apt-get --show-ugraded upgrade
```

```
Reading Package Lists...
Building Dependency Tree...
The following packages will be upgraded
  exim perl-base
2 packages upgraded, 0 newly installed, 0 to remove and 0  not upgraded.
Need to get 1256kB of archives. After unpacking 98.3kB will be freed.
Do you want to continue? [Y/n] y
Get:1 http://security.debian.org woody/updates/main perl-base 5.6.1-8.7
[497kB]
Get:2 http://security.debian.org woody/updates/main exim 3.35-1woody3 [7
59kB]
[...]
Setting up perl-base (5.6.1-8.7) ...
Setting up exim (3.35-1woody3) ...
[...]
```

The simplified algorithm uses package indices downloaded from the APT sources registered in /etc/apt/sources.list and compares the version numbers for each package that is installed on the local version. In the above example, **perl-base** was installed with version 5.6.1-8.6 prior to the update. When APT encountered **perl-base** while scanning the locally installed packages, it found that a newer version (5.6.1-8.7) was available on **security.debian.org** and thus downloaded the corresponding DEB file and called **dpkg** to install it.

Executing this update/upgrade sequence on a regular basis will keep the system running smoothly and securely. It is even possible to have **cron** do this for you automatically (see chapter 5.11.4), although I suggest that only on the rarest occasions.

Upgrading to a new Debian release

When a new *stable* release comes around, this procedure will not produce the desired effect. Even though it will update a number of packages, APT will also hold back numerous packages, due to unsatisfiable dependencies. Remember: an APT upgrade will *not* install packages previously not present on the system; it only ever updates already installed packages.

```
~# sed -i -e s,woody,sarge, /etc/apt/sources.list
~# apt-get update
[...]
~# apt-get --show-upgraded upgrade
Reading Package Lists...
Building Dependency Tree...
The following packages have been kept back:
  debconf [...]
The following packages will be upgraded
  adduser apt apt-utils base-config base-files base-passwd
  [...]
[...]
```

APT does not upgrade debconf as it would require the installation of debconf-i18n. Thus, the debconf package is "kept back". The upgrade algorithm thus enacts the requirements and guarantees of Debian *stable*.

When it is time to upgrade the entire system to *sarge* (to stick with the above example), you have to use APT's sophisticated (and slower) upgrade mechanism: apt-get dist-upgrade.

```
~# apt-get --show-upgraded dist-upgrade
Reading Package Lists...
Building Dependency Tree...
The following packages will be REMOVED:
  console-tools-libs libdigest-md5-perl libmime-base64-perl
  [...]
The following NEW packages will be installed:
  aptitude coreutils debconf-i18n dselect e2fslibs
  [...]
The following packages will be upgraded
  adduser apt apt-utils base-config base-files base-passwd
  [...]
[...]
351 packages upgraded, 100 newly installed, 6 to remove and 0 not upgrad
ed.
Need to get 200MB of archives. After unpacking 231MB will be used.
Do you want to continue? [Y/n] y
Get:1 http://debian sarge/main libdb1-compat 2.1.3-7 [30.8kB]
Get:2 http://debian sarge/main libc6 2.3.2.ds1-13 [4929kB]
[...]
Setting up libc6 (2.3.2.ds1-13) ...
Setting up libdb1-compat (2.1.3-7) ...
[...]
```

With apt-get dist-upgrade, APT can pull in new packages (like debconf-i18n) and even remove packages that have been obsoleted. The actual installation of new packages, or the removal of old ones is again handled by dpkg.

A couple of minutes[24] later, APT will have upgraded the system from *woody* to *sarge*. Since dpkg is still responsible for the actual installation, your carefully crafted configuration files will not have been modified (unless you chose to install the new versions). When a newer version of a software requires changes to the configuration files, the Debian maintainers will provide a different package so that you do not have to spend the entire afternoon getting your software to do what it should. For instance, bind9 uses a slightly different configuration paradigm than bind 8, and hence a new package is provided[25]. On the other hand, postfix

[24]This could also be hours and depends on the speed of the source medium. If you are upgrading Debian over a dialup line, it is probably best to leave it running over night. Of course, you can instead use a CD of the latest release and use that as your APT repository instead.

[25]In addition, some administrators may prefer to continue using bind and are thus not forced by APT to switch to a radically new software, but can plan for the migration themselves.

version 2.x works happily and identically with the configuration of a previous 1.x installation. Thus, the **postfix** maintainer deemed it appropriate not to produce a second package.

It should also be noted that an upgrade to the next Debian release does not require a reboot, and can easily be performed over an SSH connection on a remote server[26].

Note the use of the code names *woody* and *sarge* rather than *stable* in the above examples. By sticking to named versions, the administrator can decide precisely when a system should be updated, rather than having to follow Debian's schedule. The previous *stable* release continues to enjoy support by the security team for months (or even years) after the release of a new *stable* version. Please refer to chapter 4.3.3 for more information.

Harnessing the ease of upgrades

Debian is not the only system capable of seamless upgrading. However, it seems to be the only one that combines seamless upgrades with the concept of a *stable* archive. We return to this point in chapter 4 so for the time being let us just note that the Debian *stable* release gives you the best of both worlds: on the one hand, you get a rock-solid system with components that have been through months of intensive scrutiny; on the other, you will be able to upgrade to the next stable release without much effort. For those willing to trade off some stability against currentness, the *testing* and *unstable* releases are available via the package management system in the same way. With the great number of fluctuations in these archives (especially in *unstable*), the robustness of the package management system becomes more and more important — APT will not break a sweat.

Debian users with permanent (or at least moderately speedy) Internet connections are notoriously known to make use of the power of seamless upgrades when installing new systems. No matter how old an installation medium is available, if it can install a base system and establish a network connection, it is all downhill from there and APT can take over to update the system to the latest *stable* release, or the current *unstable* version.

5.4.8 Enacting requests with APT

As we saw earlier, deinstallation and purge requests can be registered with **dpkg** and later enacted. You may wonder if this is also possible for installations. The answer is "yes," but it requires APT to do so. After all, **dpkg** can only install DEB files,

---

[26]It is always a good idea to open a few extra SSH sessions as root when upgrading SSH itself. If the server does not come back up and due to an unfortunate circumstance, the current terminal is killed, you will not be able to get back into the machine through SSH, which can be fatal in the case of a remotely hosted server. It goes without saying that critical servers should never be upgraded remotely.

and requesting the installation of a package by its name only means that **dpkg** will not have access to the corresponding DEB file — which is no problem since this is APT's domain. Without further ado, here is how to register installation requests with **dpkg** and let APT enact them. Conveniently, APT also covers deinstallation and purging, thus replacing the **dpkg --pending ...** invocations:

```
~# echo mc install | dpkg --set-selections
~# echo apache2 deinstall | dpkg --set-selections
~# apt-get dselect-upgrade
[...]
The following packages will be REMOVED:
  apache2
The following NEW packages will be installed:
  mc
[...]
```

One interesting use of the above is to back up the package selection of a system to a file in case of a reinstallation[27], or to configure a similar system with it. Saving the output of **dpkg --get-selections** to a file is all that is needed. Assuming the file is called **selections.txt**, the following will configure the package selection on another system accordingly:

```
~# dpkg --set-selections < selections.txt
~# apt-get dselect-upgrade
[...]
```

A twist of this method relies on the fact that the selection list does not need to be complete. Just like we echo requests into **dpkg --set-selections** one by one, it is possible to create a file containing a number of such requests and then simply feed it to **dpkg --get-selections** on the target system as a whole. **dpkg** will only modify the requests for the packages included in the file, which allows for interesting applications in computer clusters (which should be using Fully Automatic Installation (FAI) instead, see chapter 8.3.5) and other areas.

There is one caveat with this method though. **dpkg --get-selections** only outputs information about packages it knows about. For a package to be known to **dpkg**, it must either be installed, or have been installed (or simply unpacked) previously. Otherwise, the package does not have an entry in **/var/lib/dpkg/status** and therefore will not be reported. This means that cloning the package selection to another system may leave the other system with *more* packages installed, if it already has some packages installed that are not known to **dpkg** on the source system.

One way to work around this problem is to run **dpkg-query** afterwards to list the installed packages on both systems, then use **diff** to find the additional ones and deinstall them manually:

[27]Which, of course, is totally superfluous with Debian...

```
~# ls -F
selections.source
~# dpkg-query --show --showformat='$Package\n' > selections.local
~# diff selections.source selections.local \
  | grep '^>' | cut -c3- | xargs dpkg --purge
[...]
```

5.4.9   APT housekeeping

APT keeps its packages in a local cache (unless the **file** or **cdrom** acquisition method is used). Over time, the cache directory can fill up and consume vast amounts of space, especially on systems tracking *testing* or *unstable*. APT does not manage the contents of its cache directory **/var/cache/apt/archives** automatically. Instead, **apt-get** provides two methods to erase files in the cache.

The first cleanup method checks each file in the cache and erases it only if it is not available on the mirrors anymore. This may seem somewhat backward at first, but if you consider that disappearance of a file from the mirror generally happens only when a newer version comes around, it makes sense[28]:

```
~# apt-get --simulate autoclean
Reading Package Lists... Done
Building Dependency Tree... Done
Del vim-common 1:6.2-532+4 [3091kB]
[...]
```

APT can also be told to leave DEB files of installed packages in the cache:

```
~# apt-get --option APT::Clean-Installed=false autoclean
```

An alternate method provided by **APT** is the complete cleaning of the cache directory, which may be necessary on small or embedded systems, or if the **/var** partition unexpectedly fills up and more space needs to be made available. **apt-get clean** removes all DEB files regardless of their availability on the mirror or not.

5.4.10   Resolving problems with APT

APT itself takes great care not to leave behind broken dependencies. However, an administrator can put the APT database into an inconsistent state by using **dpkg** parallel to APT. While APT should make direct use of **dpkg** obsolete, it is still needed

---

[28]Another possibility is the removal of a package from the archive. In such case, it would be a loss to erase the DEB file until an alternative to the software it provides has been found. http://snapshot.debian.net can help in such a situation as it mirrors the archive on a daily basis and stores the packages for later retrieval.

in some circumstances. Fortunately, the inconsistencies in the APT database are not fatal and can easily be resolved manually, or handled automatically by APT itself.

Recall that **dpkg** will refuse to install packages whose dependencies cannot be satisfied. Thus, if a package is to be installed, and its dependencies are not available locally, **dpkg** exits with an error. However, **dpkg** does not simply forget that the administrator wanted to install a certain package. The inconsistency in the APT database thus derives from the fact that the package's desired status cannot be enacted by the package management system.

```
~# apt-get install --download-only postfix
[...]
~# dpkg --install /var/cache/apt/archives/postfix_2.1.5-1_i386.deb
dpkg: dependency problems prevent configuration of postfix:
 postfix depends on netbase; however:
  Package netbase is not installed.
~# dpkg --info postfix
iU  postfix        2.1.5-1    A high-performance mail transport agent
~# apt-get install postfix
Reading Package Lists... Done
Building Dependency Tree... Done
You might want to run »apt-get --fix-broken install« correct these:
The following packages have unmet dependencies:
  postfix: Depends: netbase but it is not going to be installed
  postfix-tls: Depends: postfix (= 2.1.5-1)
E: Unmet dependencies. Try »apt-get --fix-broken install« with
  no packages (or specify a solution).
[...]
```

A similar situation arises if the administrator chooses to pass one of the **--force-depends** or **--force-conflicts** options to **dpkg**. To correct the problem, you can manually install the **netbase** package (using either **dpkg** or APT), or let APT handle the inconsistency automatically:

```
~# apt-get --fix-broken install
[...]
Correcting dependencies... Done
The following extra packages will be installed:
  netbase
[...]
The following NEW packages will be installed:
  netbase
0 upgraded, 1 newly installed, 0 to remove and 224 not upgraded.
[...]
Setting up netbase (4.19) ...
```

APT will first try to satisfy outstanding dependencies by downloading and installing the needed packages from the known APT repositories. If it succeeds, the database will be brought to a consistent state again. If it cannot download all the dependencies, because of inavailability or conflicts, APT instead removes the broken package. In all cases, APT asks for confirmation before proceeding. If the proposed solution is unsatisfactory, you can provide a better solution manually.

5.4.11 aptitude

aptitude is to APT, what dselect is to dpkg, a user interface allowing manipulation of the package selection. However, aptitude adds all the bonuses of APT, specifically dependency handling. This chapter introduces the main features of aptitude. You probably also want to read the extensive documentation the author made available in /usr/share/doc/aptitude/README.gz.

As shown in figure 5.4, aptitude presents itself in a very organised and clearly arranged layout. The top pane lists the available packages sorted by category and according to their state with respect to the local system. It is the interface used to steer aptitude. The bottom pane shows context information for to the main frame. Figure 5.4 shows aptitude's main view.

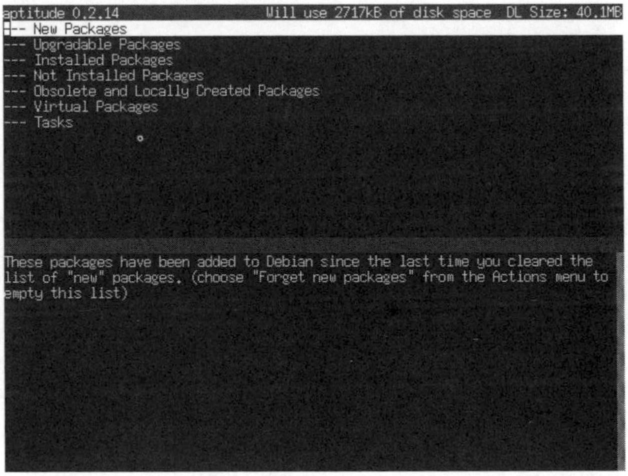

Figure 5.4:
The main view of
aptitude.

You will find up to eight sections in the main aptitude menu, depending on the state of the package selection on your system:

Security updates
> When new packages become available in the security archive, aptitude lists them in a special category for increased visibility. Similar to the other updated packages, aptitude automatically selects any security updates for installation.

New Packages

>   Following an update of the available package list (**aptitude update**, or [**u**] in
>   **aptitude**), packages which were previously unknown to **aptitude** are shown
>   under this section to allow the user to inspect recent additions to the Debian
>   archives. With every update, new packages will accumulate here until you
>   tell **aptitude** to forget and integrate the new packages into the main pool
>   by pressing [**f**].

Updated Packages

>   Packages with newer versions in the archive are listed in this section. Gener-
>   ally, these will be upgraded when the user finishes the selection process and
>   lets **aptitude** download and install desired software.

Installed Packages

>   A package which is already installed and which has no upgrade available is
>   listed here.

Not Installed Packages

>   As the name indicates, this section contains all packages which are currently
>   not installed. When you "forget" new packages without installing them, they
>   end up in this section.

Obsolete or Locally Created Packages

>   Packages which are installed locally but not available from the **APT** reposi-
>   tories configured in **/etc/apt/sources.list** are contained in this section.

Virtual Packages

>   Virtual packages are abstract concepts provided by a set of packages. For
>   instance, **mail-transport-agent** is provided by **postfix** and **sendmail**, among
>   others. Within this section, it is possible to browse the set of virtual packages
>   directly and see which packages provide the concepts.

Tasks

>   Tasks are collections of packages deemed relevant to specific applications.
>   Chapter 5.5 goes into greater detail on these. **aptitude** allows tasks to be
>   browsed and installed.

aptitude is organised in a tree structure with lines corresponding to nodes. Navigation is possible with the arrow keys, [**PageUp**] and [**PageDown**]. [**Return**] or
[**Enter**] expand or collapse a node. Figure 5.5 shows an expanded view. The listing
is split into four columns: the package status and requested action, the package
name, the currently installed version (or <none>), and the available version.

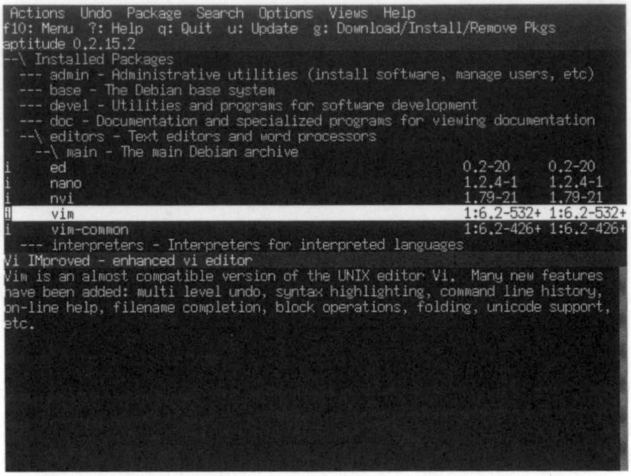

Figure 5.5:

An expanded view of aptitude's package listing.

Valid package states in **aptitude**'s package list:

v   virtual

B   broken

u   unpacked

C   half-configured

H   half-installed

c   removed but not purged

p   the package has been purged

i   installed

E   internal error

Requested actions in **aptitude**'s package list:

h   hold

p   purge

d   deinstall

B   broken

i   install

r   reinstall

u   upgrade

The bottom pane lists various different data relevant to the current selection in the top frame. Scrolling is accomplished with [a] and [z], and [i] cycles between different information views. Finally, [D] can show and hide the information area.

Searching and filtering

Using the [/] key, you can search the package names, and a number of search predicates are available. [\] finds the next match of a search. The beginning and end of a name may be anchored with ^ and $ to match the beginning and end of a name, just like in regular expressions. With [l], the user can limit the displayed package set to certain criteria, using the same predicates available for search[29]. Some of the most important predicates are:

Predicate	Effect
~ahold	held packages
~b	broken packages
~d<text>	packages with <text> in the description
~g	unused packages
~m<maint>	packages maintained by <maint>
~n<text>	packages with <text> in the name
~V<version>	packages with <version> in the version number

Table 5.4:
A selection of aptitude's search predicates.

These predicates can be combined. For instance, ~ahold ~dmail selects held packages with "mail" in their description. Using a pipe symbol (|) between the predicates causes the expressions to be logically OR'ed: ~v|~b selects all broken or virtual packages. Whitespace between the predicate and the search term is not ignored! Therefore, ~V.0 and ~V .0 are different, with the latter returning no results. An exclamation mark negates the expression: !~b finds packages that are not broken. Parentheses group expressions to allow for complex boolean logic: ~b(~mmadduck|~snet) finds broken packages either maintained by me, or in the net section.

Furthermore, regular expressions may be used at your discretion, but certain characters, like the parentheses "()", the tilde (~), and the exclamation mark must be escaped with the tilde: ~n~^(lib~)?gtk.* finds packages whose name begins with "gtk" or "libgtk."

---

[29] mutt users will quickly find themselves in familiar domains...

Manipulating the package selection

The package selection can be manipulated by browsing to a package and then pressing the key corresponding to the desired action:

[+]   Selects the package for installation.

[-]   Selects the package for removal.

[_]   Selects the package for purge.

[=]   Puts a hold on the package.

[:]   Puts a hold on the package for the duration of the **aptitude** session only.

[L]   Requests the reinstallation of a package.

[R]   Requests the reconfiguration of a package.

[I]   Requests the immediate installation of the package (and its dependencies) while putting all other upgrades or installations on a temporary hold. This has the same effect as **apt-get install <package>**.

[F]   Forbids the installation of a certain version of a package. Future versions will, however, be used regularly.

[B]   Calls on **reportbug** (see chapter 10.6.5) to file a bug against the package.

[C]   Downloads and displays a package's **changelog**.

[g]   Enters the preview screen of all requested changes. If pressed within the preview screen, it causes the changes to be enacted.

Expanding a package node yields the package detail screen shown in figure 5.6. Besides useful information about a package, this screen also allows for convenient browsing of the relation declarations and interactive dependency resolution wherever **aptitude**'s automatic resolution suggestion is not desirable. Here too, [Return] expands nodes, and the keys used to manipulate the package selection in the main list also apply to the packages listed under the relation declarations. Hitting [q] takes you up one level and closes the package detail screen to return to the package listing.

```
 Actions  Undo  Package  Search  Options  Views  Help
f10: Menu  ?: Help  q: Quit  u: Update  g: Download/Install/Remove Pkgs
aptitude 0.2.15.2
i   --\ vim                                      1:6.2-532+ 1:6.2-532+
  Description: Vi IMproved - enhanced vi editor
    Vim is an almost compatible version of the UNIX editor Vi.  Many new
    features have been added: multi level undo, syntax highlighting, command
    line history, on-line help, filename completion, block operations, folding,
    unicode support, etc.
  Priority: optional
  Section: editors
  Maintainer: Norbert Tretkowski <nobse@debian.org>
  Compressed size: 0
  Uncompressed size: 1437k
  Source Package: vim
  --\ Depends
    --- libc6 (>= 2.3.2.ds1-4)
    --- libgpmg1 (>= 1.19.6-1)
    --- libncurses5 (>= 5.4-1)
    --\ vim-common (> 1:6.2)
  p   1:6.3-013+2
  i   1:6.2-426+1
  --- PreDepends
  --- Suggests
  --\ Conflicts
    --- vim-rt
    --- vim-tiny (< 6.0)
    --- vim-perl (< 6.0)
    --- vim-python (< 6.0)
    --- vim-tcl (< 6.0)
    --- vim-tty (< 6.0)
    --- vim-gtk (< 6.0)
    --- vim-lesstif (< 6.0)
  --- Replaces
  --- Package names provided by vim
  --- Packages which depend on vim
  --\ Versions
  p   1:6.3-013+2
  i   1:6.2-532+4
  p   1:6.2-426+1
```

Figure 5.6:
The package detail screen of aptitude.

Returning to the example of the **apache2** multithreading model, here is how you would install **apache2** with a different threading model:

- After starting **aptitude**, search for the **apache2** package: /^apache2$[enter].

- Select **apache2** for installation: [+]. The status line at the top will now indicate something along the lines of:

  ```
  Will use 6644kB of disk space...
  ```

  and a new column after the package name appears showing the size difference the package selection will cause to the system.

- Expand the package node, browse to the **Depends** line and expand the line stating the dependency on one of the available multithreading models (actually called "mpm," multi-processing module). You will see **apache2-mpm-worker** selected to meet **apache2**'s dependency. Browse down to **apache2-mpm-perchild** and select it for installation: [+]. This causes **apache2-mpm-worker** to be deselected and the installation of **apache2-mpm-perchild** to be requested.

- Hit [g] to view the summary of actions to be performed, as depcited in figure 5.7.

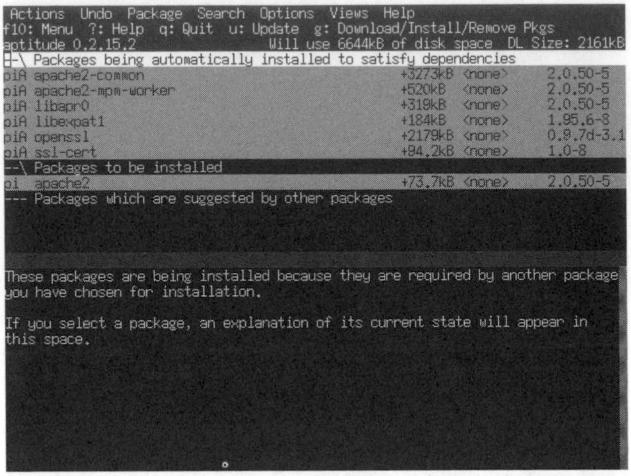

Figure 5.7:
The summary of
actions aptitude is
about to take.

- Hit [g] again to let **aptitude** do its thing and install the requested software. [q] will take you back to the selection list in case you need to make more changes

Broken packages

When **aptitude** encounters a selection with unresolved dependencies, it highlights problematic packages with a solid red background and displays the total number of errors in the title pane, as illustrated in figure 5.8.

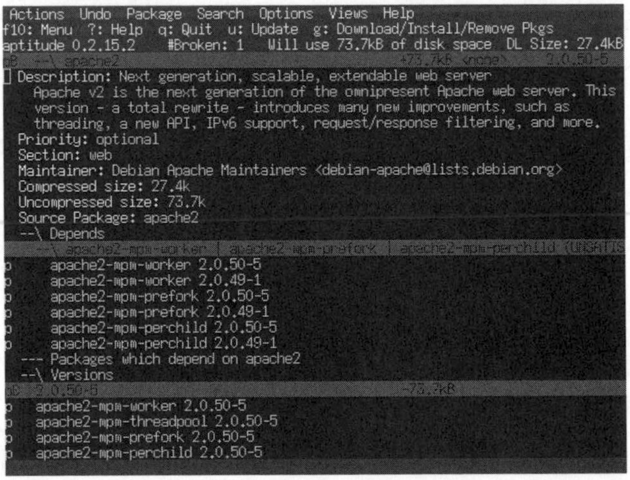

Figure 5.8:
aptitude with
unsatisfied
dependencies. Note
the #Broken: 1 count
in the title pane.

Broken packages are those with unsatisfied dependencies, or conflicting packages (in which case both packages are broken). aptitude obviously will not allow the user to commit a package selection with broken packages. Therefore, the breakage has to be fixed first, which can be done in one of two ways.

First, when the count of broken packages is non-zero and aptitude is told to perform the pending actions (the user hit the [g] key), aptitude will try to solve all problems before displaying the summary of pending actions. Generally, it takes a conservative approach to automatic fixing, so that the previous selection is favoured over other possibilities. *Always* check the count of broken packages before hitting [g], or else an elaborate set of changes resulting in one or more broken packages may be discarded in favour of the state before the changes. Fortunately, aptitude allows to undo the last action with [C-_] or [C-u] and resort to manual resolution.

When fixing broken packages in aptitude, the filter (or limit) functionality comes in incredibly handy. Hitting [l] and entering ~b as filter specification causes aptitude to limit the list to only broken packages. Using the package detail listing (accessible by expanding a package node), it should usually require little effort to fix problems by selecting missing dependencies for installation and manually resolving conflicts. Alternatively, you can simply advance to the next broken package by hitting [b].

As the count of broken packages decreases, it may be necessary to filter the list of displayed packages. Hitting [l] followed by [enter] reapplies the previous filter and should shrink the listing to a (hopefully smaller) number of packages that are still broken. Use iteratively, this procedure allows all broken packages to be fixed in a short time.

Tracking unused packages

When aptitude selects a package to satisfy another's dependency as part of its automatic dependency resolution, it marks the package as automatically installed. Consequently, these packages will automatically be selected for removal when the depending package is removed, helping to keep the system clean.

It is also possible to manually modify the "automatically installed" flag with [M] and [m]: the first adds the mark, the latter removes it. The ~g predicate can be used to search and limit according to this flag.

While this feature of aptitude is nice, deborphan provides similar functionality with greater flexibility. We will be returning to this topic in chapter 5.11.5.

Command line interaction

aptitude provides an interesting set of operations from the command line and can basically be used as a drop-in replacement for apt-get with the search capability of **apt-cache**, and adding with the search predicates available within **aptitude**'s interactive interface. The following should illustrate some of the possibilities.

```
~# aptitude search '~dsync ~dpalm !~slibs'
[...]
~$ aptitude moo
[...]
~# aptitude update && aptitude dist-upgrade
[...]
~# aptitude install pilot-link ~n^~(lib~)?gtk.*
[...]
~# aptitude purge mc
[...]
~$ aptitude moo -v
[...]
```

Just as with **apt-get**, multiple requests for different actions can be placed in a single command by appending the characters used to take the respective action in the interactive interface. In the following case, A would be installed, B removed, C purged, and D put on hold. The '+' is superfluous because the **install** action makes installation the default:

```
~# aptitude install A+ B- C_ D=
[...]
```

The advantage of **aptitude**'s command line interface is the integration of various programmes and their functionality behind a consistent interface. In addition, dependencies installed automatically by **aptitude** in response to an installation request at the command line are tracked accordingly, and **aptitude** will schedule these packages for automatic removal as soon as they are not needed anymore. This may also be explicitly requested. The following mimics **deborphan**'s (see chapter 5.11.5) default behaviour removing all unused packages from the **libs** and **oldlibs** categories:

```
~# aptitude markauto '~slibs|~soldlibs'
Reading Package Lists... Done
Building Dependency Tree
Reading extended state information
Initializing package states... Done
The following packages are unused and will be REMOVED:
  libdb2 libdb3-util libdb4.0 libgc1 libgdbmg1 libglib2.0-0
  libidentlibmagic1 libpcap0.7 libpcre3 libperl5.6 libpng10-0
  libpng2 libsas17 libsigc++0 libssl0.9.6 libstdc++2.10-glibc2.2
  libtextwrap1 libxmltok1
0 packages upgraded, 0 newly installed, 19 to remove and 0 not upgraded.
Need to get 0B of archives. After unpacking 10.6MB will be freed.
Do you want to continue? [Y/n/?] y
[...]
~# aptitude moo -vv
[...]
```

Keeping a log

aptitude writes all actions you request to /var/log/aptitude. The file can come in handy to keep track of software installations and removals. However, it goes without saying that its helpfulness depends on the exclusive use of **aptitude**. If you install packages with **apt-get** and remove them with **dpkg**, **aptitude**'s log will quickly grow out of sync. In addition, **aptitude** only logs requests. If an action fails, this is not recorded in the protocol.

5.4.12   synaptic

synaptic is a GTK-based graphical management tool, based on APT. It adequately captures the base power of APT into a front-end which is easily usable by novices. As it relies on APT for the actual package operations, it can be used in parallel to the other tools available on a Debian system. Figure 5.9 shows a screenshot of the graphical front-end featured by **synaptic**.

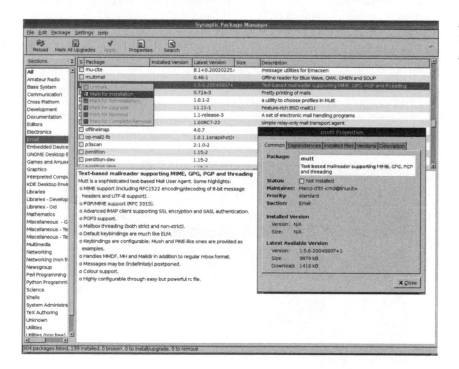

Figure 5.9:
The Synaptic Package
Manager

synaptic does not provide all the features of **aptitude**, but it sports a more intuitive and accessible interface. Nevertheless, it can perform all standard package tasks. In addition, it features a flexible search function and can lock packages to single versions, using APT pinning internally (see chapter 8.2.1). The pins do not propagate to the regular APT tools, which means that **synaptic** keeps its own pin configuration and does not touch the one in **/etc/apt/preferences**.

5.5   Debian tasks

A Debian system is usually installed to serve a certain task. For instance, you may be installing a new machine to serve as a database server, or bootstrapping a power horse to become your new desktop computer. Debian provides the concept of tasks to identify typical sets of packages for certain requirements; for the two tasks just identified, you can install a typical selection of software by installing the **SQL database** or **Desktop environment** respectively.

Traditionally, the **tasksel** programme provided an interface for the selection of these software collections, but its functionality has been integrated and extended by **aptitude**, which should thus be favoured.

The idea of a task is to select an abstract concept such as a "Structured Query Language (SQL) database" and end up with a set of installable packages which provide everything necessary to turn the local system into a typical SQL database server. In essence, tasks are similar to meta packages (or dummy packages) depending on the required packages with the sole difference that a task is actually purely virtual and does not have an associated DEB file. Furthermore, tasks are merely suggestions and the user is free to unselect some of the packages proposed as part of the task.

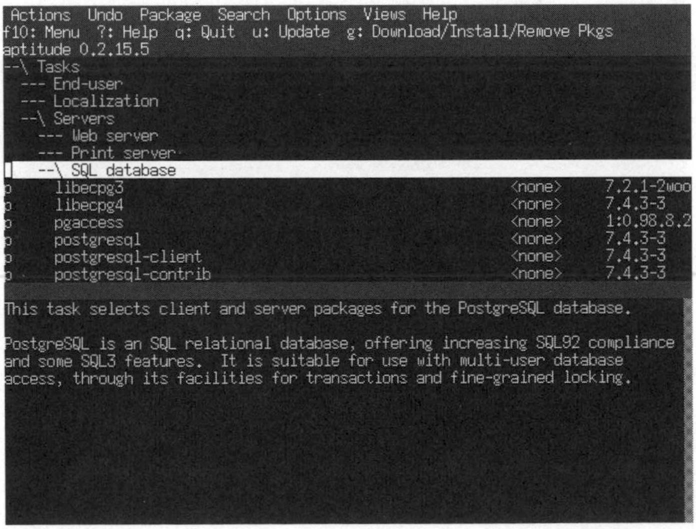

Figure 5.10:
aptitude's task
selection interface.

```
Actions  Undo  Package  Search  Options  Views  Help
f10: Menu  ?: Help  q: Quit  u: Update  g: Download/Install/Remove Pkgs
aptitude 0.2.15.5
--\ Tasks
  --- End-user
  --- Localization
  --\ Servers
    --- Web server
    --- Print server
  | --\ SQL database
p     libecpg3                        <none>      7.2.1-2woo
p     libecpg4                        <none>      7.4.3-3
p     pgaccess                        <none>      1:0.98.8.2
p     postgresql                      <none>      7.4.3-3
p     postgresql-client               <none>      7.4.3-3
p     postgresql-contrib              <none>      7.4.3-3
This task selects client and server packages for the PostgreSQL database.

PostgreSQL is an SQL relational database, offering increasing SQL92 compliance
and some SQL3 features.  It is suitable for use with multi-user database
access, through its facilities for transactions and fine-grained locking.
```

You will find the preferred interface for tasks at the very bottom of **aptitude**'s main selection screen. Similar to handling packages, tasks may be treated as singular entities, or unfolded to reveal the packages they suggest. If the local system is to become a SQL server, you can simply navigate to the "SQL server" task in **aptitude** as shown in figure 5.10 and hit [+]. Subsequently, the selection can be modified. For instance, even though **libecpg4** is considered part of a typical SQL server, it may be deselected like any other package through **aptitude**'s interface. Alternatively, a user may choose to unfold a certain task and inspect the suggested set of packages. Instead of installing the task as a whole, the user may then decide to simply install only a few of the packages the task contains. You will see that tasks in **aptitude** react just like regular packages.

It is also possible to define custom tasks by dropping task description files into /usr/share/tasksel[30]. Documentation on how to compose tasks is available in the README file installed with the **tasksel** package[31].

5.6 Package management compared

It is not the intention of this book to compare. Nevertheless, as the Debian package management system seems to be misconceived too often, it is important to establish the position of **dpkg**, APT, & co. within the field of automatic package management. The days have passed in which Debian's package management wiped the table clean. Today, various approaches exist, each with their own special features and annoying caveats. When people tout their favourite package management system and diss on the other available solutions, they effectively admit their own ignorance of the matter. In fact, it seems as if package management systems are more a question of faith.

Package management seems to encompass three aspects: the package format specification, the package handler, and the actual package manager. Many a Debian supporter will claim that Debian excels in all three of them. While the Debian package management tools have undeniable strengths, they are not perfect. The same can be said for the package management systems of other distributions. Thus, it is time for a quick comparison (without going into too much detail).

The basis for package management is the format of the package files themselves, which provides for a lot of the functionality. Flamewars rage with DEB supporters slashing RPM fans, and *vice versa*. A common belief among Debian supporters seems to be that the DEB format is largely superior to RPM, which is simply false (and certainly one of the reasons why Debian's reputation is not always positive). In fact, the RPM format is actually more feature-rich than DEB, but the additional

---

[30]Additional locations may be supported in the future, see http://bugs.debian.org/286170.
[31]/usr/share/doc/tasksel/README

features are not commonly put to use[32]. Nevertheless, in terms of the capabilities actually put to use, the two formats are just too similar to compare. The same also holds true for comparisons with other major package formats, including **pkgsrc**, **ports**, and even **.ebuilds**. Each format has its own advantages and limitations, but when it comes to package management, the administrative possibilities they support are all more or less equivalent[33].

The situation with tools handling the package files is no different. **dpkg** and the **rpm** binary are package processors (as well as other managers for other formats), provide largely the same functionality (see table 5.5): installation and removal, querying a status database, and displaying information extracted from package files; they can be told to override dependencies or disregard other rules, and they can list package contents and associate installed files with the source package. In short, what can be done with one is also possible with the other. Within each of the different implementations of package management, the boundaries between the components may shift. What counts, however, is the net result and the administrative approaches the respective toolsets enable. While **dpkg** and **rpm** and their respective package formats are fundamentally different from *e.g.* a **ports**-based system, the capabilities are more or less the same.

<table>
<tr><td>Table 5.5:
Package handling
commands available
by dpkg and rpm.</td><td>

dpkg	**rpm**
dpkg --info	rpm -qpi
dpkg --contents	rpm -qpl
dpkg --install	rpm -i
dpkg --list	rpm -qa
dpkg --listfiles	rpm -ql
dpkg --search	rpm -qf
dpkg --status	rpm -qi
dpkg --remove	n/a
dpkg --purge	rpm -E
dpkg --install --force-depends	rpm -i --nodeps
dpkg --install --force-overwrite	rpm -i --replacefiles

</td></tr>
</table>

---

[32] A good example of such functionality is the concept of RPM package triggers, which allow a package to register actions to be taken when another package is manipulated and thus go beyond the standard installation scripts. Another example is that RPM allows dependencies to be met by files installed on the local filesystem. While this practice is somewhat reminiscent of the dynamic library handling which gave "dependency hell" its name, it can be useful at times.

[33] A qualitative comparison is available online: http://www.kitenet.net/~joey/pkg-comp

The third component of a package management system is the package manager itself, which builds upon the package manager and the format specification. For a long time, APT enjoyed unrivaled precedence in this field, but the other distributions have been busy. Nowadays, tools like up2date, yum, urpmi, and emerge are hardly behind in the amount of functionality they provide (see table 5.6), and even though APT does seem to stand out in terms of maturity and robustness, it will not be long until the others are viable alternatives.

The following table attempts to list corresponding commands of the four major automatic package managers. Please note that the comparison is APT-centric, and intended to serve more as a reference than as an argument to bash the other commands, which can each do things that APT cannot. It thus primarily serves as a map to help you distinguish between the different APT commands. I purposely do not provide a map of other managers' commands to APT because APT has all the features you need for the Debian Way of package management. Concepts and approaches available with other managers but not supported by APT are unlikely to be useful on a Debian system.

Table 5.6: Package management commands of major package management systems compared.

APT	yum	up2date	urpmi
apt-cache search	yum search	http://rpmfind.net	urpmq
apt-cache show	yum info	http://rpmfind.net	urpmq -i
apt-cache showpkg	n/a	http://rpmfind.net	n/a
apt-cache depends	n/a	n/a	n/a
apt-cache rdepends	n/a	n/a	n/a
apt-get install	yum install	up2date -i	urpmi
apt-get install --download-only	yum --download-only	up2date -d	n/a[34]
apt-get remove	n/a	n/a	n/a
apt-get remove --purge	yum remove	rpm -e	urpme
apt-get update	n/a	n/a	urpmi.update -a
apt-get upgrade	yum update	n/a	n/a
apt-get dist-upgrade	yum --obsoletes update	up2date --update	urpmi --auto-select
apt-get source	n/a	up2date --src	n/a
apt-get build-dep	n/a	n/a	n/a
apt-file search	yum provides	http://rpmfind.net	urpmf

[34] urpmq --sources [...] |xargs wget

Lastly, APT is not specific to Debian. As part of Debian's commitment to the free software community, APT is publicly available and has been ported to various package formats (most notably RPM). It is already actively being used by other distributions, including Mac OS X (Fink) and Fedora.

Comparing package management systems across Linux distributions, we reach the conclusion that all major players in the field are mere mortals. But there is more to the Debian system than the aforementioned package management utilities. Those who rank APT as the true strength of the Debian operating system are wrong. The real reason is well removed from the user interfaces, deep inside the Debian system, omnipresent, but hardly noticeable.

5.7   Power from within: the Debian policy

A group of musicians does not make an orchestra. If the goal is a symphony, it does not help if each does their own thing, or small groups form to play different pieces. If the artists are willing, a little patience can lead to acceptable results, but a true symphony requires order. For an orchestra to successfully convey the energy of a musical masterpiece, it requires individual skill, a score, a conductor, and endless hours of practice.

Introducing the Debian Symphonic Orchestra

The Debian system is not unlike a symphony: the musicians are the developers who prepare numerous packages for installation on the system. If developers simply create packages to their own liking, synergy cannot emerge. Therefore, the developers have agreed on a set of rules by which to abide, just like the members of an orchestra agree on a score to follow. Within the Debian system, the role of the conductor is taken by the package management tools, which, as shown in chapter 5.3 and chapter 5.4, observe certain rules and ensure that packages harmonise. The rules as well as the tools have been around for years, and developers have had ample time to practise their use, and to correct problems.

To continue the example, the score played by the Debian developers and observed by the package management tools is the Debian policy[35]; without the policy, the Debian distribution would be Just Another Linux. But it is not. The policy is the soul of the Debian system, it is its throbbing heart, it is the reason why Debian can put the same tools to better use than others. The policy is Debian's cookbook, with years of scrutiny perfecting each single recipe.

[35]http://www.debian.org/doc/debian-policy

Restrictions for package maintainers

It is possible to administer a Debian system without knowing about the Debian policy. In fact, the guidelines put forth in the document do not impose restrictions on the users of the system. Instead, it defines what a Debian package may and must not do. Thus, it commits the Debian developers, to ensuring that all packages behave properly and that their installation or removal will leave the system in a consistent and clean state. Put differently, it helps to lessen the number of decisions a package maintainer has to make. If, in creating a package for Debian, a developer follows the rules of the policy, the package is guaranteed to be compatible with the Debian system and the tools used for its management. Furthermore, a compliant package can coexist with thousands of other packages on the same system.

All of Debian's administrative utilities obey the policy; when you tell **dpkg** to install a package, you are telling it to enact the policy. Familiarity with the policy is required of each Debian developer, and policy compliance is an important priority during the preparation of a package. However, developers do err at times, and the tools provide a safety net for such cases: rather than putting a system at risk, the package management tools will not allow an action which is in violation of the policy.

Hard rules

In general, operating systems are hardly ever policy-less. For instance, within the NetBSD project[36], rules exist to coordinate the work of the numerous coders. But upon deeper inspection, these rules do not provide the same safety as the Debian policy. Before moving on, we have to distinguish between two sources of NetBSD software. On the one hand there is the stand-alone core operating system, and on the other the NetBSD Package Collection (**pkgsrc**), containing third party software tweaked to install in a NetBSD environment without a hassle.

As the core is developed by a small and coordinated team, conflicts such as the aforementioned are extremely unlikely to happen. However, software in the **pkgsrc** archive is maintained by independent individuals, who are encouraged to follow a common set of rules. These rules, however, are "soft" rules as they are neither enforced on submission of the package to the archive, nor on installation on a NetBSD machine. If a third party package overwrites files of another software below /usr/pkg, it effectively renders the other software inoperable until the problem is fixed and the package is reinstalled. The NetBSD rules state that such a situation must be prevented with a conflict parameter, but if this parameter is wrong or has been left out (usually by human error), the conflict will not be handled gracefully.

---

[36]The NetBSD project makes a great operating system, in many ways technically superior to Linux. Thus, I feel no shame in using it as an example to illustrate the strength of the Debian policy; also, see chapter 5.12.1.

Obviously, when different pieces of software are developed specifically for a system (as in the case of the NetBSD core), it is most likely that the different pieces coexist peacefully. The majority of Debian packages, on the other hand, are pulled from external sources and possibly restructured by the maintainers to fit in with the Debian system. If you've been around the Unix world long enough, you will have seen all kinds of schemes of where to put files: the **GNU Autotools** take a standardised approach, but software such as **qmail**, **Check Point Firewall-1**, or Sun's **JDK** seems to have unusual ideas of filesystem space their component files should occupy.

The job of a Debian developer is thus that of transforming a software's intended installation footprint to one compatible with all other packages in the Debian archive. The policy serves to help the maintainer in this task by limiting the number of choices that have to be made during packaging. It also specifies clear requirements so that the developer does not have to try to cater for everything that could go wrong. This saves a lot of time and gives packages increased robustness right from the start. Similarly, the commonly used package maintainer tool enact the policy and make package creation mostly routine (see chapter 9).

A Debian maintainer cannot do much more than someone packaging third party software for NetBSD when two packages provide a file with the same name and target location on the filesystem: if the two files provide the same functionality, the meta information of the package will contain this relation (see chapter 5.7.3); if the files are functionally different, then one (or both) must be renamed. The difference is that a package that does not follow these rules will not be available from the Debian *stable* archive. In addition, to guard against the unforeseen, **dpkg** will perform meticulous bookkeeping to ensure that a maintainer error cannot inadvertently render unrelated components of your system unusable by overwriting essential parts.

The quintessence of Debian

The crucial point is that failure to abide by the policy is reason enough for a **serious** bug to be filed against the offending package (by whomever notices the violation; see chapter 10.6). As a **serious** bug prevents a package from entering Debian *stable*, a package violating the Debian policy cannot become part of an official Debian release. This is the quintessence of the Debian system: all packages available in the Debian *stable* release follow the same set of rules and constitute a system that is consistent as well as uniform throughout. In the rare case that a policy violation is discovered within the *stable* release, a new version will likely be made available with the next upgrade (even before the next official release). Nevertheless, as illustrated in chapter 4, such an upgrade must not affect the stability of the installed system.

As stated before, the policy does not impose restrictions on the administrator. However, it certainly plays an important role and accounts for some of the most important aspects of Debian system administration. In the following, the pertinent effects of the Debian policy are illustrated.

5.7.1   The sacred configuration files

We saw in chapter 5.3.3 that **dpkg** handles configuration files with special care, as it assumes local modifications are to be preserved across package upgrades. This feature is not a simple add-on, but rather a requirement imposed on the Debian package handler by the policy. In section 10.7.3, the Debian policy states that "local changes [to configuration files] must be preserved during a package upgrade." For **dpkg** to be the Debian package handler, it must ensure that the policy is not violated.

dpkg goes one step further and implements proper handling of the configuration files, placing the decision whether to overwrite local modification upon the shoulders of the administrator, not the package maintainer. By defaulting to preserve local changes, it adequatly enacts the policy, while giving a user of the system more flexibility. In addition to preventing policy violations, **dpkg** provides useful functionality and hence takes the burden of implementing similar solutions repeatedly for each package off the developers.

Identifying configuration files

It could be said that the most advanced statistical methods are only as good as the data they analyse. Along similar lines, **dpkg**'s flawless handling of configuration files is only useful if it knows which files to treat as **conffiles**. Here, too, the policy provides the rules to facilitate the maintainer's job (and responsibility): section 10.7.2 states that "Any configuration files created or used by [a] package must reside in /etc." The set of configuration files installed by a package is determined at package creation time, and **dpkg** does not enforce this rule itself (for reasons which will become obvious in an instant). However, the package creation tools used by most maintainers are aware of this clause in the policy and automatically mark every file installed to /etc as a **conffile**.

When configuration files are generated dynamically (*e.g.* through the use of **debconf**; see chapter 5.8), **dpkg**'s **conffile** handling methods may be undesirable, or even get in the way. For this reason, **dpkg** does not automatically treat all files under /etc as configuration files. In such a situation, it is the maintainer's job to provide an adequate and policy-compliant solution. The **ucf** (Update Configuration File) tool is available for such purposes and provides much the same functionality with respect to configuration files as **dpkg** itself.

A package's set of **conffiles**, which are managed by **dpkg**, is available in the section labelled "Conffiles" in the output of **dpkg --status**:

```
~# dpkg --status postfix
[...]
Conffiles:
 /etc/init.d/postfix 79ac631ecb6e3cbb1d8684aa6de101fc
 /etc/ppp/ip-up.d/postfix 0f6d12880a5f95b96037f15d658cecb0
 /etc/ppp/ip-down.d/postfix 0758469f9f1c073a53df50d9dc43c8eb
 /etc/postfix/postfix-script 43d47ae8924b92d8f929d0ffa363c84a
 /etc/postfix/post-install 9c26982c75a0500578c73a796f35c0f5
 /etc/postfix/postfix-files 4b8051f5c6101ad744f5bfbd772a29db
 /etc/resolvconf/update-libc.d/postfix 3c921a0c2447ae3e166a62411568d048
[...]
```

This list does not include configuration files managed by other tools, such as **ucf**. However, you can take it for granted that every file installed below /etc is handled correctly.

Wherever you may roam

The Debian policy protects your files by separating the areas of a system, in which the administrator may modify files at will from the areas managed entirely by the distribution. Any modifications you make under the /etc hierarchy are guaranteed to be left alone across package upgrades.

At the same time as the policy gives you full permission to roam about /etc to your heart's content, it asks you to keep your hands off the files and directories in /usr and other parts of the filesystem hierarchy. With the notable exception of /usr/local, the policy allows a package to replace any files of previous or newer versions with files from the current release. Therefore, an administrator who directly modifies *e.g.* /usr/bin/debconf is violating the policy and nobody will hear the cries when an upgrade of the **debconf** package silently overwrites all changes. Please refrain from modifying files installed by Debian packages which are not flagged as configuration files, unless you know what you are doing.

If a software actually needs modification to files in /usr (in which case the software could be said to be broken in the context of the Unix paradigm), the package maintainer should provide some way of working around the problem. Possible solutions include exporting configuration variables to files in /etc by direct modification of the software, or the use of symbolic links from the location in the /usr hierarchy to an appropriate file in /etc.

The separation of the filesystem into two partitions, one for the system and one for the user is further specified in another section of the Debian policy, to which we shall return in chapter 5.7.4.

Workarounds, cheats, and lazy maintainers

Unfortunately, some maintainers have been lazy in the past and have chosen work-arounds for the strict requirements. On your system, you may find files in /etc which warn the administrator not to make local modifications. *e.g.*:

```
~$ head /etc/fonts/fonts.conf
[...]
  DO NOT EDIT THIS FILE.
  IT WILL BE REPLACED WHEN FONTCONFIG IS UPDATED.
  LOCAL CHANGES BELONG IN 'local.conf'.
[...]
```

It is arguable whether packages owning these files are in violation of the policy. In all cases, however, it is a good idea to notify the maintainer and suggest a proper approach to handling these files. Either of the following solutions is satisfactory (and other solutions may exist):

1. As these files are usually generated automatically, the tool used to generate them should be extended to properly honour modifications. This is trivially done with files specifying variable-value pairs (such as commonly created by debconf-driven **postinst** scripts). More complex formats require more intelligent handling, if at all possible.

2. When modifications cannot be identified and/or honoured by the generating tool, the file itself must be moved to an appropriate location under /var and references with a symbolic link from its previous location under /etc.

5.7.2   Mediating between packages

The policy also lays down rules for coordinating the coexistence of packages on a system. Specifically, it prevents interference between packages by forbidding a package to touch the set of files installed by another package. In section 7.5.1 is is defined to be "an error for a package to contain files which are on the system in another package". If a package must install a file which is also contained in another package, the maintainer has to explicitly declare that it conflicts with the other package, or use diversions to move the file to be replaced out of the way (see chapter 6.1.3). As we will see chapter 5.7.3, Debian allows maintainers to replace files in other packages under special circumstances, if this intention is explicitly specified at package creation time.

Again, **dpkg** strictly enforces this rule, as we saw in chapter 5.3.6. For the curious, the following problem actually surfaced on a machine running Debian *unstable*. The developers had decided to move /bin/chgrp from **fileutils** to the **coreutils** package, but **coreutils** hit the *unstable* archive a day before **fileutils** — essentially a simple timing problem that can only affect *unstable* (see chapter 4). Noticing the availability of a new **coreutils** package, APT correctly tries to upgrade but fails because the currently installed **fileutils** package still claims ownership of **/bin/chgrp**:

```
~# apt-get upgrade
[...]
The following packages will be upgraded
  coreutils
[...]
Unpacking replacement coreutils ...
dpkg: error processing coreutils_5.0.91-2_i386.deb (--install):
trying to overwrite '/bin/chgrp', which is also in package
  fileutils
dpkg-deb: subprocess paste killed by signal (Broken pipe)
Errors were encountered while processing:
 coreutils_5.0.91-2_i386.deb
```

Declared conflicts

If two packages try to install a file to the same location, the packages are said to be in conflict. Such a conflict only constitutes a policy violation when it is not specified in the control information of all involved packages. The DEB file format allows for a conflict to be expressed as a package relation (see chapter 5.7.3).

dpkg will not allow two conflicting packages to be installed on the same system, as the following example shows. Here, **postfix** and **exim4-config** both provide **/usr/sbin/sendmail**. Thus, both maintainers registered the conflict in the package's control information:

```
~# dpkg --install exim4-config_4.32-2_all.deb
[...]
dpkg: regarding exim4-config_4.32-2_all.deb containing exim4-config:
 exim4-config conflicts with postfix
  postfix (version 2.1.5-1) is installed.
dpkg: error processing exim4-config_4.32-2_all.deb (--install):
  conflicting packages - not installing exim4-config
```

Diverting files

Several of the packages in Debian's archive extend the functionality provided by other packages. Often, such extensions are only possible by replacing an executable (which *e.g.* could be linked with additional libraries). For example, the **postfix** package installs the mail transport agent without support for Transport Layer Security (TLS). For installations requiring cryptography, the **postfix-tls** package should be used instead; it contains the executables and libraries linked against **libssl**. Rather than duplicating the work and contents of the **postfix** package, the maintainer chose to make **postfix-tls** depend on **postfix** to reuse its functionality (such as **init.d** scripts and manpages), but divert the functionality of the relevant programmes to the ones provided in the depending package. More information on diversions is available in chapter 6.1.3.

```
~# dpkg --install postfix-tls_2.1.5-1_i386.deb
[...]
Unpacking postfix-tls (from postfix-tls_2.1.5-1_i386.deb) ...
[...]
Adding 'diversion of /usr/lib/postfix/smtpd
  to /usr/lib/postfix/smtpd.postfix by postfix-tls'
[...]
Setting up postfix-tls (2.1.5-1) ...
~$ ldd /usr/lib/postfix/smtpd*
/usr/lib/postfix/smtpd:
[...]
libssl.so.0.9.7 => /usr/lib/i686/cmov/libssl.so.0.9.7 (0xb7f5e000)
[...]
/usr/lib/postfix/smtpd.postfix:
[...]
```

If **postfix-tls** is ever deinstalled, **dpkg** reverts the diversion to restore the normal operation of **postfix** without TLS support:

```
~# dpkg --remove postfix-tls
[...]
Removing postfix-tls ...
Removing 'diversion of /usr/lib/postfix/smtpd
  to /usr/lib/postfix/smtpd.postfix by postfix-tls'
```

Resolving conflicts

If two packages provide the same file, but the packages' functionalities are disjunctive, a conflict between the two packages is undesirable as it would limit the administrator to using either one or the other package, but never both. In such a situation, the respective maintainers usually find an agreement and the conflicting file is renamed in one of the packages. Usually, this will be the less popular or newer package to minimise the impact on existing users. However, if such a consensus canot be reached, then section 10.1 of the policy calls for a Solomonic resolution and requircs for both packages to change the file name.

5.7.3   Package relations

It would be a major accomplishment in artificial intelligence if package managers could deduce from a package's payload whether the contained software provides a specific feature, collides with other packages, or needs software from other packages to work properly. Unfortunately, the state-of-the-art tools are not capable of such conclusions (yet). Therefore, for **dpkg** to be able to prevent file collisions even before they occur, or for **APT** to be able to fulfill dependencies automatically, the maintainers must augment the package files with data specifying such relations. As we have seen in chapter 5.2.3, DEB files can store such information in the **control** file.

For (inherently stupid) computer programmes to make sense of the information provided in this file, a consistent syntax definition must dictate the structure of the data. In addition to the package names that make up dependency and conflict declarations, further information may be necessary to encode complex relations, or even exceptions. For instance, a certain programme may require a specific version of a library and will not work with earlier incarnations due to lack of functionality. Conversely, a maintainer may have agreed to rename a file to resolve a conflict among unrelated packages, so the second package only needs to conflict with versions of the offending package prior to renaming.

At other times, a package may require a *concept* provided by various different packages, of which one must be chosen. A classic example of such a requirement can be found in the meta data of the **at** package. The design of **at** requires the programme to be able to send electronic mail. In Debian, at least ten different mail transport agents exists, but instead of hard-coding the set into the dependency information of **at**, the package simply depends on the concept of a **mail-transport-agent**. In turn, all packages which provide the needed functionality declare that they provide the concept, which is realised by means of what is known as a "virtual package" in Debian. If any of the packages providing the virtual **mail-transport-agent** package is installed on the local system, the Debian package tools regard the dependency as fulfilled.

The Debian policy specifies a number of different types of relations, as well as the syntax required for each relation, so that specific requirements can be meaningfully represented. In addition to simple dependencies and conflicts, packages can also suggest, recommend, provide, replace, or extend other packages. Each of these relations uses a separate field in the **control** file:

Depends

> According to the policy, entries in the **Depends** field are absolute dependencies. If some of the packages listed here are not installed (and configured) on the system, a depending package may be unpacked, but it cannot be configured. Hence, it will not be usable (and not be able to satisfy other dependencies), until all the dependent packages are fully configured. Names listed in the **Depends** field of a package reference other packages that are essential to the operation of the software. Another relation, **Pre-Depends**, provides a somewhat more relaxed dependency relation and is only used in very special cases; packages listed here need only be unpacked (but not necessarily configured) to satisfy the dependency.

Recommends

> At times, a package may require another, but the requirement need not be strict; the software to be installed could work acceptably, but not without a serious limitation in its functionality. For example, the **xmms** multimedia player runs without access to the sound system, but it will only be of limited use. Therefore, **xmms** recommends the installation of a sound system interface.

Suggests

> Frequently, software is enhanced by other software. For instance, the **X server** runs without font files, but users who do not enjoy pixelated art will have their aesthetic experience greatly improved by the presence of high-resolution fonts. Therefore the **xserver-common** base package suggests the installation of font packages.

Enhances

> This is the exact counterpart to **Suggests**, but they are independent of each other. The field is supposed to communicate suggestions to the package manager, without requiring the enhanced package's meta data to be touched. Support for the Enhances field is still rather sparse, and APT does not support it at present.

Provides

> One package may provide the functionality of another, or that of a virtual package. The dependency of the aforementioned at package may be met by installing **postfix**, since **postfix** provides **mail-transport-agent** on which **at** depends.

Conflicts

> Packages listed in the **Conflicts** field cannot coexist with the package declaring the conflict, either because of file collisions or other reasons.

Replaces

> In certain cases, a package may supercede parts of another package, involving the replacement of files from the other package. **dpkg** will not allow one package to overwrite the files installed by another package, unless the new package explicitly states this intent in the **Replaces** field. Such is the situation when, for example, packages are renamed, or splitting a package into components renders the previous monolithic package obsolete. Most of the time, **Replaces** will be used together with **Conflicts** (and, in the case of a virtual package, **Provides** as well) to cause the removal of the package to be replaced.

The standard format for all the available relation fields is a comma-separated list of package names. With the exception of **Provides**, an package name may be further restricted based on the version number[37]. A package may declare a relation on one specific version number, which is usually how libraries and associated development files relate (=). Alternatively, a relation may apply to versions of a package strictly earlier (<<), earlier-or-equal (<=), later-or-equal (>=), or strictly later (>>). The following line specifies the dependency on **foo** version 2.0-1 or later as well as the requirement of **bar** prior to release 3.0:

```
Depends: foo (>= 2.0-1), bar (<< 3.0)
```

In addition, the fields can specify a set of packages, of which only one must be installed. The following encodes a preference on any version of **apache2** later than 2.0.50, or any other package providing the virtual package **httpd**:

```
Depends: apache2 (>= 2.0.50) | httpd
```

Specifying an actual package in addition to a virtual package (**apache2** actually provides **httpd**) allows a maintainer to suggest a default, rather than relying on APT to select any of the providing packages.

Gathering package meta data

We need not look very far to find other package management systems with similar capabilities. Relationship graphs are basic computer science material, and any sensibly designed package system can compute or even assemble acceptable package combinations from its database and package meta data. The fact that Debian was the first to have a consistent and robust system is not worth a pence these days.

Nevertheless, the usefulness of a relationship graph mainly relies on the data used to create the graph, just like **dpkg**'s configuration file handling relies on knowing which files to treat specially. Therefore, one of the most crucial factors of a package management system is the package maintainers' ability to specify the relations as accurately as possible. A package relation scheme as diverse as Debian's is helpful and indispensable, but providing the correct information is not always an easy task.

The policy states in section 3.5 that "every package must specify the dependency information about other packages that are required for the first to work correctly." It also calls for the use of conflict declarations, but it does not (and cannot) make a universal statement about what is to be considered a dependency, or which packages satisfy a given relation.

Debian approaches this problem from two angles. First, extensions to the policy have developed over time to coordinate practices with respect to software written in specific languages. For instance, the **Perl** policy[38] regulates aspects idiosyncratic

---

[37]Virtual packages are not versioned.
[38]http://www.debian.org/doc/packaging-manuals/perl-policy

to Perl scripts and programmes. While the Perl policy's guidelines are not as binding as the rules of the Debian policy, the document does serve as a basis for maintainers to make decisions and enable coexistence among (the much smaller set of) Perl-related packages. In the future, such sub-policies may well be integrated with the main Debian policy.

Simultaneously, the Debian maintainer utilities provide numerous helpers to encapsulate the policy and take the burden off the maintainer's shoulders. For instance, the shlibs system (see chapter 9.4.3) is a sophisticated mechanism to allow the maintainer scripts to automatically determine the set of packages required to fulfill the library dependencies of a programme. Shlibs uses automatically managed (but locally overrideable[39]) maps to help translate the output of ldd to the minimum set of Debian packages to satisfy the requirements. Rather than expecting a package maintainer to figure out which packages provide the appropriate libraries, the burden is shifted to the maintainers of packages providing shared libraries (who presumably know better which functionality and files the contained libraries provide). Furthermore, changes to a library only require modifications in one place rather than expecting the maintainers of all depending packages to amend the control data.

Along the same lines, tools exist to determine dependencies not listed by ldd, as is the case with scripts written in Perl or Python. These tools are able to harness peculiarities of the particular policy[40] and of language features that allow for automatic determination of required modules.

Beyond resolving the dependencies on dynamically linked libraries, Debian does *not* provide an automated means to determine dependencies, and probably never will, because no feasible approach exists that can simultaneously obey all requirements of the Debian policy. Obviously, you could scan a programme for all external command invocations and references to data files, and subsequently use a map structure to find associated packages. However, Debian makes it difficult not to make the set of dependencies equal to the set of resources used across all permutations of configuration options and input data of a programme. In other words, Debian packages depend on those other packages that are essential for their operation. A software that can enable additional features in the presence of a library merely suggests or recommends the package containing the library. This could be taken one step further by allowing the automatic dependency scanner to determine the context of a dependency and thus decide whether it is a hard or a soft dependency. However, this approach soon leads the infamous Halting Problem[41]. Debian maintainers therefore need not worry about being replaced by small shell scripts.

---

[39] In /etc/dpkg/shlibs.override, see chapter 9.4.3

[40] Debian's Python policy resides in /usr/share/doc/python/python-policy.txt.gz

[41] Deciding whether a software requires a certain library by parsing the code and determining whether execution will reach the places where the library is used is similar to the impossible task of determining whether a given programme will ever terminate: http://en.wikipedia.org/wiki/Halting_problem

Sane dependencies

On a tangent, it is worth mentioning that Debian takes a sane approach to indirect dependencies as well. Classic examples are programmes which come with graphical user interfaces, but which can also be used from the command line and thus do not require a graphical environment such as X. If the functionality of such a programme is useful in headless[42] or embedded setups, then it would be silly and a major inconvenience for these packages to depend on a graphical environment. In such a case maintainers will typically chose to split the package in two (if possible), separating the graphical components into an extension package. This approach allows the core components to be installed without the graphical environment, but also caters for users of the graphical components. For instance, the **isdnutils** package, which is essential on ISDN routers (which are frequently headless), can be installed without a graphical environment. Its graphical tools are contained in **isdnutils-xtools**, which uses **isdnutils** for the core functionality and depends on the X server, rather than **isdnutils** itself.

In addition, a similar logic is applied to dependent packages. With **X Window System**, programmes may rely on its resources without actually requiring a graphical display. For example, the **giftrans** package needs the **RGB** colour names from /etc/X11/rgb.txt, a file provided (indirectly) by **xserver-common**. While all X servers in Debian depend on **xserver-common**, that package may also be installed by itself. **giftrans** requires its installation but consequently does not require an X server. It is standard Debian practice to factor common parts from multiple packages into *-common packages, thereby simplifying dependency management. Similarly, most Debian maintainers split a software's documentation into a separate *-doc package, if it exceeds a (non-specified) limit. Especially for embedded and other low-resource systems, this modularity is a necessity.

5.7.4   The Filesystem Hierarchy Standard (FHS)

With 15 000 binary packages in the Debian pool at the time of writing, you may wonder how many conflicts had to be resolved between two packages each trying to install a file of the same name. Well, the answer is "very few," which may be surprising were it not again for the policy to confine packages to use very specific locations for their files, rather than installing all over the place.

Section 9.1.1 of the Debian policy specifies that "all installed files and directories must comply with the Filesystem Hierarchy Standard (FHS)." The FHS[43] is a set of guidelines drafted in the early days of Linux in an attempt to redesign the antique directory structure of Unix systems. More specifically, it provides system integrators, package developers, and system administrators with a consistent and logical

---

[42] Headless setups do not have monitors but are used exclusively through the network.
[43] http://www.pathname.com/fhs

layout of files across a Unix filesystem to improve portability and compatibility across distributions and operating systems by different vendors. While today, most Unix-like operating systems follow the suggestions the document puts forth (to varying degrees), Debian *woody* was one of the first distributions (if not the first) to almost reach full FHS compliance[44].

According to the FHS, the files installed on a system have to be placed in specific locations on the filesystem, according to their function and traits. In chapter 5.7.1, we saw that Debian requires configuration files to reside under /etc, while dpkg usually installs static files in the /usr hierarchy. This separation is a direct consequence of FHS compliance. The notable hierarchies relevant to Debian are listed in the following, along with additional restrictions imposed by the Debian policy:

/ — The root directory
> No additional files or directories than those already present may be placed in its top level. The root directory may, however, contain links to kernel files required for booting.

/etc — Host-specific system configuration
> Any file expected to be changed by the administrator of a system must reside under /etc[45].

/boot — Static bootloader files
> Files related to the bootloader are placed here. /boot must be able to sit on a read-only volume.

/usr — Shareable, read-only data
> Files under /usr must not require write permissions and be of static nature. Other than during software upgrades, the system must work regularly if /usr resides on a read-only volume. No files or directories may be placed in its top level.

/usr/lib — Architecture-specific resources
> Files needed by local software which are dependent on the system architecture (mostly binary files) must be placed here.

/usr/share — Architecture-independent resources
> Files needed by local software which are usable on any architecture must be located below /usr/share.

---

[44]I know of no Linux system that is fully FHS compliant, largely due to archaic kernel and boot-time requirements which have not been resolved in an FHS-compliant way. The classic example is /etc/mtab, which is a dynamic file required by mount, but which cannot reside underneath /var as it has to be available right after mounting the root filesystem.

[45]Exceptions exist. For instance, Grub requires its configuration to be located on the same partition as the /boot hierarchy.

/usr/local – Custom software and resources

Software and resources independent of the Debian distribution may be put into **/usr/local** and will never be touched by Debian.

/tmp – Temporary data

As a scratch space, **/tmp** may hold any type of data. Its persistence, however, is not guaranteed across different processes.

/var – Transient data

The **/var** hierarchy is the system's workspace. Files here are used for control, logging, caching and other administrative functions. No additional files or directories may be placed in the top level.

/var/log – Log files

All programmes providing logging information in Debian log to files underneath this directory.

/var/tmp – Persistent temporary data

As opposed to **/tmp**, data under **/var/tmp** is never deleted automatically by the system, but should have a temporary nature.

/var/mail – User mailbox files

If the local mail delivery agent uses the **mailbox** format, the user mailbox files reside underneath **/var/mail**.

/home – User data

User home directories generally reside in **/home**, but the layout of this hierarchy is up to the administrator. No program must rely on data contained herein.

/mnt – Temporarily mounted filesystems

This directory is provided so that the system administrator may temporarily mount a filesystem as needed. It is *not* a directory holding mount points for media.

With the release of *sarge*, Debian followed recent changes in the FHS and added the following root-level hierarchies:

/media – Removable media mount points

Mount points for removable media, such as CD-ROM drives or USB sticks are located under **/media**.

/srv – Served data

Data made available by services of the system (such as web sites) find their place within the **/srv** hierarchy.

The FHS furthermore recommends that software uses subdirectories of /usr/share and /usr/lib to guard against name clashes. These subdirectories are referred to as "compartments" in some places. For instance, architecture-independent files of the OpenOffice.org suite reside under /usr/share/openoffice while the Gimp graphics programme may store such files under /usr/share/gimp. Even if both programmes provide a file named tree.png, the packages can happily coexist.

5.7.5 Version numbers

A Debian package is identified by its name and its version number. For the package relations to allow for versioned dependencies, and for APT to be able to decide whether a package is newer or older than an installed version, the version number must follow the rules which are established by the policy. Every Debian version number takes the following format (the brackets denote optional parts of the version number):

[epoch:]software_version[-debian_revision]

When APT decides whether to upgrade a package, it compares the two strings of the previously installed version and the version of the installation candidate. Normally, the software version, which is the only mandatory component of the version number, should be enough to identify relative age of a package. When a package provides the same software version as another and the two only differ in packaging aspects, the difference must be reflected in the debian revision, which is appended to the software version following a hyphen. Packages of software written specifically for Debian generally do not have a Debian revision field.

Comparing two version numbers is done lexicographically, sorting letters before numbers. Therefore, package version 1.0.1-2 would sort before version 1.1.0-1, and APT would consider the package with the larger version number 1.1.0-1 as an upgrade candidate. At times, however, an upstream author employs a non-standard versioning scheme (e.g. 1.1, 1.11, 1.2, ...), which would utterly confuse APT's sorting algorithm. Debian works around such problems with the epoch field, which is prepended to the software version, and followed by a colon. To cater for non-standard versioning schemes, the Debian maintainer would use epochs to restore the lexicographical ordering of the version numbers (e.g. 1:1.1, 1:1.11, 2:1.2). An empty epoch is equivalent to an epoch of 0.

Epochs: normalising version numbers

The epoch field can also be used to correct errors in the versioning. For APT to consider an upgrade the newly available version must be strictly larger than the already installed version. An upstream software may decide to change its versioning scheme at some point in time: after releasing version 1 and version 2, the developer team may want to adopt a proper versioning scheme and release version 3 as 1.0 instead. Since 1.0 is smaller than 2, **APT** would not update the software packages on any Debian system until the developers released 2.0, which could be years later. Here, too, the Debian maintainer would opt to fix the situation by setting the version number of the package following the scheme change to 1:1.0.

A number of special cases exist with respect to version numbers. Frequently, upstream software is released versioned with date strings. For instance, the **postfix** mail transfer agent was versioned according to its release date until 2002. It is good practice to insert a 0.0 dummy version, such as 0.0.20011217.SNAPSHOT-1 before the date string, in the case of postfix. When the **postfix** developers chose to adopt a regular versioning scheme and released 1.0, the **postfix** package maintainer did not need to use an epoch in this situation.

Similar suggestions exist to deal with version extensions indicating pre-release states, such as alpha and beta releases, or release candidates. Consider the case of a software release candidate with upstream version 1.0-rc1. Such version strings are commonly found, but when the release candidate matures and the actual release is made, APT will find that 1.0 is smaller than 1.0-rc1 and thus not upgrade the package. Fortunately, "alpha," "beta," and "rc" compare appropriately with respect to each other, so a special scheme must be used to allow the pre-releases to sort before the final release. Within the Debian archive, it is customary to encode the real upstream version in the Debian revision. According to that scheme, a package of 1.0rc1 could be versionsed at 1.0-0+1.0rc1+1, followed by 1.0-0+1.0rc1+2, and then 1.0-1 when the final gets released. Another scheme is to use an obviously false upstream version that sorts before the final release: 0.999-1+1.0rc1, 0.999-2+1.0rc1, and finally, 1.0-1. With that in mind, it should be easy to infer the upstream version number from the Debian version, even in complex cases.

Starting with *etch*, a new character will be introduced into version strings to handle situations similar to the one mentioned earlier. As of now, the empty string is regarded as smaller than any character, and thus, 1.0-1 follows 1.0, to give a very basic example. The tilde character is defined to be even smaller than an empty string. Thus, 1.0˜1 will precede 1.0, and 1.0˜rc1-1 can be used prior to the release of 1.0-1. The *woody* package management tools do not support this new character in version strings.

The **dpkg** tool provides an interface to compare versions according to the aforementioned rules. Using literal versions of arithmetic comparison operands (**lt**, **le**, **eq**, **ne**, **ge**, **gt**), you can use it resolve any issues with Debian version numbers. Mathematical symbols may also be used, in a similar approach to the way versioned dependencies are specified (though they have to be quoted in most cases). The result of the comparison is communicated with the exit status, which will be false if the comparison is false:

```
~$ dpkg --compare-versions 1.0-0+1.0rc1+2 lt 1.0-1 && echo yes
yes
~$ dpkg --compare-versions 3:1.0-2 '<=' 1.99-15 && echo yes
~$ dpkg --compare-versions 1.0-1 '>>' 1.0~rc1-1 && echo yes
yes
```

5.7.6 Upgrading packages

Surveying the field of automatic package management, one gets the impression that automatic upgrading has lost its touch of magic and the previously prominent feature of few distributions has become a standard across all major operating systems. We have already compared the technical aspects of package management systems and found those to be roughly equal to each other. Now it is time for the Debian policy (see chapter 5.7) to enter the picture. As you may have guessed, Debian's package management differs from the other systems in that it is based on the Debian policy and works hand in hand with it.

In chapter 5.4.7, we saw that APT can upgrade a Debian system to the latest release with only two commands. Thanks to the Debian policy, it can do more. No matter which release you install or even which releases you mix (see chapter 8.2), the Debian policy lays down the necessary foundation upon which the Debian developers can produce and improve packages, which are guaranteed to be compatible with previous and future versions. It is the policy which allows you to upgrade single packages or the whole system with two commands, provided that APT can meet the dependencies for you (or you can do it manually).

The Debian policy has been in effect for almost as long as Debian exists, and it has never been subject to a major rollover. Changes have been made with great care and only after long periods of scrutiny. As a consequence, all Debian releases since *hamm* can be upgraded to the current *stable* release. It would be a lie to say that all such upgrades are painless as the main focus of the Debian developers is the smooth upgrade from one *stable* release to the next. Therefore, if you skip a couple of releases and *e.g.* attempt to upgrade a *hamm* system to *sarge*, you may need to lift a finger here or there. However, beyond some minor problems, the upgrade should complete successfully, and probably in less time and with less effort than a new installation and subsequent migration would consume.

At this time of writing, the policy has been in effect and thus tested over the period of four releases. It has reached massive inertia as one of the integral parts of the Debian system. Changes to the policy require very good reasons and large amounts of testing, to ensure that the foundation given by the policy is not put at risk. When a change is made, it usually standardises established procedures to allow future releases to build on what is being widely used now. This update strategy, bundled with the strict adherence of all parts of the Debian system to the policy, allows you to be certain that the system you are installing today can be upgraded with the same ease when the next *stable* release comes out. In management terms, this is considered a "future-proof investment;" with Debian, it's a feature.

5.8   debconf: configuration of Debian packages

One of Debian's strongest features is its configuration file management. In this domain, the system closely reflects the overall philosophy of Debian system management, which is to aid but not impose. On the one hand, the Debian system guarantees not to mess with your configuration files, keeping your modifications across upgrades and preserving the files on package deletion (but not purging). On the other hand, Debian does not provide or rely on a configuration dashboard, control panel, or other centralised form of system management. While integrated system configuration utilities, such as **linuxconf**, are usable on a Debian system (it is Linux after all), Debian does not let such a tool mess with the configuration files by default.

The complexity and flexibility of a Unix configuration file by far exceeds what can be meaningfully represented in a user interface. Therefore, configuration utilities have to make compromises, but compromises limit the ability to harness a software's full feature set. Debian's role in system management is to give the administrator full control and provide helpful back-ends facilitate ease many of the administrative tasks at the same time. While the package management tools aim to make software installation management a delightful endeavour, the software contained in a package is generally the same as if installed directly from the upstream sources. Debian does not attempt to integrate software or put configuration and/or abstraction layers between the software and the user. Thus, *e.g.*, Debian's **postfix** installs the same mail transport agent with the same configuration paradigm as the upstream tarball. In case of problems, other **postfix** users can easily help, even without knowing about Debian.

In a world of integrated products and advertised ease of management, it may seem a little backward to expect an administrator to master the software in addition to the underlying operating system. However, this precisely reflects the Debian philosophy. Rather than attempting to make administration easy for everyone, it provides shortcuts for those who already know what they want and how to achieve it. When it comes to problem solving, it pays to understand the problem rather than to be left at the mercy of a management interface.

Nevertheless, the Debian package maintainers try hard to make a software installed by a package usable once the installation has finished. Installing a software from an an upstream tarball may leave behind a software that requires substantial modifications to the default (example) configuration prior to doing anything useful. A Debian package, on the other hand, generally installs a software with sane and secure defaults, so that the administrator needs only to adapt the software to local needs rather than to understand the whole suite before getting any results.

This said, sane defaults often do not exist. Assuming a user is aiming for a functional installation, that user must be consulted to provide settings the maintainer could not foresee, or which cannot be determined automatically. For instance, when **postfix** installs, it wants to know whether to send outgoing email directly or via an Simple Mail Transfer Protocol (SMTP) relay. Similarly, a database-driven web front-end will not be much use without being told the connection details for the database to use.

In such cases, the information has to be obtained from the user installing the software. Rather than expecting every maintainer to be creative at user interaction, Debian provides **debconf**, a system intended to communicate with the user and cache the responses to package-specific questions for later retrieval by the package's own configuration scripts.

5.8.1   An overview of debconf

debconf is more than what most people think. At the same time, it is less than what is commonly believed. To deal with some of the myths up front, **debconf** is neither a system that configures packages, nor is it a central repository of configuration parameters (such as a registry).

The main purpose of **debconf** is to separate user interaction from the configuration process of a package. To use **debconf**, a package provides two files for processing by **debconf**. In the **templates** file, the package lists the questions it needs to ask the user, along with acceptable values, and longer descriptions. With the **config** script, the package instructs **debconf** when and under what conditions to ask these questions.

Contrary to popular misconceptions, **debconf** does not make any changes and does not configure any software. Its sole purpose is user interaction and the caching of a user's responses. The actual configuration and enacting of users' choices is commonly handled by a package's **postinst** script, and not by **debconf**. The **postinst** script first invokes the **config** script to make sure that all user responses are cached in the **debconf** database. Then it proceeds to query the database through **debconf**'s programming interface and process the values corresponding to the user choices accordingly.

While the **postinst** script always runs the **config** script on configuration, the **config** script may also be run at various other times during a package's life cycle. For instance, APT uses hooks (see chapter 5.4.2) to call **dpkg-preconfigure** before unpacking a package to be installed or upgraded. This comes in handy when a greater number of packages is being processed by APT. The administrator can first answer all **debconf** questions of the requested packages, and then go for a coffee or turn towards other tasks while APT zips through the unpacking and configuration phases without interrupting to wait for user input.

debconf makes sure that, unless specifically requested, questions that have already been seen and answered by the user are not presented on subsequent runs. Thus, when the **config** script is invoked by the **postinst** script after successful precon-figuration, it does not bother the user again as all responses have been cached by debconf.

5.8.2 Priority levels

Given that not all questions a package may ask are weighted equally, **debconf** provides four priority levels for its questions. For every Debian system, you can choose the level at which you want to influence a package's configuration, and **debconf** will not bother you with questions of lower levels than your preference. In decreasing order of importance, the available priority levels are:

critical
> Questions of critical priority have to be asked (and answered) by all users as they correspond to crucial choices that nobody but the system administrator can answer.

high
> Questions in the high priority class should be answered by the system ad-ministrator, since there are no sensible default answers.

medium
> Medium questions are standard questions with reasonable defaults. Thus, they only need to be answered in non-standard cases.

low
> Questions of low priority are generally trivial questions with defaults ex-pected to work in all but a few cases.

The priority of each question is encoded within the **config** file as a parameter to the **debconf** Application Programming Interface (API) call to display a question. The standard priority of a new Debian system is **high**, meaning that **debconf** only asks **high** and **critical** questions while using the defaults configured in the **tem-plates** file for questions of priorities **medium** and **low**. The environment variable **$DEBIAN_PRIORITY** may be used to change the system's default priority temporar-ily[46]. For instance, the following causes **debconf** to present all questions of the **postfix** package:

```
~# DEBIAN_PRIORITY=low apt-get install postfix
[...]
```

[46]Note that the variable is *not* named $DEBCONF_PRIORITY, but $DEBIAN_PRIORITY!

5.8.3   debconf front-ends

A major strength of the separation of user interaction from the configuration of a package's software is the ability to use different front-ends to ask the questions. The decision which front-end to use is that of the system administrator. To the package maintainer, the choice of front-end makes no difference; the **postinst** file queries the **debconf** database for cached information, regardless of the front-end used to gather the data from the user.

In addition to the standard gray-on-blue text-mode dialogs, **debconf** can also inquire for information with **KDE** or **Gnome** windows, console text mode, using text editors, or a web browser. In addition, **debconf** can also inhibit all forms of interaction for fully-automated installations.

The information presented, as well as the set of choices, is identical across all front-ends (well, with exception of the non-interactive anti-front-end). The **dialog** frontend in figure 5.11 asks the same **debconf** question as the **readline** front-end in the following:

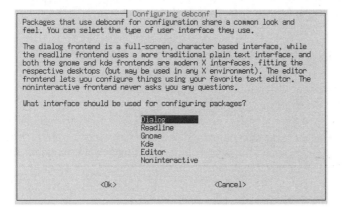

Figure 5.11:
The dialog front-end
to debconf.

```
Configuring debconf
-------------------


Packages that use debconf for configuration share a common look
and feel. You can select the type of user interface they use.

The dialog front-end is a full-screen, character based interface,
while the readline front-end uses a more traditional plain text
interface, and both the gnome and kde front-ends are modern
X interfaces, fitting the respective desktops (but may be used in
any X environment). The editor front-end lets you configure things
using your favorite text editor. The noninteractive front-end
never asks you any questions.
```

```
1. Dialog    2. Readline    3. Gnome
4. Kde       5. Editor      6. Noninteractive

What interface should be used for configuring packages? 2
```

Therefore, it is really a matter of preference, which front-end to use. During the configuration of the **debconf** package, you can select a default front-end, which may subsequently be overridden by setting the $DEBIAN_FRONTEND environment variable appropriately[47].

For unattended installations, the **noninteractive** front-end ensures that the process does not pause and wait for user input. Instead, defaults are used for all questions which have not been previously answered. Ideally, the database should be populated in advance with answers to questions with **high** or **critical** priorities, as these have no sensible defaults. Alternatively, a remote database may be used (see chapter 5.8.6).

In addition to asking questions, **debconf** can simply display messages to the user. If the ttermnoninteractive front-end is used, these messages will be sent via email to the **root** user.

5.8.4   Reconfiguring packages

Choices and settings given in response to **debconf** queries are not final. In fact, it is trivial to rerun **debconf** and provide different answers to the various questions. Previously, the standard means to reconfigure a package was its reinstallation. However, because **debconf** remembers which questions it presented and does not display them again (unless specifically requested), a reinstallation will end up using the same **debconf** parameters. Obviously, purging the **debconf** database, or at least the relevant records does the trick, but so does **dpkg-reconfigure**, a tool made specifically for this purpose.

dpkg-reconfigure takes the name of a package and tells **debconf** to ask all questions again, whether they have been previously answered or not; the **--unseen** option causes already seen questions to be skipped. As an example, the following instructs **dpkg-reconfigure** to change the default question priority and the main front-end.

```
~# dpkg-reconfigure --frontend=readline debconf
Configuring debconf
[...]
What interface should be used for configuring packages? 2
[...]
See only questions that are of what priority and higher? 4
[...]
```

[47]That is $DEBIAN_FRONTEND, and not $DEBCONF_FRONTEND (just like $DEBIAN_PRIORITY)!

Reconfiguration causes a package's hook scripts (*e.g. postinst*) to be run. These scripts must do everything required for the software to use the new configuration, while taking care not to overwrite any changes made by the administrator outside of **debconf**. The best way to accomplish this is to seed the default answers suggested by **debconf** with existing configuration files and subsequently write new files with the data held in the **debconf** cache.

5.8.5 debconf in action

Let us pause for a second and inspect an example. The **hinfo** package uses **debconf** to determine at what intervals to update its databases from the Web, and if these intervals are periodic, whether it should be verbose about the update. The package registers two parameters with **debconf**, which are available in **/var/lib/dpkg/info/hinfo.templates**:

```
Template: hinfo/autoupdate
Type: select
Choices: never, now, weekly, monthly
Default: never
Description: When would you like hinfo to download new databases?
[...]
Template: hinfo/autoupdateverbose
Type: select
Choices: quiet, nonverbose, verbose
Default: quiet
Description: How verbose should the periodic update be?
[...]
```

As you can see, the parameters are organised in a hierarchical structure, similar to a registry. With the **templates** file in place, **debconf** now knows about the parameters of **hinfo**. The display of the questions is controlled by the package's **config** script, which is stored in **/var/lib/dpkg/info/hinfo.config**. The script has been simplified for your viewing pleasure.

```
#!/bin/sh -e
# config script for hinfo

. /usr/share/debconf/confmodule

[...]

db_input medium hinfo/autoupdate
db_go
if db_get hinfo/autoupdate; then
  case "$RET" in
    daily|weekly|monthly)
      db_input medium hinfo/autoupdateverbose
```

```
        db_go
        ;;
    *)
        # added for demonstration purposes:
        db_set hinfo/autoupdateverbose false
        ;;
  esac
fi
```

db_input accumulates parameter questions and attributes one of the four priorities to the question. By not hardcoding a priority with a parameter, it is possible to vary the priority programmatically, for instance in response to a previous user choice. The question will only be registered if the priority specified as the first argument is higher than or equal to the currently configured or requested **debconf** priority. A user who configured **debconf** to priority **high** would never have to bother with **hinfo**'s parameters and **hinfo** would use the defaults instead.

The **db_go** command displays all accumulated questions, using the configured or requested front-end. This allows multiple questions to be displayed at once, should the front-end support that.

With **db_get**, the database may be queried. The command puts the parameter value into the environment variable $RET. As you can see, this variable can then be used to conditionally display the second question — which only makes sense when a periodic selection has been made in response to the first question. In case of a non-periodic selection, the **config** file uses **db_set** to write to the **debconf** database[48].

The combination of **templates** and **config** files integrates a package's parameters and their query logic with **debconf**, but none of the above accounts for the actual configuration of **hinfo** according to the user's choices. This is done in **hinfo**'s **postinst** file, which similarly queries the database and takes appropriate steps to configure **cron**:

```
#! /bin/bash
[...]
db_get hinfo/autoupdate
au=$RET
case "$au" in
[...]
  never)
[...]
    ;;
  now)
[...]
    ;;
  daily|weekly|monthly)
```

---

[48]The call to **db_set** is not present in **hinfo** and has been added for demonstration purposes only.

```
    db_get hinfo/autoupdateverbose
    verb=$RET
    temp='tempfile -p hinfo -m 0755'
    cat <<EOF >$temp
    #!/bin/sh -e
    if [ -x /usr/sbin/hinfo-update ] ; then
      su hinfo -s /bin/sh -c '/usr/sbin/hinfo-update -$verb'
    fi
    EOF
    ucf -s /usr/share/hinfo $temp /etc/cron.$au/hinfo
    chmod u+x /etc/cron.$au/hinfo
    rm $temp
[...]
    ;;
esac
[...]
```

In a nutshell, this **postinst** script reads the period of the automatic update and uses a case statement to take the steps appropriate to the user's selection. If the choice is for daily, weekly, or monthly periodic updates, it creates the upgrade script in a temporary file, and uses **ucf** to put it into place, thereby ensuring that the administrator's changes are not overwritten without consent.

By localising all configuration actions within the package scripts, all knowledge about how to turn the user's choices into a working configuration is contained within the **hinfo** package, and **debconf** does not need to know anything about **hinfo**, **cron**, or even that the former uses the latter. As opposed to configuration dashboards and control panels, the **debconf** approach can handle an unlimited number of different configuration schemata without modifications to the **debconf** core.

5.8.6   Using a remote database back-end

The **debconf** database is a flat file caching database (which resides under **/var/cache/debconf**). Despite all the disadvantages (such as performance and size) of this kind of database back-end, it is perfectly suitable as a user interface and response cache for a single machine. Nevertheless, **debconf** would not be **debconf** if it did not allow different back-ends for different requirements; at time of writing, **debconf** can use one of three local database methods in addition to an Lightweight Directory Access Protocol (LDAP) back-end: a single file (**File**, the default), a directory hierarchy (**DirTree**), or on a file-per-package basis (**PackageDir**). The LDAP back-end, while still experimental, allows the use of Secure Socket Layer (SSL) as well as the setting of a read-only attribute.

There are multiple reasons why you would want to use a remote **debconf** database. Probably the most common is because you want to use the settings of an existing Debian system during the installation of a new system. The easiest way to do so is with the **Pipe** driver and SSH to tunnel the contents of the flat file database **config.dat** from another machine (or copy it beforehand and use the local version for the pipe, rather than an SSH tunnel). I will show you how to accomplish this in an instant.

debconf provides means to combine multiple databases for this purpose. **debconf** can be told *ad hoc* to pull in parameters from another source using two environment variables: $DEBCONF_DB_OVERRIDE and $DEBCONF_DB_FALLBACK. If the first variable is set, **debconf** consults the referenced database before the local cache. Similarly, $DEBCONF_DB_FALLBACK can be used to specify a source to query in case a variable is not stored in the local cache.

Sources are specified in the form of drivers and any parameters needed by the specific driver. A driver is simply a method of accessing a database, and **debconf** comes with a number of drivers, which are described in **debconf.conf**(5). The following drivers are among the available ones:

File

> makes **debconf** use a flat file as the database. For instance: **File{/tmp/my-debconf-db}**.

Pipe

> configures **debconf** to read (and write) from the standard file descriptors **stdin** (and **stdout**). These can be pointed elsewhere with arguments.

Stack

> can stack different sources, which are then consulted in order of specification. The manpage (**debconf.conf**(5)) gives a useful example of this driver.

LDAP

> tells **debconf** to obtain values via LDAP. For example:
> **LDAP{server:localhost,basedn:dc=debconf}**

To let **APT** perform an upgrade to the next release, while obtaining all unknown settings from a remote machine rather than the user, you could use a **Pipe** transport like this:

```
~# export DEBCONF_DB_FALLBACK=Pipe
~# export DEBIAN_FRONTEND=noninteractive
~# ssh remote cat /var/cache/debconf/config.dat \
  apt-get dist-upgrade
[...]
```

APT will proceed to download all new packages and register the parameter templates with **debconf** as part of the preconfiguration. All parameters which are not yet stored in the local **debconf** database are read from **stdin**, which is assumed to be a **debconf** database in flat file format. The non-interactive front-end ensures no interruption during the upgrade process.

Alternatively, you may want to change the configuration of a number of packages on various machines. A simple way to accomplish the task is to prepare one machine with the desired configuration and then to override the **debconf** settings on the remaining systems. For instance, to enforce the same configuration for **postfix** and **apache** as on the machine **remote** (but using the **File** driver instead of **Pipe** for demonstration purposes), the following would have to be executed on each target:

```
~# scp rempte:/var/cache/debconf/config.dat /tmp/remote-config.dat
~# export DEBCONF_DB_OVERRIDE=File/tmp/remote-config.dat
~# dpkg-reconfigure --frontend=noninteractive postfix apache
```

On reconfiguration, **debconf** will use the parameters available in the file and only access the main **debconf** database when a certain parameter is not found. Since we just configured the two packages as desired on the **remote** machine, all parameters needed by **dpkg-reconfigure** will be available in the flat file we copied just before the reconfiguration.

Apart from temporary combination of database back-ends through the use of environment variables, **debconf** can also be statically configured through the /etc/debconf.conf file. Its manpage (debconf.conf (5)) provides extensive information on the configuration parameters involved.

Thanks to the read-only attribute that can be set for every database type in /etc/debconf.conf, it is also possible to use another machine's **debconf** database as reference source for a number of machines. Using the **Stack** driver to combine a local cache with a remote database containing a common set of parameters, it is possible to set up a cluster of machines all with a common set of parameters available to **debconf**, but each allowing for local modifications[49].

As the number of machines in such an arrangement increases, the flat file data structure quickly reaches its limits due to its serial nature. A hierarchical database, such as accessed over LDAP, is much better suited to serve as **debconf** back-end for a cluster or a larger set of workstations. Properly configured, LDAP allows a number of machines to pull **debconf** parameters from a shared, read-only LDAP tree while each machine has write access to an individual tree for local modifications.

The configuration of an LDAP back-end to **debconf** is straight-forward (and beyond the scope of this book). The **debconf-doc** package provides the necessary schema (for use with **OpenLDAP**) in **debconf.schema** within its documentation directory (/usr/share/doc/debconf-doc).

---

[49]This is similar to overriding variables in the local scope in programming languages (such as C), or the concept of acquisition in hierarchical databases.

5.8.7   Problems and shortcomings

Being a system that obtains and seemingly stores configuration data, **debconf** is often thought of as a configuration respository or a registry system. It does not help that its author calls it a "configuration system," when in fact it is really a user interaction framework and response caching system. Used correctly, **debconf** is a powerful and yet unobtrusive system to enable packages to install operational software without forcing the package maintainer to opt for insane defaults that could potentially result in security or integrity problems. Moreover, since packages handle their own configuration, relying on **debconf** only as a unified means to interact with the administrator, **debconf** can be used by an unlimited number of packages without requiring knowledge of these packages on the side of **debconf**. Lastly, its ability to use flexible and potentially complicated database back-ends and their combinations, allows it to scale to arbitrary complexity and even serve a cluster of Debian machines.

Nevertheless, **debconf** and its current state within Debian is less than perfect. The use of **debconf** is encouraged but not required, and no guidelines exist for when it should be used. A good rule of thumb is to use **debconf** to inquire about parameter values that are not expected to be the same across all but the most specialised installations. However, identifying parameters of this class is anything but simple and every maintainer has a different interpretation of this rule. Thus, the **debconf** experience is not consistent across the Debian package pool.

Configuration file handling is a much greater source of friction. A package whose **postinst** file merges a user's responses into the software's configuration files below /etc makes programmatic changes to the files. By the policy, files that are automatically modified in such a way must not be flagged as **conffiles** and therefore do not profit from **dpkg**'s configuration handling mechanism. They are still configuration files (since they reside underneath /etc), but not automatically handled by **dpkg**, which only treats files flagges as **conffiles** specially. This is an important distinction! Please refer to chapter 5.7.1 for more information. Also, chapter 9.4.2 provides an example of how to deal with **debconf**-managed configuration files.

Being configuration files, any manual changes by the administrator to these files must be preserved under all circumstances according to the policy. Therefore, any **postinst** script must only consider the **debconf** cache when the parameter value is not available from the software configuration under /etc. To extract the parameter value from under /etc, the configuration file must be parsed, which can be non-trivial with some configuration paradigms. Different pieces of software use different configuration file formats, and the sheer abundance of these formats makes it impossible for **debconf** to provide a common interface to the task. It remains the maintainer's job — and thus a potential source of error — to implement functionality to put local changes back into the **debconf** database so as to comply with the policy.

The **hinfo** package installed an update script under one of the **cron** directories, depending on the user's choice of interval. If the administrator selected 'daily' in response to the question, but then decides to move to a weekly schedule by moving the update script from **/etc/cron.daily** to **/etc/cron.weekly**, the **postinst** script must react appropriately. One way to achieve this is to use **db_set** to manipulate the **debconf** database to reflect the current state of the system. For instance, the following code in the beginning of **hinfo**'s **postinst** script would do the trick (although it does not cater for all possibilities, but you should get the idea):

```
#!/bin/bash -e
[...]
if [[ -f /etc/cron.daily/hinfo ]]; then
  db_set hinfo/autoupdate daily
elif [[ -f /etc/cron.weekly/hinfo ]]; then
  db_set hinfo/autoupdate weekly
elif [[ -f /etc/cron.monthly/hinfo ]]; then
  db_set hinfo/autoupdate monthly
else
  db_set hinfo/autoupdate never
[...]
```

While it is definitely possible to honour manual changes to **/etc** and update **debconf**'s database to reflect the changes, the main weakness of this approach is the extra logic required. After all, it is one of **debconf**'s main purposes to reduce the necessary logic to the bare essentials of configuration. Adding complexity to the maintainer scripts to handle manipulations gracefully introduces new potential for bugs, and the whole approach may fail horribly if the administrator's modification is not representable in the **debconf** database.

Other common problems mainly stem from the misinterpretation of **debconf**'s purpose. To reiterate, **debconf** is not a configuration storage system. All configuration resides under **/etc** and **debconf**'s sole purpose is to query the user if **/etc** does not contain enough information to piece together a usable configuration. In particular, there seems to be a common misconception about the purpose of the **debconf** database. The data stored in the **debconf** database must be treated as volatile and its presence must never be taken for granted. The database merely serves as a cache, and its complete disappearance must not have any effect on the running system other than causing **debconf** to ask the same questions the next time the **config** script is invoked.

While the problems discussed in the previous paragraphs are of particular relevance to Debian package maintainers, it is important to keep a clear view of **debconf**'s purpose and capabilities when working with a Debian system. You should know the extents of automatic configuration management within the Debian system and know what you can expect and what is unacceptable. Despite being less than perfect, **debconf** does its job, and does so quite nicely. However, when problems arise, potentially reverting manual changes to files under **/etc**, it is important to consider that it is probably not **debconf**'s fault, but rather the result of a bug in the offending package's **postinst** script.

5.9 Modifying packages

The Debian maintainers try to configure the software they package with the broadest target user base in mind. Usually, established and stable features are enabled rather than disabled, and in the face of demand, even experimental options are provided, if these can be turned off in configuration.

However, at times, an administrator may need to use different compile-time options, or make changes to the actual files installed. Of course, it is possible to simply compile the software and install it to /usr/local, or even to change the files installed to /usr by the package. However, these are not really solutions as they circumvent the package management system. For software in /usr/local, you will have to track updates, and changes to files /usr are a really bad idea anyway as these changes may be overwritten by updates (see chapter 5.7.1).

Fortunately, Debian makes it easy to modify existing packages. By intelligently setting the version number of a modified package, it is trivial to talk the package management system into integratng custom editions of packages.

In the sections to come, you will learn about two methods to modify existing Debian packages, obtaining separate packages that can be installed, tracked, and distributed. Next to the clean approach of recompilation from scratch, I will also introduce you to a tool that allows you to modify files installed by a package and to subsequently repack these files into a new DEB file.

5.9.1 Recompiling packages

The idea behind a package recompilation is to obtain the source packages, make the necessary changes, and build a new package (with a new version number) without having to understand much of what is going on. The process can be split into four steps, which will be discussed in turn.

The result of the process is a DEB file with the modified software, which installs the same package with a version number just higher than the official package, but lower than an officially upgraded package. This provides for optimal integration with the package management system without conflicting with other packages. The custom version number can be used to pin the package and thus prevent upgrades (which would not come with the appropriate modifications; see chapter 8.2.1).

Obtaining source packages

As shown in chapter 5.2, Debian distinguishes between source and binary packages. So far, we have mainly dealt with binary packages, which live in DEB files, one package per file. A source package is comprised of two or three files. Debian also distinguishes between packages needing modifications for inclusion in Debian, and packages that can be included directly. The former are known as native packages, while the latter do not have an official name and will henceforth be termed normal packages.

Native source packages consist of two files. Normal source packages provide an additional file to encapsulate the changes required between the externally available (upstream) source, and the source package. This will all become clear in a moment. The following are the constituent files of source packages:

- The Debian Source Control (DSC) file describes the package to the management tools and gives information on which files are part of the source package. It is generally clear-signed with the GPG key of a Debian developer.

- A native source package lives in a tarball, such as **apt_0.6.25.tar.gz**. Normal source packages include the original tarball of the upstream software (where possible), and include the infix **.orig** in their name: **postfix_2.1.5.orig.tar.gz**.

- The **diff.gz** file provides the information needed to turn the tree in the **orig.tar.gz** file into a Debian package tree (*e.g.* **postfix_2.1.5-1.diff.gz**). Applying this patch turns an upstream source tree into a source tree that can be easily turned into a Debian package.

Short of downloading these files from the Debian mirrors, **APT** provides a handy means to obtain all needed files and prepare the source tree as needed. To be able to do its job, it needs to be able to read the source package indices, which are stored separately from the **Packages** files we have met before. The Debian mirror structure makes it trivial to deduce the locations, and to give **APT** access to all source packages from a given mirror, you simply duplicate the appropriate line(s) in **/etc/apt/sources.list** as shown below:

```
# standard mirror for debian binary packages
deb     ftp://ftp.debian.org/debian sarge main
# same mirror, this time for debian source packages
deb-src ftp://ftp.debian.org/debian sarge main
```

The last line identifies the source package index for *sarge*'s *main* section. The line translates to the following URI:

```
ftp://ftp.debian.org/debian/dists/sarge/main/source/Sources.gz
```

Sources files are essentially the same as Packages files and identify the source packages found in the repository along with the MD5 sums of the constituent files. You will note (and not be surprised by) the absence of an architecture reference in the URI; source packages are architecture-independent.

Following an update of the indices (apt-get update), the source packages are available with a few keystrokes. Note that root rights are only needed for the update. It is good practice to rebuild Debian packages with a normal user account!

```
~# apt-get update
~$ apt-get moo
[...]
~$ apt-get source --download-only postfix
Reading Package Lists... Done
Building Dependency Tree... Done
Need to get 2399kB of source archives.
Get:1 http://ftp.debian.org sarge/main postfix 2.1.5-1 (dsc) [844B]
Get:2 http://ftp.debian.org sarge/main postfix 2.1.5-1 (tar) [1972kB]
Get:3 http://ftp.debian.org sarge/main postfix 2.1.5-1 (diff) [426kB]
Fetched 2399kB in 0s (6501kB/s)
Download complete and in download only mode
~$ dpkg-source -x postfix_2.1.5-1.dsc
dpkg-source: extracting postfix in postfix-2.1.5
```

APT automatically downloads the files belonging to the source package you requested. dpkg-source is then called automatically to extract the package. The --download-only switch prevents automatic extraction. Also, APT does not care whether you give it the name of a source or of a binary package. In the latter case, it will automatically determine the corresponding source package and work from there. If a source package generates multiple binary packages, any of the binary packages can be given to apt-get source, as exemplified in the following:

```
~$ apt-get source --download-only postfix-tls
[...]
Download complete and in download only mode
~$ dpkg-source -x postfix_2.1.5-1.dsc
dpkg-source: extracting postfix in postfix-2.1.5
```

dpkg-source knows how to handle native and normal source packages, and will automatically take all necessary steps to leave a debianised source tree in the appropriate directory (./postfix-2.1.5 in our case). With all build dependencies satisfied, it is trivial to build the corresponding DEB file(s) from the unpacked source package. However, first, we will attempt some modifications.

Modifying the source tree

A modification to a package either affects the contents, the compilation, or the packaging. The first two of these cover most needs and shall be briefly touched upon. Any deeper changes, including changes to the packaging, are best postponed until after you read chapter 9.

Changes to the contents of a package usually involve modifications to the source code. If these modifications go beyond changing simple constants or other trivial alterations, you will possibly want to attempt the compilation at various points, before finally building the package.

Most aspects of the package building process, including the compilation, are controlled by the **debian/rules** script. In most cases, the file is a **Makefile**, whose **build** target is responsible to take all steps required to build the software. To change configuration or compilation flags, this target (and any dependent targets) need to be modified. The Unix-typical *./configure; make* sequence is frequently used by these targets. For instance:

```
~$ cat wuzzah-0.53/debian/rules
[...]
config.status: configure
  dh_testdir
  ./configure --host=$(DEB_HOST_GNU_TYPE)
    --build=$(DEB_BUILD_GNU_TYPE) \
    --prefix=/usr --mandir=$prefix/share/man \
    --infodir=${prefix}/share/info

build: build-stamp
build-stamp:  config.status
  dh_testdir
  $(MAKE)
  touch build-stamp
[...]
```

From this snippet, it should be easy to see how the configuration or compilation process can be influenced. For instance, to enable the (hypothetical) "magic" feature, you could append **--enable-magic** to the *./configure* line (which should not be changed otherwise), or if you wanted to force the use of GCC 4.0, you could modify the **make** invocation by appending CC=gcc-4.0.

It is possible to invoke any of the targets from **debian/rules** directly at any point in time. To ensure that the software can be built, you need to have its build dependencies installed. Debian distinguishes between standard build tools and tools required to build specific software; you will need to make sure you have everything installed. Fortunately, Debian provides automated methods for the task. In addition, the build process requires **root** rights at various points, but the rights are actually not used. You simply need to fake the **root** rights, which should be preferred in all cases. The **fakeroot** exists for precisely this purpose (see chapter 9.2.8):

```
~# apt-get install build-essential fakeroot
~# apt-get build-dep postfix
```

Following these two commands, everything you need to build **postfix** will be installed. If you now want to attempt the compilation of the software from the unpacked source tree, you can call the **clean** and **build** targets through **fakeroot**:

```
~$ fakeroot debian/rules clean
[...]
~$ fakeroot debian/rules build
[...]
```

If you end up building multiple packages, installing all the build dependencies will slowly fill up your system. If you prefer to keep a clean system, please consider using **debfoster** (see chapter 5.11.6), or set up **pbuilder** (see chapter 9.6) to manage isolated build environments.

Logging the changes

At this stage in the process, you could just build the binary packages from the modified source tree and be done with it. However, would then have a DEB file for **postfix** 2.1.5-1 floating around, which is not the same as the official 2.1.5-1 package. To take this to an extreme, imagine that you get hit by a bug induced by your modifications, and you faithfully report the bug to the BTS, failing to identify the changes (because you forgot). The **postfix** maintainer will be driven to distraction trying to find a bug that does not exist in 2.1.5-1.

To guard against confusion and help you identify installed software, it is highly advisable to add a record of your changes to the **changelog**. At the same time, you should augment the version number with an identifier in such a way that **APT** and **dpkg** treat the custom version as newer than the current official one, but as older than the next official release. A simple recipe is to append the string +0.local.1 to the version number. You can even replace "local" with an identifier of your choice. Also, the final digit is entirely under your control and may be used to distinguish between different local versions. For instance, 1.2-3 would become 1.2-3+0.local.1. If the package is a native package and therefore the version number does not have a Debian revision, you should append one: 1.2 becomes 1.2-0+0.local.1. Please see chapter 5.7.5 for more information.

A useful tool to edit **changelog** files is **debchange** from the **devscripts** package. Invoking it with the **--increment** option automatically creates a new **changelog** stanza with an incremented Debian revision. You will need to revert the increment and append the custom version string manually. Alternatively, the **--version** option allows the specification of the full version number to use[50]. The command **dch** is provided as an alias for **debchange**.

---

[50]http://bugs.debian.org/284658 proposes an option -I to automate this process, allowing *e.g.* dch -lcustom to automatically select the next local version number.

As every **changelog** entry has an associated responsible person, you may want to be explicit about the name and email address to be used, rather than relying on the script to discover the data from your login account automatically. This can be done by setting $DEBEMAIL. For more information, please consult the **dch** (1) manpage.

```
~$ export DEBEMAIL="martin f. krafft <madduck@debian.org>"
~$ VERSION=$(dpkg-parsechangelog | sed -ne 's,^Version: ,,p')
~$ dch --version=$VERSION+0.local.1 -- Made some local changes
~$ dpkg-parsechangelog
[...]
Version: 2.1.5-1+0.local.1
[...]
   * Made some local changes.
```

If you do not specify text describing the changes, **debchange** will invoke your editor and let you edit the **changelog** by hand. Please be more descriptive about your changes than the above example.

Building the modified package

After the desired changes have been made, it is time to produce the customised binary package(s) from the source package. The process requires the set of build dependencies to be installed, a process automated by **apt-get build-dep**. We also need **fakeroot** (see chapter 9.2.8). The **dpkg-dev** package provides the **dpkg-buildpackage** tool, which automates building source and binary packages from debianised source trees. We will call it with the **-uc** and **-us** options to avoid signing the source package and the package upload. If you own a GPG key, you may want to use it; you may have to specify the key ID to be used with the **-k** switch. We can avoid building the source package by passing the **-b** switch:

```
~# apt-get install fakeroot dpkg-dev build-essential
~# apt-get build-dep postfix
~$ dpkg-buildpackage -rfakeroot -uc -us
dpkg-buildpackage: source package is postfix
dpkg-buildpackage: source version is 2.1.5-1+0.local.1
dpkg-buildpackage: source maintainer is
  martin f. krafft <madduck@debian.org>
[...]
 dpkg-source -b postfix-2.1.5
dpkg-source: building postfix using existing
  postfix_2.1.5.orig.tar.gz
dpkg-source: building postfix
  in postfix_2.1.5-1+0.local.1.diff.gz
dpkg-source: building postfix
  in postfix_2.1.5-1+0.local.1.dsc
[...]
dpkg-deb: building package 'postfix'
```

```
in '../postfix_2.1.5-1+0.local.1_i386.deb'.
[...]
dpkg-buildpackage: binary and diff upload (original source NOT included)
```

That is all. Now the parent directory contains all the DEB files generated by the **postfix** source package, and all of them use the custom version number throughout. The packages can be installed on any Debian system with the usual tools, or made available in an APT repository. If a new official release comes around, it will replace the local version. If this is not desired, configure APT to pin the package to the custom version (see chapter 8.2.1).

Building optimised packages

If you prefer to run software optimised for your local system, **apt-build** is for you. Provided in **apt-build**, the tool inquires about your architecture and desired optimisation settings and then builds packages optimised for the local architecture. To do so, it downloads the source, configures the compiler appropriately (using wrappers to guard against packages that do not allow compiler flags to be overridden), and proceeds to build the package. In addition, it can maintain a custom APT repository, containing the optimised files, and keep it up to date.

Optimisation of software is only required in very few cases, because programmes nowadays spend most time waiting for user input, network, or hard drive data. The small number of programmes which can seriously benefit from processor optimisation (such as encoders and graphics software) usually already contain code to load subsystems specific to the local architecture. In other cases, optimisations for the most common architectures are available as separate packages from the Debian archive (such as the kernels).

As **apt-build** is trivial to use, we will just mention it here instead of discussing it in depth. An article explaining its motivation and use is available online[51].

5.9.2 Repacking packages

An alternative approach is to change the files actually installed by a DEB file to your liking, and then create a new DEB file with the modified contents. This approach is fine if the desired changes do not have to be made before or during compilation (*e.g.* if they are confined to data, configuration, or script files).

The Debian archive contains a tool that can facilitate the process: **dpkg-repack**. It was designed to simplify copying of packages from one system to another, and to restore DEB files that are not available anymore, but with a little care, it can be used to create customised versions too. For instance, the following changes

---

[51] http://julien.danjou.info/article-apt-build.html

the colour used for the binary representations used by **ipcalc** and creates a new package to encapsulate the change. Here, too, we need **fakeroot**, this time with the **--unknown-is-real** option to properly package files in **ipcalc** owned by a non-root user.

```
~# sed -i -e 's/37m/32m/' /usr/bin/ipcalc
~$ fakeroot --unknown-is-real dpkg-repack ipcalc
dpkg-deb: building package 'ipcalc' in './ipcalc_0.37-1_i386.deb'.
```

As we are dealing with binary packages only, no source package is created by this method.

You may notice a problem with the resulting DEB file: it has the same version number as the official **ipcalc** package, opening doors for confusion and other problems. Unfortunately, **dpkg-repack** does not provide a means to modify the version number. For this purpose, **debedit** has been created[52], which can transform the generated DEB file appropriately. **debedit** uses **debchange** internally, so it is a good idea to explicitly configure your full name:

```
~$ export DEBEMAIL="martin f. krafft <madduck@debian.org>"
~$ debedit ipcalc_0.37-1_i386.deb Changed colour to green.
version 0.37-1+0.local.1 of ipcalc is now available in
  ./ipcalc_0.37-1+0.local.1_i386.deb
```

Please take note that **debedit** has a few issues. While it works fine in most cases, it may just not in yours. More specifically, note that it changes binary packages (only!) and hence can break strictly versioned dependencies between binary packages generated from the same source.

5.10   Integrating non-Debian software

Despite the voluminous selection of software in the Debian archive, it is necessary at times to integrate third-party software with the Debian system. While tools like **stow** provide scalable management of software installed to **/usr/local**, keeping multiple machines in sync, or integrating the external software with the rest of the system can be a nightmare.

Three tools exist to help you integrate third party software with a Debian system. **alien** converts packages from other distributions to Debian, **checkinstall** monitors an installation process and produces a DEB file to encapsulate the installed files. Both these methods create actual Debian packages that allow the package management tools to be used as before. For the few cases where neither is applicable,

---

[52]**debedit** is not yet available in the Debian archive but should be added to the **devscripts** package some time in the future; see http://bugs.debian.org/284642.

the equivs tool can create dummy packages just for the sake of satisfying dependencies. Let us look at each of the tools in turn.

5.10.1   alien

alien can convert packages between several different package formats: Debian DEB, RedHat and LSB RPM, Stampede The Slackware package format (SLP), Slackware's GZIP Compressed Tarball (tar.gz) (TGZ), and Solaris A Unix package format (used *e.g.*by Solaris and NetBSD) (PKG). Thus, it is possible to convert, *e.g.*, RPM files to DEB files for later installation on a Debian system. Alternatively, it can simply install software provided in these package formats without explicitly converting them. Obviously, alien has its shortcomings and probably does not even cover the common ground of all the different formats completely and flawlessly. Nevertheless, it does a splendid job most of the time, and generally succeeds in mapping the dependencies perfectly (if dependencies are supported by the source format).

```
~$ alien nethack-3.4.3-1.i386.rpm
nethack_3.4.3-2_i386.deb generated
~$ dpkg --info nethack_3.4.3-2_i386.deb
 new debian package, version 2.0.
 size 1250590 bytes: control archive= 1501 bytes.
      67 bytes,     2 lines         conffiles
    1237 bytes,    26 lines         control
    1498 bytes,    22 lines         md5sums
 Package: nethack
 Version: 3.4.3-2
 Section: alien
 Priority: extra
 Architecture: i386
 Depends: libc6 (>= 2.3.2.ds1-4), libx11-6 | xlibs (>> 4.1.0),
 [...]
```

The resulting DEB file can now be installed on a Debian system using dpkg and is treated just like a normal package.

Note, however, that alien does not guarantee that a package will work properly, nor does it attempt to integrate it into the Debian system with the same care with which Debian packages are tailored. A large part of the reason why Debian packages can coexist and generally work out of the box stems from the tight guidelines specified in the Debian policy (see chapter 5.7). Packages for other distributions do not have to abide by this policy, and alien can not do anything about it. alien-generated packages are thus likely to contravene the Debian policy and may cause problems and incompatibilities with other packages. As we have seen, dpkg will prevent damage, but if problems do appear, blame alien packages before you blame anything else.

5.10.2 checkinstall

checkinstall uses installwatch to determine the set of files installed and changed by an installation process (such as make install). To be able to monitor the process, it must be started as a child to checkinstall:

```
/tmp/hello-2.1.1$ ./configure --prefix=/usr && make
[...]
/tmp/hello-2.1.1# checkinstall make install
[...]
 Done. The new package has been installed and saved to
 /tmp/hello-2.1.1/hello-2.1.1_2,1.1-1_i386.deb
```

installwatch works on the level of the dynamic linker, which allows it to be used with almost any installation programme. Even the following is possible:

```
~# checkinstall /bin/sh
[...]
~# echo Welcome, stranger... > /etc/motd
~# exit
[...]
~# dpkg --info motd_1_all.deb
 new debian package, version 2.0.
 size 712 bytes: control archive= 269 bytes.
    168 bytes,      8 lines       control
 Package: motd
 Priority: extra
 Section: checkinstall
 Installed-Size: 8
 Maintainer: martin f. krafft <madduck@debian.org>
 Architecture: all
 Version: 1
 Description: Message of the day
~# dpkg --contents motd_1_all.deb
drwxr-xr-x root/root          0 2004-12-08 17:18:49 ./
drwxr-xr-x root/root          0 2004-12-08 17:18:15 ./etc/
-rw-r--r-- root/root         21 2004-12-08 17:18:13 ./etc/motd
```

checkinstall is limited in what it can do. To be precise, the packages it creates can only install files, and checkinstall does not care where it installs them. You can overwrite files in home directories with checkinstall, among other things. The generated packages cannot modify files. If the installation routine modifies existing files, they will be part of the generated package in their entirety. A horror scenario occurs when an installation routine adds a user by modification of /etc/passwd, which is subsequently included in the package. Installation of the package causes /etc/passwd to be completely replaced, and the deinstallation of the package removes the file, breaking the system in half. The generated packages also fail to register their configuration files with **dpkg**[53], therefore paving the way for upgrades that overwrite local configuration file changes.

In the light of these problems, it is probably a good idea to avoid **checkinstall** but for the rarest cases. If you end up using it, please make sure you scrutinise the packages it creates before installing them on a production system.

5.10.3 equivs

The **equivs** programme is a tool to create empty packages whose sole purpose is the satisfaction of dependencies. For instance, you may have installed your own super-duper mail transport agent under **/usr/local** and now want to get rid of the stuff Debian installed. However, since quite a number of packages depend on **mail-transport-agent**, **dpkg** will stand in your way.

The solution is to use **equivs** to create a dummy package which provides **mail-transport-agent**. The **equivs** package provides two utilities for this purpose. One creates a Debian package control file for use by the second, which then builds the package:

```
~$ equivs-control postbote.control
```

At this point, it is necessary to amend the **postbote.control** file as desired. We will delete all fields that we do not need to let **equivs** use defaults. The final version of the file looks like this:

```
Section: misc
Priority: optional
Standards-Version: 3.5.10

Package: postbote
Version: 1.0
Maintainer: martin f. krafft <madduck@debian.org>
Provides: mail-transport-agent
Architecture: all
Copyright: /usr/share/common-licenses/Artistic
Description: dummy package for the locally installed postbote MTA
 postbote is a full-featured MTA and has been installed to
 /usr/local on the local system. This package only serves to
 make other packages depending on the mail-transport-agent
 virtual package happy.
 .
 This package has been created with equivs. It is empty.
```

---

[53]But see http://bugs.debian.org/284786!

Now **equivs** can build the package:

```
~$ equivs-build postbote.control
[...]
dpkg-deb: building package 'postbote' in '../postbote_1.0_all.deb'.
~# dpkg --install postbote_1.0_all.deb
[...]
~# apt-get remove exim4
[...]
```

With **postbote** installed, **dpkg** and APT are happy because **mail-transport-agent** is provided. It is now your responsibility to provide **/usr/sbin/sendmail**, which is often hardcoded.

Let it be said that **equivs** should be a tool of last resort. It is always preferable to turn a software into a Debian package, even if the Debian package is only to be used locally. You may want to use **checkinstall**, or read up on package creation in chapter 9 and give it a shot. A true Debian package will give you less grief in the long run, but as always: your mileage may vary.

5.11   Miscellaneous package tools

5.11.1   debsums

A large number of packages register the files they install in the **dpkg** database together with their MD5 sums. These data can be used to verify the integrity of the installed files at a later point in time. The **debsums** tool is made for exactly this purpose, and can optionally augment the database with hashes for packages that did not install them. An APT hook (see chapter 5.4.2) is provided in the package to generate missing hash sums following the installation.

It should go without saying that this is *not* an alternative for a host-based intrusion detection system or file integrity checker. The data in the **dpkg** database can be trivially changed. In fact, **debsums** even provides the functionality. Thus, **debsums** is a useful administrative tool, for instance if you make changes to files in **/usr** and forget to keep track. Even though configuration files are normally ignored, **--all** includes them and can thus help to identify files that have been changed (for backup or reconstruction purposes). **debsums** should *never* be used for security purposes.

By default, **debsums** checks all files from all installed packages, which are outside of **/etc**. The **--all** option includes **/etc**, and package names may be given on the command line to restrict the checks to those specified. With the **--changed** option, the tool identifies the locally changed files to **stdout**.

As mentioned, **debsums** can create the MD5 sums for packages that do not provide them, and enter them into **dpkg**'s database[54]. To be able to do so, **debsums** needs the DEB file that installed the package. Thus, to catch up and complete the MD5 sums for all installed packages, the following two commands can be used:

```
~# PKGS=$(debsums --list-missing)
~# apt-get install --reinstall --download-only $PKGS
[...]
~# debsums --generate=keep --deb-path=/var/cache/apt/archives $PKGS
[...]
```

The **--generate=missing** causes **debsums** to read the MD5 sums from the *.md5-sums files where available, and to extract any missing sums from the appropriate DEB file in the directory specified by **--deb-path**. If you want to keep the extracted sums and merge them into the *.md5sums files, use **--generate=keep**. On the other hand, if you want to ignore the checksums in the *.md5sums files, specify **--generate=all**. For instance, if you want to verify the integrity of the **postfix** package without trusting the locally stored **MD5** sums, you can obtain the **postfix** DEB file from a trusted source, store it in **/tmp/verify.postfix** and invoke **debsums** as follows:

```
~# debsums --generate=all --deb-path=/tmp/verify.postfix postfix
```

Please note that this approach is not a failproof verification. If the system has been compromised, **debsums** and the tools it uses could have been modified to conceal any changes. Reliable verification is only possible when **debsums** is invoked from a trusted installation, where it can be used to verify packages in a mounted Debian installation against DEB files residing on the trusted system. The following verifies the files installed by the **postfix** package on the Debian installation mounted at **/mnt** against the DEB file available in **/tmp/verify.postfix**:

```
~# debsums --generate=all --deb-path=/tmp/verify.postfix \
  --root=/mnt postfix
```

5.11.2   apt-listchanges

A package upgrade necessarily drags changes to the software onto the system. A bump in the version number of a package indicates upstream changes, possibly accompanied with changes to the packaging. An increase in the Debian revision field of the version number suggests that the packaging has changed, or that some bugs filed against the package have been fixed by the maintainer. These changes are

---

[54]The hash sums will go to *.md5sums files under **/var/lib/dpkg/info**. Since **dpkg** did not put them there, they will persist when the associated package is purged.

always documented in files under **/usr/share/doc/<package>**: changelog is provided as part of the upstream software (in most cases) and contains the changes from one version to another; **changelog.Debian**, on the other hand, only describes changes done for the Debian package, such as packaging techniques, added features and patches, or modifications to the source (*e.g.* for FHS compliance). The Debian change logs generally denote a set of changes in the upstream software with a simple note such as "New upstream release," and thereby refer the reader to the other change log file.

The more productive a system, the more important it is for its administrator to know the changes caused by an upgrade. **apt-listchanges** aims to provide a convenient mechanism for an administrator to stay up to date, providing two modes of operation. First, it can read the change logs out of a DEB file and thus give the user an idea of what has changed between the previous and the current version. The second and probably more useful mode is the automatic integration with APT. When spawned by APT, **apt-listchanges** displays the change log entries corresponding to an installation or an upgrade, sorted by urgency (see chapter 9.2.7). Thus, important changes are likely to be at the top, and less important ones follow towards the end. How convenient.

Unfortunately, **apt-listchanges** only works with the Debian change logs (which every package must provide), because there is no standardised format for upstream change log files across the software packaged in Debian; the variety of formats used by the respective authors to document the changes to their code spans multiple styles. Debian change logs, on the other hand, always have the same format, which is enforced by the package maintainer tools.

Due to this limitation, Debian developers are encouraged to provide news tidbits in the **NEWS.Debian** file, which uses a format similar to the Debian change logs. **apt-listchanges** can parse these files and display news items alongside change log entries. In fact, at the time of writing, it is likely for **apt-listchanges** to be installed by default on a Debian system to display these news files for package installation and upgrades.

In any case, a simple installation of the package integrates it with **APT** through the following entry in file **/etc/apt/apt.conf.d/20listchanges**.

```
DPkg::Pre-Install-Pkgs {
  "/usr/bin/apt-listchanges --apt || test $? -ne 10";
};
```

apt-listchanges can be configured to display only unseen news and changelog entries, which is a necessity for productive use. Furthermore, it can use a number of different front-ends to display the items, and optionally email the entries to a specifiable address. Last but not least, when invoked by APT, the user can tell **apt-listchanges** to ask for confirmation after displaying the changes. This allows for easy abortion of an upgrade progress if the administrator is not yet prepared to deal with the set of changes about to be made. All these configuration parameters may be set at installation time and later changed with **dpkg-reconfigure**, as detailed in chapter 5.8.4.

5.11.3 apt-listbugs

apt-listbugs is to bug reports what **apt-listchanges** is to change logs. The script hooks into APT just like **apt-listchanges** and retrieves reports of open bugs of packages about to be installed from the Debian bug tracking system (see chapter 10.6). After filtering all but the grave and critical bugs out of the listing, **apt-listbugs** displays the bugs and asks whether the user would like to continue the process or abort.

apt-listbugs tries hard to limit the display of bugs to the ones applicable to the version currently being installed. Nevertheless, this is obviously not always possible. Even though Debian bug reports usually contain the version number of the affected package[55], the nature of a bug makes it difficult to determine other affected versions. It is thus the administrator's job to scrutinise the bug reports. Nevertheless, grave and critical bugs are fortunately not too common.

If you find a bug which you cannot tolerate, you can prevent the installation by choosing [n] at the **apt-listbugs** prompt. In addition, the tool can also add an APT pin to the previous version to prevent future updates as well (see chapter 8.2.1). Unfortunately, pinnings are initialised during APT startup and will thus not be in effect in the same session. It makes sense to restart the APT operation after setting the pins[56]

The script currently uses the HTTP interface to the BTS[57]. The author has announced work on an LDAP interface which is likely to export additional features.

5.11.4 cron-apt

The **cron-apt** tool is designed to be invoked by **cron** to perform routine APT operations. It uses several directories below **/etc/cron-apt** for its configuration. Out of the box, the tool comes to life at a random moment between 4 and 5 o'clock to update its cache and download all upgraded packages without installing them (using the **--download-only** option to **apt-get**). This behaviour is controlled by the files in **/etc/cron-apt/action.d**. The files are executed in lexicographical order

---

[55]Only usually, since bug submitters do not always follow guidelines or are not always capable of providing the necessary information. The **reportbug** tool (see chapter 10.6.5) facilitates the process and its use should thus be popularised.

[56]At time of writing, the tool had a bug which would prevent it from adding the pin. In addition, it could cause an empty **/etc/apt/preferences** file to be produced, which prevents further APT operations (see Bug #276602). If you get caught by this, simply move **/etc/apt/preferences** out of the way.

[57]http://bugs.debian.org

and specify a single command to **apt-get** per line. Here, the call to **autoclean** minimises the space used on the partition holding **/var/cache/apt**. We can insert more commands by creating the appropriate files.

```
~$ head /etc/cron-apt/action.d/*
==> /etc/cron-apt/action.d/0-update <==
update -qq

==> /etc/cron-apt/action.d/3-download <==
autoclean -y
dist-upgrade -d -u -y
~$ echo check -y > /etc/cron-apt/action.d/99-check
```

cron-apt sends informational mail about its actions to a preconfigured address (or **root@localhost**). Most aspects of this email, including its contents, special hooks to trigger in certain situations, and logging options can be configured in the **/etc/cron-apt** directory.

The **cron-apt** tool is handy for performing downloads at times when the system is not used, making the upgraded packages available locally, and allowing the administrator to supervise the upgrade. For personal machines, it can also be used to keep up to date on security upgrades. One way to do so is to create a special **sources.list** file for the security archive and use only this during **cron-apt** invocation.

```
~# cat <<EOF > /etc/apt/sources.list.security
http://security.debian.org/debian-security sarge/updates main
EOF
~# cat <<EOF >> /etc/cron-apt/config
OPTIONS='-o Dir::Etc::SourceList=/etc/apt/sources.list.security'
EOF
~# echo upgrade -y > /etc/cron-apt/action.d/10-upgrade
```

I highly discourage the use of **cron-apt** to update packages from the main Debian archive, or its use on mission-critical servers. Even though Debian is known for its robustness and package quality, software should be upgraded under supervision to be able to take appropriate action if something unexpected happens.

5.11.5 deborphan

Especially on personal systems, the number of installed packages just keeps on growing with every month. As some packages are removed, their dependencies may remain on the system (**aptitude** can track and identify superfluous dependencies, see chapter 8). An important aspect of a secure and stable system is that the set of packages should be kept to a minimum to reduce the effects of bugs (see chapter 7).

deborphan makes use of the tight dependencies between Debian packages (dictated in part by the policy, see chapter 5.7) to identify packages that are no longer used by other packages. It does not actually check for packages not being used by users of the system.

The tool has a plethora of configuration options to allow for granular searching. By default, it only scans the **libs** and **oldlibs** categories (see chapter 5.2.1). This is similar to the approach presented in chapter 8:

```
~# deborphan
libpcre3
libgnutls11
~# deborphan | xargs dpkg --purge
[...]
```

deborphan can also scan other categories (see chapter 5.2.1), and use heuristics on filenames and package descriptions to decide on the set of packages to check for orphan status (the **--guess-*** options). For instance, to remove all dummy and transitional packages, as well as all **pike** modules (in addition to the **libs** and **oldlibs** categories), you would use:

```
~# deborphan --guess-dummy --guess-pike
```

deborphan's ability to purge removed packages and clean up their configuration files is also helpful. Obviously, the configuration files persist for a reason, so you should be careful with this command. But if you find yourself **grep**ping through **dpkg-query** output and piping to **xargs** too often, this one is for you:

```
~# deborphan --all-packages --find-config --no-show-section
exim4-base
[...]
```

orphaner works in an interative way, supporting the removal of packages that have been made redundant by the previous removal step (**deborphan** merely lists them). Furthermore, **editkeep** is a graphical front-end to **/var/lib/deborphan/keep**, which keeps a list of packages which must never be suggested for removal by **deborphan**.

5.11.6 Keeping a clean system: debfoster

debfoster attempts to help you maintain a Debian system with a small footprint. It identifies packages that exist solely to satisfy dependencies and interactively assembles a list of packages to keep installed. All packages that are not essential and not explicitly wanted are then removed. The following is a simple example:

```
~# apt-get install vim emacs21
[...]
~# debfoster

vim is keeping the following 2 packages installed:
  libgpmg1 vim-common
Keep vim? [Ynpsiuqx?], [H]elp: Y

emacs21 is keeping the following 17 packages installed:
  emacs21-bin-common emacs21-common emacsen-common libice6 libjpeg62
  libpng12-0 libsm6 libtiff4 libungif4g libx11-6 libxext6 libxmu6 libxpm4
  libxt6 xaw3dg xfree86-common xlibs-data
Keep emacs21? [Ynpsiuqx?], [H]elp: N
[...]
The following packages will be REMOVED:
  emacs21* emacs21-bin-common* emacs21-common* emacsen-common*
[...]
```

Here, debfoster identified vim and emacs21 as new packages and prompted the user what to do with them. I chose to keep vim around, and to purge emacs21. Subsequent invocations of debfoster know that I want to keep vim installed and will not bother me again.

5.11.7 Caching APT archives

APT caches its downloads for the local machine. However, if you operate multiple machines, this cache is useless as you may have to download a package multiple times, once for each machine being upgraded. Depending on the upstream link, this may be time-consuming, and system administrators generally do not like to wait for progress bars to complete.

While it is possible to share APT's cache among a bunch of machines, only one machine may access it at any time. The locking required to enforce this access policy becomes unnecessarily complicated if NFS or the like is used for sharing.

To address this shortcoming, several tools have sprung up, ranging in functionality from making a local cache properly accessible to the network, through acting as a proxy cache for Debian packages, to mirroring the entire archive.

apt-proxy

apt-proxy comes as a stand-alone HTTP server (using the Python twisted server framework) and proxies access to several APT archives, as defined in its configuration file. Packages and index files are only retrieved if not already present in the cache, otherwise, the cached version is delivered instead. apt-proxy is not a proxy to be used via $http_proxy or in the APT configuration, it is a genuine APT source.

A typical (minimal) **apt-proxy** configuration might looks like this:

```
~$ cat /etc/apt-proxy/apt-proxy-v2.conf
[...]
[debian]
backends = http://ftp.de.debian.org/debian
           http://ftp2.de.debian.org/debian

[security]
backends = http://security.debian.org/debian-security

[pdo]
backends = http://people.debian.org
[...]
```

A client can access the proxy by using the following lines in the **sources.list** file, assuming that the address of the machine running **apt-proxy** is resolvable from the machine **arakis**, and **apt-proxy** listens on its default port:

```
~$ cat <<EOF > /etc/apt/sources.list
http://arakis/debian sarge main
http://arakis/security sarge/updates main
http://arakis/pdo/~madduck/packages/stage ./
```

All parts of the URL beyond the first are appended directly to the back-end which **apt-proxy** uses. Multiple back-ends can be defined and serve as fail-overs if the first is unreachable. The back-ends can also use FTP or **rsync** (which makes little sense) instead of HTTP. Lastly, it is possible to import local **APT** caches into the proxy.

Other than **APT** and its local cache, **apt-proxy** automatically takes care of house-cleaning. Its cache cleaning policy makes its tight coupling with Debian archives apparent: cleanup is attempted once a day, as the Debian mirrors only change once a day. Packages are kept until a maximum age has been reached, but **apt-proxy** also looks at the versions and purges packages as newer versions become available.

apt-proxy has a history of being buggy and causing headaches. With version 2, a complete rewrite addressed many problems, but a large number still persist. Thus, the most sensible advice is: see if it works for you. If not, then please help fixing it, or go elsewhere. In any case, you should take proper care to ensure that access to the cache is only possibly by authorised clients.

apt-cacher

With the same goal as **apt-proxy**, **apt-cacher** takes a different approach and provides a caching proxy in the form of a CGI. It uses a separate web server, such as **apache**, and can cache any **APT** archive without requiring a configuration entry for it. The following example **sources.list** file will make this clear:

```
~$ cat <<EOF >> /etc/apt/sources.list
http://apache/apt-cacher/ftp.debian.org/debian sarge main
```

apt-cacher's configuration only specifies the cache cleaning (and access) policy, which is also tailored to APT archives. All the information pertaining to cached archives is contained in the URL used by APT. Whether this is a bug or a feature is left to you to decide. apt-cacher can limit the bandwidth used for downloads, but it does not support anything but HTTP for external archive access.

Similar to apt-proxy, apt-cacher has its share of problems. Some people cannot get it working properly, others swear by it. Try it and find out. Be aware that a simple apt-get install apt-cacher pulls in a full apache2 web server. Debian's apache2 installs a sane default configuration, but you may want to further lock it down.

squid

Quite possibly, squid is to caching proxies what apache is to web servers. Therefore, the desire may arise to use it to cache requests to Debian archives. This desire can be easily satisfied, but note that squid does not have an understanding of the policy-driven Debian archive structure (unlike apt-proxy and apt-cacher). Therefore, for optimal performance, it requires some changes to its configuration. Moreover, it is advisable to run separate instances of squid for APT and general web access caching.

Without going too much into detail, the following settings in /etc/squid/squid.conf work nicely with Debian archives. You should obviously adjust the size of the cache to your needs and capacities (all changes from the Debian defaults are highlighted):

```
~# cat /etc/squid/squid.conf
[...]
maximum_object_size 150 Mb
cache_dir aufs /var/spool/squid-apt 2048 16 256
refresh_pattern (u?deb|dsc|changes|(origtar|diff)gz)$ 14400 20% 2592000
refresh_pattern (Packages(.(gz|bz2))?|Release(.gpg)?|Sources(.(gz|bz2))?
)$ 14300 20% 14400
redirect_program /etc/squid/redirector.pl
cache_replacement_policy heap LFUDA
[...]
```

The configuration adjusts the cache size as well as the maximum object size to be stored to a value appropriate for the contents of the Debian archives. If you can, increase the cache size for longer caching. The refresh_pattern is mostly needed for tracking *testing* and *unstable*, which change very often, but the Debian mirrors do not use a consistent cache expiry policy. The file names of Debian packages do not change and are not reused, which gives us the ability to tweak the storage policy of the files. Package files are now kept at least one day, but at most 30. The index files are expected to change daily and get appropriate values. One fifth of the age is used to indicate freshness, which works nicely with the advanced cache_replacement_policy chosen.

The last addition is the use of a rewriter, which prevents **squid** from caching packages twice, should they be accessed by code- and release name interchangeably. Obviously, when the next Debian release comes around, the mapping has to be amended.

```
~# cat /etc/squid/redirector.pl
#!/usr/bin/perl -w

use strict; # (somewhat) enforce good coding style
$|=1;        # unbuffer stdout

while (<>) {
  s@sid/(main|contrib|non-free|Release.*|Contents.*)@unstable/$1@;
  s@etch/(main|contrib|non-free|Release.*|Contents.*)@testing/$1@;
  s@sarge/(main|contrib|non-free|Release.*|Contents.*)@stable/$1@;
  print;
}
```

apt-move

apt-move takes the local **APT** cache and transforms it into a Debian archive. In fact, it works for any flat collection of DEB files, and can retrieve files by itself, effectively allowing it to be used to selectively mirror entire Debian archives. In its simplest form, **apt-move** makes the local **APT** cache available in a directory exportable through any of the means **APT** understands. The target directory is controlled by $LOCALDIR in /etc/apt-move.conf. For instance:

```
~# apt-move local
[...]
~# ls -Fl /mirrors/debian
drwxr-xr-x  3 root root 21 Aug 19 20:36 dists/
drwxr-xr-x  3 root root 17 Aug 19 20:27 pool/
```

The contents of these directories are what you can expect. **apt-move** uses the files in /var/lib/apt/lists to map versions to releases to index the packages contained in the pool structure accordingly. You can automate the moving of packages to the **apt-move** repository with an **APT** hook. Since that moves the files before **dpkg** would get a chance to install them, the **apt-move** has to be changed to copy rather than move the package files:

```
~# sed -i -e 's,^COPYONLY=.*,COPYONLY=yes,' /etc/apt-move.conf
~# cat <<EOF > /etc/apt/apt.conf.d/50apt-move
DPkg::Pre-Install-Pkgs  "/usr/bin/apt-move update"; ;
EOF
```

Now the files are made available in the local archive just before APT calls **dpkg** to install the packages. If you use **--download-only**, you will have to resort to a shell script two-liner.

Another mode of operation of **apt-move** is designed to allow for partial mirroring of the official Debian archive. This method can also be combined with the first. Two variables influence the way **apt-move** mirrors:

$APTSITES

> This variable lists the hostnames of the mirrors from /etc/apt/sources.list you want to mirror, or just "/ALL/" to mirror them all.

$PKGTYPE

> Here, you can specify whether to mirror just binary packages, just the sources, or both

With the right settings in place, calling **apt-move mirror** will retrieve whatever is not yet stored locally to create a mirror according to the configuration. Only packages for the local architecture will be fetched. With **apt-move sync**, the tool only mirrors the set of packages installed locally. Both commands honour the file .exclude in the mirror's root directory (**$LOCALDIR**), which can contain file name patterns identifying parts of the archive that should not be mirrored. The syntax is that of standard shell pathname expansion (wildcards).

5.11.8   Mirroring the Debian archive: debmirror

The **debmirror** package provides a script that allows complete mirroring of the Debian archive, or just parts of it. The tool has a plethora of options to allow for the exact specification of the mirror extent. It supports various download methods, including **rsync**, which is not very useful with Debian since archive changes mainly come in the form of file name changes and new files, which **rsync** cannot deal with.

The features are best demonstrated with an example:

```
~$ debmirror --arch=i386,powerpc --section=main \
  --host=debian.ethz.ch --dist=sarge --method=rsync \
  --root=:debian /srv/mirrors/debian
[...]
```

When this call completes, you will have a genuine *sarge* mirror in /src/mirrors/ **debian**, encompassing source packages and binaries for **i386** and **powerpc**. The script only mirrors *main* and uses **rsync** to access the repository at debian.ethz.ch:: debian.

The **debmirror**(1) manpage goes into great detail about the usage of this command. Among all the information, it contains a warning that cannot be stressed enough. If you specify your home directory as the target of the mirror operation, **debmirror** will do just that: it will *replace your entire home directory* with a shiny Debian mirror, which is probably not what you want. Please be careful with the command, as it can be very destructive.

5.11.9 Enhanced queries of the package database

Two tools have survived from the days of **dselect** (see chapter 5.3.9); both focus on supporting flexible searching in the **dpkg available** database, which is more or less a relic from the old days and not used, other than by these tools. Fortunately, neither of the tools you are about to meet needs the database as both can also work with the **dpkg status** database, or the **APT** cache of **Packages** files in **/var/lib/apt/lists**.

grep-dctrl

The **grep-dctrl** package provides a bunch of interesting tools to filter information out of any file that has the general format of the Debian package control file[58], thus including **/var/lib/dpkg/status**, **/var/lib/dpkg/available** and the **Packages** and **Sources** files found in **APT** repositories.

grep-dctrl acts and feels like **grep**, except it is more versatile and treats stanzas as units, not just lines. Moreover, it can limit the search scope to a number of fields and select the fields shown for matching records in the result. For instance, to scan a local **Packages** file and print out the name and version of every package maintained by my humble self, you would use the following command:

```
~$ grep-dctrl --field=Maintainer madduck \
  --show-field=Package,Version Packages
[...]
```

A number of aliases exist to allow for simpler use of the command. **grep-status** searches **/var/lib/dpkg/status**, if no other files are given on the command line. Similarly, **grep-available** searches **/var/lib/dpkg/available**, which must be updated when the list of available packages changes (which is most easily done with **dselect**):

```
~# dselect update
```

[58]which is similar (but not identical) to Request For Comments (RFC) 822: http://www.rfc-editor.org/rfc/rfc822.txt

The tools also accept regular expressions across multiple fields and thus allow for flexible searches. To give two trivial examples, the first of the following commands returns all maintainers of packages with "alpha" or "beta" in the version number, and the second returns all packages with the word "duck" in the maintainer field:

```
~$ grep-available --no-field-names --eregex \
  --field=Version '(alpha|beta)' --show-field=Maintainer

~$ grep-available --no-field-names \
  --field=Maintainer,Description duck --show-field=Package
```

ara

The **ara** tool from the package with the same name specialises on boolean queries of the database, and features a more powerful syntax than **dpkg-dctrl**. For a detailed description of the available syntax, please consult the **ara** (1) manpage.

As the tool is way too complex for a short description, sit back and relax while the following example shows you some of the possible queries (without results). **ara** merges the two **dpkg** databases with the **APT** cache of available packages in memory and then runs queries on it. While the query itself is fast, the compilation takes a while. For single commands, that is as good as it will get. If you plan to run multiple commands in a row, consider using the interactive mode by passing the **-interactive** option:

```
~$ ara -interactive
Loaded 11519 packages (processing
''debian.ethz.ch_debian_dists_unstabl...'')
Total 15754 packages...
Welcome to ara version 1.0.7 released on 2004-12-07.
Type ? for help and Ctrl-D or #quit to exit.
& Section:net
[...]
& Section:utils and !Depends:(gnome|kde|gtk)
[...]
& Maintainer:duck and (Priority:extra or Section:net)
[...]
& /boolean.*queries/ and Priority:optional
ara ara-byte bool xara-gtk xara-gtk-byte
```

The last query shows that a graphical version of **ara** is also available. The **-byte** packages install the **Ocaml** bytecode versions of the tool instead of the compiled binaries (mainly for platforms for which **Ocaml** cannot generate binary code).

At http://ara.zapto.org, the ara database can be queries and browsed.

5.11.10 Package popularity contest

The Debian system is available from numerous places and does not require any form of registration. Therefore, once you have obtained access to a source medium, you are as independent of the Debian project as you would like to be, bound only by the licence restrictions of the individual software you install. While this independence is a great advantage over some commercial operating systems, some of which only distribute security patches in exchange for information about the installed software, it also makes it difficult for the Debian developers to adjust their priorities to meet the needs of the users in an optimal way.

To give a trivial example, it may be that almost every user chooses to install the foo package, so it would be of maximum benefit to the user community if the developers spent more time improving foo. However, the developers might not know about the popularity of foo and will not place its improvement high up on their priority list.

To address this problem, the **popularity-contest** package exists. It installs a **cron** job, which will submit the list of installed packages on the local system to a dedicated server (**popcon.debian.org**) by email once a week. On the server, the submissions are processed to compute an estimated ranking of packages by their popularity. All submissions are made anonymously, but the set of installed packages is tracked for each machine set up to submit[59]. In addition, **popularity-contest** tries to include the access times of the programmes installed by packages to allow for the generation of separate installation and usage statistics.

Officially, the Debian project uses this information mainly to select the packages to be distributed on the first Debian installation CD, which is frequently the only CD distributed at fairs or with magazines. Individually, developers are free to inspect the statistics (which are available on the Web at http://popcon.debian.org) to help them make decisions. In addition, the statistics have been used to settle disputes between developers that would otherwise have had to be solved by other comparisons of size.

Unfortunately, **popularity-contest** had to be omitted from the set of packages installed by default because of a change to the package selection mechanism at an unfortunate point in time during the release preparation. As **popularity-contest** is an invaluable tool to help the Debian project improve its system, I urge you to install it and allow it to participate in the official survey; you will help improve Debian this way.

---

[59]This is accomplished by including a unique identification number for each machine in the submission. The number is generated randomly when **popularity-contest** is installed (and stored in $MY_HOSTID in /etc/popularity-contest.conf). Note that it is impossible to completely anonymise Internet email because servers in transit add headers to messages they process, thus allowing messages to be traced to the originating machines, albeit not trivially. Nevertheless, the information contained in these headers is not used by Debian.

Using the popularity contest data

The data collected by **popularity-contest** may also be used locally. Among the primary uses is the identification of packages with software that has not been used for more than a month and could thus be considered for deinstallation if space is tight:

```
~# popularity-contest | grep '<OLD>$'
1102503722 1102503725 tnef /usr/bin/tnef <OLD>
[...]
```

Furthermore, it is trivial to use **popularity-contest** for internal census: the address to which the data are sent can be controlled with the $MAILTO variable in /etc/popularity-contest.conf. Also, $MAILFROM can be set. In **/usr/share/doc/popularity-contest/examples** you will find a number of scripts to process the submissions.

5.11.11 Purposely omitted tools

Of the immense amount of available tools, a number stuck out in a particularly negative way. Thus, they are not covered in this chapter. Instead, I list them here:

auto-apt

This tool hooks in with *e.g.* a shell and intercepts errors resulting from unknown commands. It then checks to see if *any* package in the Debian archive provides the command, and if so, employs **sudo** to install the package to honour the request. Unfortunately, three attempts to make use of this install-on-demand feature resulted in shells that would only understand the KILL signal. Your mileage may vary.

cruft

The programme is designed to identify files that do not belong on a Debian system, using exclusion lists to allow a system administrator (and package maintainers) to specify additional files that are expected to be on the system. Unfortunately, **cruft** has been actively neglected since 1999 and is unlikely to see a revival. Integrity checkers, such as **aide** or **tripwire** serve the same purpose more proactively.

5.12 Debian kernels

Many aspects of the Debian system are managed with packages; the kernel, which interfaces between a machine's hardware and the operating system and software running on it, is no exception. With support for eleven different architectures (see chapter 4.5) and multiple kernels for each architecture, the kernel package maintainers have to walk the thin line between keeping down the load on the mirrors (kernel packages are big) and providing the user with all the needed flexibility.

In the following, you will be introduced to the philosophy behind the various packages that constitute the kernel and its periphery. While we first inspect Debian's support for Linux and non-Linux kernels, the remainder of the chapter is limited to the Linux packages and identifies the different packages that exist for each kernel version. Finally, the concept of extension modules and kernel patches is brushed, and Debian's approach to using packages is briefly introduced. Chapter 8.1 augments this chapter with the juicy details of building your own kernel and module packages.

5.12.1   Kernel support

When people speak of Debian, they refer to either the Debian project or its main product, the Debian GNU/Linux operating system. Thus, the name "Debian" has been established as referring to a Linux distribution. However, Debian is more than a Linux distribution, because Debian is an operating system independent of the kernel. While Debian GNU/Linux — which identifies the Debian operating system, using GNU user-space utilities and a Linux kernel — is undoubtedly the most popular and most advanced Debian operating system available, efforts are on the way to fuse the administrative paradigms of Debian with other combinations of userspace collections and kernels. The following ports to non-Linux kernels[60] are on the way:

Debian GNU/NetBSD

For administrators in favour of the NetBSD kernel, but who are used to Debian administration, or prefer Debian administration to the **pkgsrc** system, the Debian GNU/NetBSD project is porting Debian and the GNU userland to the NetBSD kernel. While support for the **i386** architecture is already well on its way, the **alpha** architecture is in its initial stages of development. With the NetBSD kernel already at production level, Debian GNU/NetBSD is expected to be a serious alternative in productive environments.

Debian GNU/kFreeBSD

The Debian port to the FreeBSD kernel uses a complete GNU userland, a GNU C library, and a FreeBSD kernel. Debian GNU/kFreeBSD currently only supports the **i386** architecture. With the FreeBSD kernel already at production level, Debian GNU/(k)FreeBSD is expected to be a serious alternative in productive environments. Another group was previously working on a FreeBSD port with a BSD userland, but the project died due to lost interest.

[60]http://www.debian.org/ports

Debian GNU/Hurd

> Efforts to use Debian with the Hurd (the GNU operating systems, which provides most its functionality via user-space processes instead of kernel-space drivers) are in progress. Unfortunately, Hurd is still immature and development is only creeping along slowly. Debian therefore serves as the Hurd reference implementation, inviting more developers to join the Hurd project. Its productive usability is questionable at the moment.

Debian GNU/Darwin

> While non-official and hosted at SourceForge[61], the Debian GNU/Darwin port is an effort to enable the Debian way on Mac OS X "Darwin." Currently, the project is inactive; I have received no response to my inquiry, and the SourceForge usage statistics seem to suggest that the project is dead.

While the Linux kernel is a powerful kernel which sports a healthy mixture of experimental code and proven features, it is far from perfect. For normal use, the kernel performs nicely and provides the stability typically found in a Unix system. However, in advanced scenarios, mysterious kernel bugs frequently drive users up the wall. While the Linux kernel definitely enjoys a number of advantages, in certain situations, other kernels provide more robust hardware support or have technically advanced approaches to common operating system tasks, such as memory management[62].

Debian's support for kernels other than Linux means that Debian users in need of other kernels for technical or other reasons do not have to leave familiar terrain. At the same time, and as with the supported hardware architectures, Debian's kernel independence allows for unified system administration across different kernels. Especially when dealing with embedded devices and eclectic hardware, the ability to employ *e.g.* the NetBSD kernel and stay with Debian's administrative paradigms comes as a big plus.

5.12.2   Anatomy of the kernel packages

In addition to supporting different kernels, the Debian archives also contain packages encapsulating the various kernels in different versions and optimised for different architectures. The Debian kernel packages install kernels which strive to support the widest possible range of hardware, making extensive use of a kernel's module support, if applicable. Nevertheless, Debian tries to limit the modifications to the kernels it distributes to a minimum. While the Debian kernels

---

[61] http://sourceforge.net/projects/debian-darwin

[62] An interesting technical comparison of Linux and the NetBSD kernel, which is interesting especially because of its portability, may be found here: http://www.wasabisystems.com/gpl/linux.htm. Also, http://www.instinct.org/~pgl/bsd-comparison-humour.txt may contain the answers you were always searching.

differ from the vanilla kernels downloadable from the official kernel distribution point[63], included kernel patches are limited to security updates and few carefully scrutinised features have been added to allow certain packages in the Debian pool to be independent of the kernel running the system[64]. Information relevant to these Debian-specific changes can be found in **/usr/share/doc/kernel-doc-<version>/README.Debian.gz**, after installing the corresponding **kernel-doc** package (**<version>** refers to the kernel version followed by architecture and flavour, *e.g.* 2.6.8-1-k7).

In the Debian archive, kernel versions are part of the package name. Therefore, each kernel version is to be treated as a separate package, and different versions can coexist. For instance, the 2.6.8 Linux kernel for modern AMD processors comes in **kernel-image-2.6.8-1-k7**. There are four important points to note about the naming of kernel packages:

- Package naming is very Linux-centric and assumes that "kernel-image" refers to the Linux kernel. As soon as other kernels gain popularity, the naming scheme is likely to change[65].

- The version number is constrained to three components. The Linux kernel team only recently started using a fourth component with the release of the Linux kernel version 2.6.8.1. Since 2.6.8.1 obsoletes 2.6.8 and the extra digit looked like a one-time deal, the Debian kernel maintainers chose to drop the final .1. With 2.6.11, the upstream kernel developers used four component version numbers again. Debian will adapt to the new scheme as soon as the practice is well established.

- Following the version number is a number encoding the kernel image's Application Binary Interface (ABI) version. A number of compile-time options and kernel configuration parameters change the kernel's ABI and render modules incompatible. Thus, the ABI version is encoded in the package name to force modules to be recompiled.

- The last part of the name identifies the sub-architecture for which the kernel was configured and optimised. It is essential for the architecture of a kernel package to be compatible to the architecture of the target system, or else the system will be unbootable. For Linux on the **i386** architecture, the available kernel package architectures are:

---

[63] http://kernel.org
[64] To give an example, the Debian 2.4 kernel series started to include IPsec support, backported from 2.5 from 2.4.20 onwards. This was done to enable users building on the stability of the 2.4 kernel series to use the range of IPsec utilities provided in the package archive.
[65] http://debian.linuxwiki.de/DebianKernel/Plan

386

Compatibility kernels, which can run on *any* x86-compatible architecture (including AMD, Intel, Transmeta, Cyrix, and others). Given the problems with the **80386** processor series (see chapter 4.5.1), this kernel may drop support for **80386** and require **80486** compatibility. It will then be renamed accordingly. In *sarge*, the **80386** processor is supported.

586-tsc

Only with the 2.4 kernel series, **586-tsc** identify packages configured for the Intel Pentium Classic, which was the first to feature the TimeStamp Counter (TSC) register.

686

These kernels are designed to be run on all 32 bit Intel processors following the Pentium. For the 2.6 kernel series, this includes the Pentium Classic. With 2.4 kernels, the **586-tsc** package must be used instead.

k6

AMD's older K6 processor series is supported by these kernel packages.

k7

All newer AMD 32 bit processors are handled by the kernels provided in these packages.

In addition, several kernels come in different flavours. For instance, the **686** and **k7** kernels do not support Symmetric Multi-Processing (SMP). Instead, the **686-smp** and **k7-smp** flavours provide this functionality and should be used when multiple processors are installed.

The upstream kernel version is part of the kernel package name. Thus, upgrading a kernel to the next upstream version requires the installation of a new package, since **APT** cannot infer the upgrade automatically. For simplicity, a number of meta packages (also known as dummy packages) allow **APT** to upgrade a kernel image when a new kernel enters the Debian archive simply by depending on the appropriate packages:

```
~$ dpkg-query --print-avail kernel-image-2.6-k7
Package: kernel-image-2.6-k7
[...]
Version: 2.6.8-1
Depends: kernel-image-2.6.8-1-k7
[...]
```

Thus, when a new upstream kernel is published and the corresponding meta package installed, **APT** will upgrade the meta package to the next version and thereby pull in the new kernel package to satisfy the dependency. These meta packages are available for every plausible combination of kernel series, architecture optimisation, and flavour:

kernel-image-2.4-386
: The latest 2.4 kernel for the **x86** architecture, without particular optimisations.

kernel-image-2.4-586tsc
: The latest 2.4 kernel, optimised for Pentium Classic (which was the first to feature the TSC register).

kernel-image-2.4-686
: The latest 2.4 kernel, optimised for all Pentium processors after the first generation.

kernel-image-2.4-686-smp
: Ditto, with multiprocessor support.

kernel-image-2.4-k6
: The latest 2.4 kernel, optimised for AMD's K6 processors.

kernel-image-2.4-k7
: The latest 2.4 kernel, optimised for AMD's Athlon and Duron processor series.

kernel-image-2.4-k7-smp
: Ditto, with multiprocessor support.

kernel-image-2.6-386
: The latest 2.6 kernel for the **x86** architecture, without particular optimisations.

kernel-image-2.6-686
: The latest 2.6 kernel, optimised for all Pentium processors after the first generation.

kernel-image-2.6-686-smp
: Ditto, with multiprocessor support.

kernel-image-2.6-k7
: The latest 2.6 kernel, optimised for AMD's Athlon and Duron processor series.

kernel-image-2.6-k7-smp
: Ditto, with multiprocessor support.

Each of these packages simply depends on the corresponding kernel package in its highest version. When a new kernel is uploaded to the archive, a new meta package is uploaded as well, with a modified **Depends** field. Therefore, an APT upgrade will pull in the new kernel package to fulfill the meta package's dependency. The old kernel image is left in place and can be manually deleted as soon as the new kernel's operation is verified. Please note that the meta packages have only been available since *sarge*. Furthermore, these packages do not exist for all hardware architectures. Therefore, users of *woody* or an earlier release, or users of a hardware architecture still without these meta packages will have to manually obtain the latest kernel image, should it be desirable. Alternatively, you could build your own kernel, as Debian makes building kernels very easy (see chapter 8.1).

In contrast to other Linux distributions, Debian kernels do not include every possible patch in an attempt to support the newest hardware. While this approach has the advantage of keeping the kernel clean and stable, and facilitates locating the source of a problem should one occur, it obviously drags along the disadvantage that the Debian kernels do not support as wide a variety of hardware as other (mostly commercial) Linux flavours. Fortunately, new hardware device drivers make it into the kernel, usually within a relatively short time period, so that support for new hardware will generally exist in the latest Debian kernel a couple of weeks later.

The Debian kernels places four files into the **/boot** directory:

vmlinuz-<version>
> The binary kernel.

initrd.img-<version>
> The ramdisk to be loaded during the initial boot phase to make drivers available needed to access the local installation.

System.map-<version>
> The translation map between memory addresses and the corresponding kernel functions, to allow debug messages to be more verbose.

config-<version>
> The kernel configuration file, included for reference purposes.

Debian's kernels aim to be as broad as possible. For workstation machines, they are usually more than adequate and deal appropriately with changing hardware and varying requirements of the box. Since most kernel features are enabled as modules rather than compiled into the box, various utilities (*e.g.* hotplug and discover) can load necessary components on demand. The kernel images are also widely used in server systems, although it may be worth considering compiling custom kernels based on the requirements. I usually compile my own kernels for server systems to be able to disable kernel modules (which are a security hazard). This approach automatically gets rid of the initial ramdisk used by the Debian kernels and thereby eliminates one point of frequent failure. In addition, third-party modules are notoriously difficult to integrate with initial ramdisks, or the integration can be easily forgotten.

Kernel modules and initial ramdisks

Almost every kernel feature and device driver is built as a module, if appropriate for the host architecture. These modules are installed under /lib/modules/<version> with the same layout as the upstream kernel. Modules which are required to boot and mount the root filesystem are also written into a compressed filesystem image (cramfs) at installation time: /boot/initrd.img-<version>. The administrator can freely influence the building of this ramdisk image with the configuration files in /etc/mkinitrd, provided by the initrd-tools package. This package is pulled in when a Debian kernel package is installed. Since the initial ramdisk is created during the kernel image's configuration phase, it will be necessary to install initrd-tools separately and in advance to be able to change its settings. Alternatively, you can reconfigure the kernel image after making the desired changes:

```
~# editor /etc/mkinitrd/mkinitrd.conf
[...]
~# dpkg-reconfigure kernel-image-2.6.8-1-k7
[...]
```

Configuration specific to mkinitrd, the programme which creates the filesystem image, may be set in /etc/mkinitrd/mkinitrd.conf. For instance, when space is tight, it may be worthwhile setting $MODULES to "dep" in the configuration file, which will cause mkinitrd consult modprobe to figure out the minimum set of modules to include. If you are using non-standard filesystems or disk controllers, it is usually a good idea to specify these in /etc/mkinitrd/modules see modules (5)) just to be sure. The manual pages mkinitrd.conf (5) and mkinitrd (8) give more information, and chapter 8.1.1 shows how initial ramdisks can be created and inspected for Debian kernels.

The initial ramdisk generated by the above procedure is a filesystem contained in a single file. With proper support from the kernel (all Debian stock kernels provide cramfs support), it can be mounted and inspected locally. If mkinitrd has been told not to include all modules, this is a handy way to ensure that all modules necessary to bring up the root filesystem are included. For instance, the following allows to check the modules included on the initial ramdisk of the custom kernel package kernel-image-2.6.8-arakis:

```
~# dpkg --install kernel-image-2.6.8-arakis
[...]
~# mount -o ro,loop /boot/initrd.img-2.6.8-arakis /mnt
~# cd /mnt
/mnt# ls -F
bin/    dev2/   lib/            loadmodules  sbin/     sys/    var/
bin2/   devfs/  linuxrc*        mnt/         script    tmp/
dev/    etc/    linuxrc.conf    proc/        scripts/  usr/
/mnt# ls -F lib/modules/2.6.8-arakis
```

```
initrd/          modules.dep         modules.pcimap
kernel/          modules.ieee1394map modules.symbols
modules.alias    modules.inputmap    modules.usbmap
modules.ccwmap   modules.isapnpmap
/mnt# ls -F lib/modules/2.6.8-arakis/kernel/security
capability.ko  commoncap.ko  root_plug.ko  seclvl.ko
```

Integration with bootloaders

After unpacking the kernel image package, **dpkg** integrates the kernel into the local system based on the settings in **/etc/kernel-img.conf**. Settings in that file include where the kernel images are installed, whether the system should maintain canonical links to the current and previous kernel binary, and how the bootloader is told of the new kernel.

By default, the kernel packages maintain a pair of symlinks to the current and previous kernel binary. The exact location of these symlinks can be controlled via **/etc/kernel-img.conf**, the default is the root directory / on most systems. **/vmlinuz** points to the current kernel binary in **/boot**. When a newer kernel image is installed, the link is renamed to **/vmlinuz.old** and **/vmlinuz** is created to point to the newly installed kernel binary.

Whether these links are necessary or useful depends largely on the bootloader employed. Debian provides no automatic management utility for the **Lilo** configuration file **/etc/lilo.conf**. Therefore, it is convenient to tell **Lilo** about **/vmlinuz** and **/vmlinuz.old** and let the kernel packages maintain the links. This is the default in Debian. The following shows the suggested contents of **/etc/kernel-img.conf** for a **Lilo**-based system. The second option, **links_in_boot** causes the kernel packages to place these links into **/boot**, which I recommend in order to keep the root directory tidy. If you choose to use this option, please make sure you update **/etc/lilo.conf** appropriately, followed by an invocation of **lilo**, or to run **update-grub** once manually. You may also want to delete the symlinks in the root directory afterwards.

```
do_symlinks = yes
links_in_boot = yes
do_bootloader = yes
```

Debian's **Grub** package provides **update-grub**, which can take over management of the **Grub** configuration file **/boot/grub/menu.lst**[66]. Therefore, the symlinks are not really necessary. The following configuration options are sensible for a system using **Grub**:

```
do_symlinks = no
do_bootloader = no
```

[66]This file may actually be in **/boot/boot/grub/menu.lst**. If you are a purist like me, you may want to move **/boot/boot/grub** to **/boot/grub** and create a symlink from **/boot** to **/boot/boot**: **ln -s . /boot/boot**

```
do_initrd = yes
postinst_hook = /sbin/update-grub
postrm_hook  = /sbin/update-grub
```

When installing the kernel image, you will be instructed to tell your bootloader about the initial ramdisk ("initrd"), which the Debian kernel uses. The **grub-update** script automatically takes care of the **initrd** option, therefore the above configuration includes the **do_initrd = yes** instruction to prevent the warning.

5.12.3   Sources, headers, and documentation

Conscious of systems with tight space requirements, Debian separates the files related to the operating system kernel into several packages. Besides the kernel image packages, there are also separate packages for the kernel sources, the headers, and the documentation. The Debian Wiki contains valuable resources about Debian's kernel packaging[67].

For each kernel version, there is a **kernel-source-<version>** package. Kernel images are packaged for each combination of kernel version, architecture, and flavour, but all use the same kernel source package, of which only one exists for each upstream kernel version. Each kernel source package installs the appropriate **bzip2-**compressed tarballs into **/usr/src**. The tarball contains the exact source code used to compile the Debian kernels, including the modifications that distinguish the Debian kernel from the upstream version. Having a tarball instead of an unpacked source tree fulfills two functions: first, the tarball greatly reduces the size requirement on the **/usr** partition, and second, it suggests to users, who need to use the kernel source, to unpack it to their own home directory. The kernel source tree is not very usable without write access to the directories (*e.g.* for object files), and therefore there is little point in providing an unpacked source tree in **/usr/src**.

Next to the **kernel-source-<version>** packages, you may find **kernel-tree-<version>** packages. These packages exist to prevent version discrepancies between kernel images and corresponding kernel sources packages in the fast-moving *unstable* archive. They serve no purpose outside of the Debian build and archive infrastructure (unless you want to build kernels with older Debian revisions, in which case you could also obtain the appropriate kernel source package from **snapshot.debian.org**). More information about the purpose and functioning of kernel tree packages is available online[68].

Before a kernel source tree can be compiled, it has to be configured. As part of the configuration, the user can choose features to enable and select the target processor type to allow for processor-specific optimisations to be put in place.

---

[67] http://wiki.debian.net/?Kernel
[68] http://wiki.debian.net/?DebianKernelTree

After the configuration, the header files found in the tree encapsulate all choices made; the source files are not modified.

As we shall see in chapter 8.1.3, additional kernel modules can be easily built for any Debian package outside of the actual kernel source tree, needing only the headers that correspond to the running kernel. To make this possible, the Debian archive provides a separate **kernel-headers-<version>** package for each kernel image it contains, to encapsulate the kernel configuration specific to the architecture and processor type used. When unpacked, the headers are installed in **/usr/src/kernel-headers-<version>**. It is the administrator's job to provide the **/usr/src/linux** symlink to one of these **kernel-headers-*** directories, if desired.

Using the appropriate kernel headers package, it is possible to build kernel modules to work with the corresponding kernel image without having to compile the kernel itself. The kernel source packages cannot be used for this purpose as the kernel trees they contain have not been configured. If you are building your own kernel from the kernel sources (see chapter 8.1), you can build any additional modules as part of the process (see chapter 8.1.3); if you are using a pre-packaged kernel image, you need the according kernel headers package to be able to build modules (see chapter 8.1.3).

Note that the kernel header files from the **kernel-header-<version>** packages are not supposed to be used when developing user-space software using kernel interfaces. For user space software, it is of utmost importance to use the same kernel headers which were used to compile the C library **libc6**[69]. These headers, which populate **/usr/include**, are provided in the **linux-kernel-headers** package.

The kernel documentation (everything under the **Documentation** directory of the kernel source) is available from the **kernel-doc-<version>** packages, which installs the files to the appropriate subdirectory of **/usr/share/doc**. The documentation has consequently been removed from the kernel source packages to conserve space on systems that only need the sources installed.

5.12.4 Kernel modules and patches

The Debian kernel packages provide the upstream kernel with a small number of Debian-specific modifications and bug fixes. Additional functionality is contained in separate packages and comes in one of three forms: precompiled kernel modules, source code for kernel modules, and kernel patches. Only the most popular kernel module extensions, such as the PCMCIA modules[70] or the Advanced

---

[69]Information on this topic may be obtained from the elaborate thread summarised here: http://www.kerneltraffic.org/kernel-traffic/kt20000814_80.html#4, and from /usr/share/doc/libc6/README.Debian.gz

[70]Debian provides two separate module package families for PCMCIA on the 2.4 kernel series: pcmcia-modules-<version> provide the mature drivers by the Linux Card Services project (http://pcmcia-cs.sourceforge.net); in kernel-pcmcia-modules-<version> are the kernel's own drivers.

Linux Sound Architecture (ALSA) drivers, are provided as pre-compiled modules for the available kernel images. For instance, **alsa-modules-2.4.27-2-k7** contains the ALSA drivers for the 2.4.27-2-k7 kernel, which it installs in the a directory below **/lib/modules/2.4.27-2-k7** for direct integration with the running kernel. At time of writing, no precompiled modules existed for the 2.6 kernel series in the official archive as most modules are available in the kernel (including PCMCIA and ALSA drivers).

Drivers developed separately from the kernel are usually provided in module source packages. These modules are provided by separate projects and are not found in the vanilla kernel sources available at **kernel.org**. For instance, **openafs-modules-source** contains the source code to build the modules needed to provide the AFS filesystem for a specific kernel version. Chapter 8.1 uncovers the details and shows how to create module packages from such sources. Generally, only the kernel headers should be needed to compile kernel modules. If a kernel module source package insists on the kernel sources, it is almost certainly a bug.

Debian distributes a number of kernel patches to allow a user to individually configure a kernel to meet certain needs. These patches come as regular Debian packages and are designed to integrate with **make-kpkg** to make building of modified kernels accessible via a single command. Crefmake-kpkg will explain how to do that. Kernel patch packages allow for a multitude of kernel customisations. For instance, with **kernel-patch-openmosix**, the Debian kernel can be easily turned into an OpenMosix-compatible kernel, and **kernel-patch-redhat** turns a Debian kernel into the RedHat kernel of the same version, including all patches that Red-Hat chose to apply to their kernel. The differences between the Debian kernel and its vanilla counterpart are also encapsulated for each version. In addition, Debian kernel patches have the ability to "unpatch" themselves. Therefore, with the help of **kernel-patch-debian-2.6.8**, a kernel source package can be used to obtain the pristine upstream kernel source code (by example of the 2.6.8 kernel). The presence and absence of the Debian revision in the output indicates whether the source tree corresponds to the Debian or the upstream kernel.

```
~# apt-get install kernel-source-2.6.8
~# apt-get install kernel-patch-debian-2.6.8
~$ tar xjf /usr/src/kernel-source-2.6.8.tar.bz2
~$ cd kernel-source-2.6.8
~/kernel-source-2.6.8$ cat version.Debian
2.6.8-1
~/kernel-source-2.6.8$ /usr/src/kernel-patches/all/2.6.8/unpatch/debian
~/kernel-source-2.6.8$ cat version.Debian
2.6.8
~/kernel-source-2.6.8$ /usr/src/kernel-patches/all/2.6.8/apply/debian
```

Having two separate packages allows the administrator to choose either one. More information is available here: **http://pcmcia-cs.sourceforge.net/ftp/README-2.4** . In the 2.6 kernel series, the Card Services drivers have been obsoleted by the kernel drivers.

```
~/kernel-source-2.6.8$ cat version.Debian
2.6.8-1
```

Obviously, the application of a kernel patch requires the compilation of the entire kernel[71], which is conveniently handled by **make-kpkg** (see chapter 8.1). **make-kpkg** can be told to automatically patch and unpatch a kernel source tree, so that a single tree can be used to create packages for different variations of the kernel.

---

[71]The 2.6 kernel series actually allows the compilation of modules independently of the rest of the kernel. Thus, if a patch provides a new device driver, that driver can be compiled as a module without recompiling the rest of the kernel. As of today, no Debian methods exist to encapsulate this functionality beyond the recompilation of the entire tree.

6

Debian system administration

rm -rf has Super Cow powers too.
— Barry deFreese

Beyond software installation management, which is the domain of the Debian package management system (see chapter 5), a Debian system can be used just like any other Linux system. Nevertheless, over the years, many useful system administration tools have been developed specifically for, and in the spirit of Debian. These tools are available under the terms of the DFSG (see appendix F) and constitute the topics of this chapter.

First, we will inspect a number of utilities that are primarily used by other tools, but which come in handy by themselves to those that know how they work. Apart from putting these utilities to work, it is a good idea to understand their concepts as they influence the way Debian systems are managed.

Following the fundamentals, we will learn Debian's approach to common system administration tasks: user management, system initialisation, automation, device management, log files, network configuration. The chapter ends with a short description of a couple of one-stop integrated management tools, and a number of pointers to invaluable resources.

6.1   Fundamentals

True to the Unix philosophy, Debian makes use of the little tools and concepts available on a Unix system, rather than providing its own approaches and reinventing the wheel. At certain times in the project's past, however, some of those wheels had not been invented, and Debian provided the reference implementations, or invented concepts to provide flexible and robust solutions to common challenges in system administration.

The concepts and tools are integral to the Debian system, and a prerequisite for anyone seriously considering managing a Debian system. They are the essential building blocks of the Debian operating system, just like the standard Unix tools are the building blocks of any Unix-based operating system.

6.1.1   Using directories instead of configuration files

One of the qualities of a Unix system is its clear-text configuration files. Often, a single file controls most aspects of a programme or a server. While this approach is favoured by many administrators, it is a nightmare when software needs to modify these files automatically. Debian does not provide a central configuration system (see chapter 5.8), any configuration changes put in place during package installation are carried out by the packages themselves; this is deemed acceptable, since the maintainer controls both the configuration file as installed by the package, as well as the script making any modifications.

Problems start arising when one package needs to make changes in the configuration domain of another package. This situation arises, *e.g.* when a package registers the software it provides with a daemon process that comes from another package. cron is a typical example. Numerous packages provide jobs to be run regularly for cleanup or maintenance purposes, and use cron to schedule them. If these packages were to just write their jobs to cron's main configuration file (/etc/crontab), imagine all the things that could go wrong as multiple packages edited the same file, or if you opened the file in an editor, edited it, installed a new package in another window, and only then saved and closed the editor.

To provide increased manageability for both the administrator and the package maintainers, the Debian system uses directories to augment configuration files where appropriate. For instance, it does not matter whether you register a job with **cron** by appending a line to **/etc/crontab**, or by dropping a file containing the line into **/etc/cron.d**, **cron** will just augment **/etc/crontab** with all the files in the directory and use the result. On a Debian system, the same goes for other tools, like **APT**, **apache**, and many others. The advantage here is that a package can drop a file into these directories and let **dpkg** handle overwrite protection and configuration file handling. While the use of this kind of directory is no longer specific to Debian, the Debian system was the first to introduce the technique and make it popular.

To accomodate the special files needed for configuration handling, as well as backup and temporary files used (and often left) by editors, only files with names made up of alphanumeric characters, the dash ('-') and the underscore('_') are considered (*e.g.* foo.dpkg-old and foo˜ are ignored). Furthermore, the convention is that packages install files named after themselves, and that the administrator should use a **local-** prefix for locally provided files.

So much for pure configuration files. Staying with **cron**, you may have noticed directories such as **/etc/cron.daily** on your system. It contains standard executables which are installed by packages based on the aforementioned rules. The idea here is that by installing a script to this directory, a package simply registers its request to have the script run once a day, rather than having to write the script somewhere else and worry about, or be limited to, the configuration syntax of **cron**. **cron** replacements can thus honour these directories as well.

The same goes for the network configuration system, which provides similar directories for scripts to be run after a connection has been established. This is discussed at length in chapter 6.8.1.

Directories like **cron.daily** are not magical in any way. In fact, if you look into **/etc/crontab**, a single line is responsible for this behaviour (slightly abbreviated):

```
~$ grep '^[[:digit:]]' /etc/crontab
17 *  *  *  *  root  run-parts --report /etc/cron.hourly
25 6  *  *  *  root  run-parts --report /etc/cron.daily
47 6  *  *  7  root  run-parts --report /etc/cron.weekly
52 6  1  *  *  root  run-parts --report /etc/cron.monthly
```

The core of this approach, and one of the most useful inventions of the Debian system, is **run-parts**. The programme simply reads a directory and executes all the executable scripts in the directory that abide by the naming scheme mentioned earlier (ignoring temporary files). With the **--test** option, it can be told to merely print the files it would execute, and by specifying **--list**, you can list any files, not just executables. This list can then be used for anything apart from execution:

```
~$ touch /etc/cron.daily/foo /etc/cron.daily/bar.dpkg-old
~$ chmod a+x /etc/cron.daily/bar.dpkg-old
~$ run-parts --list /etc/cron.daily | xargs wc -c
```

```
[...]
   0 /etc/cron.daily/foo
[...]
2571 /etc/cron.daily/standard
1307 /etc/cron.daily/sysklogd
```

Even though not all tools actually use **run-parts** to scan directories, it is commonly accepted that they should implement the same behaviour. Thus, **run-parts**' behaviour is a major part of Debian's configuration file handling strategies, and one of the most important aspects of system administration. To work with Debian's configuration paradigms effectively, you will need to internalise **run-parts**' functionality.

6.1.2   Overriding permissions

The Debian developers, assisted by the policy (see chapter 5.7) ensure that files distributed in packages from the Debian archive install with sane ownerships and permissions. At times, however, a local policy may require some files to have different owners or permissions. A somewhat antiquated but still pertinent example is the **/bin/su** group, which can be set to **wheel** along with **4754** permissions on the binary[1] to allow only members of the **wheel** group to use that file. However, whenever **login**, the package containing **/bin/su** is updated, the changes are lost:

```
~# chgrp wheel /bin/su
~# chmod o= /bin/su
~# apt-get install --reinstall login
[...]
~# ls -Fl /bin/su
-rwsr-xr-x  1 root root 23416 Sep  8 05:13 /bin/su*
```

Debian provides the **dpkg-statoverride** programme to allow the administrator to tell **dpkg** about special ownership and permission requirements for files under **dpkg** control. On upgrading, **dpkg** will honour any requests made via **dpkg-statoverride** appropriately. To tell **dpkg-statoverride** to immediately implement the proper permission settings, use the **--update** flag:

```
~# addgroup wheel
~# dpkg-statoverride --update --add root wheel 4754 /bin/su
~# ls -Fl /bin/su
-rwsr-xr--  1 root wheel 23416 Sep  8 05:13 /bin/su*
~# apt-get install --reinstall login
[...]
~# ls -Fl /bin/su
-rwsr-xr--  1 root wheel 23416 Sep  8 05:13 /bin/su*
```

[1]There is no point in making it unreadable by others as the binary is freely available in the Debian package anyway. Please see section 10.9 of the Debian policy.

6.1.3   Overriding files

dpkg-divert is a tool that can transparently rename files installed by dpkg so that dpkg subsequently uses the new location. It is used by packages which are designed to override each other's functionality but can also be used by the system administrator. For instance, the postfix package installs the postfix mail transport agent without support for TLS. If TLS support is desirable, the postfix-tls package can be installed. The package provides a number of alternate files but reuses most of the contents of the postfix package. In the following, note the existence of two smtp files (one with an extension) and the package association of the listed files:

```
~$ ls -F /usr/lib/postfix/smtpd
/usr/lib/postfix/smtpd*  /usr/lib/postfix/smtpd.postfix*
~$ dpkg --search /usr/lib/postfix/smtpd
diversion by postfix-tls from: /usr/lib/postfix/smtpd
diversion by postfix-tls to: /usr/lib/postfix/smtpd.postfix
postfix, postfix-tls: /usr/lib/postfix/smtpd
```

For dpkg's purposes, both packages own the smtpd file, but it also knows that the postfix-tls package has diverted the version installed by postfix. The important point is that when dpkg installs an upgraded postfix package, it knows that the new smtpd file should be written to smtpd.postfix; it does not overwrite the actual smtpd file, which belongs to the postfix-tls package[2].

The system administrator can make use of diversions to replace files installed by dpkg with custom versions, without running the risk of having these custom versions overwritten on an upgrade. Let us assume you want to provide a customised version of /usr/share/misc/file/magic, a database used for file type identification by libmagic1. The following call to dpkg-divert will do the trick; the --rename switch causes the file to be renamed automatically.

```
~# ls -F /usr/share/misc/file
magic  magic.mgc  magic.mime  magic.mime.mgc
~# dpkg-divert --add --rename /usr/share/misc/file/magic
Adding 'local diversion of /usr/share/misc/file/magic to
  /usr/share/misc/file/magic.distrib'
~# ln -s /etc/file/magic /usr/share/misc/file
~# ls -F /usr/share/misc/file
magic@  magic.distrib  magic.mgc  magic.mime  magic.mime.mgc
```

When dpkg is about to write a file that is diverted locally, it uses the file's "true name" instead: the name used for the diverted file. If libmagic1 is upgraded (or any other package) wants to write the magic file, dpkg makes sure that magic.distrib is used instead. It is possible to override the file name used in the diversion with the

---

[2]The exact behaviour is that if a package foo diverts a file bar, dpkg will only allow foo to write to the location of the original bar file. If any other package writes to the file, the access is diverted.

--divert option. In the following I use the **echo** commands to simulate changes to the files.

```
~# dpkg-divert --truename /usr/share/misc/file/magic
/usr/share/misc/file/magic.distrib
~# echo >> /usr/share/misc/file/magic
~# echo >> /usr/share/misc/file/magic.distrib
~# md5sum magic magic.distrib
68b329da9893e34099c7d8ad5cb9c940  magic
dd00e70107c9dc17e7fd97083b3a8c4f  magic.distrib
~# apt-get install --reinstall file
[...]
~# md5sum magic magic.distrib
68b329da9893e34099c7d8ad5cb9c940  magic
4daec1aa76b728a09b47c7ddaa6b5a69  magic.distrib
```

dpkg keeps a record of the diversions registered through **dpkg-divert**. As shown above, it also intersperses this information with the output of commands like **dpkg --listfiles** and **dpkg --search**:

```
~# dpkg-divert --list \*
local diversion of /usr/share/misc/file/magic to
  /usr/share/misc/file/magic.distrib
[...]
```

It is a good idea to keep track of which files have been diverted for what reasons. When the diversion is no longer needed, it should be removed. **dpkg-divert** can be told to restore the original file name with the **--rename** switch.

```
~#  dpkg-divert --remove --rename /usr/share/misc/file/magic
Removing 'local diversion of /usr/share/misc/file/magic to
  /usr/share/misc/file/magic.distrib'
~# ls -F /usr/share/misc/file
magic  magic.mgc  magic.mime  magic.mime.mgc
```

As a final note, be aware that diversion of configuration files can lead to subtle problems. Even though a configuration file can be diverted in theory, the diversions might bite with **dpkg**'s configuration file handling. Of course, your mileage may vary.

6.1.4 The alternatives system

One of the beauties of a Unix system is the tremendous amount of choices for each kind of application. You can take your pick between about a forty mail user agents and maybe a hundred text editors, and all these programmes will happily coexist to give each user the possibility to run their preferred application. The flexibility functionality that the huge selection of interchangeable software provides makes it extraordinarily difficult for programmes to decide which other programmes to use. For example, if a software needs a text editor for its operations, it could just force **emacs** onto the system via a dependency, but the administrator or the system's users may not want **emacs** or may not know how to use it.

Similar to virtual packages (see chapter 5.7.3), the Debian alternatives system allows the administrator to select a default out of a set of programmes that provide the same functionality. To stay with the example of the text editor, Debian systems provide **/usr/bin/editor**, and every package providing a text editor registers with the alternatives system as a provider of the functionality expected from **/usr/bin/editor**. Now, other software can rely on **/usr/bin/editor** to invoke a text editor, but the decision which editor is to be used is placed in the hands of the administrator. In addition, secondary files (such as the programme's manpage) are handled automatically.

Debian implements alternatives with double indirection via symlinks. **/usr/bin/ editor** is a symlink to **/etc/alternatives/editor**, which in turn is a symlink to the editor executable the administrator chose as the default. Obviously, **/usr/bin/editor** could point to that executable directly, but by Debian policy, aspects of the system configurable by the administrator must reside under **/etc**.

The programme to configure the alternatives system is **update-alternatives**, which is also used by the package management tools for registration of alternatives. The system administrator can register the choice for default interactively or at the command line with the **--config** and **--set** options. The **--list** option displays the possible choices, and **--display** prints the current settings:

```
~# update-alternatives --display editor
editor - status is auto.
 link currently points to /usr/bin/vim
/usr/bin/vim - priority 120
 slave editor.1.gz: /usr/share/man/man1/vim.1.gz
/bin/ed - priority -100
 slave editor.1.gz: /usr/share/man/man1/ed.1.gz
Current 'best' version is /usr/bin/vim.
~# readlink -f /usr/bin/editor
/usr/bin/vim
~# update-alternatives --set editor /bin/ed
Using '/bin/ed' to provide 'editor'.
~# update-alternatives --display editor
editor - status is manual.
 link currently points to /bin/ed
[...]
~# readlink -f /usr/bin/editor
/bin/ed
```

The alternative system supports two modes of operation for each link: links that were explicitly configured by the administrator are in the manual state, while those that have not been changed are in the automatic state. In the automatic state, the alternatives system uses priorities to determine the best candidate for any given purpose. Where necessary, the priority value is governed by the policy. To restore a manually configured link to its automatic state, you can again invoke **update-alternatives**:

```
~# update-alternatives --auto editor
~# update-alternatives --display editor
editor - status is auto.
 link currently points to /usr/bin/vim
update-alternatives --auto editor
~# update-alternatives --display editor
editor - status is auto.
 link currently points to /usr/bin/vim
update-alternatives --auto editor
~# update-alternatives --display editor
editor - status is auto.
 link currently points to /usr/bin/vim
[...]
```

Finally, it is possible to add your own entries to the alternatives link. For instance, assuming you compiled your own X terminal emulator and installed it to **/usr/local**, the following will make sure that **/usr/bin/x-terminal-emulator** invokes it. Note how the command also slaves the manpage so that a user may call **man x-terminal-emulator** and be presented with the manpage corresponding to the terminal **x-terminal-emulator** invokes.

```
~# update-alternatives --install /usr/bin/x-terminal-emulator \
  x-terminal-emulator /usr/local/bin/myterm 1000 \
  --slave /usr/share/man/man1/x-terminal-emulator.1.gz \
  x-terminal-emulator.1.gz /usr/local/man/man1/myterm.1.gz
~# update-alternatives --auto x-terminal-emulator
~# readlink -f /usr/bin/x-terminal-emulator
/usr/local/bin/myterm
```

6.1.5   The Debian menu system

A Unix system is not bound to a single graphical frontend. In fact, the Debian archive holds more than 30 window and desktop managers, giving the user ample choice as to how the desktop should look. Most of these provide a menu for easier access to the installed applications. While integrated desktop environments such as **KDE** and **GNOME** provide standardised hooks used by many programmes to register executables with the menus, there is no standard across all window managers[3]. If

---

[3]The Debian menu system is not limited to window managers. While **KDE** and **GNOME** actually render their menus independently of the window manager used, even terminal emulators such as **rxvt** can use the Debian menu system. For simplicity, we will discuss window managers here, arguably the most common field of use for menus.

the administrator needs to provide a common menu structure and still allow users the choice between multiple front-ends, a great amount of time must be devoted to managing the menu configurations. Most probably, the different frontends employ vastly different syntactic rules and paradigms, all of which have to be learnt to prevent confusion.

The Debian menu system aims to lighten the load by providing a standardised method for applications to register their user-executable binaries[4]. In turn, every Debian window manager provides a conversion specification which produces the applicable menu configuration from the Debian menu configuration. Finally, each application providing a menu entry instructs the menu system to update the menus of all menu providers during its configuration phase. For the Debian menu system to work, the **menu** package must be installed. Its documentation can be found online[5].

With the **menu** package installed, the menu system requires no further interaction to give all users of all window managers the Debian default menu. However, the administrator may override virtually any aspect of the generated menu(s), and each user can do so as well. The menu system has two configurable aspects: the first is the method used to generate each window manager's menu configuration file, and the second comprises the individual menu entries. I will limit the following discussion to the second aspect.

Menu files

To register one or multiple menu entries, a package drops a menu file into **/usr/lib/ menu**, ideally named after the source package. A good example of such a menu file is the one provided by the **dia** package:

```
?package(dia):                                                      \
  needs="X11"                                                       \
  section="Apps/Graphics"                                           \
  hints="Vector"                                                    \
  command="/usr/bin/dia-normal"                                     \
  icon="/usr/share/pixmaps/dia_menu.xpm"                            \
  title="Dia"                                                       \
  longtitle="Draw diagrams"                                         \
  description="Dia can be used to draw different kind of diagrams. \
    There is support for UML static structure diagrams              \
    (class diagrams), Entity-Relationship diagrams and             \
    Network diagrams. Diagrams can be exported to postscript."
```

---

[4]The Debian menu structure is governed by its own policy: http://www.debian.org/doc/ packaging-manuals/menu-policy

[5]http://www.debian.org/doc/packaging-manuals/menu.html

The package defines a single entry under ownership of the **dia** package, which is only made available when the X11 system is available. It resides in "Apps/Graphics" and can optionally further subclassify into the "Vector" directory. The command is specified as well as the icon to use, if the menu is capable of displaying icons. Finally, the title, long title, and description can help users to identify the application's purpose.

Assuming you would like to change the icon used for **dia**, you would drop a modified version into **/etc/menu** and run **update-menus**. This updates the global menu configuration file for all menu providers by iterating through the methods in **/etc/menu-methods**. To disable a package's menu entries, simply create an empty file under **/etc/menu**; the file have the same filename as the menu file in **/usr/lib/menu**.

Similarly, it is possible to provide custom menu entries. To avoid clashes with official Debian software, it is preferable to use names prefixed with **local.** in the **?package** clause of the menu file:

```
~# cat <<EOF > /etc/menu/local.consoles.webserver
?package(local.consoles.webserver): \
  needs="text"                       \
  section="Local/Consoles"           \
  title="Webserver"                  \
  command="ssh webserver"
EOF
```

After running **update-menus**, selecting this menu entry tells the menu provider to do everything needed to bring up an SSH session on **webserver**.

User-specific configuration

Each user can do at the user level what an administrator can do at system level. The ~/.menu and ~/.menu-methods directories completely override their counterparts in /etc (meaning that the system-wide menu configuration will be ignored). By dropping appropriate files into these directories and running **update-menus**, the user can ditch the default configuration and instead use a custom one.

To undo user-specific configurations it is usually only necessary to remove the file identified by **$userprefix** and **$genmenu** from the home directory, where the values of these variables can be obtained from the corresponding **menu-methods** file.

6.2 Users and authentication

6.2.1 System users and groups

The Debian system works with users and groups just like other Unix systems. By default, user accounts are defined in /etc/passwd, while password and account expiration data are protected in /etc/shadow. Similarly, groups are specified in /etc/group and any group passwords are hidden in /etc/gshadow. Debian uses shadow passwords exclusively, and the default password hash is MD5, rather than the less secure crypt algorithm.

Unix accounts and groups are identified by an ID number and a unique name. To be precise, an account or a group is identified by a unique ID number, which may be referenced multiple times by different names, allowing for account and group aliases (whose use is discouraged). The ID number is conventionally stored as a 16-bit integer, allowing for 65536 different accounts and groups. Even though modern kernels now use 32-bit integers and can thus accomodate more than four billion accounts, Debian still uses the smaller version. The number space is partitioned according to the following table, for both accounts and groups (see the Debian policy, section 9.2.2 for details).

ID range	Purpose
0 – 99	Globally allocated, static IDs. These are the same across all Debian systems.
100 – 999	Dynamically created IDs for system accounts and group, created and used by packages during installation
1000 – 29999	IDs for normal user accounts and local groups, used by **adduser** or **addgroup** when creating new accounts or groups
30000 – 59999	Reserved for local use by the system administrator
60000 – 64999	Globally allocated, static IDs, which are only used on demand
65000 – 65533	Reserved for local use by the system administrator
65534	User **nobody**
65535	Must not be used[6]

Table 6.1:
Partitions of the Unix account and group ID space on the Debian system

The two blocks reserved for local use are actually only marked as reserved by the policy. Since the policy governs what packages and maintainers may and must not do, this guarantees that these UIDs will never be used by components of the Debian system.

---

[6]65535 is the same as **unsigned(-1)**, which is often used as a sentinel value in programmes. To guard against possible conflicts, this ID should not be used.

System accounts

Of the statically allocated IDs, a number have a special purpose on a Debian system, while others exist merely for historical reasons. You can find a detailed description of the special users (and groups) on your system[7]. Among the special user accounts to be found on every Debian system, the following are of general relevance:

root

> The superuser, which is a Unix standard.

sync

> Logging in as **sync** causes the disk buffers to be flushed. This is a safe operation and subject only to denial of service attacks (if at all). Therefore, you may consider using a simple password to allow synchronising of the disk without logging in.

www-data

> Web servers on Debian commonly run under the **www-data** account. The web content should *not* be owned by **www-data** to prevent a compromise of the web server from affecting the data. Dynamic applications, such as Wikis and (badly designed) web applications, may still require ownership by **www-data** to be able to store data persistently.

nobody

> Daemons that do not own any files can be run as **nobody**, although a dedicated account is usually a better choice.

System groups

The following are groups with special rights:

root

> Accommodates the superuser and has no other real purpose.

adm

> Membership in this group allows for certain monitoring tasks on the local system. In particular, most log files under **/var/log** are readable by **adm**. Furthermore, **/dev/xconsole**, which receives most log messages (see **/etc/ syslog.conf**), is readable by the group members.

lp

> While primarily intended for the classic Unix print system **lpr**, the **lp** group gives its members full access to a system's parallel ports.

---

[7] In /usr/share/doc/base-passwd/users-and-groups.html

www-data

> Used by most web servers on the Debian system, status and log files generated while serving web content belong to this group. Web content itself (and parent directories) should not be writeable by this group.

dialout

> Members of this group have complete control over the system's serial ports.

dip

> Members of this group can establish connections with dial-up providers.

fax

> Membership in this group is mandatory to use fax applications.

voice

> Voice applications are usable by members of this group only.

cdrom

> Users who need direct access to CD-ROM devices must be members of this group. Note that this is not required to mount CD-ROM drives and access their ISO9660 data tracks. Members of this group can read ISO images and issue control commands to, *e.g.*, eject media in the drive.

floppy

> For direct access to the floppy drive, a user must be a member of the **floppy** group. As with CD-ROM drives, this is not requires to simply mount and access a filesystem stored on the floppy disk. However, direct access is required to create a filesystem on the floppy disk and to read and write floppy images.

tape

> Access to tape drives is exclusive to members of this group.

sudo

> **sudo** does not ask members of this group for a password.

audio

> Membership in this group is required to use audio devices.

video

> Special video hardware (beyond the basic functionality of the graphics card) is only accessible to users who belong to this group.

staff

> This group is for junior system administrators and users who can install software locally without requiring root rights. Users in this group can manipulate /usr/local, /var/local, and /home without needing root rights. This facilitates custom software management, as well as management of data stored below /home.

users
> This is a default group for plain users of a system without any special rights.

nogroup
> Accompanying the **nobody** account, this group mainly serves to accomodate daemons that do not own any files. A dedicated group is usually a better choice.

It is unlikely that you will need to add users to system groups (*i.e.* with ID numbers less than 1 000) not mentioned above. If you think you do, please make sure you know what you are doing. Practically speaking, there is no difference between low and high IDs, the distinction mainly helps to make classification easier for the administrator.

6.2.2 User and group management

User management on a Debian system is handled by a family of four tools, **adduser, addgroup, deluser, delgroup**, which are commonly referred to as the **adduser** suite, and installed with **adduser** package. These cover the most important tasks, including group membership management. All other operations, such as the modification of account data or the setting of passwords, are handled by the appropriate standard Unix tools (*e.g.* **chfn, chsh, usermod,** or **passwd**). As with most Debian approaches, you can continue to use existing tools (such as **groupadd** and its siblings).

The **adduser** suite has some advantages over tools like **useradd** as it enforces the Debian policy and provides hooks to allow *e.g.* quota to be configured for new accounts, or a custom script to be run to adjust accounts to local requirements automatically during their creation. Along similar lines, it can (optionally) back up user data when an account is purged. Moreover, the **adduser** tools meticulously log the actions they take (to **/var/log/auth.log**) to improve auditing of the system.

For the **adduser** suite members to enforce policy basically means that they know about the partitioning of the ID number space, and honour it. Both **addgroup** and **adduser** take the **--system** option to create groups and accounts with IDs between 100 and 999, but will default to choosing IDs between 1 000 and 29 000 in the absence of the option. These bounds are configurable (in **/etc/adduser.conf**) if required.

Adding and removing groups

Adding a group to a Debian system is a trivial operation. The **--system** option is usually only needed by packages, so it will not be included. The tools will use the next available ID, which can be overridden with the **--gid** option.

```
~# addgroup debianbook
Adding group 'debianbook' (1002)...
Done.
```

Deletion of a group follows a similar pattern and irrevocably eradicates all membership data for the group (unless it is available in a backup, see chapter 6.4). It is therefore probably a good idea to get into the habit of using the **--only-if-empty** option, which prevents the removal of groups that are not empty:

```
~# delgroup --only-if-empty debianbook
Removing group 'debianbook'...
done.
```

gpasswd is used to manipulate group passwords and administrators.

Adding users

The creation of new user accounts is a little more involved as the following steps are taken. **adduser** reads **/etc/adduser.conf** and uses the values defined in this file at various points to allow for greatest flexibility.

- If **$USERGROUPS** is enabled, **adduser** first creates a new group with the same name as the user. If this group already exists, an error occurs. The **--ingroup** option can be used to specify an existing group to use instead. System accounts are not treated in this way.

- Next, the Unix account is created, using **$DSHELL** as its shell. The **--shell** option can be used to override this. By default, system accounts are assigned **/bin/false** as a shell.

- If **$USERGROUPS** is enabled, the user's primary group is set to the new group with the same name as the account. Otherwise, the group identified by the ID in **$USERS_GID** is used, unless the **--ingroup** parameter is given to override this setting. Using the **--gid** option, the new account can be added to additional groups. System accounts are added to **nogroup** by default.

- The home directory location is determined by **$DHOME** and the login name. If **$GROUPHOMES** is enabled, the home directory will reside in a subdirectory for the group (**$DHOME/$GROUP**). If **$LETTERHOME** is set, another subdirectory, named after the first letter of the account name, is created. For instance, with both variables set and **$USERGROUPS** disabled, a new account for **martin** would be assigned the following home directory: **/home/users/m/martin**. With the **--home** option, the administrator can instead specify the home directory location manually.

- The home directory is created with the permissions specified by $DIR_MODE, unless the --no-create-home option is passed to adduser. If the directory referenced by $SKEL exists, its contents are copied to the new home directory. The home directory is not created for system users. Additionally, an existing home directory is left untouched. If $SETGID_HOME is enabled, the home directories setgid bit is turned on.

- Assuming that neither of the options --disabled-login or --disabled-password has been set, adduser now requests the user's new password, which is set using Pluggable Authentication Modules (PAM). If --disabled-login is specified, the new account cannot be used until a password has been set manually using passwd. The --disabled-password option configures the new account to be used with non-password authentication methods like the ones used by SSH. System accounts have disabled passwords by default.

- Now, adduser prompts for the user contact data if not specified on the command line with the --gecos switch. The command line option does not honour the commonly accepted GECOS[8] format, but expects a free-form comment instead. Use commas to separate the GECOS fields, if specified on the command line. These data are not queried for system accounts.

- If defined, adduser clones the quota information from the template user identified by $QUOTAUSER, unless the new account is a system account.

- When creating a user account, adduser invokes /usr/local/sbin/adduser.local (if present), passing it the account name, user ID, primary group ID, and home directory path as arguments. If the script does not exit successfully, the user account is removed.

The whole process looks like this (using a little debug script for the hook, to visualise what is going on):

```
~# cat /usr/local/sbin/adduser.local
#!/bin/sh -e

exec echo -e "I: $0 called with arguments:\nI: $@\n"
~# adduser martin
Adding user 'martin'...
Adding new group 'martin' (1003).
Adding new user 'martin' (1003) with group 'martin'.
Creating home directory '/home/martin'.
Copying files from '/etc/skel'
Enter new Unix password:
```

[8]GECOS is a relic from the "General Electric Comprehensive Operating System" and remains on today's Unix systems as a format specification for contact data associated with login accounts. The fifth colon-separated field of the /etc/passwd file holds a user's GECOS data in comma-separated fields: full name, room number, work phone, and home phone. The last field can be used for other free-form data.

```
Retype new Unix password:
passwd: password updated successfully
Changing the user information for martin
Enter the new value, or press ENTER for the default
  Full Name []: Martin F. Krafft
  [...]
Is the information correct? [y/N] y
Setting quota from 'template'.
I: /usr/local/sbin/adduser.local called with arguments:
I: martin 1003 1003 /home/martin
```

Removing users

The removal of users is governed by the settings in **/etc/deluser.conf**. The process consists of the following steps:

- **deluser** removes the Unix account, without touching any of the user's data (such as home directory, or mail spool).

- If **$REMOVE_HOME** is set or the command line option **--remove-home** is given, the user's home directory (and the data in it) is then purged. The same happens for system user accounts.

- If **$REMOVE_ALL_FILES** is enabled, or the option **--remove-all-files** is used, the entire system is scanned for files belonging to the user, which are then purged. This option takes precedence over (and includes) the **--remove-home** option. Again, a system user's account is treated in the same way.

- Enabling **$BACKUP**, or passing the **--backup** option to the **deluser** invocation causes the tool to archive files that would be erased by the user removal process to a tarball instead. The tarball's location can be set with **$BACKUP_TO**, or the **--backup-to** command line switch, and defaults the current directory.

- Finally, **deluser** executes **/usr/local/sbin/deluser.local** (if present), passing it the account name, user ID, parimary group ID, and home directory path as arguments. An unsuccessful exit code is echoed to the user, but otherwise ignored.

The sequence looks like this, with removal of all files and backup abilities added for extra show. Also, the same hook script as used earlier in the **adduser** example does its thing here again:

```
~# deluser --remove-all-files --backup martin
Looking for files to backup/remove...
Backing up files to be removed to . ...
/bin/tar: Removing leading '/' from member names
Removing files...
```

```
Removing user 'martin'...
I: /usr/local/sbin/deluser.local called with arguments:
I: martin 1003 1003 /home/martin
done.
~# ls -F
martin.tar.bz2
```

Group membership management

Essentially, group membership management on a Unix system can be performed in two ways: as **root**, or as a normal user with management rights for the particular group. Debian has no special provisions for the latter, so the following is all you are going to see about membership management by a user. For instance, assume a group of coders, led by Alice. The system administrator has created the group and made Alice an administrator:

```
~# gpasswd -A alice coders
```

When Bob joins the group, Alice does not need to consult the system administrator, but can add Bob herself:

```
~$ gpasswd -a bob coders
Adding user bob to group coders
[...]
```

Swapping **-a** with **-r** allows Alice to remove Bob at the end of his trainee programme.

The latter command works equally well for the system administrator. However, another approach may also be used, which requires **root** access. Exploiting the mnemonic of the **adduser** tool's name, it can also be used to add a user to a group:

```
~# adduser bob coders
Adding user 'bob' to group 'coders'...
Done.
```

The command **addgroup bob coders** has the same effect; I find the first form easier to read: "add user bob [to group] coders."

Similarly, **deluser** can be used to delete a user from a group ("delete user bob [from group] coders"):

```
~# deluser bob coders
Removing user 'bob' from group 'coders'...
Done.
```

Users and their own primary groups

For new user accounts, **adduser** creates a group with the same name and uses that group as the user's primary group. Even though it is certainly a possibility to make each user a group administrator of the corresponding group, having an explicit group for each user account may seem a waste and unnecessary.

However, consider the case of a collaborative environment, in which different sets of users cooperate on different projects. A common method to handle such situations is through the use of shared project spaces in directories belonging to the project's group, and having their **setgid** bit set. The latter causes new files to automatically assume the group of the project's directory (which is the project's group), assuming it was created by a proper member of the group.

The missing link now is the **umask**, which determines the mode of new files created by a user. To allow new files to be usable by the other members of the project group, the group permissions presumably need to be read-write on all shared files. This can be achieved by setting the **umask** of all users involved to 0007 (for instance, in **/etc/profile**, or the user-specific initialisation scripts). As the following example shows, members of the **coders** group can freely cooperate on the files in ~/coders:

```
~$ install --directory --mode=2770 --group=coders coders
~$ cd coders
~/coders$ umask 0007
~/coders$ touch hello.c
~$ ls -Fla
drwxrws---  2 alice coders  4096 Dec 21 20:40 ./
drwx--x--x  3 alice alice   4096 Dec 21 20:39 ../
-rw-rw----  1 alice coders     0 Dec 21 20:40 hello.c
```

A problem arises when, as in the classical Unix case, all users belong to *e.g.* the **users** group by default. Since the **umask** is set for the entire shell session (and if set in the initialisation script, then for every shell session), when Alice subsequently writes a private letter to a friend, all other members of **users** can read *and even edit* the letter, since it will be created with read-write permissions for the group, and the group will be **users** by default. To guard against this situation, every user gets an explicit group by default.

LDAP user management

Unfortunately, the **adduser** suite does not currently honour other user databases than **/etc/passwd**. If your users are stored in (and authenticated against) an LDAP-accessible directory, you will need to resort to other methods. The **cpu** package provides a promising framework which can perform most user management operations via LDAP. In addition, the **ldapvi** package provides **ldapvi**, which is suitable for mass-editing of user data via LDAP.

6.2.3   PAM – Pluggable Authentication Modules

It is not necessarily a Debian feature for most packages to install pieces of software that place authentication, account and session initialisation, and password changing in the hands of the PAM libraries. PAM is a flexible plugin architecture, which allows for free-form combinations of authentication methods to be used for single programmes or whole groups of programmes. It probably ranks among the most significant inventions of the last decade.

Debian's PAM does not significantly differ from the upstream libraries. It does, however, allow for an include directive. As a consequence, Debian introduced a set of common files below **/etc/pam.d** for each of the four PAM facilities: **common-account** for account management, **common-auth** for authentication, **common-password** for password management, and **common-session** for session management. The individual services then usually only add facilities specific to the service, while all services together use (and enforce) the facilities defined in the common files.

Depending on the nature of a PAM configuration change, the modification will thus be done in the common files. Two standard examples are the consistent use of LDAP (from package **libpam-ldap**) for authentication, or password checkers like **libpam-passwdqc** to force the users to choose strong passwords. As both of these modules (should) apply to every service offered by a machine, they are best added to the appropriate **common-*** files instead of the individual service control files. When a new service is installed, the specific configuration will then be automatically available, which is convenient in some cases and critical in others.

Restricting devices to local users

One special PAM module deserves special mention, even though it is not part of the official PAM distribution: **pam_console**. Its purpose is to change device permissions (and the like), depending on which user logs on locally. As this approach fails with multiple local users, and is known to expose security holes and inconsistency problems, it is not available on the Debian system. Instead, Debian makes use of groups for specific device classes. Using **pam_group**, it is possible to restrict use of *e.g.* the audio devices to users logged on locally:

```
~# echo auth optional pam_group.so >> /etc/pam.d/common-auth
~# echo '*;tty*|:*;!root;Al0000-2400;audio' >> /etc/security/group.conf
```

The same concept can be applied to protect *e.g.* CD-ROM devices. In chapter 6.2.1, the commonly defined groups on a Debian system are described. Note that the method does not protect against malicious users. To subvert the rule, the user can make a duplicate shell and use **setgid** to make it run as the **audio** group, making case the selective addition of the **audio** group with **pam_group.so** useless.

Preseeding environment variables

In many situations, the system administrator will prefer to set environment variables to some default value for all users (and possibly processes) on a system. One way to achieve the result is by modifying the global initialisation files of the respective shell. For instance, to ensure that your users all have ˜/bin in their search path, you could change /etc/bash.bashrc:

```
˜# echo 'PATH=˜/bin:$PATH' >> /etc/bash.bashrc
```

The problem with this approach is that it only works for **bash** and to make things worse, standardised files like /etc/profile are not supported by all shells. Thus, if your users collectively use more than one shell (I have seven shells installed on my largest systems), you potentially have to maintain variable default values in seven different places.

An alternative approach comes as a consequence of Debian's consistent use of PAM. The **pam_env** module reads variable-value pairs from /etc/environment. Unfortunately, the file is not interpolated, so that it is not possible to use other variables for the values. Instead, we have to hard-code the path, which is not really a problem because this happens so early in the sequence that $PATH is probably not set yet (which is why the extended configuration file /etc/security/pam_env.conf is no help either).

```
˜# cat <<EOF >> /etc/environment
PATH=˜/bin:/usr/local/bin:[...]:/usr/games
EOF
```

Unfortunately, the /etc/profile file installed by **base-files**, which is honoured by most shells, just overwrites the variable again[9], so you will have to disable the assignment, for instance by changing the lines to

```
˜# grep PATH= /etc/profile
[[ -n $PATH ]] || PATH="/usr/local/sbin:[...]:/usr/bin/X11"
[[ -n $PATH ]] || PATH="/usr/local/bin:[...]:/usr/games"
```

This has the effect of setting $PATH only if it has not been set previously.

6.3   System initialisation and automatic processes

One the most important traits of a Debian system is its transparency. A transparent system allows for efficient and secure system administration. Knowing where to

---

[9] http://bugs.debian.org/286254

look for something, or knowing what to find in a certain place is a necessity if this is your goal; the Debian policy dictates FHS-compliance to simplify that (see chapter 5.7.4). Knowing what happens on your system, whether by request or automatically, is essential to maintaining control.

On a Debian system, comparatively little happens automatically, unless explicitly requested. Few maintenance tasks are run in the background if their operation is not essential to the system's health, and their function well-contained. In addition, the system provides a large amount of power tools for use by the administrator. These tools themselves are automation tools as they perform many actions as part of fulfilling the administrator's job. However, their implementation and consistency makes them easy to understand; even though they may be next to trivial (such as **run-parts**), or as complex as various of the network configuration management tools, they do no more than they should. Most of the complexity is needed to ensure robustness, and for reasons of flexibility.

Enough of the marketing talk. Having enjoyed writing these paragraphs, I should not pass up this opportunity to say that the management tools of a Debian system could gain a lot through better integration here and there. Without the marketing connotation: improvements are being worked on in various areas. Debian has a tight set of rules to follow (see chapter 5.7), and robustness and interoperability continue to be major concerns. Therefore, progress is slow, if not pioneering. Apart from **run-parts** and APT, a couple Debian implementations of concepts and ideas have become important contributions to the broader domain of Unix system administration.

6.3.1 The system initialisation process

Let us start where the Debian system starts: at the boot prompt. After it finishes loading, the kernel executes the system's master process, **/sbin/init**. init then proceeds to start tasks and processes to get the system into a fully operational state. The entire process is documented in detail in the "From PowerUp to Bash Prompt HOWTO[10]."

The init.d scripts

System initialisation consists of little tasks that configure the system, as well as the launching of processes to be run in the background as part of normal system operations (such as a mail server). These tasks and the control of the background processes are encapsulated in scripts found below **/etc/init.d** (which is not specific to Debian). Each of these scripts is required to support at least the following five methods, which are passed to the script as arguments:

[10]http://tldp.org/HOWTO/From-PowerUp-To-Bash-Prompt-HOWTO.html

start

> starts the service.

stop

> terminates the service.

restart

> effectively just stops and starts the service.

reload

> instructs the service to reload its configuration without restarting.

force-reload

> ensures the configuration to be reloaded. That is, if the service does not support reloading, it is restarted.

For example, the following command reloads the **postfix** configuration:

```
~# /etc/init.d/postfix reload
```

For background processes, all five methods make sense. For one-off configuration tasks, only **start** and maybe **stop** make sense. It is up to the maintainer to decide what to do with the other methods.

Debian also provides a policy layer for init.d scripts, which requires a command to be run instead of calling the scripts directly. We will return to this issue in chapter 6.3.1.

The /etc/default directory

Some daemons require their configuration to be passed on the command line during initial configuration. At other times, a configuration task might depend on a system-specific configuration parameter. To be able to influence the tasks and processes started by the init.d scripts, it is sometimes necessary to edit the corresponding file. Even though the policy requires init.d scripts to be treated as configuration files (thus allowing you to modify them to your heart's content), they are primarily control scripts rather than configuration files.

To make it easier for the administrator to modify parameters, package maintainers often export the configurable aspects of the init.d script to a file (with the same name) under /etc/default. These files are actually shell script snippets to be sourced by the init.d script and usually simply define variables. For instance, /etc/default/rcS defines a number of variables that influence the system initialisation process:

```
~$ grep ^[^#] /etc/default/rcS
TMPTIME=0
SULOGIN=no
DELAYLOGIN=yes
UTC=yes
VERBOSE=yes
EDITMOTD=yes
FSCKFIX=no
```

Similarly, **/etc/default/ssh** provides **$SSHD_OPTS**, which can be used to pass command line flags to the **sshd** process on invocation:

```
~$ grep ^SSHD_OPTS /etc/default/ssh
SSHD_OPTS='-6'
```

Now, **/etc/init.d/ssh** starts **sshd** with the **-6** option:

```
~# grep SSHD_OPTS /etc/init.d/ssh
start-stop-daemon --start [...] -- $SSHD_OPTS
[...]
```

The **/etc/default** directory is gaining popularity and it is being used in similar situations for other scripts (such as scripts in **/etc/cron.***) as well.

Starting and stopping daemons

When starting a process in the background, it is not trivial to stay in control. The issue is especially difficult because there is no standard approach for background process management. Some daemons write their process IDs to temporary files, others do not. Some daemons instead spawn others, and some service programmes are not even capable of properly backgrounding themselves.

To address the problem, the Debian developers created **start-stop-daemon**, a flexible utility that can control the creation and termination of background processes. It allows programmes to be put in the background, and can identify running processes using a variety of parameters, making it easy to stop a running process properly without leaving orphans behind.

The **start-stop-daemon** (8) manpage goes into detail on usage of the command, which may also come in handy for regular users looking to run background processes (although **screen** is often a better alternative, but too clumsy for use at system level). For instance, the following has the same effect as **/usr/bin/nohup** without dropping the **nohup.out** file into the working directory:

```
~$ /sbin/start-stop-daemon --start --exec buffy --background
```

For the moment, all we need to know is that **start-stop-daemon** just does what its name suggests: it starts and stops daemon (background) processes.

System initialisation

When **init** is invoked by the kernel, it reads **/etc/inittab** and processes the file top to bottom, according to the rules described in **inittab** (5). Before anything else, **init** calls **/etc/init.d/rcS**[11], which in turn executes the scripts under **/etc/rcS.d** whose name begins with the letter **S**; S-scripts start processes upon entering a runlevel. Similarly, **K** scripts terminate (kill), also upon entering a runlevel. Scripts whose names have the **.sh** extension are sourced for speed reasons, and to be able to modify the execution environment of the initialisation sequence.

Before iterating through the files, the **/etc/default/rcS** file is sourced; the file parametrises some aspects of the boot process. The files in **/etc/rcS.d** are actually just symlinks to corresponding files in **/etc/init.d**. In the following, we inspect the symlinks to preserve the order of the boot sequence (which is sorted by file name):

S02mountvirtfs
> Mounts essential kernel file systems (such as **/proc**).

S05bootlogd
> Starts **bootlogd** to log the boot process.

S05initrd-tools.sh
> Cleans up the initial ramdisk used during boot.

S05keymap.sh
> Load the console keymaps.

S10checkroot.sh
> Checks the root filesystem, if appropriate. If a **/fastboot** file exists, the check will be skipped. The presence of **/forcefsck** forces the check even if not necessary. This script also activates any swap devices.

S18hwclockfirst.sh
> Initialises the system clock from the hardware clock. The initialisation will be redone at a later point to allow for time zones, at this point it is important to establish a reference time. If the system is configured for a time zone other than Universal Time Coordinated (UTC), please make sure you read the comments in the file.

S20module-init-tools
> Recomputes module dependencies and loads all modules listed in **/etc/ modules**.

---

[11]Unless the **emergency** boot option is given, in which case a simple shell is spawned before system initialisation proceeds.

S20modutils

> *dto.*, for 2.4 kernels.

S30checkfs.sh Checks all remaining filesystems, if appropriate. **/fastboot** and **/forcefsck** are honoured as with **S10checkroot.sh**.

S30etc-setserial

> Configures the serial devices, if you configured them manually before (see **/etc/serial.conf**). Automatic configuration happens later.

S30procps.sh

> Sets kernel variables from **/etc/sysctl.conf**.

S35mountall.sh

> Mounts all filesystems.

S36discover

> Detects and configures available hardware.

S36mountvirtfs

> Mounts remaining kernel file systems.

S39dns-clean

> Restores **/etc/resolv.conf** if it was left in an inconsistent state.

S39ifupdown

> Ensures a clean state for the Debian network configuration system.

S40hostname.sh

> Sets the machine's host name from **/etc/hostname**.

S40hotplug

> Starts **hotplug** subsystems (and thus initialises and configures attached devices).

S40networking

> Configure network devices and options.

S43portmap

> Start the port mapping daemon.

S45mountnfs.sh

> Mounts all NFS filesystems.

S46setserial

> Automatically configures serial ports on the system (if they have not been manually configured in **/etc/serial.conf**).

S48console-screen.sh

>   Loads fonts and character set maps, and finishes the configuration of the console.

S50hwclock.sh

>   With /usr mounted, the system clock can now be initialised properly from the hardware clock (time zone information is in **/usr/share/zoneinfo**).

S55bootmisc.sh

>   According to the settings in **/etc/default/rcS**, this script disables login at boot time, writes **/etc/motd**, saves **/var/log/dmesg**, and performs other miscellaneous tasks.

S55urandom

>   The Linux random number generator is always initialised with the same seed during the kernel initialisation process. To increase its strength, the Debian system generates a new (pseudo-random) seed at shutdown, which is used to initialise the random number generator in this script.

S70nviboot

>   Recovers **nvi** editor sessions.

Runlevels

Beyond basic system initialisation, **init** uses the concept of runlevels to determine what processes to start on the local system. Debian's mapping of runlevels differs somewhat from the standard configuration found on other distributions. The following table compares Debian use of each of the runlevels with the popular standard employed *e.g.* by Red Hat:

Runlevel	Debian	Other
0	halt	halt
1/S	single user mode	single user mode
2	standard (all services)	multiuser without network services
3	unused	standard multiuser mode
4	unused	unused
5	unused	standard multiuser mode with an X display manager
6	reboot	reboot

Table 6.2:
Runlevel usages on Debian and other common distributions

As the system initialises, runlevel S is active. When the initialisation scripts finish, init switches to the default runlevel (which is 2 on a Debian system, as specified at the top of **/etc/inittab**). The runlevel to use after S can also be specified at the boot prompt. For instance, to boot into runlevel 3 with **Grub**, you would edit the **kernel** line as follows (by pressing **[e]** in the menu):

```
grub edit> kernel [...] root=/dev/sda1 ro 3
```

The **single** option is the same as specifying S or 1 at the boot prompt[12]. None of the runlevels are in any way magical, not even runlevels 0 and 6 — halting and rebooting are in essence just processes that are started. For each of the numbered runlevels[13], init invokes **/etc/init.d/rc** with the runlevel as the first argument. The rc script identifies the corresponding directory (**/etc/rcX.d**, where X is the runlevel) and proceeds in three steps:

1. It runs all scripts with names beginning with **K** in the directory, passing **stop** as the argument. This stops any service that is not supposed to be running in the selected runlevel.

2. For each script whose name begins with **S**, it checks whether the previously active runlevel (which is S if the system has just booted) started the script. If it did, the script in the current runlevel is ignored.

3. If the previous runlevel did not start the script, it is invoked with the **start** argument to start the respective service in the current runlevel.

If you scan the **/etc/rc?.d** contents on a Debian system, you will notice only a few scripts whose names start with **K**, even though corresponding S scripts exist. This means that the associated processes are started but possibly not killed. If a service is not terminated upon entering a runlevel, it continues to run if that is what it did in the previous runlevel. Such processes are considered to be in a floating state, in which it is entirely up to the administrator to manually start and stop them[14]. In case of absence of an S script, the corresponding software remains dormant in Tumbolia[15].

The current runlevel can be ascertained by running the **who** utility, which also prints the runlevel preceding the current one. With the default configuration, the following shows the output after a successful boot:

---

[12]However, runlevels S and 1 are not the same. Runlevel 1 switches to runlevel S, but only after gracefully stopping (and then killing) all user-space processes.

[13]Runlevels 7 through 9 are also valid, but are not supported by Debian out of the box; if you need them, you will have to edit **/etc/inittab** accordingly.

[14]FYI: http://bugs.debian.org/243159

[15]http://en.wikipedia.org/wiki/Tumbolia

```
~$ who --runlevel
  run-level 2  Oct 26 01:15       last=S
```

It is possible to switch to a new runlevel by executing **telinit**, with the new runlevel as the argument. In fact, the **shutdown**, **reboot**, and **halt** commands essentially do not do anything else but change the runlevel to 0 or 6 (which in turn call **halt** and **reboot** with an option to circumvent **init**).

Thus, to switch the local system to single user mode (for maintenance), simply run the following command:

```
~# telinit 1
INIT: Switching to runlevel: 1
[...]
```

As this will *kill all processes* running on the system, you are should never execute this command without great care. On network-connected systems you may like to ensure that **sshd** continues to allow **root** logins, even in single user mode:

```
~# sed -i -e "/^~~/ish:S:respawn:sshd -Do 'AllowUsers=root'" /etc/inittab
```

The command adds a line to start **sshd** in single user mode, restricted to **root**, just before the line providing the single user console. Provided that **root** can actually log in via SSH[16], the above allows you to switch a system to single user mode remotely. Even though all current SSH sessions will be killed, **sshd** will wait for new connections when the switch is complete.

To return a system to normal operation, use **telinit** again (with the desired runlevel):

```
~# telinit 2
[...]
```

BSD-style system initialisation: file-rc

Debian uses the System V method for its initialisation scripts by default. An alternative scheme, similar to the one used by acsBSD systems use, is provided by the **file-rc** package, which uses a single file to control runlevel initialisation. Installing the package automatically converts an existing /etc/rc?.d hierarchy to provide the same information in a single file, /etc/runlevel.conf (and installing **sysv-rc** causes **file-rc**'s removal, which recreates the symlink tree from the information in the file. Therefore, changes are preserved.). Note that APT will complain if you try to replace **sysv-rc** with **file-rc**:

[16]It is advisable to restrict **root** login to certificate-based authentication by setting **PermitRootLogin without-password** in /etc/ssh/sshd_config for better security (and accountability).

```
~# debian:~# apt-get install file-rc
[...]
The following packages will be REMOVED:
  sysv-rc
The following NEW packages will be installed:
  file-rc
WARNING: The following essential packages will be removed
This should NOT be done unless you know exactly what you are doing!
  sysv-rc (due to sysvinit)
[...]
You are about to do something potentially harmful
To continue type in the phrase 'Yes, do as I say!'
 ?] Yes, do as I say!
[...]
```

This warning cannot be easily prevented, and while it is usually indicative of potentially harmful action, it is perfectly okay to do as instructed in this situation. When the installation finishes, **file-rc** gives you everything you need to handle system and service initialisation.

```
~# cat /etc/runlevel.conf
[...]
19  0,6     -     /etc/init.d/setserial
20  0,1,6  2,3,4,5   /etc/init.d/exim4
20  0,1,6  2,3,4,5   /etc/init.d/inetd
20  0,1,6  2,3,4,5   /etc/init.d/lpd
20  0,1,6  2,3,4,5   /etc/init.d/makedev
20  0,1,6  2,3,4,5   /etc/init.d/rsync
20  0,1,6  2,3,4,5   /etc/init.d/ssh
20  -      0,6     /etc/init.d/sendsigs
20  -      S       /etc/init.d/module-init-tools
20  -      S       /etc/init.d/modutils
21  -      2,3,4,5   /etc/init.d/nfs-common
[...]
~# ls -F /etc/rc?.d
ls: /etc/rc?.d: No such file or directory
```

As you can see, the link hierarchies under **/etc/rc?.d** have been replaced with a single file, **/etc/runlevel.conf**. Similarly, the files rc and rcS in **/etc/init.d** come from the **file-rc** package. While exporting the same interface, the two files are tailored to read **/etc/runlevel.conf** instead of the symlink hierarchy.

Controlling runlevel initialisation: update-rc.d

Debian does not (yet) specify whether a package providing a daemon can or should start this daemon automatically after installation, during the next boot, or not until the administrator enables it. A number of **init.d** scripts require you to edit a file in **/etc/default** before allowing the encapsulated process to be started, but this is not the norm. With the policy layer (see chapter 6.3.1) still in development, the way to influence which process starts when is to manipulate the **/etc/rc?.d** symlink tree (or **/etc/runlevel.conf**) directly.

Debian provides three utilities to facilitate the process. Two only work with the System V symlink tree (and conflict with **file-rc**), while the most flexible (and command line only) tool works with any initialisation process configuration scheme[17].

If you are not using **file-rc**, you can install **rcconf** and **sysv-rc-conf**. The first allows you to enable and disable services altogether on the system. If you disable a service in **rcconf**, the tool replaces all its links with K-links, which keeps the service stopped unless manually started without switching runlevels. **rcconf** remembers the previous runlevel configuration and can restore it when the service is enabled again. **rcconf** affects all runlevels and can only disable and enable services.

The second tool, **sysv-rc-conf** allows granular control over which services to start when. It features two modes: invoked without an argument, it allows individual services to be enabled and disabled for each runlevel. If you pass the **--priority** option at invocation, you can edit the priorities as well. Please note that the simple mode (without **--priority**) can only switch a service on or off, but does not honour the floating status. Additionally, simply toggling a check box makes the change persistent on the local system. Therefore, it is possible to irreversibly mess up the configuration if you are not careful[18]

If you are fond of text editors, **file-rc** is for you. Editing **/etc/runlevels.conf** is almost certainly going to be easier, safer, and more intuitive.

For package maintainers to be able to register and configure their services with the runlevel configuration, a common interface was required: **update-rc.d**. Even though its syntax is somewhat archaic, it makes sense to learn it if you will be configuring the initialisation process on a regular basis. Note that the .d extension refers to the **rc.d** directory which **update-rc.d** updates; **update-rc.d** is not a directory.

Normally, **update-rc.d** is invoked with the defaults, which configures the daemon to be started at position 20 in runlevels 2 through 5, and killed at position 20 in runlevels 0, 1, and 6. The positions can also be overridden, and it is even possible to control which runlevels start and stop a script. The four possible configurations are:

- use the defaults:

```
~# update-rc.d apache2 defaults
[...]
```

---

[17] Plans for a third package, **dependency-rc** have commenced to streamline and parallelise the boot process.

[18] See http://bugs.debian.org/285850.

- use the default runlevels, but with position 30 instead of 20:

```
~# update-rc.d apache2 defaults 30
[...]
```

- use the default runlevels, but start the daemon at position 9 and stop it at position 91:

```
~# update-rc.d apache2 defaults 9 91
[...]
```

- start the daemon at position 15 in runlevels 2 and 3, at position 45 in runlevels 4 and 5, and kill it at position 85 in the other runlevels (do not forget the final dot, it is part of the syntax):

```
~# update-rc.d apache2 start 15 2 3 . start 45 4 5 . stop 85 0 1 6 .
[...]
```

Thus, the default settings are equivalent to

```
~# update-rc.d apache2 start 20 2 3 4 5 . stop 20 0 1 6 .
[...]
```

All Debian packages that install **init.d** scripts use **update-rc.d** to do so. Thus, the package does not have to worry about which of the *-rc packages is in effect, or how the **init.d** scripts are managed under each. What is more important is that **update-rc.d** only installs the scripts if no previous **init.d** scripts for the same daemon exist. For instance, trying to install links for the **cron** daemon fails:

```
~# update-rc.d cron defaults
 System startup links for /etc/init.d/cron already exist.
```

No package upgrade will ever overwrite a previous configuration. This allows the administrator to prevent daemons from launching and ensure persistent changes. For instance, to prevent **apache2** from starting, you would first remove the existing symlinks before installing new ones. Note the use of the –f flag, which is needed because **update-rc.d** otherwise refuses to remove the symlinks if the corresponding **init.d** script still exists. The following is essentially what **rcconf** does to disable a service.

```
~# update-rc.d -f apache2 remove
~# udpate-rc.d apache2 stop 0 0 1 2 3 4 5 6 .
```

Another useful change may be to move the invocation of the **X** display manager to the front to allow you to log in while the rest of the system is configured and the processes started. In the following, replace **xdm** with the display manager of your choice (*e.g.* **kdm**):

```
~# update-rc.d -f xdm remove
~# update-rc.d xdm defaults 01
```

Note that this approach may fail if **X** needs other daemons running, such as **xfs** or **gpm**. You may have to experiment moving the display manager around within the initialisation sequence.

Policing init.d scripts

Disabling services with **rcconf** or **update-rc.d** is a good way to enact a system policy with respect to which daemons should be running. However, these tools do not prevent a daemon's **init.d** script from being called directly.

Debian packages usually try to start any daemons they provide. While this may be a questionable policy (OpenBSD, for instance, would never start anything unless requested), Debian counters this choice for usability with carefully crafted defaults, so that a daemon that starts before the administrator has had a chance to configure it to reflect to local requirements does not cause a security issue. The maintainer might only enable the bare essentials of a daemon, or bind the daemon to the loopback interface and thus not expose it to the public. Some maintainers choose to disable their daemons until the administrator has flipped the appropriate variable in the package's configuration file below **/etc/default**.

A problem arises when the administrator of a system purposely uses *e.g.* **rcconf** to disable a service, and a security update comes along. The package is upgraded and its **postinst** hook calls the **init.d** script to launch the daemon; **update-rc.d** and **rcconf** only affect the system initialisation process but do not guard against direct invocation of the **init.d** script.

invoke-rc.d addresses this long-standing problem in Debian by introducing a policy layer to decide what actions can be performed given a certain service and the current runlevel (here too, the .d extension comes from the **/etc/rc.d** directory). For a service to be started (or restarted), the following conditions must be satisfied:

1. The corresponding **init.d** script exists and is executable.

2. The daemon is configured to be started in the current runlevel, that is, there exists an **S** link in the current runlevel's startup directory (**/etc/rcX.d**).

3. The policy layer approves the start of the daemon in the current runlevel.

The stopping of a daemon only requires the first and third condition to hold.

Currently, support for this policy is very rudimentary and basically consists of the **/usr/sbin/policy-rc.d** file (which is not yet officially provided), but following the release of *sarge*, possible implementations will be discussed. Similar to **update-rc.d** and **invoke-rc.d**, the trailing .d refers to the directory upon which the tool acts: **/etc/rc.d**.

The operation of **policy-rc.d** is based on a simple idea. Whenever **invoke-rc.d** is told to take a certain action, it first runs **policy-rc.d** and checks its exit status. **policy-rc.d** receives the name of the script under consideration, the desired action, and the current runlevel and simply condenses these data into a standardised return code. The **invoke-rc.d** (8) manpage and **/usr/share/doc/sysv-rc/README.*** give you the details. The following example shows a possible implementation of the policy script which prevents **apache2** and **postfix** from being started automatically in run level 2. I use a symlink to prevent having to write to a file in **/usr**, and **dpkg-divert** (see chapter 6.1.3) to guard against accidental overwrites, in case a package provides the file some day.

```
~# cat <<"EOF" > /etc/policy-rc.d
#!/bin/bash -e

script=$1
action=$2
runlevel=$3

[[ $action != start ]] && exit 0 # we only care for action start
[[ $runlevel != 2 ]] && exit 0 # we only care for RL 2

case $script in
  apache2|postfix) exit 101;;
  *) exit 0;;
esac
EOF
~# dpkg-divert --add /usr/sbin/policy-rc.d
[...]
~# ln -s /etc/policy-rc.d /usr/sbin
```

invoke-rc.d: not for use

The **invoke-rc.d** script is Debian's way of interacting with the scripts in **/etc/init.d**. However, it was not designed to be used by the system administrator, as it does not provide the necessary flexibility. For instance, a certain daemon may be stopped, but in a floating state, suggesting that it is perfectly okay for the daemon to be running in the current runlevel, it just has not been started. If the administrator were to use **invoke-rc.d**, it would fail to start the daemon because of the lack of the corresponding S link in runlevel's **rcX.d** directory.

As soon as the policy layer is properly implemented in Debian, and other initialisation strategies (such as **dependency-rc**) enter the picture, it is likely that Debian will provide a similar tool for use by the administrator.

Lastly, it should be noted that the policy layer can only prevent an action if it has a chance to do so. With the current design, the **init.d** policy can be easily circumvented by executing the **init.d** scripts directly. Initial plans have been made to integrate the policy layer into the **init.d** scripts to prevent this, but do not expect this kind of solution to be integrated any time in the near future.

6.3.2 Regular maintenance processes

To complete the picture for regular processes that happen automatically behind the scenes, everything pertaining to the system as a whole is scheduled by **cron**. Daemons installed by packages may (and probably will) do things without waiting for the administrator, but these are specific to the functionality of the package and thus not part of the system itself. In addition, the system inititalisation process counts as an automatic process, though it is not really regular (at least I do not reboot regularly).

Let us look at the standard Debian **cron** configuration which comprises the **/etc/cron*** directories and files. Our standard system will uses packages of the first three priorities (**required** to **standard**; see chapter 5.2.2) as installed by Debian by default. Chapter 3.2 shows you how to prevent the installer from pulling **standard** packages onto the new system, in which case you will have to add **cron** by yourself.

Hourly tasks

The **cron** directory for hourly tasks, **/etc/cron.hourly** is a fairly recent addition and currently not used by the Debian system. Only a single package (**changetrack**) currently uses it.

Daily tasks

In the early morning hours (at 06:25 local time), the Debian system wakes up to do its daily tasks. If you operate a system that is not booted 86 400 ticks of the clock per day, you can install the **anacron** package to catch up with any missed jobs at boot time.

A standard installation adds the following files to **/etc/cron.daily**:

bsdmainutils
> triggers the **calendar** utility, which will mail out reminders to all users based on the configuration in **/etc/calendar** and each user's home directory.

exim4-base
> cleans the **exim4** mail spool database and removes stray locks.

find

updates the filesystem database used by **locate** to find files by pattern on the local system.

logrotate

triggers **logrotate**, which rotates and compresses log files according to the configuration in **/etc/logrotate.conf** and **/etc/logrotate.d**. Note that **logrotate** only rotates log files *not* written by **syslogd** (see below). It is possible that this will change in the future, given that **logrotate** is the canonical tool for the job.

man-db

removes cached manual pages which have not been read for a week and regenerates the manual page index database by appending new entries.

modutils

for debugging, reference, and logging purposes, this script saves the list of kernel symbols (**/proc/ksysms**) and the list of modules (**/proc/modules**) to **/var/log/ksymoops** and weeds old files. This functionality has been obsoleted and is not needed on 2.6 kernels, where **modutils** can be safely purged.

netkit-inetd

keeps the last seven versions of **/etc/inetd.conf** below **/var/backups** for back-up and later reference (see chapter 6.4).

standard

performs standard daily maintenance tasks. These include backing up **/etc/passwd** and related files (see the script) to **/var/backup**, and keeping the last seven versions of the **dpkg** status database in the same directory (see chapter 6.4). The script also scans the **lost+found** directories of **ext2** and **ext3** filesystems and alerts the administrator by email if lost blocks are found in this directory.

syslogd

identifies large log files (mainly **/var/log/syslog**) written by **syslogd**, compresses and rotates them. The number of previous log files to keep can be specified in the script[19]. See chapter 6.7 for more information. The script also ensures tight permissions on **/var/log/auth.log**. Note that permissions of other log files are not corrected if the administrator altered them.

Weekly tasks

Every Sunday morning at 06:47 local time, the Debian system runs weekly maintenance jobs. Again, the **anacron** package can be installed to catch up with these jobs

---

[19] A patch exists to export the parameter to **/etc/default/syslogd**: http://bugs.debian.org/285087.

should the machine not be running at this time. The following tasks are executed weekly by a standard installation:

lpr

> rotates and compresses the accounting and error log files used by the **lpr** printing tool.

man-db

> recreates the manual page index database, thereby weeding out non-existent pages.

syslogd

> rotates all log files which are not under daily rotation. As with the corresponding daily **cron** script, the number of previous files to keep can be configured in the script.

Monthly tasks

Finally, on the first of each month, at 06:52 local time, **cron** starts to run the monthly jobs. A standard system does not install any monthly jobs, although a single file is left in the directory: **standard**, which is empty and only exists to refer to the new approach taken to its previous purpose.

6.4 Backups

While the backup of data and configuration is left to specialised tools (such as **amanda** or **afbackup**), the Debian system does make automatic backups of the most essential data. In particular, as part of the automatic daily system maintenance tasks identified in chapter 6.3.2, the following data are maintained in /var/backups:

- The last seven snapshots of the **dpkg** database (see chapter 5.3.4). A new snapshot is made if the **dpkg** status database has changed since the last backup. The oldest snapshot is then discarded.

- The user, group, and password database, stored in the four files **passwd**, **shadow**, **group**, and **gshadown** in /etc.

In addition, packages may use /var/backup to dump snapshots of their own data as required. For instance, the **netkit-inetd** package maintains the previous version of /etc/inetd.conf in the backup directory.

What to backup

Every system should have a backup strategy. A backup strategy may range from complete filesystem dumps over selective data backups to no backup at all. The latter may not seem like a backup strategy at all, but it is, because an explicit "no" suggests that thought has been given to the question of backups, whereas the "no" implicit in the simple lack of backups does not.

It is often not clear what needs to be backed up, and what can be safely ignored. A mantra of computer science is never to store anything that can be computed, unless it is for efficiency purposes. This mantra holds just as well when it comes to backing up a Debian system: you should do your best to back up the data that you or your users create, but you should not waste space on the backup medium with bytes that can easily be restored.

In particular, there is probably very little point in backing up /usr or /lib. Both of these hierarchies are guaranteed by the FHS (see chapter 5.7.4) to be managed by dpkg only, so dpkg should be able to restore them to their current state. Note, however, that this is not guaranteed for very old systems, or systems that run something else that pure Debian *stable*, because installed versions may no longer be available when the restoration takes place.

The hierarchies of /var, /etc, and /home are valuable and cannot be restored without a backup. Therefore, these are primary candidates for backups. Similarly, you are likely to want to backup /usr/local, /opt, and /srv, but leave /bin and /sbin well alone, along with the various mount points, /dev, and /tmp. If you keep data in /root, back it up as well.

I will not attempt to present you with a failproof recipe for backing up your Debian systems. These recipes are best found in literature specific to the topic of backups and require much thought on the side of the administrator. That said, I have never backed up more than /etc, /var, /usr/local, /home, and /srv and have always been able to restore a broken system or a deleted file when the need arose.

If the system is hosed and has to be reinstalled, the generic idea behind restoring a backup is to bring up a minimal system (see chapter 3.2) and proceed to restore the old system on top of that. With a backup of /var/lib/dpkg, you can access the list of installed packages and use *e.g.* dpkg --set-selections to have these installed first. With the same packages installed, /etc can be restored, and finally, all data can be written back to the local hard disk. With a little luck, the system should be restored within a short time.

Care has to be taken when using tools such as **dpkg-divert** or **dpkg-statoverride** (see chapter 6.1.3 and chapter 6.1.2 respectively) to manipulate file nodes in system hierarchies. These modifications are recorded in the **dpkg** status library, and should be in effect following the restoration of the status database from backup. However, diversions and overrides cannot (easily) be enforced other than at installation time, so the status database should be restored at an early stage.

6.5 Device management

On a Debian GNU/Linux system, device drivers are provided by kernel modules. To support a device, the appropriate kernel module(s) must be loaded before the device can be used. These modules can be loaded in four different ways:

- by **discover** during the boot initialisation phase.

- by **hotplug** during the boot initialisation phase, and when the device is attached to a running system.

- by the kernel autoloader (**kmod**), when a certain feature is requested of the kernel and the kernel knows which module provides the feature.

- as a static list of modules to be loaded at startup; this is maintained by the administrator.

6.5.1 discover and hotplug

During the installation of the Debian system (see chapter 3.2), the **discover** tool is used to identify the available hardware and load the appropriate modules to enable them. The installation also leaves **discover1** installed on the new system to continue automatic hardware detection in day-to-day usage.

The **discover** tool maps hardware devices to the names of supporting modules; the list is compiled and administered by the **discover** maintainers (installed in /usr/share/discover by **discover1-data**, and /lib/discover if **discover-data** is installed for version 2). Thus, during installation, and when the system boots, the tool probes the available buses for devices and uses the maps to figure out which modules to load.

On new systems, **hotplug** is also installed by default, and for modern buses, it works in tandem with the kernel to determine modules to be loaded to support the available devices. Other than **discover**, **hotplug** does not use mapping but instead relies on the modules and the kernel itself to advertise which devices they support.

With the 2.6 kernel device driver model and modern hardware, **hotplug** supersedes discover. However, they do not always cover common ground, which is why the installer tries to stay on the safe side and leaves both installed on a new system. By the time **hotplug** executes, **discover** will already have completed and loaded a number of modules. **hotplug** tolerates these and simply loads any additional modules it decides are needed.

hotplug can do more than boot-time hardware detection. In particular, the tool can execute scripts when certain devices become available (or are removed), and it continues its service throughout the system's uptime, watching for new devices to appear, loading their drivers, and integrating them appropriately.

When a hardware state change occurs, the kernel notifies the hotplugging handler (specified in **/proc/sys/kernel/hotplug**). This handler is set to **/sbin/hotplug** by default. If **udev** is installed (see chapter 6.5.1), it registers the more powerful **/sbin/udevsend** handler instead.

During the boot process, the kernel initialises builtin drivers before the **hotplug** system is ready. To allow for the delayed configuration of the devices controlled by these drivers, the initialisation script of the **hotplug** package scans the local system buses upon first invocation and regenerates the notifications, a process known as "coldplugging." The files responsible for the coldplugging are the **/etc/hotplug/*.rc** files.

When **hotplug** receives a notification, it invokes an agent to handle the configuration of the device, which may include the loading of a device driver, or several other steps taken to ensure the device's proper integration into the local system. Different agents handle different classes of devices according to the scripts and configuration files under **/etc/hotplug**[20]. These agents are then responsible for loading the device drivers and initialising the device, or integrating it with the system.

For example, upon connection of a USB stick, the following sequence of actions takes place:

1. The kernel notifies **hotplug** (by calling **/sbin/hotplug**) and passes it all the information it has about the device.

2. **hotplug** determines the device class to be **usb** and passes control to any scripts found in **/etc/hotplug.d/usb**.

3. In the default configuration, no specific **usb** handlers exist, and **hotplug** thus delegates to **/etc/hotplug.d/default/default.hotplug**.

4. The default handler in turn invokes **/etc/hotplug/usb.agent**.

5. **usb.agent** then figures out the driver needed to support the new device and loads it. It gets almost all of the information it needs from the environment (where the kernel puts it). The driver (**usb-storage** in this case) actually proxies the device to the Small Computer System Interface (SCSI) layer to profit from the storage logic the layer implements.

6. The kernel now generates another (but separate) **hotplug** event for the new SCSI device.

7. The sequence repeats until **/etc/hotplug/scsi.agent** is executed, and can call further hook scripts to configure the device, assign permissions, or otherwise integrate it with the local system.

[20]**hotplug** does not call these scripts directly; **hotplug** invokes the handlers in **/etc/hotplug.d**, according to the device class. Unless a specific handler takes over, **/etc/hotplug.d/default/default.hotplug** is then responsible for invoking the appropriate agent.

The procedure is similar for network devices, which may first cause a **pci** event to be triggered because all the kernel sees at this point is a PCI card. Once **hotplug** has loaded the PCI card driver, the card will appear to the kernel as a network interface and trigger another **hotplug** event of the **net** class. A video adapter card, on the other hand, would cause only one notification to be sent, as the device itself does not contain another device corresponding to a different **hotplug** event class.

Hook scripts and custom handlers

As stated before, **hotplug** can do more than just load modules. In addition, it also has the ability to execute scripts for specific device classes, drivers, or devices, on registration and deregistration. In fact, when **hotplug** loads a kernel module in response to a new device appearing on one of the buses, it does not do anything apart from execute scripts, which are commonly called hooks.

The Debian base system does not install any hook scripts by default beyond those that handle the loading of kernel modules. Inidividual packages, however, commonly register hook scripts to allow for better integration with the system. For instance, packages providing kernel drivers often install hooks to load firmware, or to set permissions on device files according to the system configuration.

A new device causes **/etc/hotplug.d/default/default.hotplug** to execute the agent script from **/etc/hotplug** corresponding to the device class. As shown above, a new SCSI device causes **/etc/hotplug/scsi.agent** to be executed.

If you want **hotplug** to perform an automatic action upon connection of a new device, it is important to decide when the action should be executed. If the action is supposed to take place when a certain driver is loaded, you can get away with placing an executable script named after the driver into the appropriate subdirectory of **/etc/hotplug**. For instance, the following lines log the device IDs of USB storage devices:

```
~# cat <<EOF > /etc/hotplug/usb/usb-storage
#!/bin/sh -e

exec logger -t $0 -- usb-storage device $PRODUCT
EOF
~# chmod a+rx /etc/hotplug/usb/usb-storage
```

When an agent loads a device driver, it looks in the appropriate directory for scripts with the same name as the driver, and executes them.

If you need more granular control, you might prefer to provide your own handler script. For instance, to call **auto-sync** whenever your handheld is connected, a script such as the following (the name must end in **.hotplug**) would be needed:

```
~# cat <<EOF > /etc/hotplug.d/usb/auto-sync.hotplug
#!/bin/bash -e
```

```
case $PRODUCT in
  830/60/*) :;;
  *) exit 0; # unknown device
esac

[[ $ACTION != add ]] && exit 0 # we only care about new devices

modprobe visor
exec /usr/local/bin/auto-sync $DEVICE
```

In this case, it is important not to forget that this script will be called long before the corresponding agent gets a chance to load any supporting kernel modules. If the device you are trying to configure needs kernel support, you need to load the appropriate module from the hook script. When the corresponding agent is run, it will fail to load the module gracefully and not report an error.

Blacklisting kernel modules

hotplug automatically loads those kernel modules which claim to support the new device. This works most of the time, but in specific situations it may be necessary to prevent the automatic loading of a kernel module by the subsystem's **hotplug** agent. All agents installed by Debian honour a common blacklist, which can be trivially extended by the administrator. For instance, to prevent the **foobar** kernel module from being automatically loaded by any **hotplug** agent, you can add it to the blacklist as illustrated in the following. Note the choice of file name, which is in accordance with the file name scheme for locally created files used throughout Debian (see chapter 6.1.1).

```
~# echo foobar > /etc/hotplug/blacklist.d/local-foobar
```

If you now connect a device that previously caused **hotplug** to load the **foobar** kernel module, it will now instead log something along the lines of:

```
~$ tail /var/log/user.log
[...]
[...] usb.agent[20659]:      foobar: blacklisted
[...]
```

If **discover** detects a device, it needs to be told to ignore it. With **discover** 1, you can add a file to **/etc/discover.d**. To only disable the module for 2.6 kernels, add the file to the **2.6** subdirectory.

```
~# echo skip foobar >> /etc/discover.d/local-foobar
```

At time of writing, blacklisting a module with **discover** 2 required modification of /etc/discover-modprobe.conf. The file is a shell script snippet, and blacklisted modules are stored as a whitespace-separated list in the **$skip** variable. If you prefer to administer blacklisted modules in **run-parts** style (see chapter 6.1.1) instead of modifying a single file, you can insert the following line right after the assignment to the **$skip** variable:

```
~# mkdir -p /etc/discover.blacklist.d
~# cat /etc/discover-modprobe.conf
[...]
# Don't ever load the foo, bar, or baz modules.
#skip=''foo bar baz''
skip="$skip $(grep -v ^# $(run-parts --list /etc/discover.blacklist.d))"
[...]
~#
```

Now you can drop files into **/etc/discover.blacklist.d**; the files should be named in **run-parts** fashion and allow blacklisted modules to be specified, separated by whitespace. Also, comments may be used, making the syntax very similar to the /etc/modules file (see the **modules (5)**), except for the arguments. For instance, the following would cause **discover** 2 never to load the **eepro100** module:

```
~# echo eepro100 > /etc/discover.blacklist.d/local-eepro100
```

Device node management: udev

On a Unix system, **/dev** contains device nodes which are used to communicate with parts of the kernel. For instance, reading from **/dev/urandom** actually sucks bytes from the (pseudo-)random number generator available in the kernel, and writing to **/dev/fd0** causes the kernel to channel the data through to the floppy device. Each such node is identified with a pair of numbers, the "major" and "minor" device node numbers.

With an increasing number of hotpluggable devices (*e.g.* USB, Firewire, *etc.*), device node numbers are becoming a scarce. Moreover, if you inspect a standard **/dev** directory on a Debian system, you will wonder about the purpose of the hundreds of nodes present. The reason is historic: the installation creates all standard device nodes, whether a certain device is available or not.

A new development in the 2.6 kernel series is the **udev** daemon, whose job is the dynamic creation of device nodes when a device is initialised. This approach keeps **/dev** clean. It also gives the administrator a lot of flexibility. **Gnome** already depends on **udev**, and other packages are likely to follow, increasing the chances that **udev** will become a standard on the Debian system.

For instance, to have a USB stick always be available as **/dev/stick** and accessible to the group **stick**, you could configure **udev** as follows:

```
~# cat <<EOF > /etc/udev/rules.d/local-stick.rules
'BUS="scsi", SYSFS{model}="FLASH", KERNEL="sd?1",
  NAME="%k" SYMLINK="stick", GROUP="stick", MODE="0660"'
EOF
```

Note that the rule specification may have to appear on a single line. At time of writing, the udev programme had a parser bug with entries spanning multiple lines.

If you now insert the USB stick with model "FLASH", **udev** will create **/dev/stick** with the requested permissions. **BUS** and **KERNEL** are two further match specifications. A nice guide to writing **udev** rules can be found online[21]; the guide also discusses how to determine the best set of match specifications.

Unfortunately, the **udev** developers decided to drop support for **permissions.d**, a way to separate permissions from naming policy, without a real reason[22].

Dealing with removable storage devices

Having the USB stick always be available as **/dev/stick** makes writing **/etc/fstab** entries easy and allows for usage of the device without needing **root** rights (or even **sudo**).

In addition, Debian provides **pmount** (in package **pmount**), a programme that allows users to mount removable devices without requiring entries in **/etc/fstab**, provided they meet a number of criteria so as to not jeopardise the system's security.

For a user to be able to use **pmount**, that user's account must be a member of the **plugdev** group. You can then simply call **pmount** with the device node as the argument:

```
~# adduser martin plugdev
~$ pmount /dev/sda1
~$ ls -Fl /media/sda1
[...]
~$ pumount /dev/sda1
```

pmount follows symlinks and uses the device name for naming the mount point (which it removes when the device is unmounted). Thus, users will certainly benefit from the integration of **udev** and a canonical device naming scheme.

---

[21] http://www.reactivated.net/udevrules.php
[22] See http://marc.theaimsgroup.com/?l=linux-hotplug-devel&tm=110327407228756&tw=2

6.5.2   kmod, the kernel autoloader

The Linux kernel can automatically load modules when they appear to be needed. For this to happen, the kernel must receive a request for a device or feature name, which it can map to the name of the module to load. More precisely, the kernel does not do any mapping, but it invokes the tool referenced by **/proc/sys/kernel/ modprobe** with the name of the requested feature, and expects it to load the module providing the feature.

The most common tool to satisfy these requests is **modprobe**, which loads kernel modules and their dependencies according to information exported by the kernel, and configuration performed by the administrator.

For the 2.4 kernel series, the **modutils** package installs the necessary file, and the local settings are read from **/etc/modules.conf**, a single file. Because of the reasons outlined in chapter 6.1.1, which make a single file difficult to maintain, Debian provides **update-modules**, a tool that concatenates files found below **/etc/modutils** as well as files residing in the local architecture directory under **/etc/modutils/arch**. **update-modules** also generates the current dependency and module map files for use by **modprobe** (by executing **depmod -a**).

With the advent of the 2.6 kernel series, the upstream kernel departed from the single-file-approach and added functionality similar to **run-parts** (see chapter 6.1.1) to the module tools to honour files placed in the **/etc/modprobe.d** directory[23]. On pure 2.6 kernel systems, **update-modules** is no longer needed, but **depmod -a** must still be called when new modules are added, or existing ones removed.

For both kernel versions, files in the respective directories can set options to be used when loading modules with **modprobe**, defining aliases, or specifying commands to run during the registration or deregistration of modules, as specified in the corresponding manpages **modules.conf** (a)nd **modprobe.conf** (5). The syntax of the latter is much simpler than the former, because it provides more powerful directives, and because the kernel autoloader is losing importance, thanks to programmes like **hotplug**, which handle automatic module loading from user space in a much more flexible way.

Nevertheless, you may still need to control the kernel autoloader, which is enabled by default. In that case, you are advised to create files in the respective directories, named after the **run-parts** scheme (see chapter 6.1.1). Even though the tools do not use **run-parts** internally, it is a good convention to keep. Do not forget to run **update-modules** after making changes to files on a 2.4 kernel machine.

---

[23] Note that **/etc/modprobe.conf** is also honoured and *overrides* the directory. Even though the file is not officially used, it may be good to check for its existence (and delete it after migrating its contents), if things do not work as expected.

6.5.3   Loading modules during startup

During the early initialisation phase, the **/etc/modules** file is read and all modules listed in the file are loaded by **modprobe**, which automatically loads dependencies as well. The syntax of the file is trivial. Each module to be loaded during the boot sequence must be specified on a line of its own, followed by arguments, if it takes any. For example:

```
~# grep -v '^# /etc/modules
3c59x
ne2k irq=9 io=0x240
```

If you prefer not to edit the file directly, you may want to use **modconf** from the **modconf** package. The tool presents the kernel modules tree and allows you to select the desired directory by hitting [enter] to check which modules reside there. **modconf** marks modules currently loaded with a plus sign next to the description.

When using a 2.6 kernel, it may seem a little strange that most modules have their own categories. For instance, if you want Andrew File System (AFS) support, you can load the **afs.ko** module from within the category corresponding to **kernel/fs/afs**. On the other hand, cryptographic kernel modules are all contained in **kernel/crypto**. **modconf** simply uses the kernel tree hierarchy for its menus, and the inconsistent use of categories stems from the kernel itself, not from **modconf**.

When you select a module (by hitting [enter]), **modconf** asks whether you want to load the module into the running kernel, and also prompts for parameters to use. It then uses **modprobe** to load the module (and its dependencies) and, upon success, writes the module name and parameters to **/etc/modules**. When returning to the **modconf** menu, the plus sign next to the module name should indicate that the module has been loaded.

6.6   Configuring kernel parameters

The Linux kernel exports a large number of parameters to the filesystem rooted at **/proc/sys**. These parameters come in the form of pseudo-files and can be manipulated with standard tools. Thus, the following tells the kernel about the machine's identify (useful for logs and debug output):

```
~# hostname --domain > /proc/sys/kernel/domainname
~# hostname > /proc/sys/kernel/hostname
```

Any settings written to **/proc** are discarded with a reboot. To ensure their persistence, you can write them to **/etc/sysctl.conf** in **sysctl** syntax, which is quite straightforward: drop **/proc/sys** from the file name and substitute dots for slashes.

Then append an equals sign followed by the desired value. Unfortunately, **sysctl** expects static definitions and cannot interpret variables or run commands:

```
~# cat <<EOF >> /etc/sysctl.conf
kernel.domainname = debianbook.info
kernel.hostname = arakis
EOF
```

When the system boots, **/etc/rcS.d/S30procps.sh** reads the file and makes the appropriate changes, using **sysctl** (see the **sysctl** (8) manpage).

6.7   Log file management

Debian uses **syslogd** as the logging daemon by default. In the standard configuration, all logs sent via **syslogd** end up in files below **/var/log**, as specified in **/etc/syslog.conf**. In addition, **klogd** funnels kernel log messages to **syslog**, after making them human readable. The **klogd** (8) manual page gives more information.

All logs generated by programmes on a Debian system are written to files below **/var/log**. Furthermore, the standard log files are handled completely by **syslogd**. Two log files are special as their union includes all log messages generated by **syslog**:

auth.log

> receives log entries related to authentication, and other events that are critical to privacy or security issues.

syslog

> everything not related to authentication ends up in this log file. **syslog** is the catch-all log file on a Debian system.

All other files store subsets of the log messages, filtered according to the logging facility and/or priority they use. For the precise configuration, please consult **/etc/syslog.conf**. Please consider that **syslogd** can write a single log message to multiple files. In the following, you will notice that some files relate to a **syslog** facility, while others relate to a message's priority.

boot

> After changing **/etc/default/bootlogd** appropriately, log messages produced during the initialisation sequence will be logged to **boot**.

daemon.log

> Every daemon without a separate facility logs to **daemon.log**. The priority of log events is not relevant.

debug

Messages useful for debugging, which are not related to authentication **daemon.log**. The priority of log events is not relevant.

dmesg

After the kernel has booted, all kernel messages are written to **dmesg** for later reference. This file is not rotated and only exists for a single boot cycle before being overwritten. Note that the choice of name is a little unfortunate, as the **dmesg** command prints the current kernel log ring buffer, which is continuously updated as new kernel events are logged. These messages are written to **kern.log**; The **dmesg** file is not modified until the next restart of the system.

kern.log

Log messages with the **kern** facility end up in this file. The contents are mostly what the kernel spits out, after being formatted by **klogd**.

lpr.log

Log messages with the **lpr** facility end up in this file.

mail.log

Log entries related to the mail system (using the **mail** facility) go into this file. For easier parsing by scripts, mail log entries are also written to **mail.info**, **mail.warn**, and **mail.err**, according to their priority. Unfortunately, Debian's default MTA, **exim4**, does *not* use this file.

messages

Pretty much everything that is not an error or a trivial log entry, and not related to authentication, daemons, **cron** (or other automatic schedulers), mail, and news goes here.

user.log

Messages from user-space processes (but not daemonised; using the **user** facility) are written to **user.log**.

uucp.log

Somewhat antiquated but still useful in certain situations, Unix-to-Unix Copy (UUCP)-related messages (using the **uucp** facility) may be found in this log file.

news/news.*

Log messages with the **news** facility are split into three files according to their priority, and live in the **news** subdirectory.

Other programmes also drop logging information into **/var/log**. For instance, on every Debian system, the directory will probably also contain:

aptitude

> writes an entry to this log for every action the administrator requests.

base-config.*

> The debugging information dumped into these files during the second phase of the installation (see chapter 3.2.2) is of limited value.

debian-installer/*

> The Debian installer dumps the log messages it colllected during the installation here.

exim4/*

> As noted above, the **exim4** authors thought it wise to circumvent standard practice and use their own log files instead of the commonly accepted **syslogd** channel. For log entries related to **exim4**, look underneath **exim4**. Alternatively, install **postfix**.

ksymoops

> **modutils**, needed for 2.4 kernels, dumps kernel symbol information to this directory, mainly for debugging purposes. You can basically ignore it, or even delete the directory on 2.6 kernels.

In addition, the standard session log files **btmp**, **lastlog**, and **wtmp** exist to store failed (local) login attempts, the users' last login times, and each user's login history respectively.

Log file permissions

Debian tries to set the permissions of these log files in a secure and flexible way. Files are generally readable by members of the **adm** group. At time of writing, several log files with potentially sensitive information (most notably: **mail.log**) are publicly readable[24]. Unfortunately, the lack of a permissions policy can cause inconsistencies in the log file access settings. Work on formalising a policy has begun, nevertheless.

Once a log file is created, its permissions are usually kept. It is a good idea to check the contents of **/var/log** after installing new packages to make sure that no information can leak. **syslog-ng** can replace the **syslogd** log daemon, and it provides facilities to automatically choose file permissions when it creates log files. It also allows for the use of variables in log file names, paving the way for rotationless log management.

If you can take away access to **btmp**, **lastlog**, and **wtmp** from your users, consider changing the permissions on the log file directory itself to lock out non-**adm**-members. Then, use Access Control List (ACL)s to grant permissions to the users of

[24]See http://bugs.debian.org/285500, hopefully this will be fixed soon.

daemons that drop **root** privileges early during the startup phase. Obviously, you need filesystem ACL support and the **acl** package installed.

```
~# chmod g+s,o= /var/log
~# chgrp adm /var/log
~# setfacl -m user:Debian-exim:x /var/log
[...]
```

Log file rotation

To prevent log files from growing too large and possibly filling up the **/var** filesystem, the Debian system rotates log files on a regular basis. Debian uses two tools for log rotation: packages that install pieces of software with their own log files commonly use **logrotate**. The system itself uses the simple **savelog** tool in scripts to allow for greater flexibility. Log file rotation can be illustrated with **savelog**, which provides the **-t** option (among others) to create new empty log files after the rotation.

```
~$ ls -F
logfile
~$ savelog -t logfile && ls -F
Rotated 'logfile' at Fri Aug 12 17:39:24 CET 2004.
logfile  logfile.0
~$ savelog -t logfile && ls -F
Rotated 'logfile' at Fri Aug 12 17:39:27 CET 2004.
logfile  logfile.0  logfile.1.gz
[...]
~$ ls -F
logfile    logfile.1.gz  logfile.3.gz  logfile.5.gz
logfile.0  logfile.2.gz  logfile.4.gz  logfile.6.gz
~$ savelog -t logfile && ls -F
logfile    logfile.1.gz  logfile.3.gz  logfile.5.gz
logfile.0  logfile.2.gz  logfile.4.gz  logfile.6.gz
```

By default, **savelog** keeps the last seven previously rotated files. If the log file is then rotated again, the oldest file is deleted, and the second oldest takes its place. Furthermore, the tool compresses the six oldest log files. You can adjust the number of log files to keep with the **-c** option.

The two **/etc/cron.*/sysklogd** scripts use **savelog** to rotate all log files written by **syslogd**. It employs **/usr/sbin/syslogd-listfiles**, which scans **/etc/syslog.conf** and outputs a list of log file candidates for daily rotation. When the **--weekly** option is set, it only outputs candidates for weekly rotation. Whether a specific log file is subject to daily or weekly rotation is mainly a function of its size. Large files are rotated daily, while smaller files are put on a weekly schedule. **/var/log/syslog** is an exception, as it receives all log events (except for authentication-related events) and is always rotated daily.

6.7.1 Monitoring logs with logcheck

One of the strengths of a Unix system is also one of its weaknesses. Many programmes, especially daemons, write log entries for most of their actions. Most of this is informational, but it is also in the logs that problems surface. Nevertheless, the sheer volume of logging that takes place on a busy machine essentially makes it impossible for a system administrator to keep up.

When the upstream **logcheck** died, the Debian project stepped in to take over the maintenance of and improve of this tool which helps admins keep track of log entries. The way **logcheck** works is quite straightforward, but the tool turns out to be immensely useful. It is actively maintained on **alioth**[25].

Log message severities

Scheduled by **cron**, **logcheck** figures out all the log entries generated since its last invocation and runs these, line by line, through a series of filters to produce a final report. The filters are nothing more than extended regular expressions (such as understood by **egrep**) and serve to assign a log message to one of four categories. The documentation goes into greater detail on the four classes[26]:

default
> By default, all messages are classified as "system events."

ignore
> Messages matching any of the rules in **/etc/logcheck/ignore.d** are simply ignored. Here, routine messages should be identified and weeded out to keep them out of the final report.

violation
> Messages matching any of the rules in **/etc/logcheck/violations.d** are escalated to be "security events" and are assigned a special section in the final report, unless matched by a rule in **/etc/logcheck/violations.ignore.d**. For a security event to be ignored, the rule in **violations.ignore.d** must be in a file of the same name as the one containing the rule responsible for the promotion to the higher level. If **violations.d/foo** escalates log entries, the escalation can only be cancelled with an entry in **violations.ignore.d/foo**. In addition, **violations.ignore.d/local-foo** can be used (see below).

cracking
> Messages matching any of the rules in **/etc/logcheck/cracking.d** are escalated to highest priority and termed "attack alerts," unless inhibited by a

[25]http://logcheck.alioth.debian.org
[26]/usr/share/doc/logcheck-database/README.logcheck-database.gz

matching entry in the ruleset under **/etc/logcheck/cracking.ignore.d**. Here, too, the override must be in a file of the same name (with an optional **local-** prefix) as the one causing the escalated message. Attack alert messages are included most prominently in the final report.

logcheck's real power comes from its increasingly tight integration with the rest of the Debian archive. Based on the philosophy that a package maintainer knows best which of the packaged software's logging messages should be classified in which category, Debian packages containing software that writes log entries are encouraged to provide their own **logcheck** filters. To facilitate this, **logcheck** simply concatenates all files within one of the filter directories, so a package just has to drop a file named after itself in the appropriate place.

Local rules

For local rules, it is best to use the **local-** prefix to avoid clashes with files installed by packages (see chapter 6.1.1). Even though Debian's configuration file handling ensures that your files are not overwritten, a clash can still occur. Local files are treated just like those provided by packages, and can be used to override escalations, as shown above. Finally, the **local** file can contain rules not applicable to a single package. If you need to author a filter set for a certain software because the package does not install one, please consider submitting the filter with a bug report against the package for future inclusion with Debian.

logcheck itself defines a number of rules for promotion in **/etc/logcheck/*/logcheck**. For instance, any log message containing "reject" will become a security event, and a log entry containing the word "attack" will be reported as an attack alert. At times, these generic rules escalate false alarms. To prevent this, **logcheck** allows the use of files prefixed with **logcheck-**. Thus, **logcheck-postfix** could contain rules to prevent false alarms from **postfix** generated log messages, which have been escalated by generic **logcheck** rules. The **local** file can also be used for this.

Defining filters

A filter file is a collection of extended regular expressions, one expression per line. Empty lines as well as lines starting with a hash symbol ('#') are ignored. The rules should be as specific as possible, and a great way to test and author them is through the use of **egrep**. In the following, **egrep** helped in identifying a syntax error which would have caused the rule to be essentially ineffective:

```
~$ logger -t foo\[12345\] -- flushed 123 records, status=14
~$ egrep 'foo\[[[:digit:]],5\]: flushed [[:digit:]]+ records,
  status=[:digit:]+$' /var/log/syslog || echo NO MATCH
NO MATCH
```

```
˜$ egrep 'foo\[[[:digit:]]1,5\]: flushed [[:digit:]]+ records,
  status=[:digit:]+$' /var/log/syslog || echo NO MATCH
[...] foo[12345]: flushed 123 records, status=14
˜$ echo !!:1 >> /etc/logcheck/ignore.d/local-foo
```

Rule levels

logcheck also differentiates between three levels for the filters, so that maintainers can make sane choices depending on the function of the machine on which a package is installed. While the workstation level filters most messages, the server level is a lot more cautious and does not pretend to cater for local users and reports many more anomalies. The paranoid level is intended for high-security machines and probably requires quite some tweaking. The severity level to be used can be configured with **debconf** (see chapter 5.8).

6.8 Network configuration management

Nowadays, most computers are connected to others over a network. In Debian, two types of network connections exist. Note that the following are not official categories but exist for the purpose of this chapter only:

- Connections handled by kernel drivers. Standard Ethernet devices, virtual tunnels, Firewire, and USB network devices are examples of network connections of this class.

- Connections handled by user-space daemons. The best example here is **pppd**, as well as daemons using IP user-space Tunneling (TUN)/Ethernet user-space Tunneling (TAP).

Debian's network configuration management system **ifupdown** handles both kinds of interfaces, but does not attempt to reinvent the wheel. For instance, PPP connectivity is managed by **pppd** at a lower level. **ifupdown** integrates **pppd** behind the unified network configuration interface it exposes for all types of connectivity.

6.8.1 Network configuration with ifupdown

Network interfaces of the first kind are almost exclusively controlled by **ifupdown**. It consists of two commands, both driven by a single configuration file: /etc/network/interfaces.

The configuration file

The main network configuration file, **/etc/network/interfaces**, contains a number of different kinds of stanzas to describe various aspects of the network management system **ifupdown**. A stanza consists of a line starting with one of three possible directives, followed by a number of options. Additional parameters may follow on separate lines, which may be indented for clarity. A stanza ends with the beginning of a new stanza or at the end of the file. **ifupdown** knows three different types of stanzas, identified by the following three directives:

iface

Describes an interface configuration. The directive itself takes three arguments:

name

The name of the configuration (*e.g.* eth0).

address family

The network address family (*e.g.* inet)

method

The configuration method (*e.g.* dhcp). The available methods depend on the address family to be used.

Even though the **iface** directive suggests that the stanza describes a network interface, it is actually just a set of parameters to use for the configuration of an interface (the **ifupdown (8)** manpage refers to these configurations as logical interfaces, as distinct from physical interfaces. I will return to this point when I introduce the idea behind interface mappings.

auto

Takes a single type of argument: the names of one or more interfaces that should be configured during system initialisation (/etc/rcS.d/S40networking), or when the -a switch is given to one of the **ifupdown** commands. Interfaces which are not mentioned in **auto** lines are available to the administrator, but are never brought up at system initialisation.

mapping

Defines a mapping system for an interface to allow for different configuration parameter sets to be applied to the interface depending on the output of a script.

The full syntax of directives is described in the **interfaces (5)** manpage. A simple example of a typical network interfaces configuration could look like this:

```
~# grep -v '^#' /etc/network/interfaces
auto lo eth0 eth1

iface lo inet loopback

mapping eth0
  script /usr/local/sbin/get-netconfig-method.sh
  map DYNAMIC eth0-dhcp
  map STATIC eth0-static

iface eth0-dhcp inet dhcp
iface eth0-static inet static
  address 172.19.23.14
  netmask 255.255.248.0
  gateway 172.19.16.1

iface eth1 inet static
  address 192.168.0.1
  netmask 255.255.255.0
```

Configuration methods

ifupdown supports three different address families:

inet

> Internet Protocol (IP) (version 4) addressing

inet6

> Internet Protocol (Version 6) (IPv6) addressing

ipx

> Internetwork Packet Exchange (IPX) addressing

Additional address families cannot be added by the user, unfortunately. If you want to use **ifupdown** for interfaces using other addressing styles (and network protocols), you should use the **inet** address family and the **manual** method. This is possible because address families do not have a direct effect on how the interface is configured; they only serve to identify the configuration method to be used. The complete description of a configuration method includes the address family, such as **inet/static**.

Configuration methods are defined individually for each of the address families. The most important methods are:

*/static

> configures a network interface with a static address. All address families support this method. For the two IP address families, this method requires

the specification of the **address** and **netmask** to be used, and allows for other aspects of the interface or the configuration process to be configured. For instance, it is possible to define the **gateway** to be used for the default route, or to override the standard Maximum Transfer Unit (MTU) size of the interface (**mtu**).

Note that only a single interface should be configured to provide access to a gateway[27]. As **ifupdown** adds a default route to the kernel routing table for each **gateway** parameter it encounters when bringing interfaces up, multiple gateway definitions result in multiple default routes. As Linux will only use the first default route it finds, you could encounter some surprises: the effective default route will depend on the order in which interfaces are brought up: the default route set by the first interface cannot be overridden by interfaces brought up at a later point. This may seem backwards in the domain of computers to some.

inet*/loopback

configures a loopback network interface. Both IP address families have this method. The method takes no additional option.

inet/dhcp

allows for an Internet Protocol (Version 4) (IPv4) network interface to be configured with DHCP. Options include the host name to use in the lease request (**hostname**) and the hardware address to be used (**hwaddress**).

As regards to the handling of multiple default routes mentioned before, please consider that a DHCP server can communicate a gateway address to the client alongside the IP address (in the **routers** field of the response). If such a gateway is present in the DHCP offer, **ifupdown** will unconditionally configure a default route for it. If this is not desired, the **/etc/dhclient-script** (or **/etc/dhcp/dhclient-script**, if **dhcp3-client** is used) must be modified appropriately. Unfortunately, it seems to be impossible to make **dhclient** ignore the **routers** parameter otherwise.

inet6/v4tunnel

configures an IPv6-over-IPv4 tunnel. This method requires the **iproute** package to be installed.

inet/manual

does nothing at all and expects the administrator to handle configuration and deconfiguration entirely from hook scripts.

The **interfaces** (5) manual page describes all available configuration methods and the parameters they take.

[27] http://bugs.debian.org/152895

Configuration parameters

Each configuration method requires or honours any number of parameters, which are specified on lines following the **iface** directive. Not every option is available for every method. For example, specifying an address or netmask makes no sense for the **loopback** and **dhcp** configuration methods. Conversely, both **address** and **netmask** are mandatory parameters for the **static** method.

Nevertheless, it is not an error if an **iface** stanza specifying the **dhcp** configuration method contains an **address** parameter. Any options which are not relevant to the configuration method to be used are converted to environment variables (with dashes replaced by underscores, all letters capitalised, non-alphanumeric characters discarded, and **IF_** prepended) and made available during the configuration of the interface. For instance (to give a sneak preview of hook scripts, to which we will return in just a moment), the following illustrates this behaviour:

```
~# cat /etc/network/interfaces
[...]
iface eth0 inet dhcp
  [...]
  my-parameters foo bar
  up echo my-parameters are: $IF_MY_PARAMETERS
[...]
~# ifup eth0
[...]
my-parameters are: foo bar
```

Hence, an **address** parameter's value within a **dhcp** stanza would simply be available during configuration in the environment variable $IF_ADDRESS, rather than triggering something akin to a syntax error. We will see shortly how loose handling of parameters allows for maximum flexibility.

Bringing up network interfaces

To bring up a network interface in Debian, you use **ifup** and pass it the interface name(s) on the command line. Alternatively, passing -a to **ifup** causes it to sequentially bring up all interfaces specified in **auto** stanzas in the configuration file, except for those named as arguments of the **--exclude** option on the command line. Bringing up an interface entails the following steps:

- First, **ifup** looks in **/etc/network/run/ifstate** to see whether the specified interface has already been configured, in which case it aborts with an error. You can use the **--force** option to override this check.

- Next, **ifup** reads the configuration parameters for the given interface from **/etc/ network/interfaces** and obtains the method and options with which it should configure the interface.

- The tool then calls the **pre-up** hooks with any additional parameters in the environment. If any of these hook scripts exits with a non-zero return code then the interface is not configured; this behaviour cannot be overridden with the **--force** option.

- If all hooks finish successfully, **ifupdown** configures the network interface according to the specified address family and method. The configuration may consist of an invocation of a DHCP client or the immediate assignment of IP address, netmask, and corresponding routes using the appropriate network interface configuration tools. At present it is unfortunately impossible (or at least not easy) to extend **ifupdown** with custom configuration methods[28].

- Once the network interface has been brought up and configured, **ifup** runs the **up** hooks with any additional parameters in the environment.

- Finally, **ifupdown** makes a note for the interface in **/etc/network/run/ifstate**[29] to indicate that the interface has been configured.

  A problem arises when an **up** hook exits with an error. In that case, the interface will not be marked as configured even though it has been configured from the operating system's perspective in the step before calling the **up** hooks[30]. We will return to this point later when we discuss the shortcomings of the **ifupdown** system.

Deconfiguring network interfaces

ifdown takes an interface down, mostly in the same fashion as **ifup** brought it up. It honours an interface name (or multiple names) specified on the command line, or **-a** to bring down all interfaces marked **auto** other than those named after the **--exclude** command line option. The steps it takes are:

- First, **ifdown** checks whether the interface is actually configured. If an **up** hook fails during configuration, the interface can be only brought down by overriding this check with the **--force** option.

- Second, it reads the configuration information for the interface(s).

---

[28]The current **ifupdown** version in the *experimental* archive fixes this by supporting replacement configuration methods read from **/lib/ifupdown/method**.

[29]The file actually resides in **/dev/shm** which is a RAM filesystem and hence does not violate the policy anymore. This constitutes an improvement over previous versions of **ifupdown**, which used **/etc/network/ifstate** to maintain state information.

[30]See http://bugs.debian.org/286148

- Next, it calls all **down** hooks with the extra parameters available in the environment. These hooks can fail as often as they want without affecting the deconfiguration[31].

- Then it actually deconfigures the interface, based on address family and method.

- At this point, **ifdown** runs the **post-down** hooks; these can fail as often as they want without affecting the deconfiguration (unlike **up** scripts).

- Finally, **ifdown** removes all references to the now unconfigured interface from /etc/network/run/ifstate.

Using hooks

The **ifupdown** system provides four hooks for each interface, two of which are executed during configuration, and two which are run as part of the deconfiguration; one of the two hooks is run just before **ifupdown** touches the interface, and the other is called after this. In order of their usual invocation, the four hooks are: **pre-up, up, down, post-down**).

Each of these hooks receives information in the form of environment variables. Apart from any additional parameters, the relevant variables are:

$MODE
> Either **start** or **stop**, depending on whether **ifup** or **ifdown** has been called.

$IFACE
> The name of the interface, *e.g.* eth0.

$ADDRFAM
> The address family of the configuration, *e.g.* **inet**, **inet6**, or even **ipx**.

$METHOD
> The method used for configuration, such as **static**, **dhcp**, or **loopback**.

Hook scripts can be specified in two ways. First, each **iface** stanza can specify hook commands directly, as shown in the following example, which configures (and deconfigures) a masquerading router:

```
~# grep -v '^#' /etc/network/interfaces
auto lo eth0 eth1

iface lo inet loopback
  up iptables-restore < /etc/network/iptables
```

[31]A change to this behaviour has been requested: http://bug.debian.org/286166

```
iface eth0 inet static
  address 192.168.0.1
  netmask 255.255.255.0

iface eth1 inet dhcp
  up iptables -t nat -A POSTROUTING \
    -s 192.168.0.1 -o $IFACE -j MASQUERADE
  up sysctl -w net.ipv4.ip_forward=1
  down sysctl -w net.ipv4.ip_forward=0
  down iptables -t nat -D POSTROUTING \
    -s 192.168.0.1 -o $IFACE -j MASQUERADE
```

This example also shows how to initialise **iptables** when the **lo** interface is brought up, something which should probably be done in all but some special cases[32].

Obviously, loading the packet filter in the **up** hook is only one of many possible ways of configuring **iptables**; I find it one of the cleanest and most manageable. You can create **/etc/network/iptables** with the following simple command, provided you configure it to reflect your needs through various invocations of **iptables**. In appendix C.4, you will find a restrictive example to serve as a basis.

```
~# iptables-save > /etc/network/iptables
```

It may not be obvious why you want to would load the packet filter configuration when bringing up the **lo** interface, since a packet filter is only really needed when network connectivity is available; **lo** does not provide the type of connectivity which can threaten system security (unless you have local users trying to produce buffer overflows in your network server processes). The reason why I chose to initialise the packet filter when **lo** was brought up was that this ensures that the packet filter is loaded in all cases. If you were to configure it as part of the initialisation of **eth0**, you might temporarily expose the system to threats if you added a second network interface and forgot the packet filter. I only load the packet filter and never flush the rule tables simply because a packet filter should not be unloaded (and will be reinitialised during a reboot).

Following the execution of the individual interface-specific hooks, **ifupdown** invokes the scripts in the appropriate directory underneath **/etc/network**, using **run-parts** (see chapter 6.1.1). For instance, the following hook script in **/etc/network/if-up.d** would have the same effect as the **up** hook specified in the **lo iface** stanza in the above configuration example:

```
~# cat <<EOF > /etc/network/if-up.d/local-iptables
#!/bin/bash -e
```

[32]At this point, allow me to remind you that **iptables** does *not* filter IPv6 traffic. If you have IPv6 connectivity, please make sure you configure **ip6tables** as well to prevent attackers from simply using IPv6 to bypass the packet filter.

```
[[ $IFACE = lo ]] || exit 0

exec iptables-restore < /etc/network/iptables
EOF
~# chmod 755 /etc/network/if-up.d/local-iptables
```

Various packages make use of the hook directory to register the programmes to be executed when the network configuration changes. This allows package maintainers to automate many aspects of administration, such as the reconfiguration of Domain Name System (DNS) caches when the connectivity changes.

Interfaces with multiple addresses

A network device may have more than one address assigned to it. This comes in handy if you need a single server to provide multiple conflicting services in parallel, such as an SSL-enabled web server.

A common method of configuring multiple addresses is to use pseudo interfaces. While **eth0** is the main interface, **eth0:0** and **eth0:1** (and so on) are pseudo interfaces which have their own network addresses. Use of pseudo interfaces is now deprecated because a better method exists: adding multiple network addresses to a single interface. This is possible using the **ip** tool from the **iproute** package, which can be called via **ifupdown** hooks:

```
~# grep -v '^#' /etc/network/interfaces
[...]
iface eth0 inet static
  address 192.168.0.10
  netmask 255.255.255.0
  up ip addr add 192.168.0.11/24 dev $IFACE
  down ip addr del 192.168.0.11/24 dev $IFACE
```

Note that these additional addresses will not be available in the output of **ifconfig**. You will need to use **ip addr** instead. At this point, I would suggest abandoning **ifconfig** (which is deprecated and has limited support for newer features) and invest some time in learning **ip** instead (which can do everything **ifconfig** can, and more).

Interface mappings

ifupdown can also select between different configuration stanzas to be used to configure an interface. This is accomplished with **mapping** stanzas, which translate the name of the physical interface to the name of the **iface** stanza to be used. The **ifupdown** documentation refers to the **iface** stanza names as "logical interfaces", which may be confusing.

A **mapping** stanza consists of a fileglob defining its matching criterion, and a script to perform the mapping. When **ifupdown** is asked to configure or deconfigure an interface, it first checks whether a **mapping** exists whose criterion matches the requested name. It uses the first matching **mapping** to transform the name, and does so repeatedly with the result until no more matching **mapping** stanzas can be found. With the final result it then identifies an **iface** stanza to use for the configuration of the interface. The following shows a simple **mapping** definition:

```
~# cat /etc/network/interfaces
mapping eth0
  script /usr/local/sbin/map-location.sh
  map HOME eth0-home
  map UNI eth0-uni

iface eth0-home inet static
  address 192.168.0.10
  netmask 255.255.255.0
  gateway 192.168.0.1

iface eth0-uni inet dhcp
```

When **ifupdown** is asked to configure *e.g.* eth0, it successfully matches the name against the first mapping and runs the specified script with the name of the phys-ical interface as its argument. The script also receives all **map** lines (without the **map** keyword) on **stdin**. These lines allow the script to work with canonical names (such as "UNI"), and to use the data available on **stdin** to translate an internal rep-resentation to the value expected by **ifupdown**[33]. Assuming that the script would determine the current location to be "UNI", it would extract **eth0-uni** from **stdin** and write this identifier to **stdout**.

ifupdown then compares the identifier **eth0-uni** again with the matching criteria of all available **mapping** stanzas. In this case, it would not find a match and thus configure **eth0** using DHCP, which is what the **eth0-uni iface** stanza defines.

In the absence of mappings, an identity mapping is assumed, and the name of the **iface** stanza to be used is identical to the name of the physical interface. Internally, **ifupdown** identifies interfaces by the physical interface name and configuration stanza used (or to be used). More precisely, when you issue the command **ifup eth0**, **ifupdown** internally deals with the interface identified as **eth0=eth0**, which can be read as a "variable definition" to mean: "the physical interface **eth0** is assigned the configuration specified in the **iface** stanza named 'eth0." The error message issued by **ifupdown** when it encounters an unknown interface reveals this internal representation:

```
~# ifup eth1
Ignoring unknown interface eth1=eth1.
```

[33]At least this was the intended purpose. The **map** lines can also be used to pass configuration to the script. **guessnet** (see chapter 6.8.1) is an example of such an application.

You can bypass the mapping scripts and manually configure an interface with a specific configuration by using the "variable assignment" syntax to select the desired **iface** stanza. Note that a command such as **ifup eth0-uni** triggers the same error as above, as **ifupdown** cannot determine the physical interface to configure in this case. The following forces **ifupdown** to use the **eth0-uni** configuration:

```
~# ifup eth0=eth0-uni
[...]
```

In this case, the mapping is not used because "eth0-uni" is not matched by the "eth0" fileglob; a mapping with a pattern such as "eth0*" instead would cause the mapping to be applied. Another way to disable mappings is through the use of the **--no-mappings** command line option to **ifup**.

The sample **/etc/network/interfaces** file[34] contains many interesting examples of mappings, including an example of how to integrate PCMCIA schemes with **ifupdown**.

Dealing with removable network devices

As we saw in chapter 6.5.1, Debian uses **hotplug** to deal with removable hardware, which includes network devices on hotpluggable bus systems such as PCMCIA and USB. When the user attaches a network device to a machine, the kernel eventually asks **hotplug** to execute **/etc/hotplug/net.agent**, which is responsible for configuring the device.

By default, Debian's **hotplug** configures all interfaces marked **auto** in **/etc/network/interfaces** when they become available, and deconfigures them on removal. This behaviour is governed by the so-called network agent policy, which can be configured in **/etc/default/hotplug** or with **dpkg-reconfigure hotplug**. The following three policies are available:

all

> If the new network interface is configurable with **ifupdown**, **hotplug** invokes **ifup** and **ifdown** accordingly.

auto

> Only network interfaces mentioned in **auto** stanzas in **/etc/network/interfaces** are handled automatically. This raises a slight problem because removable interfaces may not be available during the initialisation sequence, and when **/etc/rcS.d/S40networking** attempts to bring up all automatic interfaces, an error occurs. Similarly, an invocation of **ifup -a** would fail even though it may have configured the available network interfaces successfully. This is the default policy.

[34]/usr/share/doc/ifupdown/examples/network-interfaces.gz

hotplug

To address the latter problem, it is possible to configure an interface with **ifupdown** so that it can be used automatically by **hotplug**, but without making it automatic in the sense of **ifupdown**'s **auto** stanzas. Since **ifupdown** does not know about **hotplug**, interface mappings are used instead. If **eth0** appears, and the **hotplug** network agent policy is in effect, **hotplug** tells **ifupdown** to deal with **eth0=hotplug** instead of the plain interface. Using **grep** and the **map** parameters, it is possible to selectively flag single interfaces as hotpluggable:

```
~# cat /etc/network/interfaces
[...]
mapping hotplug
  script grep
  map airo0
  map prism0

iface airo0 inet dhcp

iface prism0 inet dhcp

iface eth0 inet dhcp
```

When the **airo0** or **prism0** interfaces become available, **ifupdown** configures them with DHCP. If **eth0** appears, **ifupdown** ignores the request for configuration (but does not produce an error) because the call to **grep** failed. We can illustrate this by direct invocation:

```
~# ifup eth0=hotplug
Ignoring unknown interface eth0=hotplug.
```

It should be obvious that the **all** policy is equivalent to using **hotplug** as shown, but with **echo** instead of **grep** as the mapping script.

Renaming network devices

If you have been using Linux for a while now, or you are the owner of a laptop or other type of machine with removable network devices, you may well know the story: a new kernel or a different order of insertion caused the former **eth0** to become **eth1**, while **eth1** is now **eth0**; this is inconvenient if not fatal.

The **ifrename** package provides a tool that can automatically rename interfaces based on static data (such as the Media Access Control (MAC) address, or bus location) before the interface is brought up and configured. As this functionality is most useful with removable devices, the package automatically integrates with the **hotplug** system. For instance, to make sure that the PCMCIA with the shown MAC address will be named **lan** instead of **ethX**, the following line in **/etc/iftab** would cause **ifrename** to perform the name change on the next insertion:

```
echo lan mac 00:00:de:ad:be:ef >> /etc/iftab
```

Once the interface has been renamed, the new name is official and the interface will not be accessible with its old name. Therefore, you will need to amend the **ifupdown** configuration, as well as any other files that possibly hardcode the interface name (such as the packet filter definition). A recursive **grep** on **/etc** should help you.

```
~# ifconfig
[...]
lan        Link encap:Ethernet  HWaddr 00:00:de:ad:be:ef
[...]
~# ifconfig eth0
eth0: error fetching interface information: Device not found
```

After configuration, you can be sure that the network device with the shown MAC address will always be named **lan**, which should give you everything you need to make your network configuration more robust with respect to interface names.

It should be mentioned that **udev** (see chapter 6.5.1) can also rename network interfaces and thus competes with **ifrename**. The following **udev** rule achieves the same as the aforementioned entry in **/etc/iftab**:

```
~# grep lan /etc/udev/rules.d/local-netifaces
KERNEL="eth*", SYSFS{address}="00:00:de:ad:be:ef", NAME="lan"
```

udev can only rename interfaces on systems using a 2.6 kernel. On older kernels, **ifrename** has to be used. Unfortunately, to rename interfaces that are not hotpluggable, this must occur before the interfaces are configured. The **ifrename** documentation includes a patch against **/etc/init.d/networking** to do exactly this[35].

Automated location detection and configuration

If you travel between different networks, you are probably not too fond of the continuous need to reconfigure your network devices. Interface mappings go a long way to facilitate the endeavour; with the appropriate script(s) mapping interfaces to configuration stanzas according to local circumstances, you can let **ifupdown** figure out the appropriate configuration stanza to use and configure your network automatically.

[35]See /usr/share/doc/ifrename/HOTPLUG.txt.gz.

The **guessnet** package provides a tool that can integrate smoothly with **ifupdown**. Using mappings and extra parameters in **iface** stanzas, it allows for a number of tests to be run and uses the configuration stanza that specified the test to return successfully. The following example uses Address Resolution Protocol (ARP) to check if a certain host with the specified IP/MAC address combination is accessible on the network and will configure the interface accordingly if the host is found. If no such host can be found after 5 seconds, **ifupdown** will use DHCP instead. If **guessnet** concludes that the network cable is not attached, the interface will not be brought up. Note how **guessnet** uses **map** parameters to pass options to the script.

```
~# cat /etc/network/interfaces
mapping eth0
  script guessnet-ifupdown
  map default: dhcp
  map timeout: 5

iface disconnected inet manual
  pre-up false
  test missing-cable

iface uni inet static
  address 172.19.23.14
  netmask 255.255.248.0
  gateway 172.19.16.1
  test peer address 172.19.16.1 mac 00:2d:2c:33:fe:1e

iface dhcp inet dhcp
```

In addition to ARP, **guessnet** also allows for standard commands or scripts to be run as tests. Further tests include searching for PPPoE concentrators and wireless access points, although these tests are still to be considered experimental. When multiple interfaces are defined, it is possible to limit the tests to run for each interface. Unfortunately, the limit is specified somewhat non-intuitively in the **mapping** stanza. Wildcards or the like cannot be used. The following would limit the **work** profile to **eth0**, and the **home** profile to **eth1**. The **dhcp** profile is available for both (and must be specified explicitly):

```
~# cat /etc/network/interfaces
mapping eth0
  script guessnet-ifupdown
  map default: dhcp
  map work dhcp

mapping eth1
  script guessnet-ifupdown
  map default: dhcp
  map home dhcp
```

Please refer to the **guessnet (8)** manpage for more information about the configuration and its possibilities.

Further automating the network configuration

The **ifplugd** package is a useful addition to **guessnet**, especially with laptops. **ifplugd** monitors network devices and can run scripts when they appear or disappear, when the cable connection changes, or when the system is suspended or resumed. **hotplug** adequately handles the first, and **ifplugd** respects this: it uses **debconf** for its configuration and asks you for static and hotplug interfaces separately. It also allows you to specify a policy for when the system is suspended.

Since it is likely for a laptop system to wake up in a new environment, **ifplugd** simply reconfigures the interfaces it controls when the system comes back up. Similarly, unplugging the network cable causes it to take down the associated interface, and once a cable is detected again, **ifplugd** tries to configure the interface, thereby invoking **guessnet**, if so configured. A similar and equally useful daemon is **waproamd**, which is designed to facilitate roaming between different wireless networks. It can automatically select passphrases to use based on access point address or Extended Service Set Identifier (ESSID). **ifupdown** and **guessnet** provide this functionality, **guessnet** by deciding between configuration stanzas, and **ifupdown** by using **iwconfig** to configure the wireless network interface, but **waproamd** may be more mature and stable for the time being.

Shortcomings of ifupdown

ifupdown is an incredibly flexible system, and the interface mapping functionality in particular allows it to handle most common network configuration tasks. However, the **ifupdown** tools have been around for a long time, and several shortcomings have become apparent as the requirements increased.

One of the biggest problems is the need for **ifupdown** to keep track of the interface state, rather than using the kernel's interface state. When hook scripts do not do what they should, or the configuration of a network interface is modified with other tools, **ifupdown**'s idea of the interface states can quickly get out of sync. This is a problem that several people are working on, and a rewrite of **ifupdown** can be expected in the future[36], possibly based on Distributed Bus (D-BUS)[37]. You can be sure that the next version of **ifupdown** will work with your old configuration (possibly with an automatic migration path), as is customary on a Debian system.

---

[36]RedHat, for instance, has proposed the idea of "Stateless Linux," from which ideas are likely to be drawn: http://people.redhat.com/~hp/stateless/StatelessLinux.pdf

[37]**D-BUS** is a flexible message communication framework between applications, designed as part of the recent promising desktop unification efforts by the FreeDesktop.org project. More information is available on the web page: http://www.freedesktop.org/Software/dbus

Another problem is related to default routes[38]. In the current **ifupdown** system, a gateway is a parameter of a network interface. As multiple network interfaces can be configured for a system, it is possible for two network interfaces to prevent the system from communicating when configured simultaneously. Therefore, it is the administrator's job to ensure that only a single default route is configured at all times. In the future, **ifupdown** may deal with this situation, either by making the gateway parameter global (in the form of another type of stanza), or by checking for the presence of a default route before trying to configure one.

Also, the current **ifupdown** system is not extensible with respect to address families and configuration methods. It is to be expected that the next incarnation of **ifupdown** will support a modular approach, allowing the administrator to define custom configuration methods. Please refer to the **netconf** project for more information[39].

6.8.2   Using DHCP to obtain a network address

ifupdown automatically pulls in a flexible and powerful DHCP client[40], which is automatically used to configure interfaces that define the **dhcp** method. In fact, the **dhcp** method causes **ifupdown** not to do anything beyond running *e.g.* **dhclient eth0**, assuming that the DHCP client will configure the network device properly.

When **dhclient** receives a positive response from a DHCP server (a DHCP offer), it calls **/etc/dhclient-script** (or **/etc/dhcp3/dhclient-script**) to configure the device. The script itself also provides hooks. While **dhcp-client's** abilities are limited to two files, **/etc/dhclient-enter-hooks** and **/etc/dhclient-exit-hooks**, which allow commands to be executed before and after configuration, **dhcp3-client** uses the standard **run-parts** approach and honours files installed below **/etc/dhcp3/dhclient-enter-hooks.d** (and the corresponding directory for exit hooks). Thus, when **dhclient** is invoked by **ifupdown**, the **enter** hook is executed after **ifupdown's pre-up** or **down** hook, and the **exit** hook is called just before **ifupdown** runs the registered **up** and **post-down** scripts. Note that the DHCP server is contacted *before* the **enter** hook is called.

A frequent requirement when using DHCP is the customisation of the DNS search path suggested by the DHCP server. The DNS search path consists of domains which are appended to hostnames during their resolution in order of definition. For instance, with **debian.org** in your DNS search path, you can connect to *e.g.* **security.debian.org** simply by using the host name **security**. The **dhclient** documentation seems to suggest prepending custom strings to the domain name, using a special directive in **dhclient.conf** (note the trailing space):

---

[38] http://bugs.debian.org/152895

[39] http://alioth.debian.org/projects/netconf

[40] Actually, *sarge's* ifupdown pulls in **dhcp-client** 2.x, which has been discontinued. You may want to install **dhcp3-client** instead to benefit from newer features.

```
~# cat /etc/dhclient.conf
[...]
prepend domain-name "debian.org ";
[...]
```

While this works in principle, it is not advisable; the domain name returned by DHCP is supposed to be a single token and to identify the domain to be used for the Fully-Qualified Domain Name (FQDN) of the machine. The DNS search list, on the other hand, is a list of domains to consider to complete unqualified host names in connection requests.

6.8.3   Managing /etc/resolv.conf

Fortunately, the desire to specify custom search paths has been enough of a nuisance to drive the development of **resolvconf**, a software designed to get rid of the problems of managing /etc/resolv.conf in all but the simplest environments. Simply by installing **resolvconf** and making a few changes to /etc/network/interfaces (if at all required), you can wave goodbye to your /etc/resolv.conf headaches forever!

resolvconf is a framework which automatically manages /etc/resolv.conf. Applications, hooks, and even the administrator can register sets of DNS servers and domains to be searched in chunks, and remove these chunks one by one when they become obsolete. Furthermore, **resolvconf** can notify other programmes when the DNS information changes, so that *e.g.* forwarding DNS caches can reconfigure themselves.

After installing the **resolvconf** package, reconfigure your network interfaces and inspect **/etc/resolv.conf**. If you are using DHCP on at least one of the interfaces, you should see the appropriate entries for the name servers and the search path.

```
~# ifdown -a && ifup -a
[...]
~# grep -v '^#' /etc/resolv.conf
nameserver 192.168.40.5
search debianbook.info
```

This is no different from what the DHCP client configured before installing **resolvconf**. But think about what happens if you have two interfaces using DHCP, or another interface managed by **pppd** (which also automatically configures /etc/resolv.conf: one configuration overwrites the previous one.

resolvconf's job is to merge and unmerge configurations. To illustrate the point, let's register a new set of parameters. The **resolvconf** command was made for use in scripts and does not abound in usability, but it will do the job:

```
~# resolvconf -a mydomain <<EOF
nameserver 10.0.0.5
```

```
search mydomain.org
EOF
~# grep -v '^#' /etc/resolv.conf
nameserver 192.168.40.5
nameserver 10.0.0.5
search debianbook.info mydomain.org
```

In this example, the custom data are included with a lower priority (after) the data registered by the DHCP client. Sorting is controlled by the order of patterns in **/etc/resolvconf/interface-order**, and described in the **interface-order (5)** manpage. "mydomain" only matches the pattern on the last line and is thus sorted after the data gathered for **eth0**, which matches an earlier line. If we use "local-mydomain" instead, the "lo*" entry matches and sorts the custom definition before the one provided by the DHCP client.

When it comes to automating the process, hooks immediately spring to mind. Indeed, **resolvconf** drops hook scripts into all the relevant places, so that the DHCP client effectively registers its data, just like **pppd** merges in with the new management system. DHCP and **pppd** both obtain their DNS data from a server. The process requires a little more work if the data are to be provided manually, *e.g.* when a static IP configuration is used.

Recall from chapter 6.8.1 that any additional parameters in the **iface** configuration stanzas are passed to the hook scripts in the environment. **resolvconf** provides a hook for **ifupdown**, which uses four such parameters to compose **nameserver**, **search**, **sortlist**, and **domain** lines (see the **resolv.conf (5)** manpage), before feeding them to **resolvconf** for registration. Therefore, if **eth0** is defined statically, and the name server at 192.168.0.5 becomes available to provide the **local.mydomain.org** domain when the interface is configured, the corresponding **iface** stanza can be extended as follows (note the plural form of the name server parameter).

```
~# ifdown eth0
[...]
~# grep -v '^#' /etc/network/interfaces
[...]
iface eth0 inet static
  address 192.168.0.1
  netmask 255.255.255.0
  dns-nameservers 192.168.0.5
  dns-search local.mydomain.org
[...]
```

Now, bringing up **eth0** registers the additional data with **resolvconf**, and taking the interface down properly removes them again:

```
~# ifup eth0
~# grep -v '^#' /etc/resolv.conf
nameserver 192.168.0.5
```

```
nameserver 10.0.0.5
search local.mydomain.org mydomain.org
~# ifdown eth0
~# grep -v '^#' /etc/resolv.conf
nameserver 10.0.0.5
search mydomain.org
```

Permanent registration

We registered **mydomain.org** manually. It is probably not a bad idea to automate this registration so that it happens during the system initialisation, without requiring manual intervention. Moreover, custom name servers and search domains are probably provided to *override* the ones defined by the DHCP server (or the like), and should therefore always preceed the automatically obtained ones. To make a long story short, it turns out that we can simply add similar parameters to the **lo** stanza and be done with it (after removing the previous registration): name server and search domains defined for the **lo** interface take highest priority.

```
~# resolvconf -d mydomain
~# grep -v '^#' /etc/network/interfaces
[...]
iface lo inet loopback
  dns-nameserver 10.0.0.5
  dns-search mydomain.org
[...]
~# ifdown lo; ifup lo
~# grep -v '^#' /etc/resolv.conf
nameserver 10.0.0.5
nameserver 192.168.40.5
search mydomain.org debianbook.info
```

Custom settings can also be written to **/etc/resolvconf/resolv.conf.d/base** in standard **/etc/resolv.conf** format. Entries in this file are always placed before others by **resolvconf**. Thus, the following would have the same effect as configuring the name servers and search domains with the **lo** interface:

```
~# cat <<EOF > /etc/resolvconf/resolv.conf.d/base
nameserver 10.0.0.5
search mydomain.org
EOF
```

resolvconf assembles the **/etc/resolv.conf** file from files underneath **/etc/resolvconf/resolv.conf.d** and dynamic data as follows[41]: First, it includes the contents of the **head** file, followed by a unique list of resolver directives in a defined order. It then concatenates the contents of the **tail** file to the end of **/etc/resolv.conf**.

---

[41]The /etc/resolvconf/update.d/libc script actually handles the assembly.

Hooks

The /etc/resolvconf directory contains three directories which influence the processing of resolver data registered with resolvconf. However, only the update.d directory belongs to resolvconf. At time of writing, the resolvconf package provides two scripts in this directory: bind informs the Bind DNS server about changes to the set of forwarders, and libc creates the /etc/resolv.conf file. The other two directories, resolv.conf.d and update-libc.d are used by the latter script: resolv.conf.d contains files needed to assemble /etc/resolv.conf (see above), and when the file changes, the libc script invokes run-parts on the update-libc.d directory, which can inform running processes about changes to the resolver configuration.

It goes without saying that you are free to provide your own hooks. The following simple example illustrates how to process the nameserver information composed by resolvconf:

```
~# cat <<EOF > /etc/resolvconf/update.d/local-demo
#!/bin/sh -e

cd /etc/resolvconf/run/interface
for file in $(/lib/resolvconf/list-records); do
  sed -ne 's,^nameserver ,,p' $file
done > /var/run/nameservers

exit 0
EOF
~# chmod 755 /etc/resolvconf/update.d/local-demo
```

The script ensures that /var/run/nameservers will always contain the current set of name servers, one address per line, in the same order as found in /etc/resolv.conf.

6.8.4 Connectivity via PPP

In addition to kernel-driven network interfaces (most of which are Ethernet these days), PPP is a common way to access computer networks. PPP itself is actually a transfer protocol between two peers with more features than the Ethernet protocol, allowing for authentication and the negotiation of IP addresses for the calling client. PPP is used in standard Internet Service Provider (ISP) modem dial-in scenarios, as well as for DSL (PPPoE or PPP-over-Asynchronous-Transfer-Mode (PPPoA)) connections in many countries.

pppd, the PPP daemon

The most common way to use PPP is with pppd (from package ppp). Other tools can be used as well but may not be able to deal with all situations in which PPP can be used. For instance, **wvdial** is a PPP dialer for use with modems. It uses **pppd** at its core and hence is more of a wrapper programme with a different usage paradigm. **wvdial** cannot make PPP connections across DSL.

pppd itself handles the configuration of the transportation medium as well as authentication and negotiation of an IP address. In the case of an analog modem, **pppd** configures the serial port, invokes **chat** to set up the connection to the peer (by dialing the peer's number and negotiating connection parameters), and then uses the established connection to talk to the PPP server on the other side. As we will see shortly, the PPP communication steps can also be handled by external programmes.

pppd deals with the concept of peers, which are essentially bundled configuration sets that allow several different PPP connections to be configured and used with simple commands. Each connection corresponds to a file in the directory **/etc/ppp/peers**, and the file name specifies the name of the connection. The directory and its contents are only accessible to members of the **dip** group, who are allowed to establish dynamic IP connections with **pppd**.

To start a connection, you use **pon**, followed by the name of the connection you wish to establish, and an optional set of additional parameters to pass to **pppd**. **pon** then invokes **pppd call** with the appropriate arguments, which runs in the background by default. If you do not specify a connection name, **pon** uses **/etc/ppp/peers/provider** as the default connection, if present. Thus, when multiple connections are defined, **/etc/ppp/peers/provider** can be a symlink to the file containing the parameters for the default connection.

pppd logs its activity with **syslogd**, and the **plog** command filters the last couple of log messages produced by **pppd** and prints them to **stdout**. In the default configuration, only members of the **adm** group are given access to these log data. If you want your users to be able to inspect the connection process or keep track of connections in progress, one way would be to make **syslogd** channel **pppd** messages to a separate log file, which is readable by group **dip**. The following steps are required:

```
~# install --mode 0640 --group dip /dev/null /var/log/ppp.log
~# echo 'local2.* /var/log/ppp.log' >> /etc/syslog.conf
~# /etc/init.d/sysklogd reload
```

Log rotation of **/var/log/ppp.log** will be handled by **savelog** automatically every week, and permissions are guaranteed to be preserved. After the above commands, **plog** is available to all users capable of initiating PPP connections.

As an alternative, you may want to consider preventing **pppd** from running in the background and allow it to write status information to **stdout** instead. **pppd** honours two options, which can be passed via **pon**. While **nodetach** prevents it from detaching, **updetach** only backgrounds the **pppd** process when the connection has been established. The latter is particularly useful in diagnosing connection problems without affecting normal operations following a successful connection. To cut a connection, you use **poff**. It takes a connection name as the parameters and causes the appropriate **pppd** process to terminate. If no provider is specified, **poff** only closes a connection if exactly one single connection has been opened, no matter what its name may be. With the -a option, you can cause **poff** to termninate all running **pppd** connections. Alternatively, you can use **poff** to control a running **pppd** process. When option -d is specified, the corresponding **pppd** process' **debug** option is toggled. Specifying option -c tells the running **pppd** daemon to re-negotiate the compression used between the peers (which is hardly ever the case), and -r hangs up the connection and redials.

pppd configuration files

A typical file, used to dial into a provider's modem pool to access the Internet looks like this. The name is arbitrary and simply encodes country and provider name. This file can be hand-crafted or managed with **pppconfig**, to which we will return shortly. Every line is essentially just an option to **pppd**, and the **pppd** (8) manpage describes the available options.

```
~$ cat /etc/ppp/peers/ch.sunrise
debug
hide-password
connect "/usr/sbin/chat -v -f /etc/chatscripts/pap -T 0041840556666"
115200
/dev/modem
noauth
remotename ch.sunrise
user "madduck"
noipdefault
defaultroute
ipparam ch.sunrise
```

Note the lack of authentication information. While the user name to be used to authenticate with the PPP server is included, a password is not to be found. Instead of including it in the **dip**-readable configuration file, **pppd** honours **/etc/ppp/pap-secrets** and **chap-secrets** for the PAP and CHAP authentication protocols, depending on which one is used (Password Authentication Protocol (PAP) is the default). These files are only readable by **root**, and **pppd** is **setuid root**. Both files can be managed by **pppconfig**, or with any regular editor. Consisting of three columns, each password (in the third column) is bound to a user name (given to **pppd** with the **user** option) and the name of the provider (option **remotename**). For instance:

```
~# grep '^madduck[[:space:]]*ch\.sunrise' pap-secrets
sunrise    ch.sunrise    topsecret
```

Before reading connection-specific configuration files from **/etc/ppp/peers**, **pppd** reads options from **/etc/ppp/options**, followed by **˜/.ppprc** and **/etc/ppp/options. <ttyname>**, where **<ttyname>** is the name of the device in **/dev** that is to be used for the connection. Thus, global options can be overridden for each user, then for each device, then for each connection, and finally for each invocation by passing them on the command line.

Connection scripts

Much of the flexibility of **pppd** comes from the **connect** parameter, which is expected to configure the connection. **pppd** executes the specified command at an early stage, and, upon its completion, assumes that it is talking to a PPP server on the other side of the connection. If the device that provides the connectivity is an analog modem, **chat** is the tool to set up the communication. The modem (AT command) language is essentially a request-response protocol, and this is where **chat** excels: it sends a command and waits for a response, evaluates the response and conditionally selects the next command to send.

In most cases, the generic connection script **/etc/chatscripts/pap** is all you need. The script expects the number to dial to be provided to the **chat** invocation using the **-T** option (see the **connect** line in the **pppd** peer configuration file above). If your modem needs special initialisation, or you cannot use the generic script for some reason, you can create a copy and modify it to your heart's content. For instance, to prevent the modem from waiting for the dial tone, use the following script, and reference it from the peer's configuration file accordingly.

```
˜$ grep -v '^#' /etc/chatscripts/ch.sunrise
[...]
'' ATZ X3
[...]
OK-AT-OK ATDT0041840556666
CONNECT \d\c
```

After sending the initialisation commands (Z and X3), **chat** instructs the modem to dial the number of the provider and waits for the connection. In most cases, the peer automatically starts the PPP server, but even a terminal login and subsequent direct invocation of the server command are possible. When **chat** finishes, **pppd** can resume control and start its PPP dialog with the server at the other end.

Configuring PPP connections

You do not have to master the **chat** script syntax, nor know how to tell **pppd** about passwords to use, nor select the options to pass to **pppd**: In **pppconfig**, Debian provides an interactive tool to create, manage, and delete connections, which knows exactly where to put what information, and subsequently allows you to edit these data as you would expect.

Figure 6.1:
pppconfig's summary
and management
screen

When creating a new connection, **pppconfig** asks you a series of questions in the same style as **debconf** (see chapter 5.8). For standard PPP connections, no further steps should be necessary than to answer these appropriately. Nevertheless, before saving the connection, **pppconfig** drops you into the screen depicted at figure 6.1 to allow you to change parameters, or configure advanced aspects of the PPP connection (see figure 6.2). If you later choose to edit a connection, the same screen will be available.

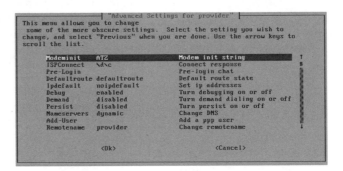

Figure 6.2:
Some of the advanced
settings configurable
with pppconfig

pppconfig takes care of all aspects of the PPP configuration and is fine for all but the most specialised tasks. In summary, the following settings are controlled. Where possible, **pppconfig** respects manual changes and does not overwrite them.

- The configuration of **pppd**. Each connection has a corresponding file in **/etc/ppp/peers**, which **pppconfig** reads and writes.

- While all configurations go to the connection-specific files, password data are stored and managed in **/etc/ppp/pap-secrets** and **/etc/ppp/chap-secrets**. **pppconfig** only makes modifications and therefore does not overwrite other credentials stored in these files.

- **pppconfig** can only be used for dial-up connections using a modem. It also controls the **chat** scripts in **/etc/chatscripts** for every connection.

Hooks

Similar to **ifupdown**, **pppd** allows for any number of scripts to run after a connection has been established, and after it has been brought down. The hooks differentiate between IP and IPv6 and reside in **/etc/ppp/ip-***, a set of scripts that invoke **run-parts** (see chapter 6.1.1) on the corresponding directories in the same location.

Each script receives six arguments: the interface name, the device name, the link speed, the local IP address, the remote IP address, and the **ipparam** configuration parameter used by **pppd**, if it has been specified. Please inspect the hook scripts for details.

Even though it is possible to integrate **pppd** with **ifupdown** (see below), **pppd**'s hooks are regularly used by tools, such as **resolvconf** or **fetchmail** to register actions to be performed on changes to the system's connectivity.

Integrating pppd with ifupdown

As the main network configuration system, it seems natural for **ifupdown** to be able to handle **pppd** connections as well. The **ppp** configuration method allows **iface** stanzas to be written for **pppd** providers. The following shows a typical example:

```
~# grep -A1 '^iface.*ppp$' /etc/network/interfaces
iface ppp0 inet ppp
  provider ch.sunrise
```

The name of the interface (**ppp0** in this case) is actually irrelevant, and could be anything (such as the provider's name). When a **ppp** interface is brought up, **ifupdown** automatically invokes **pon**, and on taking the interface down, **poff** is called as expected. If you wish to establish a PPP connection automatically at boot time, use the **auto** command in **/etc/network/interfaces** (see **ifupdown**).

When using **ifupdown** to control **pppd** connections, it is important to keep the order of hook execution in mind. As **pon** is a non-blocking call, the **ifup** hook is actually executed long before the PPP connection is actually established[42]. If you need to execute hooks only when IP connectivity is available, you should either use the **pppd** hooks instead, or append **updetach** to the configuration of the provider, which will delay the execution of **ifupdown** hooks until the PPP connection has been established.

[42]http://bugs.debian.org/287173

PPTP connectivity with pppd

Regular dial-up connections use **chat** to connect a modem to the remote provider in a connection script before **pppd** can speak plain PPP over the serial port, not having to worry about the actual connection itself. As an alternative, **pppd** can also invoke a process and use its **stdin** and **stdout** streams for the communication. This is the case with **pptp**, a user-space client to tunnel PPP traffic over existing network connections. The primary use of Point-to-Point Tunneling Protocol (PPTP) is asymmetric "dial-in" Virtual Private Network (VPN) connections, such as between a laptop and a company's gateway.

The **pptp** programme uses existing network infrastructure to wrap and deliver PPP packets to the peer. Any data it receives in **stdin** is sent to the the other side of the PPTP connection, and any packets it receives are unpacked and the payload data made available in the programme's **stdout** stream. The **pppd** daemon uses this programme in much the same way it uses the modem connection established by **chat**.

The following demonstrates how the **pptp** programme can be used in combination with **pppd** to establish a PPP connection between the local machine and the host at IP address 1.2.3.4, encrypt the channel, authenticate the user, and assign the local machine a static address on the remote network. Since **pppd** launches **pptp**, we instruct the latter not to invoke **pppd** when the connection is established (which is an alternative way of setting up the PPTP tunnel):

```
~# cat <<EOF > /etc/ppp/peers/my-vpn
hide-password
connect /bin/true
pty "/usr/sbin/pptp 1.2.3.4 --nolaunchpppd"
require-mppe-128
noauth
user "madduck"
remotename my-vpn
ipparam my-vpn
10.0.0.254:10.0.0.2
EOF
~$ pon my-vpn
```

As the above uses Microsoft Point to Point Encryption (MPPE) for the encryption of the tunnel, it requires the use of Challenge-Handshake Authentication Protocol (CHAP) for authentication. Therefore, the tunnel will only be configured if **/etc/ppp/chap-secrets** contains the correct password for the **madduck** account on the remote system.

Once the connection has been established, a route can be configured to provide (encrypted) access to the network behind the VPN gateway. Obviously, the addition (and removal) of the route is a perfect candidate for **pppd** hooks.

```
~# ip route add to 10.0.0.0/8 via 10.0.0.2
~# ping -nc1 10.1.2.3
PING 10.1.2.3 (10.1.2.3) 56(84) bytes of data.
64 bytes from 10.1.2.3: icmp_seq=1 ttl=64 time=0.368 ms
[...]
```

PPPoE (DSL) connectivity with pppd

To provide PPP connectivity over Ethernet links (as is the case with many DSL connections), **pppd** uses a kernel driver by means of a plugin which it loads when the connection needs to be established[43].

To facilitate the configuration of **pppoe**, Debian provides **pppoeconf**, which can discover PPPoE concentrators and help select the correct options to use. The tool also prompts for the user name and password and configures **pppd** for its use. While multiple modem connections make sense, machines do not have more than a single PPPoE connection in most cases. Therefore, **pppoeconf** does not allow multiple connections to be configured and simply uses the canonical name **dsl-provider** where **pon** and **pppconfig** use their connection names. The tool writes the user credentials to **/etc/ppp/pap-secrets** and drops the appropriate **/etc/ppp/peers/dsl-provider** file into place:

```
~$ grep -v '^#' /etc/ppp/peers/dsl-provider
hide-password
plugin rp-pppoe.so eth0
mtu 1452
default-asyncmap
user "madduck"
remotename dsl-provider
noauth
noipdefault
usepeerdns
defaultroute
ipparam dsl-provider
```

Note the lack of **connect** and **pty** parameters, which are not needed anymore. Instead, the **plugin** parameter tells **pppd** to load the dynamic library, which overrides the input and output channels used by **pppd** with calls to the kernel-space PPPoE driver.

6.8.5 Integrating PCMCIA network cards

The PCMCIA card services (in package **pcmcia-cs**) provide a network configuration scheme, which is not too different from **ifupdown**. In **/etc/pcmcia/network.opts**

---

[43]Previously, it used the user-space PPPoE driver **pppoe** in exactly the same way as **pptp** for the task. However, due to performance reasons, this method is deprecated.

you can set network configuration parameters and use a matching scheme to select between multiple network cards.

To remove the need to configure the network in two separate places, the Debian pcmcia-cs package extends this functionality to enable PCMCIA network cards to be configured by ifupdown. More specifically, on a Debian system, **ifupdown** will handle PCMCIA network devices if (and only if) you have not configured them in /etc/pcmcia/network.opts. In other words, the PCMCIA card services configuration takes precedence.

It is important to keep in mind that the kernel assigns network interface names in the order of driver initialisation. Therefore, in the (rare) event that you have two PCMCIA network cards, you need to make sure that you always insert them in the same order, or else eth1 may end up being configured as eth0, which may be fatal. The example **interfaces** file[44] gives you an elegant way of dealing with this problem by using **ifupdown** mappings. Please also refer to chapter 6.5.1 and chapter 6.8.1.

6.8.6   Integrating wireless network interfaces

From the administrator's perspective, most wireless network interfaces behave like regular network interfaces. Thus, controlling wireless interfaces using **ifupdown** is straightforward. Nevertheless, depending on the environment, additional configuration may be necessary in order to be able to communicate over the air. Such additional configuration can include setting the ESSID, or configuring a Wired Equivalent Privacy (WEP) passphrase. The tool to use for these configuration changes is iwconfig from the **wireless-tools** package.

Obviously, the **ifupdown** hooks seem like the perfect place for this sort of configuration, if you want it to be automated. Hence, it is hardly a coincidence that **wireless-tools** installs a **ifupdown pre-up** hook that allows all these configuration items to be specified in the **iface** stanza of the wireless network interface. For instance, the following stanza configures eth0 to use "Ad-Hoc mode", a restricted security policy, encrypt with the password 'topsecret' and join ESSID "DEBIAN":

```
~# cat /etc/network/interfaces
[...]
iface eth0 inet dhcp
  wireless-essid DEBIAN
  wireless-mode Ad-Hoc
  wireless-enc restricted
  wireless-key s:topsecret
[...]
```

[44]/usr/share/doc/ifupdown/examples/network-interfaces.gz

The iwconfig (8) manpage gives you more information about the available options. Essentially, every iwconfig option is available via ifupdown for the respective interface by prepending wireless- to its name.

6.8.7 Miscellaneous network options

Debian's netbase package (which is installed on every Debian system) allows the administrator to control a number of aspects of the network subsystem from the /etc/network/options file. This file is read just before the network interfaces are automatically configured during boot (in /etc/rcS/S40networking) and allows for the following options to be controlled:

Spoof protection
> The option ensures that packets are only accepted on an interface if the corresponding response packet would leave the machine through the same interface. This is enabled on fresh Debian installations, even though the Linux kernel does not enable this option (rp_filter) by default.

IP forwarding
> Configures the local machine to be able to route packets between interfaces. This is off by default.

SYN cookies
> Changes the Transmission Control Protocol (TCP) stack to use an extended algorithm for establishing connections, which can help guard against so called Synchronisation request packet (TCP) (SYN) flood attacks. This is enabled by default in recent kernels, but disabled in the file. Read on to find out why this results in enabled SYN cookies.

The /etc/network/options file is a throwback to an idea, which has been solved more flexibly since the original inception. If you want to use /etc/network/options, then please be aware that it can only be used to enable options. While recent kernels enable SYN cookies by default, the corresponding option in the file is set to no. However, this is never enacted, and so SYN cookies stay enabled.

The proposed way to change the three parameters is via sysctl (see chapter 6.6), by adding the following four lines to /etc/sysctl.conf. rp_filter controls the spoof protection mechanism. The last two lines should be self-explanatory.

```
cat <<EOF >> /etc/sysctl.conf
net.ipv4.conf.all.rp_filter = 1
net.ipv4.conf.default.rp_filter = 1
net.ipv4.ip_forward = 1
net.ipv4.tcp_syncookies = 1
EOF
```

6.9   Administering inetd, the Internet superserver

Some network daemons do not provide their own socket code and instead rely on **inetd** to handle the network-related stuff. For low-usage services, this is preferred as it minimises the source of errors and allows the use of access control and resource limits, which **inetd** provides.

In the Debian archive, at least two packages provide the service of the Internet superdaemon: **netkit-inetd** and **xinetd**, the latter of which is an improved and enhanced version of the former[45]. **inetd**'s configuration is specified in **/etc/inetd.conf** while **xinetd** reads settings from **/etc/xinetd.conf** and honours files in **/etc/xinetd.d** in (more or less) **run-parts** fashion (see chapter 6.1.1). As such, **xinetd** is preferable, since it allows for packages to register with the superserver without getting in each other's way.

Editing with update-inetd

Regardless, **inetd** is the standard tool, and to be able to accomodate painless autoregistration of packages, Debian provides **update-inetd**, a script that handles the management of the **/etc/inetd.conf** file. It is probably a good idea for you as the administrator to prefer this tool over direct editing of the configuration file; the utility does the best it can to honour your request and removes some of the responsibility for ensuring that configuration happens in the right place and uses the correct syntax.

I will separate edits to the file into two categories: first, services may be simply enabled and disabled. The second category includes edits that add or remove services. A service is named after the name of the port to which **inetd** binds, and must be defined in **/etc/services** to be used. The following command disable is all you need to disable the **ident** service (which is provided by the **pidentd** package and installed by default on a standard system, but not if you performed a minimal installation, see chapter 3.2):

```
~# update-inetd --disable ident
```

The tool ensures that after completion, the service is in the requested state. That is, if the **ident** service has already been disabled, nothing happens, and no error is reported. Requests for non-existent services are silently ignored.

To re-enable a service, use **--enable** instead of **--disable** in the above example. Alternatively, you may want to specify an additional pattern to match the service line to be enabled (or disabled). For instance to enable only the User Datagramme Protocol (UDP) component of the **daytime** service, specify a pattern match on

[45]http://www.xinetd.org

"udp". **update-inetd** uses a prefix of **#<off>#** to disable services by default. The standard services (of which **daytime** is one) are prefixed with a single **#** on fresh installations (and are therefore disabled by default), which has to be communicated to **update-inetd**. Check the file contents if you are unsure, or the command does not have the desired effect.

```
~# update-inetd --comment-chars '#' --pattern udp --enable daytime
```

Adding a service requires the specification of the entire configuration line, as specified in the **inetd.conf (5)** manpage. For instance, a locally installed Internet Message Access Protocol (IMAP) server can be put under the care of **inetd** with the following invocation:

```
~# update-inetd --group MAIL --add \
  'imap2 stream tcp nowait root /usr/sbin/tcpd /usr/local/sbin/in.imapd'
```

If you check the **/etc/inetd.conf** file, you will see that services are separated into categories, such as "INTERNAL" and "MAIL". To maintain the order of the file, you can use **--group** as shown above to select the specific group for the newly added service. Removing a service (although you may want to consider simply disabling it) happens analogously to disabling it, using **--remove** instead of **--disable**. **update-inetd** will silently ignore requests to add existing services, just as it will not complain about removal requests for non-existent services.

Following an update to the configuration file, **update-inetd** automatically causes **inetd** to reload the configuration, thereby stopping services to be disabled or removed and starting newly added or enabled services.

Dealing with xinetd

xinetd does not currently provide a replacement for the **update-inetd** tool. Therefore, packages are expected to register with **xinetd** by dropping a file into **/etc/xinetd.d**, following **run-parts** conventions (more or less, see chapter 6.1.1). Unfortunately, not many packages include such files, which makes using **xinetd** more difficult than it should be.

A **xinetd**-specific replacement of **update-inetd** is in the works. In the meantime, Debian's **xinetd** server provides a **inetd** compatibility mode, enabled with the **-inetd_compat** command line option which can be enabled by adding it to the **$XINETD_OPTS** variable in **/etc/default/xinetd**. In compatibility mode, **xinetd** will read and interpret **/etc/inetd.conf** after its own configuration file and therefore control any services specified only in **/etc/inetd.conf**.

As **xinetd** is capable of features that **inetd** does not provide, you may want to migrate your services from **/etc/inetd.conf** to the **xinetd** configuration to be able to make use of these extra features (such as IP and time-based access control, granular logging, redirection, rate and resource limits, and control over the environment). Two tools can be used for this job. First, **xconv.pl** can read the entire **/etc/inetd.conf** file on **stdin** and produce a valid **xinetd.conf** file on **stdout**. If you would rather migrate services selectively, **itox** is your best option:

```
~# grep ^imap2.*tcp /etc/inetd.conf \
   | itox -daemon-dir /usr/sbin > /etc/xinetd.d/local-imap2
~# update-inetd --pattern tcp --disable imap2
~# /etc/init.d/xinetd reload
~#
```

The **-daemon-dir** option is only needed for entries in **/etc/inetd.conf** which do not specify the absolute file name of the server executables; Debian packages registering with **inetd** generally do. The option will only be used if needed, so it does not hurt to provide it.

Please note that this will effectively remove the service from the package's control. In our example, the service is handled by a locally installed programme, but if a package added the entry to **/etc/inetd.conf**, the service would not be stopped on package removal. For instance, if you migrate the **ident** service to **xinetd** and subsequently remove the **pidentd** package, **xinetd** will continue to listen on port 113 until you remove the service from **xinetd**'s configuration directory by hand.

6.10   Integrated management tools

Debian package and system administration consists of more than a dozen tools working hand in hand. Learning how to use all these tools, and getting acquainted with their intricacies, is not everybody's idea of fun. For this reason, a number of integrated management tools have been developed.

The following is only a selection of integrated management tools, which come in a variety of flavours. It would be overkill to present each of these in depth. Most tools overlap with respect core functionality and extend their capabilities to other domains of system administration. You will probably have to inspect each of the tools to make up your own mind, if you are looking for one-stop system administration.

6.10.1   wajig

The **wajig** tool aims to be a Debian administration tool to provide a uniform interface to different aspects of the Debian system. **wajig** is actually just the command line interface to **jig**. **gjig** provides a **GNOME** interface.

wajig itself is really just a wrapper, hiding a plethora of other tools behind its interface. For the administrator, this means not having to remember the different commands, but rather being able to use them all through a unified interface. The tool collection includes **apt-get**, **apt-cache**, **dpkg**, **dpkg-reconfigure**, **reportbug**, **alien** and **invoke-rc.d**.

A number of commands called by **wajig** require **root** rights, but **wajig** is designed to be run as a normal user. It uses **sudo** internally to gain **root** rights. Thus, **sudo** has to be configured as detailed in **wajig**'s documentation, which is accessible by running **wajig doc**.

The following session shows some of the possible uses of **wajig**. The command output has been left out in all cases for brevity:

```
~$ wajig install apache2
~$ wajig stop apache2
~$ wajig reconfigure apache2
~$ wajig bug apache2
~$ wajig start apache2
```

6.10.2   feta

Similar to **wajig**, **feta** hides various tools behind a common interface, but restricts itself to APT, where it covers a larger set of functions. **feta** also allows the use of **sudo** to gain **root** access. Again, the outputs have been omitted for the sake of brevity.

```
~$ feta update
~$ feta install apache2
~$ feta configure apache2
~$ feta bug apache2
~$ feta purge apache2
```

On the command line, **feta** allows multiple comma-separated commands:

```
~$ feta update, install apache2, bug apache2
```

In addition to the command line functionality, **feta** provides an interactive console which can also be scripted. Another nice feature is the ability to search package descriptions by control fields and optionally display only a certain set of fields from the matching packages' control files by encapsulating **grep-dctrl** (see chapter 5.11.9).

6.11 System administration resources

System administration is more than a task. It is a fusion of skill and art, a domain in which talent and experience are the decisive factors. A system like the Debian GNU/Linux operating system goes a long way towards standardising common tasks and making life easier for system administrators. However, it does not take the entire load off the administrators' shoulders, and leaves them to face challenges and problems on a regular basis. In the following, I have put together some valuable resources which are particularly useful for Debian system administration.

First and foremost it should be noted that Debian is mostly Linux, so any resources on Linux system administration are of direct benefit to the Debian system administrator. Furthermore, system administration goes far beyond the technical aspects of the operating system, so any reasonably abstract resource is helpful. A reference such as "Unix System Administration Handbook" and "Linux Administration Handbook" by Nemeth *et al.*http://www.admin.com, in addition to this book, will provide a solid foundation for most tasks in day to day system maintenance.

The Web also holds a plethora of resources. The Debian administration forum at http://debian-administration.org is of particular interest to Debian administrators. Several Debian developers and committed users publish tidbits of knowledge for common administration tasks on the Debian system here. The site is fairly young but its potential is already showing. Articles can be trivially added, even by anonymous users (this is likely to change as the site's popularity increases — I hope my mention here will help the good cause).

In addition, the Linux Documentation Project[46] provides a listing of documents relevant to system administration and configuration[47]. The project pages also host the System Administrator's Guide[48] and a hands-on guide to using Linux[49].

Also of interest is the collection of links related to security administration found on Kurt Seifried's pages[50] as well as Davor Ocelić's Debian Hands-on Guide[51].

---

[46]http://tldp.org
[47]http://www.tldp.org/HOWTO/HOWTO-INDEX/admin.html
[48]http://www.tldp.org/LDP/sag/html/index.html
[49]http://www.tldp.org/LDP/intro-linux/html/index.html
[50]http://www.seifried.org/lasg/
[51]http://colt.projectgamma.com/debguide

7 Chapter

Security of the Debian system

> Look for opportunities, not guarantees. Hope for the best.
> — Johann Wolfgang von Goethe

In the domain of computer systems, security is a delicate topic (well, it is a delicate topic everywhere, really...). There are no recipes for securing assets, nor is there a single place where you can learn all there is to know in one go. The design of a security policy is a science of its own. Even with an appropriate security policy in place, its implementation is a demanding and catchy task. As threats are omnipresent, experience in the domain of computer and network security is paramount to the successful implementation of a security policy. The combination of affordable permanent Internet connections and cheap computer hardware have meant that far more machines are administered by users with little or no experience in computer security than by professional administrators. With the dangers resulting from today's automated attack tools and threats lingering all over the untrusted Internet, it is extremely important for operating systems to be as secure as possible out of the box.

The Debian project takes security very seriously, as is evidenced by the efforts of the security team, the design of the system's administrative paradigms, and the quality of the packages found in the *stable* archive. The Debian system is designed to face the dangers of today's networking environments and help even more experienced administrators. Hardening is a time-consuming task, and despite experience, you can never rule out human error. Furthermore, as the number of systems to administer increases, security becomes a repetitive task. Repetition can lead to boredom, and the two in combination typically increase the chance of errors.

Before possibly giving the wrong impression about Debian's security, I must state that absolute security does not exist, and while Debian's approach to security as well as the rigorous peer review process of the *testing* release (see chapter 4) provide a secure foundation, no Debian system will be immune against all possible attacks. This holds for *all* operating systems. The Debian project delivers a solid base for a secure system. Still, it is part of the administrator's job to keep it like that, which also involves the mitigation of social engineering threats through the education of the system's users.

The following chapters unfold how the Debian developers approach the challenge of security and give you the necessary information as well as some resources that you will need to setup and maintain Debian systems secure enough for most applications. The chapters do not cover applications that provide security services, such as network firewalls or intrusion detection systems. Also, advanced topics, such as hardening systems, or the configuration of mandatory access control or access control lists are not included. The goal of the chapters to come is to illustrate the Debian-specific mechanisms that provide basic security for systems *per se*.

The tasks required to maintain a secure system for years include

- monitoring relevant security channels for important announcements.

- upgrading packages in which security bugs are found in a timely manner.

- keeping the system's installation footprint down to the minimum required to fulfill the system's purpose adequately.

- keeping backups, at least of the essential files.

The Debian project and its operating system help you with all of the above. Debian delivers timely security announcements for the software it includes and provides security updates via special channels with low turnaround times. The packages provided in the Debian archive are designed to make minimal installations the default, and while Debian has no provisions to secure your data files or system configuration, it at least keeps revisions of the data needed by the system itself. In the following, we will be discussing these points (and a couple more) in more detail.

7.1 Handling security problems

The complexity of a computer environment makes it literally impossible to guarantee a programme or a library to be free from security-related bugs (or bugs at all, for that matter). Therefore, it must be anticipated for problems to surface sooner or later. When a bug that affects the security of the programme, the data it deals with or even the host system is found, it should be fixed and the users informed in a coordinated but timely manner.

Full disclosure?

One way to respond to security problems is by *full disclosure*, which calls for the immediate release of all available information, whether potentially dangerous or not, to the public. This approach enjoys great popularity in some special disclosure forums[1].

While the Debian project believes in full disclosure, it is also concerned with the negative consequences of such a radical approach. When a security bug is found and immediately published, the software or operating system distributor have to take immediate action. However, depending on the triviality of the bug, a fix may not be readily available. At the same time, however, full disclosure gives malicious hackers and script-kiddies information on an exploit which they might not have gained, had the problem not been published. The more information gets released, the easier it is for attackers to broaden the scope of their attack. On the other hand, network and system administrators are pressured into taking preventative measures, such as disabling or firewalling the affected service. Even if the administrator learns of the problem in good time, disabling a service may not be an option. For instance, if your company revenue depends on your web services, and a serious bug has been found in the web server software you employ, your options are very limited.

Another important point is that Debian works with the other major distributions to coordinate releases of security fixes. As a result, all major distributors can provide security patches at the same time as the information is made public. This agreement between the distributions is very valuable, and Debian takes care to honour its terms. Without this cooperation, distributors would risk not being able to serve their users in a timely fashion.

---

[1]The most widely known of these is Bugtraq (http://www.securityfocus.com/archive/1), but many claim to have perceived a drop in quality of the forum when it was acquired by Symantec. An alternative is the Full-Disclosure list (http://lists.netsys.com/mailman/listinfo/full-disclosure), which claims to be unmoderated (which is not entirely true). The Full-Disclosure list is fairly high volume and contains a lot of fud. Kurt Seifried provides a moderated version at http://lists.seifried.org/mailman/listinfo/security with a content to noise ratio approximating one for the price of a little delay. In addition, vuln-dev is a more technically oriented and fairly low volume mailing list: http://www.securityfocus.com/archive/82.

Responsible disclosure

The security team (in addition to many users, especially the package maintainers) closely screens established and pertinent disclosure forums for problems that could affect the Debian operating system. In addition, the BTS encourages the use of a special security tag on bugs that have security implications (see chapter 10.6.4). If the security team or a package maintainer finds a security-related problem with software from the Debian archive, or a bug report is filed, it is assumed that the report is publicly available. In that case, a rapid response is necessary. Depending on the severity of the problem, the Debian security team may release an initial advisory with general information about the problem so that administrators can choose to disable the service until a fix becomes available. Administrators of mission-critical services are advised to read the common disclosure channels for information on bugs prior to the release of an advisory by the Debian security team.

Should a problem have been reported to the Debian package maintainer or the security team directly (preferably via a secure medium), the information is probably not public yet. In the case of a trivial problem, the maintainer and security team respond similarly to the case of publicly known security bugs. However, if the problem is of a serious nature, it is treated secretly and a release is coordinated between the publishers of the major operating systems (mostly Linux). Therefore, neither the maintainer of the affected package, nor the Debian security team will release any information prematurely.

Usually, the security team is able to fix problems within a matter of hours; of course, this depends on the severity and complexity of the problem. Grave security bugs receive more attention than trivial ones. In the rare case that the security team does not have a fix available within a week after learning of the problem, a preliminary advisory is released, in which the user base is alerted to the problems, but no further details are given (if they are not already public).

Security by obscurity?

This choice of procedure, which is sometimes called *responsible disclosure*, is obviously debatable. For people fond of full disclosure, everything else is unacceptable, and responsible disclosure is just as "bad" as not disclosing any information (security by obscurity). On the other hand, proponents of security by obscurity see no value in disclosure at all, and even though responsible disclosure appears more favourable to them than full disclosure, it is still perceived to be suboptimal. Just like every approach, responsible disclosure has its advantages and disadvantages. The Debian project chose the path of responsible disclosure due to a number of reasons:

- There are often not enough details available to issue a coherent and accurate advisory at the time of problem discovery.

- The publication of an early advisory calls for advisories to follow up on the topic, correct existing data and provide new information. This results in a significant increase in volume on the advisory channel, causing administrators to scan less thoroughly and thus possibly miss important points.

- Full disclosure expects instantaneous reaction from administrators. However, administrators may not receive an advisory immediately, or not be able to tend to a machine instantly, or a company may not be able to afford to have affected services temporarily disabled.

- Full disclosure expects immediate response from publishers. While the security teams of most operating systems focus on problems as soon as possible and generally prioritise the problems according to their severity, it takes time to locate the problem, devise a fix, and then ensure that the fix does not affect the stability of the software.

- Along the same lines as the previous points, full disclosure, even without details, attracts the attention of mischievous characters, who will have an easier time finding a problem after being told where to search.

- By coordinating a release with other publishers, Debian ensures that the publication of a fix does not make the problem apparent and thus exploitable on other systems. Close cooperation ensures that Debian systems will not be left temporarily vulnerable because another publisher chooses to release a fix prematurely.

The procedure of responsible disclosure is also questionable with respect to the Social Contract. In paragraph 3, the project promises that it "will not hide problems." To a certain degree, this is violated in the case of a grave security problem that is not yet public: by keeping information restricted to the developers and other publishers involved, the Debian developers are hiding the problem from the users. Strictly speaking, the Social Contract only promises the contents of the bug report database to be public at all times, but it goes without saying that the practise of the security team with respect to grave, non-public bugs is not fully justifiable in the light of the third statement of the Social Contract. The practise is, however, justifiable with another clause of the Social Contract, in which the project promises to treat the users' interests as top priority. No approach to security response is flawless. Responsible disclosure seems to be the best compromise with respect to the Social Contract and the professional conduct many have come to expect from the Debian security team.

Reporting a security problem

If you discover a security problem in Debian or any of the software provided in the Debian archive(s), please contact the appropriate package maintainer and/or the Debian security team at **security@debian.org**, if possible using an encrypted medium. Try to provide as much information as possible. The Debian developers will then decide on the appropriate steps to take. Please do not release the information elsewhere unless you are certain that it has been disclosed through other channels already. If you consider a problem to be non-critical, you may want to discuss it on the **debian-security** mailing list[2]. You may, in any case, request the non-disclosure of a problem. The Debian developers honours such requests, unless the problem has been known for too long, or the information becomes public through other means.

Keeping up with security

It is of utmost importance for administrators of mission-critical or production machines to monitor Debian Security Announcements (DSAs)[3], and administrators of non-professional machines are encouraged to do the same. DSAs are available from the following sources:

- The **debian-security-announce**[4] mailing list, which is a dedicated, low-volume and moderated mailing list used exclusively for security-related announcements. It is the preferred method for information exchange.

- Standard disclosure forums, including **Bugtraq** and **Full-Disclosure**. If you read these anyway, it is still advisable to subscribe to **debian-security-announce** nonetheless, if only for redundancy.

- The official Resource Description Framework (RDF) feed of DSAs, linked off the Debian security web page[5].

- The official Debian security web page **http://security.debian.org**. Note that the web site may contain delayed information as it is rebuilt only once daily. Archives of previous DSAs may be found here.

Topics related to the security of the Debian system, including cryptographic issues, which are of interest to all parts of the community, are discussed publicly on the **debian-security** mailing list[2]. This is a low-volume list. Please be aware that it does *not* receive security announcements. You should subscribe to **debian-security-announce** instead, as noted above.

[2] http://lists.debian.org/debian-security
[3] The DSAs are Common Vulnerabilities and Exposures (CVE)-certified (http://cve.mitre.org/compatible/phase2/SPI_Debian.html) as of February 2004. More information on CVE is available on the official web page: http://cve.mitre.org
[4] http://lists.debian.org/debian-security-announce
[5] http://www.debian.org/security/dsa.rdf

7.2 Security updates

When a security problem is found in a software published as part of the Debian *stable* release, the Debian security team strives to release a security update in a competetive time frame. Depending on the severity of the problem, the team might independently attempt to patch the software or search for a solution or a workaround in an effort to provide the Debian user base with an update as soon as possible. If such a solution can be found, it is made available to the general public allow others to profit from the work of the security team. In most situations, however, security fixes are found in close cooperation with the software authors and other operating system publishers.

As a security fix becomes available, the update can be quickly uploaded to the *unstable* release and subsequently enjoys privileged propagation into the *testing* archive, usually taking no longer than two days. Nevertheless, the new version will not be able to enter the *stable* release until the next official Debian version is published. To accomodate security updates, the Debian security team operates a separate APT archive for security updates to software in the *stable* archive, hosted at security.debian.org.

Backporting security fixes

It is often the case that an upstream author fixes a security problem in a new release of the software and does not bother with previous versions. After all, previous versions are mostly considered obsolete and it would be a tedious job for a developer of a programme or a library to fix every version released with respect to every bug discovered. New versions often provide new functionality or drop old features, and it is not rare for such updates to contain more bugs. Therefore, providing the new version of the software via the security archive could cause massive problems on users' machines; some users may rely on features that were dropped in the new release, others may be negatively affected by bugs introduced with new features.

Debian *stable* is stable and new versions are not allowed to enter it. Rather than solving security problems by pushing fixed packages of newer versions into the security repository, the security team analyses the solution and backports it to the version available in the *stable* archive. This results in a package providing fixed software, without adding or dropping features. To help avoid a bug fixes introducing new bugs, fixes are restricted to the bare essentials and carefully audited.

Please keep in mind that only the *stable* release receives this special treatment. Neither the *testing* nor the *unstable* archive contents are supported by the security team. If system security is one of your primary concerns, you ought to stay with Debian *stable*. Along similar lines, only the *main* archive receives full attention. While packages in *contrib* and *non-free* are not actively ignored, they are treated with a lower priority than software in *main*, even if a bug's severity may be greater.

Special version numbers

As a consequence of Debian's security policy, some software on a Debian *stable* system may have version numbers that suggest a vulnerability in the installed software. For instance, **libssl** 0.9.6 is subject to a denial of service attack, a problem which was fixed in version 0.9.6l[6]. Nevertheless, the version available on *woody* these days is 0.9.6c-2.woody.7, which appears to be an older version than 0.9.6l, and thus might alert the careful administrator that the vulnerability persists. Investigating the **changelog.Debian.gz** file reveals that a prior release, 0.9.6c-2.woody.5, has dealt with the problem:

```
openssl (0.9.6c-2.woody.5) stable-security; urgency=high

  * Non-maintainer upload by the Security Team
  * Apply upstream patch to fix NULL pointer dereference in
    do_change_cipher_spec (CAN-2004-0079)

[...]
```

You should therefore never rely on the version numbers when assessing the vulnerability of installed software on a *stable* system. Generally, a version number suffix such as .woody.5 suggests the influence of the security team, and thus the presence of out-of-line security updates When *woody* became *stable*, **openssl** was at 0.9.6c-2, so the security team appended the codename and an incremental counter for each security update (see chapter 5.7.5). The **changelog.Debian.gz** file, which *every* package provides under **/usr/share/doc/<package>** will help to resolve any ambiguities.

The Debian security archive

Security updates are published in the Debian security archive, which is separate from the official Debian archive with the *stable* release among other things. Updates can be fetched and installed from this archive in one of two ways, depending on your needs.

Manual verification and installation of updates

If you have high security requirements, the best way of obtaining and installing the fixes is to download them manually from the locations specified in the DSA

[6]http://www.debian.org/security/2004/dsa-465

announcing the fixed packages. For each file, the announcement specifies the MD5 checksum and size. Prior to installation, the downloaded file must be verified against this data. The announcement itself is cryptographically signed by a member of the the Debian security team to verify the data's integrity.

For instance, DSA 588 contained the following link for the **i386** architecture:

```
[...]
http://security.debian.org/pool/updates/main/g/gzip/gzip_1.3.2-3woody3_i386.deb
  Size/MD5 checksum: 62076 536b666d29bcc648a1f105b3e5ef0708
[...]
```

The procedure for verifying and installing the file is as follows:

```
~$ cd /tmp
~$ wget http://security.debian.org/[...]/gzip/gzip_1.3.2-3woody3_i386.deb
~$ wc -c gzip_1.3.2-3woody3_i386.deb
62076  gzip_1.3.2-3woody3_i386.deb
~$ md5sum gzip_1.3.2-3woody3_i386.deb
536b666d29bcc648a1f105b3e5ef0708  gzip_1.3.2-3woody3_i386.deb
```

If the size and checksum verify correctly, the package can be installed with **dpkg** (see chapter 5.3.2).

The manual method of installation and verification is expected to become obsolete with the introduction of **APT** 0.6 (see chapter 7.5.2).

Automatic security updates with APT

If your security requirements are not so strict, you might prefert the more convenient approach of having **APT** automatically download and install these updates. Obviously, this relies on you checking for and installing updates on a regular basis (or with automatic tools, see chapter 5.11.4).

To enable **APT** to install packages from this archive, the following repository must be added to **/etc/apt/sources.list**. Instead of the canonical name *stable*, you may want to hardcode the current release in its place, as shown in the commented line. See chapter 4 for more information on this distinction.

```
deb http://security.debian.org sarge/updates main contrib non-free
```

Contrary to some rumours, the security team treats all Debian architectures (see chapter 4.5) equally. Therefore, security updates are available for all Debian architectures at roughly the same time. The Debian build infrastructure provides special, prioritised handling of security-related package updates.

The security archive is not officially mirrored, although unofficial mirrors exist on various servers. Instead, the Debian security servers are designed to handle massive quantities of requests[7]. A security update must be available to all users at the earliest possible moment. The Debian mirrors use a pull strategy to stay synchronised, and an update may take up to 24 hours to propagate to the primary servers, and even longer to make it to the secondary mirrors. Debian security updates are critical updates which must be made available at the earliest possible moment. Therefore, the mirror propagation times cannot be tolerated and security updates are served from a single location. Unofficial mirrors of the security archive exist nevertheless.

With the above two lines in **/etc/apt/sources.list**, keeping a Debian system secure is as easy as

```
~# apt-get update && apt-get --show-upgraded upgrade
```

The **--show-upgraded** option is not necessary but good practice. It will cause APT to display a list of things it plans to do, and ask the administrator whether it is okay to proceed. In fact, I suggest you make APT use this flag by default by adding APT::Get::Show-Upgraded true to /etc/apt/apt.conf (see chapter 5.4.2).

7.3   Security out of the box

Debian does not try to be as secure as possible (like *e.g.* the OpenBSD project). Instead, the Debian operating system constitutes a balance between ease of administration and security. Nevertheless, Debian is secure enough for most purposes, and its administrative paradigms make it even more applicable in situations where the security of a system is an important factor.

As the software distributed with the operating system comes mostly from external sources, a Debian system can only ever be as secure as the weakest software component installed. With this in mind, it is easy to appreciate the significance of a proper installation of a Debian system (see chapter 3.2). Rather than trying to install everything the user could possibly ever want, the idea behind installing a Debian system is to install a minimal system with respect to the requirements it should address. There is no reason to run a graphical environment on a web server, and a mail server does not need to provide DNS services. By keeping the number of installed packages low, administrators can effectively lessen the chance of a security problem affecting the system. As shown previously (chapter 5.7.3), the dependencies declared by Debian packages are chosen in that spirit and only pull in packages that are absolutely required.

---

[7]Since the arson at the University of Twente, which destroyed Debian's security server (http://lists.debian.org/debian-devel-announce/2002/11/msg00009.html), a more redundant setup has been put in place

The policy, again

In addition, the policy standardises various aspects across packages and makes it even easier for the administrator to stay in control. Even if the administrator is not completely familiar with a specific package, the package will "feel" just like any other Debian package because of the rules set forth in the policy. In addition, the policy ensures a sensible environment for administrative work no matter what the circumstances may be. First of all, every software is required to provide documentation, which is essential in case of problems. Second, the FHS imposes an order on the filesystem, which is logical and easy to keep track of. In combination with the robust database of the package management system, it is trivial to deduce the purpose of every installed file from its location and/or the providing package.

For example, the **/var** hierarchy contains variable data files. Since Debian strictly adheres to the FHS, you are highly unlikely to find an executable file with the **setuid** bit set. Thus, the following command is likely to return an empty set on any given Debian installation. Moreover, any results returned should be treated with a high degree of scepticism:

```
~# find /var -perm +4000
```

Several invaluable tools in the Debian archive make use of the consistency of the Debian filesystem layout. For instance, **deborphan** (see chapter 5.11.5) identifies packages which are not needed anymore as no other package depends on them.

The protocol governing the handling of configuration files (see chapter 5.7.1) is paramount when it comes to system security. Consider the case where an administrator modifies a software configuration to disable a troublesome feature: if an upgrade of the software were to silently re-enable the feature, the system would be at risk without the administrator noticing.

Lastly, the policy defines clear boundaries on the permissions of installed files, and regulates the creation and usage of system users and groups. Consistent use of **dpkg-statoverride** (see chapter 6.1.2) ensures that local modifications to the permissions are kept, just like configuration files.

Automation on demand

The philosophy underlying the Debian operating system ensures that nothing is done without the administrator's prior consent. This philosophy is the reason for the absence of spiffy do-it-all configuration wizards and automated administration mechanisms put in place in an attempt to enable "One-Click Administration" of criticial services. Instead, Debian provides little tools that work hand in hand to facilitate the administrator's job, but which are restricted to doing what the administrator tells them to do — a Debian administrator is not expected to figure out and catch up with the changes made by an automated administration gadget.

This philosophy has important implications for the security of a system since it ensures that the administrator and the system never get out of sync. Furthermore, with only those packages needed to satisfy a machine's requirements, the administrator has an even easier time keeping track of the system. A bird's eye view allows the administrator to spot anomalies easily and quickly. In addition, security problems can be more effectively dealt with as the administrator will have a clear idea of the affected components and be able to assess the consequences of exploits or countermeasures to the problem.

Derived works

When it comes to policy adherence, Debian's rigour enables derivative products to flourish (see appendix A.2), as they can build on an established and stable foundation. Two Debian-based custom distributions rely on the security that Debian ships out of the box to give them a head start towards publishing highly secure operating systems. The Adamantix distribution (see appendix A.2.8) adds changes at code level to bring better security to the applications that run on a Debian system, and the Debian Hardened[8] project's goal is to take the Debian system and add high security and hardening features.

In addition, the "Debian: Secure by Default" project[9] attempts to funnel the insights gained by these and similar projects right back into the core Debian system. This is perhaps the most difficult task since security often opposes usabiity. While Debian does everything to be secure out of the box, it also tries to be usable a broader sense. If restrictive features, such as mandatory access control, were to become standard on Debian systems, other projects (such as Knoppix; see appendix A.2.1) might be unable to use the Debian system as a base.

Finally, a Debian system can be converted to SELinux, which is the hardened Linux distribution published by the American National Security Agency (NSA). In appendix A.2.9, I provide some more details.

7.4   Package quality

Debian packages are governed by the rules of the policy, which ensures that they will fit in with the rest of the system without friction. Beyond policy compliance (to which chapter 5.7 is devoted), the packages in the Debian archive are generally carefully put together and scrutinised before being made available to users. Obviously, during their time in the *testing* pool, a lot of problems are identified and fixed before the package enters *stable*. However, the true quality of a package comes from the hand of the package maintainer.

[8]http://www.debian-hardened.org
[9]http://d-sbd.alioth.debian.org

A package can be put together with different motivations. For instance, you could be told to package a software, and proceed to half-heartedly slap together the files in such a way as to satisfy the packaging utilities, and then upload the results when the error level became tolerable. Actually using a package gives you a completely different motivation, assuming that you would like to be able to **apt-get install**, rather than having to build manually wherever you need the software. Furthermore, you would probably not want to spend too much time configuring, but prefer the software to work immediately after installation with just a few tweaks to mould everything into place.

Debian package maintainers belong to the second group. As a matter of fact, nobody is ever told to deal with a package. A developer maintains a package out of choice, most probably because its inclusion in the official package pool facilitates local use of the package. As a user of the package, it is in the maintainer's own interest for the package installation and configuration to be as smooth as possible. After all, many maintainers administer a number of Debian machines for fun or for profit, and at least prefer their own packages to install, configure, and then just work without requiring people to study manual pages and hack configuration files.

Package maintainers are generally aware of security issues and put a lot of time into the default software configuration installed by their packages. As a result, software distributed by Debian is very secure out of the box, allowing daemons to be started right after installation. The maintainer will have taken care of questionable, insecure or rarely used parts of a software, so as to require as little interaction by the administrator as possible and still provide a secure installation. Obviously, the administrator is free to amend the configuration, knowing that all changes will be meticulously protected by **dpkg** (see chapter 5.3.3). Furthermore, if it is not desirable for services to start automatically upon installation, a system policy can be put in place to control this (see chapter 6.3.1).

7.5   Package integrity

One of the advantages commonly attributed to open-source software is the availability of its source code to check the integrity of the software. The theory goes that since everyone can inspect the source code prior to compilation, malicious code cannot go undetected. While there is certainly truth to the argument, it sheds a different light on binary distributions such as Debian. While the DFSG requires the source code to be available for every programme distributed from the Debian archive, the software contained in the Debian binary packages is precompiled. In fact, there seems to be no guarantee that the source code available from the mirrors is in fact the exact same used to compile the binaries installed by the packages.

It is not impossible for a developer to upload a trojaned binary package along-side a source package with the malicious code removed. While someone carefully reviewing the source code in the source package would not be able to find a vulnerability, the binary code which actually executed on the system would host the trojan. While the Debian build daemons generate the binary packages from the source package for the supported architectures (see chapter 4.5) in a clean and secure environment, the binary package compiled on the developer's machine as part of the package upload is *not* rebuilt. This has been identified as a problem with a simple solution, and the build process should be amended to rebuild all packages for all architectures following the release of *sarge*[10].

In addition to the hypothetically mischievous Debian developer in the previous paragraph, the case in which a developer's GPG key is subverted and misused must also not be forgotten. It is impossible to make sure that all developers take proper care to protect their keys. Half-hearted and careless developers are unlikely to maintain important packages, however, and this further reduces the risk. Still, Debian is continuously working to improve the situation, implementing quality assurance mechanisms to further protect the integrity of the archive (see below).

Despite this, Debian is powerless when it comes to uploads of malicious code. This said, the large number of developers and the immense size of the user base allow for an efficient peer review process, in which such offences will not remain undetected for long; it can almost be taken for granted that a trojaned package will not be released as part of Debian *stable*. If a case of abuse of a developer's powers or some other form of infiltration of the Debian archive is noticed, the culprit is immediately expelled from the developer team and an updated version of the trojaned package made available with high urgency. Fortunately, no such offence has taken place since the inception of the Debian project. Although there can be no guarantees, Debian maintainer status is an asset not deliberately put at risk, and the developers are certainly aware of the threats.

A more pertinent threat than a developer gone bad is a form of man in the middle attack, in which an attacker may gain access to a Debian mirror and replace a clean package with a trojaned version. As one of the greatest shortcomings of the Debian system, this kind of attack would currently go unnoticed. When an administrator tells APT to install a package, APT will comply as long as the package to install is a valid Debian package. Since creating Debian packages is neither a secret nor difficult (see chapter 9), any moderately skilled attacker will be able to make APT install the malicious code.

Work is underway to provide an infrastructure using strong cryptography to ensure that the package about to be installed is in fact the one uploaded by a Debian developer. Two solutions have been proposed. The first, known as "Secure APT" uses chains of checksums and a cryptographic signature on the index files of the Debian archive to allow verification of the downloaded payload as part of APT's

---

[10]http://lists.debian.org/debian-security/2004/09/msg00014.html

normal operation. Manual validation is already possible, and the version of **APT** in the *experimental* archive implements the functionality. The second method, called "dpkg-sig" attempts to tag signatures directly onto the DEB files and promises to work even without **APT**.

7.5.1 Manual verification of package integrity

The current approach to package validation requires the manual traversal of checksum chains, and the verification of a cryptographic signature against the Debian archive signing key.

For instance, if you wanted to ensure the integrity of the **apache2** package you just downloaded, you'd have to go through the following set of steps. First, you would use **md5sum** to obtain the MD5 sum of the DEB file in question and verify it against the archive's **Packages** file, which indexes the archive.

```
~$ md5sum /var/cache/apt/archives/apache2-common_2.0.52-3_i386.deb
084938e1ccfde598a93501c70803479c  apache2-common_2.0.52-3_i386.deb
~$ dpkg-awk --file /var/lib/apt/lists/[...]_Packages \
   Filename:apache2-common_2.0.52-3_i386.deb -- MD5sum
MD5sum: 084938e1ccfde598a93501c70803479c
```

The above shows that the **apache2** DEB file is in fact the same file which was present when the **Packages** index file was created. However, as chapter 9.3 shows, it is trivial to create the index, and so we must assume that an attacker may have modified this file as well. Thus, we verify the index file (which resides in **main/binary-i386/Packages.gz**, relative to the **dists** directory of the archive, see chapter 4.1) against the **Release** file, which includes checksums for the available index files (see chapter 4.1.3). Unfortunately, these checksums are removed by the current version of **APT**, and we thus have to obtain the file by hand. Let us assume **getfile** can retrieve it from some Debian mirror:

```
~$ getfile /dists/sarge/Release
~$ md5sum /var/lib/apt/lists/[...]main_binary-i386_Packages.gz
99a03884619014d29a9f2d08ff1b5c24  Packages.gz
~$ grep main/binary-i386/Packages.gz Release \
99a03884619014d29a9f2d08ff1b5c24  3385272  main/binary-i386/Packages.gz
[...]
```

By now, we know that the DEB file has not changed since the **Packages** index was created, and that this index is the same as when the **Release** file was written. However, again, any attacker could create a **Release** file. To counter this problem, the **Release** files in the Debian archive are signed with a cryptographic signature, using the official Debian signing key, which is changed yearly, and which is always available from **ftp-master.debian.org**[11]. Furthermore, APT upgrades of the **debian-keyring** package are expected to provide new archive signing keys in time so that the signing infrastructure requires little interaction from the user.

The **Release** file is signed with a detached signature, located in a separate file which must first be downloaded:

```
~$ getfile /dists/sarge/Release.gpg
~$ gpg --verify Release.gpg Release
gpg: Signature made Sat Feb 12 20:27:25 2005 UTC
   using DSA key ID 4F368D5D
gpg: Can't check signature: public key not found
~$ gpg --recv-keys 4F368D5D
~$ gpg --verify Release.gpg Release
gpg: Signature made ... using DSA key ID 4F368D5D
gpg: Good signature from ''Debian Archive Automatic Signing Key (2005)
   <ftpmaster@debian.org>''
Primary key fingerprint:
   4C7A 8E5E 9454 FE3F AE1E  78AD F1D5 3D8C 4F36 8D5D
```

These results prove the authenticity of the **Release** file. Obviously, the trust-level of the key used to sign the file must be established through other means. Either, the fingerprint of the expected key can be obtained from an authoritative source, and subsequently compared locally to the output of the above command[12], or the key can be verified with the help of the Web of Trust.

Your security policy may require you to explicitly verify archive keys before trusting them. The Debian archive signing keys are themselves cryptographically signed with the developer key of at least one of the FTP masters. Thus, the authenticity of the 2005 archive signing key (with key ID 0x4F368D5D) may be verified by ensuring that one of the FTP masters has signed the archive key with the following command:

```
~# wget -q http://ftp-master.debian.org/ziyi_key_2005.asc
~# gpg --import < ziyi_key_2005.asc
[...]
gpg: key 4F368D5D: public key "Debian Archive Automatic
   Signing Key (2005) <ftpmaster@debian.org>" imported
[...]
~# gpg --list-sigs 4F368D5D | grep 'not found'
sig       1DB114E0 2005-01-31  [User ID not found]
sig 3     2A4E3EAA 2005-01-31  [User ID not found]
~# gpg --recv-key 1DB114E0 2A4E3EAA
```

[11] http://ftp-master.debian.org/ziyi_key_$YEAR.asc ("Ziyi" is the name of the script creating the **Release** files in the Debian archive, after the Chinese actress Ziyi Zhang). Alternatively, it can be obtained from the Debian key server (**x-hkp://keyring.debian.org**) with standard means, or from the **/usr/share/keyrings/debian-role-keys.gpg** file in the **debian-keyring** package.

[12] At time of writing, the Debian project does *not* publish the fingerprint of its archive signing key. See appendix C.1.1 for a current fingerprint to help you verify the keys you download.

```
[...]
~# gpg --check-sigs 4F368D5D && echo valid
[...]
sig!3    2A4E3EAA 2005-01-31  Anthony Towns <aj@erisian.com.au>
valid
```

According to the Debian organisational pages[13], Anthony Towns is in fact an FTP master, so the archive signing key can be trusted as much as Anthony's key is trustworthy. Further investigation will reveal that James' key has been signed by hundreds of other people, including Debian developers, who have all verified his identity. If that is not enough for you to trust the key, you will have to arrange to meet James in person. An ultimate trust cannot be established, nevertheless. In appendix C.1.1 you can find a list of the GPG keys relevant to the Debian archive.

Unwinding the stack, we have now shown that the **Release** file has not been modified since it was officially created for the Debian archive. By extension, since its **MD5** sum matches the **MD5** sum of the **Packages** index, and the index contains an **MD5** sum identical to the checksum of the **apache2** DEB file, the package you have downloaded is authentic and guaranteed to have been uploaded by a Debian maintainer.

Now, the only possibility for a package to become trojaned is directly on the maintainer's machine, which cannot be prevented in any sensible way. However, please keep in mind that a trojan is unlikely to go unnoticed for more than a couple of hours or days. It will probably not make it into *testing* and almost definitely not into *stable*. Of course, if the trojan lingers long enough to ensure its host has entered *stable*, it could go unnoticed and infect *stable*. Unfortunately, there are no security measures to prevent this kind of subversion and the Debian project has to rely on the low odds and the unlikelihood of the chain of events an infected package would need to make it into the *stable* release happening. This a problem affects all projects and vendors and is not specific to Debian.

7.5.2 Secure APT

It goes without question that the manual verification procedure may be acceptable for a very small number of packages, but on a larger scale, it is not a solution. One could easily script the process though, and a number of scripts exist to do exactly that[14]. In addition, work on a new version of APT has started to do the same transparently. APT 0.6, which was available in the *experimental* archive at the time of writing, essentially incorporates the steps taken during the manual verification procedure, preventing the installation of packages that fail to validate. It also adds basic keyring management. APT 0.6 is referred to as "Secure APT" in various places.

---

[13] http://www.debian.org/intro/organization.
[14] *e.g.* http://people.debian.org/~ajt/apt-check-sigs

Verifying Release files

APT uses the same MD5 sum chain we used during manual verification. As part of the **apt-get update** process, APT requests the **Release** files along with their detached signatures in **Release.gpg**. Upon successful download, it then employs GnuPG to verify its integrity. In the following, this integrity check fails because APT does not have access to the key used to sign the **Release** file.

```
~# apt-get update
Get:1 http://debian.ethz.ch stable Release [22.6kB]
Get:2 http://debian.ethz.ch stable Release.gpg [315B]
[...]
Reading Package Lists... Done
W: GPG error: http://debian.ethz.ch stable Release:
  The following signatures couldn't be verified
  because the public key is not available:
  NO_PUBKEY 6FFA8EF91DB114E0
[...]
W: You may want to run apt-get update to correct these problems
```

Given the availability of **GnuPG**, anyone could generate a key and sign the **Release** file after injecting of malicious code into the archive. Thus, it is important to tell APT which keys to trust. For this purpose, APT maintains its own **GnuPG** keyring in **/etc/apt/trusted.gpg**; the keyring may be manipulated with **apt-key**, and future versions may adopt an approach similar to **run-parts**, with a directory holding individual files for trusted keys (see chapter 6.1.1). APT 0.6 contains the official archive keys (which are rotated yearly), and new keys are available from the Debian key server[15], the **debian-keyring** package, or the Debian web page[11]. Thus, to declare that you trust the Debian archive signing key to sign packages that are authentic, you add the key to **APT**'s keyring:

```
~# apt-key add ziyi_key_2005.asc
```

With the official archive signing key added to **APT**'s key ring, the **APT** update procedure completes without a warning, as the signatures on the **Release** files are checked transparently.

If the **Release** file has been modified in transit, APT will produce the following warning:

```
~# apt-get update
[...]
W: GPG error: file: test Release: The following signatures were invalid:
BADSIG F1D53D8C4F368D5D Debian Archive Automatic Signing Key (2005)
  <ftpmaster@debian.org>
[...]
```

[15]x-hkp://keyring.debian.org

Verifying package indices

After APT has verified the **Release** files, it checks the **MD5** sums of the **Packages** files it downloads against the hashes stored in the **Release** file. If it finds a discrepancy, it reports a mismatch of the **MD5** sum and refuses to integrate the unverified **Packages** file into the local database of available packages:

```
~# apt-get update
[...]
Failed to fetch .../Packages.gz
MD5Sum mismatch
[...]
```

Thus, when **apt-get update** completes without warnings or errors, the integrity and authenticity of the **Packages** files has been successfully verified. Source package indices (in the **Sources** files) are handled similarly. Assuming that **apt-get update** completes without warnings, you can trust the APT index files in **/var/lib/apt/lists** as much as you can trust any other file on your local system.

If the update procedure fails to verify the integrity of the index files, APT will alert the user whenever told to install a package whose integrity is uncertain as a consequence. By default, it will refuse the installation and only proceed if the user explicitly tells it to.

Verifying package downloads

Recalling that APT automatically checks the MD5 sum of each DEB file it processes against the entry in the **Packages** file, package authenticity and integrity is now secured all the way between the Debian archive and a user's machine. An attempt to install a package with a checksum that not match the checksum in the index file will be refused:

```
~# apt-get install apache2-common
[...]
Failed to fetch .../apache2-common_2.0.52-3_i386.deb
MD5Sum mismatch
```

If, on the other hand, the package checksum matches, APT verifies the entire checksum chain as well as the archive signature on the **Release** file. If any link in the chain fails to authenticate (due to a missing key, or a bad signature), APT will display a warning and default to aborting the operation. APT will not install unverified packages unless the user explicitly tells it to do so:

```
~# apt-get install apache2
[...]
```

```
WARNING: The following packages cannot be authenticated!
  openssl ssl-cert apache2-common apache2-mpm-worker apache2
  Install these packages without verification? [y/N]
```

Furthermore, the installation will abort if the **--assume-yes** option was given. You have to explicitly force APT to install unverified packages, even with **--assume-yes** in effect:

```
~# apt-get install apache2
[...]
WARNING: The following packages cannot be authenticated!
  openssl ssl-cert apache2-common apache2-mpm-worker apache2
E: There are problems and --yes was used without --force-yes
```

Using Secure APT

At time of writing, APT 0.6 was experimental software, available only from the *experimental* archive on the Debian mirrors. While efforts are on the way to release APT 0.6 with *sarge*, the tight dependency between package management tools and APT may well call for APT 0.6 to be held back until *etch* is in the pipeline. Nevertheless, it is already possible to use APT 0.6, which the following demonstrates.

You can obtain APT 0.6 from the *experimental* archive by adding a line such as the following to /etc/apt/sources.list. Please consider using a closer mirror instead of ftp.debian.org[16].

```
~# cat <<EOF >> /etc/apt/sources.list
deb http://ftp.debian.org/debian experimental main
EOF
~# apt-get update
[...]
~# apt-get install --target-release experimental apt
[...]
```

Unfortunately, also at time of writing, other software depending on APT has not been updated to support version 0.6. Therefore, the installation of APT 0.6 conflicts with packages such as **aptitude** and **tasksel** and requires their removal. Obviously, when **Secure APT** becomes official, this restriction will disappear.

After installation, it is advisable to either remove or comment the *experimental* line in /etc/apt/sources.list and update APT before installing new packages to avoid inadvertedly pulling *experimental* software onto the system. While the *experimental* release automatically integrates nicely with APT and is pinned to a low priority (see chapter 8.2.1), packages unavailable in other releases will be satisfied from leaseexperimental on request.

[16]see chapter 5.4.1 and/or http://www.debian.org/mirror/list

Problems and shortcomings

The **APT** verification mechanism supported by **APT** 0.6 requires little change to the existing infrastructure and works reliably in standard usage scenarios. However, it also suffers from major shortcomings. First, it requires infrastructure support for the verification to work. An archive has to publish and sign **Release** files, and these have to be available locally at the time of verification. Additionally, the method can only verify current packages. It is impossible to verify the authenticity or integrity of *e.g.* version 1.0-1 of a package, when 1.0-2 has already hit the mirrors and replaced the older version in the pool as well as the **Packages** index.

Another related shortcoming is that **APT**'s verification mechanism only allows for the checking of packages in the archive. When a DEB file is obtained through another means, there is no way to verify its authenticity or integrity. **APT**'s MD5 sum checking mainly provides for the security of the Debian mirror infrastructure, preventing the subversion of one of the mirrors. As such, it is an adequate tool. Nevertheless, it cannot be considered a full implementation of a package signature system.

7.5.3   debsigs and dpkg-sig

While **APT** 0.6 uses index files to verify package integrity and is thus of little use when the indices are not available, two other tools use signatures attached to the DEB file for the integrity verification: **dpkg-sig** and **debsigs**. **debsigs** (in package **debsigs**) was written shortly after the release of *potato*. In the mean time, another programme, **dpkg-sig** (in package **dpkg-sig**) was authored to deal with its shortcomings[17].

A package signature is similar to the digital signatures as used in *e.g.* emails, and consist of a list of all files in the **ar** archive (see chapter 5.2.3), along with their sizes and MD5 hash sums. This list resides in a file of its own, simply inserted into the **ar** archive. This approach allows any number of signatures to accumulate for each package, and since the signatures become part of the DEB file, the distribution medium is irrelevant; the DEB file contains everything needed for verification.

Where the **APT** verification requires infrastructural support, anyone may add signatures to a DEB file with **debsigs** or **dpkg-sig**. **dpkg-sig** directly grew out of **debsigs** and should be preferred to **debsigs** for signature creation and verification. In addition to **debsigs**' features, it allows for remote signing of packages and signs all files in the DEB **ar** archive, not just the three required ones. In addition, it uses the same tools as **dpkg-deb** and thus retains policy compliance, whereas **debsigs** creates incompatible DEB files[18].

---

[17] http://dpkg-sig.turmzimmer.net
[18] http://bugs.debian.org/161593

Usage of **dpkg-sig** is trivial and assumes the presence of **GnuPG** and a secret keyring. The **-k** command-line option allows the key specification to be used for signing. **dpkg-sig** also honours $DEBSIGN_KEYID, which can be overridden with $DPKGSIG_KEYID. Each signature is identified by a signing name, which mainly serves to identify the role of the signer. For instance a person packaging a software should use "builder" as signing name:

```
~$ dpkg-sig --sign builder postfix_2.1.5-1_i386.deb
Processing postfix_2.1.5-1_i386.deb...

You need a passphrase to unlock the secret key for
user: ''Martin F. Krafft <madduck@madduck.net>''
1024-bit DSA key, ID 330C4A75, created 2001-06-20

Enter passphrase:

Signed deb postfix_2.1.5-1_i386.deb
```

Verification of a DEB file signed with **dpkg-sig** is similarly straight-forward:

```
~$ dpkg-sig --verify postfix_2.1.5-1_i386.deb
GOODSIG builder ACF49D3E1E1D5EE2B2035E53220BC883330C4A75 1093444208
```

Any modification to the DEB file is caught by **dpkg-sig** upon verification. Since the signature certifies the **MD5** sum of all data in the archive, it makes no difference whether a modification is made to the control file in **control.tar.gz**, the data in **data.tar.gz**, or by inserting new data into the DEB file. For instance, inserting a dummy file to the middle of the DEB file payload invalidates the signature:

```
~$ echo dummy > dummy
~$ ar rb data.tar.gz postfix_2.1.5-1_i386.deb dummy
~$ ar t postfix_2.1.5-1_i386.deb
debian-binary
control.tar.gz
dummy
data.tar.gz
_gpgbuilder
~$ dpkg-sig --verify postfix_2.1.5-1_i386.deb
Processing postfix_2.1.5-1_i386.deb...
BADSIG builder/
```

The signatures may accumulate, allowing authors and distributors to document the path a file takes in a cryptographically secure manner. For example, a distribution may choose to "stamp" packages with a Quality Assurance (QA) signature to certify that they have passed quality assurance tests, and an archive operator could periodically resign the available packages to prevent old packages pretending to be newer ones.

Obviously, **dpkg-sig** only checks the signatures on the package and not the authenticity of the keys used to sign the message. Before a package may be trusted, it is necessary to trust the signature of the keys used to sign it.

Apart from manual verification, no integrated verification mechanism currently exists for package signature. Following the release of *sarge*, work will begin on bringing package signatures up to speed. In addition, some developers (including myself) are already thinking about how to implement an all-encompassing policy-based signature verification mechanism.

8

Advanced concepts

Sizzling adventures!
Follow the story of J. Random Sysadmin as he battles evil,
rescues damsels in distress, and polishes his
Debian GNU/Linux installation!
— Lars Wirzenius

The concepts and techniques introduced in this book up to this point are more than sufficient to successfully administer Debian systems for most purposes. Nevertheless, special requirements exist, and the Debian archive has tools to cater for most of them. In this chapter you will learn how to build packages for customised and possibly patched kernels, create kernel module packages, mix different APT repositories in a sensible way, and install a Debian system by using alternatives to the Debian installer.

8.1   Building kernel packages with make-kpkg

make-kpkg is Debian's kernel package tool. It provides a one-stop interface to kernel compilation, creating DEB files to encapsulate the kernel, headers, sources, and
documentation in the way described in chapter 5.12.2 and chapter 5.12.3. Furthermore, make-kpkg allows for the easy compilation of modules for any Debian
kernel, as well as the application of patches to the Debian kernel sources.

The make-kpkg utility comes in the kernel-package package (what an unfortunate name). The kernel-package (5) manpage gives you a list of the advantages
and disadvantages of using make-kpkg to build kernels for Debian systems. Moreover, make-kpkg (5) includes extensive information about the programme itself,
and under /usr/share/doc/kernel-package, plenty of additional information may
be found.

Similar to make, make-kpkg works with targets. The important targets are as
follows:

kernel_image

> builds the kernel image and packages it into a DEB file.

kernel_headers

> makes the DEB file holding the kernel headers specific to the architecture
> and processor type for which the kernel source tree has been configured.

kernel_source

> bundles the entire kernel source (except for the documentation) into a DEB
> file.

binary

> does all of the above and also creates the DEB file for the documentation
> (target kernel_doc).

buildpackage

> accomplishes the same as binary, but uses dpkg-buildpackage to create the
> source package, and to augment the resulting source and binary packages
> with a cryptographic signature. Signing can be prevented by passing the -uc
> -us options to make-kpkg (see chapter 9.2.16).

modules_image

> creates DEB files for all additional kernel modules make-kpkg was asked to
> build for a specific kernel (see chapter 8.1.3).

modules

> uses dpkg-buildpackage to create the source package for the additional
> kernel modules, and adds a cryptographic signature to the resulting source

and binary packages, unless the **-uc -us** command line options have been given to the **make-kpkg** invocation (see chapter 9.2.16).

clean

restores the kernel tree to its distribution status.

The programme must be run in the top-level directory of the unpacked kernel tree. It is possible to use both the Debian kernel sources (as made available in the various **kernel-source** packages) as well as the vanilla sources from **kernel.org**. This said, it is important to note that over the past years, there has been a shift in kernel maintenance. Since almost every distribution maintains their own kernels, the vanilla kernels have established themselves as a foundation not to be used directly. The kernel team does not release a new kernel whenever a security bug has been fixed and reserves new versions for technological advancements. It is now the job of the distributors to fix holes in the kernel and provide updated packages as soon as possible. Therefore, it is advisable to base your customised kernels on the Debian **kernel-source** packages. In addition to security fixes, these include a small set of carefully selected patches which are likely not going to be in your way.

The simplest way to obtain a DEB file for a custom kernel based on the Debian sources is to install the kernel source package and unpack the tarball. Normally, **make-kpkg** expects to be run on a configured kernel tree, but it can also call the kernel's **configure** target itself, using the **--config** option. Thus, If the build tree is unconfigured (the file **.config** is not present), **make-kpkg** provides a default configuration similar to the one used in the Debian stock kernels.

Rather than installing the kernel sources in a directory, the kernel source package drops a tarball into **/usr/src**. This approach reflects the intended use of **make-kpkg**, which is supposed to be run by a normal user and *not* by **root**. Since you must have write access to the kernel source tree to build the kernel, the idea is to unpack the tarball to your home directory hierarchy and compile it there.

```
~# apt-get install kernel-source-2.6.8 libncurses5-dev
[...]
~$ tar xfj /usr/src/kernel-source-2.6.8.tar.bz2
~$ cd kernel-source-2.6.8
~/kernel-source-2.6.8$ make-kpkg --rootcmd fakeroot \
   --config menu kernel-image
[...]
dpkg-deb: building package 'kernel-image-2.6.8'
  in '../kernel-image-2.6.8_10.00.Custom_i386.deb'.
[...]
```

The resulting DEB file packages the kernel image and all modules, seamlessly integrates with Debian upon installation and integrates with any configured boot loaders (see chapter 5.12.2). Building kernels with **make-kpkg** is trivial, and the package management tools do their best to ensure a bootable system. Debian users are known to update their kernels over SSH from far away without breaking a sweat[1].

You will notice that **make-kpkg** assigned a version number to the kernel package it created. As it is always the same (10.00.Custom), it is not possible to properly integrate the generated kernel packages with an **APT** repository. **make-kpkg** allows the revision number to be specified with the **--revision** command line option. Keeping in mind that **APT** uses a comparison on version numbers (see chapter 5.7.5) and only upgrades a package when a newer version number is available, it is a good idea to use an automatic versioning scheme so as to not loose track. I use the output of **date +%Y%m%d.%H%M**, which guarantees unique, increasing version numbers (unless you use a super-computer to compile the same kernel twice within a minute...). If the revision number changes between builds, a **make-kpkg clean** is obligatory; otherwise **make-kpkg** will fail with a descriptive error (we are now in the kernel build directory):

```
~$ REVISION=$(date +%Y%m%d.%H%M)
~$ echo $REVISION
20040903.0930
~$ make-kpkg --rootcmd fakeroot --revision $REVISION kernel-image
I note that you are using the --revision flag with the value
    20040903.0930.
However, the ./debian/changelog file exists, and has a different value
    10.00.Custom.
I am confused by this discrepancy, and am halting.
~$ make-kpkg --rootcmd fakeroot clean
[...]
~$ make-kpkg --rootcmd fakeroot --revision $REVISION kernel-image
[...]
dpkg-deb: building package 'kernel-image-2.6.8'
  in '../kernel-image-2.6.8_20040903.0930_i386.deb'.
[...]
```

If you are like me, you will want to shorten the command lines to make working with **make-kpkg** easier. Skip ahead to (or wait for) chapter 8.1.6 for a way to tweak **make-kpkg** with configuration files.

Another very useful feature of **make-kpkg** is its ability to append custom strings to the upstream kernel version number. This comes in handy when building specialised kernels for multiple systems on a single machine. Since the kernel version number as well as its appendix are part of the package name, it is possible to keep specialised kernels for different systems in a single **APT** repository. Just like the revision, a change in the version appendix must be preceeded by a **make-kpkg clean**:

[1]There is obviously no guarantee. So please do not sue me. Please also check out http://colt.projectgamma.com/debian/remote-reboot.html for some inspiration.

```
~$ REVISION=$(date +%Y%m%d.%H%M)
~$ make-kpkg --rootcmd fakeroot clean
[...]
 $ make-kpkg --rootcmd fakeroot --revision $REVISION \
   --append-to-version -arakis kernel-image
[...]
dpkg-deb: building package 'kernel-image-2.6.8-arakis'
   in '../kernel-image-2.6.8-arakis_20040903.0807_i386.deb'.
[...]
```

The resulting package is named **kernel-image-2.6.8-arakis**, suggesting that it is tailored for the machine named arakis. This information will also show up in, *e.g.*, the output of **uname** when run on arakis. In fact, the appendix becomes part of the kernel name and thus also becomes part of the module directory name, among other places:

```
~# apt-get install kernel-image-2.6.8-arakis
~# reboot
[...]
~$ uname -nr
arakis 2.6.8-arakis
~$ ls -Fd /lib/modules/2.6.8*
/lib/modules/2.6.8-arakis/
~$ ls -F /boot/*2.6.8*
/boot/config-2.6.8-arakis     /boot/System.map-2.6.8-arakis
/boot/vmlinuz-2.6.8-arakis
```

With appendices, it is trivial to maintain kernels for multiple machines on a single system.

8.1.1 Using initial ramdisks

The Debian kernels use initial ramdisks to store modules needed during the kernel boot phase before the root filesystem has been mounted. **make-kpkg** makes it trivial to do the same for custom kernels. With the kernel tree from the **kernel-source** packages, this works out of the box. If you use a different kernel tree, you either have to ensure that it supports the **cramfs** filesystem, or configure **mkinitrd** to use a different filesystem instead. Please note that the initial ramdisk is created *upon installation* of the kernel package. Therefore, the filesystem change must occur on the target system, *not* the build system.

Creating a kernel image with an initial ramdisk requires no more than an addition argument to the **make-kpkg** call:

```
~$ make-kpkg --rootcmd fakeroot --initrd kernel-image
[...]
dpkg-deb: building package 'kernel-image-2.6.8'
   in '../kernel-image-2.6.8_10.00.Custom_i386.deb'.
```

The only difference between the DEB file this and the one created without the --initrd flag is the **postinst** script, since the initial ramdisk is created on the target system.

8.1.2   Patching the kernel

The Linux kernel itself provides an incredible amount of features, but a plethora of additional features or drivers only exist in the form of patches to the kernel source. Obviously, applying such patches to the kernel source tree works as expected. However, when multiple patches are to be applied, or the same source tree is to serve as a compilation basis for different machines with different patch combinations, patch maintenance quickly becomes a hassle.

Fortunately, Debian provides special packages to encapsulate kernel patches, which can be easily applied and removed from a given tree. **make-kpkg** provides all that is necessary to work with the patches provided in the Debian archive, whose package names all start with **kernel-patch** (which is just a happenstance and not required), and which install under **/usr/src/kernel-patches**. Each kernel patch is identified by its short name, which is identical to the name of the script under **/usr/src/kernel-patches/*/apply**. Some patches depend on other patches. The package management tools take care to resolve the dependencies, and **make-kpkg** ensures that all selected patches are applied in the correct order.

A Debian patch only applies to a limited set of kernel versions as the kernel patch package stores a separate patch for each kernel version to cater for upstream changes that would prevent the patch being applied. When asked to patch a kernel not supported by a specific patch, **make-kpkg** will simply output a message to this respect and continue. For some patches (most notably those created with **dh_kpatches**), it is possible to override the kernel version number to force the patch's application by setting the $KPATCH_<patchname> environment variable (with special characters replaced by underscores) to the desired kernel version number.

make-kpkg allows for two methods to select the set of patches to be applied. If the $PATCH_THE_KERNEL environment variable is set to yes, **make-kpkg** will simply go ahead and apply all installed and applicable kernel-patches before building the kernel. The **debian** target prepares the source tree and applies all the patches. It is automatically invoked by the targets that build packages (*e.g.* **kernel-image**) and thus does not need to be invoked explicitly.

```
~# apt-get install kernel-patch-skas
[...]
~$ export PATCH_THE_KERNEL=YES
~$ make-kpkg --rootcmd fakeroot debian
[...]
START applying skas patch (Separate Kernel Address Space)
```

```
Testing whether "Separate Kernel Address Space" patch for
  2.6.8 applies (dry run):
"Separate Kernel Address Space" patch for 2.6.8 succeeded
Removing empty files:
Done.
END applying skas patch
Patch /usr/src/kernel-patches/all//unpatch/skas processed fine
[...]
~$ cat applied_patches
/usr/src/kernel-patches/all//apply/skas
```

To keep track of the applied patches, **make-kpkg** writes each patch to the **applied_patches** file in the kernel source top-level directory. In addition, a similar file is distributed as part of the DEB file containing the kernel image:

```
~$ make-kpkg --rootcmd fakeroot kernel-image
[...]
~$ dpkg-deb --contents kernel-image-2.6.8_10.00.Custom_i386.deb
[...]
-rw-r--r-- root/root  19 2004-09-05 21:18:05 ./boot/patches-2.6.8
[...]
~$ dpkg-deb --fsys-tarfile kernel-image-2.6.8_10.00.Custom_i386.deb \
  | tar xOf - ./boot/patches*
skas
~$
```

As an alternative to the unconditionally applying all patches, **make-kpkg** can also take the set of patches to apply as a comma-separated list to the **--added-patches**. For this to work, the variable $PATCH_THE_KERNEL has to be set to **auto**. Thus, with a second kernel patch package installed, the following applies only the **skas** patch (and not **kernel-patch-2.6-bluez**, which we install for the sake of proving the point):

```
~# apt-get install kernel-patch-2.6-bluez
[...]
~$ ls -F /usr/src/kernel-patches/all/apply
bluez*      skas*
~$ export PATCH_THE_KERNEL=auto
~$ make-kpkg --rootcmd fakeroot --added-patches skas debian
[...]
"Separate Kernel Address Space" patch for 2.6.8 succeeded
[...]
~$ cat applied_patches
/usr/src/kernel-patches/all//apply/skas
```

make-kpkg removes the applied patches from the kernel source tree when the **clean** target is invoked[2]. It uses the information in the **applied_patches** file to

---

[2]At time of writing, a bug (#270169) causes **make-kpkg** not to unpatch reliably in all cases. In case of a problem, it may be necessary to delete and recreate the kernel tree from the kernel source tarball.

determine the set of applied patches. Automatic unpatching can be prevented by setting the environment variable $NO_UNPATCH_BY_DEFAULT:

```
~$ export NO_UNPATCH_BY_DEFAULT
~$ make-kpkg --rootcmd fakeroot clean
[...]
~$ cat applied_patches
/usr/src/kernel-patches/all//apply/skas
~$ unset NO_UNPATCH_BY_DEFAULT
~$ make-kpkg --rootcmd fakeroot clean
[...]
START unpatching skas patch (Separate Kernel Address Space)
Removing empty files:
Done.
END unpatching skas patch
Removed Patch /usr/src/kernel-patches/all//unpatch/skas
[...]
~$ cat applied_patches
cat: applied_patches: No such file or directory
```

8.1.3   Compiling modules

The Linux kernel arguably supports more devices than any other kernel these days. In addition, many devices are supported through external code, most of which compiles into kernel modules to be loaded at runtime. The Debian archive contains the most popular modules compiled against the available Debian kernels. For instance, **pcmcia-modules-2.4.26-1-k7** installs the PCMCIA modules from the pcmcia-cs project into their appropriate locations. Precompiled packages exist only for a small number of modules. The majority of module packages are available only in the form of source packages (mostly named ***-source**). Just like the kernel source packages, these packages drop a tarball into **/usr/src**, rather than installing the module source directly to the filesystem, since the build process requires write access. For instance, the package **shfs-source** looks like this:

```
~$ dpkg -L shfs-source
[...]
/usr/src/shfs.tar.bz2
[...]
~$ tar tjf /usr/src/shfs.tar.bz2
[...]
modules/shfs/Linux-2.6/Makefile
modules/shfs/Makefile
modules/shfs/debian/
[...]
```

The process of building kernel modules for Debian is somewhat confusing at first because it involves different packages at different stages of the module creation and installation process. Since modules are heavily dependent on the exact kernel version, they need to be compiled against the desired kernel headers. When the source code in (the tarball in) shfs-source is compiled against, *e.g.*, the kernel 2.6.8-1-k7, a DEB file for the shfs-modules-2.6.8-1-k7 package is generated. This package then contains the appropriate kernel modules for the desired kernel and drops them into their appropriate location when installed.

Previously, no definitive procedure for creating module packages existed for Debian. In some cases, the package would follow standard packaging rules (see chapter 9) and honour the $KSRC environment variable, pointing to the appropriate kernel headers tree under /usr/src. Unfortunately, very few module packages worked that way, some simply not supporting the standard packaging procedure and others depending on an unpacked kernel source tree. Kernel modules should not interfere with or access kernel sources but use the well-defined APIs in the kernel headers packages instead.

In recent years, the situation has improved and two methods for compiling modules have crystallised. The first uses make-kpkg, needs access to the kernel-sources and thus works best when you are compiling your own kernel. If you are using the Debian-provided stock kernels, then module-assistant is for you, a young tool that aims to settle the problems with Debian kernel modules once and for all. In an ideal world, all modules packages should work with either of the two methods. Unfortunately, there are still some modules packages that do not behave well. In such cases, please do not hesitate to file bugs (see chapter 10.6.5). Let us look at both methods in turn.

Using make-kpkg and the kernel source tree

Building modules packages with make-kpkg is very similar to applying kernel patches, except that the module sources must first be extracted from the tarball. You will notice that all module source tarballs extract their payload to the ./modules directory. Setting the $MODULE_LOC variable to the path of this module directory tells make-kpkg where to look for the module sources. make-kpkg's modules_image target, when invoked from the root of the target kernel's configured source tree, then builds all modules found under this directory. As an alternative, make-kpkg accepts the --added-modules flag, followed by a comma-separated list of modules packages to build. For instance, the shfs module can be built as follows:

```
~$ tar xjf /usr/src/shfs.tar.bz2
~$ tar xjf /usr/src/kernel-source-2.6.8.tar.bz2
~$ export MODULE_LOC=$(pwd)/modules
~$ cd kernel-source-2.6.8
~/kernel-source-2.6.8$ make-kpkg --rootcmd fakeroot \
  --added-modules shfs modules_image
```

```
[...]
Module ../modules/shfs processed fine
~$ ls -F ../*.deb
../shfs-module-2.6.8_0.35-1+10.00.Custom_i386.deb
```

As with the kernel images, it is probably a good idea to employ a sensible revision scheme and properly version the module package. Otherwise, if the kernel configuration changes and the module package has to be rebuilt, **APT** will not consider it an upgrade candidate as the version number has not increased.

module-assistant

An increasing number of module packages use **module assistant** from the **module-assistant** package, which makes package handling much easier. In fact, **module-assistant** is smart enough to figure out most parameters which the user did not specify, thus requiring only a minimum amount of information to successfully compile a package. The **--text-mode** command line option selects text mode, which is better suited for the following example:

```
~$ tar xjf /usr/src/shfs.tar.bz2
~$ module-assistant --text-mode --user-dir modules build shfs
[ldots]
dpkg-deb: building package 'shfs-module-2.6.8-1-k7' \
  in 'shfs-module-2.6.8-1-k7_0.35-1+2.6.8-1_i386.deb'.
```

Without further arguments, **module-assistant** attempts to find the kernel headers for the running kernel and proceeds to compile the modules accordingly. The kernel's version number and Debian revision are incorporated into the module's revision. The **--user-dir** option tells it to use the module sources under the **./modules** directory.

module-assistant can also be told the kernel version for which to compile, and automatically determines the location of the appropriate kernel headers. Moreover, it can be given a comma-separated list of kernel versions for which to build a module and will take the appropriate steps in sequence.

```
~$ module-assistant --text-mode --user-dir modules \
  --kvers-list 2.6.7-1-686,2.6.8-1-686 build shfs
[...]
Bad luck, the kernel headers for this kernel version could not be found
and you did not specify other kernel headers to use.

However, you can install the header files for your kernel which are
provided by the kernel-headers-2.6.7-1-686 package. For most modules
packages, this files are perfectly sufficient without having the
original kernel source.
```

```
[...]
~$ su
~# exec apt-get install kernel-headers-2.6.7,8-1-686
[...]
~$ module-assistant --text-mode --user-dir modules \
   --kvers-list 2.6.7-1-686,2.6.8-1-686 build shfs
[...]
dpkg-deb: building package 'shfs-module-2.6.8-1-686' \
  in 'shfs-module-2.6.8-1-686_0.35-1+2.6.8-2_i386.deb'.
[...]
dpkg-deb: building package 'shfs-module-2.6.7-1-686' \
  in 'shfs-module-2.6.7-1-686_0.35-1+2.6.7-2_i386.deb'.
[...]
```

Other than a local working directory, **module-assistant** does not need more than the appropriate kernel headers installed. Thus, if you are planning to use **module-assistant** with your custom kernel, you will need to create the appropriate **kernel-headers** package and install it. It may be easier just to use the **make-kpkg** method we looked at earlier instead.

8.1.4 Cross-compiling for other architectures

make-kpkg is also capable of cross-compiling for other architectures. Obviously, the appropriate cross compiling software must be available on the building system. For example, to compile a kernel for the **sparc32** architecture, **sparc-linux-gcc** must exist on the building system. Debian provides the GNU toolchain source code in the **toolchain-source** package, which can be used to create packages for the tools and libraries needed for the cross-compilation. First, we need to build the **binutils-sparc-linux** package since it is required for the compilation of **gcc**, a process automated by the **tpkg-make** tool from the **toolchain-source** package:

```
~# apt-get install toolchain-source
~$ tpkg-make sparc-linux
~$ ls -F
binutils-sparc-linux-2.15/              gcc-sparc-linux-3.4.1/
~$ cd binutils-sparc-linux-2.15
~/binutils-sparc-linux-2.15$ debuild -uc -us
[...]
dpkg-deb: building package 'binutils-sparc-linux' in
  '../binutils-sparc-linux_2.15-1_i386.deb'.
~/binutils-sparc-linux-2.15$ cd ..
~$ dpkg --install binutils-sparc-linux_2.15-1_i386.deb
[...]
```

The **gcc-sparc-linux** package also needs to be built. The build needs the **libc** development files for the target architecture. With **dpkg-cross**, Debian provides a tool to facilitate (and manage) the installation of libraries necessary for cross-compilation. Essentially, the tool takes the library for the target architecture (as downloaded from a Debian mirror) and builds a new DEB file that installs the files into /usr/<arch> (e.g. /usr/sparc32) instead of /usr. toolchain-source provides a script to automate the whole process. Setting $TPKG_SERVER allows the selection of the Debian mirror to use (please choose your closest mirror; see chapter 5.4.1)

```
~# export TPKG_SERVER=ftp.debian.org
~# tpkg-install-libc sparc-linux
[...]
Unpacking libdb1-compat-sparc-cross
Unpacking libc6-sparc-cross
Unpacking libc6-dev-sparc-cross
Unpacking linux-kernel-headers-sparc-cross
Setting up linux-kernel-headers-sparc-cross (2.5.999-test7-bk-16) ...
Setting up libc6-sparc-cross (2.3.2.ds1-13) ...
Setting up libc6-dev-sparc-cross (2.3.2.ds1-13) ...
Setting up libdb1-compat-sparc-cross (2.1.3-7) ...
```

Now **gcc-sparc-linux** can be compiled and installed:

```
~$ cd gcc-sparc-linux-3.4.1
~/gcc-sparc-linux-3.4.1$ debuild -uc -us
[...]
dpkg-deb: building package 'gcc-sparc-linux' in
  '../gcc-sparc-linux_3.4.1-1_i386.deb'.
[...]
~/gcc-sparc-linux-3.4.1$ cd ..
~$ su -c 'dpkg --install gcc-sparc-linux_3.4.1-1_i386.deb'
Password:
[...]
Setting up gcc-sparc-linux (3.4.1-1) ...
```

With the cross-compilation tools and libraries in place, **make-kpkg** can be told to compile a kernel for the **sparc32** architecture (which is the default sub-architecture for **sparc**):

```
~$ dpkg --list \*sparc\* | grep ^ii
ii  binutils-sparc 2.15-1          Binary utilities for cross
ii  gcc-sparc-linu 3.4.1-1         The GNU C compiler as cros
ii  libc6-dev-spar 2.3.2.ds1-13    GNU C Library: Development
ii  libc6-sparc-cr 2.3.2.ds1-13    GNU C Library: Shared libr
ii  libdb1-compat- 2.1.3-7         The Berkeley database rout
ii  linux-kernel-h 2.5.999-test7-  Linux Kernel Headers for d
~$ make-kpkg --rootcmd fakeroot \
  --arch sparc --subarch sparc32 kernel-image
[...]
dpkg-deb: building package 'kernel-image-2.6.8-sparc32'
  in '../kernel-image-2.6.8-sparc32_10.00.Custom_sparc.deb'.
```

8.1.5 Symlink farming

Even though **make-kpkg** can restore the kernel source tree to its clean state after a build, it is sometimes useful to keep separate source trees for different target machines. Instead of unpacking the kernel source multiple times and wasting hundreds of megabytes of storage space, it is possible to set up so-called symlink farms and for each tree store only the files that are different from the master.

Setting up a symlink farm is trivial through the use of **lndir** (from the **xutils** package[3]). For every file in the tree specified by the argument, **lndir** creates a symbolic link from the respective location underneath the current directory. If **patch** is used to apply patches to the source code, it will read the code to be patched from the linked files, then erase the symlink, and drop a regular file with the patched code in its place. This guarantess that the original tree is not modified and that the patched tree only occupies a minimal amount of space.

To prevent the created DEB files from storing the symlinks (which are of no use outside of the build context), **make-kpkg** needs to be told to follow the symlinks:

```
~$ tar xjf /usr/src/kernel-source-2.6.8.tar.bz2
~$ mkdir kernel-arakis
~$ cd kernel-arakis
~/kernel-arakis$ lndir ../kernel-source-2.6.8
[...]
~/kernel-arakis$ make-kpkg [...] kpkg_follow_symlinks_in_src=YES
  kernel-image
[...]
```

8.1.6 Configuring make-kpkg

Most of the configuration parameters used by **make-kpkg** can be set permanently in a system-wide or user-specific configuration file, using the **make** syntax. The user's file, ~/.kernel-pkg.conf is preferred over the system-wide file, /etc/kernel-pkg.conf. Thus, it is possible to maintain your own configuration without requiring **root** access or interfering with other users. Instead of the configuration file, **make-kpkg** can also be configured with environment variables, which take priority if present. The **kernel-pkg.conf** (5) manpage documents all available parameters.

It is a good idea to set **maintainer** and **email** in the configuration file, or to export the variables $KPKG_MAINTAINER and $KPKG_EMAIL appropriately so that the generated packages have appropriate maintainer information in their control data. Any other settings are optional.

With the appropriate configuration in your ~/.kernel-pkg.conf, you can use **make-kpkg** without most of the command-line parameters. For instance, I use the following setup (which is a **Makefile** snippet):

[3]See http://bugs.debian.org/301030.

```
~$ cat ~/.kernel-pkg.conf
maintainer := martin f. krafft
email := madduck@debian.org
CONCURRENCY_LEVEL := 3
MODULE_LOC := $(HOME)/debian/kernel/src/modules
debian := $(shell date +%Y%m%d.%H%M)
root_cmd := fakeroot
kpkg_follow_symlinks_in_src := YES
```

These settings remove the need to pass **--rootcmd** and **--revision** with every invocation of **make-kpkg**, or to set $MODULE_LOC when building modules. Finally, since I use symlink farms to compile for multiple machines, I tell **make-kpkg** to treat symlinks as regular files (by following them).

8.2   Mixing releases

A word of advice before we dive into this section. The following concepts allow you to mix the different Debian releases (*e.g. stable* and *testing*). However, they also give you enough ammunition to shoot yourself in the foot. In general, it is best to decide on a single release and stick with it. When newer software is needed, external archives (see chapter 4.4.5) can be consulted. With that in mind, this section introduces a powerful means to control and influence APT. When used correctly, it definitely squeezes even more out of the powerful APT utensil.

As described in chapter 4, the Debian archive sorts the available packages into three releases: *stable*, *testing*, and *unstable*. The *experimental* archive, which contains software not yet ready to be unleashed on the public, while official, cannot be considered a release as it is not complete; it is not possible to run a system with only experimental software. While a production or server system will most likely run *stable*, its contents are generally not up to date with the latest releases of the respective software. Users wishing to install Debian on their workstations are thus hardly satisfied with the offerings of Debian *stable*.

Especially in the domain of multimedia and new technologies, the software in *stable* frequently does not cut the mustard. Most of the time, newer versions, which support the desired features, reside in the *unstable* or *testing* releases, but users are frequently put off by the connotations of the release titles ("I am not versed enough to be a tester, and if I wanted an unstable system, I would not run Debian..."). In addition, even the bravest are often deterred from running anything but stable due to the high rate of fluctuation in *unstable* and the lack of security updates for *testing*.

Most of the time, the software in *stable* has a sufficient feature set and is thus generally a good choice. However, at times a particular package which is only available in *testing* or *unstable* is needed. If the desired package has only a few dependencies or non at all, you simply need to download the DEB file(s) from the Debian web site[4] and install them with **dpkg**. However, in most cases, however, dependencies are likely to thwart the attempt. Specifically, packages in *testing* or *unstable* usually depend on a newer version of the libc6 package than available in *stable*. Pulling in libc6 from *testing* calls for a plethora of other packages as well, and being a core component of the *stable* system, it is unlikely that libc6 can or should be upgraded just like that.

Even if libc6 does not need to be upgraded to be able to install another package from *testing* or *unstable*, other dependencies may have to be met. While it might be okay to install a small number of packages directly with **dpkg**, doing so essentially subverts APT's endeavours to keep the system manageable at all times. **dpkg** will still enforce the policy, but if packages that APT does not know about are installed, it may only be a matter of time until problems arise. An alternative may be to simply duplicate the repository lines in **/etc/apt/sources.list** for each release with software you wish to install.

```
deb http://ftp.debian.org/debian stable main
deb http://ftp.debian.org/debian testing main
deb http://ftp.debian.org/debian unstable main
```

Now, APT knows about all packages in all three releases, and it can correctly pull in all dependencies in response to the request to upgrade a single package to its version in *e.g. testing*.

However, there is a subtle problem with the approach. Recall that APT uses version number comparisons (as performed by **dpkg --compare-version**) to determine the set of packages to be upgraded. With the addition of the *testing* and *unstable* archives to the APT repository list, APT will, on the next **upgrade** or **dist-upgrade** attempt to upgrade *all* packages to their highest available version, which will convert the system to Debian *unstable*.

8.2.1 Pinning releases with APT

The solution to the problem is APT's pinning feature. With simple selection mechanisms, APT flags packages with priorities according to the settings in **/etc/apt/ preferences** (it "pins" a priority onto the individual packages). When it comes to the identification of upgrade candidates, APT first considers these prioritites before comparing based on version number.

The priorities use a numeric scale that is unbound at top and bottom. The most relevant range is between 0 and 1001. Packages, whether installed or not, are positioned on this scale according to three default rules. We shall see shortly how these rules can be customised:

[4]http://packages.debian.org/<package>

- Packages already installed are handled as priority 100.

- Packages available for upgrade or installation are assigned a priority of 500.

- Packages part of the target release are assigned a priority of 990.

The decision whether APT should upgrade an installed package depends on the priority of the installation candidate's priority relative to the priority of the currently installed package. If the candidate's priority is the greater of the two, its position on the numeric scale determines what APT will do. The scale is partitioned into four segments:

P <= 0
> Packages with a priority less than or equal to zero are never installed.

0 < P <= 100
> Packages with a priority in this range are only installed if a previous version of the package is not already installed.

100 < P <= 1000
> Packages with a priority in this range are automatically installed, but only if an installed version does not have a higher priority. Downgrades never happen.

1000 < P
> Packages with a priority greater than 1000 are automatically installed or upgraded, unless the currently installed version has a higher priority. Downgrades are performed as necessary.

The target release is generally undefined. It can be set in /etc/apt/apt.conf and subsequently influences APT's behaviour with respect to multiple archive sources as outlined above. For instance, having the following APT configuration file would cause all packages from the *stable* release to be pinned at 990, thereby giving them priority over the contents of other releases. Note that you cannot (currently) use code names (*e.g. etch*) here, only the corresponding canonical release names:

```
APT::Default-Release "stable";
```

Such an entry in /etc/apt/apt.conf allows several different releases to peacefully coexist in the APT sources list. However, with packages from *testing* and *unstable* pinned to priority 500, pulling in a single package from *testing* would cause it to upgrade to the version in *unstable*. All packages but the ones from *stable* would get the same priority pin (500) and APT would simply refer to the version number to determine the package candidates. The user would eventually end up in the fluctuating world of *unstable*, even if only for a few packages.

Let us look at a quick example of this. Assume that 1.0-1 is in *stable*, 2.0-1 in *testing*, and 3.0-1 in *unstable*. With the pinnings generated by the apt.conf entry and 1.0-1 installed, the resulting priorities are as follows. The **apt-cache policy** command allows us to inspect, debug, and verify the priorities pinned to the package versions in the archives:

```
~$ apt-cache policy foo
foo:
  Installed: 1.0-1
  Candidate: 1.0-1
  Version Table:
     3.0-1 0
        500 http://ftp.debian.org unstable/main Packages
     2.0-1 0
        500 http://ftp.debian.org testing/main Packages
 *** 1.0-1 0
        990 http://ftp.debian.org stable/main Packages
        100 /var/lib/dpkg/status
```

As you can see, 1.0-1 is installed, as indicated by the "Installed" line, as well as the entry for **/var/lib/dpkg/status**, which represents the version known to the package status database. The "Candidate" line as well as the three asterisks hint at the version APT would install if it were to upgrade the system at this moment. The above configuration is a stable state, which is to say that an upgrade will not do anything; 990 is the greatest priority, causing the installed version 1.0-1 to be the installation candidate due to its high priority.

If we manually upgrade the package to 2.0-1 (I'll show you how in a second), things become different. Again, we use **apt-cache policy** to inspect and debug the configuration. The output of this command includes everything there is to know about the pinning configuration with respect to the package(s) specified on the command line. It will be used in the following to illustrate the effects of various pinning configurations.

```
~$ apt-cache policy foo
foo:
  Installed: 2.0-1
  Candidate: 3.0-1
  Version Table:
 *** 3.0-1 0
        500 http://ftp.debian.org unstable/main Packages
     2.0-1 0
        500 http://ftp.debian.org testing/main Packages
        100 /var/lib/dpkg/status
     1.0-1 0
        990 http://ftp.debian.org stable/main Packages
```

Now 2.0-1 has priority 500 and even though *stable*'s priority (990) is almost twice that, 1.0-1 is a downgrade from the installed 2.0-1 and would require a pin above

1000 to take place. *unstable*'s pin is also at 500. Therefore, the comparison between the versions in *testing* and *unstable* is only based on the version number. An upgrade would cause APT to replace 2.0-1 with 3.0-1. Moreover, subsequent upgrades cause the package to remain at the *unstable* version. For instance, when 4.0-1 hits the *unstable* archive, it will immediately be selected for installation, and this is something we would probably prefer to avoid.

Fortunately, APT allows you to exercise greater control over the pinnings. In the /etc/apt/preferences file, selection criteria can be defined to pin specific priorities to packages matching the specifications. The pinning syntax allows various properties to be used in the specification of the matching set. These properties are defined in the **Packages** and **Release** files (see chapter 4.1.2 and chapter 4.1.3). While the package name and version number from the **Packages** file is relevant in the pinning of single packages, the data available in the corresponding **Release** file are best suited for selection of package sets. For instance, packages may be grouped according to the release to which they belong, the component (or section, *e.g. main*) in which they reside, and their origin (in our case, the Debian archive). Please refer to the **apt_preferences** (5) manpage for further information on the selection criteria.

Thus, if we wanted to track *stable* but still be able to pull in software from *testing* and *unstable*, and give priority to packages in *testing*, the following entries in /etc/apt/preferences would configure APT to act appropriately:

```
~# cat <<EOF > /etc/apt/preferences
Package: *
Pin: release a=stable
Pin-Priority: 900

Package: *
Pin: release a=testing
Pin-Priority: 90

Package: *
Pin: release a=unstable
Pin-Priority: 80
EOF
```

Here, we use the archive selection criteria along with the canonical release names (code names cannot be used at time of writing; use a pin on the version number instead, if desired: **Pin: release v=3.1**). **apt-cache policy** itself can be used to display the primary selection criteria (and to debug them). For instance, the above configuration produces:

```
~$ apt-cache policy
Package Files:
 100 /var/lib/dpkg/status
```

```
       release a=now
  80 http://debian.ethz.ch unstable/main Packages
       release o=Debian,a=unstable,l=Debian,c=main
       origin ftp.debian.org
  90 http://debian.ethz.ch testing/main Packages
       release o=Debian,a=testing,l=Debian,c=main
       origin ftp.debian.org
 900 http://debian.ethz.ch stable/main Packages
       release v=3.1,o=Debian,a=stable,l=Debian,c=main
       origin ftp.debian.org
[...]
```

Invoking **apt-cache policy** with a package name causes detailed information about a single package to be printed instead, which in this case will be the same as when APT::Default-Release was used. The *stable* archive has the highest pin.

```
~$ apt-cache policy foo
foo:
  Installed: 1.0-1
  Candidate: 1.0-1
  Version Table:
     3.0-1 0
         80 http://ftp.debian.org unstable/main Packages
     2.0-1 0
         90 http://ftp.debian.org testing/main Packages
 *** 1.0-1 0
        900 http://ftp.debian.org stable/main Packages
        100 /var/lib/dpkg/status
```

When the package is manually upgraded to the *testing* version, it will stay at 2.0-1 even through subsequent upgrades because *unstable*'s priority is lower than that of *testing*. Furthermore, when 3.0-1 propagates to *testing*, 2.0-1 stays installed because the *testing* pin is less than 100:

```
~$ apt-cache policy foo
foo:
  Installed: 2.0-1
  Candidate: 2.0-1
  Version Table:
     3.0-1 0
         80 http://ftp.debian.org unstable/main Packages
         90 http://ftp.debian.org testing/main Packages
 *** 2.0-1 0
        100 /var/lib/dpkg/status
     1.0-1 0
        900 http://ftp.debian.org stable/main Packages
```

Also, if we choose to manually upgrade the package to its *unstable* version, the package will stay at 3.0-1, even when 4.0-1 hits *unstable* after 3.0-1 has moved to *testing*.

The situation changes yet again when we pin *testing* to 800 (or any other number between 101 and 899). With 1.0-1 installed, APT does not consider an upgrade because 900 is greater than 800. Now, a manual upgrade to *testing* switches to another stable state:

```
~$ apt-cache policy foo
foo:
  Installed: 2.0-1
  Candidate: 2.0-1
  Version Table:
     3.0-1 0
         90 http://ftp.debian.org unstable/main Packages
 *** 2.0-1 0
        800 http://ftp.debian.org testing/main Packages
        100 /var/lib/dpkg/status
     1.0-1 0
        900 http://ftp.debian.org stable/main Packages
```

We have established that 1.0-1 will never be a candidate again because 990 is not high enough to allow downgrades. Similarly, the priority of *unstable* will prevent automatic upgrades. It starts getting interesting when 3.0-1 hits *testing*:

```
~$ apt-cache policy foo
foo:
  Installed: 3.0-1
  Candidate: 2.0-1
  Version Table:
 *** 3.0-1 0
         90 http://ftp.debian.org unstable/main Packages
        800 http://ftp.debian.org testing/main Packages
     2.0-1 0
        100 /var/lib/dpkg/status
     1.0-1 0
        900 http://ftp.debian.org stable/main Packages
```

Now, 3.0-1 has a priority of 800 and thus APT selects it for replacement of 2.0-1. Still, when 4.0-1 enters *unstable*, the package will stay at 3.0-1 until 4.0-1 propagates to *testing*.

In the above examples, the packages are selected according to the release (archive) in which they reside. Thus APT tries to satisfy installation requests first from *stable*, then from *testing*, and only consults the *unstable* release if neither of the previous two contains (any version of) the requested package. It is also possible to apply pins to single packages and thus prevent upgrades. For instance, a user may choose to delay the upgrade of a software by pinning it to a specific version:

```
~# cat <<EOF >> /etc/apt/preferences
Package: foo
```

```
Pin: version 2.0-1
Pin-Priority: 2000
EOF
```

Essentially, this is equivalent to putting a hold on **foo**, but the semantics are different. Other than pinning the package to a specific version, it is possible to pin it to
a specific version coming from a specific archive. Thus, if you maintain your own
archive with "MyOwn" as the label in the **Releases** file, you can pin a package to
only use the version from your archive:

```
~# cat <<EOF >> /etc/apt/preferences
Package: bar
Pin: release l=MyOwn, version 1.2-3
Pin-Priority: 2000
EOF
```

Another use would be to employ a zero priority to prevent a package from installing
altogether. For instance, if you wanted to prevent **qmail-src** from ever appearing
on your system, the following would do the trick:

```
~# cat <<EOF >> /etc/apt/preferences
Package: qmail-src
Pin: origin ""
Pin-Priority: 0
EOF
```

APT pinning provides a powerful means to influence APT's selection mechanism.
In addition to the features introduced here, **apt_preferences** (5) presents the full
picture, along with the complete match specification syntax and various examples.

8.2.2 Selecting target releases

APT pinning allows APT to deal with multiple releases in **/etc/apt/preferences**. The
priorities allow the system administrator to influence decision-making for installations and upgrades. It is also possible to override pinning at the command line. APT
provides two may of selecting the release to be used for an installation or upgrade.

First, it is possible to specify the desired source release of a package directly with
the package name. For instance, the following selects the **postfix** package from the
testing release.

```
~# apt-get install postfix/testing
Reading Package Lists... Done
Building Dependency Tree... Done
Selected version 2.1.4-2 (Debian:testing) for postfix
[...]
```

Similarly, packages can also be selected by version number directly (I am deliberately using a non-existent package one to allow a peek at the related error message):

```
~# apt-get install postfix=1.0-1
Reading Package Lists... Done
Building Dependency Tree... Done
E: Version »1.0-1« for »postfix« was not found
```

Both these methods have the inherent problem that the release or version selection only applies to the package for which is has been specified. If the package defines dependencies that can only be satisfied from the same source, APT gives up:

```
~# apt-get install mc/unstable
Reading Package Lists... Done
Building Dependency Tree... Done
Selected version 1:4.6.0-4.6.1-pre1-3 (Debian:unstable) for mc
Some packages could not be installed. This may mean that you have
requested an impossible situation or if you are using the unstable
distribution that some required packages have not yet been created
or been moved out of Incoming.

Since you only requested a single operation it is extremely likely that
the package is simply not installable and a bug report against
that package should be filed.
The following information may help to resolve the situation:

The following packages have unmet dependencies:
  mc: Depends: libglib2.0-0 (>= 2.2.3) but 2.0.1-2 is to be installed
E: Broken packages
```

In addition to being unclear, the error message is also misleading, advocating the filing of a bug when the problem is really within APT. While bugs have been filed about this issue, it is unlikely for a fix to appear in the near future.

A better way to control the source archive to be used for installations and upgrades is to override the default (or target) release, which can be set in **/etc/apt/apt.conf**. **apt-get** (and **aptitude**) provide the **--target-release** switch for this purpose:

```
~# apt-get install --target-release unstable mc
[...]
```

Specifying a release with **--target-release** causes the pinnings to be temporarily modified for this command only. When you installing **mc** in this way, all packages in *unstable* are be treated as having priority 990 for the duration of the call. Unless *stable* or *testing* are pinned to a higher priority, the **mc** package and all its dependencies are pulled in from *unstable*. Similarly, given a 900/99/98 pinning on *stable*, *testing*, and *unstable*, the following command upgrades an entire system to *testing* and then waits until *testing* becomes *stable* before upgrading any other packages:

```
~# apt-get --show-upgraded --target-release testing dist-upgrade
```

At any point in time, apt-show-versions (from the package of the same name) can be used to inquire which packages come from which releases. The tool works on a local cache which must be updated from time to time (this, in turn, requires root rights). Following an update, the tool can display a variety of information about the installed packages. All of this information is also accessible via apt-cache policy, but for certain applications, apt-show-versions is better suited:

```
~# apt-show-versions --initialize
~$ apt-show-versions --package=postfix
postfix/unstable uptodate 2.1.4-4
~$ apt-show-versions --upgradeable
bash/unstable upgradeable from 2.05b-22 to 3.0-5
[...]
```

apt-show-versions is also frequently advocated with mixed releases to upgrade systems without pulling in more of a less-stable distribution than wanted. For instance, if you want to install only upgrades to installed *unstable* packages, the following command will do the trick:

```
~# apt-get install $(apt-show-versions --upgraded --brief | \
   grep unstable)
```

With apt-show-versions, it is possible to maintain separate sets of packages for the three Debian releases on a single system, without running the risk of installing more of the less-stable packages than wanted (or needed).

8.2.3 Extending APT's internal cache

For performance, APT keeps information about the available packages in memory during its operation. This cache is allocated to be big enough to deal with a single release, but if you combine multiple releases and pin them accordingly, the cache may well end up being too small. APT will notify you of this:

```
~# apt-get update
[...]
> Reading Package Lists... Error!
> E: Dynamic MMap ran out of room
[...]
```

The solution is to increase the default cache size in the APT configuration (see chapter 5.4.2):

```
~# cat <<EOF >> /etc/apt/apt.conf
APT::Cache-Limit 16777216;
EOF
```

Now APT can use up to 16 Mb for its cache, which is plenty to hold *stable*, *testing*, *unstable*, and *experimental*, together with a couple of other separate repositories.

8.2.4   Mixing releases and security updates

As nice as APT's pinning abilities are, there is an inherent problem with mixing releases. As mentioned in chapter 7.2, neither the *testing* nor the *unstable* releases are tended by the security team. Due to the nature of the Debian archive and the package propagation process from *unstable* to *testing*, packages in *unstable* will receive security updates quicker than those in *testing*. Nevertheless, updates may lag badly behind the security updates for the *stable* distribution. Therefore, when mixing releases, it is of utmost importance to closely follow security announcements (at least through the **debian-security-announce** mailing list) and be prepared to take appropriate actions if a bug affects a locally installed package from *testing* or *unstable*. Depending on the severity of the problem, it may be advisable to deactivate the affected service, remove the package, or downgrade to the version made available by the security archive.

Of course, APT pinning can be put to use to honour security updates over all other versions, thereby automating such downgrades. The trick is to configure the APT pins as desired with respect to *testing* and *unstable*, and then to add a stanza pinning packages based on the label of their source archive.

Please be aware that the following method is not at all supported by Debian and can cause serious problems. If used with good care, it does provide a useful means of running software from the *testing* or *unstable* archives and still profit from the work of the security team. However, I provide the following mainly for demonstration purposes and cannot recommend deploying the approach anywhere outside of testing environments.

```
~# cat <<EOF >> /etc/apt/preferences
Package: *
Pin: release l=Debian-Security
Pin-Priority: 1001
EOF
```

Consider a package **foo** with version 1.0-1 in *stable* and 2.0-1 in *testing*. After the user manually upgraded the package to 2.0-1, the security team finds a grave bug and releases 1.0-1.sarge.1 to address the problem. Normally, APT would ignore this version because it is a downgrade from the currently installed 2.0-1. However, the above stanza causes any package distributed from the security archive (1.0-1.sarge.1 in this case) to take priority over all other packages from the archive.

This introduces three problems. First, you may rely on a feature in 2.0-1 and find yourself forced to live without it when the fixed package hits the security archive. Second, pinning prevents any further upgrades to the affected packages. Thus, if 3.0-1, which fixes the grave bug, hits *unstable*, APT will keep foo at 1.0-1.sarge.1. APT locks the package to the security archive, preventing any new features from trickling in, but assuring a secure software in exchange (see chapter 7.2).

To harness the features in 3.0-1, you could add another two stanzas to /etc/apt/ preferences to override the pinning for foo only:

```
~# cat <<EOF >> /etc/apt/preferences
Package: foo
Pin: release a=unstable
Pin-Priority: 1002

Package: foo
Pin: release a=testing
Pin-Priority: 1002
EOF
```

Now, the packages from *testing* and *unstable* take precedence again. Apart from the manual intervention (and this necessitates close screening of security advisories, as well as careful scrutiny of APT's actions), another flaw appears in the approach when a second security bug is found in 1.0-1, which is not fixed in 3.0-1. The security team will work to release 1.0-1.sarge.2 as soon as possible, but unless the two special stanzas for foo are removed from /etc/apt/preferences, APT will not consider the security update, leaving the system open for attack.

Another problem with pinning the security archive above a thousand relates to the necessity of downgrades when security *upgrades* appear. Even though downgrades work most of the time, they are officially not supported. The package maintainer scripts are carefully crafted to handle upgrades in a smart and graceful manner, but it is unusual for a package maintainer to provide the reverse path to an upgrade. Thus, it is very possible that a package which has previously been upgraded to its version in *testing* will break completely when downgraded to the version published by the security team.

All in all, multiple releases and security updates do not play along very well. This said, it is still possible to maintain a mixed Debian installation and stay secure, but it requires the administrator to keep up with security-related developments for installed software. Furthermore, every APT action must be carried out with all the more scrutiny to ensure that a security problem does not persist even though it has been fixed by the security team.

8.2.5 aptitude and multiple releases

If a system is configured to use more than one APT source, APT may have access to several versions of the same package. We have seen that **apt-get** can install specific versions of a package by appending the version to the package name with an equals sign. A powerful feature of **aptitude**'s user interface is that it displays each of the available versions at the bottom of a package detail page (see the bottom of the figure on page 193). Each of the versions can be installed separately, and the [enter] key will take you to the details page of the selected version. A package can be up- or downgraded (the latter is not necessarily supported) simply by choosing another version for installation.

While the feature is definitely a big advantage of the **aptitude** package manager front-end, it can also be a pitfall and introduce severe, unwanted changes to the package selection which first have to be undone before **aptitude** can be put to meaningful use. The key indicator of this kind of issue is the broken packages count at the top of each of the screens of **aptitude**'s user interface. When changing a package's version, or installing a specific version, keep an eye on the count. If it jumps to an unexpectedly high number, it might be a good idea to hit [C-u] to undo the last action — unless of course you know what you are doing and are ready to fix any broken packages manually.

When **aptitude** needs to automatically select a package for installation, it chooses the version with the highest pin priority, just like **apt-get** would. It is therefore sometimes a good idea to temporarily change the pin priorities with the **--target-release** option to prevent large numbers of packages breaking due to version conflicts across the releases. For instance, if you want to upgrade a number of packages to *unstable*, it is best to invoke **aptitude** as **aptitude --target-release unstable**, select the section "upgradeable packages" and cancel all pending upgrades for this invocation of **aptitude** by hitting the [:] (colon) key. Now you can freely use **aptitude** to upgrade or install specific packages from the selected target release. An alternative is to simply browse to a package or package's version to install and hit [I], which will queue the package for installation while automatically cancelling all pending upgrades.

8.3 Alternative approaches to installing a Debian system

While most Debian installations will use the Debian installer (see chapter 3.1), certain requirements may call for alterative approaches to install a Debian system. The following sections should give you enough information to be able to install Debian systems through other means than the installer, be it because the installer does not work in a given situation, or you need to install a large number of machines and need to reduce the need for installation media while automating large parts of the individual installations.

8.3.1   Bootstrapping an installation

You do not need to boot a system from Debian installation media to install it. Another way to configure a Debian system is to bootstrap it. Bootstrapping refers to the iterative process of assembly of *e.g.* a tool by using the tool itself. In the case of a Debian system, bootstrapping refers to the installation of the base system using the tools of the base system (most notably: **dpkg**). In a sense, the Debian installer does nothing else. On a newly installed system, you will notice that **dpkg** was installed as part of the **dpkg** package. This seems to be yet another instance of the infamous chicken-and-egg problem since **dpkg** cannot install itself without being installed. To overcome this paradox, Debian uses a helper to install the **dpkg** package before letting it take over and install the rest of the base system (which reinstalls **dpkg** from its package). The **debootstrap** programme integrates base system bootstrap and install.

Of all the reasons why you would want to bootstrap a Debian system, two are of particular interest. First, you may want to create an autonomous Debian installation for experimentation, to test new packages, or to accomplish temporary tasks (like taking screenshots for this book). Instead of putting your main system at risk (working as **root** is *always* a risk), you restrict the effects of all your actions to a **sandbox**.

The second reason is that of installing a new system by manually doing what the Debian installer automates. It sounds a little like reinventing the wheel, but there are good reasons for the manual route. For instance, you may be dealing with hardware that the Debian installer does not support, or you may be installing a number of systems side by side and prefer to stay in your seat and control the process from your console, with cut and paste abilities across the machines, and the World Wide Web just a click away.

Installing Debian into a chroot

A sandbox system will live inside a **chroot** and thus feel like an independent system from the user space. The kernel is shared with the host system, so a sandbox does not allow for experimentation with the kernel. Also, I should not pass up the opportunity to warn of the security implications of **chroots**. Many sources attribute greater security to software running in a **chroot** since it is confined to the sandbox and cannot touch the host system. However, breaking out of a **chroot** is trivial in Linux once **root** rights have been attained within the **chroot**[5]. While **chroots**

[5]http://www.bpfh.net/simes/computing/chroot-break.html

provide a logical separation and can ease administration, they do not constitute a security fence, but a barrier at most. For our purpose, the chroot is not supposed to provide a security jail, so we do not have to worry about above security problems.

The chroot programme starts a command with a different root directory. Therefore, the first step is to create a new designated root directory for our purposes. Note that usage of chroot is reserved for the root user, so there is no real reason why a chroot should reside under one's home directory. In the following, we designate /home/chroots/sarge as the sandbox. If you need to give your users their own sandboxes, User-Mode Linux[6] is what you are looking for. However, User-Mode Linux has its fair share of bugs and may not be suitable for all applications. An alternative is Xen, a high-performance virtual machine for Intel architectures. The xen package provides it, and documentation is available online[7].

The debootstrap tool installs the Debian base system and leaves you with the same set of packages as a regular installation from the bootable media. The necessary packages can be obtained in two ways: the easiest is to tell debootstrap to use a Debian mirror server and work its magic. An alternative method is the use of basedebs.tgz, a file containing the necessary packages for the base system. While this procedure is a relict from the boot-floppies time, debootstrap continues to support it. For *sarge* and later, you will have to create the file yourself.

The following commands install the sandbox. Please make sure you use the closest mirror[8] instead of the one quoted in the example:

```
~# cd /home/chroots
~# MIRROR=http://ftp.debian.org
~# debootstrap sarge ./sarge $MIRROR
or:
~# debootstrap --arch i386 --download-only sarge $MIRROR
~# tar cz -C sarge -f basedebs.tgz var
~# debootstrap --unpack-tarball 'pwd'/basedebs.tgz sarge ./sarge
```

When debootstrap completes, you can chroot into the new sandbox and configure the base system. We need not worry about partitions, networking hardware, kernels and the bootloader, or keyboard configuration since all that is handled by the host. The chroot is really just a namespace of its own with a separate set of installed packages, an independent /etc hierarchy, and a clean package database. It is not an independent installation. The base-config programme will ask several questions and configure the essential aspects of the base system.

```
~# rm sarge/etc/resolv.conf
~# cp /etc/resolv.conf sarge/etc
```

[6]http://usermodelinux.org, as well as the user-mode-linux package
[7]http://www.cl.cam.ac.uk/Research/SRG/netos/xen
[8]To find the closest mirror, use the official list at http://www.debian.org/mirror/list, or run the apt-spy tool (see chapter 5.4.1)

```
~# cat /etc/hostname > sarge/etc/hostname
~# cd sarge && chroot .
~# base-config new
~# apt-get install locales
```

Be careful if you set the hostname of your sandbox system, as it will affect the host system as well. Changing the hostname of a running system can have far-reaching consequences and should probably be avoided. If you do set it, you can reset it to the previous value (using the **hostname** programme).

You can now explore the sandbox to your heart's content. You will notice that it feels like a regular Debian system. Almost all of the concepts presented in this book can be tried in a **chroot**. The **chroot** itself is a normal directory on your filesystem and will thus preserve any changes you make within the sandbox.

It is important to keep in mind that a **chroot** represents a separation in the user space only. Even though the Debian installation inside the **chroot** feels like a separate Debian system, it uses the running kernel of the host installation. Several programmes (such as **ps**, to name a simple example) require access to the running kernel through the virtual filesystem mounted at **/proc**. Within the **chroot**, this filesystem is not directly accessible and must therefore be mounted inside the **chroot** (we make use of the entry in **/etc/fstab**, which **debootstrap** put there, resulting in a shortened **mount** command):

```
~# chroot sarge
~# ps
Error, do this: mount -t proc none /proc
~# mount /proc
~# ps
[...]
```

In chapter 9.6 you meet **pbuilder**, a programme for managing temporary sandboxes which cleans up after itself. **pbuilder** also handles trivial concerns such as mounting **/proc** automatically.

Bootstrapping a new system

When faced with a machine whose hardware does not support regular installation methods — perhaps because the hardware cannot boot off any medium other than the local hard disk — you will need to use an existing system to bootstrap an installation onto the hard disk to be used in the machine. You can bootstrap a new system in two ways, which I will refer to as clean and the dirty way. The dirty approach is dirty because you need to use a screwdriver to move hard disks between machines. The clean approach only requires you to remove your hands from the keyboard to insert and remove CD-ROMs. The two are technically equivalent and I will only discuss the clean approach in the paragraphs to come.

Booting a rescue system

The first step in bootstrapping a new system is to boot a rescue or live system and configure network access. I am using **Knoppix**[9] for this purpose. If you are taking the dirty approach to bootstrapping, your workstation or another machine will be the rescue system and temporary host of the new system's hard drive.

Once **Knoppix** has booted into **KDE** (which it does by default), Internet access needs to be configured. If the machine is connected to a DHCP-enabled network, a cable modem, or a sensible DSL adapter, **Knoppix** will have configured this access automatically. An external modem or a PPPoE-based DSL connection will have to be set up manually. The **pppconfig** and **pppoeconfig** tools provide guided configuration. Please refer to the manual of the rescue or live system you are using for more information.

Partitioning and filesystem creation

As soon as network access is established, the target hard drive must be partitioned and filesystems created. In appendix C.2, I provide related information. Once the filesystems are created, the new root needs to be mounted on **/mnt**[10]. The following assumes that you are using the partitioning scheme in appendix C.2.1, and that your hard disk is the master on the primary IDE channel, **/dev/hda**. The **noatime** option is not necessary but gives you minimal performance gains (probably not enough to make up for the time needed to type it, but it is a habit of mine...).

```
~# mount -o noatime /dev/hda5 /mnt
~# cd /mnt
~# mkdir -p boot usr home var tmp
~# mount -o noatime /dev/hda1 boot
~# mount -o noatime /dev/hda6 usr
~# mkdir usr/local
~# mount -o noatime /dev/hda7 usr/local
~# mount -o noatime /dev/hda8 var
~# mount -o noatime /dev/hda9 home
~# mount -o noatime /dev/hda10 tmp
```

The **/mnt** hierarchy is now prepared. Please refer to the previous section (chapter 8.3.1) for instructions on how to use **debootstrap** to install the Debian base system. The remainder of the examples in this section take place within the **chroot**!

Following the installation and configuration of the base system, we need to take additional steps to ensure proper hardware configuration, after all, we are installing an independently bootable system.

---

[9]http://www.knoppix.org

[10]Knoppix actually uses **/mnt** differently than the FHS dictates. While you can simply "overmount" the new root partition, you may want to create a new mount point, such as **/target** and use that instead.

In /etc/fstab, the partitions of the new disk must be listed. A final and valid **fstab**
for the above configuration is included below. Note the choice of mount points
for the removable media. The FHS defines /media as a replacement for /cdrom,
/floppy, or subdirectories under /mnt.

```
~# cat /etc/fstab
# /etc/fstab: static file system information.
#
# <fs>      <mount point>  <type>   <options>                    <dump>  <pass>
proc        /proc          proc     defaults                        0    0
/dev/hda2   none           swap     sw                              0    0
/dev/hda1   /boot          xfs      noatime,nodev,nosuid,noexec     0    2
/dev/hda5   /              xfs      noatime                         0    1
/dev/hda6   /usr           xfs      noatime,nodev                   0    2
/dev/hda7   /usr/local     xfs      noatime,nodev,nosuid            0    2
/dev/hda8   /var           xfs                                      0    2
/dev/hda9   /home          xfs      nodev,nosuid                    0    2
/dev/hda10  /tmp           xfs      nodev,nosuid                    0    2
/dev/hdc    /media/cdrom   iso9660  ro,user,noauto                  0    0
/dev/fd0    /media/floppy  auto     rw,user,noauto,sync             0    0
```

The mount options in the fourth column are suggestions and help to improve security, especially when users have shell access to the machine. **nodev**, **nosuid**, and
noexec prevent device nodes from being created, **setuid** bits from being set on binaries, or scripts and programmes from being executed respectively. The **noatime**
option boosts the performance a little by preventing file access time updates. I also
mount the floppy drive for synchronous access with **sync** to guard against data
loss.

The swap space referenced by the file has to be initialised before it can be used.
Please be careful with the following command, since a typo could ruin the **chroot**
you just created (or whole hard drives):

```
~# mkswap /dev/hda2
```

Installing the kernel

For a system to boot, a kernel needs to be installed. While it is possible to follow the
standard kernel installation procedure, you will also find Linux kernels of various
versions and optimisations ready to be installed in the Debian archive within regular
DEB files. The installation process of a kernel package must be able to communicate
with the running kernel, and hence requires access to the /proc filesystem, which
is a virtual filesystem provided by the running kernel (see chapter 8.3.1). Therefore,
prior to installing a Debian kernel with **apt-get**, /proc must be mounted:

```
~# mount /proc
~# apt-get install kernel-image-2.6.8-1-k7
[...]
```

If the kernel installed into the **chroot** differs from the running kernel, you might run into problems when working inside the **chroot**. For instance, **depmod** will fail to find the module tree for the running kernel. These errors should not pose serious problems, however.

The Debian kernel packages strive to be universal. While the set of applied patches is very small (especially when compared to other Linux distributions), every feature of the kernel is modularised, and Debian's module management makes most manual configuration obsolete. Nevertheless, if you need to bootstrap a new system because of special hardware requirements, the Debian kernels may not suffice. You can find information on how to build custom kernels and integrate them with the package management system in chapter 8.1. Please take care to include the necessary filesystem(s) in the kernel. If you choose to make them modules, you must create an initial ramdisk (see the **initrd (4)** manpage for more information).

Installing a bootloader

Loading the kernel at boot time is done by the **bootloader**. Debian provides the two common **bootloaders** Grub and Lilo, and the tendency is to use **Grub** in new installations because it directly supports all major Linux filesystems (see appendix C.2.2) and also handles many aspects of **bootloading** better than **Lilo**. Please note that **Grub** and **Lilo** are both specific to the **x86** architecture. Bootloading in other architectures — if applicable — is a completely different issue that we will not be looking into here.

After installing **grub** with **apt-get**, install the boot loader into the master boot record[11]. Unless Debian is the only system on the target hard disk, it is a good idea to create a backup of the MBR beforehand. Note that the call to **grub-install** can take a long time, so get up and walk around a bit! If you have not made **/boot** a separate partition, then leave off the **--root-directory=/boot** argument.

```
~# dd if=/dev/hda of=/boot/mbr.backup bs=512 count=1
~# grub-install --root-directory=/boot /dev/hda
[...]
~# update-grub
[...]
```

At times, **Grub** may appear to hang. In general, this is because it is busy probing the BIOS, which may take a very long time. However, if you do not see any activity for several minutes, it is safe to assume that **Grub** has crashed; this is a common occurrence on **XFS** filesystems. In this case, you might like to reboot and try to install the bootloader manually through the **Grub** shell:

---

[11] Grub can boot other operating systems, including Microsoft Windows. Please refer to appendix C.5 for more information.

```
~# mkdir -p /boot/grub
~# cp /lib/grub/i386-pc/* /boot/grub
~# grub --no-floppy
Probing devices to guess BIOS drives. This may take a long time.
[...]
grub> root (hd0,0)
 Filesystem type is xfs, partition type 0x83
grub> setup --prefix=/boot/grub (hd0)
[...]
grub> quit
```

Grub does not require you to run a script every time the kernel changes, since it accesses /boot directly at startup. This permits manual changes to the boot process when Grub has loaded through an interactive editor. Since it is assumed that you do not want to have to tell Grub which kernel to load whenever you boot, it can read defaults from a configuration file: /boot/grub/menu.lst, or /boot/boot/grub/menu.lst if your /boot is a separate partition.

Debian provides a means to manage this configuration file, automatically including all installed kernel images (official Debian images and packages of custom kernels alike). This is done with the **grub-update** command. The file **menu.lst** is split into three sections, which the following (abbreviated) version shows:

```
~$ cat /boot/grub/menu.lst
default   0
timeout   3
color cyan/blue white/blue
password --md5 $1$GZdc50$cdknw5Euo/ScMB..LJZSP$

### BEGIN AUTOMAGIC KERNELS LIST

## ## Start Default Options ##
## default kernel options for automagic boot options
# kopt=root=/dev/hda5 ro nmi_watchdog=1

## default grub root device
# groot=(hd0,0)

## should update-grub create alternative automagic boot options
# alternative=true

## should update-grub lock alternative automagic boot options
# lockalternative=true

## altoption boot targets option
# altoptions=(recovery mode) single

## controls how many kernels should be put into the menu.lst
# howmany=all
```

```
## should update-grub create memtest86 boot option
# memtest86=true

## ## End Default Options ##

title   Debian GNU/Linux, kernel 2.6.10-cirrus
root    (hd0,0)
kernel  /vmlinuz-2.6.10-cirrus root=/dev/hda5 ro nmi_watchdog=1
savedefault
boot

title   Debian GNU/Linux, kernel 2.6.10-cirrus (recovery mode)
lock
root    (hd0,0)
kernel  /vmlinuz-2.6.10-cirrus root=/dev/hda5 ro nmi_watchdog=1 single
savedefault
boot

title   Debian GNU/Linux, kernel 2.6.8-1-k7
root    (hd0,0)
kernel  /vmlinuz-2.6.8-1-k7 root=/dev/hda5 ro nmi_watchdog=1
initrd  /initrd.img-2.6.8-1-k7
savedefault
boot

title   Debian GNU/Linux, kernel 2.6.8-1-k7 (recovery mode)
lock
root    (hd0,0)
kernel  /vmlinuz-2.6.8-1-k7 root=/dev/hda5 ro nmi_watchdog=1 single
initrd  /initrd.img-2.6.8-1-k7
savedefault
boot

title   memtest86+
root    (hd0,0)
kernel  /memtest86+.bin
savedefault
boot

### END DEBIAN AUTOMAGIC KERNELS LIST
```

In the first section of the file, leading up to the "BEGIN" marker, you can place free-form configuration. This is where you include items for any custom (non-Debian) kernel images you have installed that should be listed before the automatically generated kernel entries. The Debian entries further down can serve as templates, but make sure you modify the entries appropriately, and remove the **initrd** line if your custom kernel does not use an initial ramdisk. The "Default Options" section contains a number of options to control the stanzas created automatically by **grub-update** and put into the third section, which immediately follows the default options. Following the "END" marker in the file, you can put in the stanzas that should be listed after the ones generated automatically.

You need to change the **groot** and **kopt** to reflect the position of your **root** and /boot partitions (which may be the same). I usually set the two **lockalternative** options to true and then rerun **grub-update**. Thus, for our example, the changed options would be[12].

```
# kopt=root=/dev/hda5 ro nmi_watchdog=1
# groot=(hd0,0)
# lockalternative=true
```

Installing or removing a kernel makes the auto-generated entries in **menu.lst** obsolete. Thus, if management of the **menu.lst** file is entrusted to **grub-update**, that command needs to be rerun anytime a kernel package is installed or removed. If this is asking too much, you can tell the kernel package system to do this automatically, by appending the following lines to /etc/kernel-image.conf:

```
do_bootloader = no
postinst_hook = /sbin/update-grub
postrm_hook = /sbin/update-grub
```

Network configuration

The next step is to configure network interfaces. First, the new kernel must be told how to access the hardware. If you have built a custom kernel with the network card driver built in, you should be all set. If the driver is configured as a module, you need to take the following steps. I am assuming your driver is the Intel EtherExpress driver. Please replace **e100** with the appropriate module name for your driver:

```
~# echo e100 >> /etc/modules
```

This tells Debian to load the **e100** module during the the boot process. If the machine has multiple network cards with different drivers, the first of the modules listed in /etc/modules causes the respective driver to claim **eth0**. As an alternative, you may want to use the kernel's dynamic module loader and add the appropriate alias to /etc/modprobe.d/local.net (/etc/modutils/local-net on a system running a 2.4 kernel):

```
alias eth0 e100
```

For the network parameters, Debian uses the feature-rich **ifupdown** system, which is mainly controlled by the /etc/network/interfaces file. The following example shows the most important configuration. More information can be obtained from the **interfaces** (5) manpage and files below /usr/share/doc/ifupdown.

---

[12]The nmi_watchdog is an interesting and helpful option for Intel architectures if you experience random lockups, and included here purely for the added value. Please refer to the **nmi_watchdog.txt** file in the kernel documentation. The kernel documentation can be found in /usr/share/doc/kernel-doc-<version> after installing the **kernel-doc-<version>** package.

```
# /etc/network/interfaces: configuration file for ifup(8), ifdown(8)

# We always want the loopback interface.
auto lo
iface lo inet loopback

# For each interface to be automatically configured, a line like the
# following is required.
auto eth0

# We assume DHCP by default
iface eth0 inet dhcp

# If you want to configure a static IP, comment the DHCP line and
# change the following to your requirements. The broadcast, network,
# and gateway addresses are optional and will be set to the defaults,
# based on the address and the netmask.

# iface eth0 inet static
#       address 192.168.1.100
#       netmask 255.255.255.0
#       network 192.168.1.0
#       broadcast 192.168.1.255
#       gateway 192.168.1.1
```

If DHCP is used, /etc/resolv.conf will be handled automatically. For a static IP, please recheck the entries in that file. Also, you will probably want to change the hostname in /etc/hostname.

Finalising the installation

Before rebooting into the new system, you should ensure that the keyboard will be configured properly. Unless you enjoy characters hiding behind differently labelled keys, quickly run **dpkg-reconfigure console-data** to guard against surprises.

Also, you will probably want to install the **ssh** package to be able to access the new installation once it has started up.

Now it is time to reboot. Before leaving the **chroot**, the **/proc** filesystem needs to be unmounted, or else the shutdown process will be unable to unmount the **root** filesystem of the target installation: **umount /proc**. Now you can **exit** the **chroot**.

If you are using **Knoppix**, tell your system to reboot: **shutdown -r now**. Other rescue and live systems may forget to unmount the target filesystems, so you should probably do it explicitly (the –l option causes busy filesystems to be scheduled for unmounting when not in use):

```
~# cd
~# umount -l /dev/hda*
```

When the BIOS has finished doing its thing, you should be greeted by **Grub**. Hitting [enter] will boot the Linux kernel, and soon you should be prompted for a login to your new Debian system. In case of problems, **Knoppix** can be used to obtain a working environment in which to mount the filesystem hierarchy as before.

Converting another Linux to Debian

A slight modification to the procedure introduced in the previous section allows for the remote conversion of a system running another Linux (or even another operating system) to Debian. It goes without saying that the following should probably never be done with a production machine, unless physical access to the machine is readily available, it is actually scheduled for migration, and backups have been made.

The trick is to use the existing system as host, but to bootstrap a temporary Debian installation into a separate partition. If the host hard disk has no free space, it is possible to use the swap partition for this purpose. Assuming **/dev/hda2** as the swap partition, the following should get you started:

```
~# swapoff /dev/hda2
~# sed -i -e 's,^/dev/hda2,# &,' /etc/fstab
~# mke2fs /dev/hda2
~# mount /dev/hda2 /mnt
~# debootstrap sarge /mnt http://ftp.debian.org
[...]
```

Take special care with the **/etc/fstab** file, which should look like this:

```
# /etc/fstab: static file system information.
#
# <fs>        <mount point> <type>  <options>        <dump> <pass>
proc          /proc         proc    defaults           0  0
/dev/hda2     /             ext2    default            0  1
```

Once this is done, the new kernel has to be added to the host's **bootloader**. Please note that the following configurations for **Lilo** and for **Grub** assume that you followed the suggestion in chapter 5.12.2 and placed the kernel symlinks into /boot on the target system (option **link_in_boot = yes** in /etc/kernel-img.conf). Otherwise you will have to adjust the paths, or Lilo will complain and **Grub** will require manual interaction during the boot process. Furthermore, it is assumed that /mnt/boot/vmlinuz and /mnt/boot/initrd.img are canonical symlinks created by the kernel package installed inside the chroot. If these links do not exist, you can either complete the filename to include the full version, or create the symlinks. Also, do not forget that we are adding the stanzas to the *host's bootloader* configuration!

Lilo requires the following addition to the host's **/etc/lilo.conf**. The **initrd** line is only necessary when an initial ramdisk is used (as is the case with Debian stock kernels), or if you have used **make-kpkg --initrd** to build a custom kernel:

```
image=/mnt/boot/vmlinuz
  label = debian
  initrd = /mnt/boot/initrd.img
  root = /dev/hda2
  read-only
```

For **Grub**, you need the following addition to the host's **/boot/grub/menu.lst**. Take a note of the number of stanzas preceeding the one you are adding. You will need this number (which is the zero-based index of the newly added stanza) in an instant.

```
title    debian
  root    (hd0,1)
  kernel  /mnt/boot/vmlinuz root=/dev/hda2 ro
  initrd  /mnt/boot/initrd.img
  boot
```

So far so good. If you have not added a regular user during the base system configuration, I suggest doing so now. The reason is that **SSH** does not always allow logins by **root**. In current versions, Debian's **SSH** *does* permit **root** login, but I am only one of many who are pushing for this to be changed. If you create a regular user, log in using that account, and then **su** to **root**, you should be on the save side.

Now for the reboot! If you are converting an existing system to Debian in this way, the system is probably hosted somewhere remotely. Therefore, if it does not boot into Debian, you have lost and may have to to call for potentially expensive support to return your system to the old state. In the following, I describe an approach that will avoid losing the system. The worst thing that can happen is kernel panic during when the Debian system boots, in which case *someone* will have to hard-reset the machine to make it return to the previous operating system. Most hosters provide this service for free.

In the event that the new Debian system boots fine but network access cannot be established, the system can automatically reset itself to return to the previous installation. This is accomplished by telling **init** to reboot the machine a certain period of time after the boot process completes. If the new Debian system comes up and connects to the network as expected, you login to the system within the period and disable the reboot mechanism. To put it in place, append the following line to **/mnt/etc/inittab** (that is, **/etc/inittab** within the new hierarchy):

```
~# cat <<EOF >> /etc/inittab
rb:2345:once:/bin/sh -c 'sleep 15m; reboot'
EOF
```

Assuming the system has rebooted and you are able to log in to the new Debian system, just delete that entry and tell **init** to forget about it:

```
~# sed -i -e '/:once:.\+sleep.\+; reboot/d' /etc/inittab
~# telinit q
```

If the system does not come back up after a while, wait fifteen minutes and then the previous installation should boot again.

The one thing left now before we finish building our safety net is to tell the **bootloader** to attempt the new image only once and return to using the default upon next reboot. Fortunately, both **bootloaders** provide this functionality:

```
~# lilo -R debian && reboot
or:
~# grub-reboot <index>
```

Now you can reboot and wait a couple of minutes, then try to log in to the machine with **SSH**. If you are not successful after five minutes, get a coffee (or another beverage of your choice) and try to get back into the old system after another fifteen minutes. If that fails too, you have no alternative but to call your hoster and ask for a reset.

An automated solution to converting a Unix machine to Debian is provided with **debtakeover**[13]. Please note that the script is in beta stage and might possibly destroy data. Therefore, please use it with care.

Running software in chroots

The potential uses for **chroot** installations are limited only by your imagination. A **chroot** is a magnificent way to try out some concepts in this book, or obtain a clean, basic installation for temporary use in which the complexity or integrity requirements of a production system would be a hindrance (make sure you check out chapter 9.6). A **chroot** also comes in handy, for instance, when you need to run 32 bit software on a 64 bit machine (and *vice versa*). For instance, to be able to run 32 bit applications (such as Sun's **Java**, tools like **MatLab**, or other software distributed in binary) on an **amd64** installation (see chapter 4.5.2), it is currently necessary to give the software 32 bit versions of all the libraries it needs as it cannot use the 64 bit libraries already installed.

The solution is to set up a **chroot**, using the appropriate 32 bit architecture, such as **i386**:

```
~# mkdir -p /srv/chroots/sid-i386
~# debootstrap --arch i386 sid /srv/chroots/sid-i386
[...]
```

[13]http://www.hadrons.org/~guillem/debian/debtakeover

When **debootstrap** has finished downloading and installing all the packages, you can copy the 32 bit software into the **chroot** and run it, after taking further steps to deal with issues such as X authentication.

Avoid the need for root rights

The approach has a major shortcoming: you need to have **root** rights to be able to access the **chroot** and run the software. It goes without saying that this is undesirable, especially given binary-only software, which many mistrust more than software for which the source code is available. Obviously, it is possible to create a user database within the **chroot** and change to a non-privileged user after entering the **chroot** and before executing the software. Now the only drawback is the need for **root** access to enter the **chroot** in the first place.

The Debian archive holds a tool designed to make executing commands in **chroots** a lot easier: **dchroot** (in the **dchroot** package). **dchroot** runs **setuid root** and drops the privileges after entering the **chroot** by switching to the user that called the tool. For this to work, the calling user must exist in the **chroot**'s user database. Moreover, the corresponding home directory needs to exist.

To avoid the administrative nightmare of manually keeping two user databases in sync, we can make use of **bind** mounts, a feature which has existed in Linux kernels since version 2.4, and use symlinks. We will go a step further and use the same technique to provide access to the **/home** and **/tmp** hierarchies as well. Using **rbind** instead of **bind** enables separately mounted filesystems within the hierarchies to be accessed from within the **chroot**. Also, **/proc** must be mounted. Instead of executing the necessary commands one by one, we enter them into the host system's **/etc/fstab** file:

```
~# cat <<EOF >> /etc/fstab
/etc   /srv/chroots/sid-i386/etc/.host auto defaults,rbind 0 3
/home /srv/chroots/sid-i386/home       auto defaults,rbind 0 3
/tmp   /srv/chroots/sid-i386/tmp        auto defaults,rbind 0 3
/dev   /srv/chroots/sid-i386/dev        auto defaults,rbind 0 3
proc  /srv/chroots/sid-i386/proc        proc defaults      0 0
EOF
~# mkdir /srv/chroots/sid-i386/etc/.host
```

We can mount these five bindings with a single command, as they are all configured to be mounted automatically:

```
~# mount -a
```

As a last step, we make the most important configuration files available, and configure the APT repositories within the **chroot**:

```
~# ln -sf .host/passwd /srv/chroots/sid-i386/etc
~# ln -sf .host/group /srv/chroots/sid-i386/etc
~# ln -sf .host/resolv.conf /srv/chroots/sid-i386/etc
~# chroot /srv/chroots/sid-i386 apt-setup
```

Having the user's home directory available inside the **chroot** also solves the problem of **X** authentication, allowing **X** applications to be run inside the **chroot**. This is also the reason why **/tmp** is needed, since **X** keeps its sockets there. If you have the **resolvconf** package installed on the host system, you also need to install it into the **chroot**.

dchroot can deal with multiple **chroot** installations, which must be listed in **/etc/dchroot.conf**, and which can be selected individually. The first **chroot** listed in the file will be used as the default.

```
~# echo sid-i386 /srv/chroots/sid-i386 > /etc/dchroot.conf
```

After letting **dchroot** know about the **i386 chroot**, commands can be executed simply by calling **dchroot**. The **-d** causes the caller's environment to be preserved (which is necessary for **X** authentication data to propagate), and **-q** avoids printing the **chroot**'s name and the command that is about to be executed:

```
~$ dpkg --print-architecture
amd64
~$ dchroot dpkg --print-architecture
(sid-i386) dpkg --print-architecture
i386
~$ dchroot -q -d xclock
```

8.3.2 Booting the installation from the network (PXE)

In network environments with PXE support in the client hardware, it may be useful to let the clients boot over the network, fetching the necessary data from a central server rather than asking the administrator to juggle media. The new Debian installer makes this quite simple, but you are encouraged to consider **FAI**, the Fully Automatic Installation system for Debian (see chapter 8.3.5) instead, if you are looking for an automated installation over the network.

The network installation requires a server capable of DHCP and Trivial File Transfer Protocol (TFTP). A Debian machine with the **dhcp3-server** and **atftpd** packages will work nicely. The following steps will prepare the server. It is assumed that you have downloaded the desired versions of the three files **initrd.gz** and **vmlinuz** from the netboot tree[14] on your nearest mirror into **/tmp**.

---

[14]The **netboot** tree may be found under **/debian/dists/stable/main/installer-i386/current/images/netboot** on the mirrors. If you need it for other architectures, make sure to modify the URL appropriately.

```
~# mkdir --mode=755 /srv/tftpboot /srv/tftpboot/pxelinux.cfg
~# cd /srv/tftpboot
~# install --mode=644 /tmp/initrd.gz .
~# install --mode=644 /tmp/vmlinuz .
~# apt-get install syslinux
~# install --mode=644 /usr/lib/syslinux/pxelinux.0 .
```

Furthermore, **/srv/tftpboot/pxelinux.cfg/default** has to be created with the following contents (and with any additional boot parameters you see fit):

```
LABEL linux
  KERNEL vmlinuz
  APPEND initrd=initrd.gz devfs=mount root=/dev/ram
```

If you wish to use a different mode of verbosity for the installer than standard mode, append the appropriate **debian/priority** setting to the **APPEND** line.

For the configuration of the DHCP server (which is included here only for convenience), the presence of an A record[15] in the DNS zone for **pxeserver** is assumed. An IP address will work equally well. The following lets your DHCP server tell the PXE clients where to get the installation image. Replace the MAC and IP addresses to reflect your local configuration.

```
host pxeclient {
  hardware ethernet aa:bb:cc:dd:ee:ff;
  fixed-address T.U.V.W;
  option host-name "pxeclient";
  filename "/pxelinux.0";
  next-server pxeserver;
}
```

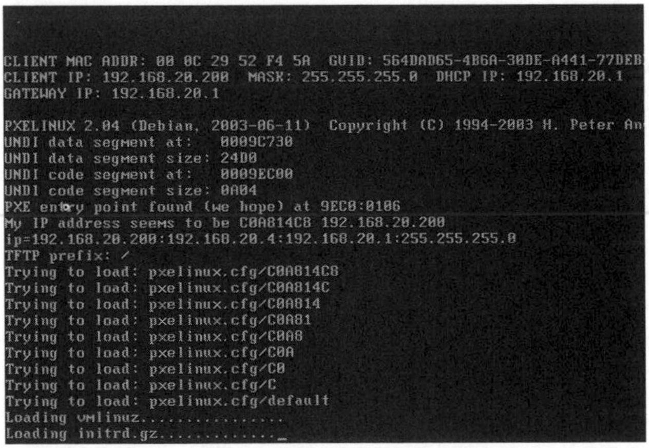

Figure 8.1:
A successful PXE
boot.

---

[15]A records map hostnames to IP addresses in DNS.

Booting **pxeclient** now should allow it to obtain a DHCP address and download the installation files from **pxeserver**. Figure 8.1 shows a successful PXE boot.

Shortly after this, the installer will launch into its familiar environment. After configuring the regional settings and the network hardware, the installer will give you the choice of loading the installer components from floppy or from the network. Generally, you will want to do the latter.

The remainder of the network installation proceeds as detailed in chapter 3.2. If you want to use a CD-ROM for the rest of the installation, the installer component **cdrom-detect** has to be loaded.

8.3.3 Customising the installer

The Debian installer (see chapter 3.1) is a modular system, which reuses much of the functionality seen elsewhere in Debian. In particular, it uses stripped Debian packages[16] and simplified package handling tools called **udpkg** and **anna** to initialise the installer, and to pull in other components during the installation process (see chapter 3).

The Debian installer in a nutshell

When an installation medium is booted, the Debian kernel loads, and a basic set of utilities in an initial ramdisk bootstraps the system to a point where it is capable of installing other UDEBs. The user interface is provided by **cdebconf**[17], which is installed and invoked after the kernel loaded. The remainder of the installation process depends on the components that are automatically loaded, or selected by the user. If an installer component is loaded, **anna** fetches it from an APT repository and hands it over to **udpkg**, which installs it and allows it to register with the main menu of the installation, handled by **cdebconf**.

It does not matter to **anna** where the APT repository resides. If network connectivity is available, installer components can be fetched from any Debian mirror. Some installation media (such as **businesscard**) include a selection of installer components in an APT repository on the medium itself. Larger installation images (such as **netinst**) also provide the regular DEB files needed for the base system to be installed in that repository. The official ISO images include popular additional packages.

---

[16] Micro DEBs (UDEBs) are Debian installer modules which use the normal Debian package infrastructure, but which do not have to comply with the Debian policy as they are only used during the installation. These packages do not include documentation or other non-essential files to minimise their size. UDEB files must not be used on a normal Debian system and can cause severe damage if installed with **dpkg**.

[17] cdebconf is a rewrite of **debconf** (see chapter 5.8) in C

Making modifications

Several reasons exist why one would want to make changes to the official installation media provided by Debian. In most cases, the selection of packages available from the installation medium (and therefore installable without a network connection) needs to be amended for a given application. For instance, a CD to be distributed at a graphics convention should probably include programmes like **The Gimp**, but does not need to provide 17 different browsers (just to give an example). Another reason may be the inclusion of a custom component to be able to influence the installation at an early stage, or to enable an automatic installation (see chapter 8.3.4) to configure the system beyond the possibilities of the standard Debian installer. While this kind of modification was possible with the **boot-floppies** installer with varying degrees of difficulty, or by using external programmes, the modifications are now a function of the installer itself, as a direct consequence of its modularity.

The possibilities are essentially endless, and there are several resources online which detail the steps involved. The Debian Wiki has two documents: while the first[18] concentrates on making modifications to an existing CD image, the second[19] details the process of building a custom installation medium from scratch. Also, a HOWTO-style document exists[20], describing how to make modifications to the installer.

8.3.4   Preseeding the installer

The Debian installer uses **debconf** (see chapter 5.8) to gather information from the user. It is possible to initialise some of **debconf**'s database directly from the boot prompt. This is known as "preseeding[21]." For example:

```
boot: linux languagechooser/language-name=English \
  console-keymaps-at/keymap=us countrychooser/shortlist=CH
```

This would preseed the language, country, and keyboard selection to the values I use. Unfortunately, the kernel accepts 8 boot prompt options at the most, so the possibilities are limited, even more so because the kernels on the installation media already provide four default options. If you specify more, 2.4 kernels just ignore the excessive options, while 2.6 kernels panic. While some of the default options can probably be removed safely (*e.g.* **vga** and **devfs**), this can only be done in a network

---

[18] http://wiki.debian.net/index.cgi?DebianInstallerModify
[19] http://wiki.debian.net/index.cgi?DebianCustomCD
[20] http://people.debian.org/~osamu/hackdi
[21] "Preseeding" is the technical term for initialising a value before its use. For what it is worth, "seeding" would have been sufficient, but the "pre" prefix (another pleonasm?) is used to emphasise the antecedence of the initialisation.

installation scenario (see chapter 8.3.2), or by customising the installer media[22]. Thus, it is possible to specify a total of four options on the 2.4 kernel prompt, and the 2.6 kernel only allows for three.

One of the boot prompt options can specify the location of a file from which to read other variable-value pairs to initialise **debconf**, and thus avoiding the need to prompt the user. This file can reside on locally accessible media, as well as on a web or FTP server. The following two lines illustrate this use:

```
boot: linux preseed/file=/floppy/preseed.cfg
boot: linux preseed/url=http://server/path/to/preseed.cfg
```

The **preseed.cfg** file (the name can be freely chosen) specifies the values to be cached for specific variables. Each line corresponds to one setting and consists of four whitespace-separated columns. The first specifies the owner of the template, followed by the template name, the type, and finally the value (which extends through the end of the line). For instance, to preconfigure the network card to use a static address, the file would need to contain the following:

```
d-i netcfg/disable_dhcp boolean true
d-i netcfg/get_ipaddress string  192.168.0.42
d-i netcfg/get_netmask string  255.255.255.0
d-i netcfg/get_gateway string  192.168.0.1
d-i netcfg/get_nameservers string  192.168.0.2 192.168.0.3
d-i netcfg/confirm_static boolean true
```

Obviously, this requires the **preseed.cfg** file to be present on a local medium. If you want to access **preseed.cfg** over the network, you have to ensure that the network can be configured with DHCP (the default), or find other means to preseed the above settings (such as a custom image).

One way to create the **preseed.cfg** file is with the **debconf-get-selections** tool (from the **debconf-utils**) package:

```
~# debconf-get-selections --installer > preseed.cfg
~# debconf-get-selections >> preseed.cfg
```

The generated file contains a dump of the entire **debconf** database and should only be used to preseed systems that will have an identical set of packages installed as the machine used to generate the file. Furthermore, the dump contains some settings which are better not preseeded (such as **base-config/main-menu** and **debconf/frontend**). If you are planning to use preseeding, it might be better to work from the example provided in the installer manual[23].

---

[22]See http://wiki.debian.net/index.cgi?DebianInstallerModify and http://people.debian.org/~osamu/hackdi

[23]http://d-i.alioth.debian.org/manual/en.i386/apcs01.html

It is, unfortunately, not (yet) possible to preseed the settings for country, language, and keyboard layout. Thus, these three items must be specified on the boot command line. In addition to the **preseed** option, the boot command will then be longer than 100 characters, which defeats the purpose of preseeding — a manual installation of Debian requires only twelve keystrokes until you are prompted for the root password. Thus, preseeding is mainly useful for use on customised installation media[22], or for network installations (see chapter 8.3.2).

8.3.5   FAI: Fully automatic installations

FAI stands for "Fully Automatic Installation"[24] and provides a scaleable solution for installation management of any number of clients. Unlike alternative solutions, such as **systemimager** or **replicator**, FAI can handle different types of hardware and install systems for different purposes all with a single, central configuration repository. A manual is linked from the FAI homepage[25], and user-contributed installation reports and documentation[26] provide valuable additional resources.

FAI uses NFS to publish a minimal Debian system which clients use to boot for the installation process[27]. To cater for different hardware and different requirements, FAI uses classes to encapsulate different aspects of the systems to be installed. An installation client may belong to any number of classes, and each class can influence partitioning, software selection, or the set of scripts run towards the end, which configure and prepare the newly installed machine.

The installation itself consists of five stages:

Class determination
> During the first stage, a set of scripts is run on the installation client to determine the classes to which the machine belongs. Every word written to **stdout** by these scripts is treated as a class, to which the install client belongs. The scripts can harness the full power of the shell, **Perl**, or any other software installed in the root filesystem (and exported via NFS) to produce the list of classes. For instance, one script may use the DHCP-assigned hostname to assign membership of a certain class, or call the **discover** utility to figure out the classes based on the available hardware. A simple example script could be:

```
~$ cat <<EOF > class/10misc
#!/bin/sh -e

case "$HOSTNAME" in
```

---

[24] FAI's homepage may be found at http://www.informatik.uni-koeln.de/fai
[25] http://www.informatik.uni-koeln.de/fai/fai-guide.html
[26] http://www.informatik.uni-koeln.de/fai/user.html
[27] FAI can also be used to install from CD-ROM; see http://www.informatik.uni-koeln.de/fai/fai-cd

```
   arakis) echo MAILSERVER;;
esac

case "$(discover --data-path=xfree86/server/device/driver display)"
in matrox) echo MATROX;;
  ati) echo ATI;;
  *) echo VESA;;
esac

echo $HOSTNAME
EOF
```

When this script runs on **arakis**, which has an ATI graphics card, it will cause the client to be placed into the classes **MAILSERVER**, **ATI**, and **arakis** (in that order). The classes **DEFAULT** and **LAST** are defined by default before and after the specific classes, respectively. Classes are ordered, and those defined later take priority over earlier ones.

Variable definition

Next, **FAI** sets all environment variables defined in **class/*.var**, according to the defined classes. In the above example, **class/MAILSERVER.var** would be sourced, but **class/MATROX.var** would be ignored. All variables defined will be available throughout the installation process to all shell, **Perl**, and **cfengine** scripts.

Partitioning

FAI reads the description of the partition table and the filesystems to be created from files in **./disk_config**, according to the defined classes. Only one configuration file is used, and this is determined by the class with highest priority (the most recently defined one) that has a corresponding file in the directory. With these configuration files, it is possible to specify filesystem options, and even to preserve filesystems across reinstallations. For instance, the following configures a standard partition table with **XFS** filesystems (except for the **/boot** partition, due to a **Grub** bug; see chapter 19)) and preserving **/dev/hda7**:

```
~$ cat <<EOF > disk_config/DEFAULT_PRESERVE
disk_config hda
primary /boot     16-48     rw,nodev,nosuid,noatime,noexec ;boot
-j ext3
primary swap      40-500
logical /         70-150    rw,noatime            ;xfs
logical /usr      200-4000  rw,noatime            ;xfs
logical /scratch preserve7  rw,nosuid,nodev       ;xfs
logical /var      90-1000   rw,noatime            ;xfs
logical /tmp      50-1000   rw,nosuid,nodev       ;xfs
EOF
```

Software installation

The hierarchy rooted at **./package_config** specifies the software to be installed, depending on the defined classes. For every defined class, the corresponding file is read (if it exists), and the collective set of all files is used to determine which packages to install, using **APT** (thus dependencies are automatically resolved). For instance, a typical package selection for the **XSERVER** class would be described like this. If the **HWDETECT** class is also defined, packages necessary for automatic configuration of the **X** server are pulled in.

```
~$ cat <<EOF > package_config/XSERVER
PACKAGES install
x-window-system-core xdm
xfonts-100dpi-transcoded xfonts-intl-european ttf-bitstream-vera
fontconfig
rxvt-unicode xterm-
menu

PACKAGES install HWDETECT
read-edid mdetect discover
EOF
```

System configuration

Finally, **FAI** executes the scripts in **./scripts**, according to the set of defined classes. For any class, the directory may contain a single file, or a directory, which causes **FAI** to run all files therein. The scripts can be standard shell scripts, use **Perl**, or **cfengine**, or whatever else is installed on the NFS-mounted root system.

By the time these scripts are run, all selected packages will have been installed in the **chroot** at **/tmp/target** (defined in the **$target** environment variable). Thus, you will need to employ **chroot** (or **$ROOTCMD**) and **$target**, but are otherwise free to do whatever you like. Depending on the nature of the installation client, it may be preferable to use **debconf** for configuration changes (see chapter 5.8), rather than editing files directly. For example, the following reconfigures the **xserver-xfree86** package, using **debconf**:

```
~$ cat <<EOF > XSERVER/S35reconfigure
#!/bin/sh -e

ifclass LCD && $ROOTCMD debconf-set-selections <<EOF || true
xserver-xfree86 xserver-xfree86/config/monitor/lcd boolean true
EOF

ifclass HWDETECT && $ROOTCMD debconf-set-selections <<EOF || true
xserver-xfree86 xserver-xfree86/autodetect_mouse boolean true
xserver-xfree86 xserver-xfree86/autodetect_monitor boolean true
EOF
```

```
$ROOTCMD dpkg-reconfigure xserver-xfree86
EOF
```

FAI is very flexible and can be used in many situations, ranging from installation management for a single workstation to clusters spanning hundreds of machines. Its flexibility stems from two features.

First, the class concept allows for granular but scalable descriptions of hosts. Since the classes are determined on the installation client itself, it is possible to service a variety of hosts, whether they differ with respect to hardware or purpose. FAI also provides numerous hooks for additional flexibility, so it is possible to influence the entire installation process, should this be desired.

Secondly, FAI combines standard Debian tools with powerful utensils, such as **Perl** and **cfengine**. Thus, a FAI installation can benefit from the robustness of the Debian package management tools and produce a consistent installation with a minimum of effort. Dependencies are met automatically, and you can rely on packages within the *stable* release to remain constant in your configuration scripts.

Apart from the FAI guide[28], you will find articles describing the setup of FAI server[29] as well as the rollout procedure[30] online.

---

[28] http://www.informatik.uni-koeln.de/fai/fai-guide.html
[29] http://www.linuxplanet.com/linuxplanet/tutorials/5667/1/
[30] http://www.linuxplanet.com/linuxplanet/tutorials/5675/1/

Creating Debian packages

The Debian design process is open to ensure that the system is of
the highest quality and that it reflects the needs
of the user community.
— The Debian Linux Manifesto

The more you integrate the Debian package management system with your administrative and system management tasks, the more likely it becomes that you will need to create custom Debian packages. Be it a modified version of an existing package, software that is not available in the Debian archive, a meta package (dummy package) to enforce a certain package selection with **Depends** and **Conflicts** relations, or more advanced uses of DEB files, acquiring the ability to create DEB files is a major step in the process of mastering the Debian system.

New users are frequently astonished and look up to the package management tools with awe. To them, the developers who put packages together are wizards, and their accomplishments unattainable works of art. I'll go out on a limb and claim that this is not the case, because there is little to no magic involved in creating Debian packages.

In fact, most of the time the need is merely to modify an existing package, to create meta packages to enforce a certain package selection, or to create dummy packages to tweak the dependency graph. Debian provides tools for these tasks, and the tools do not require you to know more than the bare essentials of Debian package creation. If you are curious, please refer to chapter 5.9. While it is often sufficient to poke at existing packages and implement hacks to attain the desired solution, the lack of a deeper understanding of the techniques involved can quite quickly turn a trivial problem into a killer.

This book adopts a bottom-up approach, which is known from various scientific domains as starting at the component level and successively integrating building blocks to create increasingly complex behaviours. Starting with the tools you already know, we will first look at the very low-level approaches to package creation before going on to meet higher-level tools. At each step, you will have all the background needed to understand what these higher-level tools actually do. If a problem surfaces later, you will have a fairly clear idea of where to look.

9.1   Manual packaging

Debian binary packages are nothing more than a set of files which can be manipulated with standard Unix archiving tools, as shown in chapter 5.2.3. In addition to the files installed by the package, which are laid out inside the package to match their installation footprint on the target system, a DEB file contains a small number of control files used by the package management tools to manage the package (see chapter 5.2.4). We saw that these are kept in separate tarballs within the DEB file, which is nothing more than a simple BSD **ar** archive.

GNU and BSD **ar** archives are not compatible, and **dpkg** brings its own minimal implementation of BSD **ar** for historic and functional reasons. While **dpkg** already knows how to handle both formats, other tools are still limited to the BSD format. It is unlikely that the standard will change anytime soon. Thus, in the following, we will assume a binary implementing the BSD **ar** format.

In the unpacked state, a Debian binary package consists of the ./DEBIAN directory, which holds the control files, along with the set of installed files spread out across a standard Unix filesystem hierarchy. The installation of the DEB file merely causes the installed files to be unpacked in the / directory, where their locations are determined by their relative location within the package.

To keep a long story short, let's build a very simple package: **gruezi**. The **gruezi** package installs a simple shell script as /usr/bin/gruezi, which will greet the caller in the four languages of Switzerland. Note that the following demonstration mainly serves the purpose of illustrating the low-level components of a Debian binary package. We will meet other methods shortly, which facilitate and automate much of the process.

The **gruezi** script is rather simple:

```
~$ cat <<EOF > script
#!/bin/sh -e

echo Hoi zämme!
echo Salut!
echo Ciao!
echo Allegra!
EOF
```

Since the script is supposed to reside in **/usr/bin**, we install it into **usr/bin** relative to the directory **./gruezi** (which we have to create first), representing the package contents. Moreover, we assume the presence of **gruezi.1**, which is the **gruezi**(1) manpage. the Debian policy requires every executable in **/usr/bin** to have a manpage, so we had better get this right too:

```
~$ mkdir gruezi
~$ cd gruezi
~/gruezi$ mkdir -p usr/bin usr/share/man/man1
~/gruezi$ install --mode=755 script usr/bin/gruezi
~/gruezi$ install --mode=644 gruezi.1 usr/share/man/man1
~/gruezi$ gzip -f9 usr/share/man/man1/gruezi.1
```

Now the script resides as **./gruezi/usr/bin/gruezi**, and its path relative to the **./gruezi** package directory identifies its final location when the DEB file is installed: **/usr/bin/gruezi**.

The Debian policy requires every package to provide copyright and change log information. The copyright file is supposed to contain all necessary licencing information (which can be given as a reference to a file in **/usr/share/common-licenses**), as well as the author, the location where to obtain the source, and ideally the maintainer who packaged it, and when.

```
~/gruezi$ mkdir -p usr/share/doc/gruezi
~/gruezi$ cat <<EOF > usr/share/doc/gruezi/copyright
This package was manually created by Wilhelm Tell <hero@suisse.ch>
on Sat, 18 Nov 1307, 11:00:00 +0100

It was downloaded from: http://www.gruezi.ch

Upstream Author: Wilhelm Tell <hero@suisse.ch>

Copyright:
```

```
Do whatever you want with this software.
But do not claim to have invented it,
Or the nation will bombard you
With Ricola candies.
EOF
```

The change log file should indicate the version, the target distribution, and give information about when which changes were made by whom (see chapter 9.2.7):

```
~/gruezi$ cat <<EOF | gzip -9 \
  > usr/share/doc/gruezi/changelog.Debian.gz
gruezi (1.0-1) unstable; urgency=low

  * The "Wer hat's erfunden?" release

 -- Wilhelm Tell <hero@suisse.ch>  Sat, 18 Nov 1307 12:00:00 +0100
EOF
~/gruezi$ chmod -R og=rX .
```

With all files in place, let's verify the layout of the installation set:

```
~/gruezi$ find . -exec ls -Fld {} \;
drwxr-xr-x  [...]   .
drwxr-xr-x  [...]  ./usr/
drwxr-xr-x  [...]  ./usr/bin/
-rwxr-xr-x  [...]  ./usr/bin/gruezi*
drwxr-xr-x  [...]  ./usr/share/
drwxr-xr-x  [...]  ./usr/share/doc/
drwxr-xr-x  [...]  ./usr/share/doc/gruezi/
-rw-r--r--  [...]  ./usr/share/doc/gruezi/copyright
-rw-r--r--  [...]  ./usr/share/doc/gruezi/changelog.Debian.gz
-rwxr-xr-x  [...]  ./usr/share/man/
-rwxr-xr-x  [...]  ./usr/share/man/man1/
-rw-r--r--  [...]  ./usr/share/man/man1/gruezi.1.gz
```

This looks fine and we are almost done. What is missing is a file to identify the package to the package management tools: the **control** file, which resides in the ./DEBIAN directory. The **control** file also specifies dependency relations and other meta data of Debian packages. The **deb-control (5)** manpage has the details of this file. For our purposes, the following abbreviated version suffices.

```
~/gruezi$ mkdir DEBIAN
~/gruezi$ cat <<EOF > DEBIAN/control
Package: gruezi
Section: misc
Priority: extra
Maintainer: Wilhelm Tell <hero@suisse.ch>
Architecture: all
```

```
Version: 1.0-1
Description: greets you the Swiss way
 gruezi is a simple script to greet its caller in all four
 languages spoken in Switzerland.
EOF
```

For completeness, let us also provide the **MD5** sums of the files that **gruezi** installs. This file is not mandatory, but since **dpkg** does not (yet) generate them on installation (see chapter 5.11.1), it might make sense:

```
~/gruezi$ find usr -type f -exec md5sum {} \; \
  > DEBIAN/md5sums
33d4beeb8e566e0b7d79358447d3856c  usr/bin/gruezi
448d7122dc9c573beba645eff495cf90  usr/share/doc/gruezi/copyright
19b6f39af548e7de4373e4568a07f8c7  usr/share/doc/gruezi/changelog.Debian.
gz
c716fb2a994740f7b1d40a4ffdb7a5fe  usr/share/man/man1/gruezi.1.gz
```

The directory is now properly prepared and the package can be created with standard Unix tools:

```
~$ tar cz -C gruezi/DEBIAN -f control.tar.gz .
~$ tar cz --exclude=DEBIAN -C gruezi -f data.tar.gz .
~$ echo 2.0 > debian-binary
~$ ar rcu gruezi.deb debian-binary control.tar.gz data.tar.gz
```

A quick inspection reveals that we did, in fact, succeed. **dpkg** identifies the package as a "new debian package" of version 2.0 because we used the current standard format as opposed to the old format from the early days of **dpkg**:

```
~$ dpkg-deb --info gruezi.deb
 new debian package, version 2.0.
 size 1788 bytes: control archive= 498 bytes.
     253 bytes,     9 lines         control
     254 bytes,     4 lines         md5sums
 Package: gruezi
 Section: misc
 Priority: extra
 Maintainer: Wilhelm Tell <hero@suisse.ch>
 Architecture: all
 Version: 1.0-1
 Description: greets you the Swiss way.
  gruezi is a simple script to greet its caller in all four
  languages spoken in Switzerland.
~$ dpkg-deb --contents gruezi.deb
drwxr-xr-x  [...]   .
drwxr-xr-x  [...]   ./usr
drwxr-xr-x  [...]   ./usr/bin
-rwxr-xr-x  [...]   ./usr/bin/gruezi
```

```
drwxr-xr-x  [...]  ./usr/share
drwxr-xr-x  [...]  ./usr/share/doc
drwxr-xr-x  [...]  ./usr/share/doc/gruezi
-rw-r--r--  [...]  ./usr/share/doc/gruezi/copyright
-rw-r--r--  [...]  ./usr/share/doc/gruezi/changelog.Debian.gz
-rwxr-xr-x  [...]  ./usr/share/man
-rwxr-xr-x  [...]  ./usr/share/man/man1
-rw-r--r--  [...]  ./usr/share/man/man1/gruezi.1.gz
```

Finally, we can become **root** and install the package just like any other DEB file:

```
~# dpkg --install gruezi.deb
[...]
Unpacking gruezi (from gruezi.deb) ...
Setting up gruezi (1.0-1) ...
~# which gruezi
/usr/bin/gruezi
~# dpkg --search /usr/bin/gruezi
gruezi: /usr/bin/gruezi
~# gruezi
Hoi zämme!
Salut!
Ciao!
Allegra!
```

Et voilà, we have created a fully-featured Debian binary package. You are likely to agree that there was no magic involved in the process. We used nothing but standard tools, and the layout of directories and files within the package seems quite logical. The result is a binary-only package without its source counterpart. Nevertheless, it can be used with the package management tools on a Debian system as expected.

9.2   Debianising with the package maintainer tools

With the knowledge of how a Debian binary package is built at the lowest level, we can ascend to using the package maintainer tools and learn how complete Debian packages are built with them. The **dpkg-dev** package installs all the tools needed to create Debian packages as simple as the **gruezi** package, or as complicated as a package may get.

The most important distinction between the previously illustrated method and the standard Debian packaging procedure is that the directory containing the filesystem archive (which the package installs) and the **./DEBIAN** directory are automatically created by the Debian tools from the data and control information found in the unpacked Debian source package.

9.2.1   A closer look at source packages

In chapter 5.9.1, you were introduced to Debian source packages, and told how to obtain them. It is now time to take a closer look at source packages. The anatomy of a source package mainly depends on the software it provides, as it contains the source code in the same layout as distributed by the author. All information required by the Debian package maintainer tools reside under the ./debian directory. In the case of a typical **autotools** package, the unpacked source package looks similar to the following:

```
~$ ls -F
aclocal.m4        configure.ac  FAQ          NEWS
AUTHORS           COPYING       include/     pkgconfig/
autogen.sh*       CVS/          INSTALL@     README
autom4te.cache/   debian/       install-sh@  ref/
ChangeLog         doc/          Makefile.am  TODO
config.h.in       Makefile.in   configure*
examples/         missing@
```

Therefore, as you can see, the normal build procedure

```
~$ ./configure && make
```

is possible in this case. In fact, a Debian source package is simply the original source package augmented with the information needed by the package maintainer tools and additional data the maintainer chose to include in the DEB package (such as extra documentation or self-authored example scripts). The maintainer might also modify the source code to make paths compliant with the FHS or to change other aspects of a software to make it fit in better with a Debian system. As a quick side note: the maintainer of a package is mostly also the author of a package, but not necessarily the author of the software the package contains. To stay consistent with common usage of the words, maintainer refers to the person packaging a software for Debian even if the software is just being packaged for the first time (and is thus not yet maintained).

A source package consists of two or three files. Debian-native source packages contain the package tool data directly. Debian source packages of third-party software provide a **diff.gz** file which encapsulates the changes needed to augment the upstream source with the Debian package information. Let us look again at **postfix**, which is a third-party software and thus consists of three files:

```
~$ ls -F postfix
postfix_2.1.5-1.diff.gz  postfix_2.1.5-1.dsc  postfix_2.1.3.orig.tar.gz
~$ diffstat -f0 postfix_2.1.5-1.diff.gz
[...]
  conf/main.cf                            |   20  14 +    6 -     0 !
```

```
conf/main.cf.debian                        |   11   11 +    0 -     0 !
[...]
debian/changelog                           | 1262 1262 +    0 -     0 !
debian/conffiles                           |    7    7 +    0 -     0 !
debian/config                              |  401  401 +    0 -     0 !
debian/control                             |   88   88 +    0 -     0 !
debian/copyright                           |  326  326 +    0 -     0 !
[...]
```

The file postfix_2.1.5.orig.tar.gz is exactly the same tarball as provided on the postfix mirrors. As you can see, the diff.gz file makes some changes to conf/main.cf, which are required for Debian, and drops a bunch of files into ./debian. The process of changing an unpacked upstream source tree into its Debian source package counterpart is known as "debianisation." Debian-native software obviously does not have to be specifically debianised.

For the diff.gz file to be created, the Debian package maintainer scripts need to have the upstream source available for comparison. There are two ways in which this can be done. The preferred method is to simply rename the tarball you down-loaded from upstream according to the following schema:

```
<package>_<version>.orig.tar.gz
```

For instance, postfix is available as postfix-2.1.5.tar.gz, and the orig.tar.gz file would have to be named postfix_2.1.5.orig.tar.gz for the package maintainer tools to find it. You can then unpack the orig.tar.gz tarball and proceed with debiani-sation in the directory it creates. The standard for tarballs is to create a directory with the following scheme:

```
<package>-<version>
```

The Debian tools require this scheme, and if the tarball uses an unconventional naming scheme for the directory it contains, you will have to manually move it into place. Thus, assuming that the postfix-2.1.5.tar.gz tarball (which we have just renamed to postfix_2.1.5.orig.tar.gz) unpacks to ./postfix and thus does not follow the guidelines (which, of course, postfix does, so this is just hypothetical), the following steps are needed to unpack the tarball:

```
~$ tar xzf postfix_2.1.5.orig.tar.gz
~$ mv postfix postfix-2.1.5
```

Now the ./postfix-2.1.5 directory, which still only contains the original upstream postfix source tree, is ready for debianisation.

Instead of renaming the tarball, you can alternatively unpack it and duplicate the directory it contains before making any changes to it:

```
~$ tar xzf postfix-2.1.5.tar.gz
~$ mv postfix postfix-2.1.5
~$ cp -a postfix-2.1.5 postfix-2.1.5.orig
```

When the package maintainer tools are invoked, the **orig** directory is used to create an **orig.tar.gz** file (overwriting any existing **orig.tar.gz**) before writing the debianisation information to the **diff.gz** file. While this method seems useful, its main drawback is that it creates a new tarball file rather than using the upstream *original*. This is not really a serious problem, but Debian users prefer the **orig.tar.gz** file to have the same **MD5** sum as the file from the official **postfix** distribution sites. After all, it is called *orig*.tar.gz.

9.2.2   Investigating the upstream source tree

Before packaging a programme or a library (or anything else), it is advisable to have a good understanding of the source tree and the installed software. Ideally, you will already have installed the software to **/usr/local** with conventional methods and understand how the software's various parts and files work.

Let's return to the **gruezi** script. In the meantime, its author has released version 1.1, which adds a configuration file in which the user can select the languages in which to be greeted. Furthermore, it now reads the greetings from a resource file rather than hardcoding them into the script.

We are about to create a complete Debian package for the **gruezi** software, including a source package. Furthermore, once the package exists, we will split it into two halves, **gruezi** and **gruezi-common**, the latter of which installs the resource file. Before we undertake the endeavour, it is necessary to inspect the source tree of the software we want to package. This allows us to get used to the software and figure out places in need of modification.

gruezi 1.1 is released as a tarball, properly named as **gruezi-1.1.tar.gz**. Unfortunately, the author did not name the contained directory **gruezi**, so we have to manually rename it and have a look at its contents:

```
~$ tar xzf gruezi-1.1.tar.gz
~$ ls -F
gruezi/  gruezi-1.1.tar.gz
~$ mv gruezi gruezi-1.1
~$ cd gruezi-1.1
~/gruezi-1.1$ ls -F
LICENCE.SWISS  ChangeLog  Makefile  greetings
gruezi.1       gruezi.in  gruezi.conf
```

The package seems simple enough. The **gruezi.in** file contains a template for the **gruezi** script, which will be parsed and substituted at compilation time.

```
~$ cat gruezi.in
#!/bin/bash -e

# read the configuration data
test -f /etc/gruezi.conf && . /etc/gruezi.conf
test -f @prefix@/share/greetings && . @prefix@/share/greetings

[[ $GRUEZI_DE -eq 1 ]] && echo $GREETING_DE
[[ $GRUEZI_FR -eq 1 ]] && echo $GREETING_FR
[[ $GRUEZI_IT -eq 1 ]] && echo $GREETING_IT
[[ $GRUEZI_RR -eq 1 ]] && echo $GREETING_RR

exit 0
```

We note that the configuration file is expected to sit in /etc, which is fine. @prefix@/share/greetings suggests /usr/share/greetings, which is too common a name for a high-volume distribution such as Debian; we will install the resources file in a different location, although we are not making any changes at this point.

The configuration file is a simple shell snippet, which specifies default values for the four variables and thus allows the user to override the preferences with environment variables before invoking the **gruezi** command.

```
~$ cat gruezi.conf
GRUEZI_DE=${GRUEZI_DE:-1}
GRUEZI_FR=${GRUEZI_FR:-1}
GRUEZI_IT=${GRUEZI_IT:-1}
GRUEZI_RR=${GRUEZI_RR:-1}
```

The resource file is equally straight forward, even though it seems to be a configuration file rather than a static resource data file. We will leave it as it is though, partly to illustrate the installation process.

```
~$ cat greetings
GREETING_DE="Hoi zämme!"
GREETING_FR="Salut!"
GREETING_IT="Ciao!"
GREETING_RR="Allegra!"
```

A manpage is also provided in **gruezi.1**. In addition, the upstream tarball provides a simple **Makefile** which produces the **gruezi** script from its template and takes care of the installation of the software.

```
~$ cat Makefile
prefix ?= /usr/local

all: gruezi gruezi.1.gz gruezi.conf greetings
```

```
gruezi: gruezi.in
  sed -e "s|@prefix@|$(prefix)|g" < $< > $@

gruezi.1.gz: gruezi.1
  gzip -9 < $< > $@

install: gruezi gruezi.1.gz gruezi.conf greetings
  mkdir -p $(DESTDIR)$(prefix)/bin/
  install --mode=755 gruezi $(DESTDIR)$(prefix)/bin/gruezi

  mkdir -p $(DESTDIR)$(prefix)/share/man/man1/
  install --mode=644 gruezi.1.gz \
    $(DESTDIR)$(prefix)/share/man/man1/gruezi.1.gz

  mkdir -p $(DESTDIR)$(prefix)/share/
  install --mode=644 greetings \
    $(DESTDIR)$(prefix)/share/greetings

  mkdir -p $(DESTDIR)/etc/
  install --mode=644 gruezi.conf $(DESTDIR)/etc/gruezi.conf

distclean: clean
clean:
  rm -f gruezi gruezi.1.gz
```

Thus, a simple **make install** will install **/usr/local/bin/gruezi**, and issuing the command **make install DESTDIR=/tmp/gruezi** will install the file to **/tmp/gruezi/usr/local/bin/gruezi**. **make install DESTDIR=/tmp/gruezi prefix=/usr** would install the package to the **/tmp/gruezi/usr** hierarchy instead of the one rooted at **/tmp/gruezi/usr/local**.

If a package provides an installation mechanism capable of relocating the destination hierarchy through the use of $DESTDIR or similar, it can easily be debianised. Software that is to be packaged for Debian must be installable to a different hierarchy than /. The $prefix variable, which is used by many programmes (such as the ones using GNU autoconf), is *not* suitable for this relocation. $prefix defines the runtime location of the programme, while $DESTDIR specifies the path used for installation, which must not have any influence on the operations of the programme once installed.

In the case of **gruezi**, the Makefile provides the relocation functionality. If a software does not, you need to add it before you can package it. First, though, let's prepare the source tree for Debian-specific modifications.

9.2.3 dh_make

The Debian archive provides the **dh_make** tool to jump start the debianisation process in the package **dh-make**. It needs to be invoked within the unpacked source directory and places templates of the most important control files for the debianisation process into ./debian. The Debian Women project has published a guide on how to create packages without the use of a helper such as dh_make[1]. Before creating these files, dh_make duplicates the current directory for later creation of the orig.tar.gz. Alternatively, it can be told which tarball to use with the --file command line switch.

Debian source packages have various forms and functions. Some source packages generate a single binary package, others a set of packages encapsulating libraries. The binary packages generated by the source package and the distribution of files among these packages is controlled by the debianisation information under ./debian. dh_make knows how to bootstrap ./debian directories for four types of source packages:

single binary
> The result is a single binary package containing all relevant files and programmes built in the source tree.

multiple binary
> The results are multiple binary packages and the maintainer later decides which files will be distributed in which package.

library
> A library source package generates at least two binary packages, one containing the runtime data necessary to run programmes linked against the library, and one containing the development files needed to write programmes that will link against the library.

kernel module
> A kernel module source package generates a binary package installing the source of the kernel module on the target system in a way to allow for a binary package to be built against the running kernel.

Here is how to jump start debianisation of the postfix source tree. Although postfix is a little more complicated in real life, we'll build a single binary package for clarity and simplicity. The maintainer name and email address fields come from the $DEBFULLNAME and $DEBEMAIL environment variables respectively.

```
~$ tar xzf postfix-2.1.5.tar.gz
~$ cd postfix-2.1.5
~/postfix-2.1.5$ dh_make --file ../postfix-2.1.5.tar.gz
Type of package: single binary, multiple binary, library, or kernel modu
le?
 [s/m/l/k] s
```

[1] http://women.alioth.debian.org/wiki/index.php/English/BuildingWithoutHelper

```
Maintainer name : martin f. krafft
Email-Address   : madduck@debian.org
Date            : Thu, 22 Jul 2004 09:40:38 +0000
Package Name    : postfix
Version         : 2.1.5
Type of Package : Single
Hit <enter> to confirm:
```

The Debian source package is now pretty much ready for you to configure it appropriately. A .*/debian* directory has been added to the unpacked source tree, and the upstream tarball has been copied to the **orig.tar.gz** file appropriately and can now be deleted (if you want):

```
~/postfix-2.1.5$ cd ..
~$ ls -F
postfix-2.1.5/              postfix-2.1.5.tar.gz
postfix_2.1.5.orig.tar.gz
~$ rm postfix-2.1.5.tar.gz
```

Finally, if you inspect the **debian/changelog** file, you will notice that **dh_make** has appended the Debian revision to the upstream version number:

```
~$ cd postfix-2.1.5
~/postfix-2.1.5$ dpkg-parsechangelog
Source: postfix
Version: 2.1.5-1
Distribution: unstable
Urgency: low
[...]
```

It is also possible to debianise a software written specifically for Debian. Even though I said earlier that Debian-native packages do not need to be debianised, the .*/debian* directory must be present, and it must get there somehow. **dh_make** can help, and if you give it the **--native** option, it will not attempt to deal with **diff.gz** or **orig.tar.gz** files. Let us assume **moo** is your worthy addition to the Debian toolbox. Since the tool is useful only in the context of the Debian system, you create a Debian-native package:

```
~/moo-0.1$ dh_make --native

Type of package: single binary, multiple binary, library, or kernel modu
le?
 [s/m/l/k] s

Maintainer name : you
Email-Address   : you@yourdomain.net
Date            : Thu, 22 Jul 2004 09:48:12 +0000
Package Name    : bla
```

```
Version       : 0.1
Type of Package : Single
Hit <enter> to confirm:
```

Looking at the change log file, we note the absence of the Debian revision. A Debian-native package does not need to track two different components (upstream software and packaging logic) for a package but instead integrates the two:

```
~/moo-0.1$ dpkg-parsechangelog
Source: moo
Version: 0.1
Distribution: unstable
Urgency: low
[...]
```

The parent directory does not contain additional files since a Debian-native package does not need a **orig.tar.gz** file for later comparison and extraction of the debianisation changes.

A final word about **dh_make**: while the tool certainly has its merits, it is also somewhat problematic due to its "wizardry." There is nothing wrong with using it, simply because it provides convenient templates for most Debian files. However, as you start seeing the bigger picture and the purpose of each of these files, you might prefer to abandon **dh_make** for a while to ensure that you completely understand what is going on. Once you start getting the hang of the **./debian** directory, by all means, use **dh_make** (or whatever else) to make your life easier.

9.2.4   Building source packages

Before continuing, I suggest verifying that the **orig.tar.gz** file is recognised as such by the package maintainer tools. **dh_make** does try its best, but it never hurts to be sure:

```
~$ dpkg-source -b gruezi-1.1
dpkg-source: building gruezi using existing gruezi_1.1.orig.tar.gz
dpkg-source: building gruezi in gruezi_1.1-1.diff.gz
dpkg-source: building gruezi in gruezi_1.1-1.dsc
```

You will recognise these three files as the components of a Debian source package. Running the same command on **moo**, **dpkg-source** generates only the two files that make up a the Debian-native source package: there is no **diff.gz** file, and the tarball's name lacks the Debian revision and the **.orig** infix:

```
~$ dpkg-source -b moo-0.1
dpkg-source: building moo in moo_0.1.tar.gz
dpkg-source: building moo in moo_0.1.dsc
```

dpkg-source might decide to treat the package as a Debian-native source package. In such a case, the Debian revision will be part of the name of the tarball generated:

```
~$ dpkg-source -b bar-1.0
dpkg-source: building bar in bar_1.0-1.tar.gz
dpkg-source: building bar in bar_1.0-1.dsc
```

If this happens, dpkg-source has been unable to find the orig.tar.gz file in the current directory, and there is no orig directory along with the directory it should build. Before going on with the debianisation process, it is best to fix this problem by checking that the name of the orig.tar.gz file conforms with the name that dpkg-source expects. If the only change you made to the source tree was the addition of the ./debian directory, then you can also easily create an orig directory and let dpkg-source recreate the orig.tar.gz file:

```
~$ cp -a bar-1.0 bar-1.0.orig
~$ rm -r bar-1.0.orig/debian
~$ dpkg-source -b bar-1.0
dpkg-source: building bar in bar_1.0.orig.tar.gz
dpkg-source: building bar in bar_1.0.diff.gz
dpkg-source: building bar in bar_1.0.dsc
```

With this approach, be aware that you are creating a non-original orig.tar.gz file. In addition, any existing orig.tar.gz files take precedence over the method with the orig directory. Therefore, you must first delete the orig.tar.gz from the current directory, or it will be used and your orig directory silently discarded.

9.2.5   Jumpstarting with dh_make

The gruezi software seems manageable and we only require a small change to the location of the resource file to make it coexist peacefully with the other packages on any Debian system. We now fire up dh_make to give us access to the control file templates in ./debian and to put the orig.tar.gz file in place as a reference reference which will allow us to isolate the changes we are about to make as part of debianisation. The --single option tells dh_make to make a single binary package and skip the question.

```
~/gruezi-1.1$ dh_make --single --file ../gruezi-1.1.tar.gz
[...]
~/gruezi-1.1$ cd ..
~$ dpkg-source -b gruezi-1.1
[...]
~$ rm gruezi-1.1.tar.gz
```

After the call to dh_make, the upstream tarball can be deleted as shown; dh_make has copied it to gruezi_1.1.orig.tar.gz.

Now we are ready to make any necessary modifications to the source tree. If **Makefile** had refused to honour **$DESTDIR**, we would add this functionality now. We also change the resource file path in **Makefile** and **gruezi.in** to use **usr/share/gruezi/greetings** instead. All the modifications we make will later end up in the **diff.gz** file and are part of the set of changes needed to debianise **gruezi**. As a courtesy to the free software community and the software authors, you should make any useful changes (such as the **$DESTDIR** addition) available to the upstream author. The next release can then hopefully include the necessary functionality, allowing us to keep the **diff.gz** file as small as possible (which should be a goal).

Inspecting the ./debian directory

It is time for us to look at the templates **dh_make** put into **./debian**. The sheer number of these files may seem overwhelming at first sight. For now, however, we can safely ignore all files ending in **.ex** or **.EX**, which are examples of specific functions. For clarity, we will remove them for the time being.

```
~/gruezi-1.1$ cd debian
~/gruezi-1.1/debian$ ls -F
README.Debian   dirs                init.d.ex          preinst.ex
changelog       docs                manpage.1.ex       prerm.ex
compat          emacsen-install.ex  manpage.sgml.ex    rules*
conffiles.ex    emacsen-remove.ex   manpage.xml.ex     watch.ex
control         emacsen-startup.ex  menu.ex
copyright       gruezi-default.ex   postinst.ex
cron.d.ex       gruezi.doc-base.EX  postrm.ex
~/gruezi-1.1/debian$ tar cf /tmp/gruezi-exfiles.tar *.ex *.EX
~/gruezi-1.1/debian$ rm *.ex *.EX
~/gruezi-1.1/debian$ ls -F
README.Debian   changelog  compat  control
copyright       dirs       docs    rules*
```

That's a lot better. The **dirs**, **docs**, and **README.Debian** files are optional and we will return to them later. The other five are essential for the creation of a DEB file so let's take a look at them:

changelog

The **changelog** file fulfills two purposes. First, every Debian package must provide a **changelog** documenting the changes to the packaging. This file is later installed as **changelog.Debian.gz** in the package's documentation directory (under **/usr/share/doc**) and constitutes one of the most important resources of a package. Second, the **changelog** file is the *only* location specifying the current version number of the package. See chapter 9.2.7 for more information.

control

> To understand the point about the version number, it is necessary to compare the **control** file with the **control** file we manufactured when we built the **gruezi** binary package from scratch in chapter 9.1:

```
~/gruezi-1.1/debian$ cat control
Source: gruezi
Section: unknown
Priority: optional
Maintainer: Wilhelm Tell <hero@suisse.ch>
Build-Depends: debhelper (>= 4.0.0)
Standards-Version: 3.6.0

Package: gruezi
Architecture: any
Depends: ${shlibs:Depends}, ${misc:Depends}
Description: <insert up to 60 chars description>
 <insert long description, indented with spaces>
```

> You will immediately notice the difference. **debian/control** contains two stanzas where **./DEBIAN/control** only had one: the first stanza identifies the source package, while the second provides limited information about the **gruezi** binary package. The package maintainer tools will later create the appropriate **./DEBIAN/control** file by merging the information from various locations. The version number, for instance, will be pulled from **debian/changelog**.

compat

> Packages created with **dh_make** use the toolset provided by the **debhelper** package by default. These are among the highest-level scripts used to prepare packages for Debian and will be explored in chapter 9.2.11. For now, it suffices to say that the **compat** file simply contains a number identifying the compatibility level which the tools should assume (which is 4 currently). Let's ignore this file for the time being.

copyright

> Also required by the policy, the **copyright** file specifies all necessary information to identify the authors of the package, the upstream software, the location where the software may be found, and the licence information. Its format is not binding but should be adhered to. Licences may be pasted, or a file reference may be used to point to one of the standard licence texts installed under **/usr/share/common-licenses** by the **base-files** package.

rules

> The **rules** file controls the building of the package and serves as the central director for all packaging-related tasks. It is usually a **Makefile**, but can also be a script in a language such as **perl**, as long as it obeys the standard interface the package maintainer tools use to call it. It has to be executable.

The **rules** file dropped in place by **dh_make** makes extensive use of the **debhelper** tools, which is why the **control** file lists **debhelper** in the **Build-Depends** field. Packages listed here provide software needed to debianise the package, to which we will return shortly.

Instead of using the provided **rules** file, we will design our own in true bottom-up fashion. As mentioned, **debian/rules** is actually a **Makefile** and as such takes two types of arguments: variable assignments of the form VAR=VAL, and target names for **make** to process, which are given below. The **configure** and **install** targets are optional.

configure

> By calling the **configure** target of **debian/rules**, you are asking the software to configure itself for the running system. This stage usually finds library and tool locations and establishes essential parameters controlling the compilation, installation, and run-time process of the software. The classic candidate for this target is **GNU autoconf**.

build

> With this target, you are effectively instructing the software to build (or compile, or make) itself. This process usually involves transforming source files to their binary or processed counterparts: C files to executables or libraries, **docbook** files to their target format, *etc.*...

install

> The **install** target then takes care to install the software into the hierarchy rooted at **debian/<package>**. Here, <package> is the name of the first package listed in the **control** file. It may, however, be any name you like. Some packages, such as libraries jump started with **dh_make** use **debian/tmp** instead. It is not a bad idea to create that directory explicitly in case the upstream installation routine assumes its existence and fails otherwise.

> Every binary package generated by a source package gets one of those directories. When multiple binary packages are created, you can install everything into the first package's directory and then later move the files belonging to the other packages into their respective directories. Alternatively, a cleaner approach would be to install everything to **debian/tmp** and move the files into each of the generated packages' installation directories. We will use this approach when we split **gruezi** into two packages. It is generally not a good idea to modify the upstream installation procedure to install into the appropriate subdirectories directly.

binary-indep

> Debian binary packages are either architecture specific or usable on all ar-
> chitectures. The **binary-indep** target takes the necessary steps to build all
> architecture independent packages from the source tree.

binary-arch

> Along similar lines, **binary-arch** prepares all architecture dependent pack-
> ages for the local architecture.

binary

> This target simply combines the two **binary-*** targets and thus produces all
> binary packages the source package generates.

clean

> The **clean** target's job is to restore the source tree to exactly the state that ex-
> isted after unpacking the **orig.tar.gz** file and applying the **diff.gz** file. There-
> fore, it usually calls the **distclean** routine of the upstream software (*e.g.*
> **make distclean**), and cleans up any files created in ./debian during the build
> process.

9.2.6   Writing debian/rules

Let us pause for a second and recapitulate what we are trying to accomplish. We
saw at the beginning of this chapter how binary packages are built from scratch
(see chapter 9.1). A binary package consists of a directory containing the filesystem
footprint of the software to be installed, and the ./DEBIAN directory. Even though
we are now using higher-level tools to package a software, the actual wrapping
into a DEB file is still accomplished by **dpkg-deb**. Therefore, we need to install
the software into a temporary directory and place the correct files in the ./DEBIAN
directory within that temporary directory.

You may start to see the connection already. Earlier, I kept emphasising the importance of $DESTDIR, and this is exactly what we need it for. For now, let **de-
bian/gruezi** be the temporary installation directory. **make install DESTDIR=$(pwd)/
debian/gruezi** will install the **gruezi** programme in the installation directory thanks
to the upstream **Makefile**. Our main task now becomes to draft a **debian/rules** file
that will chain the calls to the upstream **Makefile** appropriately, and intersperse
the calls with any necessary additional instructions. We approach this task in three
phases. First, we need to design the install process. When that is done, we will
proceed to the actual package creation. Finally, when everything is working, we
will attack the cleanup process (which is important to get right).

Installing into a temporary directory

To design the **debian/rules** file, we will use "stamp files," a common approach when writing complex **Makefiles**. Essentially, a stamp file identifies completed stages in a process just like a stamp on a document in an institution.

First though, we need to move the existing **debian/rules** file out of the way. Let's start with the **build** target, which simply compiles the software. The **configure** target is included simply for completeness. We also specify a preliminary **clean** target to remove the stamps and call the upstream **distclean** target, which should restore the upstream source tree to its distribution state. Note that the commands are all given relative to the top-level directory of the source package, even though the **rules** file resides under ./**debian**.

```
~/gruezi-1.1$ mv debian/rules /tmp/gruezi-rules
~/gruezi-1.1$ cat <<"EOF" > debian/rules
#!/usr/bin/make -f

configure: configure-stamp
configure-stamp:
  # gruezi does not use autoconf
  # ./configure --prefix=/usr
  touch $@

build: build-stamp
build-stamp: configure
  $(MAKE) all
  touch $@

clean:
  $(MAKE) distclean
  rm -f configure-stamp build-stamp
EOF
~$ chmod +x debian/rules
```

And because that was simple enough, we immediately add the **install** target. The upstream tarball provides a file **ChangeLog**, which the **Makefile** does not install. Nevertheless, it is good practice to provide this information as part of the package. Therefore, we install it manually from the **install** target and compress it to comply with the policy (and to save space).

```
~/gruezi-1.1$ cat <<"EOF" >> debian/rules

DESTDIR=$(CURDIR)/debian/gruezi
install: build
  mkdir -p $(DESTDIR)
  $(MAKE) install prefix=/usr DESTDIR=$(DESTDIR)
  mkdir -p $(DESTDIR)/usr/share/doc/gruezi/
  install --mode=644 ChangeLog $(DESTDIR)/usr/share/doc/gruezi/changelog
```

```
  gzip -f9 $(DESTDIR)/usr/share/doc/gruezi/changelog
EOF
```

So far, so good. It does not hurt to verify the progress so far and to test the installation through the **debian/rules** file:

```
~$ debian/rules install
/usr/bin/make all
sed -e "s|@prefix@|/usr|g" < gruezi.in > gruezi
gzip -9 < gruezi.1 > gruezi.1.gz
touch build-stamp
mkdir -p debian/gruezi
/usr/bin/make install prefix=/usr DESTDIR=$(DESTDIR)
mkdir -p $(DESTDIR)/usr/bin/
install --mode=755 gruezi $(DESTDIR)/gruezi/usr/bin/gruezi
mkdir -p $(DESTDIR)/usr/share/
install --mode=644 greetings $(DESTDIR)/usr/share/gruezi/greetings
mkdir -p $(DESTDIR)/usr/share/man/man1/
install --mode=644 gruezi.1.gz $(DESTDIR)/usr/share/man/man1/gruezi.1.gz
mkdir -p $(DESTDIR)/etc/
install --mode=644 gruezi.conf $(DESTDIR)/etc/gruezi.conf
mkdir -p $(DESTDIR)/usr/share/doc/gruezi/
install --mode=644 ChangeLog $(DESTDIR)/usr/share/doc/gruezi/changelog
gzip -f9 $(DESTDIR)/usr/share/doc/gruezi/changelog
```

Under **debian/gruezi** ($(DESTDIR)), you should now find the filesystem footprint of the **gruezi** software with the additional **changelog.gz** file we installed by hand.

9.2.7 Modifying the debian/* files

Half of what we need is already in the temporary installation hierarchy rooted at **debian/gruezi**. Now we need to install the appropriate control files to **debian/gruezi/DEBIAN**. All the information we need for this is contained in the files within **./debian**. Even though **dh_make** has done a fabulous job at preparing these files as well as possible, there is no way around editing some of them.

The changelog file

The **changelog** file is an essential file for both the source and the binary package. It is also instrumental during the various stages of the package life cycle (see chapter 4.2). Let us look at the current **changelog** file for the **gruezi** package:

```
~/gruezi$ cat debian/changelog
gruezi (1.1-1) unstable; urgency=low

  * New upstream release.
```

```
   * First release using debhelper.

 -- Wilhelm Tell <hero@suisse.ch>  Sat, 18 Nov 1307 13:00:00 +0100

gruezi (1.0-1) unstable; urgency=low

  * The "Wer hat's erfunden?" (initial) release

 -- Wilhelm Tell <hero@suisse.ch>  Sat, 18 Nov 1307 12:00:00 +0100
```

The **changelog** file is composed of different stanzas, each corresponding to a specific Debian revision of a specific upstream release. The stanzas are listed in reverse chronological order in the file; that is, new entries are added at the top.

Each stanza consists of a number of fields which govern different aspects of the package or its handling. We can use **dpkg-parsechangelog** (from the **dpkg-dev** package) to parse the latest stanza into its component fields:

```
~/gruezi$ dpkg-parsechangelog
Source: gruezi
Version: 1.1-1
Distribution: unstable
Urgency: low
Maintainer: Wilhelm Tell <hero@suisse.ch>
Date: Sat, 18 Nov 1307 13:00:00 +0100
Changes:
 gruezi (1.1-1) unstable; urgency=low
 .
   * New upstream release.
   * First release using debhelper.
```

The source and version fields identify the source package name and current version number. The version number is used by all Debian packaging tools to create binary packages. The distribution and urgency define the path the package takes into and through the different releases in the Debian archive. In our case, **gruezi** is intended to go into the *unstable* archive of the Debian mirrors. An experimental package would specify *experimental* here. The urgency determines how quickly the package can percolate to *testing* (see chapter 4.3.2). The maintainer field is actually mislabelled, as it identifies the person making the change, who may not be the maintainer in the case of a NMU (see chapter 10.6.10). The date of each **changelog** entry must be strictly later than the previous entry's date.

As the **changelog** has strict syntax requirements, it is best edited with **debchange**, which you may find in the **devscripts** package. Simply invoking **debchange** (which is aliased to **dch**) adds a new entry to the current stanza. The **--increment** option causes the Debian revision to be incremented, and a new stanza to be created. Finally, the **--version** option allows for the specification of the full version string to use for a new stanza. In each case it is possible to specify the change message on the command line, as you will see shortly. If it is not specified, then **debchange** invokes an editor for interactive editing of the change message.

The copyright file

With the **changelog** file in place, we next inspect the **copyright** file, which contains a couple of placeholders that need to be filled in. Also, we paste the **LICENSE.SWISS** file from the source package at the bottom of **copyright**. The result should be the same (or similar) to the **copyright** file presented in chapter 9.1. Please remove the parentheses from "Author(s)", with or without the 's' as appropriate. Obviously, this is not an important point, but when we go off to have our packages verified (see chapter 9.2.15), we can avoid a warning by getting things right at this point.

The control file

Arguably the most important file is **control**, which provides all information about the source and binary packages associated with the software we are packaging. Again, **dh_make** has done a good job of providing a workable template, but the file needs a number of modifications before it is usable. Let us step through the fields top to bottom:

Source
: The source package name identifies the source package and does not have to (but can) be the same as the binary package it generates. In our case, we will leave it as **gruezi**, but there can be compelling reasons to choose a different name. For instance, **libs11n0** and **libs11n-dev** are the two packages that make up **libs11n** in Debian. Their source package is simply called **libs11n**.

Section
: Debian packages are categorised according to the area of application of the contained software. These categories are described in chapter 5.2.1. For our purposes, **misc** seems like the best choice. Source and corresponding binary packages may exist in different categories.

Priority
: The priority field determines the importance of the package with respect to a productive system. We choose the lowest priority for **gruezi** and use **extra** here. Chapter 5.2.2 has more information on these priorities. Source and corresponding binary packages may exist in different categories.

Build-Depends
: Debian packages depend on other packages for some of their functionality. Similarly, building a package requires software provided by certain packages.

These packages must be provided in this field, using the same syntax as for the **Depends** relation.

It is important to distinguish between the software needed to produce architecture-dependent and -independent packages. **Build-Depends** specifies those packages that need to be installed to build architecture-dependent packages. All packages necessary to build architecture-independent packages must be provided in a separate field, **Build-Depends-Indep**. Since the **gruezi** package is just a script and thus applicable to all architectures, we would have to use **Build-Depends-Indep** instead of **Build-Depends**.

Looking at the upstream **Makefile**, we note that it uses **sed** in addition to core utilities of the Unix operating system. Fortunately, we do not have to specify every package providing these. A number of packages are considered "build-essential" in Debian and may be omitted from the build dependency fields. **build-essential** provides a list of the files that a package maintainer may assume to be present on every Debian system in **/usr/share/buildessential/essential-packages-list**. In addition, the **build-essential** package depends on a number of other packages specifically needed for building packages, such as **dpkg-dev**. Neither the **build-essential** package nor any of its dependencies must be included in a package's build dependencies.

Since we are not (yet) using the **debhelper** utilities (see chapter 9.2.11, the build dependency on **debhelper** may be dropped. The **gruezi** package thus does not need either of the two build dependency fields.

Standards-Version
: This field identifies the last version of the policy, against which the maintainer verified compliance.

Package
: The package field denotes the beginning of a new stanza and identifies a binary package to be built from the source package. Its name should be chosen carefully to represent the function of the package. It is very difficult to rename packages at a later point in time.

Architecture
: Here, we can specify the architectures the package is supposed to support. The special term **any** instructs the Debian autobuilders to build the package on every supported architecture. **gruezi** is an architecture-independent package, which must be indicated with an entry of **all** in this field.

Depends
: **gruezi** does not depend on any other packages, therefore it does not need a **Depends** line (nor **Suggests**, nor **Recommends**, nor **Conflicts**). The ${shlibs:Depends} and ${misc:Depends} entries are used by the package maintainer tools to place automatically determined dependencies (via the debian/substvars file).

Description

The **Description** field consists of two parts. The first part occupies the first line and must be filled with a short description (up to 60 characters) of the package, which should preferably start in lowercase and not end with a punctuation mark. Do not repeat the package name in the short description. The packages' descriptions are used on the Web[2] as well as for the output of commands list **dpkg --list**, **apt-cache search** and **apt-cache show**.

Starting at the second line, you can provide a long description, which should adequately explain the function of the package[3]. All lines in the long description must be indented by at least one space. A new paragraph may be started after a line containing a single dot (`.`) following the indent.

With all these modifications, the final **debian/control** file looks like this:

```
Source: gruezi
Section: misc
Priority: extra
Maintainer: Wilhelm Tell <hero@suisse.ch>
Standards-Version: 3.6.1.1

Package: gruezi
Section: misc
Priority: extra
Architecture: all
Description: greets you the Swiss way
 gruezi is a simple script to greet its caller in all four
 languages spoken in Switzerland.
 .
 The languages are: German, French, Italian, and Romansch.
```

Other files

The last file we have not yet encountered is **README.Debian**, which can be used to communicate Debian-specific information with the package. If a server uses a non-default port in the Debian installation, it is worth documenting the fact in this file. If you do not need this file exists, you can simply delete it.

9.2.8 Creating the DEB file

Our next step is to populate the **debian/gruezi/DEBIAN** directory with the necessary control files, which are **control**, and **conffiles**. The **control** file is a different format from the one we just encountered. **dpkg-dev** provides the **dpkg-gencontrol**

---

[2]http://packages.debian.org
[3]A good reference may be found here: http://people.debian.org/~walters/descriptions.html

tool, which can create the binary package control file from the source package control data. We will also create the (optional) **md5sums** file. The content of **conffiles** is equally straight forward:

```
~/gruezi-1.1$ echo /etc/gruezi.conf >> debian/conffiles
```

With these three files in place, we can provide the **binary-indep** target (and the other **binary** targets, which are empty) to install them into **debian/gruezi/DEBIAN** and process the directory with **dpkg-deb**. In addition, the **debian/changelog** and **debian/copyright** files must be put in the proper place. Arguably, this can be done in the **install** target as well.

The **binary-*** targets should only be concerned with the creation of the binary package. Programmes like **dpkg-source**, or post-processing of the binary packages (*e.g.* **dpkg-genchanges**, which will be introduced in an instant) have no place in this target.

```
~/gruezi-1.1$ cat <<EOF >> debian/rules
binary: binary-arch binary-indep

binary-arch: install

binary-indep: install
  install --mode=644 debian/changelog \
    debian/gruezi/usr/share/doc/gruezi/changelog.Debian
  gzip -f9 debian/gruezi/usr/share/doc/gruezi/changelog.Debian
  install --mode=644 debian/copyright \
    debian/gruezi/usr/share/doc/gruezi/copyright
  gzip -f9 debian/gruezi/usr/share/doc/gruezi/copyright

  mkdir -p debian/gruezi/DEBIAN/
  cd debian/gruezi && find * -path DEBIAN -prune -o -type f -print \
    | xargs md5sum > DEBIAN/md5sums
  cp debian/conffiles debian/gruezi/DEBIAN/conffiles
  dpkg-gencontrol -isp -Pdebian/gruezi
  dpkg-deb --build debian/gruezi ..
EOF
```

This should build the package in the parent directory of the unpacked source tree, which we should verify. First though, keep in mind that we will need to finalise the **clean** target in **debian/rules** at a later point in time. Therefore, it is a good idea to store a file listing of the source tree at this point before the Debian tools prepare the package.

```
~/gruezi-1.1$ ls -R > ls-R
~/gruezi-1.1$ debian/rules binary
[...]
install --mode=644 debian/changelog \
```

```
  debian/gruezi/usr/share/doc/gruezi/changelog.Debian
gzip -f9 debian/gruezi/usr/share/doc/gruezi/changelog.Debian
install --mode=644 debian/copyright \
  debian/gruezi/usr/share/doc/gruezi/copyright
gzip -f9 debian/gruezi/usr/share/doc/gruezi/copyright
mkdir -p debian/gruezi/DEBIAN/
cd debian/gruezi && find * -path DEBIAN -prune -o -type f -print \
  | xargs md5sum > DEBIAN/md5sums
cp debian/conffiles debian/gruezi/DEBIAN/conffiles
dpkg-gencontrol -isp -Pdebian/gruezi
dpkg-deb --build debian/gruezi ..
dpkg-deb: building package 'gruezi' in '../gruezi_1.1-1_all.deb'.
```

Faking root rights: fakeroot

The DEB file in the parent directory encapsulates the **gruezi** package. However, one subtle problem remains. The files and directories a package installs are stored in a tarball within the DEB file. **tar** stores the ownership and permission settings for each file and directory, and these data are preserved when the package is unpacked. As you may have noticed, everything so far has been done as a normal user, *i.e.* without **root** rights. Therefore, the files belong to the current user and **tar** uses the current numeric user ID in its table of contents:

```
~$ dpkg --contents gruezi_1.1-1_all.deb
drwxr-xr-x user/group    0 2004-07-28 08:42:46 ./
drwxr-xr-x user/group    0 2004-07-28 08:42:46 ./etc/
-rw-r--r-- user/group  104 2004-07-28 08:42:46 ./etc/gruezi.conf
drwxr-xr-x user/group    0 2004-07-28 08:42:46 ./usr/
drwxr-xr-x user/group    0 2004-07-28 08:42:46 ./usr/bin/
-rwxr-xr-x user/group  401 2004-07-28 08:42:46 ./usr/bin/gruezi
[...]
```

This ownership constitutes a security problem. If **user** has User Identifier (UID) 1021 on the building system, then **tar** records 1021 as the owner of all contained files. When the package is later installed on another system, the local user with UID 1021 could write to *e.g.* /usr/bin/gruezi and thus potentially introduce a trojan horse or another form of malicious code.

The files stored in the **data.tar.gz** tarball of the DEB package should therefore be owned by **root**. However, only **root** can create a tarball with files belonging to UID 0. Hence, the packaging user has to attain **root** rights on the building machine, which is frequently out of the question. To address this problem, Debian provides **fakeroot**, which uses the dynamic Linux loader to pretend an effective UID and Group Identifier (GID) of zero to its children. The caller does not actually attain **root** rights, although the programmes that are called will assume otherwise. Obviously, however, no additional rights become available with this method:

```
~$ whoami
user
~$ fakeroot sh
~$ whoami
root
~$ touch testfile
~$ ls -Fl testfile
-rw-r--r--  1 root root 0 Jul 28 13:45 testfile
~$ cat /etc/shadow
cat: /etc/shadow: Permission denied
~$ exit
~$ whoami
user
~$ ls -Fl testfile
-rw-r--r--  1 user group 0 Jul 28 13:45 testfile
```

Still, the faked **root** identity is enough to trick **tar** into storing UID 0 as the owner of the files. Thus, we use **fakeroot** to call the **binary** target of **debian/rules**:

```
~/gruezi-1.1$ fakeroot debian/rules binary
[...]
~/gruezi-1.1$ dpkg --contents ../
drwxr-xr-x root/root   0 2004-07-28 13:45:46 ./
drwxr-xr-x root/root   0 2004-07-28 13:45:46 ./etc/
-rw-r--r-- root/root 104 2004-07-28 13:45:46 ./etc/gruezi.conf
drwxr-xr-x root/root   0 2004-07-28 13:45:46 ./usr/
drwxr-xr-x root/root   0 2004-07-28 13:45:46 ./usr/bin/
-rwxr-xr-x root/root 401 2004-07-28 13:45:46 ./usr/bin/gruezi
[...]
```

As an alternative, you are free to use **su**, **sudo**, or another similar tools. However, as these actually elevate rights[4] and are thus either infeasible or too dangerous — usage of **root** rights should be kept to an absolute minimum.

9.2.9   Cleaning the source tree

We are almost done. Before we can create the source package, we must restore the source tree to the state it was in after the debianisation process. Otherwise, files generated during the build or package creation process would become part of the **diff.gz** file, which is undesirable. Furthermore, since **diff** cannot represent changes to binary files, the creation of the source package is bound to fail:

```
~$ dpkg-source -b gruezi-1.1
dpkg-source: building gruezi using existing gruezi_1.1.orig.tar.gz
dpkg-source: building gruezi in gruezi_1.1-1.diff.gz
```

[4]In fact, since **debian/rules** is writeable, having *e.g.* sudo rights to execute the file as **root** means full **root** rights on the system.

```
dpkg-source: cannot represent change to
  debian/gruezi/usr/share/man/man1/gruezi.1.gz:
  binary file contents changed
[...]
dpkg-source: building gruezi in gruezi_1.1-1.dsc
dpkg-source: unrepresentable changes to source
```

Therefore, we must identify the files which have been added since debianisation. If the upstream **Makefile**'s **distclean** target (which we call from **debian/rules**' **clean** target) properly cleans the upstream source tree, the **ls-R** file we created earlier will serve as a good reference:

```
~/gruezi-1.1$ ls -R | diff ls-R - | grep '^>'
[...]
~$ rm ls-R
```

In addition to the temporary build directory, this tells us that the Debian tools added **debian/files**. This file serves as a registry for the binary files generated by the source package and needed for the **changes** file (see chapter 9.2.12). It is created dynamically and thus should not be distributed in the source package. Therefore, we remove it in **debian/rules**' **clean** target, which can now be specified fully:

```
clean:
  $(MAKE) distclean
  rm -f configure-stamp build-stamp
  rm -rf debian/gruezi
  rm -f debian/files
```

Now it is time to build the source package and verify the contents of the **diff.gz** file to make sure that it properly encapsulates the debianisation process:

```
~$ dpkg-source -b gruezi-1.1
dpkg-source: building gruezi using existing gruezi_1.1.orig.tar.gz
dpkg-source: building gruezi in gruezi_1.1-1.diff.gz
dpkg-source: building gruezi in gruezi_1.1-1.dsc
~$ diffstat gruezi_1.1-1.diff.gz
 Makefile             |  8    4 +    4 -    0 !
 debian/README.Debian |  6    6 +    0 -    0 !
 debian/changelog     | 11   11 +    0 -    0 !
 debian/compat        |  1    1 +    0 -    0 !
 debian/conffiles     |  1    1 +    0 -    0 !
 debian/control       | 15   15 +    0 -    0 !
 debian/copyright     | 13   13 +    0 -    0 !
 debian/dirs          |  2    2 +    0 -    0 !
 debian/rules         | 39   39 +    0 -    0 !
 gruezi.in            |  2    1 +    1 -    0 !
 10 files changed, 93 insertions(+), 5 deletions(-)
```

As you can see, the **diff.gz** file seems to describe exactly what we did to debianise the package: eight files were added under *./debian* and the two files **Makefile** and **gruezi.in** containing references to the **greetings** resource file have changed to reflect the new location of the file to prevent clashes.

9.2.10 Splitting and updating a package

A source package may generate multiple binary packages. For instance, the development files of a programming library are usually in a separate package than the runtime library itself, which means that programmes that depend on the library need not pull in the development files (which would be a problem if space was tight). Similarly, many source packages generate ***-common** packages for sets of files common to multiple packages. Finally, some packages split their functionality into multiple packages to allow subsets to be used by other packages. For example, **giftrans** needs some data provided by the **X Window System**, but instead of requiring a full **X** installation, it just depends on **xserver-common**, which provides the **X** data files independently of the actual software.

Let us assume that the greetings in the four Swiss languages are needed for another package. In this case, it would make sense to split off the data into a separate package so that the greetings could be used without requiring the installation of **gruezi**. Furthermore, to make things a little more interesting, note that the upstream author has released version 1.2 and rewritten **/usr/bin/gruezi** in C.

Thus, we prepare the new source tree with **dh_make** and remove the upstream tarball, which **dh_make** has copied to **gruezi_1.2.orig.tar.gz**:

```
~$ tar xzf gruezi-1.2.orig.tar.gz
~$ cd gruezi-1.2
~/gruezi-1.2$ dh_make --multi --file ../gruezi-1.2.tar.gz
[...]
~/gruezi-1.2$ cd ..
~$ dpkg-source -b gruezi-1.2
[...]
~$ rm gruezi-1.2.tar.gz
```

Note the use of the **--multi** flag to **dh_make**: this causes the tool to add a set of templates which cause the source package to generate multiple binary packages.

Identifying the packages

The two packages we would like to produce are **gruezi** and **gruezi-common**. The first contains a compiled executable and is thus architecture dependent, the second only provides a simple data file and is thus independent of the processor architecture. The following **control** file encodes the necessary information. Take special

note of the **Architecture** fields and the new dependency of **gruezi**. The special
${Source-Version} variable is replaced by the exact version of the package and
serves to ensure that the dependency is properly met.

```
~/gruezi-1.2$ cat <<EOF > debian/control
Source: gruezi
Section: misc
Priority: extra
Maintainer: Wilhelm Tell <hero@suisse.ch>
Standards-Version: 3.6.1.1

Package: gruezi
Section: misc
Priority: extra
Architecture: any
Depends: gruezi-common (= ${Source-Version})
Description: greets you the Swiss way
 gruezi is a simple programme to greet its caller in all four
 languages spoken in Switzerland.
 .
 The languages are: German, French, Italian, and Romansch.

Package: gruezi-common
Section: misc
Priority: extra
Architecture: all
Description: Swiss greetings
 gruezi is a simple programme to greet its caller in all four
 languages spoken in Switzerland.
 .
 The languages are: German, French, Italian, and Romansch.
 .
 This package provides the actual greetings in the four languages.
EOF
```

Distributing files across the packages

The first step is to decide how the files in the package are supposed to be split. For
the current task, this is quite easy.

File	Package
etc/gruezi.conf	gruezi
usr/bin/gruezi	gruezi
usr/share/doc/gruezi/copyright	gruezi
usr/share/doc/gruezi-common/copyright	gruezi-common
usr/share/doc/gruezi/changelog.Debian.gz	gruezi

Table 9.1:
Distribution of
gruezi's files among
two packages.

continued

File	Package
usr/share/doc/gruezi-common/changelog.Debian.gz	gruezi-common
usr/share/doc/gruezi/changelog.gz	gruezi
usr/share/doc/gruezi-common/changelog.gz	gruezi-common
usr/share/gruezi/greetings	gruezi-common
usr/share/man/man1/gruezi.1.gz	gruezi

The next decision is how to perform the split. While there are many possibilities, the most popular uses **debian/tmp** as the installation target for the upstream installation mechanism. Once the software has installed, a new temporary directory is made for each binary package and each file copied (or moved) from **debian/tmp** to the temporary directory of the package that is to contain that particular file. As this method is also the clearest, we will pursue it here. To do so, we need to modify the **install** target to use **debian/tmp** as target:

```
install: build
  mkdir -p debian/tmp/
  $(MAKE) install DESTDIR=$(CURDIR)/debian/tmp
[...]
```

Splitting the files is very simple because there are only two packages, one architecture-dependent and one architecture-independent. Therefore, each of the two **binary-*** targets produces exactly one package by copying the appropriate files from **debian/tmp** to separate temporary directories: **debian/gruezi** and **debian/gruezi-common**. These two directories are then prepared for **dpkg-deb**, and in the last step, the two packages are created from their respective temporary directories.

The **gruezi-common** package will be generated by the **binary-indep** target (since it is defined as architecture **all** in the **control** file) and the package should contain the **/usr/share/gruezi/greetings** file along with the change log and copyright information required by the policy. The target may look similar to the following. Note how **dpkg-gencontrol** is now passed the **-p** option to identify the binary package for which the **control** file should be generated.

```
GCDIR=debian/gruezi-common
binary-indep: install
  mkdir -p $(GCDIR)/usr/share/gruezi/
  cp -a debian/tmp/usr/share/gruezi/* \
    $(GCDIR)/usr/share/gruezi/
  mkdir -p $(GCDIR)/usr/share/doc/gruezi-common/
  cp -a debian/tmp/usr/share/doc/gruezi/* \
    $(GCDIR)/usr/share/doc/gruezi-common/

  install --mode=644 debian/changelog \
```

```
    $(GCDIR)/usr/share/doc/gruezi-common/changelog.Debian
  gzip -f9 $(GCDIR)/usr/share/doc/gruezi-common/changelog.Debian
  install --mode=644 debian/copyright \
    $(GCDIR)/usr/share/doc/gruezi-common/copyright

  mkdir -p $(GCDIR)/DEBIAN/
  cd $(GCDIR) && find * -path DEBIAN -prune -o -type f -print \
    | xargs md5sum > DEBIAN/md5sums
  dpkg-gencontrol -pgruezi-common -isp -P$(GCDIR)
  dpkg-deb --build $(GCDIR) ..
```

On the other hand, the gruezi package contains only the binary the upstream Makefile installed into debian/tmp/usr/bin/gruezi and the configuration file. It is defined architecture any in the control file and thus needs to be built by the binary-arch target. Since the change log and copyright information are the same as installed by gruezi-common and because gruezi depends on gruezi-common, we can link gruezi to /usr/share/doc/gruezi-common symbolically instead of copying the data again. Thus, the binary-arch target will look similar to this:

```
GDIR=debian/gruezi
binary-arch: install
  mkdir -p $(GDIR)/usr/bin/
  cp -a debian/tmp/usr/bin/* $(GDIR)/usr/bin/
  mkdir -p $(GDIR)/etc/
  cp -a debian/tmp/etc/* $(GDIR)/etc/
  mkdir -p $(GDIR)/usr/share/man/man1/
  cp -a debian/tmp/usr/share/man/man1/* \
    $(GDIR)/usr/share/man/man1/

  mkdir -p $(GDIR)/usr/share/doc/
  ln -s gruezi-common $(GDIR)/usr/share/doc/gruezi

  mkdir -p $(GDIR)/DEBIAN/
  cd $(GDIR) && find * -path DEBIAN -prune -o -type f -print \
    | xargs md5sum > DEBIAN/md5sums
  cp debian/conffiles $(GDIR)/DEBIAN/conffiles
  dpkg-gencontrol -pgruezi -isp -P$(GDIR)
  dpkg-deb --build $(GDIR) ..
```

Since we are using additional temporary build directories, we must take care to delete these in the clean target.

```
clean:
  [...]
  rm -rf debian/gruezi debian/gruezi-common debian/tmp
  [...]
```

Finalising and building the packages

Before the packages can be built, we need to document the new release in the **debian/changelog** file; this involves a sneak preview of **debchange** (aliased as **dch**), which you will meet again in chapter 9.2.7:

```
~/gruezi-1.2$ dch --version=1.2-1 -- New upstream release.
~/gruezi-1.2$ dpkg-parschangelog
Source: gruezi
Version: 1.2-1
Distribution: unstable
Urgency: low
Maintainer: Wilhelm Tell <hero@suisse.ch>
Date: Sun, 1 Aug 2004 14:00:00 +0000
Changes:
 gruezi (1.2-1) unstable; urgency=low
 .
   * New upstream release.
```

Now we can use **debian/rules** to build the two packages:

```
~/gruezi-1.2$ fakeroot debian/rules clean binary
[...]
dpkg-deb: building package 'gruezi'
  in '../gruezi_1.2-1_i386.deb'.
[...]
dpkg-deb: building package 'gruezi-common'
  in '../gruezi-common_1.2-1_all.deb'.
```

Et voilà, we have successfully moved the architecture-independent data file from **gruezi** into its own package. Whenever another software needs access to the four Swiss ways of saying hello, it can depend on **gruezi-common** instead of the whole **gruezi** application. The creation of the source package is described in chapter 9.2.4. Finally, we should test the software:

```
~/gruezi-1.2$ cd ..
~$ ls -F
gruezi-1.2/                 gruezi_1.2-1_i386.deb
gruezi-common_1.2-1_all.deb  gruezi_1.2.orig.tar.gz
~$ su
~# dpkg --install gruezi*1.2-1*.deb
[...]
Setting up gruezi-common (1.2-1) ...
Setting up gruezi (1.2-1) ...
~# exit
~$ gruezi
Hoi zämme!
Salut!
Ciao!
```

```
Allegra!
~$ GRUEZI_DE=0 GRUEZI_FR=0 gruezi
Ciao!
Allegra!
```

9.2.11   The debhelper suite

Overview

Unix is the operating system of scripts and automation. It is therefore unsurprising that most of the steps and functionality needed to create a binary Debian package have been further hidden behind more abstract and simpler interfaces. The most prominent of these interfaces is **debhelper**, which provides a plethora of small scripts to handle most aspects of packaging in an intuitive and consistent way. The tools are intended for use in the **binary-*** targets of **debian/rules**.

Most of the **debhelper** tools carry out some sort of action on a set of files within the temporary installation directory (**debian/gruezi** in the above example). Examples of such actions are copying, linking, and compressing files, making directories, and fixing permissions — in short, simple actions that should require no more than a line per file or set of files. Yet, the **debhelper** scripts further facilitate these actions. For instance, the **dh_installdocs** script knows the target location without the user having to specify it, and it automatically installs *e.g.* **debian/copyright**, **debian/README.Debian** (if present), and **debian/TODO** (if present). In addition, you can tell it to install additional documentation files (or directories) by specifying the file names (or patterns) in **debian/docs** or on the command line.

By default, the **debhelper** scripts act on the first package defined in **debian/control**. The **--package** option allows a different package to be specified by name, and **--arch** and **--indep** cause the scripts to act on all architecture-dependent and -independent packages respectively. In addition, the files read by the scripts (such as **debian/docs**) can also be linked with a specific package by prefixing the package name to the filename: **debian/<package>.docs** specifies the documentation files to be installed in the package build directory of **<package>**. A package-specific file takes precedence over the file without the package embedded in its name. Any files specified on the command line augment the set of files on which a certain action is performed. The same applies to automatically installed files. For instance, if a **debian/<package>.copyright** file exists, it is installed in **<package>** rather than **debian/copyright**.

The following **debhelper** scripts are worth mentioning:

dh_testdir
      simply checks for the presence of **debian/control** to ensure that the current directory is that of an unpacked Debian source package.

dh_testroot

> checks whether the calling process has **root** rights (which may be faked with fakeroot).

dh_install

> copies files into the package build directory. The syntax is equivalent to **cp** with the final argument being the destination. If only a single source file is given, **dh_install** tries to infer the target from the source location. **debian/<package>.install** may be used in addition to the command line. File paths must be given relative to the source package root directory. The **--sourcedir** option may be used to specify an alternate source root, *e.g.* debian/tmp.

dh_installdirs

> creates directories in the package build space. The directories may be specified on the command line in addition to **debian/<package>.dirs** files. Directory paths must be relative to the package build root and contain no leading slash, *e.g.* usr/bin. The file **debian/dirs** lists directories to be created in all packages.

dh_install*

> these specialised scripts provide additional intelligence for installing specific types of files, such as manpages, fonts, init scripts, and many others. Many of these scripts provide automatic and smart handling for the file types they install. In addition to the command line arguments, these scripts also read additional files or directories to act on from special files under ./debian, similar to **debian/dirs** and **debian/<package>.dirs**.

dh_link

> allows for the creation of symbolic links within the package build directories. The links are guaranteed to be policy-conformant. In addition to the command line, **debian/<package>.links** can specify pairs of links to be created. The file **debian/links** contains links to be created in all packages.

dh_compress

> compresses all files which the policy requires to be compressed when a certain size is exceeded. Here too, **debian/<package>.compress** may be used to specify additional files, as well as the command line.

dh_fixperms

> ensures that the files installed by the package have proper permissions and conform to the policy.

dh_shlibdeps

> calls **dpkg-shlibdeps** to determine the packages which provide libraries needed by binary executables in the package. It is sometimes necessary

to use the -l option to specify a search path for libraries provided by binary packages from the same source package. For instance, if a library **libgruezi** were to provide the Swiss greetings in the **libgruezi0** package, the **dh_shlibdeps** call in the target making the **gruezi** package might need to know where to look for the library: **dh_shlibdeps -ldebian/libgruezi0/usr/lib**.

dh_makeshlibs

generates the **shlibs** file to identify libraries as provided by the current package. The **shlibs** file will be registered with the package management tools to allow **dpkg-shlibdeps** to determine dependencies automatically.

dh_installdeb

installs the control files to the **DEBIAN** directory of the package build directory or directories. Files prefixed with the package name take precedence over those without the prefix. Thus, **dh_installdeb** would install **conffiles** into the **DEBIAN** directory of the first binary package in **debian/control** and **gruezi.conffiles** into the **DEBIAN** directory of the **gruezi** package build directory.

dh_gencontrol

creates the **control** file for the specified package, passing the -isp option along automatically and also handling the -P option nicely.

dh_md5sums

computes the **MD5** sums for the files in a package and writes the **md5sums** file.

dh_builddeb

calls **dpkg-deb** to build a DEB file.

dh_clean

cleans the source tree of temporary files created by the Debian tools. The **--keep** option causes the **debian/files** file to be left in place, which is necessary when building more than one binary package.

Furthermore, the scripts will not complain when they do not have anything to do. Therefore, other than a longer build time, having more **debhelper** scripts in the **binary-*** targets (and others) than necessary does not have any negative consequences. This feature allows **dh_make** to install a **debian/rules** template, whose **debian-arch** target calls most of the scripts. To make sure that the package can be built, **dh_make** also adds a build dependency on **debhelper** to the source package definition in the **debian/control** file it prepares for the new package.

When working with **debhelper** scripts, it is useful to keep in mind that these are regular programmes that can be run from the command line, even though you are more likely to encounter them in the context of the **debian/rules** file. Nevertheless, during the design process of **debian/rules**, as well as for its debugging, it may be useful to invoke a certain script directly. Telling it to be verbose and not actually perform any actions has its merits for **debhelper** apprentices and experts alike:

```
~$ dh_installdocs --verbose --no-act --arch ChangeLog
cp -a ChangeLog debian/gruezi/usr/share/doc/gruezi
chown -R 0:0 debian/gruezi/usr/share/doc
chmod -R go=rX debian/gruezi/usr/share/doc
chmod -R u\+rw debian/gruezi/usr/share/doc
install --group=root --owner=root --mode=644 \
  --preserve-timestamps debian/README.Debian \
  debian/gruezi/usr/share/doc/gruezi/README.Debian
install --group=root --owner=root --mode=644 \
  --preserve-timestamps debian/copyright \
  debian/gruezi/usr/share/doc/gruezi/copyright
```

In addition, the **$DH_OPTIONS** variable can be set as desired before invoking the **debian/rules** targets:

```
~$ fakeroot debian/rules binary DH_OPTIONS='--verbose --no-act'
[...]
```

Build dependencies and cleaning

Let's convert **gruezi** to a package using **debhelper**. First, we need to add **debhelper** to the **Build-Depends** field of the **gruezi** source package defined in **debian/control**. Since **debian/compat** specifies **debhelper** compatibility level 4, the build dependency should be a versioned build dependency: **Build-Depends: debhelper (>= 4.0.0)** to the source package stanza (the first one) of **debian/control**:

```
Build-Depends: debhelper (>= 4.0.0)
```

Working **debhelper** into **debian/rules**, we first add **dh_testdir** at the beginnning of each target to make sure that the **debhelper** scripts execute in the appropriate directory.

Following the **dh_testdir** call, the **binary-*** targets should call **dh_testroot** to make sure that the DEB file will be created with (faked) **root** rights[5].

In the **clean** target, we previously removed **debian/files** by hand. Now, it is time to use **dh_clean** in its place. You may notice the **dh_make** template to copy **config.guess** and **config.sub** into the source directory during the cleaning process. This

---

[5]Some of Debian's build daemons require the use of **sudo** instead of **fakeroot**. Since **sudo** actually gives **root** rights to the child process, files it creates will be owned by root. Therefore, the **clean** and **install** targets will also need to be run as root, and **dh_testroot** should be called here as well.

greatly facilitates the work of the Debian build daemons in case the software is using GNU autoconf. If you are not using GNU autoconf or do not intend to submit the package to the Debian autobuilders, you can safely remove these lines.

The clean target for gruezi (which does not use the GNU autotools) thus becomes:

```
clean:
  dh_testdir
  dh_testroot # only needed when not using fakeroot
  rm -f build-stamp configure-stamp
  $(MAKE) distclean
  dh_clean
```

If a source package generates multiple packages from different binary-* targets, dh_clean should also be used in the install target to ensure that no stray files from previous debhelper invocations remain. It is important to pass the --keep option to preserve debian/files across multiple calls to the install target. Finally

```
install: build
  dh_testdir
  dh_testroot # only needed when not using fakeroot
  dh_clean --keep
  $(MAKE) install DESTDIR=$(CURDIR)/debian/tmp
```

The install target

The install target of our manually written debian/rules file installed the upstream change log file in the temporary installation directory. With the debhelper scripts, it is better to let the respective binary-* target take care of this. Let us first rewrite binary-arch to use debhelper. The binary-arch target accomplishes the following steps:

- It installs the contents of usr/bin/, usr/share/man/, and etc/ to the package build directory of gruezi. We will use dh_install and the debian/gruezi.install file for this task. dh_install will receive the --sourcedir option to allow the specification of relative paths in debian/gruezi.install.

- It links usr/share/doc/gruezi to usr/share/doc/gruezi-common. This is the task of dh_link.

- It generates the md5sums file and installs it to the debian/gruezi/DEBIAN directory. dh_md5sums is made for this job.

- It installs debian/conffiles to debian/gruezi/DEBIAN. dh_installdeb handles this, although the debian/conffiles file is not needed anymore. Starting with debhelper compatibility mode 3, all files installed in /etc are marked as configuration files automatically. Hence, we can delete debian/conffiles.

- It generates the **control** file and installs it in the **debian/gruezi/DEBIAN** directory. This is the domain of **dh_gencontrol**.

- It builds the DEB file for the **gruezi** package. **dh_builddeb** takes care of this.

In addition, **dh_changelogs** will be used to install the change log files, and a later call to **dh_compress** ensures that files in the package are compressed as required by the policy. Version 1.2 of **gruezi** comes as a compiled executable and the policy requires executables to be stripped of debugging symbols. We can use **dh_strip** for this. Finally, we let **dh_fixperms** handle the permissions of the installed files.

The binary targets

The **debhelper** scripts act on all binary packages by default; for instance, **dh_compress** inspects all files in all binary packages specified in the **debian/control** file and compresses them if acceptable. For each script, it is possible to limit a script's action to a single package. Furthermore, all **debhelper** scripts can be told to act only on the architecture-dependent or architecture-independent packages.

The **gruezi** source package generates architecture-dependent and -independent packages. The commands in the **binary-arch** target should, however, only act on the **gruezi** binary package. We can tell the scripts to skip **gruezi-common** by specifically telling the scripts to work only on **gruezi** by passing the **--package= gruezi** option, or by restricting them to the architecture-dependent packages with **--arch**. The preferable method uses **--arch** and only resorts to **--package** when the scripts need to differentiate between various architecture-dependent packages.

Along similar lines, most **debhelper** scripts use files in *./debian* in addition to the command line arguments to identify files. For instance, **debian/gruezi.install** identifies the files that **dh_install** installs when acting on the **gruezi** package. Conversely, **debian/gruezi-common.install** lists the files destined for the **gruezi-common** package. Before we string together the **debhelper** scripts, we must therefore compose **debian/gruezi.install** to tell **dh_install** what to do. Within the file, wildcards may be used, or whole directories specified. The latter is fine for our purposes. We can also remove **debian/conffiles** at this point, since it will be generated automagically by **dh_installdeb**:

```
~/gruezi-1.2$ rm debian/conffiles
~/gruezi-1.2$ cat <<EOF > debian/gruezi.install
usr/bin
usr/share/man
etc
EOF
```

debian/gruezi.install basically identifies the parts within debian/tmp which are to be copied into debian/gruezi to become part of the gruezi package. With this file in place, we can design the binary arch target using the debhelper scripts:

```
binary-arch: install
  dh_testdir
  dh_testroot # we really need this here.
  # distribute the files according to debian/*.install
  # for all architecture-dependent packages
  dh_install --arch --sourcedir=debian/tmp
  # only create the link in the gruezi package
  dh_link --package=gruezi usr/share/doc/gruezi-common usr/share/doc/gru
ezi

  # the remainder is alike for all architecture-dependent
  # packages (if there were more than one)
  dh_strip --arch
  dh_compress --arch
  dh_fixperms --arch
  dh_installdeb --arch
  dh_gencontrol --arch
  dh_md5sums --arch
  dh_builddeb --arch
```

Glancing over the binary-indep target, we find that it takes the following steps:

- It installs usr/share/gruezi to the package directory. We let dg_install handle this based on the contents of debian/gruezi-common.install, similarly to the gruezi package.

- It installs the upstream change log as well as debian/changelog and debian/copyright to usr/share/doc/gruezi-common. dh_installchangelogs and dh_installdocs (which implicitly installs the copyright file) are perfect for this.

- It generates the md5sums file and installs it in the debian/gruezi-common/DEBIAN directory. dh_md5sums is made for this job.

- It generates the control file and installs it in the debian/gruezi-common/DEBIAN directory. This is the domain of dh_gencontrol.

- It builds the DEB file for the gruezi-common package. dh_builddeb takes care of this.

The gruezi-common.install file is a simple one-liner, since only one directory has to be installed in gruezi-common:

```
~/gruezi-1.2$ echo use/share/gruezi > debian/gruezi-common.install
```

This time around, we do not need **dh_strip** because an architecture-independent package contains no strippable binaries. Of course, it would not hurt if it were put in by accident. The **binary-indep** target will thus look similar to the following:

```
binary-indep: install
  dh_testdir
  dh_testroot # we really need this here.
  # distribute the files according to debian/*.install
  # for all architecture-independent packages.
  dh_install --indep --sourcedir=debian/tmp
  dh_installdocs --indep # implicitly installs the copyright file
  # install the debian/changelog file implicitly and
  # the upstream ChangeLog file explicitly
  dh_installchangelogs --indep ChangeLog

  # the remainder is alike for all architecture-independent
  # packages (if there were more than one)
  dh_compress --indep
  dh_fixperms --indep
  dh_installdeb --indep
  dh_gencontrol --indep
  dh_md5sums --indep
  dh_builddeb --indep
```

Finally, we bump up the package version to 1.2-2 and document the change to **debhelper** in **debian/changelog**:

```
~/gruezi-1.2$ dch --version=1.2-2 -- Switched to using debhelper.
~/gruezi-1.2$ dpkg-parsechangelog | grep ^Version
Version: 1.2-2
```

And now we can build the two packages (including the source package) and admire our work:

```
~/gruezi-1.2$ fakeroot debian/rules clean
[...]
~/gruezi-1.2$ cd ..
~$ dpkg-source -b gruezi-1.2
dpkg-source: building gruezi using existing gruezi_1.2.orig.tar.gz
dpkg-source: building gruezi in gruezi_1.2-2.diff.gz
dpkg-source: building gruezi in gruezi_1.2-2.dsc
~$ cd gruezi-1.2
~/gruezi-1.2$ fakeroot debian/rules binary
[...]
dh_testdir
dh_testroot # we really need this here.
dh_install --arch --sourcedir=debian/tmp
dh_link --arch usr/share/doc/gruezi-common usr/share/doc/gruezi
dh_strip --arch
```

```
dh_compress --arch
dh_fixperms --arch
dh_installdeb --arch
dh_gencontrol --arch
dh_md5sums --arch
dh_builddeb --arch
dpkg-deb: building package 'gruezi'
  in '../gruezi_1.2-2_i386.deb'.
dh_testdir
dh_testroot # we really need this here.
dh_install --indep --sourcedir=debian/tmp
dh_installdocs --indep # implicitly installs the copyright file
dh_installchangelogs --indep ChangeLog
dh_compress --indep
dh_fixperms --indep
dh_installdeb --indep
dh_gencontrol --indep
dh_md5sums --indep
dh_builddeb --indep
dpkg-deb: building package 'gruezi-common'
  in '../gruezi-common_1.2-2_all.deb'.
```

9.2.12   The changes file

We have succeeded in creating source and binary packages, using the **debhelper** suite. The last step is the creation of a **changes** file for the version of the Debian package we just produced. Unless the package is to be uploaded to the Debian mirrors, or your own archive administration tools require it, a **changes** file is not needed. For completeness, however, we produce it nevertheless.

The **changes** file is named similarly to DEB files except that it assumes the name of the source package, followed by the version number and Debian revision, and finally the architecture on which the package was built (which can be obtained with **dpkg --print-architecture**). There is no simple way of obtaining the filename except through some scripting. We will see in chapter 9.2.16 how the process of creating source and binary packages, and generating the **changes** file can be accomplished with a single command.

The content of the **changes** file is provided by **dpkg-genchanges** command run from within the source tree. Thus, we first determine the name of the **changes** file before filling it with the output of **dpkg-genchanges**:

```
~/gruezi-1.2$ SOURCE=$(dpkg-parsechangelog | sed -n 's/^Source: //p')
~/gruezi-1.2$ VERSION=$(dpkg-parsechangelog | sed -n 's/^Version: //p')
~/gruezi-1.2$ ARCH=$(dpkg --print-architecture)
~/gruezi-1.2$ CHANGES=${SOURCE}_${VERSION}_${ARCH}.changes
~/gruezi-1.2$ echo $CHANGES
gruezi_1.2-2_i386.changes
~/gruezi-1.2$ dpkg-genchanges > ../$CHANGES
```

```
dpkg-genchanges: not including original source code in upload
~/gruezi-1.2$ cat ../$CHANGES
Format: 1.7
Date: Sat, 18 Nov 1307 14:00:00 +0100
Source: gruezi
Binary: gruezi-common gruezi
Architecture: source i386 all
Version: 1.2-2
Distribution: unstable
Urgency: low
Maintainer: Wilhelm Tell <hero@suisse.ch>
Changed-By: Wilhelm Tell <hero@suisse.ch>
Description:
 gruezi      - greets you the Swiss way
 gruezi-common - Swiss greetings
Changes:
 gruezi (1.2-2) unstable; urgency=low
 .
   * Switched to using debhelper.
Files:
 2313b6756a31b1fa108f85a7ac21398b 289 misc extra gruezi_1.2-2.dsc
 3844e3ec3c5b82fa6230180983c4d1d5 2127 misc extra gruezi_1.2-2.diff.gz
 e3212d67175c7653e52fe870ec4f95f0 1554 misc extra gruezi_1.2-2_i386.deb
 2ed625a759cfe5f280434b99c763baa1 1756 misc extra gruezi-common_1.2-2_al
l.deb
```

The **changes** file specifies which file would need to be uploaded to the Debian archive. Even though the output of **dpkg-genchanges** refers to an upload, the command does not transfer any files. It only generates a list of files that are part of the current build. The tools used to make actual uploads to APT archives (see chapter 9.3.2) then use this list to select the files to transfer.

A build will always consist of the **dsc** and **diff.gz** files, and all DEB files built from the source package on the current architecture. The **orig.tar.gz** file is normally only included when the Debian revision is 1, which is used when a new upstream version has been released. The current version of **gruezi**, 1.2-2, does not include the **orig.tar.gz** file because the changes since 1.2-1 concern Debian packaging and thus the **orig.tar.gz** file is the same as the one produced for 1.2-1. For this reason, the **orig.tar.gz** file name does not include the Debian revision as there is exactly one **orig.tar.gz** file for each upstream version. The different Debian releases are encoded in the **diff.gz** file (which includes the Debian revision), relative to the **orig.tar.gz** file.

Assuming that the **orig.tar.gz** file for **gruezi** 1.2 has already been uploaded to a distribution mirror, the upload of 1.2-2 only replaces the Debian-specific files. The **orig.tar.gz** file can be included in the **changes** file forcefully with the -sa switch to **dpkg-genchanges**; -sd forces its exclusion:

```
~/gruezi-1.2$ dpkg-genchanges -sa
dpkg-genchanges: including full source code in upload
[...]
 2313b6756a31b1fa108f85a7ac21398b 289 misc extra gruezi_1.2-2.dsc
 e72edf8c1c3d5fb45ef7f0ae359af65b 1108 misc extra gruezi_1.2.orig.tar.gz
 3844e3ec3c5b82fa6230180983c4d1d5 2127 misc extra gruezi_1.2-2.diff.gz
 e3212d67175c7653e52fe870ec4f95f0 1554 misc extra gruezi_1.2-2_i386.deb
 2ed625a759cfe5f280434b99c763baa1 1756 misc extra gruezi-common_1.2-2_al
l.deb
```

9.2.13   Verifying new packages

Before the new DEB file(s) are distributed, you should test them locally to ensure that they are complete and work properly. **dpkg --contents**, allows you to verify the listing of files contain in each DEB file, and **dpkg --install** installs the software, allowing you to test maintainer scripts and operations of the programmes. This kind of verification is essential for the high quality which Debian packages are known to have.

Both of the aforementioned **dpkg** commands need the exact name of the DEB file to inspect. Unless you know the name and are willing to enter it on the command line (tab completion is your friend), you might need to look into the directory containing the file, obtain its name, and then pass it to **dpkg**.

The **devscripts** package contains two helpers which attempt to make the process of package verification easier: **debc** displays the control information and contents of binary packages, and **debi** proceeds to install them. Both tools accept the path to a **changes** file as an argument. In the absence of such an argument, the tools use **debian/changelog** to determine the **changes** file to use.

```
~$ fakeroot debian/rules binary
[...]
dpkg-deb: building package 'gruezi'
  in '../gruezi_1.2-2_i386.deb'.
[...]
dpkg-deb: building package 'gruezi-common'
  in '../gruezi-common_1.2-2_all.deb'.
~$ debc
gruezi_1.2-2_i386.deb
- - - - - - - - - - - - - - - - - - - -
 new debian package, version 2.0.
 size 1576 bytes: control archive= 562 bytes.
      17 bytes,      1 lines         conffiles
     367 bytes,     13 lines         control
     164 bytes,      3 lines         md5sums
 Package: gruezi
 Version: 1.2-2
 [...]
drwxr-xr-x root/root     0 2004-12-30 09:02:14 ./
```

```
drwxr-xr-x root/root     0 2004-12-30 09:01:56 ./etc/
-rw-r--r-- root/root   104 2004-12-30 09:01:56 ./etc/gruezi.conf
[...]
gruezi-common_1.2-2_all.deb
--------------------------
[...]
~$ sudo debi
[...]
Setting up gruezi-common (1.2-2) ...
Setting up gruezi (1.2-2) ...
```

You will notice that **debi** is invoked with **sudo**; as it installs the packages on the local system, **root** access is required. Internally, **debi** uses **debpkg**, a wrapper which obtains **root** rights before installing the requested packages. As an alternative to using **sudo**, you can also make this wrapper **setuid root**. You should be aware that access to **debpkg** as **root**, whether via **sudo** or due to the **setuid** bit, could easily be exploited by users to obtain full **root** access to the whole system. Therefore, ensure that only trusted users are able to use the wrapper. The **setuid** bit should be configured with **dpkg-statoverride** (see chapter 6.1.2):

```
~# dpkg-statoverride --update --add root root 4754 /usr/bin/debpkg
~$ debi
[...]
```

In the following, I will assume that **debi** has been installed **setuid**.

By default, the tools operate on all binary packages listed in the **changes** file, unless the names of the binary packages to verify have been passed on the command line. Thus, if you only wanted to inspect the contents of **gruezi**, you could let **debc** know:

```
~$ debc gruezi
[...]
```

The two tools can be invoked anywhere within the package's source tree. To do their job, they iteratively move up the hierarchy until a **debian/changelog** file is found. To guard against problems or unwanted behaviour, both then check the name of the directory containing the **debian** subdirectory, and verify that it corresponds to the name of the current source package. This behaviour can be controlled with the $DEVSCRIPTS_CHECK_DIRNAME_LEVEL environment variable, or the --check-dirname-level command line option, which can take the values of 0, 1, and 2 to prevent checking, require checking only if the hierarchy has to be navigated, or always check the directory name respectively.

Another variable, $DEVSCRIPTS_CHECK_DIRNAME_REGEX (or command line option --check-dirname-regex) is used to specify the regular expression a package must match. It defaults to PACKAGE(-.*)?, where PACKAGE is replaced by the name of the source package name automatically.

Both options can also be set in the **devscripts** configuration file, which is explained in detail in devscripts.conf (5).

9.2.14 Signing the package files

If you intend to submit a package to the Debian archive, you have to cryptographically sign some of the component files so that the Debian archive tools can verify the integrity of the package after the upload. Also, since only Debian developers may upload packages to the official archive, the Debian tools can use the signature to verify the package's origin. Nevertheless, even if you simply intend to make the package available from your own server, signing the source package gives your users a means of ensuring that the package they are installing really is the package you produced. You obviously need a **GnuPG** key for that[6].

The two files to sign are the **dsc** file and the **changes** file. The first identifies the files making up the source package while the second includes the **MD5** sums of the binary packages (and thereby identifies them) as well.

Manually signing packages

The standard means to sign is **GnuPG**, and the signature should be clear-text ASCII and embedded in the file. The following command produces a **dsc** file with an embedded signature.

```
~$ gpg --armor --clearsign --textmode gruezi_1.2-2.dsc

You need a passphrase to unlock the secret key for
user: "Wilhelm Tell <hero@suisse.ch>"
1024-bit DSA key, ID B27C9467, created 1307-11-18

Enter passphrase:
~$ mv gruezi_1.2-2.dsc.asc gruezi_1.2-2.dsc
```

The **changes** file includes the **MD5** sum of the **dsc** file, which will change because of the signing. This makes it necessary to rerun **dpkg-genchanges** after signing the **dsc** file (or to sign the **dsc** file before running **dpkg-genchanges** in the first place).

---

[6]which <advocacy>everyone should have these days anyway</advocacy>

Using debsign

With the **devscripts** package comes the handy **debsign** utility, which automates the process of signing packages. At the same time, it addresses a shortcoming of the manual (and traditional) method described above: the package must be signed on the machine where the package was built, because the **changes** file includes the **MD5** sum of the **dsc** file. If the machine used to build the package does not hold the **GnuPG** key to be used for signing[7], the **dsc** has to be transferred to the local machine (where the key resides), signed, sent back to the building machine, then the **changes** file needs to be created and also signed locally.

As this process can become quite tedious, **debsign** provides an improved signing mechanism. It replaces the **MD5** sum of the **dsc** file in the **changes** file after signing and can automatically call another machine (via SSH) to do the signing. Alternatively, signing can be invoked on the local machine, fetching the two files from the building machine. Obviously, signing on the building machine is also supported:

```
~$ debsign gruezi_1.2-2_i386.changes
[...]
Successfully signed dsc and changes files
```

Assuming the files reside in ~/deb/gruezi on the remote building machine, **debsign** can be used locally to retrieve, sign, and store them remotely.

```
local:~$ debsign -r user@remote    deb/gruezi/gruezi_1.2-2_i386.changes
[...]
```

To push the files to another machine (**local**) for signing, **debrsign** may be used:

```
~$ debrsign user@local gruezi_1.2-2_i386.changes
[...]
```

9.2.15   Checking packages

Even though there is no magic behind the creation of DEB files (as I hope to have shown), there are a lot of rules to obey and potential pitfalls. As illustrated in chapter 5.7, one of Debian's core strengths is its adherence to a strict set of rules. Therefore it is paramount to check a package following its creation. The two tools **lintian** and **linda** serve this purpose. While **lintian** is likely to be the more popular (and features more tests since it has been around longer), **linda** runs faster and is easier to extend.

[7]The GnuPG key should never be stored in a place accessible by others. This includes machines managed by other people as they can become **root** and steal the key

Both can check a binary package, a source package, or the source package and all its associated binary packages by invoking the tool against the DEB file, the **dsc** file, or the **changes** file respectively. The **--info** option allows you to display verbose information for tests that fail. The tools spit out warnings and errors.

For instance, as I have forgotten to add the versioned build dependency on **debhelper 4**, **lintian** complains about this error:

```
~$ lintian --info gruezi_1.2-2_i386.changes
E: gruezi source: package-lacks-versioned-build-depends-on-debhelper 4
N:
N:    If a package sets debhelper's compatibility version to >= 1,
N:    either via DH_COMPAT, or via debian/compat, or via
N:    dh_testversion (which is deprecated), it must declare a versioned
N:    Build-Depends on the needed version of debhelper.
N:
```

Generally, a package should be free of **lintian** errors, and the warnings should be minimised if not completely eradicated. A package without any **lintian** errors or warnings is called lintian-clean. Since **linda** provides some checks that **lintian** does not (and *vice versa*), it may be a good idea to run both against the final package. While it is still possible for lintian-clean and linda-clean packages to not conform with the policy, the chances for such offences are minimised by consistent use of the checking tools.

At times, **lintian** or **linda** may report false alarms, or a package's nature might cause one or two tests to fail. If this is the case, the package maintainer may override any number of tests with **override** files to be included with the package.

9.2.16   Automating the package build

Following the development of a **debian/rules** file, the steps for building a Debian package are as follows:

1. Rid the source tree of all temporary files associated with compiling or building the package. This should be accomplished by the **clean** target of **debian/rules**.

2. Run **dpkg-source** in the parent directory to create the **diff.gz** file (for non-native packages), or the **tar.gz** file for Debian-native packages.

3. Build the software contained in the package with the **build** target.

4. Create the binary packages by calling the **binary** target.

5. Sign the **dsc** file.

6.   Generate and sign the **changes** file.

7.   Verify the package with **lintian** (and/or **linda**).

Debian would not be Debian if it did not provide at least one means of automating the process. In fact, it provides at least two: **dpkg-buildpackage** and **debuild**, which enhances the former.

dpkg-buildpackage

The **dpkg-buildpackage** tool is the basic package building tool and provides an integrated interface to the various tools used in the process: targets in **debian/rules**, **dpkg-source**, and **dpkg-genchanges**. Finally, it signs the **dsc** and **changes** file.

Signing requires a GPG key, as previously noted. **dpkg-buildpackage** will obtain the identity of the person making the last changes from **debian/changelog** and instruct **GnuPG** to select the appropriate key from its keyring. Depending on your configuration and the situation (*e.g.* when sponsoring someone else's packages), it may be necessary to use the -k option to specify the ID of the **GnuPG** key to use for signing. Alternatively, **-us** and **-uc** can be used to skip signing the **dsc** and **changes** file respectively.

```
~$ dpkg-buildpackage -rfakeroot
dpkg-buildpackage: source package is gruezi
dpkg-buildpackage: source version is 1.2-2
dpkg-buildpackage: source maintainer is Wilhelm Tell <hero@suisse.ch>
dpkg-buildpackage: host architecture is i386
 fakeroot debian/rules clean
/usr/bin/make distclean
[...]
 dpkg-source -b gruezi-1.2
dpkg-source: building gruezi using existing gruezi_1.2.orig.tar.gz
dpkg-source: building gruezi in gruezi_1.2-2.diff.gz
dpkg-source: building gruezi in gruezi_1.2-2.dsc
 debian/rules build
[...]
 fakeroot debian/rules binary
[...]
dpkg-deb: building package 'gruezi'
  in '../gruezi_1.2-2_i386.deb'.
[...]
dpkg-deb: building package 'gruezi-common'
  in '../gruezi-common_1.2-2_all.deb'.
[...]
 signfile gruezi_1.2-2.dsc
[...]
 dpkg-genchanges
dpkg-genchanges: not including original source code in upload
```

```
signfile gruezi_1.2-2_i386.changes
[...]
dpkg-buildpackage: binary and diff upload (original source NOT included)
```

The parent directory now contains all files related to the complete Debian **gruezi** package. However, the **changes** file only lists the DEB, **dsc**, and **diff.gz** files as part of the build. The **orig.tar.gz** file is not included since the build's Debian revision is larger than 1. It is assumed that the **orig.tar.gz** file was uploaded as part of the build corresponding to the -1 Debian release and is hence already present in the archive (see chapter 9.2.12). Therefore, the upload tools (see chapter 9.3.2) will not upload the **orig.tar.gz** as part of the build identified by the **changes** file.

```
~$ ls -F
gruezi-1.2/                  gruezi_1.2-2_all.deb
gruezi_1.2-2_i386.changes    gruezi_1.2-2.diff.gz
gruezi_1.2.orig.tar.gz       gruezi_1.2-2.dsc
```

debuild

debuild enhances **dpkg-buildpackage** in subtle ways. First, it uses **debsign** instead of the signing functions of **dpkg-buildpackage**. Second, it has the ability to automatically run **lintian** and/or **linda**, and third, it can be configured via configuration files and a plethora of environment variables. Finally, it writes the output of the build process to a file for later reference and assumes **fakeroot** by default, unless overridden with **--rootcmd**. **debuild** is available as part of the **devscripts** package.

The build process is largely the same as with **dpkg-buildpackage**:

```
~/gruezi-1.2$ debuild
dpkg-buildpackage: source package is gruezi
dpkg-buildpackage: source version is 1.2-2
dpkg-buildpackage: source maintainer is Wilhelm Tell <hero@suisse.ch>
dpkg-buildpackage: host architecture is i386
[...]
dpkg-buildpackage: binary and diff upload (original source NOT included)
Now running lintian...
E: gruezi source: package-lacks-versioned-build-depends-on-debhelper 4
Finished running lintian.
Now signing changes and any dsc files...
 signfile gruezi_1.2-2.dsc B27C9467
[...]
 signfile gruezi_1.2-2_i386.changes B27C9467
[...]
successfully signed dsc and changes files
```

9.3   Local APT repositories

As you build your custom Debian packages, the need for an **APT** repository for their distribution will arise. Obviously, the DEB files can be copied around and manually installed with **dpkg**, but when multiple machines enter the picture, this becomes quite tedious.

Setting up an **APT** repository is a trivial task. Whether the **APT** access method is HTTP, FTP, or any other of the supported means, the structure of the directories within the repository is always the same. Essentially, an **APT** repository is a directory (or a directory hierarchy) containing Debian binary and source packages, and providing **Packages** and **Sources** indices for APT's use. The main tool to create these indices is **apt-ftparchive**.

9.3.1   Anatomy of a personal repository

There is no stringent requirement for the directory layout of an **APT** repository. APT only needs to find the **Packages** and/or **Sources** file, which contain the relative paths to the actual data files. **APT** does not mind whether the layout uses a pool structure like the official Debian mirrors, or all files are in the same directory.

For **gruezi**, we set up a ˜/apt directory and put the **gruezi** package into the directory. This layout scales well to several dozens of packages. For our purposes, we will assume that the directory is accessible via HTTP at **http://server/apt**.

The repository will serve as a binary and source repository. Furthermore, since expect anticipate it to contain more than **gruezi** in the future, we will put all of **gruezi**'s files into a subdirectory. The **gruezi** package consists of six files: the two DEB files, the source package made up of the **dsc** file, the **orig.tar.gz** file, and the **diff.gz** file, and finally, the **changes** file. All of these can live in the same directory:

```
˜/apt$ mkdir gruezi
˜/apt$ cpio -p gruezi/
˜/gruezi/gruezi_1.2-2.diff.gz
˜/gruezi/gruezi_1.2-2.dsc
˜/gruezi/gruezi_1.2.orig.tar.gz
˜/gruezi/gruezi_1.2-2_i386.deb
˜/gruezi/gruezi-common_1.2-2_all.deb
˜/gruezi/gruezi_1.2-2_i386.changes
```

And now we create the indices, in addition to the **Contents** file, for completeness:

```
˜/apt$ apt-ftparchive packages . > Packages
˜/apt$ gzip -9 < Packages > Packages.gz
˜/apt$ apt-ftparchive sources . > Sources
˜/apt$ gzip -9 < Sources > Sources.gz
```

```
~/apt$ apt-ftparchive contents . > Contents
~/apt$ gzip -9 < Contents > Contents.gz
```

In addition, it is a good idea to provide a signed **Release** file, especially in the light of the upcoming integration of package signatures into the APT utilities (see chapter 7.5). For this, we need to create a configuration file in the same style as **apt.conf** (see chapter 5.4.2). I choose to make a separate file, but the configuration options could just be added to **/etc/apt/apt.conf**:

```
~/apt$ cat <<EOF > apt-ftparchive.conf
APT {
  FTPArchive {
    Release {
      Origin "Wilhelm Tell";
      Label "Wilhelm Tell";
      Suite custom;
      Codename helvetia;
      Architectures i386;
      Description "Unofficial Debian packages by Wilhelm Tell";
    }
  }
}
EOF
```

The **Release** file contains the **MD5** (and **SHA1**) hashes for the **Packages** and **Sources** files, which in turn contain the MD5 sums for the package files. Thus, by creating and providing a (detached) signature, we allow people accessing our repository to verify the integrity and origin of the packages. Future versions of APT will do so automatically (see chapter 7.5.2).

```
~/apt$ apt-ftparchive --config-file=apt-ftparchive.conf \
  release . > Release
~/apt$ gpg -b -o Release.gpg Release
[...]
```

The APT repository is now prepared. After adding the necessary lines to **/etc/apt/ sources.list**, it is back to business as usual:

```
~# cat <<EOF >> /etc/apt/sources.list
deb      http://server/apt ./
deb-src http://server/apt ./
EOF
~# apt-get update
[...]
Get:1 http://server ./ Release
Get:2 http://server ./ Packages [977B]
Get:3 http://server ./ Sources [385B]
[...]
```

```
~$ apt-cache show gruezi
Package: gruezi
[...]
Version: 1.2-2
Depends: gruezi-common (= 1.2-2)
Filename: ./gruezi/gruezi_1.2-2_i386.deb
[...]
```

As a side note, an interesting option to set in the **Release** file is **NotAutomatic**. Setting it to yes suggests to APT on the client machines that the contained packages of this release are to be treated with lowest priority.

```
~/apt$ echo NotAutomatic: yes >> ./Release
~/apt$ gpg -b -o Release.gpg Release
```

This causes APT to pin all packages from the release at 1, unless overridden with a manual pinning. The effect is that packages from a release marked in this way are never considered for automatic upgrades. For more information on pinning, please see chapter 8.2.1.

As a final note, it is also possible to nest APT archives. If **apt-ftparchive** is properly run in the **gruezi** directory, **http://server/apt/gruezi** becomes its own APT archive. This may be useful if your personal repository contains a larger number of packages and you want to give APT access to only single packages. My repositories at **http://debian.madduck.net/~madduck/packages** use this technique, making it possible to include *e.g.* the entire staging area (/~madduck/packages/stage), or only a single package (/~madduck/packages/stage/libhid). Both are fully-fledged APT archives, and the former includes the latter. As you would expect, however, the latter only provides access to **libhid**.

9.3.2   Upload tools

The steps required to upload files to a personal repository are few but tedious. Unsurprisingly, thus, tools exist to facilitate the process and provide useful additional features. **dupload** and **dput** are the two commonly used programmes to copy all files of a package into a repository, local or remote. Both can use different methods for the upload, including FTP and SSH. **dput** seems to be the more actively maintained of the two and has some interesting features in comparison to **dupload**. Nevertheless, both accomplish the same task in similar ways and feel more or less the same to the user.

In its simplest form, **dput** is invoked on a **changes** file. The **changes** file lists all components of a package (see chapter 9.2.12), and **dput** uses this list to determine the upload candidates. As such, an upload will usually encompass the source package (the **dsc**, **diff.gz**, and **orig.tar.gz** files), all binary packages generated from the source package[8], as well as the **changes** file itself.

dput reads the parameters governing an upload to a certain archive from configuration files. These files contain stanzas of hosts, identified by the canonical upload target name. The default upload target is the main Debian upload queue, which is only usable by developers (as the package has to be signed with a Debian developer key). Moreover, even with developer status, one should be careful using the default because it can be difficult to undo errors once automatic processing of packages in the upload queue has assumed control over a package's files. Therefore, it is not a bad idea to redefine the default to be your own repository. If the final destination of the package is the official Debian archive, it is trivial to specify the upload queue to be used with an extra argument.

In ~/.dput.cf, we can create a stanza for our local upload queue, canonically named "personal" and define it to be the default for uploads to the main Debian archive (not the *main* section of the archive, but the main archive as opposed to the *non-US* partition):

```
~$ cat <<EOF >> ~/.dput.cf
[DEFAULT]
default_host_main = personal

[personal]
method = local
incoming = ~/apt/incoming
EOF
~$ mkdir -p ~/apt/incoming
```

Now, the package can be uploaded using **dput**. Note that the **orig.tar.gz** file is not part of the upload. This is because we uploaded Debian revision 2 and since the **orig.tar.gz** file is the same as it was when revision 1 was uploaded, it is assumed to already reside at the target location. The **-sa** parameter to **dpkg-genchanges** overrides this assumption, as shown in chapter 9.2.12.

```
~$ dput gruezi_1.2-2_i386.changes
Upload package to host apt
Checking Signature on .changes
gpg: Signature made Fri Jul 30 13:28:00 2004 CEST using DSA key ID B27C9
467
gpg: Good signature from "Wilhelm Tell <hero@suisse.ch>"
Good signature on /home/madduck/gruezi/gruezi_1.2-2_i386.changes.
Checking Signature on .dsc
```

[8]For official uploads, the Debian autobuilders seem to make it unnecessary to upload the binary files too. However, aside from the load reduction, the requirement to upload binary files to the archive simply forces the uploader to verify the debianisation of a software at least up to the point of the successful DEB file creation

```
gpg: Signature made Fri Jul 30 13:27:58 2004 CEST using DSA key ID B27C9
467
gpg: Good signature from "Wilhelm Tell <hero@suisse.ch>"
Good signature on /home/madduck/gruezi/gruezi_1.2-2.dsc.
Successfully uploaded packages.
Not running dinstall.
~$ ls -F ~/apt/incoming
gruezi-common_1.2-2_all.deb   gruezi_1.2-2.dsc
gruezi_1.2-2_i386.deb         gruezi_1.2-2.diff.gz
gruezi_1.2-2_i386.changes
```

Similarly, we could define a **dput** stanza for a repository on a remote, SSH-accessible host, and use **scp** for the transfer. To tell **dput** to use this host instead of the default, we would specify the canonical name as the first argument:

```
~$ cat <<EOF >> ~/.dput.cf
[remote]
method = scp
fqdn = the.remote.server
login = username
incoming = ~/apt/incoming
EOF
~$ dput remote gruezi_1.2-2_i386.changes
[...]
```

The target directory is the **incoming** directory below the **APT** repository. Following the upload, we need to move the files to the **gruezi** directory of the repository before updating the indices. Alternatively, we could define a different stanza for each package and use the package directory (if applicable to the repository structure) directly for each package. Obviously, this will quickly get out of hand. With a small number of packages, another approach would be the use of a single directory for all files of all packages.

Once the package files are at their final location, we can update the indices. Given a script ~/apt/reindex.sh which calls **apt-ftparchive** appropriately, we can tell **dput** to automatically invoke this script following the upload by specifying a hook in the stanza of our personal repository in ~/.dput.cf.

```
[personal]
method = local
incoming = ~/apt/incoming
post_upload_command = ~/apt/reindex.sh
```

9.3.3   Automated repository management

As soon as your personal repository becomes an integral part of your Debian system management, it is worth taking a look at some of the tools that Debian provides for the management of personal archives. The Debian archives are managed by dinstall, but its complexity certainly overshoots the mark for a personal repository. Several tools are better suited for use in a smaller, unofficial archive.

mini-dinstall

mini-dinstall sports two modes of operation: manual (batch) processing, and daemon mode. Both modes process changes files (and the other files belonging to the referenced package), move them to the appropriate location in the repository (while removing files associated with an older version of the package), and update the indices. For normal requirements, batch mode is usually fine. If a repository often changes, or if uploads come from multiple sources, it might be a good idea to daemonise mini-dinstall. It will then continually check the configured incoming directory and process files as soon as they come in.

mini-dinstall requires a configuration file and uses ~/.mini-dinstall.conf by default. Of the available configuration parameters, archive_style and archivedir are the only required ones, and the latter can optionally be specified on the command line. mini-dinstall supports two different archive styles. The flat style uses a single directory for each distribution while simple-subdir separates the packages further by their architecture field. Support for package directories will hopefully be added in a future version.

Similarly to the official Debian archive, mini-dinstall can manage multiple distributions. A distribution is identified by a stanza in the configuration file. The simplest configuration file that specifies two distributions, *stable* and *unstable*, looks like this:

```
[DEFAULT]
archive_style = flat

[stable]
[unstable]
```

When mini-dinstall parses the incoming directory, it uses the Debian change log files to determine the target distribution (which is *unstable* by default, see chapter 9.2.7 for more information). The programme does not provide a way to automatically migrate packages from *unstable* to *testing*, or from *testing* to *stable* as is the case in the official Debian archive. If you need that functionality, you should look at katie and her friends (the dak scripts), which are only available via CVS[9] at present.

The hooks of dput and dupload come in very handy with mini-dinstall. For small or infrequently changing archives, the hooks can call mini-dinstall --batch to

[9]repository: :pserver:anonymous@cvs.debian.org:/cvs/dak; module: dak

process the **incoming** queue once. With multiple people uploading to a repository, or in case of frequent changes, a daemonised **mini-dinstall** process will likely cause less system load and fewer problems related to locking. The daemon process can be "woken up" and told to immediately process the **incoming** queue with the **--run** option. The daemon process writes information to **./mini-dinstall/mini-dinstall.log** at run-time.

```
~/apt$ mini-dinstall
~/gruezi$ dput gruezi_1.2-2_i386.changes
~/apt$ mini-dinstall --run
200 Reprocessing complete
```

debpool

While currently only available in the *experimental* archive, **debpool** is an effort to provide a manageable tool to maintain a full-featured Debian archive for personal use, or for use within an institution. It provides hooks for package verification, and can sign packages and releases. If you want to inspect it, install it from experimental:

```
~# echo deb http://ftp.debian.org/debian experimental main \
  >> /etc/apt/sources.list
~# apt-get update && apt-get install debpool/experimental
[...]
```

debarchiver

debarchiver is capable of automatically administering a small archive according to the Debian archive structure (using different trees for distribution, section, and architecture; see chapter 4.1). However, it does not support the **pool** hierarchy and is thus not really applicable to anything other than small archives spanning few distributions.

Configuration of **debarchiver** occurs via **/etc/debarchiver.conf** and is straightforward. Without any configuration (none is necessary, actually) packages dropped into **/var/lib/debarchive/incoming** will become available properly sorted under **/var/lib/debarchive/dists** after the next **cron** run (every 5 minutes). The **incoming** directory also contains subdirectories for the three Debian releases, which can be used to directly sort packages into those. Otherwise, the information is extracted from the package's **.changes** file.

9.4 Advanced package concepts

9.4.1 Package hook scripts

The Debian package management tools can call a number of scripts at certain points during the installation and removal process, if a package provides them. These scripts are typically called "package maintainer scripts" as they give the package maintainer more control over the package beyond its contents and meta data. A nice illustration of these scripts and their purpose can be found on the pages of the Debian women project[10]. The set of maintainer scripts consists of:

preinst
> Called right before a package's files are unpacked into the filesystem, the **preinst** script normally prepares the environment for the package. For instance, if mutable information (*e.g.* under /var) has been moved between package upgrades, the **preinst** file of the new version moves these data to ensure a smooth upgrade.

postinst
> The **postinst** script is invoked as part of the package configuration process. It is probably the most common hook script and integrates the software installed by the package with the system. For instance, **postinst** creates users and groups, initialises working directories for daemons and starts them, or incorporates the user choices cached by **debconf** (see chapter 5.8) into the local configuration. With the **postinst** script, the maintainer also registers components with the system, such as shared libraries (**ldconfig**), or plugins for other software.

prerm
> Just before a package's files are removed from the system during deinstallation, **prerm** is given a chance to run. Here, it is common to undo changes made by **postinst** script, such as the removal of users and groups, or the stopping of a daemon.

postrm
> The **postrm** script is run right after a package's files have been removed from the system, but before the configuration files are purged. The script is called *again* following the purge of a package, allowing it to remove temporary or variable data, or clear the corresponding entries from the **debconf** cache.

The scripts receive information about the current state as arguments. The first argument is the action in progress while the second usually involves the new or old version number for upgrades (whichever one is relevant). When more than a one

---

[10]http://women.alioth.debian.org/wiki/index.php/English/MaintainerScripts

package is involved (*e.g.* when one package is removed in response to the installation of a conflicting one), more arguments are available as detailed in section 6.4 of the policy (see chapter 5.7). The maintainer scripts must be idempotent, meaning that they must be callable multiple times in a row without breaking.

The scripts themselves have to be executable and should be written in shell script language or **Perl**. As the requirements for these scripts differ between all packages, we will just look at a simple example and refer to chapter 6 of the policy, section 6.4 of the developer reference, and **/var/lib/dpkg/info/*.p*** on any Debian system (for inspiration). The following **preinst** and **postinst** files handle an upgrade to 1.2.4-1 if the version of the package previously installed was earlier than 1.2.3-4. As part of the upgrade, the directory **/var/state/foo** needs to be moved to **/var/lib/foo**, and the **/usr/lib/foo/upgrade-1.2.3** has to be called.

```
~$ cat debian/foo/preinst
#!/bin/bash -e

if [[ $1 = upgrade ]]; then
  if [[ -n $2 ]] && dpkg --compare-versions $2 lt 1.2.4-1; then
    # working directory is not under /var/lib
    if [[ -d /var/state/foo ]]; then
      mv /var/state/foo /var/lib
    fi
  fi
fi

#DEBHELPER#
~$ cat debian/foo.postinst
#!/bin/bash -e

if [[ $1 = configure ]]; then
  if [[ -n $2 ]] && dpkg --compare-versions $2 lt 1.2.4-1; then
    /usr/lib/foo/upgrade-1.2.3
  fi
fi

#DEBHELPER#
```

Both scripts identify a slot for **debhelper** to paste additional commands. For instance, **dh_installinit** will make the **postinst** file call **invoke-rc.d** to start the service (see chapter 6.3.1), and dh_makeshlibs inserts a call to **ldconfig** to register the new libraries installed by the package with the dynamic loader on the target system.

9.4.2   Using debconf

As discussed in chapter 5.8, **debconf** is a caching system that supports user interactions in a programmatic and flexible way. **debconf**-enabled packages query the administrator for desired settings in a freely configurable and programmable way before the package is installed so that the configuration phase can complete without bothering the installing user.

To export this functionality, a package must provide (at least) three files which work hand in hand: **templates, config,** and **postinst.** Chapter 5.8 gives a brief overview of the purpose of these files, in the following I will be showing you how to add **debconf** to our **gruezi** package to allow the admin to select which of the four languages to display by default. To add a little complexity, the package should first ask whether to simply show all, and only display a list for granular selection if the administrator answers negatively.

Templated interaction

The first step is the authoring of the **templates** file, which governs the "looks" of **debconf's** interaction with the installing user. The **debconf-devel (7)** manpage provides in-depth documentation on the possible values and statements of a templates file[11]. The file itself uses the same format as **debian/control:**

```
~$ cat <<EOF > debian/gruezi.templates
Template: gruezi/all
Type: boolean
Default: true
Description: Should gruezi greet in all languages by default?
 gruezi knows to greet in all of the four languages spoken in Switzerland.
 Whenever invoked, should it simply greet in all of them?

Template: gruezi/lang
Type: multiselect
Choices: German, French, Italian, Romansch
Description: In which languages should gruezi greet the caller?
 Please select all languages in which gruezi should greet the caller by
 default. This can be overridden at runtime.
EOF
```

Steering the interaction

The flexibility of **debconf** comes at the expense of having to provide the logic controlling when to ask what question. This is done in the **config** file, which may be written using Perl[12], Python[13], or plain shell[14]. The commands are pretty similar across the three interfaces, and the following will use the shell interface.

---

[11]The specification is available in **/usr/share/doc/debian-policy/debconf_specification.txt.gz**
[12]Documented in the **Debconf::Client::ConfModule (3)** manpage
[13]Not documented, but pretty much the same as the Perl interface.
[14]Described in the **confmodule (3)** manpage

The basics are simple: **db_input** links a template name to a priority and a subsequent **db_go** causes **debconf** to display the template to the user and wait for a response. **db_get** fetches the cached value and puts it in the **$RET** variable, and **db_set** can be used to modify the cache. Note that most lines calling **db_*** commands use the **|| true** construct to ensure a successful execution of the line, as the shell would exit otherwise (**-e** is in effect). Non-zero return values of **debconf** commands encapsulate status information and do not necessarily indicate error conditions.

For added kicks, we make the following a state machine and use the **backup** capability to allow the administrator to return to previous questions. Remember, this is just for demonstration purposes and would be overkill for a real package with the same functional impact as **gruezi**.

```
~$ cat <<"EOF" > debian/gruezi.config
#!/bin/bash -e
. /usr/share/debconf/confmodule

STATE=0
STATE_DONE=2
LANG_ALL='German, French, Italian, Romansch'

# we support backing up, so announce that
db_capb backup

while [[ $STATE -lt $STATE_DONE ]]; do
  case $STATE in
    0)
      db_input medium gruezi/all || true
      db_go || true
      db_get gruezi/all || true
      if [[ $RET = true ]]; then
        db_set gruezi/lang $LANG_ALL || true
        STATE=$STATE_DONE;
      else
        STATE=$((STATE+1))
      fi
      ;;
    1)
      db_input medium gruezi/lang || true
      db_go || RET=$?
      if [[ $RET -eq 30 ]]; then # user chose backup
        STATE=$((STATE-1))
      else
        db_get gruezi/lang || true
        [[ $RET = $LANG_ALL ]] && db_set gruezi/all true || true
        STATE=$((STATE+1))
      fi
      ;;
  esac
done
EOF
```

debconf and configuration file handling

It is important to realise that the **config** script only controls the querying of the user. It *must not* actually make changes to the configuration. This is left to the **postinst** script.

However, we have reached a tricky situation. Based on the **debconf** responses to the two questions, we must modify **/etc/gruezi.conf** automatically. Previously we defined this file to be a **conffile**, but the policy specifies in section 10.7.3 that **conffiles** must not be modified automatically. Hence, we must work around this requirement, and there are three possible solutions:

- Add a disclaimer to the file to encourage use of **dpkg-reconfigure** instead to make changes. This is highly discouraged!

- Instead of hardcoding the default value of the variables in the configuration file, export the defaults to another file and control that with **debconf**. This file would then have to reside under **/var**, which is again difficult because /var may not be available when /etc already is. Okay, in the case of **gruezi**, this will not be a problem, but still…

- The final solution is to rip **/etc/gruezi.conf** out of **dpkg**'s **conffile** custody and implement custom configuration file management. The **ucf** package provides the Update Configuration File tool for this task. **ucf** implements **dpkg**'s configuration file handling as well as some additional features in a separate programme.

gruezi is not a quick'n'dirty package, so we will take the best route and employ **ucf** to handle the configuration file. Therefore, we must add **ucf** as a dependency of **gruezi**:

```
~$ sed -i -e 's/^Depends.*/&, ucf/' debian/control
```

Next, we remove the **/etc/gruezi.conf** file by removing etc from **debian/gruezi. install**. Now the next version will not install the file, meaning that **dh_installdeb** will not flag it as a **conffile**. Since an upgrade conveniently only removes files but leaves **conffiles** in place, the previous configuration file with its modifications stays in place and is properly picked up by **ucf**, which is invoked from **postinst**. Ideally, we would first copy the new file over the old one in case the user has not made any changes to the file yet, just to prevent **ucf** from potentially asking the user what to do. The **ucf** (7) manpage contains more information on this topic.

Actually making changes

Thus, the **postinst** script generates a configuration file from the user responses to the **debconf** queries and hands over to **ucf** to handle the replacement.

Normally, **debconf** is invoked during pre-configuration (see chapter 5.8) as well as from the **postinst** script. If all values have been cached during pre-configuration, **debconf** simply exits without any further action when invoked via the **postinst** script. However, if pre-configuration is disabled (*e.g.* because **apt-utils** is not installed), the **postinst** script ensures that **debconf** has had a chance to run.

```
~$ cat <<"EOF" > debian/gruezi.postinst
#!/bin/bash -e

set_lang() {
  lang=$1; key=$2; shift; shift
  echo $@ | grep -q $lang && local DFLT=1
  echo "GRUEZI_${key}=${GRUEZI_${key}:-${DFLT:-0}}"
}

if [[ $1 = configure ]]; then
  . /usr/share/debconf/confmodule

  TMPFILE=$(mktemp /tmp/gruezi-postinst.XXXXXX)
  trap "rm -f $TMPFILE" 0

  db_get gruezi/lang || true
  set_lang German DE $RET >> $TMPFILE
  set_lang French FR $RET >> $TMPFILE
  set_lang Italian IT $RET >> $TMPFILE
  set_lang Romansch RR $RET >> $TMPFILE

  ucf --debconf-ok $TMPFILE /etc/gruezi.conf
fi

#DEBHELPER#
EOF
```

Note the final slot for any code that **debhelper** may wish to add. We also need to provide a **postrm** file, which tells **ucf** to forget about the **/etc/gruezi.conf** file.

```
~$ cat <<"EOF" > debian/gruezi.postrm
#!/bin/bash -e

CONFIG=/etc/gruezi.conf

if [[ $1 = purge ]]; then
  test -x /usr/bin/ucf && ucf --purge $CONFIG
  rm -f $CONFIG
fi

#DEBHELPER#
EOF
```

Again, notice the **debhelper** hook. This time we actually need it, because like purging the **ucf** registration, we want a package purge to also clear the **debconf** cache of any values associated with the package. We have not taken any particular action towards incorporating the **config** and **templates** file with the package. **debhelper** provides **dh_installdebconf**, which conveniently handles all of the above in the expected manner. Thus, we insert it into the **binary-arch** package right underneath the **dh_install** call. We also need to add a dependency on **debconf**, which must be versioned because the **multiselect** control was only added in 0.2.26.

```
~$ sed -i -e '/dh_install --arch/atdh_installdebconf --arch' debian/rules
~$ sed -i -e 's/^Depends.*/&, debconf (>= 0.2.26)/' debian/control
```

Finalising the package

The final step is to log everything we did in **gruezi**'s **changelog** and prepare a new package. Since the changes are exclusive to Debian, we only need to bump the Debian revision to -3:

```
~$ dch --increment
[...]
~$ dpkg-buildpackage -uc -us
[...]
```

Interacting with the debconf cache

While the **debconf** cache is primarily designed to be used by the package management system, it is possible to interact with it directly. Doing so is mainly useful during debugging, although you are free to use your creativity to device other uses. Please try to avoid the trap of viewing **debconf** as a registry or some kind of permanent storage! As mentioned in chapter 5.8, **debconf** is a cache and its contents may be deleted at any time.

To use **debconf** directly, you have the option of writing a shell script to speak the **debconf** protocol (or using an existing **config** script), or *ad hoc* usage via the shell. While it is possible to use the **db_*** commands with the first approach, the shell utilities only speak the **debconf** protocol, which is described in detail in the **debconf-devel (7)** manpage.

The following shell extract shows how to use a shell script along with the **debconf** shell commands:

```
~# cat <<EOF > /tmp/get_prio.sh
#!/bin/sh -e

. /usr/share/debconf/confmodule
db_set debconf/priority low
db_get debconf/priority
echo $RET > /tmp/priority
```

```
EOF
~# chmod +x /tmp/get_prio.sh
~# debconf /tmp/get_prio.sh
```

The **debconf** return codes provide information about success, status, or failure. For further information pertaining to **debconf**'s operation, you may set $DEB-CONF_DEBUG to "developer," which will echo the communication between **debconf** and the script. Note that this also works when **debconf** is invoked by APT, provided you exported the variable. For maximum verbosity, set the variable to ".*" (yes, the variable is in fact the payload of a regular expression).

Alternatively, it is possible to speak the **debconf** protocol directly in the shell, using **debconf-communicate**:

```
~# echo SET debconf/priority low | debconf-communicate debconf
0 value set
~# echo GET debconf/priority | debconf-communicate debconf
0 low
```

The above methods will only work if **debconf** has access to the templates that are being accessed. These can be loaded into the **debconf** database with **debconf-loadtemplates**:

```
~# echo PURGE | debconf-communicate debconf
~# debconf-loadtemplate /var/lib/dpkg/info/debconf.templates
~# echo INPUT high debconf/priority | debconf-communicate debconf
[...]
```

It is also possible to set default values before a package has been installed or its templates loaded. The **debconf-set-selections** tool reads the values to assign to variables stored in the **debconf** database from a file. Conversely, **debconf-get-selections** (from the **debconf-utils** package) can convert the contents of the local **debconf** database into the appropriate format. For example:

```
~# debconf-set-selections <<EOF
setserial setserial/autosave-types select autosave once
EOF
~# apt-get install setserial
```

debconf-set-selections can potentially mess up the **debconf** system (and thus damage the system) if used without care. In general, it should only be used to set **debconf** values for templates belonging to packages that are or will be installed. The Debian installer uses this tool for its preseeding feature (see chapter 8.3.4).

The values **debconf** caches for a package can be displayed using **debconf-show**, which takes a package name and dumps all the variable-value pairs to **stdout**. Questions that have been asked (and marked as "seen") are prefixed with an asterisk:

```
~# debconf-show debconf
* debconf/frontend: Readline
* debconf/priority: low
```

Translating debconf templates

Debian aims to provide its operating system to as many people as possible. Since English is not comfortably understood all over our planet, this involves the translation of messages to other languages. **debconf** is no exception, and with **po-debconf**, it has a very flexible framework for localisation (also called "l10n") to different regions.

Converting a package to use **po-debconf** is trivial:

```
~$ debconf-gettextize debian/gruezi.templates
[...]
~$ rm debian/gruezi.templates.old
~$ grep ^_ debian/gruezi.templates
_Description: Should gruezi greet in all languages by default?
_Choices: German, French, Italian, Romansch
_Description: In which languages should gruezi greet the caller?
```

Localisation

debconf-gettextize modifies the **templates** file and identifies all translation candidates with an underscore. Even though the templates will probably be written in English, the messages constitute the default set for the cases when no translation is available for the user's locale. This does not affect the functionality.

The distinction becomes relevant when the **debconf** templates are translated to another language. Translation is trivial (but subject to some guidelines[15]) and basically involves the copying of **debian/po/templates.pot** to **debian/po/xx.po**, where "xx" is the two-letter language name [16] corresponding to the target locale of the translation.

Thus, to translate the **gruezi** package to German, you would create **debian/po/de.po**, edit the header in the file appropriately by filling in your name and other meta data, and then provide all the **msgstr** entries for each **msgid**. Since we are using **dh_installdebconf**, this will make sure that the German translation is used when the locale setting suggests German. The locale must be generated properly for this to work.

```
~$ dch --increment -- Switched to using po-debconf to allow for l10n.
~$ dpkg-buildpackage -uc -us
```

[15]see /usr/share/doc/po-debconf/README-trans.gz
[16]defined in the ISO 639 alpha-2 standard: http://en.wikipedia.org/wiki/ISO_639

```
[...]
~# sudo debi
[...]
~# LC_MESSAGES=de_DE.UTF-8 dpkg-reconfigure gruezi
Konfiguriere gruezi
------------------
[...]
```

If the above does not work for you, make sure that the **locales** package is installed. Then, run **dpkg-reconfigure locales** and select the wanted locales for generation.

Post-l10n changes

If you look at the .po file, you may be struck by the choice of labels. While **msgstr** makes perfect sense, **msgid** seems weird; would it not have been better to use, *e.g.* "original" and "translation" instead?

The answer is: no, but it is not quite obvious. The free-form texts you typed into the **templates** file are treated as message IDs identifying a translation at the same time as they are proper messages used by the programme; to the computer, it makes no difference if a translation is identified by an identifier such as "MSG4711" or by "Which language do you want?". Thus, using the actual messages instead of cryptic identifiers improves readability and also provides a default text when no translation can be found. Since these message IDs are already in English, it is unlikely for a package to contain an English "translation", the original messages are also used for English locales.

A problem may arise when a message is changed. If the change is of a semantic nature, then all is well, since the translations have to be adjusted anyway. Simply changing the appropriate lines in the **templates** file does the trick and automatically invalidates all previous translations of this message because the **msgid** changes. The problem only really surfaces when the change is minor, such as a typo or a punctuation fault. If the message is amended, the translations are invalidated.

Thus, all the translations would have to be updated to reflect the change in the original message. Nevertheless, with character encodings so vastly different all over the language set, maintainers are actually discouraged from touching the translations. Instead, the solution is to provide an English translation in **en.po** to correct the error for English locales. Translators can then add the new **msgid** to the .po files and allow for a smooth transition.

9.4.3   Library packages

Libraries enjoy special packaging practices in the Debian project. Most prominently, library packages are always prefixed with **lib**, and for every source package a shared library generates at least two packages. A package such as **libfoo1** contains the runtime library (the .so file), while its sibling package libfoo-dev would install the header files as well as the static counterpart (if it exists), as well as an unversioned symlink to the (versioned) .so file. The -dev packages hence depend on the corresponding runtime packages and contain everything needed to develop applications that link against the library.

It should be noted that packaging libraries for Debian is not for the faint-hearted and definitely should not be attempted before you have mastered normal Debian packages and fully understand the ins and outs if libraries and their effects on dependent packages. If you consider yourself ready for library packaging, set your sights low, and pick a library that is unlikely to be needed by many. Without doubting your care and abilities, it is likely that there will be glitches. The definitive library packaging guide for Debian is available online[17] and must be read by everyone intending to maintain library packages.

Package names

You will also notice the trailing number in the name of the runtime package, but not in the name of the development package. This number encodes the SONAME of the library. When a library changes its ABI, it becomes binary incompatible with previous versions and indicates that with a change in the SONAME. New applications written with that library will then depend the new version, but older applications cannot be expected to make the switch immediately (or at all). Thus, several versions of a library must be able to coexist on a Debian system, and having the SONAME be part of the library package name allows just that.

Most -dev packages do not have this kind a number in their names. The few that do encode the API version (not the ABI) to allow developers to compile their software against different API versions, rather than just the latest. This may be necessary particularly with respect to security bugs. Nevertheless, very few -dev packages in the Debian archive actually encode the API version in the package name, which is less than perfect but not really relevant in most cases. When the API version is not encoded, the -dev package claims to be compatible with all previous and future versions, which is rather rare, especially for small libraries.

The shlibs system

The shlibs system shifts the responsibility of deciding which library package provides the necessary functionality from the user to the provider of the library. In the process of building a package containing one or more executables, dpkg-shlibdeps uses objdump to figure out the libraries with which the executables (and other shared libraries) are linked. As no standard for library file and package names ex-

---

[17]http://www.netfort.gr.jp/~dancer/column/libpkg-guide/libpkg-guide.html

ists, **dpkg-shlibdeps** then uses the **shlibs** database to map the sought filename to the providing Debian package.

Conversely, the maintainer of a library package includes a **shlibs** file with the runtime package; **dpkg** automatically merges this with the **shlibs** database on the system where the library is installed. Since every **-dev** package depends on its corresponding runtime library package, a system used to compile the aforementioned executables will have all the necessary entries in its **shlibs** database.

Mapping to package names

Let's look at an example. The **libcurl2** and **libcurl3** packages provide the following two entries in the **shlibs** database:

```
~$ cat /var/lib/dpkg/info/libcurl?.shlibs
libcurl 2 libcurl2 (>= 7.11.2-1)
libcurl 3 libcurl3 (>= 7.12.1-1)
```

curl links with **libcurl** and needs its ABI identified by SONAME 3 (**ldd** could also be used):

```
~$ objdump -p /usr/bin/curl | grep NEEDED                      [321]
  NEEDED       libcurl.so.3
[...]
```

dpkg-shlibdeps uses this data to query the **shlibs** database to obtain the needed dependency: "libcurl3 (>= 7.12.1-1)".

```
~$ dpkg-shlibdeps -O /usr/bin/curl                             [334]
shlibs:Depends=libc6 (>= 2.3.2.ds1-4), libcurl3 (>= 7.12.1-1), [...]
```

The **libcurl3** maintainer, who authored the record, is telling us that any package depending on ABI 3 of **libcurl** must install the Debian package **libcurl3** 7.12.1-1 or later to ensure binary compatibility.

dh_makeshlibs

The **debhelper** suite (see chapter 9.2.11) provides **dh_makeshlibs**, which attempts to generate the **shlibs** file automatically. By default, it will create an unversioned dependency, which may not be desirable. Generally, different versions of a library with the same SONAME are guaranteed to be backwards-compatible, but forwards-compatibility can never be guaranteed. Thus, the versioned dependency identifies the minimum library version which satisfies the requirements of its ABI.

If the API grows, the library will need to use versioned dependencies with the **shlibs** system. However, it is not enough to use the current version of the library. For instance, if **libcurl** 7.12.1 simply fixes some documentation issues over 7.12, a versioned dependency on the latter should be used instead. **dh_makeshlibs** provides the -V option to give full control to the maintainer. Maintaining a library package thus requires a solid understanding of the library's API and ABI, and also means tracking changes in the two across releases to be able to give the right hints to **shlibs**.

Overriding shlibs

The policy requires every package containing a shared library to drop an appropriate **shlibs** file during installation. Thus, a library package missing a **shlibs** record should be filed as a serious bug. Given that **shlibs** is required well before *buzz*, it is highly unlikely that non-conforming packages still exist in current releases. What is far more likely is that a provided **shlibs** file does not properly represent the package's ABI requirements. In such a case it may be necessary to override another package's **shlibs** data locally.

The local system administrator can specify **shlibs** overrides in **/etc/dpkg/shlibs.override**, and each package can finally override the **shlibs** entries with **debian/shlibs.local**. Thus, if the libfoo1 package published a **shlibs** entry with an unversioned dependency, but version 1.2.3-4 or greater of libfoo1 was required to satisfy the ABI needed by the software, the package would have to override the **shlibs** records manually:

```
~$ echo 'libfoo 1 libfoo1 (>= 1.2.3-4)' > debian/shlibs.local
```

Now **dpkg-shlibdeps** would simply ignore libfoo1's **shlibs** entries and use the locally provided ones. It goes without saying that a bug should be filed against libfoo1 in the process (see chapter 10.6).

9.5 Alternative build tools

Traditionally, the **debian/rules** file has been a **Perl** or **make** script. However, other approaches are also possible. Two alternatives have been gaining popularity in the past: **cdbs** and **yada**.

9.5.1 cdbs

cdbs is the "Common Debian Build System," which aims to factor out parts of **debian/rules** to shared **Makefiles** using **Makefile** inheritance. It provides a sane set of default rules which can build most standard packages. The rules may be overridden individually to customise just about every aspect of the build process.

The best display of **cdbs**'s power is a full-featured **debian/rules** file, which does everything needed to build a Debian package from a tarball that uses the **GNU** autotools:

```
~$ cat debian/rules
#!/usr/bin/make -f

include /usr/share/cdbs/1/rules/debhelper.mk
include /usr/share/cdbs/1/class/autotools.mk
```

Done. **cdbs** provides similar ease for packages with plain **Makefiles**, **Perl** or **Python** modules, **GNOME** or **KDE** applications, and packages using **ant** or **hbuild** — and the collection is growing.

The juicy details of customisation are best left to the **cdbs** documentation (**/usr/ share/doc/cdbs**) as the package is still under development and evolving quickly. The project's web page is hosted on **alioth**[18].

Let's convert the ubiquitous **gruezi** package to use **cdbs**:

```
~$ cat <<"EOF" > debian/rules
#!/usr/bin/make -f

DEB_MAKE_INSTALL_TARGET := install prefix=/usr DESTDIR=$(CURDIR)/debian/
tmp
DEB_DH_INSTALL_SOURCEDIR := debian/tmp

include /usr/share/cdbs/1/rules/debhelper.mk
include /usr/share/cdbs/1/class/makefile.mk
EOF
```

Since **Makefiles** are not standardised, we have to help **cdbs** in determining what to do. It needs to know what **make** arguments install the software; we can copy them from our previous **debian/rules** file. Finally, since we are using **debian/tmp** as temporary storage before letting **dh_install** sort the files into the corresponding package build spaces, we have to tell **dh_install** about the source directory. These two lines are all the customisation required, the rest is just **cdbs** default for **Makefile**-based packages.

Before we can build the package with **cdbs**, we have to modify the build dependencies. Obviously, **cdbs** itself is required. In addition, since will be continuing to use **debhelper**, we must keep it in the list as well. The only change required here is to the version number, since **cdbs** will only work with **debhelper** 4.1.0 or newer:

```
~$ grep ^Build-Depends debian/control
Build-Depends: debhelper (>= 4.1.0), cdbs
~$ dpkg-buildpackage
[...]
```

[18]http://alioth.debian.org/projects/build-common

9.5.2 yada

yada is Yet Another Debianisation Aid which takes a somewhat different approach from **cdbs**. Using the information in **debian/packages**, **yada** creates the files in the **debian** directory prior to creating the package. Thus, a package is basically controlled via a single file.

The following **debian/packages** file would build **gruezi** without requiring manual maintenance of **debian/rules** or **debian/control**. For brevity, the example does not handle **debconf** integration:

```
~$ cat <<"EOF" > debian/packages
Source: gruezi
Section: misc
Priority: extra
Maintainer: Wilhelm Tell <hero@suisse.ch>
Standards-Version: 3.6.1.1
Upstream-Source: <URL:http://www.gruezi.ch>
Description: Swiss greetings
Copyright: .
 Do whatever you want with this software.
 But do not claim to have invented it,
 Or the nation will bombard you
 With Ricola candies.
Build: sh
 make all
Clean: sh
 make distclean

Package: gruezi
Section: misc
Priority: extra
Architecture: any
Depends: gruezi-common (= ${Source-Version})
Description: greets you the Swiss way
 gruezi is a simple script to greet its caller in all four
 languages spoken in Switzerland.
 .
 The languages are: German, French, Italian, and Romansch.
Install: sh
 make install prefix=/usr DESTDIR=$ROOT
 yada remove -dir /usr/share/gruezi
Doc-Depends: gruezi-common

Package: gruezi-common
Section: misc
Priority: extra
Architecture: all
Description: Swiss greetings
 gruezi is a simple script to greet its caller in all four
 languages spoken in Switzerland.
```

```
  .
 The languages are: German, French, Italian, and Romansch.
  .
 This package provides the actual greetings in the four languages.
Install: sh
 yada install -data -into /usr/share/gruezi greetings
 yada install -doc -as changelog ChangeLog
EOF
```

As you can see, the file contains pretty much what there is to know about **gruezi**, including special build and installation rules. To build a package with **yada**, you would need to create the **debian/rules** file first before invoking **dpkg-buildpackage** as before:

```
~$ yada rebuild rules
~$ dpkg-buildpackage -uc -us
[...]
```

9.6   Automating clean builds with pbuilder

pbuilder is a personal build system, which comes in handy at other times as well. The principal idea is that it creates a minimal Debian base system, downloads and installs a package's build dependencies, and then compiles your package in this tidy environment. Using **pbuilder** is not necessary as you can build packages on your main system. However, it handles build dependencies automatically and does not clutter your system with them. Moreover, since the minimal base system it installs is the lowest common denominator of all Debian systems, it ensures that the package will build on any system, and not just your own.

pbuilder allows for two modes of operation. The simplest involves using tarballs to store the root filesystem. An advanced use is with a User-Mode-Linux (UML) kernel[19] and a filesystem image. Here, **pbuilder** "boots" an emulated Linux instance and thus provides physical separation of the build system from your workstation, which may be beneficial. The root filesystem is immutable in that it restores itself to the original state when the build process has finished. **pbuilder** provides methods to upgrade the root filesystem with **APT** however, and it has hooks for user-provided scripts to make additional modifications. Finally, since the root filesystem is stored in a tarball or a filesystem image, it may be manipulated with the standard tools (do not tell anyone I told you so...).

Finally, **pbuilder** provides a method to log in to the build system it creates. Although intended primarily for debugging purposes, it proves to be equally valuable for use as a system for quick tests. In fact, most of the tests for this book were done in **pbuilder** base systems.

[19] http://user-mode-linux.sf.net

An important notice up front: with the tarball method, **pbuilder** must be invoked as **root** because it needs to be able to use **chroot**. It is probably best to use **sudo** for this purpose. However, be advised that access to pbuilder should only be given to trusted users as it is fairly trivial to break out of a **chroot** jail[20]. If you are planning to provide **pbuilder** to normal users, please consider the UML method instead. Unfortunately, the UML patches and software were in a buggy and unsupported state at time of writing. Moreover, read chapter 9.6.4 for a trivial way for a **pbuilder** user to get (write-)access to **/etc/shadow** or virtually any other file on the host system.

9.6.1   Setting up a base tarball

By default, **pbuilder** uses Debian *unstable*, but the **--distribution** option allows it to use any other Debian release, even ancient ones[21]. For most purposes, the *sid* distribution is fine, however. Packages intended for the Debian archive must be built against *sid*. Nevertheless, **pbuilder** can obviously also be used to backport packages to *woody* or *sarge*. In the following, I will explicitly work with *sarge*, to make it explicit.

Before **pbuilder** can do anything useful, it has to assemble the base system. This is easier done than said, it seems. Unless overridden, **pbuilder** uses the Japanese Debian mirror to download the packages. You will definitely want to override this (see chapter 5.4.1 for a tool to help select the best mirror to use):

```
~# pbuilder create --distribution sarge \
   --mirror http://ftp.debian.org/debian --othermirror \
   'deb http://security.debian.org/debian-security sarge/updates main'
Distribution is sarge.
Building the build environment
 -> running debootstrap
[...]
I: Base system installed successfully.
[...]
 -> creating base tarball [/var/cache/pbuilder/base.tgz]
[...]
~# ls -Fla /var/cache/pbuilder/base.tgz
-rw-r--r-- 1 root root 43136583 Oct  7 18:31 /var/cache/pbuilder/base.t
gz
```

The **base.tgz** file now contains a plain *sarge* base system ready to be used. Note how we added the security mirrors so that the **pbuilder** system does not expose known security bugs. From time to time, it will be necessary to upgrade the base

---

[20] http://www.bpfh.net/simes/computing/chroot-break.html

[21] pbuilder uses debootstrap to create the base system. The earliest Debian release supported by debootstrap for use with pbuilder is *woody*. If you want to use older releases, you will have to create the tarball yourself. debootstrap can help back until *slink*, but it has to be run separately since pbuilder uses special buildd scripts (under /usr/lib/debootstrap/scripts).

system to allow security upgrades (or any other upgrades in the case of *testing* or *unstable*) to trickle in:

```
~$ sudo pbuilder update
Upgrading for distribution sarge
[...]
Refreshing the base.tgz
 -> upgrading packages
Get:1 http://ftp.debian.org sarge/main Packages [3121kB]
Get:2 http://ftp.debian.org sarge/main Release [81B]
Get:3 http://security.debian.org sarge/updates/main Packages [200kB]
Get:4 http://security.debian.org sarge/updates/main Release [110B]
[...]
0 upgraded, 0 newly installed, 0 to remove and 0 not upgraded.
[...]
Copying back the cached apt archive contents
[...]
 -> creating base tarball [/var/cache/pbuilder/base.tgz]
[...]
```

9.6.2   Building packages with pbuilder

Its main purpose is building packages in a clean environment. To do this, **pbuilder** spawns a base system, copies the source package specified on the command line into the base system, invokes **chroot**, installs all the build dependencies, and subsequently calls **dpkg-buildpackage** to build the package.

When the build is complete, **pbuilder** drops the source package files along with the DEB files it generated into **/var/cache/pbuilder/result**. The files are owned by **root**, which makes it a little difficult if you (or your users) are invoking **pbuilder** with **sudo**. Therefore, it is best to configure **pbuilder** to **chown** the resulting files to your current user and drop them somewhere else. The following entries in ~/.pbuilderrc accomplish this. We also specify the mirror to use for future **pbuilder --create** invocations (using shell variables for line brevity). Other uses of ~/.pbuilderrc are documented in **pbuilderrc(5)**.

```
~$ cat <<"EOF" > ~/.pbuilderrc
MIRRORSITE=http://ftp.debian.org/debian
DEBSECSERVER=http://security.debian.org/debian-security
OTHERMIRROR="deb $DEBSECSERVER sarge/updates main"

BUILDRESULT=$(pwd)/result.$$
# make sure the directory exists:
DUMMY=$(mkdir -p $BUILDRESULT)
echo The result will be in ${BUILDRESULT}...

if [[ -n $SUDO_USER ]]; then
  BUILDRESULTUID=$SUDO_UID
```

```
    BUILDRESULTGID=$SUDO_GID
fi
EOF
```

Now, without further ado, let us build **gruezi** from earlier in this chapter, using **sudo**
to invoke **pbuilder**. I assume that you have already configured **sudo** appropriately:

```
~$ sudo pbuilder build gruezi_1.2-2.dsc
The result will be in /home/gruezi/result.2592...
[...]
Building the build Environment
[...]
Installing the build-deps
 -> Attempting to parse the build-deps : pbuilder-satisfydepends[...]
[...]
0 upgraded, 15 newly installed, 0 to remove and 0 not upgraded.
[...]
 -> Finished parsing the build-deps
[...]
Copying source file
    -> copying [gruezi_1.2-2.dsc]
    -> copying [./gruezi_1.2.orig.tar.gz]
    -> copying [./gruezi_1.2-2.diff.gz]
[...]
Extracting source
dpkg-source: warning: no utmp entry available and LOGNAME
  not defined; using uid of process (0)
dpkg-source: extracting gruezi in gruezi-1.2
 -> Building the package
[...]
dpkg-deb: building package 'gruezi' in '../gruezi_1.2-2_i386.deb'.
[...]
dpkg-deb: building package 'gruezi-common' in
  '../gruezi-common_1.2-2_all.deb'.
[...]
dpkg-buildpackage: binary and diff upload (original source NOT included)
[...]
    -> removing directory /var/cache/pbuilder/build//2592[...]
~$ ls -Fl result.2592
-rw-r--r-- 1 gruezi users 1740 Aug  8 10:58 gruezi-common_1.2-2_all.deb
-rw-r--r-- 1 gruezi users 2138 Aug  8 10:57 gruezi_1.2-2.diff.gz
-rw-r--r-- 1 gruezi users  325 Aug  8 10:57 gruezi_1.2-2.dsc
-rw-r--r-- 1 gruezi users  725 Aug  8 10:58 gruezi_1.2-2_i386.changes
-rw-r--r-- 1 gruezi users 1548 Aug  8 10:57 gruezi_1.2-2_i386.deb
```

As you can see, the **orig.tar.gz** file is not included in the list of files belonging to the
build because the Debian revision of the build was larger than 1 (see chapter 9.2.12.
If we wanted to force the inclusion, we could tell **pbuilder** to pass the **–sa** option
to **dpkg-buildpackage**, either on the command line, or with the **$DEBBUILDOPTS**
environment variable. The following illustrates both, although only one is needed:

```
~$ export DEBBUILDOPTS=-sa
~$ sudo pbuilder --debbuildopts '-sa'
[...]
```

The **pbuilder** package also provides **pdebuild**, which is a convenience wrapper of **pbuilder build**, which creates the source package from the current tree, obtains the appropriate rights using **sudo** or **fakeroot**, and builds the package in the **chroot**.

That is all there is to it. Using **pbuilder** forces you to set the build dependencies correctly and ensures that the package builds in a clean environment. Now validating the package with **lintian** and **linda** (see chapter 9.2.15 and chapter 9.2.15) is the last step on the way to creating proper Debian packages.

9.6.3 Using pbuilder to set up test systems

pbuilder provides two other methods which come in particularly handy if you want to test something or explore certain depths of Debian without having the changes stick. When you are done, **pbuilder** simply deletes the sandbox.

The first method allows you to log in to a **pbuilder**-managed base-system. You will be left to the graces of a shell and are free to do whatever you can do on a normal Debian system[22]. When you exit the shell, **pbuilder** will simply delete the workspace and all your changes will be lost. This is a feature:

```
~$ sudo pbuilder login
Building the build Environment
[...]
 -> entering the shell
File extracted to: /var/cache/pbuilder/build//20982
pbuilder:/# ls
bin   dev home    lib   mnt  proc sbin  sys  usr
boot  etc initrd  media opt  root srv   tmp  var
pbuilder:/# apt-get install vim
[...]
pbuilder:/# exit
[...]
    -> removing directory /var/cache/pbuilder/build//20982[...]
```

Another method to use the **pbuilder** base system is simply for the execution of a script. **pbuilder** copies the script into the **chroot**, executes it, and then cleans up the sandbox again:

```
~$ cat <<EOF > exec.sh
#!/bin/sh -e
```

---

[22]Do not set the host name within the **chroot** as it can potentially break the host system.

```
echo executing exec.sh...
exec cat /etc/apt/sources.list
EOF
~$ chmod +x exec.sh
~$ sudo pbuilder execute exec.sh
Building the build Environment
[...]
executing exec.sh...
deb http://ftp.debian.org/debian sarge main
#deb-src http://ftp.debian.org/debian sarge main
deb http://security.debian.org/debian-security sarge/updates main
#deb-src http://security.debian.org/debian-security sarge/updates main
[...]
    -> removing directory /var/cache/pbuilder/build/[...]
```

As mentioned before, the **login** method is intended merely for debugging **pbuilder** itself. Nevertheless, it proves very helpful for testing aspects of the Debian system. However, you must be extremely careful, since exiting the shell will remove the environment and discard all your changes. If you are like me (and have tripped over this too many times before), you might like to combine the two methods:

```
~$ cat <<"EOF" > phoenix-shell.sh
#!/bin/bash -e

while true; do
  /bin/bash -il < /dev/tty &> /dev/tty
  echo 'Are you sure you want to exit'
  echo 'and LOSE ALL CHANGES? If yes,'
  echo -n 'please answer with "yes": '
  read -e ans
  [[ $ans = 'yes' ]] && break
done
EOF
~$ sudo pbuilder execute phoenix-shell.sh
[...]
```

You can even use **pbuilder** to run **X** clients, including completely different desktop environments, such as **GNOME**. The following snippet in ~/.pbuilderrc will set it all up for you in the normal case (assuming you use **sudo**):

```
~$ cat <<"EOF" >> ~/.pbuilderrc
MYHOME=$(getent passwd $SUDO_USER | cut -d: -f6)
if [[ -d /tmp/.X11-unix ]] && [[ -f $MYHOME/.Xauthority ]]; then
  BINDMOUNTS="$BINDMOUNTS /tmp/.X11-unix"
  install --mode=600 $MYHOME/.Xauthority /tmp/.X11-unix/.Xauthority-${SU
DO_USER}
  export XAUTHORITY=/tmp/.X11-unix/.Xauthority-${SUDO_USER}
  export DISPLAY=:0
fi
EOF
```

9.6.4 Mounting host directories inside the chroot

pbuilder allows you to access directories from the host inside the **chroot** by bind-mounting them. This allows you to share files between the two systems.

```
~$ mkdir /tmp/mnt
~$ echo Hello, world\! > /tmp/mnt/hello
~$ sudo pbuilder login --bindmounts /tmp/mnt
[...]
pbuilder:/# cat /tmp/mnt/hello
Hello, world!
```

The option to bind-mount directories also gives you everything you need to shoot yourself in the foot, and if you give **pbuilder** to your users, it makes it even easier for them to gain root access on the machine.

As a warning, here is the story of the obsessive system administrator who bind-mounted **/home** to be able to work effectively within the **pbuilder chroots**. After a particularly rough day, he logs in to his **pbuilder chroot** and executes the command that cures the senses and the soul, and paves the path to enlightenment: **rm -rf /**. Knowing that **pbuilder chroots** are not persistent, he sits back, takes a deep breath, and feels as if a giant stone had been lifted from his chest... until he finds out that the bind-mounted **/home** directory inside the **chroot** is in fact the same as the one holding all his data.

9.6.5 Modifying the tarball

pbuilder normally just deletes the base system after having done whatever the user requested. Making permanent changes to the base system is arguably not as easy as it should be; **pbuilder** was designed to build packages in a minimal base system environment, and expecting more from 'login' than it currently does it certainly not justified.

Nevertheless, **pbuilder** features hooks to allow scripts to act on the unpacked base system. The full set of hooks is documented in **pbuilder (1)**; the following demonstrates how to use hooks to obtain an interactive shell just before the update process finishes and **pbuilder** repacks the tarball. Some example hooks can be found in **/usr/share/doc/pbuilder/examples**:

```
~$ mkdir -p hooks
~$ cat <<"EOF" > hooks/E99shell
#!/bin/bash -e

PROMPT='do you want to spawn a shell [y/N]? '
TIMEOUT=$SHELL_TIMEOUT
```

```
read -p"$PROMPT" -t$TIMEOUT -n1 ans < /dev/tty > /dev/tty || echo -n tim
eout.
echo

if [[ $ans = y ]] || [[ $ans = Y ]]; then
  /bin/bash < /dev/tty &> /dev/tty
  rm -f /root/.bash_history
fi
EOF
~$ chmod +x hooks/E99shell
~$ echo export SHELL_TIMEOUT=60 >> ~/.pbuilderrc
~$ sudo pbuilder update --hookdir ./hooks
```

Hooks of type **E** are invoked just before the base system is repacked, and priority 99 suggests that the shell hook executes last. If you invoke the **update** method with the **--hookdir** set appropriately, **pbuilder** will first update the sandbox and then drop you into it to allow for custom manipulation. Any changes you make in this shell session will be written to the tarball and used in further invocations of **pbuilder**. You may also set the **$HOOKDIR** variable in ~/.pbuilderrc to your hook directory to use the hooks permanently.

Recent versions of **pbuilder** support the **--save-after-login** and **--save-after-exec** options to achieve much the same effect. I prefer the hooks approach because it allows for more prominent notification that changes are being preserved. For instance, it is trivial to change the shell prompt in the above to warn about persistency[23].

---

[23]Of course, this may not be relevant if you do not juggle around 50 shell sessions at once, like my wonderful **fluxbox** instance has to on a daily basis.

10

Documentation and resources

Let's say the docs present a simplified view of reality...
— Larry Wall

Debian, like most other open source software, does not come with a printed manual. In addition to books like the one you are reading right now (which tries to be more than a manual), documentation is spread all over the local system and the Internet.

In the following, I attempt to compile a list of useful resources for any level of Debian expertise, including references to more social content among the pure technical stuff.

An important point to keep in mind is that the software found in the Debian archive is kept as close as possible to the upstream release. Debian maintainers try to limit the changes made during Debianisation to a minimum. As a result, the software you install is very similar (if not identical) to the software released by its upstream authors. Thus, all the resources that are available upstream (including mailing lists and documentation) apply to the product as installed on a Debian system. Thus you can get the best of both worlds: software installation and maintenance managed by Debian, and the ability to peruse the same resources as if installed from source.

10.1 Local documentation

The available documentation for Debian can be categorised into three groups: installed documentation, documents available in separate packages, and online documentation. Between the three, a vast amount of resources exist, and there is more.

The Debian policy (see chapter 5.7) encourages maintainers to provide manpages for every programme, utility, or function, and even configuration files (in section 5) associated with a package. Absence of a manpage is to be considered a bug. The documentation of protocols and auxiliary aspects of a package is optional.

In addition to the manpages, many packages provide documentation and other useful resources in their directories under **/usr/share/doc**. Thus, *e.g.***/usr/share/doc/ cron** contains information to augment the **cron** manpages. It is not mandatory for a package to provide any files other than **changelog.Debian.gz** and **copyright** in this directory.

Even though no strict rules exist, it is customary for packages to use subdirectories for specific types of addditional information. HyperText Markup Language (HTML) documentation (if it exists) can usually be found under *./html*. Examples, including example and template configuration files reside under *./examples*. If applicable, *./contrib* may contain scripts and utilities related to the software contained in the package, but not part of it (usually contributed by users instead).

Some source packages generate separate binary packages for software and documentation. For instance, the **debconf** package provides the programme, while all documentation except the manpages may be found in **debconf-doc**. The rationale is obvious: virtually every Debian machine has **debconf** installed, but the documentation is only required by a few. Separation helps to the installation footprint of a Debian system as low as possible, which is particularly important for embedded systems. Note that there is no standard for the naming of document packages. Although **-doc** is the most common, **-docs** is also used, and there may be others.

10.2 Online resources

As a distribution that primarily lives on the Internet, a plethora of Debian-related resources are available online. On the one hand, the **debian.org** domain hosts numerous pages with helpful information. On the other hand, many unofficial web sites are devoted to Debian and serve as inexpendable repositories. The **debian.net** domain provides subdomains for Debian-related use to its developers.

Rather than listing all possible resources, the following attempts to pick the most important, while ensuring that everything is up to date (outdated documentation is often worse than no documentation). I make no attempt to cover all available resources on the Net.

Also note that many of these online resources are available as Debian packages, effectively adding them to the set of local documentation. I make an effort to mention the corresponding packages where appropriate.

10.2.1 Official documentation and manuals

The one-stop source for documentation about Debian is the DDP[1], which attempts to unify the vast amounts of documentation that exist about Debian. In particular, the project strives to weed stale documentation and unify existing ones to improve the user experience.

The following lists the most important resources under supervision by the DDP. All these documents are available online at **http://www.debian.org/doc**, so in the following, only the relative path will be used. Where a document is available as a Debian package (most are), this is noted:

manuals/reference/reference.en.html
> The Debian reference is intended to serve as a post-installation user's guide, covering many aspects of system administration with a large number of examples. The document is also available in the **debian-reference** package. It is developed collaboratively at **http://qref.sf.net**.

manuals/debian-faq
> A large number of common questions are answered in this FAQ before you even have to ask them. Make sure you give it a read! The **doc-debian** package provides the list for offline use.

manuals/securing-debian-howto
> With viruses and hackers, it is paramount these days to secure a system connected to the Internet. The Securing Debian Manual provides an excellent resource with instructions on how to harden the distribution, and beyond. You can find this document in the **harden-doc** package.

manuals/apt-howto
> A good understanding of the **APT** system and its tools is an important prerequisite for the successful administrator. The file can be installed with the **apt-howto** package.

[1] http://www.debian.org/doc/ddp

manuals/project-history

> If you are into history, this one is for you. The document also describes the goals of Debian, and can be locally installed with the **debian-history** package.

debian-policy

> As one of the most important documents of the Debian system, the policy (see chapter 5.7) is also available in the **debian-policy** package. Even though the policy should be unnoticeable, reading this document will further your understanding of the Debian system and its philosophies.

manuals/developers-reference

> Whether you are maintaining packages for yourself, or for Debian, you will find best practices and other helpful information here, or in the **developers-reference** package.

books

> A number of books have been written about the Debian system. This document attempts to list, evaluate, and categorise them.

The release notes[2] and installation manual[3] are invaluable resources for the current *stable* release.

The BTS (see chapter 10.6), which stores information about almost every known bug that exists in Debian, is an important resource. The BTS allows you to verify whether a problem is due to a fault in your local configuration, or whether you are at the mercy of the upstream maintainer to provide a fix (or go and fix the software yourself, see chapter 5.9). In addition, entries in the BTS often provide workarounds or temporary solutions.

The Debian Desktop project[4] focuses on bringing Debian to the Desktop, and "to the mainstream world." The group concentrates on usability improvements without limiting their target audience to a certain skill level.

The Debian Accessibility Project[5] aims to make Debian a suitable operating system for people with disabilities. The goal is a completely accessible system which offers users with disabilities the highest possible amount of independence, bundled with the strengths and freedom of the Debian system.

Finally, the Debian International pages[6] are the starting point for non-English-speaking Debian users. Here, you may find information on how to see translations of the Debian web pages, and links to resources in the supported languages.

[2] http://www.debian.org/releases/stable/releasenotes
[3] http://www.debian.org/releases/stable/installmanual, the newest version is always available at http://d-i.alioth.debian.org/manual
[4] http://www.debian.org/devel/debian-desktop
[5] http://www.debian.org/devel/debian-accessibility
[6] http://www.nl.debian.org/international

10.2.2 Semi-official resources

A Debian "executive summary" may be found online[7]. Although somewhat out-dated, the page still serves as a quick reference about some of the most important points of the Debian system.

At **http://wiki.debian.net**, some developers maintain a Wiki, which is a public, collaborative scratchpad, intended to be "the simplest online database that could possibly work." In a Wiki, everyone has read and write rights, can modify, add, and delete pages. All changes are logged and can be undone. A Wiki thus allows everyone to work together and to assemble tidbits of information in a central location. As such, the Debian Wiki serves as a useful resource to which everyone can contribute to make it even better.

If you are interested in the Debian community, you may want to visit **http://planet.debian.org** once in a while (or set up your RDF Site Summary (RSS) reader appropriately). The site unifies the web diaries[8] of all developers that run them. Non-developers may well be included if they have made a name for themselves with quality contributions. Reading "Planet" every now and then will give you a good idea of what is going on behind the lines.

The Debian Women project, a rather recent yet prosperous effort, aims at increasing women's visibility in the project. While the project's incentive was to turn the Debian project into a more attractive environment for women, it is now going beyond to set a precedent on how to improve integration of minority groups with Debian, and to facilitate joining the project for everyone, men and women alike. The Debian Women web site[9] aims at providing helpful documentation, and the community around the project tries to maintain a warm and friendly environment.

Finally, Debian is also a language with special words, abbreviations, and acronyms. Whether your native tongue is English or not, sometimes it is hard to follow a document or discussion when the author or participants bandy jargon about. The Debian Women project has started to put together the Debian dictionary[10] which offers a glossary of Debian terms, translations of common words to and from non-English languages, and expands abbreviations and acronyms.

10.2.3 Unofficial resources

As one of the biggest Linux distributions, Debian is present in many places on the Web. The following attempts to highlight some of the most useful bookmarks.

---

[7] http://people.debian.org/~osamu/newbie.html
[8] No, I will *not* use the b* word…
[9] http://women.alioth.debian.org
[10] http://women.alioth.debian.org/dicts

http://debianplanet.org

Titled "News for Debian. Stuff that *really* matters"[11], this site aims to provide the latest news for the Debian World. The future of the site is not certain. With http://planet.debian.org and the Debian Weekly News (DWN)[12], the authors seem to be unable to find a remaining niche[13]. However, it seems that the moderators are continuing...thus, if you like the site, write to them and encourage them, or even consider helping out!

http://newbiedoc.sf.net

newbieDoc is an exchange platform for "documentation by newbies for newbies." Even though the project started out as a Debian project, the documentation extends beyond the Debian system to include tips and useful information about common software and Linux or even Unix paradigms. The newbiedoc package contains a snapshot of the available documentation.

http://colt.projectgamma.com/hands-on/hands-on.html

The Hands-on Guide to Debian aims to be an introductory guide to Debian GNU/Linux, targeted at users new to the Unix operating system. It features recipes and tips on how to accomplish common tasks on Unix-like operating systems, and on Debian especially.

http://melkor.dnp.fmph.uniba.sk/~garabik/debian-utf8/HOWTO/howto.html

This document is a detailed description of Unicode/UTF-8 status in Debian, and how to enable it. A UTF-8-enabled system allows for special characters from all over the world to be used. Thus, it should also eliminate the need for the the configuration of Euro support, for which a separate document is available[14].

http://debianhelp.org

This site hosts a plethora of information about the Debian system, as well as user support forums, news, and user-contributed documentation. In addition to solutions for common problems, you will find articles here documenting the installation of Debian on all kinds of hardware, or the configuration of Debian-based appliances.

http://aboutdebian.com

About Debian Linux aims to assemble all there is to know about Debian GNU/Linux. There you will find background information, explanatory documents, and recipes for performing common tasks with the Debian system.

[11] see http://slashdot.org
[12] http://www.debian.org/News/weekly
[13] http://debianplanet.org/node.php?id=1100
[14] http://www.debian.org/doc/manuals/debian-euro-support, or the euro-support package.

http://www.debianhowto.de/en/howtos.html

> This site aims to be for Debian what The Linux Documentation Project (TLDP) HOWTOs[15] are to Linux. The page hosts numerous documents that explain how to perform various aspects of system administration and configuration with the Debian system.

http://debian-administration.org

> Although a young site, its potential already shows. The forum is intended to collect articles on random aspects of system administration, geared towards generic Linux and Debian-specific topics.

http://www.linuks.mine.nu/workstation

> This site documents the configuration of a Debian machine as a workstation, including screen shots and configuration hints for different packages to get day-to-day tasks done on a Debian system: from word and graphics processing, through CD recording and sound editing, to networking applications, everything is briefly presented.

http://people.debian.org/~enrico/survey/survey.php

> Enrico Zini has evaluated a survey conducted in April 2004 about how Debian users use the system. The results are available for the curious giving to give various insights into the Debian community. In addition, the information presented here may come in useful during decision-making.

http://people.debian.org/~psg/ddg

> Dale Scheetz wrote "Dwarf's Guide to Debian GNU/Linux", a book about Debian, which he published online (as well as in print). The book is now somewhat outdated as it is largely based on the Debian *potato* release.

http://liw.iki.fi/liw/texts/debian-lessons

> This page documents project management lessons learnt from the Debian project. While many processes in Debian are undoubtedly less than perfect, the overall performance is astonishing. Maybe other projects can learn from the mistakes made by the Debian project, and embark on a new endeavour with proper preparation, thanks to the points mentioned here.

http://people.debian.org/~bap/dfsg-faq.html

> The page aims to answer some common questions about the DFSG. If licencing is of any importance to you, this document is a must.

http://www.pseudorandom.co.uk/2004/debian/ipsec

> The Debian kernels provide native Internet Protocol Secure (IPsec) support, even in the 2.4 kernel series (it was backported from 2.5). The site attempts

---

[15] http://tldp.org/HOWTO

to serve as glue between the Debian system and the upstream documenta-tion[16].

http://debian.fabbione.net

This site hosts the Debian IPv6 project, which aims to help administrators run IPv6-capable systems without much effort, harnessing the power of the package management tools. Essentially, the project provides enhanced pack-ages for all those programmes in the Debian archive that do not support IPv6 in a separate **APT** repository (with a custom versioning scheme), so that it can be trivially integrated with **APT**. Another site related to Debian and IPv6 is also available[17].

10.3   Printed resources

Even though the book you are holding in your hands is not the first or only book about Debian, it is difficult to find printed and up-to-date material on the oper-ating system. In October 2004, Raphaël Herzog (a Debian developer) published a book called "Debian," which covers the administration and use of Debian *sarge*[18]. The book was only available in French at the time of writing.

Two Debian developers, David B. Harris and Benjamin Mako Hill, are writing the "Debian GNU/Linux 3.X Bible", which is to be released in the second quarter of 2005. The book introduces the basics of Debian system administration and focuses mainly on how to get daily jobs done on a Debian system[19].

Frank Ronneburg maintains an online book in German, targeted at users of the Debian system[20], which he plans to have printed one day. The second edition of Peter H. Ganten's book "Debian GNU/Linux-PowerPack" was released in the mid-dle of 2004. Also written in German, the book deals with the fundamentals of installation, administration, and use of Linux and the Debian system.

In addition, several older titles exist which deal with older versions of Debian and have not been maintained since, including the aforementioned "Dwarf's Guide to Debian GNU/Linux". However, these books are based on earlier versions of the De-bian system and do not cover recent developments, such as the new installer, de-vice management, or several aspects of the network configuration system. A list of books about the project and/or the operating system is maintained on the official Debian web site[21].

[16]found at http://ipsec-howto.org
[17]http://people.debian.org/~csmall/ipv6
[18]http://www.ouaza.com/livre/admin-debian
[19]http://www.wiley.com/WileyCDA/WileyTitle/productCd-0764576445.html
[20]http://www.openoffice.de/linux/buch/
[21]http://www.debian.org/doc/books

10.4 Discussion forums

As an instance of open source software, Debian is developed around the clock and all over the globe. It is therefore no big surprise that the project makes intensive use of synchronous and asynchronous discussion forums, perhaps more so than many other projects. Synchronous discussion takes place mainly on in IRC channels, and over 180 mailing lists provide the asynchronous back-end that supports the project's operations across all timezones.

10.4.1 Mailing lists

Most of Debian's development takes place via email, and mailing lists are the preferred medium of communication in the project. The lists range in granularity from huge catch-all lists to small lists that are very specific in their topics.

The project operates two primary mailing list servers:

lists.debian.org

> With over 180 mailing lists, **lists.debian.org** is the primary list server of the project. Here, coordination and discussion lists are found, as well as support lists for users and aspiring developers. The server is powered by **smartlist**, and hosts some other project lists besides the Debian ones. All lists associated with the Debian project are prefixed as such, *e.g.* **debian-user**.

lists.alioth.debian.org

> **alioth** is Debian's dedicated projects server, which hosts Debian-related projects as well as other free software projects, providing each project with mailing lists upon request. Lists related to Debian packaging efforts are prefixed with **pkg-**. The lists are provided by **Mailman**.

While the lists on **alioth** are probably mostly of interest to those contributing to the individual projects, the primary mail server hosts a number of lists aimed specifically at Debian users (remember: every developer is also a user). While it is very possible that any discussion will reach technical levels, these lists are where most user support happens. Spending a bit of time on these lists, it is interesting to see that questions come from everywhere, even from developers. The same applies to answers: the Debian lists are just not there to allow users to put questions to the developers; instead, users ask each other, and whoever can help, will gladly do so.

Discussion lists

The majority of Debian lists are discussion lists, to which anyone can subscribe. General information about these lists is available online[22]. The lists all have an open posting policy. Thus, you do not have to be subscribed to post to the list. To handle the large volume of spam the lists receive, the list servers employs **SpamAssassin** (with a conservative configuration). In addition, the main list server also runs a custom software called **crossassassin**, which attempts to filter out posts sent to multiple lists at once — spam is often sent to multiple lists simultaneously. It is possible to get excluded from these filters by subscribing to the **whitelist**[23].

Apart from the normal rules of Netiquette[24], one of the most important considerations about posting to the Debian lists is to choose the one most closely matching the topic and level of the issue at hand. To facilitate the decision, I describe the most prominent lists in the following. All lists are linked online[25].

debian-user

> The **debian-user** mailinglist is the principal support forum for the Debian system. It is essentially open to all topics and thus serves as a catch-all for all kinds of problems and discussions about the administrative and user side of the Debian system. It relays several hundred mails per day and serves as an excellent resource to learn about the system as you gradually shift from reading to submitting your own answers here and there. Nevertheless, there are often more appropriate lists where the advice may be more timely or more competent.

debian-security

> Anything related to the security of the Debian system should be discussed on this list. There is often no clear separation between usage and development as the issues circulating here often touch both aspects. In general, the level of discussion is fairly advanced. This mailing list is sometimes confused with the email address of the Debian security team: **security@debian.org**. The mailing list is open to the public; emails to the security team are only read by members of the team.

debian-firewall

> The Debian system makes an excellent basis for a firewall. Topics on this list range from packet filters to intrusion detection and content filters.

debian-isp

> This list unites people running Debian in an ISP environment. As ISPs usually battle with advanced issues, the level of this list is generally kept high.

---

[22] http://www.debian.org/MailingLists
[23] http://lists.debian.org/whitelist
[24] http://www.albion.com/netiquette
[25] http://lists.debian.org/completeindex.html

debian-legal
> Any discussions about legal matters, such as licences, are held here. Discussions can grow rather fierce at times, such is the law...

debian-doc
> Anything related to documentation in Debian is on topic here.

debian-kernel
> This list is exclusive to discussions about the kernels used with Debian (not just Linux), patches, bugs, tools, modules, and kernel packaging issues. Note that issues about **kernel-package** are better discussed with **kernel-package @packages.debian.org** first.

debian-bsd
> Debian is not just Linux. Several sub-projects exist to make the Debian system available on top of a BSD kernel. This list is dedicated to issues related to BSD ports.

debian-mentors
> As chapter chapter 9 shows, developing and maintaining packages for Debian is not an act of wizardry. However, it is not trivial either. Many users develop their own packages for later inclusion in Debian (see chapter 2.5.2), or just to profit from the robustness of the package management tools. The **debian-mentors** list provides a productive forum for people new to Debian packaging, and new and prospective developers alike. Many competent and experienced developers ready to help, and the atmosphere is not as daunting as can be the case on the **debian-devel** mailing list. A detailed FAQ document is available online[26].

debian-devel
> What **debian-user** is to usage and administration of the Debian system, **debian-devel** is to its development. This is a high-volume list which handles all topics related to the technical side and inner workings of the operating system and its tools. It should not be used for support questions, but remains open to everyone to participate and possibly influence future development of the project.

debian-qa
> On this mailing list, quality issues and topics of quality assurance are discussed.

debian-testing
> If you are interested in the next Debian release, one great way to contribute is to take the packages from *testing* for a test drive and report problems. The **debian-testing** mailing list is dedicated to this.

[26]http://people.debian.org/~mpalmer/debian-mentors_FAQ.html

debian-release

> The upcoming Debian release is coordinated on this mailing list, including discussions on issues that hold up the release or should be addressed in time.

debian-boot

> The development of the **debian-installer** takes place on this mailing list, which is open for discussions about any aspects regarding the Debian boot sequence, including device auto-detection and architecture compatibility.

debian-project

> Anything related to the project, which is not of a technical nature, has its place on this mailing list.

debian-private

> This mailing list is closed and accessible to developers only. It is intended to be used for non-technical discussions that are not suitable for the public, such as absence announcements. Rest assured that technical issues are highly discouraged and pushed to public forums as soon as possible.

Chapter 2.4.2 gave you an overview of the social aspects of the Debian community. Understanding the community and how it works is an important step. Learning how to ask smart questions[27] is important to your experience on these lists.

The Debian mailing lists are also governed by a code of conduct[28], by which you should try to abide. If you do not, you risk being flamed or simply ignored. In addition to the guidelines, you should try not to break threading, either by starting a new topic by replying to an existing topic (and changing the subject header), or by using a mail programme that does not understand how Email works[29].

Announcement lists

While the aforementioned lists are discussion forums, a number of "read-only" mailing lists are available to stay up to date on Debian issues:

debian-announce

> This list receives major news and announcements of very important changes in the project. It is advisable for everyone using Debian to subscribe here. The list has very low traffic.

[27] http://www.catb.org/~esr/faqs/smart-questions.html
[28] http://www.debian.org/MailingLists/#codeofconduct
[29] If you have no preference about the mail client, you may want to have a look at Mozilla Thunderbird (http://mozilla.org/products/thunderbird) and mutt (http://mutt.org).

debian-security-announce

> Any announcements about security issues are released to this mailing list. It is advisable to subscribe here. The list has very low traffic.

debian-news

> Every Tuesday, the Debian project releases the DWN newsletter, which is published online[30] and also delivered to this list. The DWN is an entertaining and informative read, a must for those with a serious interest in the project. It is also a good way to contribute, so if you have a journalistic vein, please consider helping out.

Subscribing and unsubscribing

The lists are run with standard mailing list software. For both servers, you can use a web interface to subscribe, or send a simple email request to manage your subscription. Please *do not* send these requests to the mailing list address!

lists.debian.org

Each mailing list hosted in **lists.debian.org** has a web page of its own. For instance, **debian-user**'s home is at **http://lists.debian.org/debian-user**, which prominently displays a simple form to subscribe and unsubscribe. Upon entering your desired subscription email address and hitting **subscribe**, the server will send a message to the address. To confirm your subscription, you have to reply to this email, keeping the subject field intact (prefixes such as "Re:" are fine). If successful, the server sends a welcome message.

Unsubscribing works in the same, except that you need to hit the **unsubscribe** button instead. It is important to use the same address as used to subscribe. The following command can extract the message used for subscription from a message you received via the list, in case you have forgotten it:

```
~$ sed -ne 's,.*bounce-debian-[^=]*=\(.*\)=\([^@]*\)@.*,\1@\2,p'
```

Assuming that **$EMAIL** holds your email address, the following two commands should illustrate how to use the mail interface instead. In fact, the web interface does nothing more than compose these messages for you. Please note that **lists.debian.org** has been abbreviated as **l.d.o** for brevity[31].

```
~$ mail -s "subscribe $EMAIL" debian-user-request@l.d.o < /dev/null
~$ mail -s "unsubscribe $EMAIL" debian-user-request@l.d.o < /dev/null
```

[30] http://www.debian.org/News/weekly

[31] It is quite common for Debian machines to be referenced similarly, if unambigious. For instance, **d.d.o** is the LDAP server, **p.d.o** is **people.debian.org**, and **b.d.o** is **bugs.debian.org**. An email address like **madduck@d.o** is then what you would expect.

The Debian mailing list server has had its fair share of bad publicity. Many people seem to be unable to unsubscribe, but the problem is almost always with the user. The list managers have assembled a list of common glitches to avoid[32] to help people get on and off the project's lists.

lists.alioth.debian.org

alioth runs **Mailman**, which provides a comprehensive information page for each list, accessible through the index at **http://lists.alioth.debian.org**. **Mailman** requires a subscription password to be entered below the email address. Please do not use an important password as it will be transmitted as plain text. Also, make sure you remember the address used for subscription! Even though **Mailman** sends monthly reminders, there is no universally easy way to find out the address used for the subscription *ad hoc*.

Shortly after hitting **subscribe**, you will receive a confirmation message to which you must reply. The server waits for this message before adding you to the list and welcoming you with yet another email.

Unsubscriptions are done through the subscription management page, which is available online after logging in using the form at the bottom of the list information page, using your email address. Depending on the version of **Mailman**, you have to enter your subscription password if you want to make changes directly on the configuration page, or log in first to see the available options. For every list, you can then disable mail delivery (among other options), or unsubscribe yourself altogether.

Mailman also provides a mail interface for subscription management, which is somewhat easier to use than **smartlist's**. The following two lines should be enough to illustrate its use. Again, I assume that $EMAIL holds the email address to be subscribed:

```
~$ /usr/sbin/sendmail -f $EMAIL listname-join@l.a.d.o < /dev/null
~$ /usr/sbin/sendmail -f $EMAIL listname-leave@l.a.d.o < /dev/null
```

More information on how to use the **Mailman** mailing lists is available on the **Mailman** web site[33].

List archives

The archives of the various Debian mailing lists are some the most valuable resources there are. With archived posts dating back more than ten years, the archives not only hold timeless gems, but frequently the answers to many questions. In fact,

---

[32] http://www.debian.org/MailingLists/#subglitches
[33] http://www.list.org/mailman-member

if the archives were used more rigorously as a knowledge resource, it would cut the volume of traffic on the Debian lists by half.

The official Debian archives are part of the problem as they provide threaded and sortable views of the traffic, but have no search function. Instead, Debian relies on Internet search engines to index the archives, and they do so, although with a delay of several days. Fortunately, alternatives exist. For people fond of Usenet, **gmane.org** provides all the Debian lists via Network News Transfer Protocol (NNTP). In addition, the **lurker** package provides a software specifically designed for the Debian lists, providing many useful features that make its archives far more convenient to use than regular list archives. You can see it in action over at its author's page[34].

Please try to make use of these resources before contacting the list for assistance. Very often, the answers are already available in the archives.

10.4.2 Web forums

For those who prefer to to interact with the community over a web interface, http://forums.debian.net hosts a number of user support forums and knowledge channels. Forums accessible over the browser have some advantages over mailing lists, even though their nature largely overlaps. This said, web forums require you to go out and fetch discussions and replies while mailing lists deliver them right to your doorstep.

On the one hand, web forums are more independent of the user agent, as all modern browsers can handle the forum web sites and thus allow interaction. On the other hand, an astonishing number of new email clients are not ready for effective mailing list usage[35]. Web forums can hence be used even in the absence of a sensible mail client, which is often the case while travelling, or in companies with restrictive policies.

Since web forums are not based on email messages, you can get by without disclosing your email address to the public. The Debian mailing lists are all archived without any obfuscation of email addresses, so spammers may harvest them. Not obfuscating the email addresses is a choice made in favour of convenience. Considering that the Debian mailing lists are also available from a plethora of other sites without a consistent obfuscation policy, the difference is miniscule.

In addition, the software used for the Debian web forums (**phpBB**) adds some synchronous features to the otherwise asynchronous discussion boards by tracking users' online status and allowing for personal messages to be sent between two

---

[34]http://people.debian.org/~terpstra

[35]To give just an example: only few email clients handle replying properly (see chapter 10.4.1), and some fail to display messages with digital signatures, which are quite common the the Debian mailing lists.

parties. Furthermore, web-based forums make it easier to join an existing discussion, or to submit a one-time post. The entire thread is available, so you need not have followed it from the start. You may prefer the ability to read a whole thread in chronological order. The mailing list archives are not ideal for everyone, and while lurker[34] does not allow threads to be listed chronologically[36], web-based forums may be preferable.

If you are interested in following every discussion in a forum, you will be better served by mailing lists. Lists also enable you to harness the filtering and categorisation features of your mail client, integration with your address book, and other local tools. Along the same lines, mailing lists can be trivially read offline (*e.g.* on a plane), while doing so with web-based forums is not easy.

Lastly, it should be noted that the communities of both media are different and hardly overlap. Based on experience, web forums are infrequently used by the same users over long periods of time, while mailing lists tend to have considerably less fluctuations in discussion peers.

10.4.3   IRC — Internet Relay Chat

IRC is a chat system, which uses a large number of globally-spaced, but synchronised servers to provide a robust infrastructure with close to real-time performance. To use IRC, you log in as a user with a **nickname** and then send private messages (also known as **privmsgs**) to others, or join **channels** to participate in group discussion. The channels are usually specific to certain topics, and varying degrees of guidelines apply. These are usually announced in the channel's **topic** message.

Debian runs a couple of channels on two separate IRC networks. The first, accessible through **irc.freenode.org** is more or less the official Debian IRC network (**irc.debian.org** points there), but **irc.oftc.net** is actively used at the same time. Some channels exist separately on both networks. As they are not synchronised, a channel is mostly identified by both name and network. If the network identifier is absent, **irc.freenode.org** is probably assumed.

IRC channels are easy to register, and come and go faster than one could keep track. An (unofficial) web site is in the works[37], and intended as a reference for the official or semi-official channels supported by Debian developers. In the following, I attempt to list the most important channels. The parallels between channel names and mailing lists are obviously intentional, and most of the rules of a mailing list apply to the respective channel, and *vice versa*. When people refer to a forum, they will either *e.g.* talk of a list (**debian-boot**), or the IRC channel (**#debian-boot**); the leading pound sign identifies the medium.

---

[36]see http://bugs.debian.org/280603
[37]http://channels.debian.net

#debian

As Debian's main IRC channel, **#debian** serves as the primary user support forum, and also hosts general discussions among members of the community. A channel by this name is present on both IRC networks (but not synchronised). An unofficial FAQ for this channel is available online[38].

#debian-<language>

Several non-English channels exist to accomodate Debian users, and to coordinate localisation (translation) efforts at the same time. Most of the time, the channel name will consist of **debian-** followed by the two letter country code[39] (like **#debian-es** and **#debian-fr**). Others use the full (English) name of the language (like **#debian-catalan** and **#debian-japanese**). Others use a dot, such as **#debian.de**.

#debian-mentors

New maintainers, and maintainers who are not interested in deep, technical discussions are invited to ask their questions related to packaging here.

#debian-devel

Discussions in this channel focus on development issues of the Debian system, and the channel also serves as a hangout for developers. A channel by this name is present on both IRC networks, but the two are not synchronised.

#debian-boot

This channel is dedicated to the development of the Debian installer.

#debian-kernel

Debian kernel issues are up for discussion in this channel.

#debian-bugs

During bug squashing parties, this channel serves as the primary electronic communication medium. The channel exists on both IRC networks.

#debian-private

Similar to the mailing list, **#debian-private** is exclusive to developers and almost never used. I am mentioning it here for completeness.

Conduct on IRC channels is generally rougher than on mailing lists, and not for the faint-hearted. Most of the same rules as for mailing lists apply, and Netiquette[24] should also be obeyed. In addition, it is generally considered polite to ask first before sending someone a private message. Also, only send private messages if the issue is really private; keep in mind that Debian is about open development, so let other people hear what you have to say (within the expected bounds of conduct).

[38] http://www.linuks.mine.nu/debian-faq-wiki
[39] http://en.wikipedia.org/wiki/ISO_639

Lastly, the FAQ of the **#debian** channel[40] largely applies to all Debian channels (and most other IRC channels) too; please make sure you have read it.

Also note that it is generally not a good idea to paste more than a few lines of text into a channel. If you want to share a command's output with the rest of a channel, it is best to use a "paste bot," such as **http://rafb.net/paste**. Alternatively, special bots exist for the Debian channels on **freenode.org**[41] and **oftc.org**[42], and will automatically announce your pasted text in the specific channel.

A list of the most important IRC commands is provided in table 10.1.

Command	Function
/connect irc.debian.org	establishes a connection to the server
/join #debian	joins the **#debian** channel
/part	leaves the current channel
/quit	quits IRC
/topic	displays the current channel topic
/msg madduck hello!	sends "hello!" to **madduck**

On **#debian**, two robots attempt to field common questions. Thus, if **dpkg** or **apt** suddenly start talking to you, do not be surprised. You can interactively use this by sending a private message to them.

```
#debian: /msg dpkg help
[...]
```

Start with "help" to get an overview of the commands offered by the bot.

10.5 Contacting people

The primary means of communication between members of the Debian community is email. While mailing lists (see chapter 10.4.1) are an excellent medium for discussion, there are times when you would want to reach out only to a single person, or exactly the set of people responsible for a certain task or aspect of the project.

One of the strong points of Debian packages is that each and every package has at least one maintainer, listed in the package's meta data:

```
~$ apt-cache show ipcalc | grep ^Maintainer:
Maintainer: martin f. krafft <madduck@debian.org>
```

[40]http://www.linuks.mine.nu/debian-faq-wiki
[41]http://channels.debian.net/paste
[42]http://channels.debian.net/paste2

Additionally, a package may have any number of co-maintainers ("Uploaders"), which are listed in the control information of the source packages. Therefore, you need to have source repositories listed in **/etc/apt/sources.list**, see chapter 5.9.1:

```
~$ apt-cache showsrc wmaker | grep ^Uploaders:
Uploaders: [...] martin f. krafft <madduck@debian.org>
```

Rather than fiddling with command-line tools, these data are also available from the package's homepage (accessible from **http://packages.debian.org**, or via the PTS, see chapter 10.6.9).

Alternatively, every package has an email forwarder of the form **<package>@packages.debian.org**, which reaches the package's maintainer (but not the co-maintainers). To also reach the co-maintainers, you can use the PTS addresses, such as **<package>@packages.qa.debian.org**. Any message sent to this address will be forwarded to all people who have expressed an interest in the package by subscribing to its PTS status tracker (see chapter 10.6.9). Please note that the PTS uses a header checking mechanism to weed out spam. For a message to pass the checks, it must contain the **X-PTS-Approved** header (which can be added automatically, using *e.g.* a **mutt** hook):

```
~$ mutt -e 'my_hdr X-PTS-Approved: sure thing' \
  <package>@packages.qa.debian.org
```

Each Debian developer may also register additional means of contact (specifically, the "I Seek You" (ICQ) UID and IRC nickname), which may be viewed using the LDAP search form at **http://db.debian.org** (or with any LDAP browser, using **ldap://db.debian.org** and base **ou=users,dc=debian,dc=org**), or accessed using **finger**:

```
~$ finger madduck@db.debian.org
[db.debian.org]
uid=madduck,ou=users,dc=debian,dc=org
First name: Martin
Middle name: F.
Last name: Krafft
Email: Martin F. Krafft <madduck@debian.org>
URL: http://people.debian.org/~madduck
IRC nickname: madduck
ICQ UIN: 4883537
Fingerprint: ACF4 9D3E 1E1D 5EE2 B203 5E53 220B C883 330C 4A75
Key block: finger madduck/key@db.debian.org
```

Furthermore, **http://qa.debian.org/developer.php** provides access to a summary of the packages managed for each developer, as well as some useful links.

10.6   The bug tracking system

The Debian BTS is one of the pivot points of the Debian system and its development. Everything, from a grave bug, through minor inconveniences and simple feature requests, is kept in the bug tracking system; each issue is filed against a single package[43], and indexed with a unique ID. While bugs are primarily viewed using the web interface[44], email is the primary means to manipulate bug reports, including the addition of further information to a filed bug.

When a bug is first reported, it enters the bug tracking system in the open state. After the described problem has been fixed by the maintainer and a new version hits the **incoming** archive, the bug is marked as done. While in the open or closed state, additional information may be posted to a bug, or the bug state manipulated using control commands (see chapter 10.6.7). A closed bug is archived 28 days after the last comment was added. Once a bug is archived, it becomes immutable[45]. Figure 10.1 illustrates this cycle.

Figure 10.1:
A bug's life in Debian

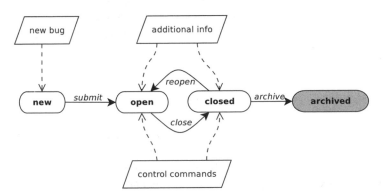

The BTS is a great resource for end users, but it primarily serves to track bugs until fixed versions of affected packages eventually make it to the *unstable* archive. When a bug has been closed by a package in the *unstable* archive, it is marked as closed even though it may continue to apply to the package's versions in *stable* and *testing*. It is thus not a bad idea to check the archived bugs for packages in these archives as well when seeking more information about a problem on the local machine.

---

[43]Actually, a single bug can belong to multiple packages after being reassigned to a comma-separated list of packages (without spaces). This option is not documented and should probably not be used except for the most special cases.

[44]http://bugs.debian.org

[45]Even though it is possible to manually un-archive a bug, this is very rarely done.

10.6.1   Querying the BTS

The Debian BTS can be accessed in a number of ways[46]. The two most relevant to users are through its web and its mail interface. There is also an experimental LDAP gateway as well as a **rsync** server, which is only really useful for mirroring, statistical analysis and status reports.

Using a web browser

The web interface is the most common means of querying the BTS. While its front page[47] presents various search forms, allowing many settings to be configured, the following shortcuts are some examples of how to specify the search criteria as part of the URL:

http://bugs.debian.org/<bug-id>
:   accesses a single bug by ID.

http://bugs.debian.org/<package>
:   shows all bugs of a binary package.

http://bugs.debian.org/src:<package>
:   displays all bug related to the specified source package.

http://bugs.debian.org/from:<submitter@email.address>
:   queries the BTS for all bugs submitted by the owner of the specified email address.

http://bugs.debian.org/<maintainer@email.address>
:   retrieves a listing of all bugs filed against packages belonging to the maintainer with the specified email address.

Browsing bug reports as mbox files

In addition, you can download a bug report and the follow-up thread as a **mbox** file for offline viewing, and to facilitate commenting. Apart from the link at the top of each bug's web page, a shortcut can also be used. Assuming you use **mutt**, this allows you to read the bug report just as if it were regular email. **mutt** correctly threads the comments, and replying to messages works as expected:

```
~$ wget -qO debbug.241343 http://bugs.debian.org/mbox:241343
~$ mutt -f debbug.241343
[...]
~$ rm debbug.241343
```

[46]http://www.debian.org/Bugs/Access
[47]http://bugs.debian.org

Using the LDAP BTS gateway

The BTS can also be accessed using LDAP, using graphical and command line LDAP clients alike. While browsing the bug reports is probably most convenient with a graphical user frontend like **gq**, the command line tools from the **ldap-utils** are ideal for complex searches from the shell.

For instance, you can use the following command to list the all open bugs with the **security** tag:

```
~$ ldapsearch -x -H ldap://bugs.debian.org \
  -b dc=bugs,dc=debian,dc=org \
  '(&(debbugsState=open)(debbugsTag=security))'
[...]
```

You will find more information about the available search criteria, as well as the LDAP schema in use, on the **bts2ldap** gateway page[48].

Unfortunately, the gateway was almost unusably slow at time of writing. Hopefully the future will bring a more powerful implementation to allow for quick and efficient interaction with the BTS via LDAP.

10.6.2   Querying bugs from the command line

The **bts** tool from the **devscripts** package is a command line interface for querying the BTS. Given a criterium, it can download a single bug, or a package's or maintainer's bug listing page and display it in a browser. The browser to use is set by the **$BROWSER** environment variable[49] and can contain a list of different browsers, which are tried in turn. By default (if the variable is not set), the tool uses **sensible-browser**, which should invoke a reasonable browser given the circumstances of its invocation (see chapter 6.1.4).

The following examples should sufficiently illustrate the use of **bts** to obtain bug reports from the command line:

```
~$ export BROWSER=w3m
~$ bts bugs ipcalc
[...]
~$ bts show 241343
[...]
~$ bts bugs tag:sarge
[...]
```

If you prefer to read bug reports with *e.g.* **less**, you can exploit the flexibility of the **$BROWSER** variable:

[48] http://people.debian.org/~aba/bts2ldap
[49] See http://catb.org/~esr/BROWSER

```
~$ BROWSER='w3m -dump' bts show 241343 | less
[...]
```

The bts tool also comes with caching functionality, allowing you to download and cache bug reports for offline use. For instance, if you wanted all bugs related to ipcalc be available without a network connection, you could issue the following command (we are using src:ipcalc to obtain bugs filed against all binary packages generated by the ipcalc source package):

```
~$ bts cache src:ipcalc
[...]
```

Now, to access the cache, you have to force bts into offline mode, using the --offline option, or by setting the $BUGSOFFLINE environment variable; it does not use the cache automatically. Otherwise you may use it as before:

```
~$ bts --offline bugs src:ipcalc
[...]
```

Once the cache has been filled (and ~/.devscripts_cache/bts exists), bts will cache all downloaded data. To prevent the user's home directory from filling up, it also automatically expires outdated cache data, just as it also keeps the cache in sync by updating cached data whenever bugs are requested in online mode. The cache can be cleaned at any time with cleancache, which either takes the same selection criteria as the bugs command, or the keyword ALL to purge the entire cache:

```
~$ bts cleancache src:ipcalc
~$ bts cleancache ALL
```

The querybts tool

Another notable programme is querybts, which installs with the reportbug package. querybts takes a package name or one or more bug numbers, goes out to fetch the associated bug reports and their comments, and displays them with a special pager. The pager allows the bugs to be browsed (by entering a number or index in the pager), and even filtering with Perl regular expressions is available with the [f] key. Just pressing [enter] shows the next screenful of bugs, or exits the programme if no more bugs are to be listed.

Once a bug has been selected, subsequent hits on the enter display the bug's comments in turn. The [o] key returns to the bug listing and allows another bug to be selected. In both menus, the [?] key causes a short command listing to be displayed to refresh the user's memory of the available keystrokes.

Through the mail interface

The option to query the BTS via email is rather appealing, especially for disconnected clients. The usage of the request server is trivial and will appear very familiar to those who have interacted with mail request servers (such as mailing list managers) in the past.

The requests are sent via email to **request@bugs.debian.org**. The subject of the request mail only serves to determine the subject of the response. Commands to the request server go into the mail body, one command per line. For instance, to request the full bug report for **#241343**, the bug index of the **ipcalc** package, and the help document with further commands understood by the request server, the following email is all you need:

```
From: a.n.other@email.co.uk
To: request@bugs.debian.org
Subject: bug report requests

send 241343
index packages ipcalc
help
thank you so very much
```

Within a short while, you should receive three emails with the requested information as dumps from the corresponding web pages. The help document for the request server is also available online[50]. The **thank you** command is not really needed, but it never hurts to be polite.

The BTS request server may be discontinued in favour of **bts** (see chapter 10.6.2) at one point.

10.6.3 Bug severities

Each Debian bug is rated with one of seven severity levels to indicate its importance. In increasing order of seriousness, these levels are:

wishlist

>   Wishlist bugs mark feature requests, but are also used for any bugs that are very difficult to fix due to major design considerations, unless they have serious implications.

minor

>   Minor bugs relate to problems which do not affect a package's usefulness. Furthermore, they are presumably easy to fix.

[50]http://www.debian.org/Bugs/server-request

normal
: New bugs are of severity normal by default. Most bugs can be rated with normal severity.

important
: Important bugs have major effects on the usability of a package, but they do not render a software completely unusable to everyone.

serious
: Bugs with severity serious identify violations of the Debian policy (see chapter 5.7), or faults that render the software mostly unusable, according to the package maintainer. Please leave it up to the maintainer to promote a bug to **serious** when the policy is not being violated.

grave
: A grave bug makes the package in question unusable or mostly so, causes data loss, or introduces a security hole allowing access to the accounts of users who use the package.

critical
: Bugs of criticial severity break unrelated (local) software or the whole system, cause serious data loss, or introduce a security hole on systems where the containing package is installed.

The package maintainer can use the severity to prioritise bugs. Furthermore, bugs of the last three classes (**serious**, **grave**, and **critical**) constitute the set of RC bugs. No package with an open bug of the RC class can ever enter the *stable* release.

When reporting a bug, it is not always easy to decide on the right severity. In general, the lowest four severities are enough for normal use. An RC bug should only be reported after consulting with Debian developers, *e.g.* on a mailing list. Nevertheless, if you are certain that a problem is of release-critical severity, then you should not hesitate to file an appropriate bug. By the way, the **rc-alert** tool in the **devscripts** package allows you to check whether any of the locally installed packages have open RC bugs against them. The **apt-listbug** tool notifies you of any bugs filed against packages you are about to install (see chapter 5.11.3).

Within the lowest four, you should almost always opt for the **normal** severity. The severity can be raised to important following careful consideration and investigation. It is always a good idea to verify the symptoms and possible causes of the bug to make sure that you are looking for the solution in the right place. Furthermore, a bug report with severity **important** should include all relevant information and be crafted with even greater care.

Downgrading a bug to the **minor** severity is less problematic. That said, one should avoid opting for a severity that does not fit the problem. If the problem at hand is a problem with a certain option (or menu item, or process) of a programme, it is probably a **normal** bug. If the problem is an inconvenience (*e.g.* a text box clearing the previous entry, or the user interface not behaving properly), the bug is likely to be **minor**. If, on the other hand, the problem affects a whole subsystem of a programme, do not hesitate to report an **important** bug. If you are simply missing a feature, make it a **wishlist** bug. Choosing a severity level is not final and the developer (or you) may freely change it later (until the bug is archived).

10.6.4 Bug tags

A bug report can also be marked with a set of tags. These tags identify certain properties of a bug. Although mainly reserved for the package maintainer, each tag provides useful information about the problem and is thus also relevant to people researching a problem. The most important tags are the following:

patch
> A patch fixing the problem is included in the bug report or its follow-up messages.

wontfix
> This tag plainly states that the bug will not be fixed. It could be that the maintainer disagrees with the bug report, or that a fix would be too invasive and could cause other problems. Also, this tag is often used to identify **wishlist** bugs that go beyond the scope of the package.

moreinfo
> The maintainer cannot work to solve the bug without more information. If such information is not made available within a reasonable time period, the maintainer may opt to simply close the bug, ideally after trying a few more times to establish contact.

unreproducible
> The maintainer cannot reproduce the bug. If you can reproduce it, maybe you can provide more information on the circumstances of the bug.

help
> The maintainer is at a loss and needs help with fixing the bug (see also chapter 2.5.1).

pending
> A solution has been found and an upload will be made soon. If the maintainer seems to have forgotten about the upload, feel free to send a (polite) reminder.

fixed

> This indicates that the bug has been fixed in a recent NMU, but it has yet to be acknowledged, or that some issues remain (*e.g.* because the fix was merely a hack).

fixed-in-experimental This tag identifies bugs fixed in a package available from the *experimental* archive (see chapter 4.4.1).

security

> The **security** tag identifies security problems and should only be used for such. **security** bugs will be treated with greater priority. Make sure that you only tag security bugs as such since the usual rules of "the boy who cried wolf" apply[51]

upstream

> The problem exists in the upstream source rather than in the Debian packaging. This is similar to marking the bug as **forwarded** (see below).

potato, woody, sarge, etch, sid, experimental

> The bug only applies to the particular Debian release. Efforts are on the way to support bug reports to apply to single versions (or even version ranges) of packages. As soon as this feature is available, these tags will be deprecated.

forwarded

> Although not really a tag, a bug can be marked as forwarded to indicate that the bug has been brought to someone else's attention, most likely the upstream developers'. Forwarded bugs will almost always be accompanied by the **upstream** tag, but the BTS does not automatically connect the two.

10.6.5 Reporting bugs

Bugs are reported using the BTS's mail interface. The format of bug submission mails is straightforward. For instance, to report a minor bug against **postfix**, version 2.1.4-4, the following email to **submit@bugs.debian.org** is all you need:

```
From: a.n.other@email.co.uk
To: submit@bugs.debian.org
Subject: postfix takes ages to start

Package: postfix
Version: 2.1.4-4
Severity: minor

Ever since upgrading to 2.1.4-4, postfix takes 10 seconds to start.
```

---

[51]"The boy who cried wolf" called for help too many times without there being a danger. So when the wolf really came one day, nobody listened.

```
It took only 1 before. Please fix that.

Sincerely,
Ashley Other
```

After many hours of brain racking and hundreds of emails sent back and forth (yes, I am exaggerating), the problem was found to be in the Berkeley database code in libdb4.2, version 4.2.52-16; an upgrade to 4.2.52-17 got rid of the startup delay. Part of why it took so long was that the maintainer did not consider the possibilities of a faulty libdb4.2 version, and the bug reporter did not provide all relevant information.

This bug report and its diagnosis is purely fictitious but it serves to illustrate an important point. A bug is usually the result of a very specific interaction of various factors. To be able to diagnose and fix a bug, the developer must have access to as much information as possible. The poster did report a bug, but left out important data, such as the versions of the packages involved. Obviously though, it is impossible to expect Ashley N. Other to properly collect all relevant pieces of information, or even to know what is relevant and what is not.

The reportbug tool

The reportbug tool has been written to ease the process of reporting bugs for both, the submitter and the receiving maintainer. It reads its configuration from /etc/reportbug.conf but allows per-user modifications in ~/.reportbugrc.

reportbug supports four operating modes, which determine the number of questions asked and the expertise expected from the user. In increasing order of complexity, these are

novice
: This is the default mode and shifts the triage burden onto the maintainer by asking for only the absolute minimal set of information. Furthermore, it checks for updated packages only in the *stable* release. It is the default mode.

standard
: In standard mode, the user can also select from a set of patches to be applied to the bug report.

advanced
: Advanced mode differs from standard mode mainly in that it queries the incoming queue for updated packages, and allows bugs to be filed against so-called "dependency packages," which are those packages that exist for the sole purpose to depend (and thus pull in) others (such as transitional and dummy packages).

expert

> In expert mode, **reportbug** assumes that you are fully aware of the Debian policy and have extensive experience with the bug tracking system. It is advisable not to use this mode unless you really know what you are doing.

Reporting a bug with the tool takes the user through a series of steps, depending on the selected mode. **reportbug** goes out to fetch several bits of information automatically, expecting the user to supply others:

1. Unless a package has been specified as the first argument on the command line, **reportbug** prompts for a package name. Entering "other" will display a screenful of pseudo packages (see chapter 10.6.8) with their descriptions.

2. Once the package name is known, the tool first gathers information about the locally installed package, such as the version number and its installation status. Also, some data relevant to **APT**'s configuration and the system in general is collected.

3. If no package by the name given to **reportbug** is installed, **reportbug** offers to search for files with similar names, automatically selecting the appropriate package when a match is found.

4. Next, it checks whether newer versions of the package are available in the archive. In novice mode, only the *stable* archive is consulted. In standard mode, the *testing* and *unstable* archives are checks as well. For advanced and expert mode, even the **incoming** queue is considered. If a newer version is found to be available, **reportbug** alerts the user of this fact and queries whether it should go on. Unless upgrading is not an option, the bug prevails throughout versions (*e.g.* feature requests). Unless you already know that the newer version does not include a fix, please consider upgrading and verifying the bug's existence in the newer version before continuing to file a bug.

5. Then, any bug reports already filed against the package are displayed using the **querybts** tool (see chapter 10.6.2). When viewing a bug, the [x] key allows you to submit additional information for the bug (rather than filing a new bug), using **reportbug**.

6. If none of the existing bugs relate to the problem you are trying to report, **reportbug** goes on to determine the package's dependencies (and their versions) for later inclusion in the report.

7. **reportbug** then prompts for a subject, which should be a concise summary of the problem. The subject will have the package name (or absolute filename, if that was specified) prepended (unless you are using expert mode).

8.   In advanced mode or above, the programme asks you for additional addresses that should receive the bug report. Please specify third parties involved in the bug here, rather than in the Cc header of the email.

9.   Next, you are prompted for the severity of the problem. Please take good care to make sure you use the right severity level.

10.   In modes standard and above, **reportbug** gives you the opportunity at this moment to add tags to the report. Tags not included in the selection list may be entered verbatim (see chapter 10.6.4).

11.   Finally, **reportbug** spawns your mail user agent or a simple editor to allow you to write the bug report. It should appear after the pseudo header (listing package name, version, and severity), but before the (automatically generated) section with system information.

Authoring the bug report

Using the responses to the various prompts, **reportbug** pieces together an email message that will submit the bug report with a good amount of useful information. It is still up to you to properly describe the bug. Writing a good bug report is an art, and the better a bug report is, the better the odds are that the problem will be found and solved. The Internet has plenty of information on how to report bugs effectively[52]. In general, it is important to be as precise and verbose as possible. Instead of simply claiming that a certain feature does not work, your description of the problem should include the following:

- What do you want to do? What is the desired result of the action that fails due to the alleged bug?

- What do you expect to happen as you perform a certain action, and how does the actual result differ from your expectation?

- What are the exact steps that you are taking? Try to be as specific as possible.

- What circumstances could affect or even cause the problem? Are there certain constellations in which the problem does not appear? If possible, try different ways of achieving your desired result and attempt to pinpoint the conditions under which the bug exists.

- What other information do you consider relevant to the problem? Include whatever comes to your mind. However, try to be reasonable and limit the information to relevant bits. Nevertheless, if you are unsure, it is always better to include more information than to leave out some vital data.

[52]A document by Simon Tatham is a must-read for everyone serious about contributing to the open source community; filing bugs *is* contributing. http://www.chiark.greenend.org.uk/~sgtatham/bugs.html

Writing bug reports also involves the social skills from real life. A bug report is probably going to be ignored or deprioritised if you flame the maintainer or the software's author. Instead, it is important to be polite. Furthermore, keep in mind that a bug report generally puts you in the position of requesting something from someone else. Granted, having bugs fixed is also in the interest of the maintainer, but you are the one establishing contact. Some maintainers may respond to a bug report inappropriately. Do not feel offended. Try to stay calm and polite, and do your best to follow the maintainer's instructions. If you do not see the discussion going anywhere, feel free to contact a mailing list (presumably **debian-user**) for assistance.

As a last note, please do not report multiple problems in a single bug. As the maintainer may be able to immediately fix one issue, but maybe not another, progress cannot be meaningfully represented in the BTS. Instead, if you find multiple problems, file multiple bugs.

Special headers for bug reports

X-Debbugs-No-Ack

Once a bug report has been files, the BTS sends an acknowledgement mail. This email can be suppressed by setting the **X-Debbugs-No-Ack** header to any value (it just has to be present) in the initial email to the BTS. It is also possible to use a mail filter to weed out the acknowledgement replies. For instance, with **procmail**:

```
:0
* ^X-Debian-PR-Message: ack-info [0-9]+$
/dev/null
```

However, this will also eradicate acknowledgements in response to messages sent under your name, by accident or by malicious intention. Obviously, the truly mischievous will just set the header themselves, so there is no cure. The one thing preferable about feature of the mail filter approach (which is **procmail** in the above example) is the entry in the log, which allows you to verify the bug's reception. Of course, you could always confirm the bug submission by checking the bug record online; the record is updated every 15 minutes.

The **X-Debbugs-No-Ack** header (if used) must appear in the email header, not the pseudo header created for the BTS:

```
From: a.n.other@email.co.uk
To: submit@bugs.debian.org
Subject: postfix takes ages to start
X-Debbugs-No-Ack: please keep them to yourself

Package: postfix
[...]
```

X-Debbugs-Cc

Some bug reports may be of interest to a third party. You may have found a bug on a colleagues system and offered to report it (since you have read this book and thus know everything there is to know about bug reporting in Debian), or you may have worked with someone on the problem to be reported and would like to keep that person in the loop. The obvious thing would be to add the individual to the Cc header of the submission email, but this approach has an inherent problem: the BTS assigns the unique ID to each new bug upon submission. For later reference, the third party will probably want to know that ID to be able to track the bug. However, if the individual is sent a carbon copy of the submission email, the ID cannot be included, for it has not been assigned. The solution is to set the **X-Debbugs-Cc** header in the same way as the **X-Debbugs-No-Ack** header, and let the BTS send a carbon copy to the specified addresses once the ID has been assigned:

```
From: a.n.other@email.co.uk
To: submit@bugs.debian.org
Subject: postfix takes ages to start
X-Debbugs-Cc: postfix-bugs@postfix.org

Package: postfix
[...]
```

The BTS will acknowledge the carbon copy (unless **X-Debbugs-No-Ack** is set, in which case acknowledgements are dropped even though the carbon copy is still sent) and send the bug report together with its ID on to **postfix-bugs@postfix.org**.

10.6.6 Mail traffic following a bug report

In addition to using **reportbug**, follow-up information or comments may be appended to a bug record by sending a normal email message to **<bug-id>@bugs. debian.org**. The BTS will append all messages that arrive at these addresses to the corresponding bug records. In addition, it will forward the message on to the package maintainer (or the owner of the bug, see below), and to the **debian-bugs-dist** mailing list[53].

Appending **-maintonly** to the bug number (*e.g.***241343-maintonly@bugs.debian. org**) tells the BTS not to forward the information to the mailing list. If the system is supposed to file the message without forwarding it to the maintainer (or owner), use: **241343-quiet@bugs.debian.org**. It is generally better to avoid using **-quiet**, whereas the use of **-maintonly** for minor additions or corrections is fully justified. Using **-quiet** makes sense for minor additions or corrections to previous messages, or to log information extracted from private discourse with the maintainer.

[53] http://lists.debian.org/debian-bugs-dist

Yet another suffix, -submitter, allows a message to be sent to the submitter of a bug. The message is filed in the bug record by the BTS, and subsequently forwarded to the address that is currently listed as the submitter. Messages sent to -submitter are not forwarded to the maintainer or the debian-bugs-dist mailing list.

The BTS sets the Reply-To header on the bug report forward to the submitter's address as well as the bug address. Thus, when the maintainer replies, the submitter receives a direct mail, and the BTS files the reply. Then, the BTS forwards the reply back to the maintainer as well as the debian-bugs-dist mailing list.

So far, so good. A slight inconvenience arises when the reporter then replies to the maintainer's reply. If the user replies to all correspondents of the message, the maintainer receives the reply twice, once directly, and once via the BTS. Clearly, this is a case for procmail or the like, but it does not hurt for the user to exercise some care in selecting the recipients. As a rule of thumb: delete the maintainer's address (and possibly your own) from the recipient list and send your replies only to the bug address. If the comment is minor, you may opt for the -maintonly suffix. Third parties should be kept on Cc though. For follow-up messages to a bug report, the X-Debbugs-Cc header is ignored.

10.6.7 Interacting with the BTS

The Debian BTS is open to everyone. Not only are bugs and all their follow-up posts freely available via HTTP, bugs may also be manipulated by anyone. While the Debian project has had problems in the past with spam closing bug reports, openness has never been a problem. Every action is logged and the package maintainer is notified via email. Thus, everything, including acts of vandalism, can be detected and reverted. The BTS is an open, collaborative platform and has served the project well.

Almost every aspect of a bug report may be changed via the BTS control interface. However, it is not possible to change or delete comments once they have been posted to the bug. Furthermore, as previously mentioned, every action is logged to the bug record and publicly visible via the web and mail interfaces. In fact, the only way to manipulate a bug report is through a mail request server similar to the request server (see chapter 10.6.2), and every received mail is logged in raw format (including all headers). In case of an abuse attempt, this information can be used to track down the offender.

The control server knows all of the request server commands, and adds the commands used to manipulate bug reports. While most of the BTS control commands are mainly of interest to package maintainers, a number of them are relevant to users cooperating with the package maintainers and interacting with the BTS directly. Each command occupies a line by itself. The first argument is always the bug ID of the bug that is to be modified. Following the ID are the arguments for the specific commands. Control commands of general interest include:

package

Not really a command by itself, the **package** command limits the commands that follow until the end of the request email or the next **package** statement to a specific package. Using this command is highly encouraged as it limits the consequences of typos in bug numbers.

retitle

Changes the bug's title to the new title specified in the argument.

severity

Modifies the bug's severity to the severity specified in the argument.

tags

Alters the set of tags recorded for the bug. The first argument can be a plus, minus, or equals sign (+/-/=) to request the addition, removal, or absolute specification of the set of tags that follows. If no sign is specified, a plus is assumed.

reopen

Reopens a bug report that has not been archived yet. The command takes a new submitter address as argument, which may be '!' to use your mail address. If no argument is specified, the submitter is left unchanged.

owner

By requesting the owner of a bug to be set to the email address specified in the argument (where '!' is shorthand for your email address), you transfer responsibility of the bug to the reader of the address. The BTS will send further mail regarding this bug to the owner address. If you are planning to help out by fixing a bug and you have coordinated this with the maintainer, you may use this command.

close

The use of this command is deprecated. Use the **-done** suffix to the bug's email address instead (see below).

quit, stop, thank...

Any of these commands (as well as two dashes at the beginning of a line) tell the control server to stop processing the message.

For instance, the following email would increase the severity of bug #241343 to minor[54], add the **pending** tag, set the owner to the requester's address, and ensure that all commands only apply to the **wnpp** (pseudo-)package against which #241343 was filed:

---

[54]Setting the severity to minor would be a definite mistake, given the nature of the bug report. It is okay for demonstration purposes, but do not try this at home!

```
From: a.n.other@email.co.uk
To: control@bugs.debian.org
Subject: this space intentionally left blank

package wnpp
severity 241343 minor
tags 241343 + pending
owner 241343 !
```

Logging changes

The above control commands are enough for the BTS to know what to do. However, a human reader may not be able to deduce the reasons of why the changes were made. Instead of sending such plain control emails, it is advisable to provide reasons for the changes. The best way to do so is to append human-readable reasoning to the control commands and sending the email to both, the bug and the control server. In that case, the control server email address must be included in the Bcc header. Please avoid the Cc header, since the control server then usually becomes part of the ensuing correspondence — people prefer to reply to all recipients rather going to the trouble of trimming the recipient list appropriately.

```
From: a.n.other@email.co.uk
To: 241343@bugs.debian.org
Cc: 241343-submitter@bugs.debian.org
Bcc: control@bugs.debian.org
Subject: upload pending

package wnpp
severity 241343 minor
tags 241343 + pending
owner 241343 !
thankyoueversomuch

I heartily agree and think that the reported issue deserves
more attention than a simple wish. I have prepared a solution
and an upload is pending.

Sincerely,
Ashley N. Other
```

The control mail server parses the mail up until it sees the **thankyoueversomuch** command (or any other command starting with "thank"). The rest of the message serves as a record to account for the manipulation. The maintainer of the package to which the bug belongs will receive two emails, the forward of the follow-up post, and the transcript of the actions the control server carried out.

The BTS supports a load of additional commands, which are documented online[55].

---

[55]http://www.debian.org/Bugs/server-control

Closing bugs

When an issue has been resolved, the corresponding bug should be closed. This can happen in one of three ways:

- In the **changelog** entry of the new version, the maintainer can specify that the version closes certain bugs. The Debian archive scripts will automatically extract the bug numbers and close them by submitting the **changes** file to the BTS with an appropriate note.

- A bug can also be closed by sending an explanation to its email address with the **-done** suffix: **nnnnnn-done@bugs.debian.org**.

- Using the **close** BTS control command, a bug can be closed without an explanation. This is discouraged and the command deprecated.

The bts utility

In the **devscripts** package, you can find the **bts** utility, which allows you to interact with the BTS from the command line, rather than expecting you to author cryptic mail control messages (which are not so cryptic after all). Its use is trivial and requires no extra knowledge if you are already familiar with the mail interface. To use **bts** you simply specify the mail interface command in the arguments. Multiple commands can be given, separated by dots or commas:

Each invocation of **bts** produces a separate email message to be sent to **control@bugs.debian.org**, as if you had created it manually.

```
~$ bts severity 241343 wishlist . tags 241343 + wontfix
```

The tool tries hard to figure out the right sender address to use, consulting the standard variables $DEBFULLNAME and $DEBEMAIL, among others. The bts (1) manpage has more information.

10.6.8 Bugs against pseudo-packages

As a bug is normally conceived to be a problem with a software, bugs are generally filed against packages containing software. In fact, the concept of a package is completely hardwired into **debbugs**, the Debian BTS[56]. While it is possible to reassign bugs to other packages, a bug must always belong to a package and cannot exist by itself.

The Debian BTS is an integral part of the Debian project and also serves as a problem tracking system. For instance, errors on the Debian web pages are handled via bugs,

[56]Which is available in the **debbugs** package

as well as problems with the various servers, the policy, the installer, the kernel, the archives, mirrors, or lists, or a plethora of other aspects of the project. To cater for such problem reports, the BTS knows about a number of pseudo packages[57] that it treats as normal packages, but which do not have corresponding files in the archive. The following lists the most important pseudo packages:

Package name	Problem categories
bugs.debian.org	Problems with the Debian BTS.
ftp.debian.org	Problems with the content of the Debian archive (e.g. removal requests due to licence problems).
mirrors	Problems with Debian archive mirrors.
general	General problems that do not fit another category or package, or which apply to too many packages at once.
install	Problems with **debian-installer**.
kernel-image	Problems with the Debian kernel images.
listarchives	Problems with the Debian list archives.
lists.debian.org	Problems with the Debian list servers.
policy	Problems with or proposed changes to the Debian policy.
project	Problems with the project and its administration.
www.debian.org	Problems with **www.debian.org** or other ***.debian.org** web pages (unless the footer specifies contact information.

Table 10.2:
The most important pseudo packages of the Debian BTS

reportbug can assist you with pseudo packages. Calling it with the name of a pseudo package works as expected. Calling it without an argument causes it to prompt for the package. If you enter "other", it will display a list of pseudo packages to help you select.

Work-Needing and Prospective Packages

While most pseudo packages have a "maintainer" or a set of people responsible for addressing or forwarding the issue, one pseudo package is somewhat special in that it belongs to everyone. The **wnpp** package's bugs enumerate the "Work-Needing and Prospective Packages," which is the list of packages in need for help or a new maintainer, as well as packages that are being worked on or which have been requested for inclusion in Debian. The **wnpp** package also has a special web

[57] http://www.debian.org/Bugs/pseudo-packages

page[58] enumerating the status of the various requests which serves as a central switchboard for new package and package transfer coordination. There are six different types of Work-Needing and Prospective Packages (WNPP) records, which can be split into two categories:

Bugs about prospective packages

Request For Package (RFP)

> A "Request For Package" is filed by someone who would like to see a software included in Debian and seeks someone else to package it. The request should contain a proposed package name (which must not clash with an existing package), the version, a package description, the URL, the software's copyright information.

> You do not have to be a Debian developer to file such a request, or prepare packages in response. In fact, fulfilling such requests is a great way to get involved with Debian.

Intent To Package (ITP)

> This describes an "Intent To Package" and should include the same information as a RFP, ideally in addition to a statement on the plans for completion, or where finished packages can be downloaded for inspection. When the new package is uploaded, the ITP should be closed with an appropriate message in the **changelog** (see chapter 9.2.7).

> If a package has been previously requested with a RFP, the ITP should be created by retitling the existing bug report, and do not forget to set the bug owner (see chapter 10.6.7).

> Note that you do not have to be a Debian developer to file ITPs. If you have succeeded in creating a package and find an interested Debian developer to upload it to the archive, you become the maintainer of a package distributed as part of the official Debian archive.

Bugs about existing packages

Request For Help (RFH)

> When a package maintainer is overloaded and cannot maintain a package satisfactorily (but would like to continue as maintainer of the package), a "Request For Help" can be filed to call for assistance or co-maintainers. Such a request is another excellent way of getting involved with Debian, especially because you do not have to start from scratch.

---

[58] http://www.debian.org/devel/wnpp

Request For Adoption (RFA)

A "Request For Adoption" indicates a maintainer's wish to transfer the responsibility for a package to someone else. In the meantime, the maintainer will continue to maintain the package.

Before adopting a package, it is important to understand the package and ensure that the maintainer's reasons for putting the package up for adoption will not get in your way either.

Also, the current maintainer has to agree with the adoption, or might first require some proof of competence. Before adopting a package, it is thus important to inform the maintainer of your intent.

Orphan (O)

When a maintainer cannot continue maintenance of a package, it is "Orphaned" and transfered to the custody of the Debian QA team until a new maintainer can be found. Here also, please ensure that you understand the package and are able to maintain it. Otherwise there is more damage done than good.

Intent To Adopt (ITA)

An O or RFA is ideally answered with an "Intent To Adopt" by another maintainer interested in taking over the package. The new maintainer retitles the previous report to an ITA, transfers ownership of the bug (see chapter 10.6.7), and closes the bug with the next upload.

The bug records for **wnpp** use the bug title to store the actual package name to which they apply. The syntax of the field is

```
<requesttype>: <package> -- <short summary>
```

A double hyphen with surrounding spaces must separate the summary from the package name. It is a good idea to use **reportbug** (see chapter 10.6.5) to file bugs against **wnpp**, since it provides templates asking for all the necessary information for a well-formed **wnpp** bug report.

Changes to the status of these requests are made through retitling or closing the bug report. ITPs and RFPs are acknowledged in the **changelog** of the package upload when done. If the reporter of an ITP ends up not being able to work on the package, the bug should be closed or retitled to become an RFP:

```
~$ sendmail control@bugs.debian.org <<EOF
retitle 345678 RFP: foobar -- software to do something cool
thanks
EOF
```

Similarly, a RFA or O request should be renamed to ITA if you intend to adopt the package to signalise your intent to other interested parties and prevent duplicated efforts.

Keeping an eye on WNPP

The WNPP pseudo package is an important organisational component of the Debian project. It allows for the coordination of new packages, and the transfer of packages to new maintainers. However, the WNPP list is also useful for system administrators.

Software is inherently buggy. To put it differently, problems are to be expected in any kind of software. With an active upstream and responsible package maintainer, users need not worry too much about a package, since updates and security fixes are going to make it to the local machine eventually. However, if you rely on a certain software and the maintainer cannot allocate sufficient time to the package, you may be in the unfortunate situation of having to make a move and consider alternatives, take on maintenance of the package yourself, or urge someone else to assume responsibility for the package.

At the very least, you will want to know when a package that you have installed somehow enters the WNPP list. In the **devscripts** package, the **wnpp-alert** tool has been written exactly for this purpose. It fetches the WNPP list and compares it to the list of locally installed package, printing any intersecting information to the console. On criticial systems, it is a good idea to run the package regularly and keep an eye on its output.

10.6.9   Subscribing to a package's bug reports

The BTS only knows a single maintainer address for each package. Thus, it only ever sends bug reports to that one person, unless this address is a mailing list (see *e.g.* the **dpkg** package). The thought that someone may want to track the bug reports for a package is not far fetched. The Debian PTS[59] provides a subscription interface to opt to receive mail related to the activity of a source package. A subscription can be requested either through the web interface, or by mail:

```
~$ echo subscribe postfix a.n.other@email.co.uk \
  | mail pts@qa.debian.org
```

The default subscription includes more than just the bug reports. You will also be notified when a new source package has been uploaded and accepted, and receive warnings and errors resulting from an upload, as well as all mail sent to <package>@packages.qa.debian.org. In addition, you will receive regular summary emails about the package status as soon as this feature has been implemented in the PTS.

If you just want to follow bug reports and possibly be alerted of new versions, you can modify your subscription (this is assuming that **mail** sends out messages with the proper sender address):

[59] http://packages.qa.debian.org

```
~$ echo keywords postfix = bts bts-control upload-source \
  | mail pts@qa.debian.org
```

In addition, you can choose to be notified of binary uploads, commit emails by the package's version control system (if it uses one), and translation submissions. The PTS web page offers an advanced mode of subscription (by selection box) that allows you to control exactly the type of mail you want to receive for a package. In addition, the mails sent out include well-defined headers for processing by mail delivery agents (*e.g. procmail*). More information is available in the developer reference[60].

Subscribing to a single bug is not currently possible. Look for this feature some time in the distant future. For now, please subscribe to receive all bug reports through the PTS and use a mail processor such as **procmail** to filter out all messages but the ones concerning the bug:

```
:0
* ^X-PTS-Keyword: bts(-control)?$
* ! ^Subject:.*Bug#(241343|654321)
/dev/null
```

10.6.10   Fixing bugs

If you find a bug in a software packaged for Debian, you should always file a bug against it. Depending on the urgency of your problem, you may consider investing time and resources to fix the problem yourself. One of the irreplaceable advantages of open source software is your ability to obtain the source code and attempt to figure out the root of a problem you are experiencing. Granted, hacking around in programme code is not everyone's idea of fun, but if it is yours, all the better.

The procedure of how to prepare patches to fix bugs in packages is not documented, nor is there really a standard. Some maintainers prefer what others hate. Considering that your fixes must be approved by the maintainer, it is important to work with, rather than against, the maintainer. Due to the wide variety of preferences and approaches, a universal recipe does not exist, but the following guidelines on how to fix and submit bugs should get you started. Always keep in mind that you want to make it as easy as possible for the maintainer to review and accept your patch.

- Try to understand the maintainer's practices by reading the README.developers file (if provided) and inspecting the code and/or the package layout. Then, make

[60]http://www.debian.org/doc/developers-reference/ch-resources.en.html#s-pkg-tracking-system

sure that your changes smoothly blend in with the rest. Please consider that developers can be quite pedantic, so that small things such as indent size actually do matter.

- Fix one bug per patch. If you are fixing multiple bugs at once, then it is considerably easier for the maintainer to inspect them if they are physically separate.

- In particular, do not attempt to sneak in features or make changes to the software (such as default settings). If you are "fixing" wishlist bugs, make sure to clearly mark the patches as such.

- Provide context-sensitive patches by passing the **-u** flag to **diff**. This adds robustness to the patch and makes it easier for the maintainer to assess the fix.

- Provide documentation with your patch, unless your changes are trivial.

In addition, unless you are sure to have the bug fixed and uploaded to the BTS within a short time, it is good practice to notify the BTS of your intention to prevent duplicate work. Moreover, if you are planning to fix a number of bugs, or your fixes involve some non-trivial changes, it is probably a good idea to consult with the maintainer and agree on a strategy.

The standard methods of creating patches are perfectly applicable to Debian packages, of course. An interesting alternative is the preparation of a fixed package with an increased version number. Rather than using the next available Debian revision, you are advised to simply append .1 (or increment the version number following the dot in the Debian revision, if it already exists). If the package has been built with **dpkg-buildpackage** or the like, you can use **debdiff** to extract the changes by comparison with the downloaded source package.

```
~$ apt-get source foobar
[...]
dpkg-source: extracting foobar in foobar-1.23
~$ cd foobar-1.23
[...]
~/foobar-1.23$ dch --version=1.23-1.1 -- fixing a bug
~/foobar-1.23$ dpkg-buildpackage -us -uc
[...]
dpkg-deb: building package 'foobar' in '../foobar_1.23-1.1_all.deb'.
~/foobar-1.23$ cd ..
~$ debdiff foobar_1.23-1.dsc foobar_1.23-1.1.dsc > foobar.diff
```

In this approach, **foobar** 1.23-1.1 only really exists for the purpose of creating the patch. Using **filterdiff** from the **patchutils** package, it is possible to filter out the changes to the **changelog** file to allow the package maintainer to apply the patch without intruding on the official **changelog**:

```
~$ debdiff foobar_1.23-1.dsc foobar_1.23-1.1.dsc ~
  | filterdiff -x '*/debian/changelog' > foobar.diff
```

If you were careful to restrain the changes made by the patch to fixing the problem, then the above patch, together with an adequate explanatory note, constitute a proper submission to the BTS. Please do not forget to set the **patch** tag (see chapter 10.6.4) when including a patch in a follow-up to the BTS.

NMU – Non-Maintainer Upload

If the maintainer of a package does not respond to a bug report, you might opt to announce a NMU. An upload of this kind consists of a version of a package that fixes a bug to be uploaded to the Debian archive by another developer. In such a case, the version number is modified as if the patch had been created (see the previous section), to ensure that the upload does not interfere with any efforts by the maintainer. A NMU does not constitute an abduction of the package, and while it will be regularly available from the archives, the maintainer is generally free to acknowledge or reject it with the next upload (which will use the next higher Debian revision).

NMUs are acceptable under a number of conditions. Primarily, if a NMU fixes a bug of **normal** severity (or greater) and the maintainer is unresponsive or on vacation, a NMU is justified. In addition, during especially announced bug squashing periods, NMUs are encouraged. Like to regular uploads, NMUs also need to be authenticated with a Debian developer signature. If you are building or planning to build a NMU as a non-developer, you will need to find a sponsor for the actual upload, that is a Debian developer willing to make the upload for you (see chapter 2.5.2).

Appendix

A

Debian flavours and other Debian-based operating systems

The robustness and universality of the Debian system has allowed a plethora of projects of all kinds to build upon Debian and profit from the solid foundation. Such projects can generally be split into two categories: while a Custom Debian Distribution (CDD) exists within the official Debian system in form of a two-way relationship, Debian derivatives usually fork or snapshot the contents of the Debian archive and produce an independent product.

A.1   CDDs – Custom Debian Distributions

A CDD is a version of Debian tailored for a specific user groups, or a niche, and designed to work out of the box. CDDs are a fairly recent development within the Debian project, which grew out of what were formally known as Debian Internal Projects. The endeavour is gaining popularity and new CDDs are emerging at a fast rate. A paper describing the ideas behind CDDs and giving additional information is online[1].

The main problem CDDs are trying to solve is to facilitate installation, pre-select package sets (and sometimes pre-configure them) for specific user groups. Due to the vast amount and variety of packages available in the Debian archive, this is not always an easy task. While the task system (see chapter 5.5) aims at doing the same, CDDs try to provide a more fine-grained selection.

A CDD does not constitute a fork from Debian. A complete Debian GNU/Linux distribution includes all available CDDs, and developments in the main distribution are available instantaneously in all CDDs, just as much as general-purpose improvements made within a CDD flow right back into the main Debian archive. As such CDDs differ substantially from derivatives of the Debian distribution (see appendix A.2).

In the following, I give a brief summary of each of the official CDDs that existed at the time of writing.

Debian-Junior
>   The goals of Debian-Junior, a CDD designed for "children from 1 to 99" is to make Debian an operating system that children of all ages will want to use. It strives to be easy to use while providing the most important applications of high quality from a child's perspective. Debian-Junior was the first CDD.

Debian-Med
>   The CDD tries to provide an integrated software environment for all medical tasks. As part of the effort, the project focuses on integrating new medical software into Debian, improving the quality of existing software, and generally furthering the use of Free Software in the field of medicine.

Debian-Edu
>   The Debian-Edu CDD has merged with the Skolelinux, a network computer solution designed for schools. Please refer to appendix A.2.7 for more information.

---

[1]http://people.debian.org/~tille/debian-med/talks/paper-cdd

DeMuDi

> The Debian Multimedia Distribution is on its way to becoming a CDD. It tries to be the distribution of choice for musicians and multimedia artists. The DeMuDi project grew out of the European Agnula project[2].

Debian-Desktop

> Labelled "Debian for Everyone," the Debian-Desktop CDD tries to make Debian the best possible system for home and corporate workstation use by providing "software that just works." The project tries to make Debian easy to use and configure, while not sacrificing the flexibility wanted by expert users.

Debian-Lex

> The Debian-Lex project strives to build a complete system for all tasks in legal practice. In particular, the CDD adds value to the Debian system by providing customised templates to existing packages like **OpenOffice.org** and **SQL-Ledger**, and sample database schemas for **PostgreSQL** which are specific to the world of lawyers.

Debian-NP

> This CDD addresses the needs of non-profit organisations by tailoring the system specifically to their requirements. Among several improvements, the project tries to improve and provide solutions that solve non-profit tasks such as fund raising, membership lists, and conference organisation.

Debian Accessibility Project

> As another attempt to bring Debian to everyone, the Debian Accessibility Project works on making Debian usable by blind and visually impaired people. The CDD has enhanced support for screen readers and speech software.

Debian Enterprise

> This CDD wants to merge Debian into the enterprise world, making it compatible with industry driven shared-cost development models. It aims at providing professional documentation, certification, pre-configured servers, and intends to stand up for Free Software in legal affairs.

A.2   Debian derivatives

Debian GNU/Linux is not only an operating system by itself, it also aims to be the foundation for an increasing number of derived works. A Debian-derived operating system builds on Debian technology and infrastructure, and commonly adds features not available in the main Debian distribution. Such features include graphical

---

[2]http://www.agnula.org

and/or automated installers, a cutting-edge software collection, extra security features, or other enhancements or specialisations. In most cases, these additions to the Debian core do not meet all of Debian's requirements for inclusion in the main archive and are thus maintained as separate products.

The following is a selection of derivatives which does not try to be comprehensive. During the process of writing this book, I contacted the team behind every reasonably mature derivative I could find. I chose only to cover those that proved responsive. Natural selection in action...

A.2.1   Knoppix

Knoppix[3] is a Debian derivative that is designed to run entirely from read-only media, such as CD or DVD. The system boots from the media, detects and automatically configures the available hardware, and drops the user into a pre-configured and spiffy looking **KDE** desktop with plenty of software to satisfy most needs. For instance, aside from browsers, email readers, and productivity software like **OpenOffice.org**, Knoppix also features multimedia applications, development environments for various languages, network and security tools. In addition, Knoppix includes a plethora of diagnostic utilities for Linux and other operating systems, making it a perfect rescue system. Of course, Knoppix can connect to the Internet using various means, including Ethernet, PPP, DSL, and ISDN. Knoppix also supports various other graphical interfaces, such as **IceWM**, **WindowMaker**, **Xfce 4**; it does not, however, support **Gnome** (Gnoppix does, however; see chapter A.2.3).

For variable data, such as configuration files, the system uses ramdisks. To preserve these configuration data across reboots (when ramdisks are cleared), it allows the ramdisk contents to be swapped to removable media or the local hard disk. This greatly increases the system's security and stability and ensures that the user cannot break the system by accidentally deleting or overwriting a file. Alternatively, Knoppix may be installed to the hard drive and subsequently treated like a regular Linux installation. As it is based on Debian, the Debian tools are available as if Debian had been installed directly.

Knoppix uses parts of the *testing* archive for its base system. The desktop, especially **KDE**, come from the *unstable* archive, which includes more current usability features and the latest bells and whistles, in which users are very interested. In addition, it integrates a variety of software from other distributions, like **libkudzu** from RedHat, and scripts and programmes written by Klaus Knopper add hardware autodetection and configuration abilities. Also, handlers for services like terminal servers, Internet connectivity and configuration storage have been added by the Knoppix author and founder.

[3] http://knoppix.org

Klaus Knopper developed Knoppix mainly for his own use in lectures, remote work, presentations, and to jump start a Debian installation (see chapter 8.3.1). By now, Knoppix is mainly used by Desktop users for office work or Internet access. It also powers Internet cafes and computer pools in schools. In addition, the live system enjoys great popularity among system administrators as rescue system, as well as for forensic purposes. Yet another popular application of Knoppix is getting to know Linux. The booted system allows access to Windows partitions and thus gives the user an opportunity to experiment with the Linux tools, using real data. Nevertheless, an underlying Windows installation is not affected by a Knoppix boot. Thus, Knoppix has established itself as *the* Linux demonstration system.

Since its inception, about a dozen Knoppix derivatives have sprung to life, each specialising in certain application areas or languages. For instance, Morphix attempts to modularise Knoppix to make its specialisation easier. ClusterKNOPPIX has **Open-Mosix** enabled, Quantian sports many applications for scientific use, KnoppixSTD focuses at information security and network management tools, and INSERT aims to be a powerful rescue system.

The CD's software collection and all programmes written by Klaus Knopper that are included, are licensed under the GNU General Public License. Individual software packages that are present on the Knoppix CD, however, may use a different license, and some of them are even "binary-only, but freely distributable for non-commercial as well as commercial use", like **acroread4**, **Java**, and some binary-only firmware files for certain hardware. The reason for this is that they are needed by the main target users, and there is unfortunately no usable free software alternative available yet.

A.2.2   Ubuntu

Ubuntu[4] is a very young Debian-based distribution. The company behind the endeavour, Canonical Software, is steered by some of the most active Debian, Gnome, and Python developers, who are spread all over the planet. Their goal is to release Debian *unstable* twice a year, with security support for 18 months following the release. In contrast to Debian, it will be a Gnome- and Python-based distribution with plans for very strong integration (using Python, mostly) and focusing on the Gnome desktop. As such, Ubuntu trades currency and security for variety of choice, which is a necessity for usability. Nevertheless, an offspring project by the name of Kubuntu works on the integration of the popular **KDE** desktop.

The Ubuntu software archive is available at no cost[5] and is comprised exclusively of free software, although Canonical Software does plan to include documentation and binary-only firmware. The available packages are spread across four sections:

[4] http://www.ubuntulinux.org; Ubuntu is the Zulu word for community and contribution
[5] In fact, Canonical Software plans to ship CDs of their software to anyone at no charge.

base, desktop, supported, and universe. The first three contain almost 3 000 packages and are fully supported in terms of security updates. Universe contains the remaining packages from the Debian *unstable* archive built against the distribution, but without support. The developers are expecting the pool of supported packages to increase in size. If enough people end up using a package from the universe section, it will be considered for inclusion in the supported archive. Ubuntu also features a bootable live CD, allowing it to be used without having to install it.

A.2.3 Gnoppix

Gnoppix[6] is a live distribution, which runs off read-only media similarly to Knoppix. Unlike Knoppix, it uses the Gnome desktop environment, but otherwise provides the same or similar features, including automatic hardware detection, and a large selection of common, pre-configured software. The software is available in three versions: the stable version is intended for production use, the testing release for, well, testing and possibly daily use by the more adventurous. The last version, called beta, is mainly used for development.

The Gnoppix project plans to produce specialised versions of Gnoppix for development machines, desktop machines, firewalls, multimedia stations, cluster machines, for game playing, and for system recovery. Furthermore, the project wants to support the **amd64** and **powerpc** architectures.

A.2.4 MEPIS

MEPIS[7] is a Debian-based operating system designed for everyday home and office desktop computer users. MEPIS pulls software from Debian's *unstable* archive and packages it into a ready-to-use Linux system. It is intended to be a complete replacement for Microsoft Windows.

MEPIS develops and continues to improve special components designed to make installation and configuration easier for users. The MEPIS Installation Center allows for easy installation and related tasks. With the MEPIS System Center, the user has control over input and output devices, network interfaces, the package management system, and various system tweaks. The MEPIS Auto Configuration components and scripts automatically load drivers for most hardware and also detect and facilitate the use of fixed and removable drives, and USB and Firewire devices.

While the company behind the MEPIS system publishes commercially available versions of their operating system, together with preconfigured packages and books

---

[6]http://gnoppix.org
[7]http://www.mepis.org

for Linux beginners[8], the system and all additional software is also freely available from their mirrors, although somewhat delayed in comparison to the commercial version.

A.2.5 MNIS

MNIS[9] is a Debian-derived embedded systems development system. It uses Debian for the base system and adds the Ocera real-time extension[10] to provide a framework, development and integration tools, and documentation for generating embedded systems with industrial real-time efficiency. MNIS contains the necessary tools to develop embedded systems following industrial standards.

The MNIS distribution is especially adapted to real-time developers and engineers in need of a very fast real-time operating system. MNIS provides latencies and task switching in the order of microseconds. At the same time, it profits from Debian's large software collection and its robust administrative toolkit.

The MNIS distribution, its addons, documentation, and derivative work is licensed under the GNU General Public License. The OCERA part is based on RTLinux-GPL and also licensed under the terms of the GPL. The software stemming from the Debian archive is available in accordance with the DFSG.

A.2.6 Quantian

Quantian[11] is a Knoppix/Debian-derived operating system tailored to numerical and quantitative analysis. Quantian adds a large number of programmes to Knoppix, which are mostly of interest people working in the field of applied or theoretical data-driven analysis. In addition, Quantian sports a number of scientific applications, such as **Octave, Maxima, OpenDX, CRAN, Alliance VHDL**, and various emulators to run Windows software. Quantian also draws from clusterKNOPPIX to add **OpenMosix** support, allowing it to be used in clusters for distributed computation.

A.2.7 Skolelinux

Skolelinux[12] is a project targeted at providing a complete computer solution for schools. It became an official part of the Debian project after merging with the Debian-Edu CDD (see appendix A.1). The system is based on a network architecture

---

[8] http://pointandclicklinux.com
[9] http://www.mnis.fr/en/services/opensource/linux
[10] http://www.ocera.org
[11] http://dirk.eddelbuettel.com/quantian.html
[12] http://www.skolelinux.org

with centralised user management and storage. Skolelinux uses **Webmin** to provide an administration and maintenance interface available through a web browser. Software installation and maintenance is left to the graces of **APT**.

The default means of installing Skolelinux is through the use of a terminal server and a bunch of thin clients. The low hardware requirements of thin clients help keep the cost down, and having a central server used by everyone helps cut administration to a minimum. Nevertheless, the network architecture allows the integration of workstations (fat clients), laptops, and even offers users the ability to install the system at home, using the Internet for authentication and file storage on the central server. Windows machines may also be integrated into a Skolelinux network through **Samba**.

Being a subproject of Debian, Skolelinux is available under the terms of the DFSG.

A.2.8 Adamantix

The Adamantix project[13] (formerly known as Trusted Debian) aims to create a highly secure but usable Linux platform. Adamantix uses Debian as a basis and provides its own archive of hardened packages. Ideally, all software installed on an Adamantix system comes from their archive, but the Debian mirrors may be easily integrated.

Adamantix adds various security-related patches to the kernel and attempts to increase the security of the software by recompiling Debian's packages with special compiler extensions. The kernel patches include RSBAC and PaX, and all its packages (including the kernel) are compiled with a compiler patched to use IBM's stack smashing protector as well as PaX address layout randomisation, which makes buffer overflow attacks a lot harder.

The distribution is available under the same licence as Debian itself, and therefore completely free in terms of the DFSG. Moreover, it is possible to turn an existing Debian *woody* system into an Adamantix system simply by pointing /etc/apt/sources.list to their mirrors and letting **APT** do a **dist-upgrade**. Following the release of *sarge*, it is only be a matter of time until Adamantix moves to the new Debian release.

A.2.9 SELinux

SELinux[14] is a project started by the American NSA to enhance the Linux kernel with a strong, flexible mandatory access control (MAC) architecture incorporated into the major subsystems of the kernel. The system provides a mechanism to enforce the separation of information based on confidentiality and integrity requirements. A system with an SELinux kernel and supporting applications mitigates the

[13] http://adamantix.org
[14] http://www.nsa.gov/selinux/

risk of the **root** account and effectively confines the damage that can result from tampering and attacks to small, contained domains of the system. For instance, if a mail server running as **root** is exploited on an SELinux-enabled system, the attacker will not be able to gain access to other parts of the system.

SELinux is available for Debian on the i386 architectures, and for the ARM processor. It can be installed on any Debian *stable* system through the addition of appropriate lines to **/etc/apt/sources.list** to allow APT to retrieve SELinux kernels and packages enabled for the security features of SELinux. To make the integration with an existing system possible, it uses a custom version numbering scheme designed not to clash with official Debian packages (see chapter 5.7.5). Details on the use of SELinux for Debian are available from the Debian SELinux web page[15].

---

[15]http://www.coker.com.au/selinux

B

When is Debian the right choice?

A number of traits distinguish users who will profit from Debian from those who would be better off with a different distribution or operating system, or maybe simply a different Debian release (see chapter 4). The following are suggestions to help you discover whether Debian is for you or not.

B.1   You should run Debian if...

- you are an experienced user and know what you want. Furthermore, you want a system that is stable, easy to administer, and non-autonomous in that it never does anything you did not tell it to do.

- you are the administrator of a computer cluster of a similarly large number of workstations. Rather than spending considerable time keeping each workstation up to date, you would prefer to rely on the consistency of the Debian package management system and possibly employ FAI (see chapter 8.3.5) in addition to cluster management software (*e.g.* cfengine) to automate the maintenance of the machines.

- you or your team are in charge of machines spanning multiple hardware architectures. Instead of expending more time than you have staying on top of different operating systems and keeping them up to date, Debian unifies system administration across many architectures and allows you to apply your knowledge everywhere, independently of the processors powering your systems.

- you are looking to select an operating system for a controlled environment with a finite set of requirements. If a system administrator is available to assist users with their installations, Debian provides the best for both: ease of maintenance for the administrator, and indirectly, the stability of the Debian system for the users.

- you prefer stability to the bleeding edge. While the software available in the official Debian distribution is undoubtedly outdated, it works and has been tested extensively. If you need a machine to enhance productivity, Debian is for you. If you need newer software, you may want to consider using packages from the *testing* and *unstable* archives (see chapter 4).

- along similar lines, you need a secure system rather than one with the latest bells and whistles. It is impossible to combine a state of the art system with security, which is why Debian *stable* consciously provides mature software and provides timely fixes should a security update still have gone unnoticed.

- you want to get down to the core of Linux. Since Debian only puts very thin layers between you and the low level operating system, you are free to dive into the depths of all aspects of the system. Moreover, the Debian layers are not required. In fact, removing Debian to leave a bare-bones system can be accomplished by removing a couple of packages (which I will not show you).

- you have many friends running Debian. After all, Debian (or Linux in general) is simply more fun With A Little Help From Your Friends. In addition, resources such as mailing lists (see chapter 10.4.1) are friendly in that you can always find people eager to help. Often, these are not strangers, but well-known personalities in the free software arena, or regular visitors of the lists.

- you are willing to invest some time and work now for later ease of maintenance. Debian seems to have a steeper learning curve than many other operating systems, but the efforts pay off quickly, especially when in charge of multiple installations.

- you are a perfectionist or purist. Debian allows you to stay in control and it does not interfere with your ideas of system administration. Moreover, strict conformance to the policy results in a system that is concise and easily manageable over years.

- you are socially sensitive with respect to freedom of software. Debian's strict adherence to the DFSG is an implementation of idealism in practice, without making big compromises.

- you are curious to know what Debian is all about and do not mind climbing the Debian learning curve.

- you are curious to learn about the Debian community and experience the mixture between diversity, and the determination causing thousands of people to work towards a common goal.

- you want to use Debian for whatever reason, and you are self-confident about the desire.

B.2 You should probably choose something else, if...

- you are new to Unix. Obviously, if you are willing to jump in at the deep end and invest a lot of time, nobody is going to stop you. But you might be better off with another distribution. You can always come back to Debian when you have gained enough experience with Linux[1]

- you need to use top-of-the-line hardware. While the Linux kernel supports a variety of modern hardware, the latest drivers may not be available in the official kernel source yet. These often exist as external patches, but Debian tries to minimise the number of patches applied to the kernel. Other distributions add most available drivers to the kernel and thus support a larger set of modern hardware, at the expense of reduced stability and security. Even though they may be missing during the install (and thus call for an advanced method of installation; see chapter 8.3), most drivers are available as packages and can be easily installed on a running Debian system (see chapter 8.1).

- you want to run Debian because "it is cool". Obviously, if you want to run Debian, you should, but you will not be "cool" without making some stellar contributions to the project. Also, keep in mind that "cool" users should probably make sure they recompile all software locally[2].

---

[1]Or you can ignore what I just said; the Debian Hands-On Guide will be of help: http://colt.projectgamma.com/hands-on

[2]http://funroll-loops.org

- you want a working system and are unwilling to figure out how it works. Debian is a complex system with virtually limitless possibilities. However, to harness its power, you need to invest time in it (*e.g.* by working through this book). If you are rather looking for something that just works, try one of its derivatives (see appendix A.2), or another distribution.

C

Miscellaneous

C.1 Important GPG keys related to Debian

The Debian project makes extensive use of GPG keys (see chapter 2.4.3). The reliability of these keys increases with the number of sources of information that can be used to verify them. Therefore, this book provides the fingerprints and other key data for some of the most important keys related to Debian.

THE FOLLOWING INFORMATION IS PROVIDED HERE ACCORDING TO THE BEST OF MY KNOWLEDGE AND CAPABILITY. IT COMES WITHOUT ANY WARRANTY OF CORRECTNESS OR INTEGRITY.

C.1.1   Official Debian archive signing keys

The following list contains the official Debian archive signing keys (see chapter 7.5). These keys are available from **ftp-master.debian.org**, as indicated. Alternatively, they are available from the Debian key server[1], and in the **/usr/share/keyrings/ debian-role-keys.gpg** file of the **debian-keyring** package. Each of these keys is connected to the Debian Web of Trust through the signature of at least one Debian developer (see appendix C.1.2).

Archive key 2005

```
       URL: http://ftp-master.debian.org/ziyi_key_2005.asc
        ID: 4f368d5d
      Date: 2005-01-31
Fingerprint: 4c7a 8e5e 9454 fe3f ae1e  78ad f1d5 3d8c 4f36 8d5d
   Creator: Anthony Towns (key 0x2a4e3eaa)
```

Archive key 2004

```
       URL: http://ftp-master.debian.org/ziyi_key_2004.asc
        ID: 1024R/1db114e0
      Date: 2004-01-15
Fingerprint: d051 fe3a 848d cabd 4625  787a 6ffa 8ef9 1db1 14e0
   Creator: James Troup (key 0x27141bb0)
```

Archive key 2003

```
       URL: http://ftp-master.debian.org/ziyi_key_2003.asc
        ID: 1024D/38c6029a
      Date: 2002-12-20
Fingerprint: eb2f a2af 170d 2359 26a7  7bf3 b629 a24c 38c6 029a
   Creator: James Troup (key 0x27141bb0)
```

Archive key 2002

```
       URL: http://ftp-master.debian.org/ziyi_key_2002.asc
        ID: 1024D/722f1aed
      Date: 2002-01-11
Fingerprint: 8fd4 7ff1 aa93 72c3 7043  dc28 aa7d eb7b 722f 1aed
   Creator: Anthony Towns (key 0x7172daed)
```

[1]x-hkp://keyring.debian.org

Archive key 2001

```
        URL: none
         ID: 1024D/b8ae9b77
       Date: 2001-07-20
Fingerprint: e16c d067 c97a 1f4f 7a88  1f81 ae10 f9db b8ae 9b77
    Creator: Anthony Towns (key 0x7172daed)
```

C.1.2   Other relevant signing keys

The Debian security team contact key

With security-sensitive issues, it is best to contact the Debian security team at security@debian.org with an encrypted mail (see chapter 7.1). You may use the following key for the encryption.

```
         ID: 1024R/363ccd95
       Date: 1998-11-24
Fingerprint: cb 34 33 b3 6f 3b c9 6e  ca c2 87 e3 e1 c6 a4 82
```

Principal signers of the archive key

The integrity of these keys is in the hands of the signers mentioned. For completeness, the keys of the people who created the archive keys are included below. Note that other Debian developers may have also signed a given archive key to indicate their endorsement of its integrity.

I have not verified these keys myself, but I trust a large part of the signatures on their keys. These signatures serve to certify that numerous people, including several Debian developers, have met with these two signers in person and verified their identity. In turn, these peoples' keys have been signed by others, and so on. The integrity of the keys is therefore guaranteed as much as the Web of Trust can guarantee identities, and as much as the security of the asymmetric encryption algorithms used in creating the keys and signatures can be trusted.

Anthony Towns

```
         ID: 1024R/2a4e3eaa
       Date: 2004-06-04
Fingerprint: c135 f6a8 6d8f 7d25 f040  e7b4 3b17 bc74 2a4e 3eaa
```

Prior to this key, Anthony used the following key, which has since expired:

```
         ID: 1024R/7172daed
       Date: 1996-06-15
Fingerprint: 70 b6 04 9b a2 c8 7d aa  00 5d dc 82 58 9d 49 6e
```

James Troup

```
        ID: 1024D/27141bb0
      Date: 1998-11-24
Fingerprint: 2458 e71a 1950 7b3f 4388  8da6 803f ee12 2714 1bb0
```

The volatile.debian.net archive key

The archive at **volatile.debian.net** (see chapter 4.4.2) uses its own key to sign the index files (see chapter 7.5):

```
       URL: http://volatile.debian.net/ziyi-2005.asc
        ID: 1024D/276981f4
      Date: 2004-12-24
Fingerprint: 90c5 d4a2 d7b1 30d2 36f7  49a9 7ef7 fff4 2769 81f4
   Creator: Andreas Barth (key 0xec36a185)
```

The amd64 archive key

The archive for the **amd64** architecture (see chapter 4.4.3) uses its own key to sign the index files (see chapter 7.5):

```
       URL: http://amd64.debian.net/archive.key
        ID: 1024D/b5f5bbed
      Date: 2005-04-24
Fingerprint: c20c a1d9 499d ecbb d8bd  acf9 e415 b2b4 b5f5 bbed
   Creator: Joerg Jaspert (key 0x7e7b8ac9)
```

My key

I use my GPG/ key to sign all outgoing email[2], the Debian packages I create (using **dpkg-sig**; see chapter 7.5.3), the keys of my public **APT** repositories (see chapter 7.5.2), and any other sensitive data. I shall thus not pass up the opportunity to include the data of my current key at this point to provide an additional means of verification:

```
       URL: http://people.debian.org/~madduck/gpg/330c4a75.asc
        ID: 1024D/330c4a75
      Date: 2001-06-20
Fingerprint: acf4 9d3e 1e1d 5ee2 b203  5e53 220b c883 330c 4a75
```

---

[2]I use the PGP/MIME standard. Several ancient or inferior email programmes do not support this (old) standard, causing my emails to be blank. The actual text is to be found in a text-only attachment, which you can safely open. Mail readers broken in this way should be banned in favour of modern replacements.

C.2 Setting up the filesystems

C.2.1 A sensible partition table

Although a little outside the scope of this book, the following is a general purpose partitioning scheme, which works well with Debian. I have used this scheme successfully for servers and workstations alike over the past years. Numbers correspond to sizes in Gigabytes, unless otherwise noted.

In the following tables, a dash (–) denotes suggested size ranges. The symbols $<$ and $>$ corresponds to optimal maxima and minima respectively. Finally, RAM/2 stands for half the size of the available working memory[3] (RAM).

Partition	Size	Mount point
primary	48 Mb	/boot
primary	RAM/2, $<$ 512 Mb	<swap>
logical	256 Mb	/
logical	2 – 7%, $>$ 2 Gb	/usr
logical	1 – 10%	/usr/local
logical	1 – 10%, $>$ 1 Gb	/var
logical	remainder	/home
logical	0.5 – 2%	/tmp

Table C.1:
A generic partition table for Debian

Please note that this table may be too complicated (and restrictive) for generic purposes. For single-user system desktops, the following scheme may be preferable:

Partition	Size	Mount point
primary	5%, $>$ 3 Gb	/
logical	remainder	/home
logical	1 – 2%	/usr/local
logical	RAM/2, $<$ 512 Mb	<swap>

Table C.2:
A simplified partition table for Debian

Each partition has a type associated with it. All data partitions should be of type 0x82. The swap partition must be of type 0x83.

---

[3]If you want to make use of the kernel's software suspend technology to hibernate a system, provide a swap partition of about 150% of the size of the available RAM.

You may have to mark the filesystem to which you installed the **bootloader** as **bootable** (or **active**). Generally, the **bootloader** should be placed into the MBR, but in multi-boot setups, you may choose to place it into a partition.

C.2.2 Supported filesystems

What some other operating systems call "formatting" is the process of making filesystems within the partitions. Debian supports all filesystems that Linux supports, some of which are:

ext2

> the traditional Linux filesystem and provides adequate performance and robustness for most applications. **ext2** carries forward a long history of stability and reliability.

ext3

> the successor to **ext2** adds journaling to provide for faster recovery after unexpected reboots. **ext3** builds on **ext2**'s proven reliability. Furthermore, it is possible to switch transparently between the two without the need to back up or recreate data.

XFS

> SGI's journaling filesystem supports very large files, **B-tree** indices, and native access control lists. It has only been added to Linux lately but builds on years of experience as the filesystem of the Irix operating system. It comes with a great number of utilities.

JFS

> IBM's journaling filesystem provides large file support, native access control lists, but only a somewhat sparse toolset. **JFS** came to Linux from AIX, where it performed in demanding environments for years.

ReiserFS

> the only filesystem that is not entirely free, according to the DFSG (see appendix F). It also supports journaling and its **B-tree** indexing is optimised for large numbers of small files. **ReiserFS** was developed specifically as a Linux journaling filesystem and version 3 is now used in stable, productive environments. Its successor, version 4, is considered experimental by many.

The choice of filesystem depends on many factors[4]. I have taken a liking to **XFS** and can warmly recommend it[5]. Debian provides the full set of goodies for **XFS** in the **xfsprogs** package. The ACLs may be controlled with the utilities in the **acl** package.

---

[4]Data from a quantitative comparison are available here: http://www.fortunecity.com/skyscraper/romrow/935/jfs_xfs_rfs_ext.html

[5]If you are using XFS, you may be familiar with the problem of a file's contents being replaced by binary zeros after a system crash. What happened was that XFS managed to write the file's meta-

C.3 Extra packages

The minimal installation of Debian (see chapter 3.2) leaves only a small number of packages installed. Depending on your requirements, some of these packages may even be removed. The following attempts to list all packages from a minimal installation that are not essential to the operation of the system. If you remove these packages, you are left with the smallest possible Debian system that can still be called a Unix system. Note that the list does not try to be complete. Also, please make sure that you know what you are doing when removing any of these packages.

dash	dhcp-client	exim4
exim4-base	exim4-config	exim4-daemon-light
info	initrd-tools	ipchains
iptables	libgcrypt1	libgnutls7
libident	liblockfile1	liblzo1
libnewt0.51	libopencdk8	libpcap0.7
libpcre3	libsigc++-1.2-5c102	libssl0.9.7
libtasn1-0	libtextwrap1	locales
mailx	makedev	nano
pcmcia-cs	ppp	pppconfig
pppoe	pppoeconf	setserial
tasksel	telnet	wget

When running a 2.4 series kernel, you can also remove **module-init-tools**. Similarly, if you use a 2.6 series kernel, you can safely drop **modutils**. With monolithic kernels (*i.e.* kernels that do not use modules), both packages can be purged.

data but never got around to flushing its contents. When accessing the data, the filesystem takes the precautionary measure of returning zeros instead of random data (which could lead to to problems, or expose sensitive information). If existing files were affected by this phenomenon after a system crash, it meant that the application writing the file unlinked the old file and wanted to write a new one (the proper thing to do would be to truncate the file and reuse it). Unfortunately, in such a case, the data cannot be recovered through other means than raw access to the storage medium, and I do not know of a tool to automate the process. The problem is not specific to XFS but may be aggrevated by the long delay XFS uses between metadata and file contents flushing (for performance reasons, and because the internal log structure is optimised for it). The flushing interval can be controlled with files in /prov/sys/vm (see the kernel documentation), and a call to sync() (*e.g.*through the use of /bin/sync) ensures that all metadata and contents up to the point of the call are flushed.

C.4   Configuring a local packet filter

Starting with the 2.4 kernel series, the Linux kernel provides a powerful packet filtering framework known as **netfilter**. Its front-end user space utility **iptables** is often used as a synonymous name. The Debian kernel includes complete support for **netfilter**, and **iptables** is installed on every system by default. Therefore, it is trivial to protect every Debian host with a restrictive packet filter. The small amount of effort required to configure this kind of packet filter justifies the relatively small gain in security the filter provides.

Packet filters should always be designed to deny everything which is not explicitly allowed. Therefore, you should always start with a restrictive policy and poke holes only where needed. The following configures **iptables** to accept only traffic on the lo interfaces as well as SSH connections to a valid local address. Everything else, including **broadcast** and **multicast** traffic, is dropped. You can uncomment the lines relating to **broadcast** and **multicast** packets to let them through. Remember that in the case of a router, the following would only protect the router while actually preventing any packets from traversing the machine due to the **DROP** policy on the **FORWARD** chain. Rules for the shielded network should go into the **FORWARD** or **PREROUTING** chain, depending on whether they are applicable to the network, or both, router and network respectively. The **netfilter** HOWTO[6] provides more information.

```
~# cat <<EOF > /etc/network/iptables
*filter
:INPUT DROP [0:0]
:FORWARD DROP [0:0]
:OUTPUT ACCEPT [0:0]
:drop-not-to-me - [0:0]

# allow localhost traffic
-A INPUT -i lo -j ACCEPT

# drop everything not intended for me
-A INPUT -j drop-not-to-me
-A drop-not-to-me -m addrtype --dst-type LOCAL -j RETURN
#-A drop-not-to-me -m addrtype --dst-type BROADCAST -j RETURN
#-A drop-not-to-me -m addrtype --dst-type MULTICAST -j RETURN
-A drop-not-to-me -j DROP

# accept packets of established connections (stateful)
-A INPUT -m conntrack --ctstate RELATED,ESTABLISHED -j ACCEPT

# drop invalid packets, or non-SYN packets of unknown connections
-A INPUT -m conntrack --ctstate INVALID -j DROP
```

---

[6]http://www.netfilter.org/documentation/HOWTO/packet-filtering-HOWTO.html

```
# accept incoming SSH connections
-A INPUT -p tcp --dport ssh -j ACCEPT

COMMIT
```

In chapter 6.8.1, you will find one method of automatically loading the packet filter definition during the configuration of the network interfaces. It uses **iptables-restore** to load the configuration, which can also be done manually:

```
~# iptables-restore < /etc/network/iptables
```

A packet filter such as defined above fulfills two main purposes:

1. Any daemon started by accident will not be accessible from the network. Therefore, the problem which **invoke-rc.d** is trying to solve (see chapter 6.3.1) is somewhat mitigated by the packet filter. In addition, you may want to provide services only locally, but not over the network. While you should configure the respective daemon to only listen on the loopback interface, keeping the packet filter closed on the corresponding port(s) is another layer of security.

2. None of your users, whether intentionally or by way of a trojan horse, will be able to provide a daemon accessible from the outside; the packet filter drops all connection requests to ports other than the few defined by the administrator (only **ssh** in the above example). Obviously, should a local user (or trojan horse) gain **root** access on the local machine, the packet filter will be no help as it can be trivially modified.

Depending on your environment and the purpose of the system, you may also want to consider restricting outgoing traffic accordingly, using the **OUTPUT** chain, which has an **ACCEPT** policy in the above example and therefore does not filter anything by default.

Please keep in mind that **iptables** only filters IPv4 traffic. If your host has IPv6 connectivity, you will have to use programmeip6tables to configure the appropriate filters too, or else an attacker could simply bypass your filters with IPv6 traffic.

Finally, it must be stated that a packet filter by itself only provides a minimal increase in security. If security is a concern to your system(s), please take other precautions, such as the use of content filters, host- (and possibly network-) based intrusion detection systems, process accounting and logging, a restrictive account and password policy, filesystem quota, backups, and the meticulous use of a log book to keep track of changes. The "Securing Debian HOWTO"[7] provides a vast amount of useful information.

[7] http://www.debian.org/docs/manuals/securing-debian-howto

The Debian archive contains a number of firewall builder applications designed to make the process of firewall rule design more intuitive[8]. Two more popular examples are the **fwbuilder** and **shorewall** packages. While their use certainly facilitates the design process, there is some danger in the false sense of security when the user does not fully understand what these front-ends piece together. My advice is to stay with the lowest level and define the packet filter with the plain definition shown above. However, there is nothing wrong with using the builders to create templates and examples to help understand and design the rules.

Other firewall builders, such as **ferm** (and also **fwbuilder**) can be used from the command line. They do not attempt to automate the process of firewall design, but rather provide syntactic sugar, such as loops, variables, and conditions. Also, they are capable of generating rules for various firewalls and can thus be used to deploy the same ruleset on **iptables**, **ipf**, or even Cisco routers. Another package worth mentioning is **firehol**, which provides a higher-level language for the configuration of an **iptables**-based packet filter.

C.5   Dual-booting with other operating systems

The Debian system can coexist with other operating systems on the same machine. Bootloaders, like **Grub** or **Lilo** can easily be configured to offer the choice between Debian and other operating systems at boot time.

While the order of installation of the operating systems theoretically does not matter, some operating systems like to pretend that they are the only ones in the world and will render all previously installed systems unbootable. Since Linux takes a more liberal approach, it is usually a good idea to install it last. In any case, an unbootable Linux system can easily be repaired by using a boot disk to gain access to the system, and reinstalling the bootloader (see chapter 8.3.1). If Linux is installed last, the bootloader will be installed automatically.

Most other operating systems provide their own bootloader. Some of these are capable of bootling Linux, but it is not always easy. Therefore, the idea is to install **Grub** (or **Lilo**) into the MBR, and to let them chain-load any other bootloaders required by other operating systems. While **Lilo** requires other operating systems to provide their own bootloaders and can only pass control over to them, **Grub** can actually boot other operating systems directly. More details are available in chapter 4 of the **Grub** manual[9]. In the following, I discuss only chain-loading.

---

[8]The definition of firewall is unclear; generally, a firewall is conceived to be a separate machine, separating two networks of different trust levels. Often, a firewall includes content filtering and gateway components. However, simple packet filters, such as the one described here, are also often refered to as firewalls. Firewall builder software can usually generate the appropriate configuration for packet filters too.

[9]The manual is available in the **grub-doc** package; chapter 4 is to be found in **/usr/share/doc/grub-doc/html/grub_4.html**

C.5.1 Chain-loading other bootloaders

The Debian installer automatically detects other operating systems and offers to add appropriate entries to the boot menu, while configuring the bootloader. The same can be achieved manually. For instance, an installation of NetBSD /dev/hda1 (the first partition of the primary master disk) can be added to the Grub boot menu by appending the following stanza to the Grub menu file:

```
~# cat <<EOF >> /boot/grub/menu.lst
title         NetBSD
rootnoverify (hd0,0)
makeactive
chainloader  +1
EOF
```

Similarly, for Lilo, the following has to be added to /etc/lilo.conf, and lilo has to be run.

```
~# cat <<EOF >> /etc/lilo.conf
other    = /dev/hda1
  label  = NetBSD
  table  = /dev/hda
  loader = /boot/chain.b
EOF
~# lilo
[...]
adding NetBSD...
```

Other operating systems can be loaded similarly. Please refer to chapter 4 of the Grub documentation for details about each of the supported operating systems[9].

C.5.2 Dealing with Windows peculiarities

The Microsoft Windows boooloader (ntldr) can be chain-loaded by Grub and Lilo, using the aforementioned method. However, once control is passed to ntldr, it may fail to load the Windows operating system due to a number of criticial deficiencies in the design of the Windows boot process. Fortunately, the free software tools make it relatively easy to work around the pitfalls.

Garbled partition tables

The most common difficulty arises when Linux is installed onto a disk which was partitioned by Windows, and which holds an installation of that operating system. Often, the Windows installation garbles the partition table, causing partition numbers and their relative positions on the disk to be inconsistent. When the Linux partition managers rewrite the partition table, they restore consistency. Unfortunately, Windows hardcodes the the (inconsistent) partition numbers in the boot configuration, rather than using logical addressing. Therefore, a proper partition table may prevent Windows from booting.

The situation can be dealt with in three possible ways: by creating the partition table with free software tools before installing Windows, by taking precautions before installing Linux, or by fixing the solution at a later point in time. While the first two are the preferred ways, the latter should only be used as a last resort.

An easy way to deal with the peculiarities of the way the Windows installation writes the partition table is to use a free software tool to partition the disk, prior to installing Windows. Any partition tool can prepare partitions to be used by the Windows installation[10], thereby preventing the chance of inconsistent partition tables. The natural way here is to install Linux first, and to leave some space for Windows, to be installed second[11].

If the partition table already exists, and Windows is already installed, the preferred way to prevent an unbootable Windows installation is to edit the %SYSTEMDRIVE%\boot.ini file prior to installing Linux, and add new entries for each possible partition. Later, when the default selection produces an error about ntoskrnl.exe not being found, the other entries can be tried in turn. For instance, the following depicts a boot.ini with the relevant lines duplicated. Note how the value of the partition parameter increases[12]:

```
[boot loader]
timeout=30
default=multi(0)disk(0)rdisk(0)partition(1)\WINDOWS
[operating systems]
multi(0)disk(0)rdisk(0)partition(1)\WINDOWS=
  ''Microsoft Windows XP 1'' /fastdetect
multi(0)disk(0)rdisk(0)partition(2)\WINDOWS=
  ''Microsoft Windows XP 2'' /fastdetect
multi(0)disk(0)rdisk(0)partition(3)\WINDOWS=
  ''Microsoft Windows XP 3'' /fastdetect
[...]
multi(0)disk(0)rdisk(0)partition(9)\WINDOWS=
  ''Microsoft Windows XP 9'' /fastdetect
Professional'' /fastdetect
```

When the correct partition has been found and Windows has finished booting, the boot.ini file should be properly modified. Please make sure you change the default line as well.

[10]NTFS partitions should be created with parititon type 0x07; FAT32 partitions use the type 0x0e. You should mark the partition destined to be the c: drive as bootable/active.

[11]If you spend some time in Linux before rebooting to install Windows, you may even find out that you do not need to dual-boot after all...

[12]The lines have been broken for readability. The whole "multi ... fastdetect" string must appear on a single line, however.

The second solution to Windows' inability to produce partition tables is to test your luck, and use a rescue disk to change the **boot.ini** file afterwards. Note that this typically requires write access to an **NTFS** filesystem. Even though Linux is capable of writing files to the filesystem, it should be avoided wherever possible, as write support is not deemed stable yet.

Windows on a secondary hard disk

Windows is only capable of booting off the first hard disk. To enable it to boot off another disk, we have to make the bootloader juggle hard disks. For instance, to boot an installation of Windows on the second hard disk with **Grub**, the following line needs to be inserted before the **rootnoverify** option:

```
map (hd1) (hd0)
```

With **Lilo**, this is achieved by swapping the BIOS IDs with some extra options added to the stanza.

```
map-drive = 0x80
       to = 0x81
map-drive = 0x81
       to = 0x80
```

Multiple Windows installations

Microsoft would like Windows to be the only operating system installed. The developers thus chose a rigorous method of enforcement, which makes it impossible even for two Windows installations to coexist independently of one another. Or, put differently, if with more than one set of DOS/Windows on a single disk, the operating system easily gets confused over which one to use.

If you need to operate two independent installations, you can use the bootloader to hide one partition. For instance, with two installations of Windows on **/dev/hda1** and **/dev/hda4**, the following lines have to be added to the corresponding **Grub** configuration stanzas, before the **rootnoverify** option (but after any **map** options). Note that the partitions have to be reversed for one of the two stanzas to which you have to add these lines:

```
  hide (hd0,3)
unhide (hd0,1)
```

In Lilo's configuration, this is also possible, albeit a little more elaborate:

```
change
  partition=/dev/hda1
     activate
     set=DOS16_big_normal
  partition=/dev/hda4
     deactivate
     set=DOS16_big_hidden
```

D

The Debian Linux Manifesto

Written by Ian A. Murdock, Revised on 6 January 1994.

What is Debian Linux?

Debian Linux is a brand-new kind of Linux distribution. Rather than being developed by one isolated individual or group, as other distributions of Linux have been developed in the past, Debian is being developed openly in the spirit of Linux and GNU. The primary purpose of the Debian project is to finally create a distribution that lives up to the Linux name. Debian is being carefully and conscientiously put together and will be maintained and supported with similar care.

It is also an attempt to create a non-commercial distribution that will be able to effectively compete in the commercial market. It will eventually be distributed by The Free Software Foundation on CD-ROM, and The Debian Linux Association will offer the distribution on floppy disk and tape along with printed manuals, technical support and other end-user essentials. All of the above will be available at little more than cost, and the excess will be put toward further development of free software for all users. Such distribution is essential to the success of the Linux operating system in the commercial market, and it must be done by organizations in a position to successfully advance and advocate free software without the pressure of profits or returns.

Why is Debian being constructed?

Distributions are essential to the future of Linux. Essentially, they eliminate the need for the user to locate, download, compile, install and integrate a fairly large number of essential tools to assemble a working Linux system. Instead, the burden of system construction is placed on the distribution creator, whose work can be shared with thousands of other users. Almost all users of Linux will get their first taste of it through a distribution, and most users will continue to use a distribution for the sake of convenience even after they are familiar with the operating system. Thus, distributions play a very important role indeed.

Despite their obvious importance, distributions have attracted little attention from developers. There is a simple reason for this: they are neither easy nor glamorous to construct and require a great deal of ongoing effort from the creator to keep the distribution bug-free and up-to-date. It is one thing to put together a system from scratch; it is quite another to ensure that the system is easy for others to install, is installable and usable under a wide variety of hardware configurations, contains software that others will find useful, and is updated when the components themselves are improved.

Many distributions have started out as fairly good systems, but as time passes attention to maintaining the distribution becomes a secondary concern. A case-in-point is the Softlanding Linux System (better known as SLS). It is quite possibly the most bug-ridden and badly maintained Linux distribution available; unfortunately, it is also quite possibly the most popular. It is, without question, the distribution that attracts the most attention from the many commercial "distributors" of Linux that have surfaced to capitalize on the growing popularity of the operating system.

This is a bad combination indeed, as most people who obtain Linux from these "distributors" receive a bug-ridden and badly maintained Linux distribution. As if this wasn't bad enough, these "distributors" have a disturbing tendency to misleadingly advertise non-functional or extremely unstable "features" of their product. Combine this with the fact that the buyers will, of course, expect the product to live up to its advertisement and the fact that many may believe it to be a commercial operating system (there is also a tendency not to mention that Linux is free nor that it is distributed under the GNU General Public License). To top it all off, these "distributors" are actually making enough money from their effort to justify buying larger advertisements in more magazines; it is the classic example of unacceptable behavior being rewarded by those who simply do not know any better. Clearly something needs to be done to remedy the situation.

How will Debian attempt to put an end to these problems?

The Debian design process is open to ensure that the system is of the highest quality and that it reflects the needs of the user community. By involving others with a wide range of abilities and backgrounds, Debian is able to be developed in a modular fashion. Its components are of high quality because those with expertise in a certain area are given the opportunity to construct or maintain the individual components of Debian involving that area. Involving others also ensures that valuable suggestions for improvement can be incorporated into the distribution during its development; thus, a distribution is created based on the needs and wants of the users rather than the needs and wants of the constructor. It is very difficult for one individual or small group to anticipate these needs and wants in advance without direct input from others.

Debian Linux will also be distributed on physical media by the Free Software Foundation and the Debian Linux Association. This provides Debian to users without access to the Internet or FTP and additionally makes products and services such as printed manuals and technical support available to all users of the system. In this way, Debian may be used by many more individuals and organizations than is otherwise possible, the focus will be on providing a first-class product and not on profits or returns, and the margin from the products and services provided may be used to improve the software itself for all users whether they paid to obtain it or not.

The Free Software Foundation plays an extremely important role in the future of Debian. By the simple fact that they will be distributing it, a message is sent to the world that Linux is not a commercial product and that it never should be, but that this does not mean that Linux will never be able to compete commercially. For those of you who disagree, I challenge you to rationalize the success of GNU Emacs and GCC, which are not commercial software but which have had quite an impact on the commercial market regardless of that fact.

The time has come to concentrate on the future of Linux rather than on the destructive goal of enriching oneself at the expense of the entire Linux community and its future. The development and distribution of Debian may not be the answer to the problems that I have outlined in the Manifesto, but I hope that it will at least attract enough attention to these problems to allow them to be solved.

E

Debian Social Contract

The Social Contract is a foundation document of the Debian project. During the release period of *sarge*, a number of changes were proposed but delayed until *sarge*'s release (see chapter 2.3). As a result, two slightly different versions of the social contract are floating around[1], which shall be referred to as the current and the future version. The current version governs the release of Debian *sarge*. The future version will only come into effect when *sarge* becomes *stable*, a decision made by majority vote[2].

[1] http://www.debian.org/vote/2004/social_contract_reform.3
[2] http://www.debian.org/vote/2004/vote_004

E.1   The current Social Contract

The following corresponds to the offical version of the Debian Social Contract as applicable to Debian *sarge*. It can be obtained from the Debian web page at http://www.debian.org/social_contract.

Debian Will Remain 100% Free Software

We promise to keep the Debian GNU/Linux Distribution entirely free software. As there are many definitions of free software, we include the guidelines we use to determine if software is "free" below. We will support our users who develop and run non-free software on Debian, but we will never make the system depend on an item of non-free software.

We Will Give Back to the Free Software Community

When we write new components of the Debian system, we will license them as free software. We will make the best system we can, so that free software will be widely distributed and used. We will feed back bug-fixes, improvements, user requests, etc. to the "upstream" authors of software included in our system.

We Won't Hide Problems

We will keep our entire bug-report database open for public view at all times. Reports that users file on-line will immediately become visible to others.

Our Priorities are Our Users and Free Software

We will be guided by the needs of our users and the free-software community. We will place their interests first in our priorities. We will support the needs of our users for operation in many different kinds of computing environment. We won't object to commercial software that is intended to run on Debian systems, and we'll allow others to create value-added distributions containing both Debian and commercial software, without any fee from us. To support these goals, we will provide an integrated system of high-quality, 100% free software, with no legal restrictions that would prevent these kinds of use.

Programs That Don't Meet Our Free-Software Standards

We acknowledge that some of our users require the use of programs that don't conform to the Debian Free Software Guidelines (see appendix F). We have created "contrib" and "non-free" areas in our FTP archive for this software. The software in these directories is not part of the Debian system, although it has been configured for use with Debian. We encourage CD manufacturers to read the licenses of software packages in these directories and determine if they can distribute that software on their CDs. Thus, although non-free software isn't a part of Debian, we support its use, and we provide infrastructure (such as our bug-tracking system and mailing lists) for non-free software packages.

E.2 The future Social Contract

Debian Will Remain 100% Free

We provide the guidelines that we use to determine if a work is "free" in the document entitled "The Debian Free Software Guidelines" (see appendix F). We promise that the Debian system and all its components will be free according to these guidelines. We will support people who create or use both free and non-free works on Debian. We will never make the system require the use of a non-free component.

We Will Give Back to the Free Software Community

When we write new components of the Debian system, we will license them in a manner consistent with the Debian Free Software Guidelines. We will make the best system we can, so that free works will be widely distributed and used. We will communicate things such as bug fixes, improvements and user requests to the "upstream" authors of works included in our system.

We Won't Hide Problems

We will keep our entire bug report database open for public view at all times. Reports that people file online will promptly become visible to others.

Our Priorities are Our Users and Free Software

We will be guided by the needs of our users and the Free Software community. We will place their interests first in our priorities. We will support the needs of our users for operation in many different kinds of computing environments. We will not object to non-free works that are intended to be used on Debian systems, or attempt to charge a fee to people who create or use such works. We will allow others to create distributions containing both the Debian system and other works, without any fee from us. In furtherance of these goals, we will provide an integrated system of high-quality materials with no legal restrictions that would prevent such uses of the system.

Programs That Don't Meet Our Free-Software Standards

We acknowledge that some of our users require the use of works that do not conform to the Debian Free Software Guidelines. We have created "contrib" and "non-free" areas in our archive for these works. The packages in these areas are not part of the Debian system, although they have been configured for use with Debian. We encourage CD manufacturers to read the licenses of the packages in these areas and determine if they can distribute the packages on their CDs. Thus, although non-free works are not a part of Debian, we support their use and provide infrastructure for non-free packages (such as our bug tracking system and mailing lists).

F

The Debian Free Software Guidelines

The following corresponds to the official Debian Free Software Guidelines as applicable to Debian *sarge*. The document is available from the Debian website at http://www.debian.org/social_contract#guidelines.

Free Redistribution

The license of a Debian component may not restrict any party from selling or giving away the software as a component of an aggregate software distribution containing programs from several different sources. The license may not require a royalty or other fee for such sale.

Source Code

The program must include source code, and must allow distribution in source code as well as compiled form.

Derived Works

The license must allow modifications and derived works, and must allow them to be distributed under the same terms as the license of the original software.

Integrity of The Author's Source Code

The license may restrict source-code from being distributed in modified form *only* if the license allows the distribution of "patch files" with the source code for the purpose of modifying the program at build time. The license must explicitly permit distribution of software built from modified source code. The license may require derived works to carry a different name or version number from the original software. (This is a compromise. The Debian group encourages all authors not to restrict any files, source or binary, from being modified.)

No Discrimination Against Persons or Groups

The license must not discriminate against any person or group of persons.

No Discrimination Against Fields of Endeavor

The license must not restrict anyone from making use of the program in a specific field of endeavor. For example, it may not restrict the program from being used in a business, or from being used for genetic research.

Distribution of License

The rights attached to the program must apply to all to whom the program is redistributed without the need for execution of an additional license by those parties.

License Must Not Be Specific to Debian

The rights attached to the program must not depend on the program's being part of a Debian system. If the program is extracted from Debian and used or distributed without Debian but otherwise within the terms of the program's license, all parties to whom the program is redistributed should have the same rights as those that are granted in conjunction with the Debian system.

License Must Not Contaminate Other Software

The license must not place restrictions on other software that is distributed along with the licensed software. For example, the license must not insist that all other programs distributed on the same medium must be free software.

Example Licenses

The "GPL", "BSD", and "Artistic" licenses are examples of licenses that we consider "free".

Notes

The concept of stating our "social contract with the free software community" was suggested by Ean Schuessler. This document was drafted by Bruce Perens, refined by the other Debian developers during a month-long e-mail conference in June 1997, and then accepted as the publicly stated policy of the Debian Project.

Bruce Perens later removed the Debian-specific references from the Debian Free Software Guidelines to create "The Open Source Definition."

Other organizations may derive from and build on this document. Please give credit to the Debian project if you do.

Index

open
source
PRESS

```c
int main(int argc, char **argv) {
    Writer *you;

    you = good_writer_create("<insert your name here>");

    if ((is_specialist(you, "Linux/Unix") ||
         is_specialist(you, "Open Source Software")) &&
        TRUE == want_to_write_book(you) &&
        TRUE == need_a_good_publisher_for_book(you)) {
      get_in_contact(you, "Open Source Press");
    }

    /* don't free 'you' as we want to re-use 'you'
       for another book */

    return 0;
}
```

www.opensourcepress.de

Electronic Frontier Foundation
Defending Freedom in the Digital World

Free Speech. Privacy. Innovation. Fair Use. Reverse Engineering. If you care about these rights in the digital world, then you should join the Electronic Frontier Foundation (EFF). EFF was founded in 1990 to protect the rights of users and developers of technology. EFF is the first to identify threats to basic rights online and to advocate on behalf of free expression in the digital age.

The Electronic Frontier Foundation Defends Your Rights!
Become a Member Today!
http://www.eff.org/support/

Current EFF projects include:

Protecting your fundamental right to vote. Widely publicized security flaws in computerized voting machines show that, though filled with potential, this technology is far from perfect. EFF is defending the open discussion of e-voting problems and is coordinating a national litigation strategy addressing issues arising from use of poorly developed and tested computerized voting machines.

Ensuring that you are not traceable through your things. Libraries, schools, the government and private sector businesses are adopting radio frequency identification tags, or RFIDs – a technology capable of pinpointing the physical location of whatever item the tags are embedded in. While this may seem like a convenient way to track items, it's also a convenient way to do something less benign: track people and their activities through their belongings. EFF is working to ensure that embrace of this technology does not erode your right to privacy.

Stopping the FBI from creating surveillance backdoors on the Internet. EFF is part of a coalition opposing the FBI's expansion of the Communications Assistance for Law Enforcement Act (CALEA), which would require that the wiretap capabilities built into the phone system be extended to the Internet, forcing ISPs to build backdoors for law enforcement.

Providing you with a means by which you can contact key decision-makers on cyber-liberties issues. EFF maintains an action center that provides alerts on technology, civil liberties issues and pending legislation to more than 50,000 subscribers. EFF also generates a weekly online newsletter, EFFector, and a blog that provides up-to-the minute information and commentary.

Defending your right to listen to and copy digital music and movies. The entertainment industry has been overzealous in trying to protect its copyrights, often decimating fair use rights in the process. EFF is standing up to the movie and music industries on several fronts.

Check out all of the things we're working on at http://www.eff.org and join today or make a donation to support the fight to defend freedom online.

ELECTRONIC FRONTIER FOUNDATION · 454 SHOTWELL STREET · SAN FRANCISCO, CA 94110 · 415.436.9333